AFRICAN HISTORICAL DICTIONARIES
Edited by Jon Woronoff

1. Cameroon, by Victor T. Le Vine and Roger P. Nye. 1974. *Out of print. See No. 48.*
2. *The Congo,* 2nd ed., by Virginia Thompson and Richard Adloff. 1984. *Out of print. See No. 69.*
3. *Swaziland,* by John J. Grotpeter. 1975.
4. *The Gambia,* 2nd ed., by Harry A. Gailey. 1987.
5. *Botswana,* by Richard P. Stevens. 1975. *Out of print. See No. 70.*
6. *Somalia,* by Margaret F. Castagno. 1975.
7. *Benin (Dahomey),* 2nd ed., by Samuel Decalo. 1987. *Out of print. See No. 61.*
8. *Burundi,* by Warren Weinstein. 1976. *Out of print. See No. 73.*
9. *Togo,* 3rd ed., by Samuel Decalo. 1996.
10. *Lesotho,* by Gordon Haliburton. 1977.
11. *Mali,* 3rd ed., by Pascal James Imperato. 1996.
12. *Sierra Leone,* by Cyril Patrick Foray. 1977.
13. *Chad,* 3rd ed., by Samuel Decalo. 1997.
14. *Upper Volta,* by Daniel Miles McFarland. 1978.
15. *Tanzania,* by Laura S. Kurtz. 1978.
16. *Guinea,* 3rd ed., by Thomas O'Toole with Ibrahima Bah-Lalya. 1995.
17. *Sudan,* by John Voll. 1978. *Out of print. See No. 53.*
18. *Rhodesia/Zimbabwe,* by R. Kent Rasmussen. 1979. *Out of print. See No. 46.*
19. *Zambia,* 2nd ed., by John J. Grotpeter, Brian V. Siegel, and James R. Pletcher. 1998.
20. *Niger,* 3rd ed., by Samuel Decalo. 1997.
21. *Equatorial Guinea,* 3rd ed., by Max Liniger-Goumaz. 2000.
22. *Guinea-Bissau,* 3rd ed., by Richard Lobban and Peter Mendy. 1997.
23. *Senegal,* by Lucie G. Colvin. 1981. *Out of print. See No. 65.*
24. *Morocco,* by William Spencer. 1980. *Out of print. See No. 71.*
25. *Malawi,* by Cynthia A. Crosby. 1980. *Out of print. See No. 84.*
26. *Angola,* by Phyllis Martin. 1980. *Out of print. See No. 52.*

84. *Malawi*, 3rd ed., by Owen J. Kalinga and Cynthia A. Crosby. 2001.
85. *Sudan*, 3rd ed., by Richard A. Lobban Jr., Robert S. Kramer, Carolyn Fluehr-Lobban. 2002.
86. *Zimbabwe*, 3rd ed., by Steven C. Rubert and R. Kent Rasmussen. 2001.

Historical Dictionary of the Sudan

Third Edition

Richard A. Lobban Jr.
Robert S. Kramer
Carolyn Fluehr-Lobban

African Historical Dictionaries, No. 85

The Scarecrow Press, Inc.
Lanham, Maryland, and London
2002

SCARECROW PRESS, INC.

Published in the United States of America
by Scarecrow Press, Inc.
A Member of the Rowman & Littlfield Publishing Group
4720 Boston Way, Lanham, Maryland 20706
www.scarecrowpress.com

4 Pleydell Gardens, Folkestone
Kent CT20 2DN, England

British Library Cataloguing in Publication Information Available

Library of Congress Cataloging-in-Publication Data

Lobban, Richard.
　Historical dictionary of the Sudan / Richard A. Lobban, Jr., Robert S. Kramer,
Carolyn Fluehr-Lobban.—3rd ed.
　　p. cm.—(African historical dictionaries ; no. 85)
Fluehr-Lobban's name appears first on the 2nd edition.
Includes bibliographical references.
ISBN 0-8108-4100-2 (alk. paper)
　1. Sudan—History—Dictionaries. 2. Sudan—History—Bibliography. I.
Kramer, Robert S, 1956- II. Fluehr-Lobban, Carolyn. III. title. IV. Series.

DTI55.3 .V64 2002
962.4'003—dc21   2001057614

First edition by John Voll, African Historical Dictionaries, No. 17, Scarecrow Press,
Metuchen, N.J., 1978   ISBN 0-8108-1115-4
Second edition by Carolyn Fluehr-Lobban, Richard A. Lobban Jr., and John Obert
Voll, African Historical Dictionaries, No. 53, Scarecrow Press, Metuchen, N.J., 1992
ISBN 0-8108-2547-3

To peace, justice, and unity in Sudan

Contents

Maps

Illustrations

Editor's Foreword

The Republic of Sudan is Africa's largest country, and regrettably one of its least successful in many ways. The main problem is not so much its size as that it straddles an uneasy divide where the Arabized, Muslim north comes into contact with the still largely animist or Christian ethnic groups of "black" Africa. The relations between North and South frequently resulted in conflict and slave raiding during the centuries before British colonization, and again for the more than four decades since independence. To this inherent instability has been added ideological quarrels between established regimes and their opponents (now, between supporters of a stricter Islamist polity and their opponents). These strains inevitably not only stifled political and social progress, they also undermined an economy that, given the relatively poor natural endowment, could only prosper with more suitable policies and considerable aid. Although it might be tempting to dismiss Sudan, it is too large and strategically placed a country to ignore, and while the inner tensions persist they can only generate further friction with its many neighbors.

This is now the third edition of the *Historical Dictionary of the Sudan*. It differs from its predecessors in that this volume only covers the period from the rise of Islam on, while the earlier period will be included in a forthcoming volume on Ancient Nubia. This means more space could be devoted both to other eras, many of them still poorly researched, and also to more recent developments that, despite their significance, are scarcely known abroad. The information is provided in various ways. First, the introduction brings the overall story up to date. Then the chronology follows crucial events as they take place. The dictionary includes entries on significant persons, places, institutions, and events. The bibliography leads to other sources of information for those who wish to follow up one aspect or another.

This third edition of the *Historical Dictionary of the Sudan* was written by Richard A. Lobban Jr., Robert S. Kramer, and Carolyn Fluehr-Lobban. Richard Lobban and Carolyn Fluehr-Lobban authored the second edition, which grew out of a first edition by John Obert Voll. Both Dr. Lobban and Dr. Fluehr-Lobban are Professors of Anthropology at Rhode Island College, with the former also Director of the Program of African and Afro-American Studies and the latter also Director of General Education. Dr. Kramer is Associate Professor of African and Middle Eastern History at St. Norbert College. All three have spent considerable time in Sudan, on which they have written extensively, and are active in the Sudan Studies Association of North America. This substantially expanded and updated work is a result of close collaboration and an abiding dedication to furthering knowledge on Sudan.

Jon Woronoff
Series Editor

Acknowledgments

Richard Lobban and Carolyn Fluehr-Lobban would like to record their appreciation to John Voll for producing the first edition of this work in 1978. This gave us a strong base for this continuing project. In the coauthored second edition in 1992, we added new sections and entries that carried residual material from the first edition. We have certainly benefited from the foundation he laid more than twenty years ago.

We are also grateful for the contribution of Gregory A. Finnegan, reference bibliographer at Dartmouth College, for aiding us with the bibliography for the second edition. The newly expanded bibliography for the present third edition has been developed through the Internet searches assisted by the reference librarians at Adams Library, Rhode Island College.

The scope of this present work has become so vast that we have had to draw upon the expertise of many colleagues and friends. We are most grateful for this service to Sudanist scholarship. We wish to thank them here for their guest entries; their individual authorship is noted at the end of their specific contributions. These include Constance E. Berkley, Anita Fabos, Albrecht Hofheinz, W. Stephen Howard, Ann Lesch, Mahgoub Al-Tigani Mahmoud, Gerasimos Makris, Baqie Badawi Muhammad, Heather J. Sharkey, Richard Skidmore, Knut S. Vikor, and William Young. Above all, Robert Kramer's anchor role as the new author gives the volume more historical depth, and his entries have brought a new and rich dimension to the volume.

Rhode Island College, our home institution, and its Faculty of Arts and Sciences have regularly expressed their confidence in us by giving broad freedom in course content, sabbatical leaves, study leaves, and faculty research grants. Without all of this assistance for over a quarter of a century, it would have been impossible to consider writing this book describing such a huge country with its long and complex history and very diverse cultures. Much of the writing for the third edition was done while Richard and Carolyn were on sabbatical leaves generously awarded by Rhode Island College, for which we are most grateful indeed.

Robert Kramer would like to acknowledge St. Norbert College's Office of Faculty Development, whose assistance has enabled him to write, rewrite, and edit this volume over the past three years. Andrew Kauth provided extremely valuable research and editing assistance as this project neared completion. Finally, my colleagues at St. Norbert College, especially Dr. Victoria Tashjian, have given invaluable support and encouragement during the many difficulties that such a project entails. My heartfelt thanks to them all.

Preface

By adding new authors to the third edition of this *Historical Dictionary of the Sudan*, we have expanded upon the breadth of topics that formerly were included. We have also devoted considerable attention to the necessary updating of recent history since 1978, especially highlighting the renewal of civil war in 1983, the institution of Shari'a law in the same year, the fall of Nimeiri in 1985, and up to the al-Bashir government that has ruled from 1989 to the present. An outline of these more recent developments is contained in the chronology and introduction.

Thus this new edition includes important people, events, and publications that were not known at the time of the former work. It has revised or expanded previous entries, or it created new synthetic and/or analytic essays on a selected variety of topics. Some of the more important new entries are on the following topics: British administrators, major ethnic groups, European explorers, foreign relations, histories of individual cities and towns, Islam, Islamic law, Islamic revival, minorities, Sudanese literature, the SPLA/SPLM, the civil war and efforts at peace negotiations, slavery, the anti-slavery movement, trade unions, women, women leaders and women's rights, as well as new maps, charts, and tables. New material has been introduced on the complexities of Sudan's civil war in terms of major leaders, movements, and conferences. These may all be found in the dictionary section.

The selection of topics is a difficult matter for a variety of reasons. First, we have sought to include the main people(s), places, and events that have defined the historical experience of the Sudan since the arrival of Islam. Naturally there may be disagreements about this, but the problem becomes more challenging when for some important figures and events there are few written records, while others are well chronicled. For half of the twentieth century the Sudan was governed by Great Britain, and its records naturally are from the British rather than Sudanese point of view. Moreover, Sudanese may also have conflicting views, especially relative to Islam and North-South politics. Such are the usual problems of historiography. When in doubt, we have sought to project a Sudanese point of view to avoid or minimize Eurocentrism; where Sudanese judgments differ we have tried to present multiple and sometimes contradictory views.

We have made use of the disciplines of anthropology and history to create a comprehensive dictionary that considers the experiences and achievements of the famous as well as the obscure, the powerful as well as the marginal, the well-documented and the not well-documented. Ultimately all researchers, whether historians, political scientists, or anthropologists, are limited by their access to data and by their analysis of these data. For information on recent times, we have used the *Sudan Democratic Gazette*, National Democratic Alliance press releases, Sudan-oriented homepages on the World Wide Web (which were not even imagined in the second edition), as well as official Sudanese sources. Like all academic writers, we accept credit or blame for what is contained in this volume.

Beyond the updates and expansions, this present third edition has completely restructured the former second edition. The second edition had large portions devoted to Sudanese antiquity. These mainly have been removed to create a forthcoming, separate book entitled *Historical Dictionary of Ancient Nubia*, which is recommended for readers concerned with topics such as ancient foreign relations with Egypt and Assyria, A-Group, C-Group, and X-Groups, Christianity in Nubia, ethnohistory, Greek influences, Jews in the Nile Valley, Kerma, Kushites at Meroë and Napata, prehistoric Nubia, Roman influences, the Twenty-Fifth Dynasty, women in antiquity, as well as new maps, charts, and tables. In short, the revised scope and chronology has very substantially reduced or eliminated the sections on prehistory, the Kushitic period, and the Christian kingdoms in Nubia, since these are now covered in a separate book. Some ties to this earlier period are left in the chronology and introduction as they serve to provide a background and context for the arrival of Islam.

Therefore, this third edition focuses mostly on the Sudan in Islamic times from about the fourteenth century to the present. There is more on the sultanates of Sinnar and Dar Fur, the Mahdiya, and the history of Islam in the Sudan in general, and especially on the chronology and analysis of significant events of the past decade, which has seen a radical Islamist movement in power in Khartoum.

At the same time, Sudanese are clearly in a personal and political struggle to determine their relationship toward Africa and the Arab world. This has taken the form of a protracted civil war that has most heavily involved the southern region, so this part of the book is also expanded to portray southern movements and leaders in much greater detail.

The revised bibliography contains new sections built upon the recent proliferation of literature on women in the Sudan, minority and human rights, Islamism, opposition movements, and refugees and exiles from the Sudan. New sources relating to the Sahelian drought and famine as it affected Sudan can be found within the geography and environment section, while the war-related famine conditions would be found within the section on the southern Sudan. Updated sources on the renewed civil war since 1983 also would be found in the section on southern Sudan. There are now sections and references to the later years of the Nimeiri regime, the popular *intifada* that overthrew the May Revolution in 1985, the Transitional Military Council of 1985–1986, the civilian government of Sadiq al-Mahdi of 1986–1989, and especially the military government of Gen. 'Umar al-Bashir in alliance with the National Islamic Front since June of 1989.

We have revised the *Historical Dictionary of the Sudan* in an effort to make it a more comprehensive reference and research tool for undergraduate students and generalist researchers. Specialists in Sudan or African/Middle Eastern studies should find many of the former and new entries of interest and available for access in their own teaching or scholarship.

Spelling and Alphabetical Conventions

There are always difficult problems with spelling conventions of non-Western languages, which are often reported phonetically through the ears of speakers of still greater numbers of languages. These approximations may replicate the sounds heard by one observer but not another. Standard transliteration orthography is one way out, but these "precise" forms appear awkward for the nonspecialist. In this respect we have very largely followed the standard transliteration guide for Arabic of the International Journal of Middle East Studies (IJMES). A further problem is raised by the many nonliterate Sudanese societies whose languages are neither Arabic nor European.

There are also forms in established usage that are not "proper" transliterations. An excellent example of this much-debated problem is the variety of ways in which persons spell their own names. Shall we inform a Sudanese person that his or her name is spelled incorrectly? For example, should it be Abdel Wahhab Mohamed or 'Abd al-Wahhab Muhammad? Then, in this confusion, how does one alphabetize? Should this example be alphabetized under "A," "al," "W," or "M"? We have sought to solve this problem guided by most common usage and spelling, and by the individual's spelling of his or her name when widely known. We have not used the embedded article "al-" or "el-" for alphabetization, but have used the first letter after it. Similarly we have decided to use the term "Sudan" rather than "the Sudan" when referring to the period following independence in 1956.

We have placed cross-references in the dictionary with inserted (q.v. and qq.v.) citations. These will guide the reader from a possibly confusing name they are searching for to our version in its alphabetical location. We have elected the simpler and more common form of names, for example Ja'aliyin, Mahdiya, Nimeiri, Turkiya, and Qadiriya, rather than the "correct" forms of Ja'aliyyin, Mahdiyya, Numayri, Turkiyya, and Qadiriyya. This may offend linguists, Orientalists, and Arabists but should make the book more user-friendly and intelligible to the generalist audience for which it is mainly intended.

Abreviations and Acronyms

ACNS	Advisory Council for the Northern Sudan
ADB	African Development Bank
AH	*Anno Hegira* (i.e., Islamic calendar date)
AID	(U.S.) Agency for International Development
AIDS	Acquired Immune Deficiency Syndrome
ALF	Azania Liberation Front
ARG	Anyidi Revolutionary Government
BCE	Before the Common Era (i.e., before Christ)
CBR	Crude Birth Rate
CDR	Crude Death Rate
CE	Common Era (i.e., AD)
DUP	Democratic Unionist Party
ECA	Economic Commission for Africa
FAO	Food and Agricultural Organization (UN)
GDP	Gross Domestic Product
GNP	Gross National Product
GUN	General Union of Nubas
IBRD	International Bank for Reconstruction and Development (World Bank)
IDR	Infant Death Rate
IGAD	Intergovernmental Authority for Development
IGADD	Intergovernmental Agency for Drought and Development
ILM	Islamic Liberation Movement
IMF	International Monetary Fund
KUSU	Khartoum University Students Union
LDC	Least Developed Country
NAM	Non-Aligned Movement
NANS	National Alliance for National Salvation
NDA	National Democratic Alliance
NGO	Non-Governmental Organization
NIF	National Islamic Front

NPG	Nile Provisional Government
NUP	National Unionist Party
OAU	Organization of African Unity
OLS	Operation Lifeline Sudan
PDF	Popular Defense Forces
PDP	Peoples Democratic Party
RCC	Revolutionary Command Council
SACDNU	Sudan African Closed Districts National Union
SAF	Sudan Alliance Forces
SAF-LC	Sudanese Armed Forces-Legitimate Command
SALF	Sudan African Liberation Front
SANU	Sudan African National Union
SAP	Structural Adjustment Program
SBA	Sudan Bar Association
SCP	Sudanese Communist Party
SHRO	Sudan Human Rights Organization
SNC	Sudan National Congress
SPDF	Sudanese Peoples Democratic Front
SPLA	Sudanese Peoples Liberation Army
SPLM	Sudanese Peoples Liberation Movement
SPS	Sudan Political Service
SRP	Socialist Republican Party
SRWU	Sudan Railway Workers Union
SSA	Sudan Studies Association
SSIM	Southern Sudan Independence Movement
SSLM	Southern Sudan Liberation Movement
SSPG	Southern Sudan Provisional Government
SSSUK	Sudan Studies Society of the United Kingdom
SSU	Sudanese Socialist Union
SUP	Sudan Unity Party
SUS	Sudan Union Society
SWTUF	Sudanese Workers' Trade Union Federation
SWU	Sudanese Women's Union
TMC	Transitional Military Council
UDSF	United Democratic Salvation Front
UN	United Nations
UNDP	United Nations Development Program
UNESCO	United Nations Educational, Scientific, and Cultural Organization
UNHCR	United Nations High Commissioner for Refugees

USSR	Union of Soviet Socialist Republics
WAA	Workers' Affairs Association
WFTU	World Federation of Trade Unions
WHO	World Health Organization

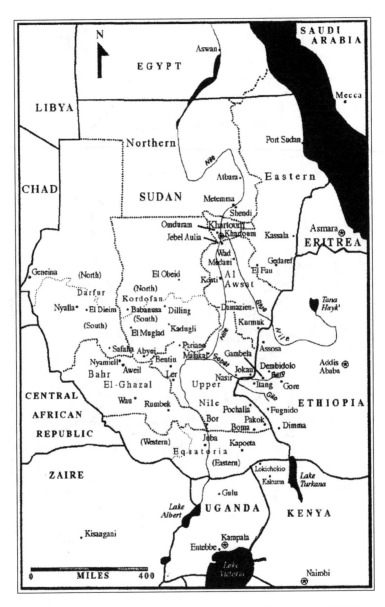

1. Map of Modern Sudan with Current Provincial Borders and Neighboring Nations.

Designed by Richard Lobban. Drawn by Jason Martin.

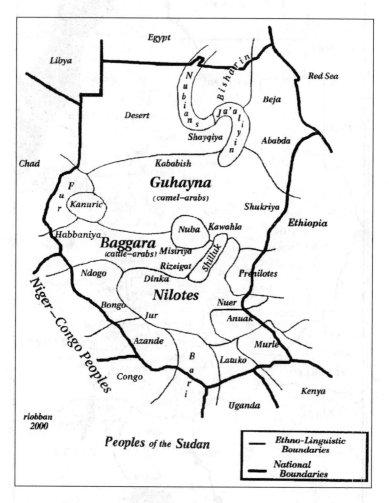

2. Map of the Peoples and Cultures of Sudan.

Designed by Richard Lobban. Drawn by Melissa Talbot.

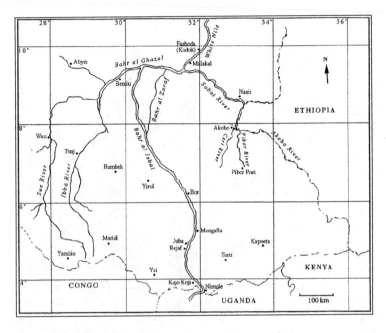

3. Map of the Southern Sudan with Main Towns and Rivers.

Designed by Richard Lobban. Drawn by Jason Martin.

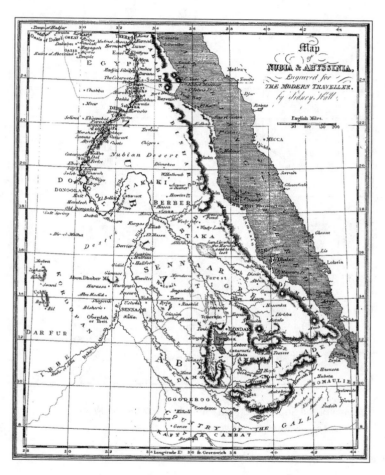

4. Map of Nubia and Abyssinia.

By Sidney Hall, London, 1827.

**Detailed Section from J. Arrowsmith,
Map of Nubia and Abyssinia, London,
15 February 1842.**

Richard Lobban Map Collection.

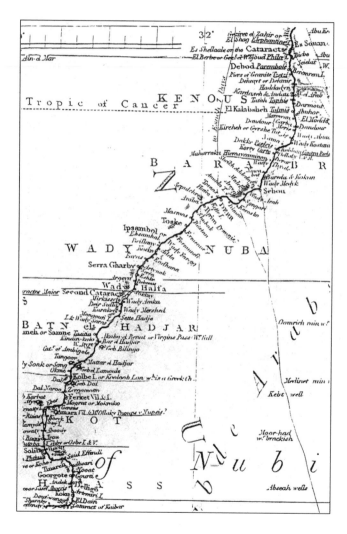

5. Detail for Lower Nubia, ca. 30° to 33° East Longitude
and 20° to 24° North Latitude.

**Detailed Section from J. Arrowsmith,
Map of Nubia and Abyssinia, London,
15 February 1842.**

Richard Lobban Map Collection.

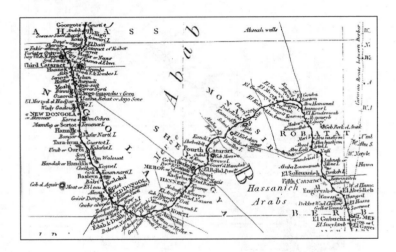

6. Detail for Region between 3rd and 5th Cataracts, ca. 30° to 34°
   East Longitude and 18° to 20° North Latitude.

**Detailed Section from J. Arrowsmith,
Map of Nubia and Abyssinia, London,
15 February 1842.**

Richard Lobban Map Collection.

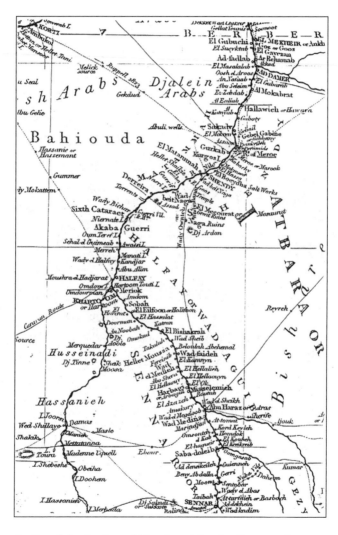

7. Detail for Region of Meroë and the Confluence of
White and Blue Niles, ca. 32° to 34° East Longitude
and 14° to 18° North Latitude.

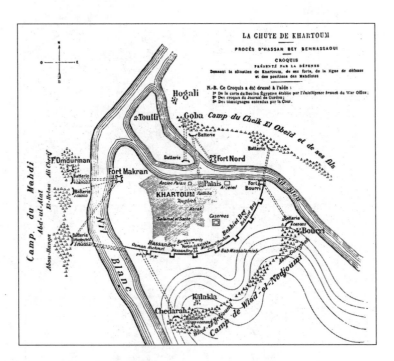

8. Map of the Fall of Khartoum.

From O. Borelli-Bey, la Chute De Khartoum, 26 Janvier 1885. Paris, 1893, Annex B, Figure 12.

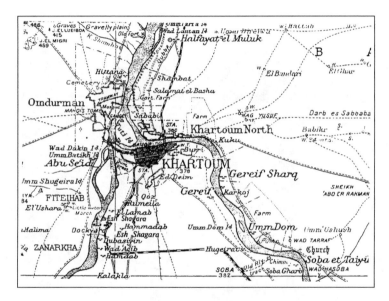

9. Detail of Khartoum [Province] Map, Sudan.

Sheet ND-36-B, Sudan Survey Department, 1940 (1967). 1:250,000.

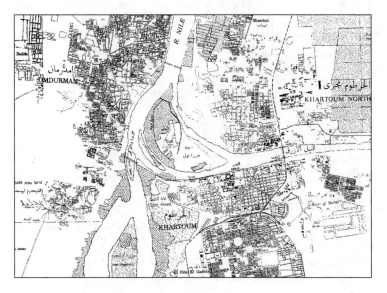

10. Detail of the Map of the Three Towns.

Provisional Edition, Sudan Survey Department, 1965. 1:50,000.

Chronology

[The prehistoric, ancient, and Christian history of the Sudan (Nubia) is covered far more fully in the *Historical Dictionary of Ancient Nubia*. These events are presented here in abbreviated form to link the two works.]

Some Early Turning Points

5000–3500 B.C.E.   Very late Mesolithic or very Early Neolithic, as in Kadero, Kadada, and Al-Shaheinab sites, pastoralism and agriculture.

3250 B.C.E.   Classic A-Group in lower Nubia.

3100 B.C.E.   Unification of Upper and Lower Egypt. Raiding against the Ta-Seti in Sudanese Nubia.

2700–2100 B.C.E.   Period of growing contact with Egypt and some Egyptian attacks in Nubia.

2300–1900 B.C.E.   Rise of C-Horizon and relative decline of Egyptian influence in the Sudan.

2250–2050 B.C.E.   Rise of Kerma at the third cataract. Africa's oldest state outside of Egypt.

2065–1780 B.C.E.   Reunification of Egypt in the Middle Kingdom.

1900–1575 B.C.E.   Expansion of Kerma Culture.

1887–1850 B.C.E.   Pharaoh Senwosret III raids Nubia.

1786–1567 B.C.E.   Hyksos seek Nubian allies against Egypt.

1570–1090 B.C.E.   Egyptian New Kingdom pharaohs rule the northern Sudan reaching the fourth cataract.

1069–715 B.C.E.   Third Intermediate Period in Egypt.

Kingdom of Kush Emerges at Napata

ca. 950 B.C.E.   Kushites seek to expand into Egypt.

ca. 800 B.C.E.   Kush expands northward due to a weak Egypt. Piankhy claims Thebes as province of Kush.

Kushite Rule of all of Egypt as Dynasty XXV

760–656 B.C.E.   Reunification of Egypt under the Kushite "Ethiopian" Dynasty XXV.

656–590 B.C.E.   Kushite withdrawal back to the Sudan. The worship of Amun continues at Jebel Barkal and Napata.

Kingdom of Kush Moves to Meroë

590 B.C.E.–ca. 325 C.E.   Period of Kush at Meroë. The kings of Kush continue to be "Lords of Two Lands."

Greeks Enter Nile Valley

332 B.C.E.   Conquest of Egypt by Alexander of Macedonia. Expeditions sent to Nubia; Greek language and culture introduced to Meroë.

323 B.C.E.   Rise of the Ptolemies.

270 B.C.E.   Napatan period of Kush comes to an end.

47–30 B.C.E.   Reign of Cleopatra VII and Ptolemy XV, initially as coregents, then Cleopatra VII rules alone.

Romans Enter Nile Valley

30–28 B.C.E.   Roman conquest of Egypt under Octavian; suicides of Cleopatra and Antony. The end of the Ptolemies.

24 B.C.E.   Meroites raid Elephantine Island and Philae at Aswan.

21–20 B.C.E.   Peace treaty between Romans and Meroites.

Christianity Enters Nile Valley

37 C.E.   First Christian enters Nubia.

61   Nero sends "explorers" to Nubia.

64   Expansion of Christian persecution.

ca. 260–300   Widespread introduction of Coptic Christianity.

284–304   Diocletian withdraws from Nubia. Persecution of Christians.

312   Emperor Constantine accepts Christianity as the Roman religion.

ca. 325   King Ezana begins Christianity in Ethiopia and destroys Meroë.

350–550   Period of X-Group at Ballana, Tanqasi, and Qustul.

ca. 536   Nubian King Silko drives out Blemmyes from Nobatia. Isis cult at Philae suppressed by Justinian. Silko is considered to be the first Christian king of Nubia.

543   Faras established as Christian capital of Nobatia.

ca. 560   Missionary Longinus at Nobatia and Alwa.

ca. 569   Dongola established as capital of Mukurra.

579   Conversion to Christianity of the kingdom of Alwa.

580   Missionary Longinus at Alwa or Meroë.

Islam Enters Egypt

639–640   Arab Muslim conquest of Egypt and beginning of Muslim contacts with the northern Sudan; Nubians forced to pay tribute in slaves and livestock and promise no aggression against Egypt.

639   'Amr ibn al-As reaches north of Dongola but fails to capture it.

646   Egyptians attack Nubia.

652   *Baqt* treaty established between Nubia and Egypt under 'Abdallah ibn Sa'ad ibn Abi Sahr. Nubia would provide 360 slaves each year, promising no attacks; Egypt would provide 1,300 *kanyr* of wine. Old Dongola is captured for a period. Conflicts noted between Makuria and Nobatia.

661–750 Umayyad Dynasty in Egypt.

697–707 Merger of Nobatia and Mukurra under King Merkurius.

720 *Baqt* established between Egyptians and Beja.

740–750 Cyriacus, king of Dongola, lays siege to Umayyad capital at Fustat (Cairo).

750–870 Abbasid Dynasty in Egypt.

758 Abbasids complain of no *baqt* payments and Blemmyes attack Upper Egypt.

819–822 King of Dongola and Beja refuse to pay *baqt* tribute and mount attacks on Egypt.

835 George I (816–920) crowned king of Dongola. George I travels to Baghdad and Cairo.

868–884 Ahmad ibn Tulun rules Egypt; large numbers of Nubians in Tulunid army.

920 Christian King Zakaria starts his reign at Dongola.

950 Some Muslims reported at Soba.

951, 956, 962 Nubian raids into Upper Egypt.

969–1171 Fatimid rule in Egypt; Arab adventurer al-'Umari attacks Nubia.

969 King George II attacks Egypt.

ca. 1000 Nilotic cattle pastoralists expand into southern Sudan.

ca. 1050 Some 50,000 Nubians serve in Fatimid army.

1171–1250 Ayyubid Dynasty in Egypt.

1172 Saladin (Ayyubid) forces Nubians to withdraw to Upper Egypt; George IV is Nubian king.

1140–1150 Christian kingdom of Dotawo (Daw) noted in Nubia.

1163 Crusaders attack Ayyubids and ally with Nubian Christians.

1172 Crusaders attack Ayyubids in Cairo and Delta towns; Turanshah attacks Nubia.

ca. 1200   Rise of the Daju Dynasty in Darfur. Movement of Dinka and Nuer populations into Bahr al-Ghazal and Upper Nile.

1204   Nubian and Crusader leaders meet in Constantinople.

1235   Last priest sent to Nubia from Alexandria.

1250–1382   Bahri Mamluk Dynasty in Egypt.

Islam Penetrates Nubia

1260–1277   Forces of Mamluk Sultan Al-Zahir Baybars attack Nubia.

1264   Nubians again pay *baqt* tribute to Mamluks.

1268   King of Dongola, Dawud, pays *baqt* to Mamluks.

1275   King Dawud raids Aswan.

1275–1365   Period of warfare between Mamluks and Nubians.

1276   Mamluk Egyptians sack Dongola, with forced conversion to Islam and King Dawud captured.

1289   Last Mamluk military campaign against Dongola.

1317   Defeat of the last Christian king in Nubia, and the first Muslim king, 'Abdullah Barshambu, accedes to the throne in Dongola; *baqt* reestablished and first mosque built at Dongola.

1372   Bishop of Faras consecrated by the patriarch in Alexandria.

1382–1517   Circassian (Burji) Mamluk Dynasty in Egypt.

1400s   Probable time of the replacement of the Daju by the Tunjur Dynasty in Darfur. Luo migrations from the southern Sudan lead to creation of Shilluk groups.

Islam in the Central Sudan: Rise of Funj and Fur Sultanates

1504   The fall of Soba, capital of the last Christian kingdom of Alwa, and the beginning of the Islamic Funj Sultanate at Sennar.

1517–1805   Sultan Selim I comes to power in Egypt; Mamluks defeated; rule of Ottoman prefects.

1520 Portuguese Francisco Alvares visits Ethiopia; Nubians appeal for help from Ethiopian priests.

1521 Jewish traveler David Reubeni visits Soba and Sennar. He then meets the pope and Spanish king, offering a plan to resist Turks.

1535 Tunjur defeated by Bornu from Nigeria.

1580–1660 Beginning of Keira rule in Darfur.

1610 Alliance of the Funj and 'Abdallab.

1647 Portuguese priests, Giovanni d'Aguila and António da Pesco-pagano, visit Sennar.

ca. 1660 Shayqiya revolt against the 'Abdallab.

1699–1711 Three papal missions to Ethiopia, via Dongola and Sennar.

1742 Practicing Christians still reported in Nubia.

1750s–1890s Azande people spread southeast and north into the Sudan.

1761 Muhammad Abu Likaylik takes control of the Funj Sultanate, beginning the Hamaj dominance over subsequent sultans.

ca. 1770 'Abdallab revolt against the Funj.

1772 Scottish explorer, James Bruce, visits Bejrawiya, Qerri, Sennar, and central Sudan.

1782 End of Funj influence at Dongola.

1805–1848 Rule of Muhammad 'Ali in Egypt.

1813 J. L. Burckhardt, a Swiss explorer, visits Nubia (Abu Simbel) and elsewhere in the Nile Valley.

1819 First Meroitic transcription published by F. C. Gau.

The Turkiya

1820–1822 Ottomans from Egypt conquer much of the northern part of the Sudan, ending the Funj Sultanate and establishing the Turco-Egyptian regime. Heavy tax burden in slaves imposed on riverine Sudanese.

1822 November. Isma'il Pasha and retinue killed at Shendi by Mek Nimr and his Ja'aliyin followers. Short-lived revolt against Turkiya.

1823–1824 Muhammad Bey Khusraw ("Daftardar") harshly puts down uprising, burning towns and massacring their inhabitants throughout the Nile Valley.

1824–1825 'Uthman Bey governs with the assistance of professional soldiers of slave origin (*jihadiya*). Beginnings of Khartoum as a military, later administrative, center. Harsh taxation prompts flight of riverine Sudanese from the Nile. Depopulation, smallpox, drought, and famine abound.

1825–1826 Mahu Bey as governor, with reconciliation of Sudanese, reduction of taxes, and restoration of order.

1826–1838 'Ali Khurshid Agha governs, developing civil administration. Cultivation increases, fugitives from regime granted amnesty, and Sudanese serve as advisors to government. Khartoum develops, trade increases, and prosperity returns. Failed raids in South, East, and Ethiopian borderlands.

1834 Ferlini raids the jewel hoard of the pyramid of Queen Amanishakhete at Bejrawiya cemetery.

1838–1843 Abu Widan is governor-general (*hukumdar*). Fiscal and land regulation. Shayqiya resistance to tax policies. Extension of government control toward Red Sea coast.

1838 Successful penetration of *Sudd* swamp in southern Sudan by Captain Salim Qabudan, a Turkish sailor.

1840s Period of weak administration in Sudan: frequent changes of government and reorganizations of administrative districts. Trade in ivory and slaves on Upper Nile and Bahr al-Ghazal by Europeans and riverine Sudanese *Jallaba*. Christian missions in south.

1844 Birth of Muhammad Ahmad (the Mahdi) on Labab Island near Dongola. The Prussian Egyptologist Carl Richard Lepsius (1810–1884) begins serious Meroitic archaeology.

1851 Coptic church built in Khartoum.

1863–1879 Reign of Khedive Isma'il in Egypt. Largely unsuccessful efforts to suppress slave trade and establish Khedival control in south. European Christians in employ of government, including Samuel Baker (1869–1873) and Charles Gordon (1874–1876). Rise of "merchant princes" in Upper Nile and Bahr al-Ghazal. Government steamers introduced on Nile; telegraph system links Khartoum with Egypt, Suakin, Kassala, and el-Obeid.

1863 Suakin and Massawa ceded to Egypt by Ottoman Empire. Official opening of the Suez Canal in Egypt.

1873–1874 Zubayr Rahma Mansur is governor of Bahr al-Ghazal, conquering Darfur for Turkiya.

1877–1880 Charles Gordon is governor-general, as the first Christian and European to hold this office. Further attempts to suppress slave trade.

1879 Bishop of Nubia and Khartoum established in Khartoum.

The Mahdiya

1881 Muhammad Ahmad reveals himself to be the "Expected Mahdi" and invites followers to Aba Island. A government force sent to arrest him is defeated, and Mahdists (Ansar) make famous emigration to Jabal Qadir in Nuba mountains. A second government force is defeated: Ansar win booty and arms and give the Mahdi prestige.

1882 Third government force under Yusuf Pasha al-Shallali is destroyed. Failed Mahdist attack at el-Obeid ("Friday Battle"); Ansar now include *jihadiya* soldiers with rifles.

1883 Bara and el-Obeid capitulate to Mahdi. Expedition of Col. William Hicks annihilated at Shaykan. Slatin Pasha, governor of Darfur, surrenders; Mahdi now controls virtually all territories of the west. 'Uthman Diqna leads Mahdist revolt in the east, aided by Majadhib of al-Damer and Hadendowa people. Sieges of Sinkat and Tokar on the Red Sea.

1884 January. Gen. Charles Gordon leaves Cairo for Sudan as governor-general.

February. Gordon reaches Berber, publicly reveals Egypt's intention to abandon Sudan, and revokes ban on slavery. Sudanese loyalists are alarmed. Gordon arrives in Khartoum determined to "smash the Mahdi."

May. Berber taken by Mahdists and Khartoum isolated. Most of the East is now under Mahdist control.

August–October. Gordon Rescue Mission approved by British parliament, but army tarries in Egypt. Khartoum is besieged by Mahdists under 'Abd al-Rahman al-Nujumi. Mahdi encamps south of Omdurman.

1885 January. Fort Omdurman capitulates; Khartoum is taken by Mahdists, and Gordon is killed.

June. Mahdi dies in Omdurman, probably of typhus. 'Abdullahi al-Ta'aishi ("The Khalifa") succeeds him as ruler of the Mahdist state.

1886–1887 The Khalifa neutralizes Dongolawi opposition, removing enemies from power. Western revolts suppressed. Ansar faithful make pilgrimage to "holy city" of Omdurman. Northern Egyptian threat diminishes.

1886 January. Mahdists invade Ethiopia and enter Gondar.

May–December. Migration of Baqqara tribes (Rizayqat, Habbaniya, Ta'aisha) to Omdurman; increased friction between riverine (*Awlad al-Balad*) and western (*Awlad al-Arab*) peoples. Failed harvest in Sudan.

1889 Famine: Khalifa resolves to feed Baqqara and city population from the Gezira; thousands perish.

March. Mahdists defeat Ethiopians at Qallabat; King John IV is killed.

August. Mahdist army destroyed at battle of Tushki and al-Nujumi is killed; effective end of northern *jihad*.

1891 Revolt of Mahdi's kinsmen (*Ashraf*) in Omdurman is settled by mediation; Khalifa punishes Dongolawi opponents and imprisons junior *khalifa* Muhammad Sharif until 1896.

1894 Italians attack and occupy Kassala; Italians in Eritrea since 1890.

1896 Anglo-Egyptian invasion of Sudan commences. King Menelik defeats Italians at Adowa.

1897 The French Marchand expedition to Upper Nile commences. Ja'aliyin of Matamma defy Khalifa and seek Anglo-Egyptian support; Matamma destroyed by Ansar under Mahmud Ahmad, sealing Ja'ali hatred of Mahdist regime.

September. Anglo-Egyptians occupy Berber.

November. Trans-Nubian railroad reaches Abu Hamad, ensuring Anglo-Egyptian military supply line.

1898 April. Mahmud Ahmad's army defeated at Atbara.

2 September. Mahdist forces destroyed at battle of Karari; Omdurman taken. Khalifa flees with small following. Mahdiya ended.

Anglo-Egyptian Condominium

1899 British and French forces almost fight at Fashoda in imperialist rivalry for control of the Upper Nile Valley. Condominium Rule of the Sudan established by Great Britain and Egypt. Khartoum restored as capital; Suakin enters decline. Final destruction of Mahdiya. Muhammad Sharif and two sons of Mahdi executed at Shukkaba; Khalifa 'Abdullahi, 'Ali wad Hilu, and last of the loyal Ansar killed at Umm Dibaykarat in Kordofan.

1900–1912 Period of Messianic/anticolonial revolts in western and central Sudan.

1904 Foundation of new Coptic cathedral in Khartoum.

1905 Sudanese Antiquities Ordinance passed; Construction of the Atbara-Port Sudan railroad.

1905–1919 Missionaries return to southern Sudan.

1905 Work begins on building Port Sudan, replacing Suakin as the major Sudanese harbor on the Red Sea.

1909 J. Garstang excavates at Meroë; F. Griffith transcribes numerous Meroitic texts.

1913–1923 Egyptologist George Reisner excavates at Kerma.

1914 2 August. Turks enter World War I on side of Germany.

18 December. As war begins, Britain establishes formal protectorate over Egypt and continues its military rule of the Sudan.

1916 Sultan 'Ali Dinar in Darfur defeated, bringing an end to the Keira Dynasty and resulting in the full incorporation of the province into the Anglo-Egyptian Sudan.

1922 28 February. Egypt establishes a monarchy independent of Turkey but under British protectorate status.

1923 24 July. Treaty of Lausanne is ratified by Turkey, nullifying its claims to Egypt and the Sudan.

1924 Major nationalist outbreaks in the Sudan. White Flag League and other groups lead anti-imperialist demonstrations. Egyptian influence reduced in the Sudan, military mutineers defeated, and nationalism temporarily suppressed.

19 November. British reaction to nationalist outbreaks intensified by the assassination of Lee Stack, governor-general of the Sudan in Cairo.

1925 Completion of the Sennar Dam and opening of the Gezira agricultural scheme.

1930 Introduction of policy of separation of North and South.

1931 Student strike at Gordon College over pay cuts for Sudanese employed by the government.

1935 Fascist Italy invades Ethiopia; the Sudan remains under British control.

1936 Anglo-Egyptian Treaty signed, reducing the restrictions on Egyptians in the Sudan.

1938 Formation of the Graduates Congress.

1940–1942 World War II fighting in North Africa: Italian and British forces fight in Libya and German Field Marshal Rommel begins Axis Powers' offensive in North Africa. British General Montgomery wins victory at El Alamein after huge losses.

1942 Presentation of the Graduates Congress memorandum speaking in the name of the Sudanese; British reject claims of the Congress.

1943–1945 Formation of the first political parties in the Sudan: Ashigga, Umma, and others.

1943 Creation of the Advisory Council for the Northern Sudan.

1946 Reversal of the southern policy of separation.

1947 Juba Conference, where southern leaders accept the idea of unification of the southern and northern parts of the Sudan.

1948 Opening of the Legislative Assembly; establishment of two Coptic Dioceses in the Sudan.

14 May. Proclamation of the State of Israel; Arab nations muster unsuccessful military opposition.

1952 Enactment of the Self-Government Statute, providing for Sudanese self-government after an indefinite period.

23 July. Egyptian Free Officers Movement deposes King Faruq.

1953 Anglo-Egyptian Agreement prepares the steps toward self-government. The first Parliament is elected with a majority of seats won by the National Unionist Party (NUP) led by Isma'il al-Azhari. Southern Sudanese generally excluded from these agreements by northern parties and politicians.

1954 Formation of the Southern Liberal Party (SLP).

1954–1955 Sudanization of the army and administration with a cabinet led by Isma'il al-Azhari.

1955 18 August. Equatoria Corps of the Sudan Defense Force mutinies in Torit with many northerners and southerners killed, a result of southern fears of northern dominance. This launches decades of civil war between North and South.

The Independent Sudan

1956 1 January. Anglo-Egyptian Condominium rule is terminated and Sudanese independence proclaimed. In a political shift resulting from the creation of the People's Democratic Party (PDP), a PDP-Umma coalition government led by 'Abdallah Khalil replaces the government of al-Azhari.

26 July. Egypt nationalizes the Suez Canal.

29 October. Britain, France, and Israel invade Egypt over the issue of Suez access. Conflict is terminated by United Nations and United States intervention.

1957 Mission schools placed under the authority of the Ministry of Education. The Constituent Assembly rejects the Federation of the South and insists on unity.

1958 New Parliamentary elections held; the PDP-Umma coalition continues.

22 February. Egypt and Syria form United Arab Republic, representing radical Arab nationalism.

17 November. Fearing regional destabilization and Arab radicalism, a military coup in the north by General Ibrahim Abboud terminates parliament.

1959 Nile waters agreement with Egypt outlining Egyptian compensation for lands flooded by waters rising above the Aswan Dam.

1960 Formation of the Sudan African Closed Districts National Union, in exile; vigorous Arabization and Islamization of the South.

1960–1964 International UNESCO Campaign to Save the Monuments of Nubia.

1961–1962 New constitutional law promulgated, creating provincial councils and a national council.

1963–1963 Intensification of the conflict in the South, accompanied by the establishment of Anya-Nya and Sudan African National Union (SANU).

1964 October Revolution ousts Abboud regime after a series of demonstrations and strikes. A transitional government is formed by Sirr al-Khatim al-Khalifa. Restoration of civilian government.

1965 New elections for parliament. National Unionist Party (NUP) and Umma Party alliance results in a government headed by Muhammad Ahmad Mahjoub. Southern Front representatives in cabinet agree to have elections in the North only, but NUP and Umma do not address their issues.

26 March. Khartoum Round Table Conference attempts to find a solution to conflict in the southern Sudan, but Umma and NUP fail to provide opportunities for southerners and soon turn to military "solutions" for the South. Southern politician William Deng returns from exile and is promised amnesty.

1966 Split within the Umma Party brings down Mahjoub government, which is replaced by a cabinet led by Sadiq al-Mahdi.

1967 Muhammad Ahmad Mahjoub becomes prime minister again.

May. United Nations forces withdraw from Israeli frontier. Outbreak of "Six Day War" between Israel and Arab coalition led by Egypt. Sudan sends forces to fight in this war. Israel gains territory from contiguous Arab nations that suffer humiliating defeat. Sudan hosts an Arab summit conference in Khartoum to map a new Arab strategy.

1968 General election held and the Mahjoub government, with some changes, continues.

April. William Deng assassinated by government soldiers in Rumbek.

1969 25 May. Military coup in Sudan is led by Colonel Ja'afar Nimeiri. His government begins with radical Arab nationalism and leftist orientation:

new policies of amnesty and regional autonomy for the southern Sudan and a broad socialist program for economic and social development, including widespread nationalization of private holdings.

9 June. Declaration of "regional autonomy" for southern Sudan to resolve the intermittent civil war.

1970 March. Revolt of the Ansar under Imam al-Hadi al-Mahdi is defeated by Nimeiri.

May. Banks and businesses nationalized and a five-year development plan is initiated.

28 September. President Nasser of Egypt dies of a heart attack and is replaced by Vice-President Anwar Sadat.

November. Sudan agrees with Egypt and Libya on basic steps to be taken for eventual tripartite federation.

1971 May. First steps to create the Sudan Socialist Union (SSU) and new constitutional regime. Joseph Garang helps form the Sudan African Socialist Union (SASU).

July. Government briefly taken over by a group of Communist-backed officers. In aftermath of the abortive coup, Communist Party leaders and others are jailed or executed.

September. Referendum confirms Nimeiri as president.

1972 January. SSU officially established, with first SSU Congress giving its approval to the National Charter. Basic outline of the permanent constitution approved, and the SSU Political Bureau formed.

March. Addis Ababa accords contain a settlement between Sudanese government and southern leaders by recognizing regional autonomy.

September. Elections held for the new People's Assembly.

1973 March. Palestinians in Khartoum capture and kill foreign diplomats.

Summer. Discontent over economic conditions; state of emergency declared briefly.

6 October. Yom Kippur War between Israel and Egypt.

December. First Popular Regional Assembly for the southern region created. Ratification of Constitution.

1974   4 March. Israel returns Suez Canal control to Egypt.

April. Egypt and Sudan announce measures for closer cooperation.

May. Nimeiri charges Libya with attempting to overthrow Sudanese government.

Fall. Many agreements with other Arab countries announced to help finance Sudanese agricultural and industrial development. Juba mutiny.

1975   March. Incident at Akobo reveals some southern unrest, but basic lines of southern settlement continue in effect.

May. Major development budget announced.

June and July. Further measures of Egyptian-Sudanese cooperation announced.

1976   January. $700-million plan for agricultural development announced, involving more than 60 projects in the next decade.

June. Nimeiri visits United States for talks on economic and political cooperation.

July. Attempted coup, blamed on Sadiq al-Mahdi and Libya.

August. Nimeiri forms new cabinet, relinquishing post of prime minister to Rashid al-Tahir.

October. Continuing Sudanese–Saudi Arabian cooperation affirmed during state visit to the Sudan by King Khalid of Saudi Arabia.

1977   January. Continuing crisis over Sudanese-Ethiopian territorial incursions. Nimeiri announces support for Eritrean independence.

February. A major cabinet reorganization, with Rashid al-Tahir remaining prime minister. National Congress of the SSU is held and Nimeiri reelected president of the SSU. Policy of "National Reconciliation" incorporates Sadiq al-Mahdi and Muslim Brothers in government. Committee established to conform Sudanese law to the teachings of Shari'a. Mutiny at Juba airport.

September. Sadiq al-Mahdi returns from exile.

November. President Sadat of Egypt visits Israel.

1978   18–22 July. Organization of African Unity meetings held in Khartoum.

1979   January. Meeting of High Ministerial Committee on Integration between Egypt and Sudan.

26 March. Egypt and Israel sign peace accords; Egypt is suspended from the Arab League.

April. Sudan and Iraq break diplomatic relations.

9–12 August. Urban riots over price increases; Nimeiri becomes secretary-general of the SSU and promises to punish 'Communist' agitators.

September. Sudan and Uganda restore diplomatic relations.

1980   February. Nimeiri issues decree dissolving Parliament and regional legislative assembly of southern Sudan.

March. University of Khartoum closed following student rioting.

November. Sudanese-French agreement signed for oil and gas exploration in southern Sudan.

1981   6 October. President Sadat of Egypt assassinated by Islamic extremist group and replaced by Husni Mubarak.

November. International Monetary Fund economic reforms are instituted by Nimeiri as prerequisite for $230 million in aid; prices of sugar, petrol, and cooking oil rise.

1982   January. Students protesting economic reforms burn 120 shops in Khartoum; all universities and other schools closed; schools reopen forty-five days later. Chad-Sudan border conflict resolved and relations normalized. Nimeiri dissolves Central Committee and high-ranking leadership of the SSU and appoints seventy-eight new members; coup attempt reportedly foiled.

May. Egyptian Defense Minister Abu Ghazala in Khartoum for discussion of integration of Egyptian and Sudanese armed forces.

June. Joseph Lagu sworn in as vice-president of Sudan; Muslim Brother 'Abd al-Rahman Abu Zayd appointed vice-chancellor of Juba University.

October. Husni Mubarak arrives in Khartoum to sign political and economic treaty that stops short of Egypt-Sudan union.

November. People's Assembly endorses Egyptian-Sudanese integration.

1983   February. Sudan accuses Libya of massing troops near its border.

26 April. Nimeiri elected for third term as president by national referendum.

16 May. Kerubino Bol and William Bany revolt from Sudanese Army Battalion 105 (former Anya-Nya) at Bor and Wat in Jonglei area.

18–19 May. Sudan army claims defeat of mutiny by a battalion of the Southern Command at Pibor and Bor.

22 May. Nimeiri divides the southern region into three subregions.

25 May. Opening session of joint Sudanese-Egyptian Parliament of the Nile Valley with Presidents Mubarak and Nimeiri presiding.

5 June. Amidst stalled southern governments, Nimeiri issues Republican Order No. 1, which abrogates the 1972 Addis Ababa Accords and self-government for the South.

31 July. The Sudanese Peoples Liberation Movement (SPLM) is founded under John Garang. The SPLM resumes military activity against the government of Sadiq al-Mahdi.

8 September. Islamic Shari'a introduced to replace civil penal codes.

29 September. Nimeiri releases 13,000 convicted prisoners; secular laws now superseded by Islamic criminal codes.

30 September. Sadiq al-Mahdi arrested for opposing the process of Islamization.

28 October. Nimeiri holds that some Islamic laws apply to non-Muslims.

November. Southern antigovernment forces hold eleven foreign workers hostage, demanding repeal of Islamic law.

December. Sudanese Peoples Liberation Army (SPLA) briefly captures the southern town of Nasir.

1984 February. Southern rebels overrun Chevron oil drilling site at Bentiu. Chevron halts its operation to protect its workers. Rebels attack Jonglei canal construction site, kidnapping seven French workers. Nile river barges attacked 104 kilometers south of Malakal.

March. Nimeiri threatens to go to war with Libya and Ethiopia for alleged support of rebels; United States agrees to airlift supplies to Sudan for use in south. Omdurman bombed and Nimeiri blames Libya. United States charges Libya with attack and promises aid to Sudan. Two thousand Sudanese doctors resign to protest poor wages and working conditions; Nimeiri responds by dissolving their union.

April. Professors at the University of Khartoum join the physicians' strike; Nimeiri imposes state of emergency to control unrest, corruption, opposition to Islamic law, and southern rebellion.

May. Two public limb amputations for thieves, bringing the total to nine.

June. Chevron oil resumes its operations in South.

August. Opposition parties form the National Salvation Front (NSF).

September. Nimeiri lifts state of emergency.

2 November. SPLA Radio begins transmission in English and Arabic.

December. Heavy fighting around Juba; government holds town.

1985 January. Sudan cancels its cooperation with Israel to airlift Ethiopian Jews. Mahmud Muhammad Taha and four others sentenced to death for opposing Islamization of law.

18 January. Taha executed at Kober prison; the others renounce their leader and are released.

8 February. Hasan al-Turabi resigns as assistant to President Nimeiri.

17 February. University of Khartoum closed indefinitely after student protests. United States announces delay in $194 million aid.

4 March. U.S. Vice-President George Bush visits Khartoum for drought relief.

11 March. Police arrest 100 Muslim Brothers, including Hasan al-Turabi.

16 March. Nimeiri appoints Suwar al-Dahab as defense minister.

27 March. Nimeiri leaves for visit to Washington, DC. Three killed and many wounded in Khartoum protests against price increases.

3 April. The largest demonstration in Sudanese history demands Nimeiri's ouster and a return to democracy; President Reagan and Nimeiri meet in Washington, DC, and the United States releases $67 million in aid. Telephone and telex communications cut and Khartoum airport closed. President Mubarak announces that Egypt will not intervene to save Nimeiri.

6 April. General Suwar al-Dahab seizes power in coup for "an interim period"; hundreds of thousands celebrate in Khartoum. Prison doors are forced open. Suwar al-Dahab pledges to keep Sudan on pro-Western course and Reagan announces no change in policy. Southern opposition hails the ouster of Nimeiri.

8 April. Thousands demonstrate for democracy and civilian rule; Nimeiri informs Suwar al-Dahab that he understands the reasons for the coup and wishes the new regime well.

9 April. John Garang announces truce and asks for civilian rule in seven days.

10 April. Suwar al-Dahab and the professional unions agree to one-year interim period before election; the SPLA is not consulted.

13 April. Suwar al-Dahab pledges to "amend" Islamic law in order to eliminate "incorrect" and "excessive" punishments.

14 April. Hasan al-Turabi addresses large rally in Khartoum, calling for an "Islamic Front" to protect Shari'a law in Sudan.

16 April. Transitional Military Council (TMC) includes southerners.

18 April. Muslim Brotherhood rally of 30,000–40,000 in support of Shari'a law, "the only real achievement of the Nimeiri regime."

25 April. TMC invites Anya-Nya II to discuss the "Southern Problem."

26 April. Suwar al-Dahab declares cease-fire in south and general amnesty.

30 April. The SPLA denounces "new militarists" in Khartoum.

11 May. Founding of the National Islamic Front (NIF). Nimeiri's "Courts of Prompt Justice" abolished.

24 June. Egypt will not extradite Nimeiri to Sudan, despite the case against him for Taha execution.

22 September. Government bans demonstrations during state of emergency.

27 September. Garang supporters revolt in Khartoum and Omdurman but are defeated. Philip Ghaboush arrested in connection with the uprising.

3 December. Government introduces tough measures to stop illegal strikes.

30 December. Attorney General 'Abd al-Ati amends penal code to nullify September laws but still adheres to principles of Shari'a.

1986 Formation of the Intergovernmental Authority on Drought and Desertification (IGADD), a significant forum for cease-fires and peace negotiations in Sudan.

February. The International Monetary Fund (IMF) refuses more credit to Sudan.

1 March. Umma Party elects Sadiq al-Mahdi as leader.

5 March. SPLA troops capture Rumbek; Juba airport closed.

24 March. Koka Dam Declaration signed in Ethiopia by major Sudanese parties, excluding the NIF and proposing a peace framework.

30 March. TMC Cabinet dissolves integration agreement with Egypt.

1–11 April. First multiparty election since 1968 held with 30 parties competing for 301 seats in National Assembly.

17 April. Umma Party wins 97 of 207 seats in Constituent Assembly to form coalition government.

6 May. Sadiq al-Mahdi becomes prime minister for a second time.

18 October. Operation Rainbow airlifts 232 tons of relief to southern Sudan.

31 October. Government expels UN official for contact with SPLA to expedite food shipments to the South.

2–3 November. Police fire on student demonstrators in Khartoum, but protests continue; NIF blamed for the riots.

19 November. Prime Minister al-Mahdi announces new laws to replace the Shari'a law introduced by Nimeiri.

9 December. Prime minister says Sudan will export a food surplus.

1987 Al-Mahdi government uses militias to war in the South. SPLA captures Kurmuk, but government forces recover it.

January. "Sudan Charter: National Unity and Diversity" issued by NIF.

27 March. Philip Ghaboush, leader of the Sudanese National Party (SNP), is arrested and charged with "illicit wealth, swindling, and forgery."

28–29 March. As many as 1,000 southerners massacred by northern militias at al-Da'in in southern Darfur.

April. Former U.S. President Carter initiates IGADD talks between North and South to bring the Sudanese conflict to an end.

26 April. Two days of mourning declared in memory of "mysterious" death in 1970 of Imam al-Hadi al-Mahdi, uncle of the prime minister.

1 May. Ansar leaders announce Sadiq al-Mahdi nominated as spiritual leader of the sect succeeding his uncle.

24 August. Addis Ababa "Struggle for Peace and Democracy" forum held in Ethiopia; joint statement of SPLM/SPLA and Anya-Nya II, supporting Koka Dam Declaration.

8 September. Quest for Peace Communiqué, issued by Sudan African Parties and SPLM/SPLA, supporting Koka Dam Declaration.

1988 15 May. Palestinian *fedayeen* attack Sudan Club killing seven British and Sudanese. Relations sour between Khartoum, the United Kingdom, and United States.

27 July. The minister of finance indicates Sudan's $3 billion debt will rise to $5.5 billion in 1990. Worst floods in Sudan in four decades.

8 August. Government announces 1.5 million are homeless due to flooding.

9 August. Prime Minister al-Mahdi declares state of emergency due to flooding; 80 people dead and 83,000 homes destroyed.

18 August. SPLM/SPLA meet in Addis with DUP delegation.

4 September. Thousands die of starvation in South due to war and flooding.

16 September. SPLA forces capture Jebel Lado 25 kilometers north of Juba.

19 September. Non-Muslim African parties leave Constituent Assembly to protest introduction of new Shari'a codes.

6 October. National Assembly withdraws plan to introduce new Shari'a codes.

13 October. United States airlifts food and supplies to southern Sudan.

25 October. Government says it controls all major southern towns.

30 October. Demonstrations in Khartoum and Omdurman over food shortages.

13 November. DUP leader Muhammad al-Mirghani meets John Garang in Addis Ababa, signing agreement with framework to end civil war.

19 November. The NIF rejects DUP-SPLA agreement.

22 November. Thousands of NIF supporters and southerners battle in Khartoum street due to DUP-SPLA agreement.

14 December. Prime Minister al-Mahdi supports DUP-SPLA agreement and requests Assembly authorization to implement agreement.

21 December. Constituent Assembly rejects al-Mahdi's request but authorizes convening of constitutional conference.

26 December. Government price hikes result in strikes that paralyze Khartoum.

29 December. Government rescinds price rises.

1989 2 January. Judges and magistrates resign nationwide to protest "interference" of executive authorities in legal affairs.

9 January. The SPLA charges chemical weapons are being used in the South; al-Mahdi establishes committee to contact SLM/SPLA.

24 January. Prime minister asks to extend the constitutional conference.

31 January. Hasan al-Turabi appointed deputy prime minister.

1 February. United States offers to mediate civil war.

21 February. Armed forces commander and 150 officers ask Prime Minister al-Mahdi for action on economic deterioration, a balanced foreign policy, and an end to civil war.

22 February. International Red Cross resumes relief flights to the South.

26 February. SPLA captures Torit, near Juba. Constituent Assembly introduces emergency preventive detention for up to ten days. The United States and DUP offer to mediate an end to the war.

3 March. The SPLA captures Nimule, near Ugandan border.

4 March. Leaders of major parties, except the NIF, trade associations, and labor unions sign the "Seven-Point Program, National Declaration for Peace."

6 March. DUP, trade associations, and labor unions call for resignation of prime minister. SPLA shells Juba and controls most of Equatoria.

9 March. Food relief convoy of 230 trucks arrives in Wau.

10 March. Broad political coalition issues ultimatum that Prime Minister al-Mahdi submit government's resignation within twenty-four hours.

12 March. State Council accepts resignation of cabinet, but the prime minister does not resign.

17 March. Demonstration at British embassy protests Salman Rushdie's *Satanic Verses.*

2 April. Prime Minister voids Sudan-Egypt defense agreement void.

10 April. NIF Speaker of Constituent Assembly resigns to protest shelving of debate on implementation of Shari'a.

11 April. SPLA captures Akoba in Upper Nile. Government ends three-day talks with SPLA representatives in Addis Ababa.

24 April. Imam, in Omdurman, sentenced to two months in prison for inciting worshippers to attack a Christian "charity compound."

26 April. International aid workers expect 100,000-ton food shipment to fall short of needs, placing 100,000 Sudanese in danger of starvation.

7 May. Prime minister announces new experiment in application of Shari'a that would preserve the rights of non-Muslims.

1 June. SPLA leader John Garang announces three conditions for peace: freezing Shari'a laws, canceling emergency laws, and ending all defense agreements with Egypt and Libya.

28 June. Prime minister demands that Egypt expel Nimeiri after allowing him to speak to Egyptian press about his political aspirations.

30 June. Al-Mahdi government toppled in a coup led by Brigadier General 'Umar Hasan Ahmad al-Bashir and his fifteen-member Revolutionary Command Council (RCC) that dismisses senior commanders and places government officials under arrest. Bashir moves quickly to ban all trade unions and political parties. Property owned by political parties is confiscated. Foreign currency can no longer be held by private citizens. It is widely understood that Islamist intellectual and lawyer Hasan al-Turabi and his NIF played the "king-maker" role, providing ideological underpinnings of the government.

2 July. Government closes all trade unions, political parties, and associations, ending Sudan's third period of democracy; most former high-ranking government officials are arrested.

4 July. Al-Bashir declares a brief cease-fire in the civil war, offers amnesty to opponents, and asks Garang to discuss an end to the war.

6 July. Former Prime Minister al-Mahdi arrested by security forces in Khartoum. Al-Bashir announces that al-Mahdi will be tried for corruption and economic sabotage and could face the death penalty.

9 July. New government is announced. New investigative committees, price courts, and appeals courts established with the RCC Council of Ministers as highest constitutional authority.

13 July. Al-Bashir says issue of Shari'a should be settled by referendum; he does not object to "separation" of the South, as long as a federal system of government is enacted; RCC spokesman denies report.

19 July. Garang announces conditions for meeting al-Bashir, including clarification of the government's attitudes toward national unity and the Arab world and its ability to respect future agreements.

30 July. Al-Bashir states that there will be "no return for the political parties." Discussions and shaky cease-fire with SPLA continues into August.

8 August. Restrictions put on travel abroad, including medical treatment.

14 August. Garang accuses new regime of planning an Islamic state with partition for the South. Garang calls for resignation of al-Bashir and the formation of a broadly based government to end civil war.

16 August. Two new government publications appear, *Al-Sudan al-Jadid* and *Al-Inqaz al-Watani*.

30 August. Brief visit to Khartoum by Egyptian President Husni Mubarak restores 1976 military treaty between Sudan and Egypt, which had been abrogated by al-Mahdi.

13 September. Government ends ban on foreign volunteer organizations.

14 September. RCC allows defense lawyers to represent people accused before the new special courts.

20 September. Khartoum University students disrupt speech by RCC member and demand restoration of democracy.

30 September. Al-Bashir extends cease-fire for another month.

October. Fighting resumes in South after seven-month cease-fire. The Charter for Democracy is signed by the National Democratic Alliance (NDA).

November. The Sudanese militias are renamed the Popular Defense Forces (PDF).

17 November. Al-Mahdi, DUP leader Muhammad 'Uthman al-Mirghani, and NIF leader Hasan al-Turabi freed from prison and put under house arrest. The NDA calls for further resistance.

December. Former President Carter restores relief efforts and mediates talks between SPLA and Khartoum, but Shari'a proves to be a basic barrier. Widespread famine in southern Sudan.

4–6 December. Four students are killed in disruptions at the University of Khartoum between NIF supporters and other students.

17 December. A young businessman is hanged for alleged currency offenses.

28 December. Reports of at least 600 southerners, mostly Shilluk, massacred by "Arab" militia at al-Jabalein.

1990 January. In Shilluk massacre, government troops shown idle. The SPLA captures many garrisons and attacks Juba.

22 January. SPLA holds claims to garrison in Kordofan. Government attacks at Yei and Juba, whose population has swelled; relief efforts hampered.

1 February. Chief Justice Kamil 'Ali Lutfi blocks amputation orders for twelve prisoners' limbs, but Shari'a laws remain. SPLA and Umma Party agree to coordinate overthrow of the government.

March. Coup attempt in Khartoum. SPLA joins NDA to pledge democracy.

17 March. Africa Watch condemns al-Bashir government as worse than Nimeiri. Torture, detention, arbitrary justice, and execution all cited.

April. Coup attempt includes the Umma Party. Twenty-one senior army officers are among fifty arrested. Twenty-eight officers executed.

11 April. Sudan and Libya sign accord for binational integration.

June. Bona Malwal, editor-in-chief of the banned *Sudan Times*, starts the *Sudan Democratic Gazette* in London.

18 June. Eighteen officers arrested for plotting on behalf of Nimeiri.

30 June. Government stages huge rally calling for implementation of Shari'a.

13 July. Police move thousands of southern refugees out of Khartoum; 600,000 may have returned to Bahr al-Ghazal.

2 August. Iraq invades Kuwait; Khartoum offers support to Iraq.

September. Government confiscates 40,000 tons of U.S. grain for South, but Sudan bombs South where UN and Red Cross relief efforts are active. Donor nations refuse aid because of noncooperation. Sudan trades 300,000 tons of sorghum for war materials from Iraq and Libya.

20 September. Sudanese Air Force bombs Bor, Yirol, Waat, Akon, and Ayod.

October. Libyan President Qaddafi visits Khartoum and warns of mixing religion with politics.

22 October. Egypt charges Sudan with training and financing Egyptian terrorists.

28 October. Al-Bashir insists that Sudan has no food shortages, contrary to foreign reports; he continues forced relocation of 1.8 million refugees.

7 November. Nimeiri seeks aid from Gulf and African states to topple al-Bashir. Hundreds of Khartoum University lecturers fired. Failed coup results in arrests of former ministers. Protests against al-Bashir in provinces.

16 November. United States says that Sudan needs one million tons in food aid due to poor harvests and will provide 100,000 tons if fairly distributed.

26 November. Government says students admitted to universities and high institutes in 1990 will be trained at PDF camps. UN appeals for one million tons of food aid fearing devastation in 1991.

27 December. Al-Bashir in Lagos for talks with Nigerian President Babangida.

1991 January. Government issues clothing code for women.

8 January. Five Palestinians convicted of killing two Sudanese, three British aid workers, and two children in Khartoum attack in May are freed; the British are outraged and cut economic aid, while urging its citizens to leave Sudan. UN delays major relief, angered by Sudan's support of Iraqi invasion of Kuwait. U.S. Embassy in Khartoum is closed.

February. Al-Bashir government declares a new nine-state federal system, eliminates the Council of the South, and promises to implement Shari'a in the North as of 22 March 1991; the South is to maintain the standing legal system until it chooses its own law. Michael Gassim, a southern youth, is the first to suffer cross amputation (right hand and left foot) since Nimeiri era.

16 March. Council of Ministers declares three years of compulsory national service for all Sudanese between eighteen and thirty years of age.

16 April. French news sources report another coup attempt foiled by the Khartoum government; twenty officers executed.

29 April. UNESCO conference in Namibia criticizes the human rights record of the Khartoum government.

May. President Mengistu is forced out of Addis Ababa, putting SPLA base areas in Ethiopia in jeopardy.

June. Ethiopian rebel groups seize power in Addis Ababa, and SPLA loses its strongest regional ally, its radio broadcasts, and its safe haven. Some southern Sudanese driven out of Ethiopian refugee camps to face starvation and air attacks in the South by Khartoum planes.

July. Two students killed at the University of Khartoum during peaceful demonstration against the government.

22 August. Hundreds of military officers and civilians are arrested in Sudan. Claims of torture soon follow.

28 August. Group at Nasir claims to overthrow SPLA leader Garang, who is accused of Dinka favoritism. New SPLA-United is initially led by Dr. Lam Akol, a Shilluk, and Gordon Kong. Riek Machar, a Nuer, joins them until breaking away as the Southern Sudan Independence Movement (SSIM).

31 August. Divisions within the SPLA weaken support from the NDA. Widespread southern factional fighting in Bor district.

September. Government bans the Student Union at the University of Khartoum. Widespread arrests, disappearances, and killings in Kadugli in the Nuba Mountains are attributed to the PDF.

October. PDF continue arrests and attacks in the Nuba Mountains.

29 November. The SPLA attacks in southern Darfur.

26 December. Sudan military enters village near capital to kill about seventy refugees.

1992 Khartoum government declares *jihad* against "apostates." Government takes Kapoeta, towns in the East, and Nuba Mountains.

February. USAID worker executed in Juba by military court. A 300-member Transitional National Assembly is appointed to enact laws. IMF threatens to expel Sudan for nonpayment of debt.

15 February. Government air and army offensive in South is backed by Iranians.

March. Army retakes Pachala after confusion in SPLA bases in Ethiopia.

28 March. Women protesters enter Presidential Palace to commemorate the execution of their loved ones in the Ramadan Murders of 1990.

April. Two commanders from the Nasir faction, Deng Ayuen and Telar Ring Deng revolt and break away from Lam Akol. Large protests against high inflation in Khartoum. Two Sudanese soldiers killed in Halayeb border dispute with Egypt. Hasan al-Turabi is subject to hostility on European and American speaking tours.

4 April. Government forces retake Bor, held by the SPLA for several years.

May. Brigadier Hasan Bashir Nasr sentenced to die for ties to the NDA.

25 May. Al-Turabi is beaten in Ottawa by an exiled Sudanese opponent of the regime. Al-Turabi recovers from a coma.

26 May. Talks at Abuja, Nigeria, fail to solve the Sudanese civil war despite hopes from Khartoum that the southern divisions would make agreement possible. Al-Bashir charges Saudi support for the SPLA.

6–8 June. The SPLA attacks the outskirts of Juba.

15 June. Chevron relinquishes concessions to oil production in Sudan.

20 August. UN food relief flights reach Juba.

September. Egyptian troops take over Halayeb border area.

October. U.S. Congress condemns Sudan for widespread human rights abuses. Nasir faction of the SPLA claims to have captured Malakal, but it is soon brought back to government control.

November. UN states that Khartoum is blocking Operation Lifeline Sudan (OLS), which provides relief for the South. Widespread arrests and executions of southerners in Malakal. The Sudan Human Rights Organization holds a conference in Cairo.

December. Antigovernment protests in Kordofan and northern cities.

1993 January. Wau under siege by SPLA forces.

February. Pope John Paul II visits Khartoum and criticizes its human rights abuses. The Sudan Human Rights Organization is abolished. Publications and press are restricted. Talks at Abuja, Nigeria, break down without resolution of Sudan conflict. The Khatmiya is banned; its assets are seized. One element of the Nasir faction of the SPLA breaks off, seeking secession for the South. Riek Machar and Lam Akol fight the SPLA not Khartoum. Machar works with Khartoum, and Akol creates the Shilluk-based SPLA-United faction. Khartoum offensive stopped by joint SPLA/NDA forces, causing deteriorating relations with Eritrea and Ethiopia. Khartoum backs the "Lord's Resistance Army" and "West Bank Nile Front" attacks on Uganda.

26 February. World Trade Center in New York is bombed by Shaykh Omer 'Abd al-Rahman. He is linked to some Sudanese agents at UN.

August 18. United States accuses Sudan of being a "terrorist nation" and cuts its aid.

September. Seven East African nations meet in Addis Ababa under the auspices of IGADD to discuss issues, including the Sudanese conflict.

October. The RCC is dissolved and General al-Bashir becomes a "civilian." "Islamic" principles are institutionalized for all government agencies. The NDA accepts the principle of self-determination for the SPLA, achieving unity and restoring the SPLA as a full member of the NDA.

21 October. John Garang and Riek Machar meet in Washington, DC, under a U.S. House of Representatives' effort to bring peace. The effort fails but the possibility of unity between them worries the NDA and NIF.

December. The Umma Party attends the Chukudum conference and agrees to the principle of self-determination for the South.

27 December. NDA members sign the Asmara Declaration, which reaffirms the Chukudum Accords as a public expression of democracy and unity against the Khartoum government.

1994 January. The Archbishop of Canterbury and his wife visit southern Sudan. The "Dry Season Offensive" is launched by Khartoum government forces.

6 January. Riek Machar signs an accord with John Garang of the SPLA-Mainstream in support of the IGADD agenda.

4 February. Muslim radicals of the *Takfir wa al-Hijra* group attack a mosque in Omdurman, killing sixteen worshippers. (*Takfir* claimed credit in 1981 for the assassination of Egyptian President Sadat.)

14 February. Sudan redivided into twenty-six states, with some undetermined borders.

17 March. Meeting of IGADD to focus on the Sudanese civil war.

May. Declaration of Principles (DOP) by the SPLA at IGADD meeting.

18–29 July. Third IGADD meeting in Nairobi.

July–August. Khartoum launches offensive in Equatoria and uses soldiers of William Bany in this effort, while Kerubino Bol, also a Dinka, attacks SPLA in Bahr al-Ghazal.

September. Machar renames his organization Southern Sudan Independence Movement/Army (SSIM/A).

5–7 September. Fourth IGADD meeting fails.

October. Massacre of Akot Dinka at Rumbek by Nuer forces of Riek Machar.

15 October. Sixteen squatters killed in the Khartoum "slum clearance program."

21 October. In Cairo, southern Sudanese women protest treatment of refugees.

November. Shanty towns outside Omdurman demolished and refugees relocated. Sudan orders compulsory military training for high school students.

7 November. Al-Turabi declares the war is won and all problems are solved.

10 November. Singer Khojali Osman is murdered in Omdurman.

December. The "Dry Season Offensive" is stalled, and the SPLA attacks at Nimule and Kapoeta. The PDF suffers great losses. Arbitrary arrests of doctors, lawyers, journalists, students, and members of the military and trade unions. Sudanese suffer from hyper-inflation and spiraling debt. Resumption in the domestic slave trade by PDF. Public flogging is administered for slight offenses. The Beja people of eastern Sudan are repressed, while the Nuba people are subject to "ethnic cleansing."

5 December. Eritrea breaks diplomatic relations with Sudan.

12 December. Umma Party and SPLA agree to work together to restore democracy in a meeting at Chukudum, Sudan. Both accept the DOP of the IGADD, and the Umma Party accepts the principle of self-determination.

Mid-December. About 200 arrested in Atbara following elections. Reports of torture and beatings follow. Forced recruitment into the PDF in eastern Sudan.

27 December. All members of the NDA sign the Asmara agreement, including the Umma Party, DUP, SPLA, and Sudan Allied Forces (SAF).

1995 January. Four IGADD members discuss peace in the Sudan in Nairobi. Eritrea breaks relations with Sudan. Tensions with Uganda mount when Sudanese forces cross border in pursuit of SPLA.

February. 'Ali Osman Muhammad Taha, deputy leader of the NIF, appointed foreign minister. Ghazi Salah al-Din, NIF hard-liner, appointed minister of state. John Garang announces creation of New Sudan Brigade to extend civil war into the North.

March. The IGADD talks led by former President Carter reach a cease-fire and a Guinea worm-eradication program, while both sides rearm. The IGADD principles remain endorsed by the SPLA and the NDA.

April. William Bany reunites the SSIM faction with SPLA-Mainstream.

11–12 April. Uganda and Sudan dismiss diplomats from their embassies.

23 April. Uganda breaks diplomatic relations with Sudan.

16 May. Sadiq al-Mahdi arrested after denouncing al-Bashir in Omdurman.

20 May. Umma Party calls for al-Mahdi's release in ultimatum.

15–23 June. President Afwerki of Eritrea gives NDA the use of the Sudanese Embassy in Asmara. The NDA reaffirms its commitment to a democratic, secular Sudan. Garang is made overall commander of the opposition military forces. Sudan and Egypt clash in Halayeb.

26 June. Sudan implicated in assassination attempt on President Mubarak in Addis Ababa.

August. New military offensive by Khartoum. Riek Machar seeks membership in NDA after the latter agrees to self-determination for the South and armed struggle. Ministry of Health reports epidemic of malaria due to deterioration of health and sanitation services.

September. Relations with Ethiopia worsen in wake of Mubarak assassination attempt. Allegations surface that al-Turbai was the architect of the plot. Ethiopia expels Sudanese diplomats from Addis Ababa. Libya orders mass expulsion of Sudanese workers.

9–14 September. Demonstrations and rioting in capital put down by government.

October. SPLA conducts a major offensive against Equatoria.

23–25 October. SPLA takes the garrison of Parajuok. Abel Alier and other southern leaders launch peace appeal.

December. Khartoum resumes military operations in the South.

1996 1 January. Sudan celebrates forty years of independence, amidst political isolation and hostility from most neighboring states.

12–15 January. The NDA meets in Asmara with the main Sudanese political parties, Beja Congress, and the legitimate commander of the Sudanese military. Independent of the NDA, the Sudan Allied Forces (SAF) conducts borders raids near Kassala.

31 January. The UN Security Council adopts Resolution 1044, condemning Sudan's "terrorism."

February. The United States suspends diplomatic presence in Sudan, claiming fear of terrorism. Twice, the Sudanese Air Force bombs sites in the South where Red Cross personnel are delivering food aid.

29 February–3 March. Misiriya Arabs and PDF attack Dinka in Gogrial and Abyei, taking cattle and capturing slaves.

March. SSIA attacks SPLA after agreeing to a cease-fire with government. Former Vice-President Abel Alier is arrested in Khartoum.

6–17 March. Parliamentary and presidential elections held under emergency military rule, civil war, and political repression. Victories go to NIF loyalists al-Turabi and al-Bashir.

9–12 March. The SPLA takes the town of Yei in Equatoria.

13 March. Congressional hearings in the United States on slavery in Sudan.

10 April. Riek Machar and the SPLA faction, led by Lt. Col. Kerubino Bol, sign the "Political Charter" agreement with NIF officials in Khartoum, ending any reconciliation between the NDA, the NIF, and the SPLA.

27 April. UN Security Council approves sanctions against Sudan.

10 May. UN sanctions are brought into force when the deadline expires for Khartoum to hand over those charged in the Mubarak attack.

16 May. SPLA-United of Lam Akol, largely a Shilluk force, signs a peace agreement with the government.

June. The internal opposition including former Vice-President Abel Alier meets in Khartoum to draft protest of policies of the NIF regime.

12–13 July. The Khartoum-backed "Lord's Resistance Army" attacks southern Sudanese refugees at Kitgum. Ninety are reported killed.

August. Coup attempt is broken up. Ten high-ranking officers arrested.

September. Bread riots after Nile floods ravage capital area and towns along the Nile. Squatter camps devastated.

October. The vice-chancellor warns that Khartoum University might close due to financial problems; large numbers of faculty have already left.

26 October. Third coup attempt of the year, following those in March and August.

1997 January–February. Offensive opens in eastern Sudan by the NDA, the SAF, and the SPLA. The SAF threatens Damazin and the hydro-electric dam at Roseires.

13 January. Allied effort of the NDA, the SAF, and the New Sudan Brigade of the SPLA in eastern Sudan takes border towns.

15 January. The government closes the University of Khartoum, calling for faculty and students to help the war effort in the South.

5 February. World Health Organization announces that Sudan has 77 percent of the world's cases of Guinea worm disease.

April. Riek Machar, Kerubino Bol, and four other factions create Southern Sudan Defense Force, allied with the government.

28 April. Death of General Fathi Ahmed 'Ali, head of NDA Military.

May. Riek Machar attracts Nuer supporters and attacks the SPLA in Upper Nile, while Kerubino Bol attacks SPLA forces in Bahr al-Ghazal. Khartoum issues military conscription plan for 120,000 students.

June. Presidential order that unmarried males must perform twelve to eighteen months compulsory military service to qualify for admission to the University of Khartoum.

14 June. The SPLA takes Yirol and blocks river transport to Juba.

26 July. Sudanese conscripts flee barracks in Omdurman.

August. Al-Bashir and Ugandan President Museveni meet President Mandela for peace talks in South Africa. Garang is present; he and Museveni are long-time allies. The meeting closes without progress.

7 August. Al-Bashir appoints Riek Machar as Chairman of the Southern States Coordination Council.

1 September. Chinese sign agreement to finance the Kajbar dam hydroelectric project in Sudanese Nubia.

November. The United States applies sanctions against Sudan for "sponsorship of terrorism and human rights abuses." Sudanese assets in United States blocked and most financial transactions barred. More inconclusive IGADD talks held.

3 November. Members of *Takfir wa al-Hijra* group attack worshippers at a mosque in Wad Medani, killing two.

4 November. The United States halts all commercial dealings with Sudan.

17 November. Egyptian terrorists massacre fifty-eight tourists in Luxor. Egypt in bid to release Shaykh Omer 'Abd al-Rahman from prison in the United States.

1998 January. UNICEF reports that at least one million Sudanese children died of polio and malnutrition in 1996–1997. Machar named chair and assistant president of the Southern Sudan Coordination Council. Al-Bashir appoints Kerubino Bol as deputy president and minister for local government and public security in the South.

25 January. Sudan and Russia sign trade agreement in Moscow.

28 January. Kerubino's troops revolt against government in Bahr al-Ghazal.

12 February. Plane crashes at Nasir and kills thirty-one, including the first vice-president, al-Zubayr Muhammad Salih, and General Arok Thom Arok.

17 February. Foreign minister 'Ali Osman Muhammad Taha appointed first vice-president; Mustafa Osman Isma'il named new foreign minister.

18 February. Kerubino Bol allegedly rejoins the SPLA.

19 February. Hasan al-Turabi elected secretary-general of the Sudan National Council (SNC), the sole legal political organization in Sudan.

20 February. NDA rejects bilateral negotiations with the government, calling for multiparty democracy.

22 February. Sudan signs $600 million accord with companies from Argentina, China, and Britain for 1,600-kilometer oil pipeline to the Red Sea.

5 March. Government bombs a hospital in Yei run by Norwegian Peoples Aid, killing seven and wounding forty-six. IMF decides to reopen Khartoum office, suspending threat to expel Sudan in recognition of Sudan's economic reforms and increased debt payments.

8 March. Al-Bashir reshuffles cabinet, making Ibrahim Sulayman Hasan the minister of defense, 'Abd al-Rahim Muhammad Husayn the minister of the interior, 'Ali Muhammad 'Uthman Yasin the minister of justice, and Lam Akol the minister of transport, and adding two Umma Party supporters, Mahdi Babo Nimr (Health) and Sharif al-Tuhami (Irrigation). A new ministry, International Cooperation and Investment, headed by former Bank of Sudan governor 'Abdallah Hasan Ahmad, is created. NIF hardliner Ghazi Salah al-Din Atabani is named minister of information and culture.

24 March. The Supreme Council for Peace is dissolved and replaced by the Southern States' Coordination Council.

29 March. The government of Sudan resumes IGADD negotiations.

23 April. Government referendum on new constitution that retains Shari'a.

3 May. The government allows food relief into southern Sudan.

4 May. Renewed talks between the government and the SPLM in Nairobi.

7 May. The government claims that both sides have reached an agreement on a referendum on southern self-determination; the SPLA disagrees.

9 May. Voting begins on new Constitution in Khartoum.

24 May. Armed units of the Umma Party attack Sudan along Eritrean border.

June. Sudan's Parliament passes new Constitution, but only members of the NIF are in the Parliament.

June–July. Threat of famine mounts gravely in southern Sudan.

14 June. SPLA attacks the Blue Nile Province, near the strategic road between Port Sudan and Khartoum.

8 July. The United States announces shipment of $16 million of food aid to southern Sudan and additional sums for infrastructure development.

12 July. Sudanese government allows access to relief agencies.

15 July. The SPLA declares a cease-fire so that relief agencies can operate in the South.

3 August. The government declares a cease-fire in Bahr al-Ghazal for famine relief.

7 August. The U.S. Embassies in Nairobi and Dar es Salaam are bombed; at least 260, mainly Kenyans, and 12 Americans are killed; hundreds are wounded, and Osama bin Laden is suspected.

20 August. U.S. Cruise missiles bomb the Al-Shifa pharmaceutical plant in Khartoum, alleging that Osama bin Laden manufactures the chemical EMPA, which is used to make VX nerve gas bombs. Crowds protest at the U.S. Embassy in Khartoum, which was closed in January.

22 August. Al-Bashir promises retaliation for U.S. attack on Al-Shifa.

September. Terrorist plot to blow up the U.S. Embassy in Uganda is thwarted; the chief suspects have ties to Sudan.

10 September. The government bombs Labone refugee camp and breaks cease-fire.

5 October. Twenty men charged with the June bombings in Khartoum.

7 October. The government claims fifty SPLA soldiers killed in southern Kordofan.

11 October. The SPLA claims Chadian forces have joined government troops in Juba.

12 October. The SPLA and government cease-fire is renewed for three months.

4 November. Parliament leader al-Turabi forms a Constitutional Court as a "liberal" reform, but all court members are appointed by al-Bashir.

14 November. Plotters fail in Nairobi attack on SPLA leader John Garang.

1 December. The government retakes Tekuk and Toqan, near Eritrea, from the SPLA.

9 December. Al-Bashir passes a law to restore multiparty democracy.

1999 1 January. New law provides for the organization of political associations in Sudan. The DUP organizes a rally to protest this new law.

January. OLS anticipates famine in Sudan.

5 January. Kerubino Kwanyin defects again to the government side. The government decrees that women must wear "Islamic" dress.

15 January. The SPLA and the government announce three-month "cease-fire."

28 January. Government offensive in Blue Nile Province kills 157 SPLA troops.

8 February. Chemists state that Al-Shifa was not producing EMPA.

21 February. Al-Bashir would allow secession to end fifteen-year war.

26 February. Progovernment militias attack Dinka in Bahr al-Ghazal.

March. Eight parties recognized by National Congress.

5 March. Red Cross workers held hostage by SPLA.

23 March. Garang addresses the UN Human Rights Commission.

31 March. The SPLA claims killing 405 government troops in eastern Sudan.

6 April. The UN condemns the NIF for human rights abuses.

13 April. The SPLA and the government agree to three-month cease-fire.

16 April. Journalists arrested for links to foreign intelligence.

20–25 April. Round of IGADD talks scheduled.

2 May. Sudan and Eritrea sign peace accord and renew diplomatic ties.

17 May. The United States asserts that Khartoum has violated cease-fire in bombing the South.

22 May. Nimeiri returns to Khartoum after fourteen years in exile to lead the Alliance of Working Forces with the NIF government.

June. Christian Solidarity International movement raises money to purchase the freedom of Sudanese slaves.

10 June. Sudan willing to cooperate with the United States to control terrorism.

25 June. Sudan and Britain restore diplomatic staffs to their embassies.

October. Founding of the National Congress to isolate al-Turabi. The Sudanese government seeks oil production of 20,000 barrels a day.

December. President al-Bashir declares state of emergency, dismisses al-Turabi from his post, and dissolves the Parliament.

2000 The SPLA claims 600 government troops killed in Upper Nile and in southern Blue Nile; arms and equipment seized, curbing Chinese and Canadian oil production in the Higleig oil fields.

3 May. Amnesty International publishes *Sudan: The Human Price of Oil*, criticizing the Sudanese government for using oil to make arms purchases.

9 May. Al-Turabi supporters sack President Al-Bashir and other leaders from the ruling National Congress, calling on followers to oppose the president's efforts to exclude al-Turabi.

10 May. Al-Turabi predicts armed rebellion against al-Bashir.

12 May. Major Ethiopian offensive initiated against Eritrea.

18 May. Ethiopians seize Eritrean territory near Barentu.

23 May. Former Sudanese slave, Francis Bok Bol, meets antislavery groups in Washington, DC, to appeal for support for the "Sudan Day" program.

31 May. Ethiopia declares an end to its offensive actions against Eritrea.

4 June. Pro al-Turabi faction led by Ibrahim al-Sanousi declares breakaway party to oppose President al-Bashir.

5 June. Al-Bashir promises free presidential and parliamentary elections in Sudan in October. Eritreans counterattack Ethiopians at Barentu.

6 June. Turkish tanker departs from Port Sudan with a load of 20,000 tons of refined benzene from Sudan.

9 June. A "Day in Solidarity with Sudan" is declared in the United States, Canada, and Europe. A pro-Turabi youth demonstration broken up by police.

10 June. The United States welcomes a cease-fire between Eritrea and Ethiopia.

11 June. Eritreans force Ethiopian withdrawal, with heavy casualties.

12 June. UN refugee officials visit Eritrean refugee camp in Sudan. Sudan claims that the United States favors the SPLA in Sudanese IGADD peace talks.

13 June. SPLA claims attack in eastern Sudan on Qufa garrison in Blue Nile.

15 June. SPLA attacks Gogrial, but government troops hold town. Guffa falls to SPLA attack, and SPLA seizes trucks, tanks, howitzers, and jeeps. Eritrea and Ethiopia close to new cease-fire.

16 June. Bashir marks 11th coup anniversary with heavy arms production.

September. 'Umar al-Bashir has exploratory talks with NDA leader Muhammad 'Uthman al-Mirghani in Eritrea.

November. NDA attacks and claims to capture Kassala.

December. 'Umar al-Bashir is reelected president, winning 86.5 percent of the vote in an election marred by an opposition boycott. Fighting prevents voting in three southern provinces.

2001 January. SPLA attacks and destroys Canadian oil installations in western Upper Nile state, warning that oil wells are a legitimate target.

18 February. Hasan al-Turabi signs memorandum of understanding with the SPLM, signaling an alleged change in his political thinking.

20 February. Umma Party is offered a place in the Bashir government and refuses, calling for free elections and a resolution of the civil war.

21 February. Al-Turabi and senior members of his party, the Popular National Congress, are arrested. Al-Turabi is imprisoned in Kober prison in Khartoum North. The Bashir government seeks charges of sedition and "inciting hatred against the state."

22 February. SPLA forces attack town of Nyal in western Upper Nile. Nuer-Dinka ethnic tensions threaten to erupt.

March. Catholic bishop of Rumbek warns of impending disaster, as one million people in Bahr al-Ghazal face starvation.

4 April. Deputy Defense Minister Ibrahim Shams al-Din, a close aide to President Bashir, is killed with thirteen other high-ranking officers in a plane crash in Upper Nile province blamed on bad weather. The dead are proclaimed martyrs by the government.

[N.B.: The above chronology has been extensively updated since the second edition. Contemporary Sudanese, Egyptian, European, and American newspapers, magazines, and journals have been consulted. The following have been especially helpful: *Al-Ahram Weekly*, *The Egyptian Gazette*, *Africa Report*, *The Middle East Journal*, *Sudanow*, *Sudan Studies Association Newsletter*, *Sudan Studies Society of the UK Newsletter*, *Sudan Democratic Gazette*, and the various Web sites that focus on Sudan.]

Introduction

The Republic of Sudan is the largest country in Africa, stretching from sandy deserts in the north to tropical rain forests in the south. It contains a complex diversity of peoples with differing origins, religions, languages, and lifestyles. This diversity reflects Sudan's geographical location in northeast Africa, sharing borders with nine other African nations.

Sudan shares aspects of its history and culture with both the Middle East and Africa. Arabic is the national language, with English firmly established as the second language as a result of the colonial experience. Arabs, as a matter of self-identification, are a minority of the population, while non-Arab Muslims constitute the majority, and a significant one-third of the population is Nilotic and other central African groups.

Sudan straddles a number of significant cultural frontiers as well as ethnic ones: it historically has been on the frontier between Muslim and Christian Africa, between Nile Valley civilizations and African Sudanic cultures, between Arabic-speaking and English-speaking Africa, and, at the same time, between English-speaking and Francophone Africa. It is a transitional zone between the cultural units of West Africa and East Africa, and it is a bridge between the Arabian Peninsula and Africa. Some scholars suggest that the Sudan may have had an important historical role as a bridge for ideas and technology passing from the ancient Near East into Africa. Bridging a number of frontiers and including a tremendous diversity of elements, Sudanese society has emerged with profound links to other societies and yet has had consistent difficulties in forging its own distinctive identity. Civil war has repeatedly plagued the nation since independence, due to unresolved issues of national unity between north and south, and between the central riverine peoples, who have traditionally dominated power and economics, and the remaining peoples of the west, east, and south.

GEOGRAPHY

The name "the Sudan" comes from the Arabic expression *Bilad al-Sudan*, meaning "the land of the blacks." In medieval Muslim literature, it was applied generally to Africa south of the Sahara. The term "the Sudan" also has been used in this general way to refer to the broad belt of plains and savanna land stretching from the Atlantic to the Red Sea and lying between the Sahara and the forest areas. In English and Arabic the term is also used specifically to refer to the territory south of Egypt, which formed the Anglo-Egyptian Sudan (1899–1955) and the contemporary independent Republic of Sudan. It was first used in this sense during the nineteenth century and applied to the African territories ruled by Muhammad 'Ali, the Ottoman governor of Egypt, and his successors.

The Republic of Sudan has an area of 2,503,890 square kilometers or 967,500 square miles. It shares borders with Egypt, Libya, Chad, the Central African Republic, Democratic Republic of the Congo, Uganda, Kenya, Ethiopia, and Eritrea, and has a coastal frontier on the Red Sea. Its boundaries were drawn largely by the imperial powers, with only minor adjustments being made since independence in 1956. Its future integrity is a projected goal, but protracted civil war in the country has pitted various ethnic and religious groups and classes from the North against those in the South. There have been intermittent demands for secession, autonomy or federation being a part of the political agenda during successive political regimes in Khartoum.

Sudan is a country of great geographical diversity. The climate includes the deserts of the North, where rainfall is rare, a semi-arid belt in the central plains, and increasing rainfall further to the south. Up to 1,520 millimeters or 60 inches of rain falls per year near the southern border. Vegetation tends to match this, with sparse desert growth in the North and, moving south, belts of acacia scrub and short grasses, then woodland savanna, and finally, swamps, floodlands, and rain forest areas. Occasional mountain or high hill areas, especially Jabal Marra, the Red Sea Hills, the Nuba Mountains, and the Ethiopian border highlands, interrupt these belts and have distinctive mountain vegetation.

The Nile and its tributaries are the most dominant single feature of the physical landscape. The river system cuts across the climatic and vegetation belts, providing water for irrigation, a major means of transportation, and the locus for most of the settled agricultural life and economy of the country. The Nile itself is formed by two great rivers, the Blue and White Niles, which have their confluence at the *Mogren* in Khartoum. The Blue

Nile rises in the Ethiopian highlands and contributes rich volcanic silt as well as most of the floodwaters, since the White Nile loses a great percentage of its water by evaporation in the Equatorial swamps (*Sudd*). The only major tributary north of Khartoum is the seasonal Atbara River.

Different regions of the Sudan can be identified in a variety of ways. In geological terms, one can see the dominant topological features as follows: the Nile drainage system; the great eroded region of the Red Sea mountains; vast plains with occasional sharp hills; volcanic uplands in Darfur; and southern and southeastern highlands.

Geographers have combined geological with other features and have defined as many as twelve basic regions (with many subregions), thus reflecting the great diversity of the country. A classification should include the Nile Valley in the north and central parts, where most people farm with the aid of irrigation; the western Sudan as an area of mixed nomadism and peasant agriculture; the eastern Sudan as primarily an area of nomadism but with some irrigated agricultural areas; and the southern region with a wide variety of pastoral and complex agricultural societies.

Within Sudan, certain areas have been defined by historical experience as much as geographical features. The Nile Valley in the northern Sudan and southern Egypt, approximately from Aswan in Egypt to Dongola, is Nubia, a region whose people have maintained a cultural distinctiveness since ancient times. In southern Nubia was the central area of the ancient kingdom of Kush around the city of Meroë. It was bounded on three sides by the Nile and Atbara rivers and was known as the "Island of Meroë."

Further up the river valley, the area between the Blue and White Niles came to be called the Gezira (from the Arabic *jazira*, "island"). Finally, the southern third of the country has in the twentieth century come to be spoken of as a separate region, "The South." This area became recognized as constituting the three colonial provinces of Equatoria, Bahr al-Ghazal, and Upper Nile.

POPULATION

The Sudanese population must, first of all, be viewed in the light of the huge territory of this nation. It stretches about 2,050 kilometers north to south, and about 1,600 kilometers at its widest point. As Africa's largest country, its population varies tremendously by region: some desert regions are essentially uninhabited, while the Nile Valley and especially the Three Towns area (Khartoum, Khartoum North, and Omdurman) have a high and rapidly increasing population density.

The population of Sudan has changed dramatically in the years since independence in 1956. Two factors mainly account for this radical demographic transformation. Typical of Third World nations, Sudan has a high rate of natural increase, that is, an excess of births over deaths. (However the opposite has been true in the civil war–ravaged southern regions of the country, where the population loss among some ethnic groups in the 1980s and 1990s has been precipitous.) The other cause of rapid population increase has been high rates of migration. This migration has resulted from a variety of internal factors, such as uneven regional development of the economy, severe ecological degradation and regional desiccation, and an influx of refugees into the North from southern regions wracked by persistent civil war.

Additionally, the Sudanese population has grown markedly with an influx of refugees from neighboring Eritrea, Ethiopia, Uganda, Democratic Republic of Congo (Zaire), and Chad, all seeking shelter from civil strife. Some estimates state that as much as 20 percent of the present population of Sudan has arrived in the last fifteen years alone, refugees from their own nations and regions. In Africa as a whole, Sudan is considered to have the largest proportion of refugees relative to total population.

The Sudanese population at independence was 10,262,536 and by the 1973 census it had reached 14,872,000. The most recent census, in 1983, determined that the national population had reached 21,103,000. Estimates in the 1990s suggest that the population of Sudan has now reached 29,419,798 (July 1994), but with much of the nation at war it is impossible to calculate with any accuracy. Although precise censuses were not conducted during earlier times, the Sudanese population just after the turn of the century may have been as low as five million people as a result of protracted famine and warfare during the Mahdiya. The rebuilding of the Sudanese population during the colonial period was a result of improved health care and food supply as well as a substantial in-migration from West Africa. In this respect, the Sudan has long been on a major route of easterly migration across the Sahel by migrants and pilgrims to Mecca.

All Sudanese demographic statistics must be viewed with some skepticism given the country's vast size, the presence of nomadic populations, and the state of war in the southern region. The rate of natural increase is usually put in the vicinity of 2.5 percent per annum (a typically high Third World rate). In 1994 the Crude Birth Rate was put at 42/1,000, and the Crude Death Rate at 12/1,000. Here the great excess of births over deaths is readily apparent, and both rates are far more than double those in most Western nations. The rate of increase would be even higher were it not for an Infant

Death Rate of 79/1,000, which is especially tragic since most infants die from easily avoided intestinal and respiratory infections. As a consequence of these factors, plus endemic parasitic diseases and generally poor medical services, the life expectancy in Sudan is only about fifty-four years.

Amidst these general trends there is also a notable drain from rural areas to the national and provincial capitals. In the case of the Three Towns the growth rate has been staggering. At independence the total population was about 250,000; by 1970 it had tripled to about 750,000, and with the factors noted above the population in 1980 was in the vicinity of 1.5 million. The population of course continues to grow: Some estimates, including the thousands of squatters and refugees living at the peripheries of each of the Three Towns, suggest a total capital region population of 3.5 million or more. Except for Nubia in the far north, most provincial capitals have also experienced tremendous growth ranging from 9 to 11 percent per year. In the case of Juba, the capital of Equatoria, the urban population is living under siege and the surrounding hinterland is contested militarily by government and rebel forces. Juba became a city of 84,000 by 1983 and in 1990 it may have surpassed 150,000. Malakal leaped from 33,000 in 1983 to as many as 80,000 today, and Wau has grown from 58,000 in 1983 to perhaps 100,000 at present.

Population growth along the Blue Nile and the cities of the eastern Sudan, especially Kassala and Port Sudan, has also been notable. These areas have experienced their own internal growth by natural increase, but have also received thousands of refugees from Ethiopia and Eritrea as well as resettled Nubians from the northern Sudan. Nubia is the only region not to experience such prodigious growth, as it was subject to the inundations of Lake Nasser and also by-passed by the main rail, river, and road networks.

The ethnic composition of Sudan is very roughly one third "Arab," one third "Southerners," and one third "Others" (such as Beja, Nubians, Fur, and Nuba). Within these crude groupings there is very considerable ethnic heterogeneity, and in fact the numbers themselves are disputed for a variety of political reasons. In still other terms, the majority of Sudanese consider themselves Muslims, though this can include a variety of syncretic beliefs as well. Most southern Sudanese are adherents of traditional religions (often identified as "animism"), although many southern leaders consider themselves followers of various Christian denominations. Clear and sharp delineation of ethnicity and religion are useful at a general level, but the complex history and movements of Sudanese people means that all such generalizations must be related or confirmed with reference to specific circumstances. For those who are Muslim there are also various *turuq*, or politico-religious brotherhoods, reflecting regional and historical differences, even though virtually all Sudanese follow the Sunni Muslim beliefs rather than Shi'ite.

Another significant transformation of the Sudanese population has been caused by an out-migration of educated and skilled people, who have elected to leave the country for personal, economic, and/or political reasons. This "brain drain" has had the effect of further confounding plans for economic development, but has also become an important source of hard currency and petrodollars for the ailing Sudanese economy.

EARLY HISTORY

The history of the Sudan is as diverse as its people. Unfortunately much of its ancient history is either poorly known or dimly seen through the lens of oral tradition. Most available information concerns the development of the central and northern areas of the Nile Valley, but even there much remains to be learned. In the 1960s much information came to light from archaeological efforts in Nubia to study sites before they were covered by the waters of the Aswan High Dam reservoir, Lake Nasser; perhaps the renewed threat to Nubia in the 1990s from the Kajbar Dam project at the third cataract will prompt further archaeology. Elsewhere in Sudan many important sites remain to be studied. The vigorous activity of the Sudan Department of Antiquities and of other scholars means that new information on the ancient Sudan is constantly being made available.

Ancient Times

Evidence of early human activity is scattered throughout the Sudan. Early Stone Age or Paleolithic sites suggest dates as early as 250,000 BCE to some scholars. The most thoroughly studied sequences of early tool industries and settlement sites are in Nubia. There, around Wadi Halfa and now covered by Lake Nasser for example, a series of cultures has been found with dates of perhaps 50,000 years ago. Local social evolution and the immigration of new peoples are both postulated as sources for gradual changes in Sudanese Paleolithic cultures.

The techniques of plant and animal domestication began to appear in the Sudan and by 4000 to 3000 BCE the Shaheinab or Khartoum Neolithic in the central Sudan had emerged. Neolithic groups in the Sudan may have had relations with a wide range of cultures in north and northeast Africa.

The closest affinities were with inhabitants of predynastic Egypt. What is known of the subsequent ancient history of the Sudan is closely tied to Egyptian history.

The modern study of ancient Sudanese history has been concentrated in Nubia in salvage archaeology to rescue sites before they were flooded. The first major survey was begun in 1907 and directed by G. A. Reisner. This work made it possible to construct an outline of Nubian cultural history. Reisner used a simple terminological scheme, which is still partially used, naming the various cultures with a letter, so that the earliest one, related to predynastic and early dynastic Egypt, is called the A-Group and dates roughly around 3100–2600 BCE.

A-Group or Ta-Seti people were independent but strongly influenced by emerging Egyptian civilization. Then, around 2500 BCE, the Egyptians conquered some of northern Nubia and local Sudanese culture changed. As long as Egypt was in an Intermediate Period of political disorganization, Sudanese Nubia flourished. Beyond the control of Egypt, the ancient Lower Nubian C-Group people developed, and the contemporary state now known as Kerma or Yam grew in strength as an autonomous trading center. C-Group people were influenced by Egypt but had their own distinctive cultural dynamism. This era came to an end when the revived Egypt of the New Kingdom conquered and established firm control over much of Nubia around 1500 BCE. The Egyptian viceroy of the province of Kush, as the area was then called, held firm sway until the eleventh century BCE.

As the Egyptian empire weakened, especially after 1070 BCE, Sudanese states reemerged and even became a refuge area for Egyptians fleeing civil war and foreign conquest. By 950 BCE the Sudanese city of Napata had recovered as a major temple of Amun, the god of the most important priesthood. A distinctive Egyptian-Kushite culture evolved. Napata became the capital of Kush and several of its kings conquered Egypt, forming the 25th Dynasty from 750 BCE. When the Assyrians conquered Egypt in 656 BCE, the Kushites were driven back but maintained their independent Nubian state for another millennium. The attacks on Napata by Psammetichus II, who invaded from Egypt in 591 BCE, and by the Roman Petronius in 23 BCE, encouraged the capital to be moved farther south to Meroë but did not destroy the state.

Meroë was a vibrant state influenced by Hellenistic, Roman, Ethiopian, and ancient Egyptian ideas. However, it developed its own cultural traits and may have been the gateway for some Middle Eastern ideas and technologies into Africa. Meroë eventually began to feel pressure from growing states around it, especially Axum in Ethiopia, and it came to an end certainly before 350 CE.

Medieval History

Comparatively little is known about Nubian history in the period of disorganization following the collapse of Meroë. This is the time of the X-Group or Ballana culture, which was a post-Meroitic mixture of Roman, Kushite, and new elements. Out of the confusion, three states emerged: Nobatia, Mukuria, and Alwa. Their rulers converted to Christianity between 543 and 580 CE and Nobatia and Mukuria merged into the kingdom of Dongola by 700 CE.

The best-known aspect of the history of these states is their relationship with Egypt, which became one of the early Islamic conquests in North Africa in 640 CE. There were battles, treaties, attacks, and counterattacks, with the long-term trend in favor of the Muslims. Tradition holds that the first Muslim became king of Dongola in 1315 and that Soba, the capital of the last Christian kingdom, Alwa, fell in 1504. Some scholars think that this event may have taken place earlier. Meanwhile, Arab Muslim merchants and teachers gradually moved into the Sudan where they intermarried and settled. As a result, the end of the medieval period and the spread of Islam and the Arabic language in the Sudan was more a gradual transition than fully the result of conquest.

The Islamic States

The three centuries between the traditional date for the fall of Soba and the Turco-Egyptian conquest of the Sudan in 1820–1821 are of great importance in Sudanese history. The movement of people and establishment of new institutions confirmed both the Islamization and Arabization of much of the northern Sudan. During this time the major movement of Nilotic peoples into the south was also completed and the Azande kingdoms were firmly established. During this period it is possible to trace with greater accuracy the main outlines of the history of the whole country. The best-known features relate to the emergence of larger, regional states within the area of the modern Sudan.

The Funj Sultanate was established in the central and northern Sudan in the early sixteenth century with its capital at Sinnar. The origins of the Funj are still the subject of scholarly dispute; however, they probably comprised a non-Muslim, non-Arab group coming from the south or southeast. The state they established followed traditional African patterns of kingship, although Islam rapidly became an important political and cultural force and the Funj converted to Islam. They defeated the earlier major Arab state of the 'Abdallab and incorporated that group into the Funj political system as viceroys of the northern provinces. The sultanate was a major force in the Nile Valley and extended its control on occasion both east into the Red Sea hills and west into Kordofan.

The political system of the Funj experienced a gradual evolution, with Islamization undermining the bases of the African kingship. In the late seventeenth century, Sultan Badi II created a slave army and tensions developed, with the old Funj aristocracy feeling threatened. In 1720 the old nobility revolted and deposed the sultan. Other revolts occurred during the century as groups broke away from control by Sinnar. In 1761 a successful general, Muhammad Abu Likaylik, and his kin group the Hamaj, became the real rulers in Sinnar, naming and deposing sultans. The final years of the sultanate were filled with internal conflict, and the control of the Hamaj regents and their puppet rulers was increasingly restricted to the area around the capital. Localized kingdoms emerged throughout the region, and it was a divided and anarchic Sudan that the Turco-Egyptian forces invaded in 1820.

In Darfur, in the western Sudan, other sultanates were also emerging. Small states were created in medieval times though little is known of their history. The Daju gained control over part of the area before 1200 and were followed by Tunjur. They were succeeded in turn by the Keira Dynasty, which created a sultanate controlling most of Darfur from the mid-seventeenth century until 1916. From the time of Sulayman Solong in the late seventeenth century, the Keira state was Islamic, although keeping many pre-Islamic features. The last of the Keira sultans was 'Ali Dinar, who was defeated by the British during World War I.

Islam was firmly established in the northern Sudan during the Funj and Keira periods. Traveling merchants and teachers opened the region to the rest of the Islamic world. Local schools were created and the great Islamic Sufi orders or *turuq* gained a firm foothold. Holymen and their families came to wield important influence in all areas of life. In this way the basic Sudanese Islamic pattern was set, focused around individuals in a personalized, socioreligious order. The religious brotherhood joined the primary ethnic group, kin, and family as the bases for social identity.

The period from the fifteenth to the nineteenth centuries was also of crucial importance to the development of the southern regions of the Sudan. It is during these centuries that ethnic migrations brought the major groups to their modern locations and institutional structures were defined. The Nilotic peoples moved into and out of a possible original cluster in central Bahr al-Ghazal. The Dinka and Nuer moved a relatively short distance and their patterns of decentralized political organization were established. Other Nilotic groups found their modern homes; those who settled on the White Nile became the Shilluk. They developed a more centralized monarchical tradition and achieved unity under their king or *reth*, which enabled them to retain much of their cultural integrity during the foreign onslaught of the nineteenth and twentieth centuries.

The largest state to emerge in the southern region during this period was created by a non-Nilotic group, the Azande. These people, speaking a language of the Equatorial subfamily of the Niger-Congo linguistic group, began to enter the southern Sudan in the sixteenth century. At first this movement had little cohesion and created only a pattern of small, scattered groupings. However in the eighteenth century the Avungara arrived as a new wave of invaders and, as a military aristocracy, succeeded in imposing their authority over the various Azande-speaking groups. The result was the creation of a well-organized and expanding state system. The key to expansion was the vigor and rivalry of the royal princes who would leave the center and carve out domains of their own. In this way internal division was minimized and the weaker peoples in surrounding areas were conquered and assimilated. This basic pattern was not altered fundamentally until the British consolidated their conquest in the early twentieth century.

These postmedieval experiences created the foundations for modern Sudanese society. The major states of both North and South had provided more than simply a localized ethnic identity. In the North the Islamization of society was confirmed and its Arabization was far advanced. However, the geographical differences and sheer distance across the Sudan meant that these factors were more confined to the northern regions. This period for the southern regions saw the decentralized, egalitarian peoples, such as the Dinka and Nuer, become established in their modern locales, and the creation of the monarchical states of the Shilluk and Azande.

Turco-Egyptian Rule

During the nineteenth century a number of circumstances emerged that began to bring the disparate peoples and regions together into a single unit called the Sudan. Economic, religious, and political organizations broadened to countrywide activity at times and provided elements of integration that would coexist, and sometimes conflict, with the elements of diversity.

In politics, a dramatic change was brought about by the conquest of much of the Sudan by Turco-Egyptian forces. Muhammad 'Ali, the virtually independent Ottoman governor of Egypt, decided to invade the region to his south. A variety of explanations are given for this, including his desire to "pacify" troublesome elements on the southern border, the search for gold and slaves, and the extension of his own name and reputation. For whatever motivations, his army moved into the Sudan under the command of his son Isma'il in 1820. The noncentralized peoples and disintegrating Funj armies were no match for the relatively modernized army from Egypt. The central and northern areas of the Sudan were quickly conquered.

In 1822 Isma'il was murdered in a clever ruse designed by the leader of the Ja'aliyin people, Mek Nimr of Shendi, and a period of revolt against the new conquerors ensued. The Turco-Egyptian forces did not face another major local threat until the Mahdist movement in 1881. A civil and military administration was established with its capital in Khartoum, at the confluence of the White and Blue Niles. A bureaucratic structure emerged with provincial and district officers for land registration and tax collection, as well as central services for river steamers, post, and telegraph. In this way a centralized, protonational government system was established, and the modern political framework of the Sudan was begun.

The Turco-Egyptian rulers expanded the area under their control. By 1840 at least nominal control was won over the peoples of the Red Sea hills, gaining access to the ports on the coast. Meanwhile expeditions to the south created a military presence there, if not control over the region. The final expansion was completed in 1874 with the inclusion of Darfur.

Perhaps the most drastic changes were caused by the expansion of the slave trade during the early and mid-nineteenth century. At first officially condoned, the trade destroyed many small population groups and created a tradition of violence and mistrust between peoples of the south/southwest and outsiders. Only the largest, best-organized, or most isolated ethnic groups survived the massive onslaught of the nineteenth-century slave trade. The trade also created a group of powerful merchants with private armies. These people (known locally as *jallaba*), and those who profited with them, came to oppose Egyptian rule when it eventually attempted to limit and then abolish the slave trade.

By 1880 the Egyptian regime was growing unpopular. Since midcentury administrative officials had sometimes been recruited from among Europeans, a situation that antagonized the religious sensibilities of more pious Muslims. Even the Egyptian Muslim officials frequently offended local opinion, due to their foreign (and relatively Europeanized) ways, lax religious habits, and reputation for corruption. Most Egyptians viewed a posting to the Sudan as a form of punishment, and indeed many who were sent there had fallen out of favor with their superiors in Cairo. Consequently, the

Egyptian officials in the Sudan were not of the highest caliber: those who were not openly corrupt were usually ineffectual.

The Egyptians were, however, able to secure the cooperation of some important local groups such as the Shayqiya, who after a strong but brief resistance provided irregular cavalry for garrisons throughout the Sudan. A few tribal leaders, like the Abu Sinn family of the Shukriya, became important figures in the governmental structure itself. Some religious teachers received training and help from the government, which sought to create an "orthodox" religious leadership as an alternative to the local teachers (*fekis*) and Sufi orders. The most important group to cooperate was the Mirghani family, whose Sufi *tariqa*, known as the Khatmiya, was widespread and tremendously influential in northern and eastern portions of the Sudan.

Ultimately, many local religious leaders and tribal shaykhs opposed Egyptian rule, though generally this was expressed through noncooperation rather than active resistance. Growing discontent reached a climax in the late 1870s; this coincided with the end of the thirteenth Islamic century, a time when many Muslims were expecting the arrival of a special restorer of the faith. The various opponents of the regime found an effective vehicle for expressing their discontent in the movement of Muhammad Ahmad, the Sudanese Mahdi.

The Mahdiya

Among those Sudanese distressed by what they believed to be the impiety of Turco-Egyptian rule was a religious man with a broad reputation for ascetic rigor, Muhammad Ahmad ibn 'Abdallah. Initiated at a young age into the Sammaniya *tariqa*, he had had a dispute with his original shaykh over the luxury of that man's lifestyle before attaching himself to a new teacher. Living as a recluse on Aba Island in the White Nile, Muhammad Ahmad began to attract many followers. Eventually he became convinced of the need to restore the purity of Islamic society, and believed himself to be the divinely appointed guide, or *mahdi*, chosen to bring about this final purification. He traveled about the northern Sudan gathering support and gauging the popular mood before proclaiming his mission in 1881 (1298 by the Muslim calendar), a time of great millenarian excitement.

The government at first underestimated the scope of popular resentment and potential popularity of the Mahdi. Forces sent to arrest the Mahdi at Aba Island were defeated and the momentum of revolt built rapidly. Mindful of the symbolism of his actions, the Mahdi emulated the experience of the Prophet Muhammad. Calling his followers *Ansar* (helpers), he led them in a withdrawal to Kordofan that he proclaimed a *hijra* (emigration); to better accord with popular beliefs in a *mahdi*, he renamed the hill at which they gathered Jabal Qadir. As victory followed victory, people flocked to the Mahdi's banner, drawn to the uprising either out of religious zeal, resentment toward Turco-Egyptian policies, or plain opportunism. Soon the Mahdi controlled most of the northern Sudan save Wadi Halfa in the north, Khartoum and its vicinity, and the Red Sea port of Suakin. In 1884 General Charles Gordon, a former Sudan governor-general and British military hero, was sent by the British government to Khartoum to evacuate Egyptian forces and officials. Gordon, for his part, understood his mission differently and stubbornly resolved to "smash the Mahdi." Finally isolated in the capital, he died as the city fell to the Mahdi, after a long siege, in January 1885.

For the next six months the Mahdi lived at Omdurman, opposite Khartoum on the Nile, while elements of his army pursued the *jihad* throughout the Sudan. The Ansar now comprised a great many ethnic and tribal groups, including settled riverine Arabs, nomadic cattle and camel herders of the western and eastern regions, West African migrants and Egyptian refugees, and the Beja peoples of the Red Sea coast. A rudimentary administration was begun, while leadership of the Ansar was divided among three lieutenants, termed *khalifas*: 'Abdullahi ibn Muhammad of the Ta'aisha cattle herders, 'Ali ibn Muhammad Hilu of the White Nile Arabs, and the Mahdi's young cousin Muhammad Sharif ibn Hamid of the Danagla people. It was the former who was of primary importance: an early adherent, he was the Mahdi's chief advisor and commander-in-chief of the army. When the Mahdi died suddenly at Omdurman in June 1885, 'Abdullahi succeeded him as leader of the movement; henceforth he was to be known simply as "the Khalifa."

Khalifa 'Abdullahi faced the difficult task of consolidating and protecting the new state while keeping diverse factions unified. Between 1885 and 1898 he put down a number of challenges to his authority, including two serious threats posed by the Mahdi's kinsmen and their leader the *khalifa* Muhammad Sharif. The *jihad* against unbelievers continued as before, though to little effect. An expedition against the British was destroyed at Tushki in 1889 and the border with Egypt remained Wadi Halfa. To the east the Ansar enjoyed limited success against the Ethiopians, though in the long term this cost them an important alliance; while in the southern Sudan the Mahdists utterly failed to garner new recruits to their army. Despite the Khalifa's attempts to encourage unity among the Ansar, social tensions simmered and occasionally exploded: most notable was the antagonism between the Khalifa's own people, the Baqqara cattle nomads of the west, and the settled riverine Arabs such as the Ja'aliyin and Danagla. Adding to the Khalifa's woes were such ecological disasters as a locust invasion, drought, and consequent famine in 1888–1889. On a more positive note, the Khalifa oversaw the establishment of a capital at Omdurman, which quickly grew to contain an enormous and diverse population and served as both marketplace and administrative hub. Among many Ansar Omdurman acquired the status of a holy city, and thus became the symbol of a nascent Sudanese self-consciousness.

Drawing upon a loyal coterie, and utilizing an administrative structure and personnel largely taken from the former Egyptian regime, the Khalifa was able to achieve a measure of security and stability for the Mahdist state by the early 1890s. However, by then a major threat to the state had already been hatched at the Berlin Conference of 1884–1885, where the partition of Africa by the dominant European powers was approved. Great Britain, France, and Italy all had interests in the Sudan, though it was the British who ultimately succeeded, neutralizing Italian ambitions in Eritrea and French ambitions in the upper Nile. In 1896 the British invaded the Mahdist state with an Anglo-Egyptian army, supposedly to suppress the slave trade (and, it was popularly believed, to avenge the death of General Gordon). The invasion faced meager opposition until the British had completed a railway across the Nubian Desert to Abu Hamad, and by then a British victory was all but assured. The decisive battle was fought at Karari north of Omdurman in September 1898, where over 10,000 Ansar were mowed down by the British machine guns. The Khalifa managed to flee the battle before Omdurman was occupied; within a year he was hunted down with the last of his followers and killed.

The Anglo-Egyptian Sudan

In 1899 an Anglo-Egyptian agreement defined the new regime for the Sudan. Devised by Lord Cromer, the British representative in Egypt, it provided for joint Anglo-Egyptian control, with flags of each country to be flown side by side and officials drawn from both nations. The term for this arrangement was a "Condominium" (from the Latin, co-domini). The governor-general was to be appointed by the Egyptian ruler on the recommendation of the British government; in practice, the Sudan was controlled by the British.

The organization of the new government initially relied on nineteenth-century Turco-Egyptian precedents for central and provincial organization.

At first most governors, inspectors, and officials were drawn from the Egyptian services, consisting largely of British officers on secondment to the Egyptian army. However, a civil service was soon recruited directly from British universities, and medical, veterinary, educational, and other services were created especially for the Sudan. By 1920 the Condominium regime had begun to employ a form of indirect rule in the provinces, empowering tribal shaykhs and village headmen with administrative and judicial authority under the supervision of British district commissioners and governors. This style of governance, already proven successful in British Nigeria, was deemed both necessary (given limited government resources and the vast territories involved) and politically expedient.

The early years of British rule were occupied mainly with establishing military control and maintaining order. In the North, messianic movements continued to appear, but these were forcefully put down and Mahdist writings and observances were outlawed. Nonetheless, many Sudanese cherished their adherence to Mahdism, and the Mahdi's posthumous son Sayyid 'Abd al-Rahman provided the locus for their loyalty. An eminently practical man and astute leader, he was willing to cooperate with the British authorities, especially in avoiding revolts during World War I, and Mahdism ceased to be a threat to the colonial state by the 1920s. Meanwhile in the South there was protracted resistance: More than 170 military patrols, each involving more than 50 men, were required in the first 3 decades of British rule to establish control. This early resistance was almost completely localized rather than nationalist in style and content.

In economic terms, the integration of the country continued in the form of an expanded railway system. A new port, Port Sudan, was built on the Red Sea, and plans were made for a large agricultural project in the Gezira. By the time of independence in 1956, there was considerable economic development in the North, though little had been done to encourage comparable growth in the South.

The 1920s were important years of transition. By then the relatively limited educational development had created a small but articulate educated class in the Sudan. After early cooperation with the colonial system, this group began to grow dissatisfied with their prospects and the lack of possibilities for self-rule. With the emergence of an educated class of Sudanese, resistance to British rule began to shift away from traditional definitions of identity to nascent political parties.

Initially the major religious and ethnic leaders were compelled to cooperate with the British. Early nationalism found its expression in small, usually secret organizations of educated Sudanese, like the Sudan Union

Society (*al-Ittihad*) and the better-known White Flag League. Because of their anti-British tone, they found a natural alliance with the Egyptian nationalists. The first phase reached a climax in 1924 when a series of demonstrations ended in a military mutiny led by two Muslim southern soldiers, 'Ali 'Abd al-Latif and 'Abd al-Fadil al-Maz. Startled by the vigor of this movement, the British reacted strongly by crushing the White Flag League, expelling all Egyptian officials, and limiting the governmental role of educated Sudanese.

For the next two decades there was little overt national political activity. The British encouraged traditional leaders to take a more active role in government through its policy of Indirect Rule. The two largest religious groups, the Ansar and Khatmiya sects, were the most effectively organized mass associations in the country, and their leaders emerged as a focus for political action. Meanwhile, members of the educated class formed a Graduates Club in which two groups emerged, that of Shaykh Ahmad al-Sayyid al-Fil (the "Filists") with the support of 'Ali al-Mirghani, and the group around Muhammad 'Ali Shawqi (the "Shawqists"), which had 'Abd al-Rahman al-Mahdi's sympathy. In addition to the sectarian division, sides were taken in the British-Egyptian rivalry, and the two competing slogans of Sudanese nationalism became either "Unity of the Nile Valley" for the former group, or "Sudan for the Sudanese" for the latter.

In terms of national growth the era leading up to party politics at the end of World War II was filled with more than partisan struggles. Sudanese journalism emerged as a force independent from government control. Literature and literary criticism prospered. Two journals appeared that, though short-lived, had an impact on the evolution of Sudanese intellectual life. They were *al-Nahda*, appearing in 1931–1932, and *al-Fajr*, which began publication in 1934 and became more politically active later in the decade. An important issue of debate at this time was whether or not there was such a thing as a unique Sudanese culture, given the country's historical ties both to the Arab world and Islam and to the cultures of central, Equatorial Africa.

A Sudanese political triangle eventually developed, consisting of members of the educated class, Sayyid 'Abd al-Rahman al-Mahdi and his Ansar sect, and Sayyid 'Ali al-Mirghani and the Khatmiya. By 1930 a number of themes were emerging: Ansar-Khatmiya rivalry and their competition for educated support; the educated sector mobilizing for an effective nationalist movement, but being forced to seek support from one of the two religious sects; and the struggle between Britain and Egypt for patronage of both sectarian leaders and the educated class. The theater for working out these issues was primarily the northern Sudan. Increasingly, the South was isolated from the North by British policies, especially with the Closed Districts Ordinance of 1933.

The educated Sudanese made an attempt to create a nonsectarian nationalist group in 1938 when they formed the Graduates Congress. However, the need for mass support soon caused the Congress to turn to the traditional "Sayyids," while the sentiment for independence forced a choice between cooperating with either Britain or Egypt.

The Graduates Congress gave impetus to political activity in 1942 by presenting a petition to the British for speedy Sudanese self-government. The abrupt rejection of the Congress memorandum precipitated a split in that group. The activists, whose leaders included Isma'il al-Azhari, demanded a vigorous response and a policy of noncooperation with the British. This meant they came to be allied with Egyptian nationalism and thus became proponents of Nile Valley unity. The activists formed their own political party, the Ashiqqa, which was the first and most outspoken of a number of parties supporting unity with Egypt. Meanwhile the moderates in Congress mistrusted Egyptian aims and felt that independence might be more rapidly achieved by working with the British. As both groups sought mass support they turned to the religious organizations, and nationalist politics became sectarian. 'Ali al-Mirghani and the Khatmiya gave support to the unionists, while 'Abd al-Rahman al-Mahdi and his Ansar worked with the more moderate nationalists in support of a separate, independent Sudan, creating the Ansar-affiliated Umma Party.

In this growing turmoil the British were also active, trying to create instruments for controlling political developments. An early step was the creation of the Advisory Council for the Northern Sudan in 1944. The activists objected that it had only advisory functions, excluded the southern Sudan, and consisted largely of traditional leaders, so they boycotted the Council. A Legislative Assembly was formed in 1948 as an elected body including both northern and southern representatives. Unionists boycotted it as well, and the Assembly was dominated by the Umma Party. On the international level, an Anglo-Egyptian stalemate over the British role in Egypt made agreement on the status of Sudan impossible.

Resolution came suddenly with the Egyptian revolution of 1952. The new Egyptian leadership was more flexible regarding the Sudan, and an agreement was signed in 1953 defining the steps toward Sudanese self-government and self-determination. Local politics were also simplified when most of the small unionist parties joined together, creating the National Unionist Party (NUP) led by Isma'il al-Azhari. Elections for a new parliament were held late in 1953 and the NUP won a majority. The Umma Party also won a large number of seats, while the only other large block of representatives was made up of southern members who were organized into the Liberal Party. Most of the smaller parties gradually disappeared.

Isma'il al-Azhari thus became the first Sudanese prime minister, and under his leadership the Sudanization of the administration rapidly progressed. Meanwhile the NUP membership, which had supported a unity-of-the-Nile platform, found its perspective changed with the new political developments. As the Sudan moved toward the time of self-determination, the unionists became convinced of the viability of a separately independent Sudan. Independence was endorsed by the NUP-led parliament, and on 1 January 1956 the British withdrew and the Sudan became an independent state. However, one cloud had arisen on the horizon in 1955. Southerners were upset by the limited role given them in the Sudanization of the government, and they feared northern domination. Rumors and mistrust spread in the South, and in August 1955 a mutiny broke out among southern army troops in Equatoria. Many people were killed in the fighting that ensued and a number of southern soldiers fled into exile. The issue of integrating the South into a unified Sudan hence arose as a major problem before the country had even achieved its independence.

POSTINDEPENDENCE

The new state of Sudan inherited a parliamentary structure from the Anglo-Egyptian regime, but the political system had little stability. Old cleavages and new problems emerged during the first two years of independence. The economic situation was troublesome, with Sudan having difficulty marketing its major export, cotton. Questions about the permanent form of the political system—parliamentary or presidential, centralized or federalist—were never resolved to the satisfaction of the major political forces. The problem of the South remained unaddressed and southern leaders began to withdraw in discouragement. Finally, even among the northern politicians the minimum consensus for effective government began to dissipate, with politics becoming little more than an arena for personal, factional, and sectarian feuds.

The political forces that interacted after independence were continuations of earlier groups. The activist, educated Sudanese, with solid support in the more modernized urban areas, generally looked to Isma'il al-Azhari for leadership, although small radical groups existed, especially the well-organized Sudanese Communist Party (SCP). The Khatmiya under the leadership of 'Ali al-Mirghani had joined with al-Azhari in the formation of the National Unionist Party (NUP). This alliance soon broke and in 1956 Sayyid 'Ali's followers formed the Peoples Democratic Party (PDP). The Ansar, following 'Abd al-Rahman al-Mahdi, continued to be the mainstay of the Umma Party.

When the PDP was formed, a major reversal in Sudanese politics took place. Until 1956 the Mahdi-Mirghani rivalry had been strong enough for the Khatmiya, though quite conservative, to ally themselves with the more radical Sudanese nationalists. However, the tensions between the Khatmiya leadership and al-Azhari that led to the breakup of the NUP also led to a PDP-Umma alliance, pitting the traditional religious forces against al-Azhari and the NUP. The PDP-Umma cooperation created a coalition government with 'Abdallah Khalil (Umma) as prime minister, and put al-Azhari into opposition. But since the Umma and PDP agreed on little more than opposition to al-Azhari, the effectiveness of governmental policy formation suffered. After new elections in 1958 failed to clarify the political picture, and the economic situation grew worse, the army chief of staff, Ibrahim Abboud, took control of the government through a military coup in November 1958.

It is widely believed that both the PDP and Umma received the coup willingly. However, Abboud made parties illegal and the Ansar soon lost most of the influence they had within the military regime. 'Ali al-Mirghani, who was never as directly active in politics as the Mahdist family, was able to maintain contact with the Abboud group although the PDP was outlawed along with the other parties. Northern politicians became restive and some were jailed briefly, but it was the southern leadership that suffered the most. The Abboud government attempted to "solve" the southern question militarily. This turned a bad situation into a major civil war. By the end of the Abboud era in 1964 most southern leaders were either in exile or prison, or were fighting openly against the Khartoum government. Southern resistance had become organized into a guerrilla movement, with the Anya-Nya, as well as a number of political organizations in exile.

Repression, lack of imagination, inability to handle the southern problem, and other factors created widespread discontent with the Abboud regime. In October 1964 student demonstrations, strikes, resistance by professional and legal leaders, and other activities forced the removal of the military regime. It was replaced by a transitional government led by Sirr al-Khatim al-Khalifa. Radical educated groups had an influential role in the new civilian government because of their prominent place in the October

Revolution. However, as elections and parliamentary government resumed, the older political parties regained control.

By 1965 the balance of political forces was different, although the actors were familiar. The radical intelligentsia was actively represented, especially in the small but influential Sudanese Communist Party (SCP). They had few seats in parliament but influenced at least the tone of political rhetoric. The NUP reemerged under al-Azhari and proved again to be a good vote winner. The PDP's position was less clear. It allied itself for a time with the Communists and boycotted elections. As a result, its position was rather insecure. 'Ali al-Mirghani's age and ill health reduced his role in national affairs so that the Khatmiya leadership was less concentrated than before, although it maintained cohesion even after his death in 1968.

The leading party in the elections following the revolution was the Umma, benefiting from the continued mass support of the Ansar movement. The problem facing the Umma was a split in the Mahdist family leadership. 'Abd al-Rahman had died in 1959 and his experienced son and successor, Siddiq, died unexpectedly in 1961. Ansar leadership roles became divided: Siddiq's son Sadiq became the head of the Umma Party, while al-Hadi, a more conservative son of 'Abd al-Rahman, became the *imam* or religious leader of the Ansar sect.

In parliament following the revolution, the Umma and NUP formed a coalition. Muhammad Ahmad Mahjub (Umma) became prime minister, while al-Azhari gained the post of president of the Supreme Council, which legally functioned as head of state. Divisions soon appeared among the Ansar as the Oxford-educated and more modern Sadiq disagreed with the more traditional Imam al-Hadi. This dispute carried over into politics as Mahjub tended to support al-Hadi. Sadiq engineered the ouster of the Mahjub-Imam wing of his party from power and became prime minister himself in 1966–1967. A reconciliation between Sadiq and the Imam brought Mahjub back into office, but by then it seemed clear to many Sudanese that the old pattern of personal and factional bickering had returned to dominate politics. This was perhaps only emphasized by the reunion of two bitter rivals, al-Azhari's NUP and the PDP, into the Democratic Unionist Party (DUP) in 1969.

The ineffectiveness of the parliamentary regime in resolving the southern problem also created discontent. Its solution had been a high priority matter for the civilians who overthrew Abboud. An important step was taken in 1965 when many southern leaders returned from exile for a Round Table Conference. However, southern divisions and northern inflexibility proved to be major stumbling blocks. As northern factional politics reemerged, leaders in Khartoum reverted to the attempt to solve the problem militarily and the war continued.

By May 1969 the feeling of unrest paved the way for a group of younger soldiers, led by Col. Ja'afar Nimeiri, to take over the government. The old parties were declared illegal, a Revolutionary Command Council (RCC) was set up, and a new cabinet including younger and independent civilians was formed. The May Revolution saw itself as a continuation of the October Revolution of 1964. Its leaders adopted domestic socialist programs and aimed at curbing conservative elements in Sudanese politics. Finding a solution to the southern question was announced as a major goal.

The Nimeiri revolutionary government faced a wide variety of challenges. It worked to create a new political structure for Sudan that would avoid the problems of the old system. Initially, although the RCC was the real center of power, a civilian cabinet had an important role in the operation of the government. Then more formal political institutions were created. In May 1971 the Sudanese Socialist Union (SSU) was formed as a mass organization to replace political parties. In January 1972 the first SSU congress approved a national charter and also the basic outline for a permanent constitution. After extensive discussions, this constitution was formally promulgated in May 1973 and a new government was formed under now-President Nimeiri.

Dealing with the southern question was a key element in the constitutional development. The northern insistence on a centralized political system had been an obstacle since the achievement of independence. The early announcement by the RCC that it recognized southern autonomy was an important step. In addition, the evolution of southern leadership also helped to pave the way for a settlement. In the 1960s, a large number of short-lived southern political organizations had made southern unity of action difficult. However, in 1969 much of the southern resistance, especially the military activities, became effectively coordinated by Joseph Lagu. With relatively unified southern leadership, more effective negotiations were possible. Early in 1972 northern and southern negotiators met in Addis Ababa, Ethiopia, and created a peace agreement that was formally signed late in March. Both sides were able to enforce the cease-fire and in a surprisingly short time the northern and southern military and administrative systems were integrated. There were some incidents, but by mid-1977 the basic outlines of the settlement were still in force.

Regional autonomy for the South was recognized in the permanent constitution. A broader decentralization of government in general was the stated goal of the Nimeiri regime. The hope was to create structures that would encourage popular participation without losing the benefits of centralized efficiency in planning. One of the continuing series of efforts in this direction was the reorganization of provincial government, changing from a system of a few large provinces to one having a greater number of smaller ones.

The Nimeiri regime also brought a new economic approach. Its first months were rather disorganized, but soon a more extensive state socialism was instituted: there was the nationalization of banks (May 1970), cotton marketing (June 1970), and newspapers (August 1970). However, especially after disagreements with the radical left, there was a feeling that the expansion of the government's economic role had been too rapid and there was some loosening of early control measures.

In political terms the revolutionary government initially appeared as a radical regime. Members of the Communist Party and officers sympathetic to the party were active and influential in government. The first real challenge came from conservative forces, especially the Ansar. The Imam al-Hadi led an open revolt in March 1970, which was quickly crushed at Aba Island and in the Wad Nubawi section of Omdurman (an Ansar stronghold). Organized conservative opposition within Sudan was destroyed, and the Ansar leadership and groups like the Muslim Brothers began to work in exile. In the next year, Nimeiri worked to avoid moving too far to the left and began to clash with the Communists. This reached a climax in July 1971 when a coup led by leftist officers took control of Khartoum for three days. After Nimeiri quickly regained control he began a campaign to crush the left opposition. Those leftist leaders who avoided execution were forced underground or into exile. Even through 1977, major opposition to the Nimeiri government came from both ends of the political spectrum: those who thought him too radical and those who thought him not radical enough.

During the Nimeiri years Sudan was identified in its constitution as a democratic republic ("democratic" being perhaps loosely defined). The central government was the basic focus of political power and policy making. A single mass political organization, the Sudanese Socialist Union, was the legal basis for popular participation in politics. Of course important steps were taken in the direction of decentralization, especially in the establishment of regional autonomy for the southern provinces. There was a High Executive Council for the Southern Region that had some power to determine action on the local and regional level. In the country as a whole, there were eighteen provinces for regional and local administration.

Economically Sudan was (and continues to be) primarily agricultural. Many Sudanese still worked within the traditional, subsistence sector, though a modern agricultural sector had arisen as well. The core of this was the Gezira Scheme, which was established as a major cotton growing area in the 1920s and was poised to become one of the most successful large-scale schemes in Africa. Throughout the 1970s there was considerable investment in agricultural development, with some seeing Sudan as the future "breadbasket of the Arab world."

Poor central planning, insufficient local coordination, and widespread corruption eventually dashed hopes for the economic development of Sudan's agricultural potential, and the economy progressively devolved instead of evolving. Domestic inflation rates soared while foreign indebtedness increased. As the World Bank and International Monetary Fund (IMF) tried to control and regulate the economy, the burden was made to fall upon the beleaguered Sudanese consumer, as prices for basic commodities like petrol and sugar rose beyond the reach of the ordinary citizen. Periodic popular demonstrations erupted over the final years of the Nimeiri regime, culminating in a popular uprising (*intifada*) that led the military to intervene in April 1985, bringing an end to the May Revolution government for its political as well as economic failures. Nimeiri, on an official visit to the United States at the time, settled into political exile in Egypt.

The most serious political failure of what increasingly was referred to as the Nimeiri "dictatorship" was the disintegration of the Addis Ababa Accords, leading to a renewed deterioration of relations between North and South and the resurgence of civil war in 1983. A number of grievances led to the outbreak of fighting, the most basic of which was the failure to fulfill the spirit of the Addis Ababa agreement, which was to have brought about economic development in the South and real, not token, political representation. Trust began to break down with the discovery of oil in the South, which Chevron Oil Company planned to develop. The decision by the government to locate the oil refinery in the North, near Kosti, and to pipe most of the oil outside Sudan for the generation of hard currency was received with hostility in the South. When southern protest became more organized and unified, Nimeiri responded with a plan to redivide the South, which amounted to an act of political "gerrymandering."

While these events shaped the more recent North-South relationship, Nimeiri took steps to move the government and the nation away from its secular path toward an Islamic emphasis in law and society. This state-supported Islamization began in 1977 with a plan to gradually Islamize laws, and there was some limited success in the banning of alcohol and the institution of *zakat*, a form of religious taxation. However, as secular forces from the South and their northern allies objected, this gradual approach was abandoned and Nimeiri took the bold step of imposing Islamic law upon the Sudanese state by decree. This occurred in September 1983, and thereafter the new Islamic civil and criminal codes became known as the September Laws. With opposition to this move coming from the Judiciary and even staunch Muslim advocates such as Sadiq al-Mahdi, Nimeiri sought greater control of the application of these laws through newly appointed judges who served in the regime's "Courts of Prompt Justice." Harsh application of the *hudud* (criminal) penalties resulted in the use of these courts as tools of repression, as the jails filled and many lost limbs to Nimeiri's version of Islamic "justice."

The popular *intifada* of spring 1985 brought about a massive democratic upsurge with a broad united opposition to the Nimeiri government, and literally millions were mobilized to bring down the regime. In the end, it was a relatively simple coup d'etat, led by General Suwar al-Dahab, that finished the May Revolution. It promised, keeping to its word, that civilian rule would be restored. By the spring 1986 elections had been held and the Umma Party won, forming a government with Sadiq al-Mahdi again as prime minister. As democracy dramatically returned to Sudan, the older parties revived, but in the process over three dozen new political parties also took shape.

ISLAMIST RULE

Sudan's third brief period of democracy (1986–1989) finally bogged down with a failure of leadership and initiative. Prime Minister al-Mahdi did not act decisively on either the bitterly divisive issue of Shari'a and Islamization or the urgent need to begin negotiations with the chief southern organization, the Sudan Peoples Liberation Movement (SPLM). Intensified fighting in the South and incidents of unrest in other areas of the country encouraged profound economic and social decay. With tensions in the capital rising and the government on the verge of collapse, the military stepped in once again to "solve" the problems of the country, only this time the coup-makers and coup-backers were strongly influenced by the National Islamic Front (NIF) and its parent organization, the Muslim Brotherhood.

The regime of General 'Umar Hasan al-Bashir that came to power in the coup of 30 June 1989 was committed to a Sudan unified under Shari'a law. It immediately acted to ban all political parties except religious ones and shut down all newspapers and other media, instituting its own publications. One, *al-Inqaz al-Watani* ("The National Salvation"), lent its name to the new regime, which indeed saw itself as the country's only answer to the failure of sectarian-influenced party politics and Western-style secular democracy. A large number of politicians and intellectuals representing a broad political spectrum were arrested, and allegations quickly arose of political repression and torture, bringing the regime unwanted attention from the international media and organizations such as Africa Watch and Amnesty International.

In the face of deteriorating political conditions and harsh repression, unprecedented alliances were formed among the banned political parties, which formed the National Democratic Alliance (NDA) and found common cause in opposing the al-Bashir regime, some from places of exile. All major parties, including the SPLM, were signatories to the National Democratic Charter in Cairo in March 1990. A consensus was reached that the civil war could only be negotiated to an end by the removal of Shari'a as the state law. Also needed was the convening of a constitutional conference, whereby a secular and democratic state, justly representing all of Sudan's diverse regions and minorities, would be constructed.

Offsetting the newfound cooperation of the major political parties has been the intransigence of the al-Bashir regime. In its twelve years of power, it has relentlessly pursued a military solution to the civil war, while its domestic and foreign policies have been guided by the strict Islamist principles of its chief ideologue, Dr. Hasan al-Turabi.

Upon first coming to power in 1989, the regime proclaimed itself free of any ideological predilection, and among those it placed in detention were Sadiq al-Mahdi, Muhammad 'Uthman al-Mirghani of the Democratic Unionist Party, and al-Turabi of the NIF. Within four months all three were released, and though the official chief authority in the state was the Revolutionary Command Council, Turabi's influence soon became apparent. By 1993, the RCC had been dissolved and al-Bashir was ruling as a "civilian" president, with the assistance of a 300-member Transitional National Assembly appointed to enact laws. In the parliamentary elections of March 1996, held under the most dire conditions, both al-Bashir and al-Turabi won seats, and the NIF emerged as the sole party in government. Al-Turabi's governmental role was further consolidated in February 1998, when he was elected secretary-general of the National Congress, the sole legal political organization.

In its attempt to reorganize national politics, the al-Bashir regime has been adamant from the start that there would be no return to political parties. In 1991 a federal system of government with nine states was announced; almost exactly three years later, Sudan was redivided into twenty-six states. Just what these units of administration meant to the governance of the country is unclear, particularly since governance has played a secondary role to the pursuance of the civil war and the imposition of authority. Popular protests in the towns and at the universities have been met with force, and occasionally deadly force. At least nine coup attempts have been thwarted, leading to the arrest and execution of scores (and perhaps hundreds) of army officers.

Social conditions in Sudan have declined precipitously since 1989, due to both the civil war and government policy. Well before the al-Bashir regime came to power, refugee settlements ringing the capital area had grown to township size. Since 1990 many of these areas have been destroyed in the name of "slum clearance," while their inhabitants—mainly non-Muslim southerners—have been either relocated to desert settlements equally lacking in amenities or on some occasions killed outright. Behind the government's public health and civil engineering concerns lies a well-documented agenda to forcibly convert these people to Islam, while the young men, with increasing frequency, are impressed into the popular militias to fight the civil war in the South.

Throughout the country health conditions have declined, as war-related famine, rampant malnutrition, appalling sanitary conditions, and a shortage of both doctors and medical equipment have exacerbated an already bad situation. Khartoum experienced bread shortages and riots in 1995 and 1996, while Guinea worm infection and such diseases as polio, malaria, and *Leishmaniasis* have been rampant throughout the South and Ethiopian borderlands. Devastating flooding in the capital area and along the Nile Valley in 1996 added to these miseries.

In the face of such disasters the al-Bashir regime has stood firm, committed to its Islamist policies and intolerant of dissent. Widespread arrests and torture in so-called ghost houses have been reported since the early years of its rule; this and the failing economy have driven many professionals and educators out of the country. Residents of the capital naturally have come under the closest scrutiny. Islamic dress has been imposed on all women, and on at least one occasion female students were flogged for wearing pants on a school bus. The *hudud* (penal) laws of the Shari'a have been applied, including amputations, while several prostitutes were sentenced to death in Khartoum in November 1997. In such a political atmosphere, religiously inspired criminal acts have claimed a number of lives, including the murder of a popular singer in Omdurman in 1994.

Related to the civil war and the breakdown of social and political order is the revival of slavery practices. Though the government has steadfastly denied accusations of slavery within Sudan, numerous victims have come forward over the years to relate their experiences. For the most part they have been Dinka or Nuba people, inhabiting the cultural transition zone between North and South, whose villages were attacked by either elements of the Popular Defense Forces (PDF) or Arab tribal militias armed by the government. In some cases they have been sent to the far north of the country to serve as laborers and sexual slaves; other times they have served masters from the cattle-herding tribes that abducted them. The SPLA, for its part, has also practiced coercive measures on a vulnerable civilian population, impressing abandoned or orphaned children into its ranks.

In the realm of foreign policy, the al-Bashir regime has found itself isolated in the region, while internationally Sudan has been labeled a "terrorist" state. Relations with Egypt, already tense over a dispute over the Halayeb region on the Red Sea, worsened as Iran began giving military aid to the government in 1991 to pursue a jihad in the South. In 1995, Sudanese were implicated in an assassination attempt on the Egyptian president in Addis Ababa; Sudan's unwillingness to surrender the suspects in the case led to a breakdown in diplomatic relations with both Egypt and Ethiopia. In 1996, the UN condemned Sudan for harboring terrorists and approved punitive sanctions, while the United States suspended its diplomatic presence in Khartoum. Meanwhile, Eritrea had broken off diplomatic relations with Sudan in 1994, giving the NDA use of the former Sudanese embassy for its headquarters. Libya, a onetime ally of the al-Bashir regime, began expelling Sudanese "guest workers" in 1995, allegedly fearing Islamist subversion. Finally, to the south, Sudan and Uganda have accused one another of aiding their respective insurgencies: while Uganda has apparently given support to the SPLA, Khartoum has aided Osama bin Laden and the "Lord's Resistance Army." In 1995 Sudan and Uganda dismissed each other's diplomats, amid reports of Sudanese bombing within Ugandan territory and threats of war.

With regard to the civil war itself, the al-Bashir regime managed in 1996 to attract a number of renegade SPLA commanders to its side, most notably Riek Machar (of the Southern Sudan Independence Movement), Lam Akol (of SPLA-United), and, at least temporarily, Kerubino Bol. The advantage of these alliances seems negligible, however, as the war follows its decades-old pattern of dry season offensives and rainy season entrenchment. Opposition forces under the NDA umbrella, including the main faction of the SPLA led by John Garang, have succeeded in extending the civil war into southern Darfur and Kordofan as well as portions of eastern Sudan. On the other hand the SPLA has been riven with factionalism, hampering its effectiveness.

While there are as yet no winners in Sudan's civil war, there are clearly losers. Those southern Sudanese and Nuba who have succumbed to the attacks of the Sudanese Army, PDF, and government-armed tribal militias are all losers. Likewise are the vulnerable population of the borderlands who have been abducted and enslaved by Arab militiamen, and the rest of the country's population, North and South, that has suffered directly and indirectly from the costs of the war. As the casualty figure climbs above one and a half million, the true cost of the war to the nation is beyond calculating.

THE ECONOMY

The economies of the vast territory known as the Sudan were based chiefly upon subsistence production, including cultivation, pastoralism, and foraging (hunting and fishing), until the rise of the states of Sinnar and Dar Fur in the sixteenth and seventeenth centuries. The Funj state of Sinnar developed a system of "administered trade," wherein the ruler organized and dominated an external trade with Egypt in order to obtain luxury goods, either for his own use or to maintain his power. Caravans leaving the capital at Sinnar carried mainly gold and slaves north, but also amounts of gum arabic, ivory, ostrich feathers, and other goods; caravans arriving from Egypt brought spices, soap, perfumes, sugar, and cotton goods. From the mid-seventeenth century the Keira state of Dar Fur also practiced an administered trade with Egypt, exporting slaves, ivory, and other goods across the desert route known as the "Forty Days Road" and receiving in return weapons, saddles, cloth, soap, and spices. In both states there existed as well groups of merchants practicing domestic and foreign trade, though their activities were subordinated to those of the ruler.

The eighteenth century saw the dissolution of the administered trade system in Sinnar, as political troubles weakened the Sultan and groups of local and foreign traders began to assume more economic power. Aiding the rise of this new merchant class was the implementation of aspects of Islamic law (Shari'a), which regulated the commercial system. The use of foreign currencies also facilitated trade, as did the spread of trading centers (later towns) and organization of traders under a chief merchant. As the economic system evolved, land became privatized and commoditized, replacing the earlier communal ownership of land, while the rise of huge estates made possible (and even desirable) large-scale slave production as well as share-cropping.

The Turco-Egyptian conquest of the northern Sudan (1821–1822) was undertaken to obtain large quantities of gold and slaves. In this respect the conquerors failed, though Turco-Egyptian rule expanded considerably the trade between Sudan and the rest of the world. Among their many achievements, the new rulers improved Sudan's systems of transportation and communication, provided political stability and security for trade to flourish, introduced new crops, and brought more land under cultivation. The administrative capital at Khartoum quickly became the commercial center as well, where local traders were joined by Egyptians and foreigners of European and Mediterranean origin, many representing commercial companies abroad. Chief among Sudan's exports at this time were gum arabic, ostrich feathers, and ivory. As the search for ivory spread south and southwest into territories ungoverned by the Turco-Egyptians, slave raiding of the local peoples grew, changing from an ancillary to a primary economic activity. By the middle of the nineteenth century Khartoum was an important slave market, exporting slaves to Egypt and the Arabian Peninsula.

The development of Sudan's economy under the Turco-Egyptians had many ramifications. Large trading concerns developed on the Upper Nile and in Bahr al-Ghazal, sometimes dominated by freebooters such as al-Zubayr Rahma Mansur, who controlled vast territories with the aid of slave armies. The ruthless activities of these individuals laid waste whole communities of stateless peoples and initiated a long history of antagonism between northern Muslims and southern non-Muslims. Meanwhile the expansion of slave and ivory hunting by Khartoum-based merchants undermined the activities of the Keira sultanate of Dar Fur, which fell to al-Zubayr in 1874 and was joined to the Turco-Egyptian Sudan. The spread of a market economy, aided by the wider circulation of currency, sharpened social and economic distinctions in Sudanese society. Among the dispossessed were petty traders of the riverine north, while among the disempowered were northern Sudanese women, victims of both market forces and Islamic mores. At least in Khartoum and the larger towns, imported European goods could now be purchased, sold by merchants who enjoyed considerable prosperity, while exported Sudanese gum arabic was fast becoming an important commodity in Britain.

Many of the social and economic forces unleashed by the Turco-Egyptians encouraged the rise to power of Muhammad Ahmad, the Sudanese Mahdi, who in 1885 sealed his victorious revolt with the capture of Khartoum. The hostility of the Mahdist era severely curtailed Sudan's foreign trade, though some small degree of trade with Egypt continued during the reign of Khalifa 'Abdullahi (1885–1898), mostly in gum arabic and ostrich feathers (exports) and perfumes (imports). Just as affected by the upheavals of the period was the domestic trade, which suffered triply from political instability, environmental disasters, and poor economic planning. As the Khalifa struggled to affirm his authority, he relied heavily on the support of his Baqqara kinsmen of the West, whose settlement in Omdurman he required and with whose sustenance he was charged. Seizing grain from the rich Gezira region to feed his soldiers and the booming population of Omdurman, the Khalifa alienated many followers; he did so again with his attempt to revive a form of administered trade, exercising enormous personal control over the economy. With the shortage of reliable currency came black marketeering, while excessive trade duties encouraged smuggling and cronyism encouraged corruption.

The sole vital market of the Mahdist period was in Omdurman, which the Khalifa intended as the political, economic, and popular center of his state. With the abandonment, destruction, or suppression of other market towns, Omdurman grew enormously, and its market—despite difficult conditions and a dominant ethos of Mahdist asceticism—offered a wide degree of goods and services. Separate from the formal economy of the city was a barter economy of handicrafts and food items conducted chiefly by women in the neighborhoods of the capital. Meanwhile, immune from the privations suffered by others, Mahdist elites employed large contingents of slaves to farm rural estates along the Blue and White Niles.

The Anglo-Egyptian Condominium that came into being in 1899 governed a society that was still mainly involved in subsistence production, and from which little money could be raised. Responding to Britain's need for new sources of cotton as well as the Condominium's need for revenues, the government embarked on a program of centrally organized, highly supervised cotton-growing schemes along the Blue, White, and main Niles. In 1904 the Sudan Plantation Syndicate was established to oversee pump irrigation schemes on the main Nile and in several locations in the Gezira. Increasing the scope and profitability of these schemes was the construction of the dam at Sinnar on the Blue Nile (1914–1925), whose integrated, dam-irrigated plots came to be known as the Gezira Scheme. In allocating land for development in the Gezira, the government favored local elites such as tribal and religious leaders, whose loyalty was deemed necessary to pacify the country and minimize the appeal of antigovernment uprisings. However, much of the actual labor in cultivating the Gezira's cotton was provided by immigrant West Africans (*Fellata*), who entered Sudan in search of labor or en route to pilgrimage in Mecca. Farther east, the government initiated cotton schemes in the deltas of the seasonal Gash and Baraka rivers, respectively near Kassala and Tokar.

Among the other economic developments in the early years of the Condominium were improvements in Sudan's infrastructure and an expansion of the cash-based economy. The extension of the railroad to Khartoum in 1899, and thereafter south to the Gezira, west to El Obeid, and east to the Red Sea, opened up Sudan's productive regions to more efficient exploitation and marketing. Meanwhile the construction of Port Sudan as the country's main port ensured the rapid transport of goods to foreign markets. With the increase in productivity and trade, Sudan became the world leader in gum arabic production by 1930 as well as a major supplier of long staple cotton for fine cloth. Meanwhile the growing population of the Three Towns area (Khartoum, Khartoum North, and Omdurman) provided a large market to encourage the cash economy, while government tax and payment policies did the same.

Reinvestment of capital derived from the earlier developments provided the chief impetus for Sudan's economic growth in the years 1930–1956. While the government continued to invest in agricultural schemes, veterinary services, communications, transport, and power facilities, the most significant investments were from the private sector. Of these, investments in pump schemes were the most important, realizing large profits in the 1930s and 1940s in cotton and food crops. Complementing these were private investments in mechanized farming, real estate, commerce, and petty manufacturing, leading in particular to the rise of numerous trading companies across the country. By the time of independence in 1956, Sudan had realized very little industrialization, and much of the economy remained unchanged from pre-Condominium times (i.e., subsistence). On the other hand, the level of cash-based market exchanges had grown considerably, while the country's emphasis on cotton production made it increasingly dependent upon foreign trade.

Sudan's economic development during the first thirteen years of independence largely followed the pattern established during the Condominium: productive investment from the private sector in pump schemes or mechanized farming, with limited state investment in industrial development. A radical jolt to Sudan's economy and politics came with the Free Officers coup of May 1969 and the rise to power of Ja'afar Nimeiri. Dedicated to a socialist plan of strengthening the state's control over the economy and restricting the power of the private sector, Nimeiri's regime announced the formation of two state companies in 1969 to monopolize international trade. Next, in May 1970, the government announced its intention to nationalize most privately held companies: In short order the state took over virtually all trading, industrial, and financial companies, including all banks and import-export companies. A five-year development plan in 1970 sought to involve the state further in the economy with state investments in productive activities, while legislative measures attempted to restructure Sudanese society along more egalitarian lines.

Nimeiri's economic plans necessarily entailed a reorientation of foreign policy. In 1969 Sudan officially recognized the German Democratic Republic and began trade talks with East Bloc countries in order to strengthen economic ties with other socialist nations. These talks led to a number of trade agreements as well as promises of long-term, low interest loans for Sudan. Closer to home, Nimeiri negotiated a plan for economic integration with Egypt and Libya, including joint economic policies and the lifting of customs barriers. As negotiations moved in a more overtly political direction, including a plan for the creation of federal institutions with both countries and Syria as well, Nimeiri deferred agreement pending further consideration.

The Nimeiri government's experiment in radical social and economic transformation was ultimately short-lived. Differences between the ruling RCC and the Communist Party flared over the issue of political organization and developed into a contest for power. In November 1970 the RCC began a purge of Communist-affiliated individuals from government positions. After a brief Communist coup in July 1971, Nimeiri regained power and had the leaders of the CP executed. This event occasioned a transformation in Nimeiri's thinking: Now, injections of capital into the economy were regarded as the key to successful development, rather than socioeconomic transformation. The state's role would be to create the necessary infrastructure while leaving the private sector to develop the productive sphere. As the attraction of capital was now the state's chief concern, Nimeiri sought to pursue policies acceptable to the IMF to reassure investors.

A portion of Nimeiri's hopes were pinned on investments of petrodollars from the Arabian gulf, which he assumed would be mutually beneficial to the Sudan (in agricultural development) and the Arab countries (in a new food source). An IMF stabilization program undertaken in 1972 represented a significant about-face for the May regime, involving privatization measures, reducing the role of the public sector, liberalizing trade, eliminating subsidies, implementing anti-inflationary policies, and devaluing the Sudanese currency. Meanwhile, government expenditures rose in the 1970s as agricultural schemes and infrastructure improvements continued. A new and promising branch of the economy was the oil sector, developed from 1974 by Chevron Corporation in Bahr al-Ghazal, where commercially exploitable amounts of oil argued in favor of a pipeline to the Red Sea.

By the late 1970s it was apparent that Nimeiri's economic program was failing. A vicious cycle of increased foreign debt and declining production undermined the economy's ability to grow out of its quagmire; while inflation rose, the Sudanese currency lost value and the standard of living declined. In 1978 the national debt was $3 billion; by 1982 it had reached $5.2 billion. The actual causes of the country's economic problems were twofold: deficient government planning exacerbated by corruption and external factors such as the rise in oil prices and flight of skilled labor to the Gulf countries, adding to inflationary pressures. Nimeiri chose to view matters differently, seeing in a program of Islamization the means to repair Sudanese economy and society as well as salvage his regime.

As early as 1978 the Saudi-based Faisal Islamic Bank had begun successful operations in Sudan, enjoying government exemptions from taxes and normal banking regulations to quickly outstrip other banks in both growth and profitability. Other Islamic banks soon followed, lending support to the political program of Hasan al-Turabi and the Muslim Brothers organization, which sought to cultivate a Shari'a-based society in Sudan. The implementation of Shari'a law by Nimeiri in 1983 did little to aid Sudan's economy, driving away foreign investments even as it sparked a deadly (and expensive) new cycle in the country's relentless civil war. As Sudan's economic and political problems mounted, resistance to Nimeiri's rule grew, until he was overthrown by the military while on a visit to the United States in 1985.

The Islamist regime of 'Umar Hasan al-Bashir that came to power in a coup in 1989 has presided over the further dissolution of Sudan's economy. The regime's decision to back Iraq in the 1990 Gulf crisis cost Sudan an enormous amount of financial aid, as Saudi Arabia immediately suspended all grants, project loans, and concessionary oil sales. Other forms of development aid were cancelled amid accusations of Khartoum attempting to export an Islamist program in Africa and the Middle East. The continuation of Sudan's civil war has not only drained the economy of much-needed capital, but also ruined the country's economic potential and prevented the further development of oil reserves in Bahr al-Ghazal. In the eyes of the IMF and other international financial institutions, Sudan is bankrupt and mismanaged; in the eyes of the United States and other Western powers, it is a rogue state dedicated to terrorism. While the Bashir regime now operates a major oil pipeline to the Red Sea and optimistically forecasts oil production for the coming years, the political conditions that would allow Sudan to harness its resources and develop economically continue to diminish.

* Much of the information in this section on the economy is drawn from T. Niblock, *Class and Power in the Sudan* (1987) Albany: State University of New York Press.

1. African dress in Shendi, Sinnar, and Shayqiya.

I Bd., II Abth, Taf 31, German polychrome print, ca. 1740.

2. Dinka House near Wau.

Photo: Richard Lobban.

3. Sir Samuel Baker.

Hugh Craig, *Great African Travelers*. London; Routledge, 1890, p. 58.

4. Negro soldiers in battle engagement positions.

Richard Buchta Album, Photo No. 99, 1881. Courtesy of the Boston Public Library, Print
Department.

5. General Charles Gordon Pasha.

James P. Boyd, *Stanley in Africa*. Stanley Publishing, 1889.

6. Original Palace of the Governor General in Khartoum. (The building where Gordon Pasha was killed.)

Richard Buchta, 1881. Courtesy of the Boston Public Library, Print Department.

7. Muhammad Ahmad al-Mahdi.

By Montband (the Mansell Collection).

8. The Qadi of Khartoum.

Photo: Richard Buchta, 1881.
Courtesy of the Boston Public
Library, Print Department.

9. Display of Plundered Trophies of Sulayman Zubayr.

Richard Buchta Album, Photo No. 100, 1881. Courtesy of the Boston Public Library, Print
Department.

10. General Horatio Herbert Kitchener, Commander in Chief
of the Egyptian Army, age 46.

Illustrated London News, 1896.

11. Emin Pasha.

J.W. Buel, *Heroes of the Dark Continent.* Philadelphia; Historical Publishing Co., 1889.

12. Omdurman landing place in the early 20th century.
Victoria Bookstore: Khartoum.

13. "Nubian Dancers" (probably slaves) in 1881.
Photo: Richard Buchta. Photo 9, Courtesy of the Boston Public Library, Print Department.

14. Baqqara woman, ca. 1971.

Sudan Government Photo: Ministry of Information.

15. The Nubian Guard (in Cairo).
Ludwig Deutsch, 1895 painting.

16. Shaqiya Woman, 1881.
Photo: Richard Buchta, Courtesy of the
Boston Public Library, Print Department.

17. Leaders of the White Flag League, 1924 (right to left: Hasan Sharif, 'Ali 'Abd al-Latif, Salih 'Abd al-Qadir, 'Ubayd al-Haj al-Amin).

Courtesy of the University of Durham, Sudan Archives.

18. Gordon Memorial College, Khartoum, ca. 1930.

Courtesy of the University of Durham, Sudan Archives.

19. 'Uthman Ibn Abi Bakr Diqna (Osman Digna), ca. 1925.

20. Suakin, 1905.

Courtesy of the University of Durham, Sudan Archives.

Shelluks-Fashoda. (Sudan)

21. Three Shilluk men from Fashoda, postcard, ca. 1930s.
R. Lobban Collection.

22. View of Deim Sulayman in Dar-Fertit, 1881.

Photo: Richard Buchta. Courtesy of the Boston Public Library, Print Department.

23. Hasan al-Turabi.
Photo: C. Fluehr-Lobban Collection, 1992.

24. Sadiq
al-Mahdi.
Sudan Government
Photo, c. 1979.

25. Ja'afar Nimeiri.

Sudan Government Photo, c. 1980.

26. Sayid 'Ali al-Mirghani.

Courtesy of Kegan Paul, Ltd.

27. John Garang.

Courtesy of Kegan Paul, Ltd.

The Dictionary

– A –

ABA ISLAND. An island in the White Nile near Kosti (q.v.), about 270 kilometers south of Khartoum (q.v.), to which the family of Muhammad Ahmad al-Mahdi (q.v.) was drawn to harvest timber ca. 1870, and that was the site of the Mahdi's manifestation and first battle against the Turco-Egyptian (q.v.) regime in 1881. After the Anglo-Egyptian (q.v.) conquest the Mahdi's son 'Abd al-Rahman al-Mahdi (q.v.) was allowed to begin cultivation there, and by 1918 the island had become a place of annual pilgrimage for thousands of West African and western Sudanese Ansar (q.v.), much to the discomfort of the British authorities. Sayid 'Abd al-Rahman attempted to create a "rightly ordered" society among his followers on Aba based on the ideals of the Mahdist period, including a comprehensive social welfare system, strict hierarchical structure, and quasi-military pattern of organization. Aba also formed the base of the Mahdi family's vast agricultural holdings and political influence.

In 1970 the Ansar opposition to Ja'afar al-Nimeiri (q.v.), led by Imam al-Hadi, withdrew to Aba Island and threatened revolt. On 27 March 1970 the island was attacked by government forces by air and from land, resulting in many Ansar fatalities and the confiscation of Mahdi family land. Since the overthrow of Nimeiri, Aba Island has resumed importance as an Ansar center.

ABABDA. A nomadic group with some sedentary sections in upper Egypt and the northern Sudan. They are Arabic-speaking and are associated with Beja (q.v.) origins. They were traditionally important as the guardians of the caravan routes from Korosko to Abu Hamad and served as irregulars in the Anglo-Egyptian (q.v.) army in the nineteenth century, aiding in the initial conquest and in fighting against the Mahdist movement.

1

ABBAS (1813–1854). This Ottoman ruler of Egypt and the Sudan was the son of Touson and grandson of Muhammad 'Ali. (q.v.). During his reign (1848–1854) a railway connection between Cairo and Alexandria was begun, and the private European expeditions to the southern Sudan took place. In conjunction with legitimate trade for ivory were also extensive raids in the Upper Nile into Shilluk and Dinka (qq.v.) territories for capturing slaves (q.v.).

ABBAS HILMI (1874–1944). This Ottoman ruler of Egypt and the Sudan was the son of Muhammad Tewfik, son of the Khedive Isma'il (q.v.) (i.e., the great grandson of Muhammad 'Ali). He ruled from 1892 to 1914, thus during the end of the Mahdiya (q.v.) through the "Reconquest" by General H. H. Kitchener (q.v.) and into Condominium (q.v.) rule.

ABBAS, MEKKI (1911–1979). Educated in Gordon Memorial College (q.v.) and England, he served in the Ministry of Education (1931–1946) and was active in the Advisory Council for the northern Sudan (q.v.), which helped lead to Sudanese self-government. He edited a small but influential newspaper after World War II and wrote an important study, *The Sudan Question*. After 1958 he worked outside Sudan in international agencies and in the mid-1960s he was assistant director general of the United Nations Food and Agriculture Organization.

ABBOUD, IBRAHIM (1900–1983). Sudanese soldier and prime minister (1958–1964). He was educated in Gordon Memorial College (q.v.) and the Khartoum Military College, entering the Sudan Defense Force in 1925. After serving in many areas in World War II he was promoted to general in 1954. He was commander in chief of the armed forces after independence when Prime Minister 'Abdallah Khalil (q.v.), with the tacit support of Sayid 'Abd al-Rahman al-Mahdi and Sayid 'Ali al-Mirghani (qq.v.), supported his seizure of power to relieve the country of its political squabbles. The Western-backed military coup came on 17 November 1958, elevating Abboud to the office of president of the Supreme Council of the Armed Forces, prime minister, and leading figure in the military government. Committed to a conservative policy of maintaining the economic and social status quo, and lacking a coherent vision for the nation as a whole, his regime failed to address the serious problems of development and national integration. The eruption of the southern problem, which he had left to fester, led to the demonstrations of the October Revolution (q.v.) of 1964, forcing him to retire.

'ABD AL-FADIL AL-MAZ. One of the main leaders of the 1924 White Flag Revolt (q.v.) in Khartoum (q.v.). This movement sought to oust the British from the Sudan in a secret alliance with Egyptian forces. This Muslim southerner and his colleague 'Ali 'Abd al-Latif (q.v.) were betrayed at the last moment when the Egyptians failed to join the revolt. In protracted resistance at the old Blue Nile railway bridge and in government buildings nearby, 'Abd al-Fadil refused to surrender; at last the building he was in was dynamited. When his body was found it is claimed that his fingers were still on his machine gun. The story of 'Abd al-Fadil has now entered Sudanese nationalist folklore.

'ABD AL-KHALIQ MAHGOUB (?–1971). This important Sudanese political leader was a founder of the Sudanese Communist Party (SCP, q.v.) in 1946, which was based among workers, peasants in the Gezira (q.v.), and students at Gordon Memorial College (q.v.) and Cairo University extension in Khartoum (q.v.). The SCP created a youth wing in 1948. By 1949 'Abd al-Khaliq became the SCP secretary-general amidst the Cold War, serving until his death in 1971. Among the many activities and united fronts of the SCP under his leadership was the Movement for National Liberation formed in 1947 that was linked to its counterpart Egyptian Democratic Movement in Egypt.

In the late 1940s and early 1950s period of labor and nationalist agitation, the SCP and especially the Sudan Railway Workers Union (SRWU) in Atbara (q.v.) were finally able to call a general strike. The SRWU was a member of the Sudanese Workers Trade Union Federation (q.v.), then headed by his fellow SCP-member al-Shafi' Ahmad al-Shaykh (q.v.). The SCP followed the more orthodox Moscow orientation. As top official of the party 'Abd al-Khaliq was jailed by the Ibrahim Abboud (q.v.) military regime and after his release played a very active role in the period following the 1964 October Revolution (q.v.). In 1968 he won a parliamentary seat running as an independent, although his party affiliation was very well known. In the early years of the Ja'afar al-Nimeiri (q.v.) government, the SCP was given access to power and had a collaborative role, but 'Abd al-Khaliq was jailed in late 1970. He escaped and went underground in Sudan in 1971 and was alleged to have been involved in the July 1971 coup led by Hashim al-Atta (q.v.). When Nimeiri was quickly restored to power 'Abd al-Khaliq and other leading members of the SCP were executed.

'ABD AL-MAHMUD, FATMA. Prominent woman leader during the Ja'afar al-Nimeiri (q.v.) years. She was named to the newly created post of minister of state for social welfare in 1975, became minister of social affairs in 1976, and was active in the affairs of the Sudanese Socialist Union (q.v.).

'ABD AL-LATIF. *See* 'ALI 'ABD AL-LATIF.

'ABD AL-MUN'IM MUHAMMAD (1896–1946). Sudanese business-man. He formed a large import-export firm in the early twentieth century. He was a founder of Printing and Publishing Company, Ltd., publisher of *al-Nil* newspaper, associated with Ansar (q.v.) interests. He was an early member of the Graduates Congress (q.v.).

'ABD AL-QADIR WAD HABUBA (?–1908). This religious revolution-ary was an active follower of the Mahdi (q.v.). After the fall of the Mahdist state he returned to his home in the Blue Nile area. Continuing religious fervor and local land ownership disputes caused him to lead a revolt in 1908 against British control. Although his movement was quickly crushed and he was executed, the revolt pointed up the continu-ing potential for religious uprisings of a Mahdist nature.

'ABD AL-RAHMAN, 'ALI (1904–). Sudanese politician. He was a judge in the Shari'a (q.v.) courts until he was elected to parliament in 1953 as a member of the National Unionist Party (NUP, q.v.). He was closely as-sociated with the Khatmiya (q.v.) leadership and became president of the Peoples Democratic Party (PDP, q.v.) when it was formed in 1956. He served in many cabinets as minister of justice (1954–1955), minister of education (1955–1956), minister of interior (1956–1958), and minister of agriculture (1958). After the 1964 October Revolution he was again president of the PDP and became vice-president of the Democratic Unionist Party (DUP, q.v.) formed by the PDP-NUP merger in 1967. His political activity came to an end with the 1969 revolution.

'ABD AL-RAHMAN AL-MAHDI. *See* MAHDI, AL-.

'ABD AL-RAHMAN, SHAYKH OMER. *See* SHAYKH OMER 'ABD AL-RAHMAN.

'ABD AL-RAHMAN WAD AL-NUJUMI. *See* NUJUMI, AL-.

'ABDALLAB. An Arab (q.v.) group descended from a fifteenth-century leader, 'Abdalla Jamma of the Qawisima Arabs, who united all Arabs of what became the northern Sudan to destroy the Christian Nubian kingdom of Alwa (q.v.). The 'Abdallab controlled the area around the confluence of the Niles and conquered Soba, the capital of Alwa. This was achieved in alliance with Amara Dunqas (q.v.), leader of the Funj (q.v.) peoples who likely included the Shilluk (q.v.) from the White Nile along with other indigenous Sudanese in the region. Dunqas established the Funj Sultanates in Sinnar (q.v.).

The 'Abdallab established and maintained their Arab sheikhdom in Qarri (Gerri) until the late eighteenth century. Their kings carried the title *manjil* (q.v., or *manjiluk*), which may be understood to mean "we venerate you, and only you, as our leader." Later the 'Abdallab moved to Halfayat al-Muluk.

The political power of the 'Abdallab virtually encompassed all the inhabited areas of the riverine northern Sudan, parts of Kordofan (q.v.) to the west, and to the east up to Suakin (q.v.) on the Red Sea. Their relationship with Sinnar continued as a loose political alliance, but the *manjil* of the 'Abdallab was actually independent throughout the 'Abdallab dynasties from its founder Jamma and his strong oldest son, *Manjil* 'Ajib. The 'Abdallab rule gradually weakened from continuous wars with the Shayqiya (q.v.), who finally assumed their own *mek* (q.v., local king) rule. Conflicts also broke out with their southern neighbors the Hamaj (q.v.) of Sinnar. Taking advantage of these divisions, Isma'il Pasha (q.v.) conquered the entire country in 1821. The 'Abdallab descendants are now allegedly living as the Adarkojab and Ingriyab of the northern province and the 'Abdallab of the Central Sudan and the Blue Nile. [by Mahgoub el-Tigani]

'ABDALLAH DAFA'ALLAH AL-ARAKI. *See* ARAKIYIN.

'ABDALLAH JAMMA' (?– ca. 1560). This regional Arab leader succeeded in conquering the northern riverine lands of the Sudan and establishing a capital at Qarri. He was the founder of the 'Abdallab (q.v.) and was known as its *manjil* (q.v.) in the loose political alliance they had with the Funj (q.v.) sultans. During the later dynasties of the 'Abdallab their position eroded relative to the Shayqiya (q.v.) to the north and to the Hamaj sultans, who were the last to prevail over Funj lands until the Turco-Egyptian (q.v.) conquest of the Sudan.

'ABDALLAH AL-TAYYIB (1921–). Sudanese scholar, poet, and intellectual, and a leading expert on Arabic language and classical Arabic poetry. After studying at Gordon Memorial College and the University of London, he worked as a teacher of English, and in 1956 was appointed professor of Arabic in the University of Khartoum (q.v.). Apart from holding leading positions at the University (dean of the Faculty of Arts, 1961–1964 and vice-chancellor, 1974–1975), and being founding director of Juba University (1975–1976), he taught Arabic literature in Kano, Nigeria (1964–1966), and Fez, Morocco (1978–1986). Since 1990 he has served as president of the Arabic Language Council at the University of Khartoum. He is the author of many literary studies, volumes of classicist poetry, memoirs, plays, a commentary on the Qur'an in Sudanese dialect, and recollections of Sudanese folk traditions. Through his many contributions to newspapers, radio, and television, his views became influential in shaping the national attitude toward Sudan's heritage. [by Albrecht Hofheinz]

'ABDULLAHI AL-TA'AISHI, AL-KHALIFA (1846–1899). Successor to Muhammad Ahmad al-Mahdi (q.v.) and commonly known as "the Khalifa" (q.v.). His father was Muhammad wad 'Ali al-Karrar (aka *Tawr Shayn*, "Ugly Bull"), a holyman of central Sudanic origin, and his mother was Umm Na'im, of the Ta'aisha branch of the Baqqara cattle-herding nomads (qq.v.) of southern Darfur (q.v.). Enthused with the millenarianism of his time, 'Abdullahi is said to have identified Zubayr Rahma Mansur (q.v.) as the "Expected Mahdi" after the latter's conquest of Darfur in 1874. Later he migrated to the White Nile where he became a loyal disciple of the then-Sammani shaykh (q.v.) Muhammad Ahmad, who revealed himself first to 'Abdullahi as Mahdi in 1881. He was present at all of the major battles of the early Mahdiya (q.v.) and served as advisor to the Mahdi and general of the Black Flag division, which included Ta'aisha and other western tribal levies. His formal title of *Khalifat al-Siddiq* indicated his spiritual (and hence political) equivalence to the Caliph Abu Bakr; similarly, the other *khalifas*, 'Ali wad Hilu and Muhammad Sharif (qq.v.), were respectively styled *Khalifat al-Faruq* (Successor to the Caliph 'Umar) and *Khalifat al-Karrar* (Successor to the Caliph 'Ali). As early as 1883 the Mahdi emphasized the preeminence of 'Abdullahi as his deputy and overall commander of the army. This notwithstanding, 'Abdullahi was deeply resented by Muhammad Sharif and the Dongolawi Ashraf (q.v.), who viewed him as an uncouth upstart. Upon the Mahdi's death in 1885, 'Abdullahi was proclaimed leader by an assembled elite, though not until the party of Muhammad Sharif had challenged him for power. For the remainder of the period, 'Abdullahi was known simply as *Khalifat al-Mahdi*.

Never truly secure in power, 'Abdullahi withstood serious challenges from the Ashraf in 1886 and 1891; the latter event nearly developed into an armed conflict and threatened the security of the capital. Ever suspicious of intrigues against him, he frequently dismissed administrators and military commanders, to the detriment of the state, while his reliance on his Ta'aisha kinsmen (whom he forcibly resettled along the Nile in 1888–1889) upset the social and economic order of the region and engendered considerable tensions between westerners (*Awlad al-Arab*) and riverine Sudanese (*Awlad al-Balad*). During his reign, Omdurman (q.v.) grew into a huge capital city; Khartoum (q.v.) had been abandoned, and other towns had declined as resources and population had become centralized. 'Abdullahi continued the jihad begun by the Mahdi, though this was largely unsuccessful, and in the campaign against Egypt in 1889, suicidal. Added to his woes was a serious famine in 1888–1889, which decimated the rural population of northern Sudan.

The Khalifa's central administration borrowed heavily from its predecessor the Turkiya (q.v.) despite Mahdist rejection of the "unbeliever Turks," and many of its personnel had served under the previous regime. Provincial administration lay in the hands of military governors, who were directly responsible to Amir Ya'qub, the Khalifa's brother and chief executive of the Mahdist state. If his institutions were unstable and administrators inefficient, the Khalifa nonetheless was more shrewd and pragmatic than his adversaries gave him credit for; meanwhile, Sudanese who disliked the policies of his government still tended to view him ideally, as the repository of the Mahdi's *baraka* (q.v.) and leader of the Mahdiya. By the early 1890s an amelioration of conditions in the northern Sudan had begun to restore popular support for the Khalifa's rule. By this time, however, external forces in Europe had begun to arrange his downfall.

The Anglo-Egyptian (q.v.) conquest of Sudan began in 1896 with the capture of Dongola (q.v.) province. In 1897 a railroad link was built across the Nubian desert to the Nile at Abu Hamad, ensuring the conquerors' supply route. Meanwhile, a revolt by the Ja'aliyin (q.v.) people of Matamma in July 1897, harshly suppressed by the Khalifa's kinsman Mahmud wad Ahmad (q.v.), cost the Khalifa considerable support among the riverine Sudanese. As the Anglo-Egyptian forces approached the Khalifa vacillated, uncertain how best to respond and perhaps overly confident of divine intervention. Mahmud Ahmad's army was defeated at Atbara (q.v.) in April 1898. On 2 September 1898 the Anglo-Egyptians under Gen. H. H. Kitchener (q.v.) crushed the Mahdist army at Karari (q.v.) outside Omdurman, inflicting over 11,000 casualties with a prototype of the machine gun. The Khalifa himself escaped from Omdurman with a small group of followers, fleeing into Kordofan (q.v.) province where the Mahdiya had won its early victories. After a year as a refugee, the Khalifa was hunted down at Umm Dibaykarat west of the White Nile on 24 November 1899 by a cavalry force under Col. F. R. Wingate (q.v.). He died seated on the ground surrounded by 'Ali wad Hilu (q.v.) and other loyalists, waiting a martyr's death. His tomb near Kosti (q.v.) continues to attract Ansar visitors, though his reputation in Sudan as a whole is mixed.

'ABDELWAHHAB AL-AFFENDI. *See* AL-AFFENDI.

ABU AL-KAYLIK. *See* LIKAYLIK, MUHAMMAD ABU.

ABU HASSABO, 'ABD AL-MAJID. Sudanese politician in the National Unionist Party (NUP, q.v.) who held a number of cabinet posts in the democratic period following the October Revolution (q.v.) of 1964 and who was an important figure in NUP decision making. After the May Revolution (q.v.) of 1969 he was tried and convicted of misuse of funds and was jailed. After his release in 1975 he was accused by the Ja'afar al-Nimeiri (q.v.) regime of involvement in various coup attempts.

ABU ISSA, FARUK. Sudanese lawyer and politician. He was a member of the Sudanese Communist Party (SCP, q.v.) Executive Committee and was active in the October Revolution (q.v.) of 1964. After the May Revolution (q.v.) of 1969 he was active in various cabinets, serving at times as minister of labor and foreign affairs. He was part of the SCP group that worked closely with the Ja'afar al-Nimeiri (q.v.) regime and opposed the SCP leadership of 'Abd al-Khaliq Mahjub (q.v.). He continued to be a prominent figure in the 1990s within the National Democratic Alliance (NDA, q.v.) against the Islamist Turabi/'Umar Bashir regime (qq.v.).

ABU JOHN. A southern Sudanese soldier of Zande (q.v.) origin who was British trained and active in southern resistance in the late 1960s. After the Addis Ababa Agreement of 1972 (q.v.) he served in the Sudanese army.

ABU LIKAYLIK. *See* LIKAYLIK, MUHAMMAD ABU.

ABU RANNAT, MUHAMMAD AHMAD (1902–1977). Abu Rannat was a lawyer, civil court judge, and chief justice. He attended the Gordon Memorial College (q.v.) and graduated as an accountant in 1922. Later he studied at the School of Law in Khartoum (q.v.) and joined the Condominium (q.v.) government judiciary as a civil court judge. He rose to become a judge of the High Court (1950–1955) and then chief justice of Sudan (1955–1964). During the regime of Ibrahim Abboud (q.v.) he helped to devise the Local Council system, and was important in the legal transition involved in the 1964 Revolution. He later joined the legal division of the United Nations (q.v.), where he drafted reports for the UN Commission on Human Rights and the UN Sub-Commission on the Prevention of Discrimination and Protection of Minorities. In 1973 he was chosen as the head of the Sudanese Court of Appeals. [by Heather J. Sharkey]

ABU RAWF GROUP. This literary society was founded in about 1927 in the Abu Rawf neighborhood of Omdurman (q.v.). It was active throughout the 1930s among a group of nationalist intellectuals, many of whom were graduates of Gordon Memorial College (q.v.). Its members tended to come from Khatmiya (q.v.) backgrounds, to sympathize culturally and politically with Egypt, and to be wary of cooperating with the British or with the Mahdists (q.v.). Its members read English literature extensively and were strongly influenced by Fabian socialism and by the writings of the Indian nationalist Jawaharlal Nehru. The Abu Rawfians participated actively in social improvement charities such as the Ahliya Schools project (q.v.) and the *Malja al-Qirsh* ("Piaster House") orphanage, and were active in the formation of the Graduates Congress (q.v.) in 1938. Prominent among them were Isma'il al-Atabani (q.v.), the brothers Hasan and Husayn Ahmad 'Uthman al-Kid, Ahmad Khayr, Muhammad Ahmad Abu Rannat (q.v.), Khidir Hamad (q.v.), 'Abd Allah al-Mirghani, Hamad Tawfiq Hamad (q.v.), Makkawi Sulayman Akrat, al-Nur 'Uthman, Ibrahim Anis and others. [by Heather J. Sharkey]

ABU SINN, AHMAD AWAD AL-KARIM (ca. 1790–1870). Leader of the Shukriya (q.v.) ethnic group in the nineteenth century and member of the Abu Sinn family (q.v.). He was an important advisor to the Turco-Egyptian (q.v.) rulers and was one of the few local notables to gain high rank in their regime. He served as governor of Khartoum (1860–70, q.v.)

and had authority over the nomad peoples between the White Nile and Ethiopia.

ABU SINN, MUHAMMAD AHMAD HARDALLU (1830–1917). Leader of the Shukriya (q.v.) people and a son of Ahmad Awad al-Karim Abu Sinn (q.v.). He was a recognized local leader under the Turco-Egyptian (q.v.) government, joined the Mahdist movement, and was a Shukriya leader during the Anglo-Egyptian (q.v.) regime. He was also a poet whose works gained wide acceptance in the Sudan.

ABU SINN FAMILY. The Abu Sinn family is a leading group among the Shukriya (q.v.) of the eastern Sudan. The traditional founder of the family is Sha'a al-Din, who lived in the sixteenth century. However, the family and the Shukriya people gained importance in the eighteenth and nineteenth centuries under the leadership of Awad al-Karim and his son, Ahmad (q.v.). At the end of the Funj (q.v.) era Ahmad Abu Sinn became an ally of the Turco-Egyptian (q.v.) regime and his family and people became dominant in the central part of the country. The Abu Sinn tried to remain aloof from the Mahdist movement and suffered from famine and fighting in the last quarter of the nineteenth century.

During the twentieth century the family again had a position of influence as major traditional notables, such as Muhammad Awad Abu Sinn. After World War II members of the Abu Sinn family were active in politics, working in the Socialist Republican Party (SRP, q.v.), the National Unionist Party (NUP, q.v.), and later the Peoples Democratic Party (PDP, q.v.). Members of the family have been elected to parliaments and assemblies and have served occasionally in cabinets. The family continued to have some influence in the assemblies formed after the 1969 May Revolution (q.v.).

ABU-WIDAN, AHMAD PASHA (?–1843). Second governor-general of the Sudan under Turco-Egyptian (q.v.) rule (1838–1843) and son-in-law of Muhammad 'Ali (q.v.). During his term of office, penetration and exploitation of the upper White Nile took place. The Turkish sailor Salim Qapudan (q.v.), commissioned by Abu-Widan, made three expeditions between 1839 and 1842 as far south as Bari (q.v.) territory, near present day Juba (q.v.). At this time the non-Muslim, non-Arabized peoples south of the Funj and Darfur (qq.v.) sultanates were raided and enslaved.

ABU ZAYD, MAMOUN AWAD. Sudanese political leader who was a member of the Revolutionary Council of the 1969 May Revolution (q.v.)

and served in its early cabinets. He was named the secretary-general of the Sudanese Socialist Union (SSU, q.v.) when it was formed in 1971 and served in that post for a year. In 1975 he was appointed to the SSU Political Bureau and became minister of interior in 1976. He is believed to support policies of close Sudanese-Egyptian cooperation.

ABUJA CONFERENCES. The Abuja conferences were convened by the government of Nigeria on 26 May 1992 (Abuja I) and 26 April to 18 May 1993 (Abuja II). The government of Sudan and the Sudanese Peoples Liberation Movement (SPLM, q.v.) participated in both conferences. The SPLM-Nasir group (q.v.) participated in the 1992 negotiations, but not the 1993 talks. The escalation of the civil war after the military coup d'etat in Khartoum (q.v.) in 1989 had caused deepening concern in Africa, which prompted the president of Nigeria, Ibrahim Babangida, to attempt to resolve the basic issues dividing the parties.

The principal issues involved questions of national identity and the relationship between religion and politics. Although the parties agreed that Sudan's identity was multiethnic, multilingual, multicultural, and multireligious and that there should be constitutional guarantees for that diversity, they disagreed on how to operationalize those concepts. The government argued that the Muslim majority had the right to establish an Islamic constitutional system; religious diversity should be expressed by exempting the South from the *hudud* (prescribed Islamic punishments) but not from other Islamic laws (q.v.), including those relating to business, property, and taxes; and in the long term, assimilation would transform Sudan into an Arab-Islamic country. Moreover, the government delegation refused to mention the possibility of there being no official state religion in the final communiqué.

Both wings of the SPLM rejected the government position. The SPLM maintained that the "multi"ness of Sudan must be upheld by a secular, democratic system that would encompass political pluralism and equality before the law. SPLM-Nasir's delegation, led by Dr. Lam Akol (q.v.), argued that Sudan was composed of two nations, one in the North and the other in the South, that were separate culturally and ethnically and should not attempt to retain their artificial unity. At most SPLM-Nasir would accept the establishment of two states in a loose confederation, which would enable the North to rule itself according to Islamic law.

The issue of self-determination was equally contentious. The head of the government delegation, Muhammad al-Amin Khalifa, declared that "separation comes from the mouth of a gun," not from debates around the conference table. Nonetheless, the two SPLM delegations argued that a referendum must be held at the end of any interim period to ascertain whether the people in the South wished to remain within Sudan or to secede. The government also refused to discuss issues of security, such as a cease-fire and foreign monitors. The government argued that security was an internal matter that it would handle. In contrast, the SPLM sought an immediate cease-fire that would lead to an interim period in which the South would control its own security. Neutral foreign observers would supervise and monitor the process of disengagement and withdrawal by the armed forces.

Despite the impasse over basic principles and security arrangements, the parties devoted considerable time to discussing political and economic arrangements during a possible interim period. Government delegates sought to concentrate authority at the federal level, whereas the SPLM wanted to maximize the powers of the states over social, cultural, and economic policies.

When the government and SPLM reconvened in Abuja in 1993, the government of Nigeria insisted that the first agenda item focus on the issue of religion and state; if that could be resolved, the other issues would fall into place. But if that could not be resolved, no accord was possible on any issue. The delegates immediately deadlocked on that crucial issue, with the government of Sudan insisting that Islamic law had to be maintained and the SPLM arguing that the government must choose between Islamic law and territorial unity. Given that polarization, there could not be fruitful negotiations on interim arrangements or on security matters. The government continued to deny that the South had the right to self-determination, an issue upon which the SPLM delegation, led by Salva Kiir Mayardit (q.v.), became increasingly insistent. The talks, therefore, adjourned without any positive result. They illustrated the pitfalls of negotiating in a polarized political context, in which talks served to heighten mistrust rather than to bridge differences. [by Ann Lesch]

ACHOLI. The Acholi and Luo (q.v.) are Nilotic (q.v.) peoples found mainly in Uganda and southernmost Sudan, however, political and military events in Uganda caused some to flee farther into Sudan. They are members of the Luo cluster of the Sudanic language family. *See also* DINKA; SHILLUK.

ADAMAWA-EASTERN. A linguistic subfamily of the Niger-Congo language group, whose major representative in Sudan is the Azande (q.v.).

Some other linguistic classification systems call this the Equatorial cluster.

ADARISA. *See* IDRISIYA.

ADDIS ABABA AGREEMENT OF 1972. Agreement between the Sudanese government and the Southern Sudan Liberation Movement (SSLM) and Anya-Nya (qq.v.) with Ethiopian Emperor Haile Selassie as official mediator. The main features of this historic agreement included the concept of a unified Sudan with a representative government, allocation of revenue for regional self-rule in the South, and economic development with regional security in the hands of southerners. A caretaker government, to manage the transition, included mechanisms for regional repatriation, resettlement, and incorporation of Anya-Nya forces into the Sudan army, police, prison forces, and regional civil service. After the peace agreement for regional autonomy was implemented, over one million Sudanese returned home. The Addis Ababa accords officially recognized the solution to the "southern problem" as one of a federal system of government. Its greatest achievement was the attainment of political autonomy; its greatest weakness the failure to ensure economic development and a viable southern economy. The renewed outbreak of civil war in 1983 signaled the political failure of the Addis Ababa accords.

ADDIS ABABA PEACE FORUM (1988). One of the peace efforts of the mid-1980s, after the renewal of civil war in 1983. This meeting brought together leaders of the Sudanese Peoples Liberation Movement/Army (SPLM/SPLA, q.v.) and the Union of Sudan African Parties, a body of political parties organized after Sudanese democracy was restored in 1985. The result of this forum was a call for a National Constitutional Conference in the spirit of the Koka Dam Declaration of 1986 (q.v.). The SPLA guaranteed safe conduct for international relief agencies trying to alleviate the war-related famine in the South. The forum reiterated its commitment to a secular state for Sudan.

ADVISORY COUNCIL FOR THE NORTHERN SUDAN (ACNS). The ACNS was created by the British to provide a channel for expression of Sudanese opinion. It had only advisory powers, but was a formal step toward self-government. It soon became dominated by the Umma Party (q.v.) and 'Abdallah Khalil (q.v.). Its first session was in 1944 and it was dissolved with the creation of the Legislative Assembly (q.v.) in 1948. *See also* ABBAS, MEKKI.

ADWOK, LUIGI (1929–). Southern Sudanese politician of Shilluk (q.v.) origin elected to Parliament in 1958. After the 1964 October Revolution (q.v.) he was on the Executive Committee of the Southern Front (q.v.) and was its representative in the Supreme Council of State (1964–1965). He left the Front and was elected to Parliament in 1967. After the 1969 May Revolution (q.v.) Adwok served in the cabinet for a time as minister of public works (1971) and then in the Southern Region High Executive Council created by the Addis Ababa Agreement of 1972 (q.v.). He served for two years (1974–1976) in the Sudanese Socialist Union (SSU) Political Bureau. He was originally a schoolmaster, educated at the Bakht Al-Ruda Institute of Education.

AL-AFFENDI, 'ABD AL-WAHHAB. One of the prominent intellectuals associated with the National Islamic Front (NIF, q.v.), al-Affendi was educated as a philosopher and political scientist. He began his writing career at age eighteen working as a reporter for the Khartoum daily newspaper, *Al-Sahafa*. He edited *Arabia,* the Islamic World Review, and wrote a definitive insider's book on Hasan al-Turabi (q.v.). He had a brief career as a diplomat working for the NIF regime in the foreign service. After dissociating himself from direct involvement in NIF politics, al-Affendi positioned himself as a leading Islamist intellectual.

AFRICAN NATIONAL FRONT. *See* NILE PROVISIONAL GOVERNMENT.

AFRO-ARAB, AFRO-ARABISM. A concept that developed early in Sudanese nationalist writings, especially those of Muhammad Ahmad Mahgoub (q.v.), that Sudanese national identity is based on Islam (q.v.), Arabic culture, and African soil. The term has been used in a scholarly as well as a political context to describe the racial and cultural diversity of postindependence Sudan. However, the reference has been accepted as more accurately reflecting the identity of northern Sudanese, and has generally not been adopted by southern intellectuals and politicians who may be more apt to describe northern Sudanese as Arabized Africans. With questions of national unity and national identity still to be resolved, the future of the Afro-Arab concept is uncertain.

AGRICULTURE. Sudan is overwhelmingly an agricultural nation. This is both a heavy liability and a great potential. To the extent that the Sudanese economy is linked to agriculture it is an economy of primary export of crops and livestock and heavily reliant on imported manufactured goods. If agricultural production is weak because of civil or climatological problems Sudan suffers greatly. If agricultural production is adequate or favorable Sudan has a vast ability to produce for its own national needs and have a very large surplus. The potential and vulnerability of Sudanese agriculture is a tormenting feature of this part of the national economy. In the early 1990s about one quarter of the development budget was spent on agriculture. From 60 to 80 percent of the national labor force is formally or informally engaged in agriculture.

There are three main types of agriculture. First, about 85 percent of Sudanese agriculture rests in traditional rain-fed cultivation, which varies greatly by region, crop, technique, and amount of rainfall. These small rain-fed and small-scale irrigated gardens and plots produce domestic cash and subsistence crops.

Second are commercial irrigated farmlands and plantations for about 10 percent of the total, including small private farms along the riverbanks and the vast Gezira scheme (q.v.) of over 1.2 million *feddans*. Costs of fertilizer, farm labor, and agricultural credit have complicated and diminished Gezira production in recent years. After the huge Gezira scheme there are large-scale agricultural projects at Gash, Gedaref (q.v.), Geneid, Jongeli (when completed, q.v.), Kenana, Khasm al-Girba (q.v.), Manakil, New Halfa, Rahad, Roseires, Sinnar (q.v.), al-Suki, Tokar, and Zande (q.v.).

The third type of agriculture is found on mechanized, rain-fed lands, but this counts for only 5 percent of the total agricultural land. Such farming is known especially in the area of Gedaref, Upper Nile (q.v.), and South Kordofan and this is regulated through the Mechanized Farming Corporation, which aims toward private commercial usage of lots no less than 1,000 *feddans* each. Mechanized agricultural projects are often under private ownership and in areas of clay soils, which are highly vulnerable to degradation without fertilizing and crop rotation. Sudan is steeply graded by widely differing amounts of rainfall and access to irrigation canals.

Agriculture accounts for 80 to 90 percent of all national production and from 30 to 35 percent of the Gross National Product (GNP) or about 15 percent of the Gross Domestic Product (GDP). It was estimated in 1989 that Sudan had 18,900 square kilometers of land that was arable by rain or irrigation. About two million hectares are supported by gravity-fed irrigation and the vast majority of this is under government authority. Natural forests abound in the southern region. With adequate rainfall the middle and southern sections of Sudan can also support extensive grazing of cattle, goats, and sheep.

The leading crops are cotton, oilseeds, sorghum, millet, wheat, and gum arabic from the Acacia tree. The colonial monocrop dominance of Gezira cotton has been reduced by other cash crops, especially including sugar cane, grains, and peanuts (*ful Sudani*). Despite some government subsidies and incentives, the mobilization of adequate agricultural labor is a recurrent problem in production. Among the exports of Sudan, cotton alone accounts for 43 percent of all revenues. Sudan produces about three fourths of the world supply of gum arabic, which also accounts for 29 percent of the Sudanese export economy. Recently this production is reduced because of drought and political boycotts.

The commercial production of livestock for meat, hides, milk, and cheese rests upon sheep (about 20 million) and goats (about 14 million), especially in the Gezira scheme. Darfur and Kordofan (qq.v.) are the chief producers of cattle (about 20 million). Cattle are also raised in great numbers by the Nuer and Dinka (qq.v.), but they are not as fully involved with the market economy. Cattle play a very important social role in southern and central Sudan as a means of moveable wealth to settle disputes, marry, and gain prestige. The camel herd (about 3 million) is centered in Kordofan. Perhaps 50,000 camels are exported each year, including thousands smuggled across the Forty Days Road (q.v.) to Egypt.

Fodder crops and beasts of burden such as camels, horses, and donkeys are also present in significant numbers. There are also sizable numbers of poultry used in the domestic economy throughout the nation. Pigs are raised in the southern non-Muslim areas. Sudan potentially has one of the largest livestock populations in all of Africa. Livestock and dressed meat account for another 24 percent of exports.

Other exports include sesame, peanuts, *kerkedeh*, incense, hard woods, and animal hides. Small-scale artisanal fishing and some limited industrialized fishing on Lake Nasser and on the Red Sea contribute to the subsistence and local economy. Generally Sudan should be self-sufficient in animal and plant foods if war, man-made famine, natural drought, and animal diseases were better controlled and did not severely disrupt this potential. Wide fluctuations in cotton and sugar cane production are common.

The timber industry is devoted to modest amounts of sawed lumber and major amounts of timber depletion for fuel used; this is causing serious ecological problems since there is no broad reforestation program. The predicament of Sudanese agriculture is compounded by a weak system of transportation, which has three gauges of railroad, poor or seasonal roads, and limited river transport. These systems are further challenged by recurrent political and military instability. Overall, the agricultural potential of Sudan is immense, but the predictions that it will become the food-producer for the Arab world have not yet become realized. *See also* FAMINE; HUNT, S. J.; KASSALA; KOSTI; WAD MEDANI.

AHFAD UNIVERSITY COLLEGE FOR WOMEN. The first, and still only, university for women in Sudan, and the only women's (q.v.) university in Africa. Founded in 1907 by the pioneer of girls' education in the Sudan, Babikir Badri (q.v.), it opened originally as a private primary school at Rufa'a. In 1933 Ahfad became an intermediate school; in 1943 a secondary school; and in 1966 it became a university college for women. At present it is a comprehensive university with five colleges: family sciences, medicine, organizational management, psychology and early education, and rural development. Still operated by the Badri family, it remains a vanguard institution promoting women's education and advancement. At present it enrolls 4,500 students, about 40 percent of whom receive scholarship aid or other forms of financial aid toward its full tuition payment of $1,000 per year. As a nonsectarian institution, it enrolls students from all over Sudan and especially recruits southern women. It contributes locally to women's studies through its curriculum, and its academic publication, the *Ahfad Journal,* has been published since 1983 and circulates internationally.

AHLIYA SCHOOLS MOVEMENT. This movement was started in the late 1920s by northern Sudanese intellectuals, religious notables, and other leading citizens in response to the inability of government schools to meet a growing public demand for education. The term "*ahli* education" or "*ahliya* schools" referred to its nature as a national project for the populace at large. The first Ahliya boys' elementary school opened in Omdurman (q.v.) in 1926. Other elementary, intermediate, and secondary schools, for boys and later for girls, subsequently opened throughout the northern Sudan. Although the Ahliya schools were subject to government supervision, they received few government subsidies.

Supported through proceeds from charity fund-raising activities, they reflected a successful case of northern Sudanese self-help and social improvement. As a nongovernmental educational system, the Ahliya schools had a parallel in the Ahfad (q.v.) schools for boys and girls, founded by Babiker Badri (q.v.). [by Heather J. Sharkey]

AHMAD AL-TAYYIB IBN BASHIR. *See* SAMMANIYA.

AHMAD FUAD. *See* FUAD, KING.

AHMAD IBN IDRIS (1750–1837). A religious teacher who influenced the Sudan through his students. He was born in Morocco and taught in Arabia. His ideas of Islamic revival and of using religious brotherhoods (*turuq*, q.v.) are instruments that inspired a number of religious leaders important in the Sudan. These include Muhammad 'Uthman al-Mirghani (q.v.), Muhammad Majdhub, Ibrahim al-Rashid, and his own family who lead the Idrisiya (q.v.). *See also* MAJADHIB; RASHIDIYA. [by Albrecht Hofheinz]

AHMAD, JAMAL MUHAMMAD (1915–1986). J. A. Ahmad was a diplomat, an educator, and a writer. He attended Gordon Memorial College in Khartoum (qq.v.), the University of Exeter, the University of London, and Balliol College, Oxford. With the British educator Robin Hodgkin, he coedited *al-Sibyan*, a pioneering magazine for young people that stressed basic literacy. He was an active participant in the Graduates Congress (q.v.) and later served as the Sudanese ambassador to Iraq (1956–1959), Ethiopia (1959–1964), the United Nations (1965–1967), and Great Britain (1969), and as minister of foreign affairs (1975–1976) during the Ja'afar al-Nimeiri (q.v.) era. He published many works of a political and literary nature, including studies on Afro-Arab relations, Sudanese diplomacy, and African drama. He also translated many works, some from English into Arabic and others (including a collection of stories) from his native Nubian (q.v.) language into Arabic. His scholarly writings also include *The Intellectual Origins of Egyptian Nationalism*, and in 1992 a compilation of his writings appeared under the title *Rasa'il wa-awraq khassa* (Letters and Private Papers). [by Heather J. Sharkey]

AHMAD MUMTAZ PASHA (ca. 1825–1874). An officer in the Turco-Egyptian (q.v.) army and administration in the nineteenth century. He is best known for having initiated large-scale cultivation of cotton in the

Sudan. He was briefly governor-general but was accused of corruption and died soon after his dismissal.

AHRAR. *See* LIBERAL PARTY.

AKOBO INCIDENT (MARCH 1975). A mutiny of some southern troops at Akobo in Upper Nile Province. The cause was minor but indicated the continuing potential for unrest in the South after the Addis Ababa Agreement (q.v.) of 1972.

AKOL. *See* LAM AKOL AJAWIN.

AL-. The definite article in Arabic (q.v.). To find a word beginning with "Al-," look under the word following it. For example, to find "Al-Mahdi" ("the Mahdi") look under "Mahdi." Some texts use an "El-" form and others use "nunated" or liaison letters, which may transform "Al-" to "Ar-," "Ash-," or "En."

'ALI, GENERAL FATIH AHMAD (1939–1997). This soldier, diplomat, politician, and national democrat was the deputy chairperson of the National Democratic Alliance (NDA, q.v.) and leader of the Legitimate Command of the Sudanese Armed Forces at the time of his death in April 1997. He was a former commander-in-chief of the Sudanese army when 'Umar al-Bashir (q.v.) seized power in a coup d'etat in June 1989 backed by the National Islamic Front (NIF, q.v.). He was arrested at the time and was briefly detained before being released and retiring from the army. His growing opposition to the regime forced his exile from Sudan to Egypt where he set up the Legitimate Command with other exiled officers. He was a founder of the NDA and leader of the *Ana al-Sudan* military campaign to overthrow the NIF rule since 1990.

A professional army officer, he was once the military attaché to the United States. He first came to public attention in February 1988 when he signed a strongly worded memorandum to the democratically elected Sadiq al-Mahdi (q.v.) government calling for a peaceful political solution to the civil war. This was widely interpreted as a thinly veiled warning to the government to take some action or risk a takeover. It has been theorized that the June 1989 coup d'etat was engineered by Fatih 'Ali and supported by army units around the country because of his credibility.

One of his first acts in exile was to visit Colonel John Garang (q.v.) at his headquarters in Torit in 1991, although they had been military opponents previously. This fostered a positive working relationship between the two and ultimately between the NDA and Sudanese Peoples Liberation Army (SPLA, q.v.). General 'Ali acted as a driving force within the NDA to reach the Asmara Agreement of June 1995 (q.v.), which recognized for the first time the right of self-determination for the South, the Nuba Mountains (q.v.), and the Ingessana.

Following the capture of Yei by the SPLA in spring 1997, General 'Ali visited Colonel Garang again, where he recruited 1,000 Sudanese Armed Forces captives of the SPLA to join the NDA forces under the general command of Garang, newly appointed commander of the NDA Joint Military Command. He died in Alexandria, Egypt, only a few days after his return from this trip to southern Sudan (q.v.). His wife and family insisted that his body be flown back to Sudan for burial; however, the NIF regime prevented a prominent public funeral fearing General 'Ali as a symbol of the opposition. [by Mahgoub al-Tigani and *Sudan Democratic Gazette*, Number 85, June 1997]

'ALI 'ABD AL-LATIF (1897–1937). A Sudanese nationalist leader in the 1920s. An army officer of Dinka (q.v.) origin, 'Ali was dismissed for political reasons. At first he advocated Sudanese independence through his own Sudan United Tribes Association, for which he was jailed briefly in 1922. This gave him some fame and, on his release in 1923, he worked to create the White Flag League (q.v.) advocating union with Egypt. 'Ali was centrally involved in the anticolonial revolt in Khartoum (q.v.) in 1924. A Sudanese postage stamp commemorates this early nationalist figure. *See also* 'ABD AL-FADIL AL-MAZ.

'ALI DINAR IBN ZAKARIYA IBN MUHAMMAD FADL (ca. 1865–1916). The last sultan of Darfur (q.v.), ruling from 1898 to 1916. A member of the reigning Keira Dynasty (q.v.), he inherited the title of sultan in 1890 upon the death of Abu'l-Khayrat. Suspected by the Mahdists of disaffection, he was brought to Omdurman (q.v.) where he spent from 1892 to 1898 as a "guest" of the Khalifa (q.v.). Immediately after the Anglo-Egyptian (q.v.) conquest he eliminated his rivals and received British recognition as the autonomous ruler of Darfur. He ruled relatively effectively, though he resented French annexation of western territories formerly under his sway, as well as the Sudan government's refusal to sell him sufficient arms to defend his realm. Governor-General

F. R. Wingate (q.v.), for his part, had long sought the extension of government control over Darfur, a development that he regarded as inevitable. The outbreak of World War I and subsequent Anglo-French agreements of cooperation might have hastened this development; in any case, 'Ali Dinar renounced his allegiance to the Sudan government in 1915 and called for jihad, thereby inviting a government invasion of Darfur in 1916. The sultan's army was defeated and al-Fasher (q.v.) quickly occupied; after brief resistance 'Ali Dinar was hunted down and killed in November of that year.

'ALI WAD MUHAMMAD HILU (?–1899). One of the Mahdi's (q.v.) three *khalifas*, considered the spiritual successor of the Caliph 'Umar and entitled *Khalifat al-Faruq*. Born in the White Nile region of mixed Kinana and Dighaym parentage, he developed a reputation for piety and is rumored to have studied at Egypt's al-Azhar University (q.v.). He met Muhammad Ahmad (q.v.) at Aba Island (q.v.) in the 1870s and became an early disciple. After the latter's manifestation in 1881 he brought over to the Mahdi's side the Kinana and Dighaym ethnic groups, who formed the basis for the Green Flag division that 'Ali nominally commanded. Never ambitious, he avoided the political squabbles of the period and hewed to the Mahdi's publicly stated preference for 'Abdullahi al-Ta'ayshi (q.v.) as successor, supporting the Khalifa against his Ashraf (q.v.) opponents during the succession crisis of 1885 and the crises of 1886 and 1891. Known for his modesty (he frequently mediated between the Khalifa and the headstrong Muhammad Sharif, [q.v.]) and piety, he personally supervised the education of the women of the Mahdi's household and earned the nickname *al-Zahid*, or "The Ascetic." A loyalist to the end, he fled Omdurman (q.v.) after the battle of Karari and died seated next to the Khalifa at Umm Dibaykarat in 1899. *See also* MAHDIYA.

ALIER, ABEL (1933–). Sudanese political leader and lawyer of Dinka (q.v.) origin. He studied law in Khartoum (q.v.) and London and joined the Sudanese judiciary as a magistrate, becoming the first Sudanese judge of southern origin. He was an active member of the Southern Front (q.v.) from its beginning in 1964, and served in the historic Round Table Conference (q.v.) of 1965 that almost succeeded in bringing peace between northern and southern Sudan (q.v.).

Alier was elected to the national Parliament (1968–1969) from his home region of southern Bor. He continuously held posts of cabinet rank after the Ja'afar Nimeiri "May Revolution" (qq.v.) of 1969, serving as minister of housing (1969), supply (1969–1970), public works (1970–1971), and southern affairs (1971). In 1971 he was named a vice-president and represented the Sudanese government in the negotiations leading up to the Addis Ababa Agreement of 1972 (q.v.) and the first period of protracted peace since 1955. He is widely regarded as the principal architect of this significant peace agreement.

From 1972 to 1977, and again from 1980 to 1981, Alier served as the president of the newly created Southern Region High Executive Council. For most of this time he also served as the second vice-president of Sudan, a post he held until 1981. In 1990 he authored the book *Southern Sudan: Too Many Agreements Dishonored*, which carefully chronicled the long history of distrust between northern and southern Sudan.

Since 1989 Alier has suffered harassment from the National Islamic Front (NIF, q.v.) regime because of his support for self-determination of the southern conflict and the pursuit of a negotiated peace. He and four colleagues presented a memorandum to the government of 'Umar al-Bashir (q.v.) in October 1995 to recognize the South's right to self-determination. Alier is a member of the International Court of Justice at The Hague; however, he is unable to serve in this court since his diplomatic passport was revoked by the NIF government.

ALWA. The kingdom of Alwa first emerged in the central Sudan after the fall of Meroë (q.v.). Its capital was at Soba near modern Khartoum (q.v.). The rulers were converted to Monophysite Christianity by Longinus around 580 CE and Alwa survived as a Christian state far longer than the northern Christian kingdoms in Nubia (q.v.). According to tradition, Soba finally fell to the Funj (q.v.) in 1504, although the kingdom may have collapsed before then.

AMARA DUNQAS. The founder of the Funj Sultanate of Sinnar (qq.v.), ruling from 1504 to 1534. Possibly of the Hamaj (q.v.) people whose homeland was on the Blue Nile, he created the city of Sinnar in 1504 and became the first ruler since ancient times to unite the riverine North with the Equatorial swamps. The state he built was a federation of local rulers under Funj overlordship. Amara may have originally been animist or Christian, but after 1523 all Funj rulers were officially Muslims.

AMIN, NAFISA AHMAD AL-. Sudanese political leader who was named deputy minister for youth and sport in the first Sudanese Socialist Union

(SSU, q.v.) cabinet, formed in 1971. Under Ja'afar Nimeiri (q.v.), she was the first Sudanese woman to attain an office of this rank. She has remained a leading voice for women's rights in Sudan.

AMIN MUHAMMAD AL-AMIN. *See* GEZIRA TENANTS UNION.

AMINA BINT FATIMA. *See* AWLAD JABIR.

ANGLO-EGYPTIAN AGREEMENT OF 1953. This agreement outlined the steps to be taken for Sudanese self-rule and self-determination. It provided the basis for the parliamentary elections of 1953 and the first Sudanese cabinet, formed by Isma'il Al-Azhari (q.v.).

ANGLO-EGYPTIAN SUDAN. The name for much of the land of the current Republic of Sudan during the period 1899–1955. The regime was defined by the Anglo-Egyptian Agreement of 1899 and was often called the Condominium (q.v.). In theory both Egypt and Great Britain participated in ruling the Sudan at this time, but in practice it was the British who ruled, the Egyptians who supplied the main military force, and the Sudanese who were taxed.

ANGLO-EGYPTIAN TREATY OF 1936. This treaty redefined Anglo-Egyptian relations in light of the development of Egyptian nationalism. The Sudan was covered in an article which reaffirmed the existing administrative arrangements but opened the way for somewhat increased Egyptian participation in the administration of the Sudan. The British and Egyptians promulgated this treaty without consulting the Sudanese. This helped to arouse nationalist feelings in the Sudan and was a factor in the creation of the Graduates Congress (q.v.) in 1938.

ANSAR. The Arabic term for "helpers," which was applied to some of the early companions of the Prophet Muhammad. During the Mahdiya, the Mahdi (qq.v.) also styled his followers Ansar, seeking to model his movement on the earliest Muslim community at Medina. All followers of the Mahdi were considered Ansar and expected to adhere to his (and later, the Khalifa's, q.v.) teachings. As an outward sign of their disregard for worldly things, the Ansar wore a patched robe (*jibba*); though affecting a look of poverty, these could be quite elaborate. Additionally the Ansar wore a large turban, tied in a particular fashion, which could serve as a burial shroud. In principle at least, the Ansar were dedicated to holy war on behalf of the Mahdi and his *Khalifa*.

With the Anglo-Egyptian (q.v.) conquest of 1898 the Ansar ceased to exist in an organized fashion. During World War I they reemerged as a religious sect, supporting the personal ambitions of Sayyid 'Abd al-Rahman (q.v.), whose support the British needed, and providing a counterweight to the influence of Sayyid 'Ali al-Mirghani and his Khatmiya sect (qq.v.). In 1945 the Umma Party (q.v.) was created to serve as the political arm of the Ansar, though the distinction between the two was often hazy: Sayyid 'Abd al-Rahman served as Imam (q.v.) or spiritual leader of the Ansar as well as patron of the Umma. Frequently the Ansar were mobilized for political demonstrations, including in 1954 against union with Egypt, 1965 against the transitional government, 1970 against Ja'afar Nimeiri (q.v.), and 1980 against the Assembly elections. These demonstrations often led to significant loss of life, most particularly in 1970 in the Omdurman (q.v.) riots and subsequent government attack on Aba Island (q.v.). After the death of Sayyid 'Abd al-Rahman (1959), the leadership of the Ansar passed to his son Sayyid Siddiq (q.v.); upon his premature death in 1961, his brother al-Hadi became Imam. The death of al-Hadi following the Aba attack of 1970 left the Ansar without an Imam, as disputes split the Mahdi family. Since the 1980s Sadiq al-Mahdi (q.v.), son of Sayyid Siddiq, has assumed the role of de facto Imam of the Ansar. *See also* AL-MAHDI FAMILY.

ANTI-IMPERIALIST FRONT. A party formed in 1953 that acted as the public vehicle for the then-clandestine Sudanese Communist Party (SCP, q.v.). The Front's president was Hasan Tahir Zarruq (q.v.) and its leftist viewpoints appealed to some of the educated Sudanese. It won one parliamentary seat in 1953 and participated in various commissions, such as the National Constitutional Commission of 1956. In 1957 it joined the anti-Umma (q.v.) alliance called the National Front (q.v.). It urged its supporters to vote for National Unionist Party (NUP, q.v.) candidates in the 1958 elections and ceased to operate as a legal entity after the Ibrahim Abboud (q.v.) coup in November 1958.

ANTISLAVERY MOVEMENT. The impact of the world antislavery movement on the Sudan is tied to the interaction between European reformers and the imperial designs of the British in the Turco-Egyptian regions. The return of the British explorers John Speke and James Grant (qq.v.) to England in 1863 did much to expose the slave trade in the Sudan, and with the broad negative reaction in Europe, Muhammad 'Ali (q.v.) was moved to declare his ignorance of the trade and deny that his armies were comprised of slaves. In a memorable trip to the Sudan in 1838, Muhammad 'Ali declared the abolition of slavery (q.v.) and that the pay of soldiers was no longer allowed to be made in slaves. Circulars were sent to the governors to stop the practice of slaving, and Muhammad 'Ali's entourage, which included a number of Europeans, were convinced of his sincerity to stop the commerce in human beings. In 1840 the General Anti-Slavery Convention in London declared that Muhammad 'Ali was committed to the cause of antislavery, and Great Britain, eager to have good relations with Muhammad 'Ali to keep open the steamship navigation to India via Egypt, was satisfied. Indeed, British policy toward the Ottoman Empire was to maintain the integrity of its economic foundations, one of which was the size and commercial success of the slave trade. Publicly, Britain promoted the idea of a legitimate trade that would replace the slave trade.

Contrary to official optimism about the end of the trade, R. R. Madden of the Anti-Slavery Society told the 1840 Convention that the slave trade was still flourishing in the Sudan and that the number of slaves captured by the end of the summer of 1840 was 10,000. It gradually became clear that Muhammad 'Ali was more interested in good publicity in Europe than in the actual abolition of the Sudanese slave trade.

In 1856, after the reign of Muhammad 'Ali, Sa'id Pasha issued a decree freeing all slaves in Egypt, and he visited the Sudan in 1857 where he issued a similar decree abolishing slavery and declaring the traffic in slaves illegal. But after his return to Cairo he issued an order for a bodyguard of 500 "Negro" soldiers, thus giving impetus to the trade he had just abolished. Meanwhile, continuing reports of the slave trade in the Sudan were a regular feature from travelers to the region, and the British public was especially aroused by Samuel Baker's (q.v.) publications between 1866 and 1872. Antislavery sentiment in Britain saw little difference between Western slavery as an institution, and that which was practiced in the Ottoman Empire. Whereas the former was tied to agricultural production and capital accumulation, the latter was an expression of surplus wealth and luxury.

During the period that Charles Gordon (q.v.) was officially linked to the Sudan, British public attention was preoccupied with slavery and the slave trade in the Sudan. This and the usual economic factors caused Britain and the Ottoman Empire to enter into a formal Convention for the Suppression of the Slave Trade in 1877, but the effective end of the slave trade (though not slavery) occurred with the ouster of Turco-Egyptian rule and Mahdist conquest of the Sudan in 1885. Slavery was officially abolished in 1899 with Condominium rule (q.v.), and a Repression of Slavery Department was created by the British in 1900. This notwithstanding, slavery as a domestic practice continued quietly under the British, who had no desire to undermine the social and economic order of a territory they struggled to govern. Alarmingly, the revival of civil war hostilities in southern Kordofan (q.v.) since the 1980s has brought allegations of a resurgence of slave raiding between Arabs and southerners.

ANUAK. The Anuak are a pre-Nilotic group speaking a Nilotic (q.v.) language in the Sudanic language family. They live along the Blue Nile in the frontier region with Ethiopia. Like other pre-Nilotes, they are sedentary herders of sheep and goats and small-scale cultivators. They have local-level political organization, and with this decentralization of authority and their remote location they mounted a substantial resistance to British colonialism until 1921.

ANYA-NYA. Southern guerrilla military organization formed in 1963. It was related to the Sudan African National Union (SANU, q.v.) but became a virtually autonomous military organization operating within the Sudan. As southern politicians in exile were unable to create a unified resistance movement, Anya-Nya leaders became increasingly active in political affairs. Finally in 1969 the Anya-Nya commander, Joseph Lagu (q.v.), succeeded in bringing together various factions in the Southern Sudan Liberation Movement (SSLM, q.v.). Under Lagu the SSLM was a principal agent in negotiating the 1972 settlement of the southern conflict. After the Addis Ababa Agreement of 1972 (q.v.) Anya-Nya soldiers were integrated into the Sudanese army and government services.

ANYA-NYA II. Revived after the renewal of the civil war in 1983, Anya-Nya II has differed with the Sudanese Peoples Liberation Movement (SPLM, q.v.) over such issues as its support for the transitional government that took power after the toppling of Ja'afar Nimeiri (q.v.). In 1987 the two groups met officially in Addis Ababa and issued a joint communiqué calling for the convening of a constitutional convention in the spirit of the Koka Dam Declaration (q.v.).

ANYIDI REVOLUTIONARY GOVERNMENT (ARG). A southern political group. It was formed in 1969 as a result of a split within the Nile Provisional Government (q.v.). The ARG was led by Emidio Tafeng (q.v.), a commander in the Anya-Nya (q.v.). The ARG became a part of the Southern Sudan Liberation Movement (q.v.) in 1970.

ARAB. Strictly speaking, an Arab is a pastoral nomad who speaks the Afro-Asiatic (Semitic) language, possesses "Arabic" culture, and after the seventh century, is likely, but not necessarily, a follower of the Islamic religion. Islam (q.v.) was rather slow in reaching the Sudan; it spread from the Arabian Peninsula into Egypt, across North Africa and, by separate routes, into western and eastern Europe, all within one or two centuries after the prophet Muhammad. However, the Christian kingdoms in Nubia (q.v.) blocked the spread of Islam into the central Sudan until the early sixteenth century. Today, the vast majority of people who consider themselves Arabs are neither nomadic nor of purely Arab ethnic origin.

In the Sudanese case one also finds variation by herding cattle rather than camels; many are fully sedentary or only seasonally migratory; and there are numerous degrees of Africanization of Arabs expanding southward, and of Arabization of southern slaves brought northward. There are also Sudanese people such as the Daju, Fur, and Nubians (qq.v.) who are heavily Arabized and Islamized, but still speak their own non-Afro-Asiatic languages, not to mention native Arabic speakers who are Christians and Jews (q.v.). Thus, the broader definition of an Arab is a matter of cultural self-awareness and self-identity, rather than strict terminology. Perhaps a third of Sudanese are "Arabs" in the general sense and claim descent through the Ja'aliyin, Khazraj, or Juhayna (qq.v.) Arab groups.

ARAB-ISRAELI CONFLICT. Sudan joined the Arab League immediately after independence in January 1956 and publicly has supported the Arab position against Israeli seizure of Palestinian and other Arab lands. Nonetheless, Sudan's involvement in the Arab-Israeli conflict has been complicated by the fractious nature of the Sudanese state, as well as limited by its scarce economic resources. Arab unity, like Pan-Africanism and other foreign policy options, has been neither easy to implement nor effective in a country beset by sectarianism and civil war.

During the 1956 Anglo-French-Israeli invasion of the Suez Canal, Sudanese volunteers were sent north to help the Egyptians, though Sudan refused to sever its diplomatic ties to Great Britain and France. Sudan did join nine other Arab states in severing ties to the Federal Republic of Germany in 1965 after the latter's exchange of ambassadors with Israel.

The June 1967 Arab-Israeli war elicited a stronger reaction from Sudan: Military contingents were sent to support Egypt, and diplomatic ties were severed with Britain (restored in 1968) and the United States (restored in 1972). An important Arab summit was convened in Khartoum (q.v.) in August 1967, and Sudan began to increase its military and economic cooperation with the Soviet Union. In December 1969 Sudan agreed to coordinate its foreign policy with Egypt and Libya in a short-lived "Federation of Arab Republics." Related to the Arab-Israeli conflict, the American ambassador to Sudan was killed by Palestinian gunmen in Khartoum in 1973. Though President Ja'afar al-Nimeiri (q.v.) agreed to release the killers to the Palestine Liberation Organization (PLO), he had already begun to appreciate the need for closer ties to the West, particularly in light of the damaging rise in oil prices following the 1973 Arab-Israeli war.

In 1977 Sudan signed a mutual defense pact with Egypt. One year later, in 1978, Sudan reluctantly supported Egypt's signing of the Camp David peace accords with Israel. Camp David placed Sudan in a difficult position: on the one hand, Egypt had broken ranks with the other Arab League members; on the other hand, Egypt and Sudan shared many common interests, including the Nile waters and exporting of cotton. Perhaps tempering Sudan's involvement in the Arab-Israeli conflict was the knowledge that Israel was simultaneously supporting southern Sudanese rebels: from 1965 to 1972 Israel armed the Anya-Nya (q.v.) soldiers from Uganda in an attempt to draw Sudanese forces away from the Suez Canal zone; Israel has also been rumored to supply and arm southern insurgents from Kenya and Eritrea since the 1980s. Sudan was embarrassed by the disclosure that it had assisted the transport of Ethiopian Jews (Falashas) to Israel in 1985.

Since Nimeiri's overthrow that same year, Sudanese governments have maintained a steady anti-Israel (and increasingly, pan-Islamic) rhetoric. As a serious political concern, however, the Arab-Israeli matter has remained subordinate to the resolution of the Sudanese civil war. *See also* KHARTOUM SUMMIT OF 1967.

ARAB SOCIALISM. This ideology of progressive social and political development that was an outgrowth of the Arab nationalist movement was most closely associated with Gamal 'Abdel Nasser of Egypt. The Ba'athist movements of Syria and Iraq, as well as Mu'ammar Qaddafi's "Green Revolution" in Libya, are examples of Arab socialist regimes. In Sudan, Ja'afar al-Nimeiri (q.v.) was closely allied with the Sudanese

Communist Party (q.v.) from 1969 to 1972, but after the abortive coup of 1971, he turned toward Arab socialism and Pan-Arabism with the founding in 1972 of the Sudanese Socialist Union (SSU, q.v.). The founding of the SSU had a similar effect in Sudan as the 1961 founding of the Arab Socialist Union had in Egypt. The Communist parties of each country suffered isolation at home as they developed closer ties with the Soviet Union and its allies. Arab socialism thus provided a nationalist alternative to the progressive political spectrum, based upon the Arabic language (q.v.) and identity, while avoiding the stigma of association with the international communist movement.

The Pan-Arabist rhetoric of Arab socialism proved more stirring in theory than in practical politics, and several attempts to unify the "Arab Nation" under the banner of socialism failed, including a proposed union among Sudan, Egypt, and Libya. The SSU at its first national congress opposed any federation between Sudan and other Arab states, specifically mentioning the Arab Socialist Union of Egypt. Effectively, Arab socialism ceased to have any significant impact on Sudanese politics after Nimeiri's courtship of the religious right-wing movements in the late 1970s and played a limited role in the national uprising that ousted Nimeiri in 1985 and in the democratic elections thereafter.

During the period of democracy from 1985 to 1989, remnants of Arab socialist parties and the Iraqi-backed Ba'ath Socialist Party attacked the National Islamic Front (NIF, q.v.), while the Libyan backed Popular Revolutionary Committees joined with Nasserites and pro-Syrian Ba'athists to form a National Progressive Front that had little electoral success. Their view, pan-Arab and secular, privileged Arabic speakers and those of "Arab" (q.v.) lineage although their secular view acknowledged the need for a democratic pluralist Sudan in which the rights of non-Arabs and non-Muslims would be protected.

ARABIC LANGUAGE. This widely spoken language of the Middle East and North Africa belongs to the Semitic or Afro-Asiatic family of languages and as such is based upon an ancient system of grammar and lexicon. In its written form, Arabic only became widespread for the *literati* in the region well after the spread of Islam in the seventh century to Egypt, but only after the sixteenth century in the Sudan. Historically, writing in the Sudan prior to Arabic was in hieroglyphics, Meroitic, Greek, Latin, Old Nubian, and Coptic. Indeed Arabic languages, like other Semitic languages such as Berber or Hebrew, are closely related historically, structurally, and semantically. Arabic language has been undergoing a process of development and Sudanization (in the broad African sense) for over a thousand years. Sudanese Arabic, which is closest in form and content to Egyptian Arabic, is the only Sudanese language that has a modern literary history, and it is the national language available for communication among the majority of Sudanese. After the Closed Districts Ordinance (q.v.), the Condominium (q.v.) forbade its use for teaching in the southern regions. Since the holding of the 1972 political negotiations between North and South under the Addis Ababa Agreement (q.v.), it has been agreed that Arabic is the official administrative and literary language of Sudan, while English is to be used in the translation of national and international communication.

The Modern Standard or Classical form of Arabic is used today in Sudan and the region for nearly all written communications such as newspapers and books and in formal oral presentations, including radio and television. It is the official language of instruction in the educational system, but is usually replaced by its colloquial form. Those with formal training in Arabic take great pride in its rich vocabulary, nuances, and poetic expression.

Despite its distribution in the Sudan, Modern Standard Arabic is the first language for inhabitants of the riverine central Sudan only. The formal nature of this language makes it barely intelligible for Sudanese with only colloquial Arabic, and barely at all with Sudanese Creole-Arabic. This language carries a special importance to Islam because it is the language of the prophet Muhammad and the Qur'an. In the non-Islamic regions of the Sudan, it is much less used and even resisted by those who find it isolates them from the wider Anglophone world and non-Muslim identities. Thus, many Sudanese governments have projected Arabic as the language of national unity while important minorities throughout the country have seen it as a manifestation of Arab cultural domination.

On the other hand, facility with Sudanese colloquial Arabic as a vernacular language is very widespread throughout the nation, especially in the north and central regions. It functions as a *lingua franca* and trade language for the nation and the wider region in the Horn of Africa, in Egypt, and across the Sahel. It is certainly related to classical Arabic but includes simplified grammar and many loan words from European and African languages. Regional dialects of Sudanese colloquial Arabic can be recognized.

Finally, there is a form of Creole or Pidgin Arabic, which is widely used in the south and other frontier areas, including the east among Beja speakers, to the north among Nubians, and among the Furawis in the west. Through the multilingual southern regions and adjoining nations, especially in refugee camps and urban areas, this language functions well. It is used widely in elementary education, in local commerce, and in religious services. Sometimes heavily accented, it is not very intelligible with northern Sudanese colloquial Arabic, and virtually fails to communicate with Modern Standard Arabic. [by Constance E. Berkley]

ARAKIYIN. A religious family with influence centered in the Blue Nile area. The traditional founder of the family was 'Abdallah Dafa'allah al-Araki. He lived around 1570 and was one of the first *khalifas* (q.v.) in the Sudan of the Qadiriya (q.v.). Around 1800 some leaders of the clan switched to the Sammaniya (q.v.). Many Arakiyin fled from Turco-Egyptian (q.v.) rule, returning gradually in the nineteenth century. The tomb of the founder and its custodian-patrons maintain local religious prestige in Abu Haraz.

ARCHER, SIR GEOFFREY (1882–1964). This British governor-general of the Sudan, who is most noted for his short-lived and failed administration from 4 December 1924 to 17 October 1926, assumed his position in the wake of the assassination of Sir Lee Stack (q.v.) in 1924. Still reeling from this shock, the administration could not quickly swing its support behind Archer, and his rival Sir John Maffey (q.v.) moved into the vacuum created by the British Foreign Office.

ARMENIANS. One of the first known Armenian visitors to the Sudan was a certain 'Abu Salih' (actual name unknown), who flourished in the thirteenth century and wrote an account of Nubia (q.v.). By the late seventeenth century there were Armenians trading in Sinnar (q.v.) as part of a foreign merchant community. The Armenian presence increased considerably during the Turco-Egyptian (q.v.) period, with many Armenians involved in trade or else serving as tax and finance officials. Higher in the administration, Arakil Bey (a relative of the Egyptian prime minister Nubar Pasha Boghos) became the first Christian governor in the Sudan when he was appointed governor of Khartoum (q.v.) and the Gezira (q.v., 1856). Concerned with improving health conditions in the capital, he died prematurely in 1858. His relative, Arakil Bey Nubar, served Egypt as governor of Massawa and connected the telegraph from that port to Kassala (q.v.) in 1874. Meanwhile, Artin Arakilian (d. 1889) introduced the growing of tobacco in Gedaref (q.v.) in 1859, from whence it was shipped to Khartoum for curing by other Armenians and packed for export. Most Armenians seem to have fled the Sudan with the rise of the Mahdist (q.v.) movement. The few who remained behind are known to have lived in Omdurman (q.v.) during that period, entrenched in the Masalma (q.v.) community and working as jewelers or watchmakers. The British found only three Armenians when they entered the city in 1898.

Along with the Greeks, Syrians, and Jews (qq.v.), the Armenians returned to the Sudan in the wake of the Anglo-Egyptian (q.v.) conquest, some even accompanying the invading force. One merchant, Soukias Vanian (1840–1915), opened his shop in Omdurman immediately after the conquest, moving it to Khartoum in 1899. Like other minority communities, the Armenians were chiefly involved in trade in the Three Towns (q.v.) and other commercial centers. They were issued Sudanese passports during the Condominium (q.v.) period as well as Sudanese nationality certificates after independence. Their exodus from Sudan began with the nationalization policies of the Ja'afar al-Nimeiri (q.v.) regime in the 1970s, and intensified with the "September Laws" of 1983 (q.v.) and rise of political Islam. Few Armenians have remained in Sudan since the 'Umar al-Bashir (q.v.) coup of 1989.

ASHIGGA PARTY. A minor political party in the World War II period and major actor as a political broker in the turbulent nationalist period of the 1940s and early 1950s. Meaning "full blood brothers," this group was formed in late 1940 by a militant nationalist faction within the Graduates Congress (q.v.) that was known as the Committee of Sixty and aimed at forming a National Front (q.v.). In early 1941 the position of the Khatmiya *tariqa* (qq.v.) had weakened within the Graduates Congress and the more militant nationalist position in the Ashigga-Mahdist alliance was briefly more dominant. By late 1941 and into 1942, divisions among the Mahdists led to an erosion of their relative strength within the National Front and within the Graduates Congress.

Because of the divisions of the member parties and leaders by 1943 the Ashigga controlled the Congress executive committee and played an active role in negotiations with Egypt for Sudanese independence at a time when Great Britain was hugely preoccupied with the World War. Although still a main partner in the Graduates Congress elections of 1944 the Ashigga Party gained more strength as a brokerage political party under the leadership of Isma'il al-Azhari (q.v.). The Congress (a proto–National Assembly) still held the Unionist and Liberal Parties (qq.v.) within the national framework of decolonization. The party continued to support a general sense of unity with Egyptian King Faruq (q.v., a tolerable Khatmiya objective); and it opposed official cooperation with the British (a Mahdist objective).

As the Mahdist influence waned within the Congress in 1944 it rose within the Advisory Council of the Northern Sudan so the Mahdists could still function as main actors in the political arena. The Mahdists finally broke free from these political struggles within the National Front and with the Ashigga by forming the Umma Party (q.v.) in 1945. Although inherently fearing the legacy of Mahdism, the British also saw that Mahdist domination of the Sudan would weaken Sudanese links to Egypt, which could enhance British imperial interests. So by 1946–1947 the brokerage role of the Ashigga had been somewhat diminished, while the British ability to maneuver was enhanced as they still controlled power, albeit on a "lame duck" basis. In this temporary power vacuum the Sudanese Communist Party (SCP, q.v.) and its associated Sudanese Workers Trade Union Federation (q.v.) had their greatest influence. While certainly not a majority party, the SCP managed to control critical nodes in the Sudanese political economy and reenergized political debates and the timetable for independence with protests and strikes, especially in 1947–1948. As the Cold War mentality emerged the British could charge (falsely) that the "Communist menace" lay behind the Ashigga. It is alleged that the British created a puppet socialist Republican Party (q.v.) to counter the growing strength of the SCP.

In 1948 the Ashigga again received the cautious support of 'Ali al-Mirghani (q.v.) who wanted to block the influence of the Mahdists by any means. The plurality of other small parties still left al-Azhari in control of not only the Ashigga but also of the Graduates Congress and its short-lived Internal Struggle Front. The influence of the Ashigga Party began to decline by 1949–1950 when much Khatmiya support went directly to the National Front (q.v.). At the same time, the British-sponsored elected assemblies gained more popular recognition. In this way, the still-active British undermined the power base of the Ashigga Party that they could not otherwise effectively control.

The Ashigga Party split into two factions. A dissident group led by Muhammad Nur al-Din (q.v.) opposed al-Azhari and his supporters. The party was dissolved when both factions joined the National Unionist Party (NUP, q.v.) in 1952. This was the year of the Egyptian revolution, which toppled the monarchy and installed a revolutionary military government and also accelerated the process of decolonization in the Sudan. To a notable degree 1952 also witnessed a volatile struggle for power within the movements and parties in the Sudan over who would actually hold power at the moment of the now-inevitable independence. Specifically the 1953 Anglo-Egyptian Agreement (q.v.) abrogated the 1899 and 1936 agreements of Condominium (q.v.) rule in the Sudan and cleared the way for full Sudanese independence following the 1953 elections to create a legislative assembly. These many dramatic events restored the initiative to the Ashigga Party and dramatically weakened the British negotiating position in the end game of decolonization.

On 6 January 1954 the Parliament elected al-Azhari as the first prime minister of the Sudan, but the path to independence was still rough with a violent demonstration backed by the Umma and constitutional crises that almost brought down the government. Perhaps worst of all was the 1955 revolt in the southern Sudan (q.v.), which opened a wound still unhealed. Nonetheless it was al-Azhari of the Ashigga Party who was in control on 1 January 1956 when the British formally departed. By July 1956 al-Azhari was himself brought down in interparty wrangling while Ashigga politics and leadership continued to be an important force within the NUP. This first period of Sudanese multiparty democracy was terminated in 1958 with the Ibrahim Abboud (q.v.) military coup that suspended all political parties. In the second period of democracy from 1964 to 1969, al-Azhari did not play a very active role. He died in 1969, the same year as Ja'afar al-Nimeiri's "May Revolution" (qq.v.) and thus the symbolic end of the old era and the start of a very different one in Sudanese politics.

ASHRAF. An Arabic term (sing. *sharif/sharifa*) referring to descendants of the Prophet Muhammad or the Prophet's uncles among the Hashimite clan. This lineage historically has bestowed high social status, and hence it is a title that many have laid claim to in Muslim societies throughout the world. Among Sudan's Ashraf are prominent families such as the al-Hindi (q.v.), Mikashfi, and Mirghani (q.v.). The holyman Muhammad Majdhub (q.v.) denied being a *sharif* and claimed only a symbolic link to the Prophet, though he promoted the *sharifi* status of some of his influential followers (who in turn insisted on his direct descent). In various circumstances individuals have "discovered" *sharifi* roots or else earned the honorific title through their piety and learning.

Otherwise, al-Ashraf is the name of a distinct ethnic group in eastern Sudan who claim descent from "Sharif Muhammad," said to have arrived in Suakin (q.v.) between the fifteenth and seventeenth centuries. The family of the Mahdi (q.v.) claimed *sharifi* status through an ancestor, al-Hajj Sharif Satti 'Ali (ca. early seventeenth century). During the Mahdiya (q.v.) the head of these Ashraf, Ahmad Muhammad Sharfi, supported the Khalifa 'Abdullahi (q.v.), while a faction led by Khalifa Muhammad Sharif (q.v.) challenged the Khalifa's rule on a number of occasions, most notably in the insurrection of 1891. At least since the Mahdiya, the families of 'Ali wad Hilu (q.v.) and Khalifa 'Abdullahi have hinted at their *sharifi* status. *See also* SAYYID.

ASMARA DECLARATION OF 1995. The leaders of the National Democratic Alliance (NDA, q.v.) held a historic meeting in Asmara, Eritrea, in June 1995. Eritrea, which had broken relations with the Sudanese government earlier that year over Khartoum's efforts to export its Islamic revolution and destabilize its government, took this occasion to recognize the NDA as the legitimate representative of the Sudanese people.

Five main agreements emerged from the Asmara conference, including bringing about a peaceful settlement to the civil war; overthrowing the National Islamic Front (NIF, q.v.) regime in Khartoum (q.v.); the nature and duration of an interim government; the nature of the future Sudanese state; and the structure of the NDA as it prepared itself for these tasks. A basic agreement by the NDA on the right of the southern Sudanese to self-determination preceded the formal organization of the conference, the first time that all of the Sudanese political parties (excluding the NIF) signed a document recognizing self-determination, conceived of as being implemented through a regional referendum. One of the most controversial issues hammered out at the Asmara conference was the status of certain border areas between the North and South, including Abyei, the Nuba Mountains (q.v.), and Ingessana Hills, whose future as part of the South may be determined by referendum. It was agreed that these regions would be jointly administered by the Sudanese Peoples Liberation Army (SPLA, q.v.) and the administration of southern Kordofan (q.v.) during the interim period. In the end the future structure of the Sudan envisions six federal states of the North with a confederated state of the South having its own governance and standing army.

On the matter of the most effective means of overthrowing the NIF government, the Asmara conference agreed that the military opposition of the SPLA has been more effective than political opposition. The singular role of the SPLA as the leading opposition force was recognized, as was the role of Colonel John Garang (q.v.).

The conference defined the future Sudan as one based upon multiparty pluralism, democracy, human rights, and the rule of law. As a thoroughly secular state, religion will have no role to play in politics, thus there is to be no state religion. The setting of a future political agenda, based on peace and unity, justice, and democracy, to which all of the leading opposition parties and leaders will be held accountable, is viewed as the major significance of the Asmara conference and declaration.

'ATABANI, ISMA'IL (1910–?). Al-'Atabani was a journalist, newspaper entrepreneur, and nationalist intellectual. He graduated from the Gordon Memorial College (q.v.) in 1931 and served as a government accountant until 1939. He was a leading member of both the Abu Rawf (q.v.) literary society and the Wad Medani (q.v.) literary society, and later of the Graduates Congress (q.v.) executive committee. His most important contribution, however, was in the field of journalism. He was an early contributor to the journal *al-Nahda* (q.v.). Later, in 1941, he accepted a position as editor-in-chief of the Khatmiya-supported (q.v.) newspaper, *Sawt al-Sudan* (Voice of the Sudan). In 1945 he left to start his own daily independent newspaper, *Al-Ra'y al-'Amm* (Public Opinion). *Al-Ra'y al-'Amm* became one of the Sudan's largest and most successful Arabic newspapers; by 1956, it had an estimated circulation of 4,000 copies. *Al-Ra'y al-'Amm* ceased publication after twenty-five years when Ja'afar al-Nimeiri (q.v.) nationalized it in 1970. [by Heather J. Sharkey]

ATBARA. This northern Sudanese town is located between the fifth and sixth cataracts on the east bank of the Nile. Its name is a corruption of the Romano-Nubian word "Astaboras," referring to the river that meets the Nile at this point (at best, only a seasonal river). In ancient times the Atbara was also the corridor from Ethiopia to ancient Meroë (q.v.), through which King Ezana passed to complete the destruction of that ancient Sudanese civilization in about AD 325.

In modern times Atbara functioned as a small-scale trade center along the river and to the Red Sea. Since Atbara is simultaneously located on the North-South railroad as well as the track east to Port Sudan, it has gained a dominant regional position in size and strategic importance.

Atbara was damaged in 1884 by Mahdist attacks. What was not wrecked then was subsequently leveled by British shelling in April 1898 during the Battle of Atbara against the Mahdist leader Mahmud Ahmad. Using vastly superior weaponry, the British killed some 2,000 Mahdist soldiers and gave a savage defeat to Mahmoud. This British victory led directly to an expansion of the railway network for military, administrative, and economic needs and Atbara was often central to these concerns.

Dating from this period, Atbara also has a number of colonial-style dwellings and a wooden Anglican church.

In 1924 an Egyptian work force revolted in Atbara concurrent with a strike of cadets at the Khartoum military school. The Atbara revolt was put down with loss of life and with evacuation of the Egyptians. In the 1930s British troops were stationed at Atbara as a security measure against further revolts, and relations between British and Sudanese were often tense. On the other hand, the need for low-paid colonial staff led to the creation of two small elementary schools and a small hospital in Atbara by this time.

During World War II the British were concerned about Italian attacks against Atbara, given its strategic position on the railway. In fact, in July 1940 Atbara was bombed by Italian military aircraft, but without substantial damage. After the battle of Keren in Eritrea the British transported Eritrean soldiers to prison camps in Atbara. In 1940 the schools were briefly closed, but by 1943 they had not only been reopened but also were augmented by intermediate schools as well.

After the war during the period of intense nationalist agitation for independence, Atbara again played an important role because of the well-organized railway and telegraph workers, the Workers' Affairs Association (WAA, q.v.) and the nascent Sudanese Communist Party (SCP, q.v.) in this town. The railway had its central office in Atbara, where over 20,000 workers lived by the 1940s. Attracted by this strategic labor force, in November 1945 Atbara was visited by Jamal al-Din Sanhuri of the Egyptian Muslim Brothers (q.v.) movement, who succeeded in establishing a branch of his organization in Atbara. In 1946 during widespread strikes throughout the Sudan, the Atbara Technical school was closed as both Sudanese and Egyptians were intensifying their anticolonial drives. In July 1947 and in January and March 1948 the WAA in Atbara was able to organize effective and widespread strikes about labor concerns that were implicitly anticolonial. By March 1949 the WAA and the Sudan Railway Workers Union (SRWU) had launched a Workers Congress that was the springboard for the formation of the Sudan Workers Trade Union Federation (SWTUF, q.v.), founded there in 1950.

As independence approached the British were well aware of the threat posed by Atbara, but they were dependent upon the railway for their own economic and military needs and were politically powerless to stop the movement. At independence Atbara had 36,500 inhabitants, by 1964 it had reached 50,000, and estimates for 1987 were 75,000.

ATIYAH, EDWARD (1903–1964). Atiyah was a Lebanese teacher, Intelligence Department official, and pan-Arabist intellectual. Born in Suq al-Gharb, Lebanon, he came from a family with employment connections in the Sudan. His father, Salim, was a Sudan government doctor; an uncle, Farid, was an education department inspector; and a second uncle, Samuel, was a high-ranking intelligence official. Atiyah spent his early childhood in Khartoum (q.v.), then studied at Victoria College in Alexandria, and finally at Oxford. He returned to the Sudan in 1926 and worked as a teacher at the Gordon Memorial College (q.v.). Embittered by the poor treatment of Sudanese and Lebanese teachers by their British colleagues, he left the education department to succeed his uncle in intelligence, where he worked until 1945. He developed contacts with northern Sudanese nationalists and even participated in the Hashimab (q.v.) literary society, sharing with them an interest in Fabian socialism. He supervised the development of Sudanese radio during World War II. Atiyah wrote a novel called *Black Vanguard* (1952), which depicted the plight of the young, Western-educated northern Sudanese struggling to come to terms with the traditions of Sudanese society. Atiyah left the Sudan to head the Arab Office in London, where he served as a spokesman for Arab issues. He died on the floor of the Oxford Union, while defending the Palestinian cause. [by Heather J. Sharkey]

ATTA, HASHIM AL-. Sudanese soldier and political leader. He was a member of Ja'afar al-Nimeiri's (q.v.) original Revolutionary Command Council in 1969, and served in early cabinets. He was dismissed from his civil and military posts in November 1970. In July 1971 he led the short-lived pro-Communist (q.v.) coup and was executed.

AVUNGARA. *See* AZANDE.

AWADALLAH, BABIKER (1917–). Sudanese judge and political leader. After studying law in Khartoum (q.v.) and London he served as a lawyer and district judge. He resigned to become speaker of the Parliament (1954–1957) and then rejoined the judiciary. He served as chief justice of Sudan (1964–1967) after being active in the 1964 Revolution. Awadallah resigned as chief justice in protest over the issue of banning communists from Parliament. After the 1969 Revolution of Ja'afar al-Nimeiri (q.v.) he was named the first prime minister in the new regime. He also served, at various times, as minister of foreign affairs and of justice, and as deputy prime minister before resigning for health reasons in 1972 and taking up residence in Cairo.

AWLAD JABIR. "The children (descendants) of Jabir" were major religious leaders in the Nilotic Sudan from the sixteenth until the mid-eighteenth century. They, their kinsmen through marriage, and their descendants formed a complex of holy families that maintained important schools and provided religious leadership in the Sudan. Their ancestry is traced back traditionally to a wandering fifteenth-century scholar, Ghulamallah ibn Ayid. Little is known about Jabir, but his offspring gained fame: Ibrahim al-Bulad, 'Abd al-Rahman, and Isma'il all established major schools in the Shayqiya (q.v.) area, while his scholar-daughter was the teacher and mother of the continuing line of scholars in the family. Her most famous children were Muhammad al-Sughayarun, who was granted land by a Funj (q.v.) sultan and was a political as well as religious force in the sultanate, and Amina, a learned woman whose sons set up schools in the Shendi (q.v.) area.

AZANDE. The Azande are members of the Equatorial cluster of the huge African family of Niger-Congo languages. Like their relatives the Bantu, the Azande had been expanding in the last thousand years. Their economy is based on cultivation of millet and Malaysian crops such as yams and bananas. They began migrating into the southwestern Sudan as early as the sixteenth century. In the eighteenth century the Azande created a military aristocracy, the Avungara, which imposed itself upon all Azande people in addition to others such as the Bongo, Madi, Ndogo, and Mundu. In the eighteenth and nineteenth centuries these conquests were related to acquiring slaves whom they traded with Danagla (q.v.) merchants coming from the northern Sudan or slave traders who operated for Ottoman interests.

As a result of this expansionist phase a number of related kingdoms or small states was formed and these dominated the region through the twentieth century. Azande leaders like Yambio (q.v.) resisted British rule, while others like Tambura (q.v.) cooperated.

After World War II an attempt was made to organize a large-scale cotton production project, the Azande Scheme. Although it had initial success it has no long-term impact. Azande people also live in the neighboring countries where their total number is probably well over one million. *See also* ABU JOHN; LANGUAGES.

AZANIA LIBERATION FRONT (ALF). A southern political organization formed in 1965. Following the split in the Sudan African National Union (SANU, q.v.) members of SANU in exile formed the ALF under Joseph Oduho and Father Saturnino (qq.v.). The Sudan African Liberation Front (q.v., SALF), formed by Aggrey Jaden (q.v.), merged with the ALF late in 1965. Personal and interethnic rivalries divided the ALF and most of its leadership went to the Southern Sudan Provisional Government (q.v.) when it was formed in 1967.

AL-AZHAR UNIVERSITY. The world's leading Islamic university in Cairo, arguably the intellectual seat of the Islamic world. Sudanese are known to have studied at al-Azhar at least as early as the sixteenth century, and Azhar-trained *fekis* and merchants played a role in the spread of Islam (q.v.) in the sultanates of Sinnar and Darfur (qq.v.). The Turco-Egyptian (q.v.) regime sought to encourage a more orthodox form of Islam in the Sudan and brought Azhari jurists with its invasion force in 1820. Sometime during the nineteenth century special hostels at al-Azhar were created for Sudanese students, the *Riwaq Sinnariya* and *Riwaq Dar Fur*. The Egyptian ruler Khedive Isma'il (1863–1879, q.v.) further encouraged Sudanese study at al-Azhar by issuing grants to students. Nonetheless the actual influence of al-Azhar on the formation of Sudanese Islam is debatable. In the twentieth century students at al-Azhar were one conduit of nationalist ideas following World War I. *See also* AL-AZHARI.

AZHARI, Al-. This means "from al-Azhar," the great Islamic university in Cairo. In the Sudan, "al-Azhari" is associated most frequently with a branch of the family of Isma'il al-Wali. Isma'il's second son, Ahmad (ca. 1810–1882), was educated at al-Azhar (q.v.) and was a prominent nineteenth-century Sudanese legal scholar. In contrast to his older brother Muhammad al-Mekki, who succeeded his father as leader of the Isma'iliya (q.v.) and was an advisor to the Khalifa 'Abdullahi (q.v.), Ahmad al-Azhari opposed Mahdism and was killed in an early battle in 1882. Ahmad's son Isma'il al-Azhari (1868–1947) became a judge of Islamic law (q.v.) and served as *Mufti* of the Sudan (1924–1932). Isma'il's grandson, another Isma'il al-Azhari (q.v.), became the first prime minister of the independent Sudan. Other members of the family, like Ibrahim al-Mufti, were also prominent in modern Sudanese politics.

AZHARI, ISMA'IL, AL- (1902–1969). Isma'il al-Azhari was the first prime minister of the independent Sudan. He was born in Omdurman (q.v.) in 1902, grandson of a noted *mufti* and from a family long involved in religion and politics in the Sudan. He had his early schooling at Gordon Memorial College (q.v.) and from 1921 to 1927 was a teacher of mathematics. From 1927 to 1930 he attended the American University in Beirut. When he returned to the Sudan it was for a lifetime of public service and politics, as a major figure in the development of a Sudanese nationalism that favored unity with Egypt, at that time still ruled by King Faruq (q.v.).

Al-Azhari was a founder of the Graduates Congress (q.v.) in Omdurman (q.v.) in 1931 and was elected as its president in 1938, despite the majority being supporters of the Ansar (q.v.) sect. The rivalry of the traditional leaders was evident in the 1941 election, which was largely divided between the Khatmiya (q.v.) and the Ansar. The resultant compromises within the Committee of Sixty gave rise to their 1942 proclamation calling for Sudanese independence, while Great Britain was otherwise preoccupied by World War II and trying to determine a new relationship with Egypt. Becoming the leader of the Ashigga Party (q.v.), al-Azhari took advantage of Ansar internal divisions to dominate in the 1943 elections and begin to shift the postcolonial debate toward unity of the Nile Valley, rather than full independence advocated by the Ansar at the time. The 1944 elections in the Congress only strengthened al-Azhari's position, both because of continued divisions among the Ansar, and with the solidification of ties between his Ashigga Party and the traditional leadership of the Khatmiya *tariqa* (q.v.). The determination of the Sudanese relationship with Egypt remained a point of disagreement within Sudanese elites, as seen in the small Unionist and Liberal Party divisions. Thus, this alliance was no small achievement since al-Azhari was not a member of that *tariqa*, but of the Isma'iliya *tariqa*, which had been founded by his great grandfather, Isma'il al-Wali. The Ansar anticipated further isolation in the Graduates Congress elections for 1945 and so they withdrew, placing al-Azhari and the Ashigga in full power of a somewhat more narrowly defined body. Ansar strength was maintained in their dominance of the Advisory Council of the Northern Sudan (q.v.), which had independently charted a path toward independence.

The British sought to apply some restraint to al-Azhari, who became a full-time politician in 1946 based with the Ashigga Party. Al-Azhari was reconfirmed in 1948 as the president of the Graduates Congress, largely from his skills in keeping the pro-union parties together; putting pressure on the British who briefly held him in jail; and having enough ambiguity about the nature of "Nile unity" so as not to antagonize the Ansar any further, while keeping his rivals from that party off the track to independence under their administration. In fact, the very survivability of al-Azhari at this critical crossroads in Sudanese history was because he thrived as a power broker between the Ansar and Khatmiya, on one side, and between his Ashigga and the Khatmiya, on the other. His ability to find an independent route made him quite unpopular with the waning British establishment, hoping to build upon a model of pliant neo-colonial leaders. It was ironic that the more the British opposed al-Azhari, the more popular he became as a public figure.

After intraparty wrangling for leadership in 1951, al-Azhari emerged as the president of the National Unionist Party (NUP, q.v.) when it was formed in 1952. After the NUP victory in the 1953 parliamentary elections, al-Azhari became the first Sudanese prime minister, but through February relations between al-Azhari and the British had soured seriously and on 1 March 1953 rioting led by the Ansar broke out in the capital with over a score killed. Modest advances in the process of Sudanization in 1954 helped to restore calm and broaden the credibility of al-Azhari during the last year of the Robert Howe (q.v.) administration. The next major crisis to be faced was the bloody revolt in the southern Sudan in August and September 1955, with southerners deeply apprehensive about being excluded from the independence process conducted by northern elites. Realizing that they had only months left to serve as colonialists, the British reacted to this sudden emergency and supported al-Azhari at a time of grave political weakness and protracted parliamentary crisis in November 1955.

This rough road led Isma'il al-Azhari to become the first prime minister of an independent Sudan, which was granted full independence on 1 January 1956. This was the first time a Sudanese was head of government since the defeat of the Khalifa 'Abdullahi (q.v.) in 1898. However his unstable cabinet fell in July 1956 after another split between the Khatmiya and the Umma Party (q.v.).

Following the Ibrahim Abboud (q.v.) military coup in November 1958, al-Azhari was formally out of politics but active in opposition. After the 1964 October Revolution (q.v.) he again led the NUP to political importance, often in a precarious alliance with the Umma Party. He was elected as the permanent president of the Supreme Council, serving until the 1969 May Revolution (q.v.), the year in which he died.

AZMIYA. A Muslim group established by Muhammad Madi Abu al-Aza'im (1870–1936). The founder was an Egyptian school teacher in the Sudan who was deported in 1915 because of his political views. He was influenced by Wahhabi teachings and advocated a vigorous reform of Islam (q.v.) and opposition to the influence of the hereditary religious leaders. Membership in his organization reached a peak in the 1920s.

– B –

B. Between two proper names, b. stands for *ibn* . . ., meaning the "son of . . ."

BA'ATH PARTY. The Ba'ath Party has long been one of the smaller parties in Sudan. Its size is chiefly measured during the several periods of democratic elections. This local expression of Pan-Arabism was compelled to choose sides in the Baghdad-Damascus split that has long rent the movement. The Sudanese branch supported the Iraqi Ba'ath Party. As a Pan-Arabist party, the Sudanese Ba'athists have tried to link Sudan alternatively with Egypt or Libya in their step-by-step approach to unify all Arab and Muslim nations. Since Egypt, Libya, Iraq, and Syria have all had their own problems in maintaining cordial ties, the Ba'ath Party of Sudan can not point to many successes.

Indeed the zealous objectives of the Ba'ath have often meant that it was strongly critical of the very regimes with whom it sought political association. This is also the case in Sudan itself, where the local Ba'athists have wavered between hot and cold relations with various military governments, especially those of Ja'afar al-Nimeiri and 'Umar al-Bashir (qq.v.), which have sometimes welcomed, sometimes tolerated, and sometimes persecuted Sudanese Ba'athists, depending upon the political climate between Khartoum and Baghdad. Al-Bashir banned all parties after 1989 and this included the arrest of almost four dozen Sudanese Ba'athists in 1990. However, when Sudan chose to back Iraq in the Gulf War, the Ba'athists were given greater political freedom.

BADI II, ABU DIQN. This Funj (q.v.) sultan of Sinnar (q.v.) ruled from 1645 until 1681. His reign marked the peak of the dynasty's power and prosperity. He defeated potential enemies in the White Nile and Nuba Mountain (q.v.) areas, built the royal palace and first major mosque in Sinnar, and encouraged trade and religious scholarship. Using slaves (q.v.) from his conquests he created a corps of slave troops, which later caused tensions with the old Funj aristocracy.

BADRI, BABIKIR (1861–1954). Sudanese educator and intellectual and pioneer in women's (q.v.) education. As a young man he was a soldier in the Mahdist army. In the twentieth century he became a pioneer in modern education in a traditional context. He created an extensive network of boys' schools, which thrived into the 1950s. He is also called the "father of girls' education in the Sudan," establishing the first of many Sudanese girls' schools in 1908, that is today the Ahfad University College for Women in Omdurman (qq.v.). He and his family were active in twentieth-century intellectual developments in the Sudan. His three-volume memoirs are published (two volumes of which are in English). These fascinating first-hand reports of events such as the fall of Khartoum (q.v.) and life during the reign of Khalifa 'Abdullahi (q.v.) make an important contribution to Sudanese historiography.

BAGGARA. *See* BAQQARA.

BAHR AL-GHAZAL PROVINCE. Region and former province (q.v.) located in the southwest of the Sudan and named for the Bahr al-Ghazal ("Gazelle Waters") river on its eastern boundary. Comprising approximately 82,530 square miles, its population was estimated at 1,427,000 in 1970. The dominant ethnic group, perhaps 90 percent, is the Dinka (q.v.). In the nineteenth century it was raided frequently for slaves (q.v.) and ivory. It was known in the twentieth century for cattle rearing and some farming prior to the devastation of the civil war. Its principal city is Wau (q.v.).

BAKER, SIR SAMUEL (1821–1893). British author, hunter, and traveler. As a member of the adventuring crowd in England, Baker was familiar with John Hanning Speke and James Grant (qq.v.), who were eagerly engaged in the search for the headwaters of the White Nile from east Africa. Baker imagined that he could have a great game-hunting experience and meet Speke in the southern Sudan. Setting off from Cairo in 1861 with his wife, Florence, he advanced up the Nile to Berber and Khartoum (qq.v.) where he also explored and hunted along the Atbara River (q.v.), the Blue Nile, and in Ethiopia between 1861 and 1862. He departed from Khartoum in 1862 and headed south hacking his way through the dense swamps of the *Sudd* before reaching Gondokoro (q.v.). His timing was excellent as Speke arrived a few weeks later to report on his historic discoveries.

By 1863 the Bakers sought to confirm the claims of Speke. Facing grave attacks of malaria and wild animals they advanced south of Gondokoro on 26 March 1863 (about 1,250 kilometers south of Khartoum), to travel across the Madi Mountains to the great basin of the upper Nile through Bunyoro and Kitwara territory and to Albert Nyanza (or Lake Albert, named for the recently deceased husband of Queen Victoria), which Sir Samuel discovered on 16 March 1864 at Vacovia. After a thirteen-day canoe trip along the northeastern shore of Albert Nyanza he went upstream on the Victoria Nile to the Murchinson Falls and Karuma Falls before heading back through Fatiko and returning to Gondokoro on 23 March 1865. He slowly regained Khartoum and then went east to Suakin to get back to Egypt. He finally reached England to receive the Gold Medal from the Royal Geographical Society and was knighted in 1866 for his discoveries. His book *The Albert Nyanza, Great Basin of the Nile and Explorations of the Nile Sources* was also published in 1866. This well-illustrated, 516-page work gave meticulous documentation of his movements and elevations to offer convincing proof of his (and Speke's) discoveries.

In 1869 the ruler of Egypt appointed him governor-general of the southern provinces of the Sudan, under the wishes of the British government, which had adopted an active antislavery (q.v.) policy by this time in order to establish commercial entrepots in central Africa and force the local people to submit to British governmental control.

The British government determined that Baker's knowledge of the southern Sudan, the main area of slave supply, would be highly suited to this mission. Accordingly, he was authorized to form a uniformed and armed bodyguard, which came to be known as "The Forty Thieves," in order to support this effort. Baker and his detachment struggled southward and regained the strategic river port of Gondokoro from where he organized raids against the local slavers. Serious problems with supplies and desertion made his task extremely difficult. He sought to control this southern section of the White Nile with river patrol forts to make a secure route to Masindi, the Bunyoro capital, now under King Kabarega (Kavarega). The Bunyoro state was heavily involved in the slave export business to the East African coast, so Baker's forces were resisted at the Battle of Masindi on 8 June 1872. Although Baker's small force had been further reduced in number, these "Forty Thieves" were now a hardened and relatively disciplined force, which was temporarily able to force a retreat of the soldiers of Kabarega with a rocket attack at Masindi.

Sensing his vulnerability however, Baker began his retreat from Uganda to the comparative security of Gondokoro. The Bakers returned to England in 1873, when he was replaced at his post by General Charles Gordon (q.v.). He died in Devonshire in 1893. *See also* SLAVERY.

BAKHEIT, JA'AFAR MUHAMMAD 'ALI (?–1976). Sudanese intellectual and political leader active in political and ideological affairs after the 1969 May Revolution (q.v.). He was one of the drafters of the permanent constitution, editor of the official newspaper, *al-Sahafa,* and at various times minister of local government, assistant secretary-general, and secretary-general of the Sudanese Socialist Union (SSU, q.v.). His excellent but unpublished 1965 Cambridge Ph.D. thesis, entitled *British Administration and Sudanese Nationalism, 1919–1939*, was published in Arabic as *al-Idara al-Baritaniya wa'l-haraka al-wataniya fi'l-Sudan, 1919–1939* (translated from the English by Henry Riyad; 3rd edition, 1987).

BAKHITA, MOTHER JOSEPHINE (1869–1947). Catholic saint born in southern Sudan and sold into slavery in El-Obeid and Khartoum (qq.v.). Bakhita was the Arabic name given to her in slavery, and Josephine was the name she took after her conversion to Catholicism in Italy, where she was sent after being purchased by the Italian Consul in Khartoum. Bakhita took her vows to become a nun in December 1896 at the Institute of St. Magdalene of Canossa and died in Schio, near Venice, in 1947. Twelve years after her death the process of canonization began for "our black mother," as she was popularly known in Italy. Mother Josephine was beatified by Pope John Paul II on 17 May 1992, one of the last steps toward sainthood in the Catholic faith. In his sermon delivered to over one million people, the Pope praised Mother Josephine's virtues and prayed that her grace would guide the Sudanese peoples to peace and reconciliation. Attending her beatification were Sudanese Archbishop Gabriel Zubeir Wako of Khartoum and Bishop Makram Max Qassis of El-Obeid, along with a delegation of some fifty other Catholics from Sudan. She was canonized a saint on October 1, 2000.

BANAGGA, BAN AL-NAQA. A form of Ban al-Naqa. *See* YA'QUBAB.

BANY, WILLIAM NYUON (?–1996). This soldier and politician of both Dinka and Nuer (qq.v.) origins was born in Ayot. He was a veteran of the Anya-Nya I (q.v.) forces from the 1960s, which were later integrated into the Sudanese army after the 1972 Addis Ababa Agreement (q.v.). He was assigned to Battalion 105 in Bor in May 1983 when a mutiny took place that he and Kerubino Kwanyin Bol (q.v.) led. The revolt was put down with great loss of life, but they escaped to return to the lives of guerrillas under the Anya-Nya II and Sudanese Peoples Liberation Army (SPLA, qq.v.) under the leadership of John Garang (q.v.). Bany served as Garang's chief of staff and was the commander of the 1989 SPLA attack on Kurmuk on the Ethiopian frontier.

Bany reluctantly joined the Nasir faction formed in August 1991. Disagreeing with Garang on 6 September, Bany freed political prisoners (including Martin Majerg, Kerubino Kwanyin Bol, and Arok Thon Arok) held by the SPLA, and on 28 September 1992 claimed to have taken full control of the SPLA in coordination with the Nasir faction. However, Garang was able to maintain his position and Bany was placed in an awkward circumstance, which found him attacking or resisting SPLA troops in Equatoria (q.v.) in the summer of 1994. By April 1995 Bany sought to regroup his followers in the Southern Sudan Independence Movement (SSIM, q.v.) with Garang's SPLA-Mainstream. Bany's political judgment at this stage was correct, since Garang was placed in command of the National Democratic Alliance (NDA, q.v.) military in June 1995. However, in January 1996 Bany was assassinated at Gul by forces of the SSIM in circumstances that seem to relate to his effort to rejoin the SPLA.

BAQQARA (BAGGARA). A large Sudanese ethnic group of Arab (q.v.) descent, principally found in Darfur and Kordofan (qq.v.), which belongs to the larger category of Juhayna (q.v.) Arabs. They are primarily a nomadic, cattle-herding (q.v.) people. They gave active support to the Mahdist movement, and the Khalifa 'Abdallahi (q.v.) was from the Ta'ishi branch of the Baqqara. Other major Baqqara subgroups are the Rizayqat, Humr, and Misiriya. *See also* MAHDIYA.

BARAKA. An Arabic term denoting a divinely given beneficent force possessed by certain holy people following the traditions of folk Islam (q.v.). Many of the *fekis* (q.v.) who helped to spread Islam in the Sudan, including the heads of the various Sufi orders or *tariqas* (q.v.), were thought to possess *baraka*. Because it is transmittable by contact, people flocked to their schools or settlements to receive it, and visited their tombs (*qubbas*, q.v.) after their death. *Baraka* might be sought to cure an illness, ward off misfortune, or bring good luck. It is also inheritable, hence the leadership of Sufi orders were usually hereditary. Muhammad Ahmad al-Mahdi, Muhammad 'Uthman al-Mirghani (qq.v.), and all other great religious leaders were thought by their followers to possess *baraka*, and their descendants are considered the present-day repositories of it.

BARI. A large ethnic group of the southern Sudan (q.v.). The Bari are members of the Nilotic (q.v.) subgroup of the Eastern Sudanic language family. Their territory is in Equatoria (q.v.) province along a 100-mile stretch of the White Nile, southeast of the main groups of Nilotes- (i.e., around the modern city of Juba [q.v.]). Bari speakers can be found east of the White Nile (like the Latuko, Mondari, and Taposa), while related groups are west of the White Nile (like the Fajulu, Kakwa, and Kuku). Linguistic evidence suggests an Ethiopian origin for these people; however, evidence from food crops suggests a more complicated mix of Ethiopian (millet), southeast Asian (bananas and yams), and other regional influences.

The Bari are southern neighbors of the Dinka and Nuer (qq.v.) and are much influenced by these Nilotic peoples, with whom they have complex relations. The predominant role of pastoral cattle culture for the Nilotes exists for the Bari, but to a lesser degree, while the role of sedentary horticulture is increased. Cattle are still very significant for Bari bridewealth and conflict resolution payments.

Bari groups have a relatively egalitarian but segmentary clan structure within their traditional society. High positions were the "Rain Chief" and the "Earth Chief," whose influence rested upon their spiritual or magical powers (especially in stone and spear rituals), but they did not exceed the authority of the council of elders where even broader powers were invested. Common to such egalitarian societies, the Bari have age-grades and initiation rituals to provide additional order to their social and political structure. Initiation rituals include removal of the incisors like other Nilotes. At the same time the Bari are sufficiently stratified to have a type of caste endogamy among the two main layers of their society. Traditionally among the lower castes were ironsmiths, hunters, and farmers. Some anthropologists believe these subordinated caste groups may be the remnants of a population of hunters who predated the Bari.

The Bari's first contact with non-Africans is probably dated to 1841, when the Turco-Egyptian (q.v.) explorer Salim Qapudan (q.v.) arrived looking for cattle, ivory, slaves, and the headwaters of the White Nile. Subsequently the Bari and their neighbors were repeatedly raided for cattle and slaves, the latter being used for both domestic and military service. This difficult situation continued under the Mahdiya (q.v.). During the Anglo-Egyptian (q.v.) era a major missionary (q.v.) influence brought widespread conversions to Christianity (q.v.) and especially to Catholicism and Anglicanism. In the postindependence period the Bari region, like other parts of the South, has been hugely disrupted by decades of civil war, in which ethnic affiliation plays a role in political and military dynamics. Bari have fled to the relative security of Juba or East African exile, or have joined various rebel groups in the countryside.

BARING, EVELYN, EARL OF CROMER (1841–1917). A British colonial administrator and financier. Baring became the British agent and consul-general in Egypt in September 1883, following the British occupation of 1882, and remained the virtual ruler of the country until his retirement in May 1907. Parallel with his administration in Egypt were the following Egyptian prime ministers: Nubar Pasha (1884–1888 and 1894–1895), Riaz Pasha (1888–1891 and 1893–1894), and Mustafa Pasha Fahmi (1891–1893 and 1895–1908). Baring was, at least in principle, the immediate superior to General Charles Gordon (q.v.) during the latter's mission to the Sudan in 1884 to relieve the Egyptian garrisons. Gordon's impulsive and irascible nature made him unsupervisable and thus relieved Baring of any blame for the disastrous failure of Gordon's mission.

Baring's long and influential administration allowed him to dominate British policy toward the Sudan from prior to the Mahdiya (q.v.) through the early Condominium (q.v.), of which he was the principal architect. He conceived of the elite administrative corps that became the Sudan Political Service (q.v.).

BASHIR, 'UMAR HASAN AL- (1944–). Islamist military ruler of Sudan since 1989. A graduate of Sudan Military College and paratroop commander, he fought with distinction alongside Egyptian forces in the 1973 Arab-Israeli war and later served as a senior battlefield commander in southern Kordofan (q.v.) against the Sudanese Peoples Liberation Army (SPLA, q.v.). On 30 June 1989 he led a coup that overthrew the coalition government of Prime Minister Sadiq al-Mahdi (q.v.). Bashir created the Revolutionary Command Council for National Salvation as the ruling body, banned all political parties except the National Islamic Front (NIF, q.v.), and arrested government leaders and more than a 100 military officers. Insisting that his regime was nonsectarian, nonpartisan, and anticorruption, he nonetheless abolished the constitution, national assembly, and trade unions while periodically closing down private newspapers.

While it was announced that a priority of the new government was to end the civil war, within a year of the coup no direct peace talks with the Sudanese Peoples Liberation Movement (SPLM, q.v.) were underway. Moreover, the issue of Sudan's Islamic law (q.v.), a major grievance of southerners, was manifestly non-negotiable. From almost the beginning of Bashir's regime, NIF leader Hasan al-Turabi (q.v.) was regarded as its principal theorist.

The Bashir regime soon received international attention and criticism for its broad political repression, especially of professionals and intellectuals, as well as its human rights violations. The office of the Sudan Human Rights Organization (SHRO, q.v.) was shut down soon after the regime came to power and its leaders forced into exile in Egypt and elsewhere. An apparent coup attempt against Bashir in April 1990 resulted in the immediate execution of twenty-eight army officers; later coup attempts were similarly crushed. For the decade of the 1990s Bashir held onto the reins of military power while frequently promising a return to civilian rule. The creation of a National Transitional Assembly in 1992 and the holding of local elections for "people's congresses" were in partial fulfillment of this promise. However, the continuation of civil war meant the exclusion of the southern Sudan (q.v.) from the political process; and elections to the national assembly in 1996 predictably resulted in the presidency for Bashir, while Hasan al-Turabi was elected speaker. In 1998 the Bashir regime introduced constitutional reforms that conditionally allowed the formation of political parties and freedoms of speech, assembly, and the press. A call for political rivals to cooperate in building a "democratic Sudan" yielded the return to Sudan of former leaders Ja'afar al-Nimeiri (q.v.) and Sadiq al-Mahdi. No political resolution of Sudan's many problems resulted from this development.

In the realm of foreign policy, Bashir forged ties with Iran, Iraq, and China, while attempting to improve relations with neighboring countries. More ominously, his apparent support for Islamic terrorist groups earned Sudan international condemnation and isolation, further compounding the country's already-catastrophic political and economic problems.

In December 1999 a power struggle erupted between Bashir and Turabi, sparked by Turabi's introduction of constitutional amendments to limit Bashir's power. In response, Bashir dissolved the NIF-dominated Parliament, removed state governors from office, and appointed a new cabinet. With Hasan al-Turabi politically isolated (though still strongly supported by the NIF), Bashir maintained the army's supremacy and control of Sudan. In December 2000 he was reelected president with 86.5 percent of the vote in an election marred by an opposition boycott; Bashir's nearest challenger was former president Nimeiri, with 9.6 percent of the vote. Matters came to a head in February 2001 with Turabi signing a memorandum of agreement with the SPLM and Bashir arresting the NIF leader under charges of sedition.

BASHIR, AL-TIJANI YUSUF (1910–1937). This Sudanese poet graduated from the *Mahad al-'Ilmi* (the forerunner to Omdurman Islamic University), worked briefly for the Singer Sewing Machine Company in the Khartoum (q.v.) area, and contributed poetry to journals, including *al-Fajr* (q.v.), *Multaqa al-Nilayn* ("Nile Junction"), and the Egyptian periodical, *al-Risala*. He achieved lasting recognition, not only in the Sudan but also in the Arabic-speaking world as a whole, for his development of a style of Romantic Arabic poetry that was inspired by English Romantics such as Percy Bysshe Shelley and John Keats. Numerous literary studies have been written on his poetry. [by Heather J. Sharkey]

BEHEIRY, MAMOUN (1925–). Sudanese banker and economist. He was educated at Oxford University and worked in the Ministry of Finance. He was governor of the Bank of Sudan (1960–1964), minister of finance (1964), and first president of the African Development Bank (1965–1970). After the Addis Ababa Agreement of 1972 (q.v.) he was named chairman of the Relief and Resettlement Fund for the South and in 1975 became the minister of finance.

BEIR CLUSTER. The Beir and related culturolinguistic groups are "typical" Nilotes. Since they live in a rather remote frontier region near the Ethiopian Sidamo people and the Sudanese town of Pibor, their language group became a distinct branch of Nilotic languages. Members of the Beir cluster mix pastoralism and agriculture as conditions permit. *See also* DINKA; LANGUAGE; NUER.

BEJA. The Beja and related groups are members of the northern branch of Cushitic languages that belong to the Afro-Asiatic family of languages. The generally egalitarian, pastoral Beja are probably derived from the Arabian peninsula, but at a very remote period in the past, as the Beja and their ancestors have occupied the region between the Red Sea and the Nile for as much as 4,000 years. The Blemmyes (q.v.) are considered the ancestral group and relations between dynastic Egyptians, Kushites, and Nubians show repeated reference to trading or raiding of the Blemmyes.

After the seventh century they gradually converted to Islam (q.v.) and Arab social customs; however, they have also retained various pre-Islamic cultural practices. In the last few centuries the modern Beja subgroups began to emerge. In the Sudan, these groups include the Ababda (on the coast), Amarar, Bisharin (along the Nile near Atbara), Beni Amer (next to Eritrea), and Hadendowa. During the Mahdiya (q.v.) some were militarily active in the support of the Mahdist Ansar (q.v.) especially around Suakin (q.v.), while other sections who followed the Khatmiya (q.v.) leadership in Kassala (q.v.) were opposed to the Mahdiya. In most of the twentieth century the Beja people were peripheral to mainstream Sudanese politics with the exception of the Beja Congress (q.v.), which sought to represent their interests in the period of parliamentary government. In the 1965 election the Beja Congress won ten seats and in the 1968 election three seats. Electoral opposition was suspended by the Ja'afar al-Nimeiri (q.v.) government after May 1969. *See also* CHRISTIANITY IN NUBIA.

BEJA CONGRESS. A political organization representing regional interests of the Beja (q.v.) peoples in the eastern Sudan. It won ten seats in the parliamentary elections of 1965. The Congress remained in existence until the abolition of political parties in 1969 but had won only three seats in the elections in 1968.

BELZONI, GIOVANNI BAPTISTA (1778–1823). This flamboyant Italian adventurer, painter, and archaeologist had thought of careers in engineering or the priesthood, but it was his fascination for the Orient that earned him his fame. He met John L. Burckhardt (q.v.) in Egypt and both inspired each other. He "claimed" a number of major pieces of Upper Egyptian antiquity for the British Museum. In Nubia (q.v.) he researched the great New Kingdom temple at Abu Simbel and the Greco-Roman Isis temple at Philae as well as the contemporary port town of Berenice, which linked Nubia to the classical world. His publications and illustrations drew widespread interest then and now.

BERBER. Before the twentieth-century importance of Atbara (q.v.), Berber had been the leading trade town in the North. Its products were mainly based in animal and agricultural exchange and in the production of local handicrafts. During the time of the Funj Sultanates (q.v.), Berber had a minor center for religious learning, especially with the Mirafab section of the Ja'aliyin (q.v.) people who are the most numerous inhabitants. In 1820, the Turco-Egyptians (q.v.) passed through Berber and later came back to massacre local people in a "punitive action." In the 1860s and 1870s an elementary school, post office, and telegraph station were constructed, but in 1884 Mahdist troops entered the town and destroyed it.

Since the twentieth century Berber's hopes for development have rested on small-scale trade and increased agricultural production. Berber's population today could be estimated at about 21,000, but the now-larger town of Atbara draws off some of Berber's potential development.

BERTI. The Berti, Zaghawa (q.v.), and Bideyat are Sudanese remnants of the Garamantes people who controlled trans-Saharan trade with North Africa, in this case along the Selima Trail to the Selima Oasis. These three groups have linguistic and cultural affinities through their common membership in the Kanuric language family. They are mainly found in western Darfur (q.v.) where they express their commitment to Islam (q.v.) in various syncretic ways.

BESHIR, MOHAMED OMER (1926–1992). Mohamed Omer Beshir was born in Karima and educated at Gordon Memorial College, later the University of Khartoum (qq.v). Upon graduation he joined the Ministry of Education as a teacher, but later continued his studies at Queen's University in Belfast and Oxford University. He joined the University of Khartoum's teaching staff where he became academic secretary in the 1960s. He helped to found and headed the new Institute of African and Asian Studies in the 1970s.

Professor Mohamed Omer Beshir, known to colleagues, friends, and admirers affectionately as "M.O.B.," was a scholar-patriot whose boundless energy inspired generations of students, Sudanese and expatriate alike. Over the span of his sixty-five years he served the cause of Sudanese education, scholarship, and foreign relations with an unparalleled variety of posts and publications. He helped in the promotion of many colleges and departments through his work as registrar of the University of Khartoum; he established the Graduate College and became its first dean in the late 1970s. At the Institute he edited its publications series, which produced something of a golden era of young Sudanese scholarship under his tutelage. The series included works on the Nile Basin countries, especially Egyptian-Sudanese relations. He taught at the Institute until his death.

As a consummate nationalist he hailed Sudanese accomplishments in his writings and activism, and criticized its shortcomings, always with passion. He was an early supporter of the Sudan Studies Association (q.v.) in the early 1980s and fostered its international expansion throughout that decade with critical support for the first International Conference of Sudan Studies in Khartoum (q.v.) in 1988.

A prolific writer, M.O.B.'s works covered a wide range of topics from education to history, politics and national unity. Among his better-known works were several concerned with the history of conflict between southern and northern Sudan. His works were based on close personal observations and relationships with the parties involved, including his significant role as secretary-general of the Round Table Conference (q.v.) in 1965. He was a Sudan government delegate to the peace talks in Addis Ababa in 1972 (q.v.), which led to a successful end of the seventeen-year civil war by negotiating regional autonomy for the South. He was among a handful of prominent northern notables to voice opposition to Ja'afar al-Nimeiri's (q.v.) unilateral abrogation of the Peace Accords a decade later because he believed this to be the only formula for a lasting peace and national unity. He predicted the renewal of the civil war.

Following the 1972 agreement M.O.B. was appointed director of the African Department of the Ministry of Foreign Affairs while he enjoyed the role of roving ambassador explaining the Addis Ababa agreement to African nations. He returned to the University of Khartoum where he remained throughout the Nimeiri years and post-Nimeiri democratic period based at the Institute for African and Asian Studies. His greatest effort and life accomplishment in his own view was his founding of the first privately funded university in Sudan, the Omdurman Ahliya College in the mid-1980s, whose main hall now bears his name. He actively recruited students of both sexes from all over Sudan and arranged for support for needy students, with special attention paid to southerners.

M.O.B. founded the Sudan Human Rights Organization (SHRO, q.v.) in 1983 in exile and helped to establish SHRO branches in Juba, Atbara, Port Sudan, El-Obeid, and Kosti (qq.v.). His extensive contacts with Arab, African, and Western human rights groups fostered the growth and reputation of the SHRO. After the National Islamic Front (NIF, q.v.)–backed coup d'etat he intensified his human rights activities and was harassed, and even assaulted, for his staunch support for the maintenance of basic civil rights by any Sudanese government, Islamist or otherwise. Already ailing with cancer his health seemed to worsen with the retreat from democracy and human rights and the resulting political isolation Sudan suffered in the 1990s. Despite a number of treatments outside the country he died in Khartoum in January 1992. [by Mahgoub al-Tigani Mahmoud]

BEVIN, ERNEST (1881–1951). Ernest Bevin was the British foreign secretary during the rule of Hubert Huddleston (q.v.) as the governor-general of the Sudan. These war years were very challenging for the British who were being battered in Europe and faced increased nationalism in the Sudan and other overseas colonies. Determining British and Sudanese relations with Egyptian King Faruq (q.v.) only made the situation more complex at this tumultuous time. The king turned to Isma'il Sidqi (d.1950) to form a new government in the wake of major riots and demonstrations in Egypt. Fears of a repeat of the 1924 White Flag Revolt (q.v.) and the assassination of Governor-General Lee Stack (q.v.) brought alarm to the Foreign Office. In a sense of appeasement, Bevin began to discuss, in general terms, the possibility of Sudanese independence, which fueled Sudanese nationalist sentiments further while provoking the Sidqi government to protest British colonial occupation. An antagonized Egypt was a horror to British military planners who recalled the great strategic value of Egypt in the Allied war effort against Germany. Playing off Britain's fears, Sidqi saw an opportunity to increase Egyptian autonomy while preserving the monarchy of Egypt. As relations between Cairo and London worsened, Sidqi and Bevin met in October 1946 and the resulting agreement is termed the Sidqi-Bevin Protocol, which accepted Egyptian King Faruq's continuing condominium rights over the Sudan.

Governor-General Huddleston, now in London, greatly feared the Sudanese response, which soon came in the form of public demonstrations led by the Ansar (q.v.) against the Protocol. In early December 1946 the Sidqi government fell and was replaced by that of Mahmud Fahmi al-Nuqrashi (d.1948), who was not able to hold the Protocol together. Although short-lived, the Protocol was a sign of things to come, sooner than expected: the resignation of Bevin in 1951 following the defeat of the Labour Party; the overthrow of the King Faruq in 1952; and the rapid evolution of Sudanese independence led by Isma'il al-Azhari (q.v.) in 1956.

BEY. A civil and military title below pasha (q.v.) in rank in the old Ottoman and Egyptian administrative systems.

BIDEYAT. *See* BERTI.

BINT AL-MAKKAWI (Daughter of al-Makkawi). Bint al-Makkawi was a great poetess of the Mahdiya (q.v.) period (1881–1898) who composed many praise songs that included political and cultural elements. Describing the Mahdi's (q.v.) victory in one of her songs, she used the image of a drum as a symbol of joy, pride, and victory. Through the metaphor of wool that must be trimmed when it becomes too long, she urged the Mahdi to cut back those who had exceeded their limits, such as the Turks. Bint al-Makkawi likened the Mahdiya revolution to the flooded Nile: when the Nile floods, ducks proliferate; similarly, by liberating the Sudan, the Mahdi enabled people to live a full but strictly decorous life. The song ran as follows:

> *Tabla'l-'izz drab,*
> *Hawayna fi'l barza.*
> *Wa ghayr tabl Umm Kubban,*
> *Ana ma badur 'izza.*
> *In tall al-wabar,*
> *Wasiyhu bi'l-jazza.*
> *In ma 'amma Nil,*
> *Ma farrakhat wizza.*

Translation:

> The drum of pride and joy: was beaten,
> This elevated us to a high status.
> My only joy and pride is Umm Kubban's drum.
> If the wool is getting long, trim it!
> Without the Nile's generosity,
> The ducks will never hatch.
> [by Baqie Badawi Muhammad]

BISHARIN. According to tradition this nomadic Beja-related (q.v.) people moved into part of their present area on the western slopes of the Red Sea hills in the fifteenth century and moved into the Atbara River area under a great chief, Hamad Imran, around 1760. There are two major sections, the 'Umm 'Ali and the 'Umm Naji. They were not very active in the Mahdiya (q.v.) or twentieth-century national developments.

BLACK FRONT. A group reported to be working in the southern Sudan (q.v.) in 1948 among southern government staff. It advocated no interference by northerners in the South and demanded "the South for the Southerners."

BLEMMYES. The Blemmyes are a very early, pastoral group on the east bank of the Nile at least by the last years of the ancient kingdom of Kush (q.v.). Expanding their area they came into conflict with the Romans in Egypt. The Romans attempted to create a buffer state in Nobatia but the Nobatae later fought beside the Blemmyes against the Romans. The Blemmyes did not convert readily to Christianity (q.v.) and were destroyed by wars with the kingdom of Dongola (q.v.) in the 500s CE. Some scholars trace the origins of the modern Beja (q.v.) people to the Blemmyes.

BLUE NILE PROVINCE. Former province (q.v.) encompassing the Gezira (q.v.) region between the White and Blue Niles, or approximately 54,880 square miles. A 1970 census estimated its population at 3,156,000, including a variety of Arab (q.v.) groups as well as West Africans (Fellata, q.v.), Ingessana, Berta, Gule, and Uduk. The Funj Sultanate of Sinnar (qq.v.) was located here from the sixteenth century. In Anglo-Egyptian (q.v.) times the important Gezira Scheme (q.v.) was established to grow cotton. The region is also known for its sheep and cultivation of durra. Wad Medani (q.v.) is its most important town.

BOL, KERUBINO KWANYIN (KUANYIN). This Dinka (q.v.) soldier had been a member of the Anya Nya I (q.v.), which was integrated into the Sudanese army after the Addis Ababa Agreement in 1972 (q.v.). He was serving in Battalion 105 at Pibor in March 1983 and from there led the mutiny at Pibor, Pachala, and Bor in May 1983. Although this was put down, Bol escaped and was an early high-ranking member of the Sudanese Peoples Liberation Movement/Liberation Army (SPLM/SPLA, q.v.) when it was formed in July 1983.

From 1983 to 1986 Bol was a top member of the SPLA under John Garang (q.v.), but after that he and others began to oppose Garang. This culminated with his arrest and imprisonment until 1991, when he was freed during an attempted coup against Garang by William Nyuon Bany (q.v.), which led to the breakaway Nasir movement and Bol's flight to Uganda. There President Yoweri Museveni, a friend of Garang's, placed him under house arrest until 1993. Thus, after years of service to the SPLA, Bol found himself in active military opposition to its mainstream branch. By July–August 1994, Bol's substantial forces were attacking

SPLA-Mainstream forces at Mayen Abun in Bahr al-Ghazal (q.v.). In April 1996 Bol and the Nuer (q.v.) breakaway leader Riek Machar (q.v.) were signatories to the "Political Charter" sponsored by the National Islamic Front (NIF, q.v.) in Khartoum (q.v.). In May 1997 Bol was still militarily engaged in anti-SPLA attacks in Bahr al-Ghazal in support of Khartoum.

BOL, MANUTE (1962–). Southern Sudanese basketball player, also known as the "Dinka Dunker" in American professional basketball. He retired in the mid-1990s to devote time and aid and to relieve the war-torn southern Sudan (q.v.). He was reportedly a member of the Sudanese Peoples Liberation Movement (SPLM, q.v.). He returned to Uganda in 1996 using Kampala as a base for these efforts, but soon fell on hard economic times. In October 1997 he accepted an offer to become minister of sports for the 'Umar al-Bashir (q.v.) government, which drew criticism from government opponents.

BONGO. *See* AZANDE; MADI; GEORGE A. SCHWEINFURTH.

BORI. *See* ZAR.

BROWNE, WILLIAM (1768–1813). This British explorer traveled from Asyut in Middle Egypt across the *Darb al-Arba'in* (Forty Days Road, q.v.) to reach Kobbei and al-Fasher (qq.v.). From there he went south to Dar Fungara, Dar Fertit, and Hoffrat al-Nahas, and to Donga country. His travels took place between 1793 and 1796, when he returned by the same route. He was among the earliest explorers of that region.

BRUCE, JAMES (1730–1794). This Scottish traveler began his life as a wine merchant in Portugal, but found that the study of the Middle East was far more engaging. At the age of thirty-eight he arrived in Egypt, visiting important sites in Luxor and Karnak as well as clearing the tomb of Ramses II in the Valley of the Kings. He ventured into the Sudan "in search of the headwaters of the Blue Nile," which were, in fact, already known. For some reason Bruce also considered that both the White and Blue Niles flowed from Lake Dembea (Tana); this basic error misinformed many cartographers of the eighteenth century.

Bruce reached Ethiopia in 1768 in time for the Timkat festival, allegedly because of his interest in tracking the Ark of the Covenant, which he believed to be in Axum. After circumambulating the entirety of

Lake Tana (Dembea) he finally reached the source of the Blue Nile above the lake on 4 November 1770. He then went to Sinnar, Halfaya, and Shendi (qq.v.) and crossed through the Nubian desert and arrived in Aswan by November 1772. His famous book, *Travels* (1790), is an important document for eighteenth-century central Sudanese history.

BURCKHARDT, JOHN L. (1784–1817). This early nineteenth-century Swiss traveler to Nubia (q.v.) explored the region on behalf of The African Association, which was founded in England to explore the interior of Africa. He began his adventures in 1810 as a student of Arabic at Cambridge and Islamic law (q.v.) in Aleppo, and traveled through Palestine and Arabia to Egypt. In 1813 he traveled along the Nile to Aswan, where he set out across the desert route of James Bruce (q.v.). He advanced as far as Shendi (q.v.) from whence he went east to Suakin (q.v.) and on to Jedda and the Muslim holy places of Mecca and Medina in 1814–1815, under the assumed character of a religious pilgrim. He returned to Cairo where he died and was buried as a Muslim. The account of his journey was published posthumously as *Travels in Nubia* (1819).

BURTON, SIR RICHARD FRANCIS (1821–1890). An Irish-born adventurer, soldier, linguist, diplomat, and explorer who, as a young veteran of the Indian army, earned attention for his clandestine 1853 "pilgrimage" to Mecca and Medina. Burton was fluent in perhaps thirty languages. His remarkable linguistic skills in French, Latin, Italian, Arabic, Farsi, and several Indian languages led him to translate *The Arabian Nights,* which has often been edited and reprinted from his original. The work was published in sixteen volumes from 1885 to 1888, just two years before his death.

Burton's explorations in Africa grew out of his travel adventures with John Hanning Speke (q.v.), which began in northern Somali at Zaila. They were among the first Europeans to locate Harrar in Ethiopia. Upon exiting Ethiopia near Berbera, Burton and Speke were seriously wounded by a Somali attack in April 1855. Both published books to recount this trip; Burton's was entitled *First Footsteps in East Africa.*

In late 1856 Burton was sent by the Royal Geographical Society to lead an expedition to determine the headwaters of the White Nile. In June 1857 he and Speke left Zanzibar for the east African coast at Bagamoyo to begin their inland journey through central Tanganyika (Tanzania). In February 1858 they reached Ujiji on Lake Tanganyika and traveled across and to the north of this lake. Leaving an ill Burton at Ujiji,

Speke set a new course northward and in August 1858 reached Lake Victoria, becoming the first European to see this vast body of water. Speke believed that he had discovered the source of the Nile, but broken instruments prevented any certifiable proof. Burton and Speke returned to Zanzibar and sailed for England in March 1859. These exploits were recorded in Burton's book *The Lake Regions of Central Africa*, published in 1860. But because the expedition was led by Burton but the lake reached by Speke, the seeds of controversy were sown.

Speke continued to explore for the source of the Nile to substantiate his claim. Traveling with another British officer, James Grant, he explored new territory west of Lake Victoria and exited by the southern Sudan, but still failed to locate the river's precise outlet.

Meanwhile, accepting a diplomatic post in Fernando Po, Burton and his wife took a steamer down the West African coast. During this period from 1861 to 1864 Burton's duties allowed him to write other books: his *Wanderings in West Africa* was published in 1863; *A Mission to Gelele* (the king of Dahomey) in 1864; *Wit and Wisdom from West Africa* in 1865; and his *Selected Papers on Anthropology, Travel, and Exploration* in 1866.

Back in London Speke was honored by a Royal Medal and credited with discovering Lake Victoria. Deep jealousy arose as Burton tried to disprove Speke's claims. In order to answer criticisms, Speke had taken measurements of the lake's elevation at 3,740 feet; Lake Albert (2,296 feet) and Lake Tanganyika (2,756 feet) were lower and consequently could not be at the head of the Nile. A public debate moderated by David Livingstone was arranged between these now contentious explorers. The day before the forum in September 1864, Speke died in either a hunting accident or suicide.

Burton served as consul in Brazil from 1864–1868, when he was appointed consul in Damascus. He continued to write of his adventures. *Zanzibar: City, Island, and Coast* appeared in 1872, and as a result of his time in Brazil he published *The Captivity of Hans Stade* in 1874. After he died in 1890, his wife edited and published his *Personal Narrative of a Pilgrimage to Al-Madinah and Meccah* in 1893.

– C –

CAMEL-HERDING ARABS. The camel-herding group of Juhayna Arabs (q.v.) of the Sudan include the Kababish, Humr, Shayqiya, Shukriya (qq.v.), and Dubaniya. They range in their respective territories and watering places in the eastern Butana, in parts of the Bayuda steppe, and in northern Darfur and Kordofan (qq.v.). Their ecological region represents the East-West frontier between desert and grasslands. In recent years their patterns of intraterritorial migration have been severely disrupted by increased desertification, causing either loss of their stock or an adjustment or abandonment of their way of life. In areas of water supply or rivers the camel-herders have placed additional pressure on sedentary agriculturalists. All speak Arabic (q.v.) and follow the practice of Islam (q.v.).

"CARLOS THE JACKAL," ILYICH RAMIREZ SANCHEZ (ca. 1949–). This "professional revolutionary" of many aliases was born in Venezuela to a revolutionary family. In the 1970s "Carlos" pursued an anti-Zionist, pro-Palestinian program, which led him to support the Popular Front for the Liberation of Palestine. Some alleged that he had ties to the Russian KGB. Among the many crimes of which he is accused are bombings; at least eighty murders; and kidnapping of eleven Arab OPEC oil ministers in Vienna in 1975, two French secret police, and a supposed Lebanese informant in Paris in the same year. In 1976 he planned the hijacking of an Air France jet to Entebbe, Uganda, where the hostages were freed by an Israeli commando raid. "Carlos" fled to Sudan after the National Islamic Front (NIF, q.v.) government came to power in 1989. He was hosted in Khartoum (q.v.) for many years, and apparently was there while Sudanese authorities also welcomed Shaykh 'Umar 'Abd al-Rahman (q.v.), convicted of bombing the World Trade Center in 1993. The French pursued "Carlos" to Khartoum, and in secret negotiations convinced Sudanese authorities to allow him to be drugged and transported back to France in 1996. He stood trial in Paris in December 1997, was found guilty, and sentenced to life imprisonment.

CATTLE-HERDING ARABS. The cattle-herding group of Juhayna Arabs (q.v.) of the Sudan are more numerous than their camel-herding relatives to the north and east mainly because their pasturage is more productive and can sustain larger populations. At times of drought they are pressed from the north by the camel-herders and they themselves press upon the cattle-herding Nilotics (q.v.) in the southern provinces. Grazing territories have often been hotly contested and fiercely defended. The majority of the cattle-herders, living closer to the Nilotic south, are sometimes considered more "Africanized" Arabs although all are Arabic-speaking Muslims. Most are found in the central and southern portions of Darfur and Kordofan (qq.v.), although there are sedentary relatives in the Nile valley. In central Kordofan north of the Nuba Hills are the Bidayriya, Hawazma, Kawahla, and Misiriya; farther south are the Habbania, Rizayqat, and Ta'aisha.

CELEBI, EVLIYA (1611–ca. 1685). A seventeenth-century explorer of the Sudan whose travel accounts, *Seyahatname*, exist in many volumes in Turkish. Celebi was close to the royal court in Istanbul and served in numerous nations throughout the Ottoman Empire. In 1671 he traveled to Egypt, Sinnar (under Sultan Badi II, q.v.), and Abyssinia. These travels were recorded in his *Book Ten*.

His work is accepted critically and consists of both original observations as well as details from accounts of other seventeenth-century travelers to the region. He certainly visited the Turkish fortress at Sai Island and his four-meter-long map of the area drawn by his cartographer, Hikemizade, is quite accurate. Celebi reported that Sai had just been seized by Kor Hussein, a vassal of the Funj sultans (q.v.), in an effort to suppress a revolt by Hardokan. Celebi also passed through the 'Abdallab (q.v.) area then under the authority of Shaykh Ajib ibn Areiji in about 1671. From there he traveled on to Sinnar (q.v.) where he spent two months in the court of Badi and was much impressed by the size of the surrounding wall of Sinnar (3,000 paces) and the mosque of Kakan Idris.

CENTRAL SUDANIC PEOPLES. A linguistic grouping of southern Sudanese peoples who speak languages (q.v.) of the Central Sudanic subfamily of the larger Nilo-Saharan family. They are scattered in the Bahr al-Ghazal and Equatoria (qq.v.) regions and include the Njangulgule, Shatt, and Kreish.

CHAILLÉ-LONG, CHARLES (1842–1917). An American explorer and author, born in Maryland and educated at the Washington Academy. He enrolled in the Maryland State Guard at the outbreak of the American Civil War. Later Chaillé-Long was mustered into a regiment of Maryland Infantry that saw action in the battles at Gettysburg, Pennsylvania, and Monocacy, Maryland. In 1864 he was appointed captain of the 11th Maryland Infantry and he served at Fort Delaware, a prison for captured Confederate soldiers.

Following the Civil War, Chaillé-Long became a New York businessman until 1869, when he and colleague William Wing Loring (q.v.) were engaged by the Khedive Isma'il (q.v.) to serve in the modernization of the Turco-Egyptian (q.v.) military, then in control of the Sudan. His first rank was that of *kaimakam* (lieutenant colonel) while he was engaged in planning the military defenses of Cairo. In February 1874 he became the chief of staff to *Miralai* (Colonel) Charles Gordon (q.v.), who died in the sack of Khartoum (q.v.) in 1885.

Chaillé-Long departed from Cairo on 21 February 1874 with Gordon Pasha. They reached Khartoum on 9 March 1874, with a great distance still to travel for Gordon to begin his service as the governor of Equatoria (q.v.) in the unsuccessful effort to curb the slave trade (q.v.) in the southern Sudan. They reached Lado and Gondokoro (qq.v.), the capital of Equatoria, on 16 April 1874. From there Chaillé-Long was sent on a mission by the Khedive to carry presents to King Mutesa of Uganda and to explore the Lakes Region. There he discovered Lake Ibrahim, now renamed as Lake Kioga, which forms a passage between Urundogani and Foweira and is thus a part of the tributary headwaters of the White Nile. This area and the source of the Nile in Lake Victoria (Nyanza) had been visited for the first time by the Europeans John Speke, Richard Burton, James Grant, and Samuel Baker (qq.v.) only a few years earlier. Chaillé-Long returned to Gondokoro on 18 October 1874 to receive praise from Gordon Pasha.

After these travels Chaillé-Long left Egypt in 1877 amidst rumors that he had reported a drinking habit of Gordon Pasha. In 1882 Chaillé-Long returned to Alexandria, Egypt, as the provisional chief of the U.S. Consulate. In the 1880s and 1890s he held various diplomatic and high-level international political appointments for the United States, including his appointment to the International Geographic Congress (1904–1910), which awarded him the distinguished Daly Gold Medal. He authored eight books, including *Central Africa: Naked Truths of Naked People* (1876); *The Three Prophets* (1884); and his autobiography, *My Life on Three Continents* (1912). [with Richard Skidmore]

CHEVRON OIL CONCESSION. Commercial oil exploration by the Chevron Oil Company yielded information that viable reserves existed in southern Sudan (q.v.), near Bentiu. Oil drilling began in the early 1980s, expected to reach 50,000 barrels a day by 1986. However, the renewal of civil war in the south caused Chevron to abandon its concession in 1992 once its workers were killed, captured, or held hostage by the Sudanese Peoples Liberation Army (SPLA, q.v.). The discovery of oil in the South that was to be refined and exported in the North is one of many simmering grievances among southerners in the renewed outbreak of hostilities in 1983.

CHRISTIANITY IN NUBIA. A few Christian disciples may have reached Nubia (q.v.) from the first to third centuries C.E. just as this "secret religion" found a few early Egyptian adherents. But it was not until after the acceptance of Christianity by Emperor Constantine in 312 C.E. that Christianity spread more widely in Nubia. Active missionizing activity took place in 324 C.E. in Nubia and with the Axumite King Ezana in Ethiopia. The destruction of Meroë by King Ezana at the same period created a vacuum into which the missionary activities could take place. Officially it was not until 391 C.E. that Christianity became the state religion of Egypt. In Nubia the seeds of Christian states were sown between 350–550 C.E. with the formation of the kingdoms of Nobatia, Mukurra, and Alwa (q.v.).

In 325 C.E. the Council of Nicaea met to resolve the issue about the "oneness" of a Monophysite Christ. This gave momentum to Christian missionizing in Nubia. When the Roman, Papal view of Christ as a "single person with two natures" succeeded, the Egyptian Bishop was exiled. This early Christian schism isolated the Egyptian, Nubian, and other eastern Orthodox branches from the western (Roman) branches of the Christian church. Despite this, the Orthodox church in Egypt and Nubia made a more aggressive attempt to spread the Christian message from Egypt to the Sudan after 452 C.E.

By 524 C.E. a political and religious alliance was established between Byzantium in Egypt and the Axumites in Ethiopia. When Emperor Justinian came to rule Byzantium in 527, this alliance gained greater force. During the period 543–569 C.E. the first Monophysite Christian kingdoms were organized in Nubia; in 543 Faras was established as the capital of Nobatia. Faras later received a visit from missionary Longinus in 569, when he went on to recognize Dongola (q.v.) as the capital of Mukuria. In 579 Longinus was associated with the conversion to Christianity of the Kingdom of Alwa, with its capital at Soba near modern Khartoum (q.v.).

Meanwhile in 640, Arab Muslims conquered Egypt and moved across North Africa. Islam (q.v.) also spread quickly southward to Lower Nubia and by 641 the forces of 'Amr ibn al-As reached the plain just north of Dongola but failed to capture this Christian capital. North of this point the Nubian populations were forced to pay a regular tribute in slaves (q.v.) and livestock and to promise no aggression against Egypt. Frustrated by this barrier, Egyptian Muslims tried again in 646 to penetrate Nubia without success. At last, in 652 a famous *baqt* (treaty) was established between Christian Nubia and Muslim Egypt under 'Abdallah ibn Sa'ad ibn Abi Sahr.

While Christian Nubians were put in a tributary status, they were also guaranteed autonomy with an annual payment of 360 slaves and nonaggression toward Egypt. With conflicts between Makuria and Nobatia, this *baqt* was acceptable and its principles lasted for some six centuries. A similar *baqt* in 720 between the Egyptians and the Blemmyes (q.v.) did not fare nearly as well. By 697–707 the conflict between the two Christian kingdoms was resolved with the merger of Nobatia and Mukurra under King Merkurius. About this same time the existence of a combination of Greek, Arabic, and Coptic languages signaled the end of Meroitic language and writing.

Egyptians were not always successful in military affairs and in the middle of the eighth century, Cyriacus, King of Dongola, attacked the Umayyads and besieged their capital at Fustat (Cairo). Similarly, in 819–822 the Christian king of Dongola (George I, 816–920?) and the Beja (q.v.) both refused to pay *baqt* tribute and mounted joint attacks on Upper Egypt. A degree of mutual respect may also be seen following the coronation in 835 of Mukuria King George I, who, in the following year traveled to Cairo and Baghdad through Cairo.

During the reign of Ahmad ibn Tulun in Egypt (868–884) the relations between the two states were so favorable that thousands of Nubians enlisted in the Tulunid army. Some were converted to Islam while the two states coexisted. By the mid-tenth century some Muslims were as far south as Soba, the capital city of the Christian kingdom of Alwa. Yet Nubian raids into Upper Egypt took place in 951, 956, and 962.

In 969 Tulunid Dynasty and its successors were replaced with the Fatimids (969–1171) and relations deteriorated with attacks waged on Nubia by al-'Umari. Yet up to 50,000 Nubians served in Fatimid army. Coming to power at the same time, in 969, King George II of Dongola also is reported to have attacked Egypt.

Once the Fatimids were replaced by the Ayyubid Dynasty (1171–1250) the Nubians were forced to withdraw to Upper Egypt and Lower Nubia. Playing upon the hope of a Christian alliance, the European Crusaders sought a tactical alliance with Nubian Christians in Upper Egypt. This Nubian-Crusader alliance against the Ayyubids resulted in clashes in Cairo and Delta towns and were followed by Turanshah's attacks in Nubia. In 1204 various Nubian and Crusader leaders met in Constantinople, but were finally defeated in their plans to topple the Ayyubids.

Thus Christian Nubia and Islamic Egypt had fought to a standoff with the Fatimids and Ayyubids, but this would not be the case during Mamluk rule. Under the Bahri Mamluks (1250–1382), especially during the reign of Sultan al-Zahir Baybars (1260–1277), the Nubians were again forced to renew *baqt* tribute. For example in 1268 King Dawud of Dongola reluctantly paid the *baqt*, but in 1275 showed his opposition with raids against the Mamluks in Aswan. The following year the Mamluks organized a punitive attack that captured King Dawud and sacked Dongola. Its citizens were forced to convert to Islam. Resistance continued, and in 1289 still another major attack was waged upon Dongola by the Mamluks. Even in the first decades of the fourteenth century skirmishes continued, but by 1317 the first mosque was built at Dongola and 'Abdullah Barshambu was installed as the first Muslim King. *Baqt* payments to the Mamluks were reestablished.

With these events, the formal presence of Christianity in Nubia was at an end, although Christian symbols and small communities of believers lingered. Nevertheless Christianity in the Sudan still had almost two more centuries of life in the kingdom of Alwa until its collapse in 1504, brought on by the rise of the Funj sultanate farther south at Sinnar (qq.v.).

Although the Christian kingdoms had been defeated, isolated Christian communities in Nubia were still reported as appealing for support from Christian Ethiopia as late as 1520. Such was the case during the visit to Ethiopia of the Portuguese missionary Francisco Alvares. Another visitor in 1522 was the Jewish traveler David Reubeni, who visited both Soba and Sinnar and later met with the Pope and Spanish king with a plan to resist the Ottomans who had only come to power in Egypt a few years before.

For much of the following two centuries Christians in Ethiopia, backed by Portuguese seeking to avoid Arab control of the Eastern Mediterranean, managed to maintain a rather stable frontier between the Funj and Ethiopia. During the sixteenth and seventeenth centuries several religious missions took place. In 1541 there was a mission to neighboring Ethiopia. In 1647 Sinnar was visited by the Portuguese priests Giovanni d'Aguila and António da Pescopagano. From 1699 to 1711 there were three papal missions to Ethiopia that passed through Dongola and Sinnar.

CHRISTIANITY IN THE SUDAN. After the fall of the Christian kingdoms in Nubia (q.v.), Islam (q.v.) spread by state control and popular means, and Christianity was not reintroduced until the beginning of the modern colonial period. In 1842 the Catholic Mission of Central Africa opened a small school and church for foreign Christians. In 1846 the Holy See established the Vicarate Apostolic of Central Africa whose mission territory comprised the entire Sudan. In Khartoum (q.v.) the missionaries under Father Ryllo established a school for boys and foreign residents and appointed Dr. Ignaz Knoblecher (q.v.) his successor. Knoblecher extended their vision of a Christian mission to the south in 1849, reaching Gondokoro near present day Juba (qq.v.) and establishing a formal mission site with European priests in 1852. The early mission effort took the lives of twenty-two missionaries between 1851–1858, including Knoblecher himself. The continuation of the mission fell to the Franciscan Friars who opened a mission at Shellal in 1860–1862 but also failed due to a high number of casualties.

In 1864 Daniele Comboni (q.v.) reopened the Mission of Central Africa to be run on new lines using more African personnel. In 1867 he founded in Verona a seminary for the training of priests and laymen to work in Christian mission work in Central Africa, and in 1872 he opened a society for religious women to aid in the effort and to promote African women. In 1873 Comboni established himself in Khartoum as head of the Mission of Central Africa. Deng Surur, a Dinka (q.v.) from Abyei, escaped from enslavement, assisted Comboni, and became the first southern Sudanese priest, while "Mother" Josephine Bakhita (q.v.) led an exemplary religious life in Christian education and missionizing in El-Obeid (q.v.). In 1900 the Comboni Sisters opened the first schools for girls in Omdurman (q.v.) and Khartoum, and mission activities increased dramatically in the southern regions after the British conquest in 1898. Prefectures were established in the major towns at Juba, Wau, and Malakal (qq.v.).

After independence the Catholic missions underwent Sudanization of their basic institutions and leadership, and the Catholic Church is an important factor in the multiconfessional character of contemporary Sudan.

The Episcopal Church was founded in the Sudan with the active intervention of General Gordon (q.v.) between 1877–1879, who urged that an Anglican mission come to the Sudan. The first successful Protestant mission is attributed to Bishop Llewellyn Gwynne, who began his effort in 1899. The Anglican church followed its Catholic predecessors by expanding its mission activities to the south as well, especially after 1905. Major Anglican churches were established in Khartoum, Omdurman, and Wad Medani. The church was placed in Sudanese hands in 1974.

Eastern Rite Christians came to the Sudan after the Turco-Egyptian (q.v.) conquest of 1821, mostly as traders. Greek Orthodox, Greek Catholic, Chaldean and Syriac rites, Maronites, Armenian Catholics, and Egyptian and Ethiopian Coptic Christians have all been significant eastern Christian minorities within the Sudan. *See also* ARMENIANS; COPTS; PAPAL VISIT TO SUDAN; SYRIANS.

CIRCUMCISION (MALE/FEMALE CIRCUMCISION, ALSO FE-MALE GENITAL MUTILATION). Circumcision *(tahur)* is performed routinely on Sudanese Muslim males and females as a rite of passage in the preadolescent years. Male circumcision is celebrated, while the practice of female circumcision has been controversial and illegal since 1946. Nonetheless, female circumcision is widespread in the Muslim areas, but since its practice is found among non-Muslims and Christians in Egypt, Ethiopia, Somalia, Kenya, and other parts of Africa and its local designation is "pharaonic" circumcision, the suggestion that the practice is pre-Islamic seems quite sound.

Sudanese practice includes the most severe operation, infibulation, or "pharaonic" circumcision, as well as the modified forms of intermediate and *sunna* types of circumcision, which may include partial or total clitoridectomy. The type that has been approved by the Islamic jurists is the modified, *sunna* form, which places official Islam (q.v.) with the traditional reformers of the practice. In recent years female circumcision, usually termed Female Genital Mutilation (FGM, q.v.), has been actively opposed by Sudanese and Western doctors and feminists, who view the practice as hazardous to women (q.v.) both medically and psychologically and as an issue of human rights (q.v.). Their efforts to reduce or eliminate the practice have been largely unsuccessful given the continuing prevalence (placed at 95 percent in a sample of over 3,000 women studied in Khartoum).

CLOSED DISTRICTS ORDINANCE. Following the military defeat of Mahdism in the northern Sudan, the British instituted a campaign of military and political "pacification" in the southern Sudan (q.v.). Elsewhere in Africa the British developed a system of "indirect rule" (q.v.), which worked relatively well for societies that had a hierarchical political structure. Among southern Sudanese cultures this type of political organization was not developed and the system of indirect rule was difficult to apply. Moreover the vast size of the Sudan, the few southern natural resources, and difficult transportation and communication caused the

British to develop a policy of separation and indifference that was formally promulgated as the Closed Districts Ordinance. This imposed great restrictions of trade and travel into the southern Sudan and even sought to block the wearing of Arab clothing and the spread of the Arabic language (q.v.), a lingua franca even in the South.

This ordinance and its practice were developed by H. A. MacMichael (q.v.) in the 1930s. It led not only to internal separation of the Sudan but also to a mentality of institutionalized primitivism, and according to Stewart Symes (q.v.) the southern Sudan was administered with the objective of simple maintenance, not development. The southern "Bog Baron" officials of colonial rule were granted a high degree of local autonomy and authority in this extreme form of indirect rule. At the same time, their staff and facilities were grossly inadequate to provide even basic services for the colonized South. In the context of a long history of slaving (q.v.) by northerners and of a lively nationalist movement in the 1940s, southerners inevitably were drawn into the regional events despite the British effort to keep them in a state of laissez-faire backwardness.

By 1940 the Closed Districts Ordinance was perceived to have failed, or in other words, the political costs of backwardness were rising. In the North the Advisory Council for the Northern Sudan (q.v.) began to function and northern elites struggled for power; there was not a counterpart group for the southern region, which had been left further and further behind by indifference, neglect, and paternalism.

By 1947 the old southern policy was halted and the British sought to reverse course and integrate the two sections of the Sudan so as to balance Egypt and secure the Nile waters. Very modest efforts were initiated to educate a few southerners through missionary education and in the very late 1940s at Gordon Memorial College (q.v.). The Azande agricultural scheme was launched to try to develop some cash crops. However, the seeds of distrust and division had been deeply sown, and as the 1950s process of Sudanization began to be implemented southerners found themselves again neglected and marginalized. It is not surprising that in 1955, on the eve of independence, the southern Sudan broke out in a widespread mutiny and revolt that, aside from the Addis Ababa Agreement (q.v.) period (1972–1983), has continued as the protracted Sudanese Civil War. Clearly there were major divisions by ethnicity, economy, polity, and religion within the Sudan before the British arrived, but the practice of the Closed Districts Ordinance certainly added to this.

COBBE. *See* KOBBEI.

COLSTON, RALEIGH EDWARD (1825–1896). American Civil War veteran who in 1873 accepted a general staff position under Khedive Isma'il of Egypt (q.v.) along with such other Americans as Charles P. Stone and Charles Chaillé-Long (qq.v.). Colston was thus a part of the ambitious African expansion of the Khedive, which included the opening of the Suez Canal in 1869.

Colston traveled down the Red Sea to Suakin (q.v.) where he disembarked with Charles Gordon (q.v.) to ride to Berber (q.v.) by camel and then travel upstream by steam barge to Khartoum (q.v.), which he reached on 13 March 1873. However, Colston considered Khartoum to be a graveyard for Europeans and was appalled by the unhealthy conditions. He noted in his official reports that it was a major commercial center for Europeans and Egyptians, which even then commanded a trade of $65 million dollars annually. He observed that there were large homes and rich bazaars based on a lively trade in livestock, grain, fruit, and other agricultural products.

He also reported that Gordon Pasha had been clearly informed of the mission to suppress the active slave trade in the Sudan by any means possible. However, the deeply rooted practice of the slave trade and of domestic slavery (q.v.) meant that it was very difficult to halt, and Colston stated that slaves could easily be purchased in Khartoum for $35 to $50 dollars. By 1875 Khedive Isma'il's plans were being slowed down by inflation and overspending. Nevertheless, Colston served the Khedive for six years, during which he had a serious fall from a camel that resulted in the paralysis of his legs. He rose to the rank of general or *lewa*, led two noteworthy expeditions, and was awarded the "Knight Commander of the Turkish Imperial Order of Osmanieh" for distinguished and meritorious service.

Frustrated by European manipulation of Egypt, Isma'il dismissed his "European Ministry" in April 1879, but Isma'il was himself replaced by his son in June. This political turbulence was likely a factor in Colston returning to the United States in the same year. Disabled and suffering financial reverses, he lived out his remaining years at the Confederate Soldiers' Home in Richmond, Virginia. [by Richard Skidmore and Richard Lobban]

COMBONI, DANIELE (1831–1881). An Italian missionary in the Roman Catholic Church, who first came to the Sudan in 1857 and worked under the auspices of the Central African Mission and the Mazza Institute. He proposed a program for missions to Africa utilizing an African priesthood. Comboni gained support and recognition, and from 1867 to 1872 he established two seminaries in Verona, Italy. In 1872 he was appointed pro-vicar apostolic for Central Africa and returned to the Sudan where he established missions and schools. In 1873 he resided in Khartoum (q.v.) as the head of the mission of Central Africa, and by 1877 he was appointed bishop with a special authority granted him to free Sudanese slaves (q.v.). After his death on 10 October 1881 the work of the Verona Fathers (q.v.) continued to be an important force in Sudanese missions and education. Comboni College in Khartoum is named in his honor. *See also* CHRISTIANITY IN THE SUDAN; ZENAB, CATERINA.

COMMUNIST PARTY OF SUDAN. *See* SUDANESE COMMUNIST PARTY (SCP).

CONDOMINIUM. The term is usually used to describe the governmental structure of the Sudan in 1899–1956. It was defined in the Anglo-Egyptian Agreement of 1899, with some later modifications in the Anglo-Egyptian Treaty of 1936 (q.v.). Although it theoretically provided for some governing role for Egypt, in practice the structure ensured full British control over the Sudan. The Anglo-Egyptian Agreement of 1953 (q.v.) defined the steps leading to the end of the Condominium arrangement. *See also* BARING, EVELYN.

COPTS. Egyptians of the Coptic Christian faith began settling in the Sudan at least as early as the sixth century, both to avoid religious persecution in Egypt and to proselytize. Their community seems to have disappeared with the downfall of the Christian Nubian kingdoms (fourteenth century), and it is not until the late seventeenth century that Copts are again observed in the Sudan, this time as part of a large foreign merchant community in Sinnar (q.v.). Significant Coptic migration to the Sudan resumed with the Turco-Egyptian conquest, with many Copts serving as civil servants (especially tax and finance officials) in the Turkiya (q.v.) regime. Coptic merchants settled in many of the towns of the northern Sudan, while others were active as middlemen in the ivory trade of the Upper Nile and Bahr al-Ghazal (qq.v.) in the 1850s–1860s. A Coptic Orthodox church was built in Khartoum (q.v.) by 1852, and it is likely that Coptic communities in towns such as Bara and El-Obeid (q.v.) had their own churches as well. There is evidence that by the late nineteenth century many Copts were well assimilated, even thinking of themselves as "Sudanese," which may explain why so many Copts were reluctant to leave the Sudan during the years of the Mahdist revolt.

When the Mahdi (q.v.) came to power, he and the Khalifa 'Abdullahi (q.v.) recognized in the Copts a ready-made administrative corps: From the earliest days of the Mahdiya (q.v.), Copts served as an indispensable clerical class that allowed the *Bayt al-Mal* (public treasury) to function relatively smoothly. Obliged to convert to Islam (q.v.) and take wives from among the Sudanese, the Copts formed the largest segment of the Masalma (q.v.) community of Omdurman (q.v.). Some Copts were allowed to continue long-distance trade during the Mahdiya, importing needed goods into the Sudan from Egypt. Known as "Nagada" (after a town in Upper Egypt), these were accorded a quasi-"tribal" status almost equivalent to that of the other Sudanese ethnic groups. After the conquest of the Sudan in 1898, the British numbered some 600 Copts, including families, present in Omdurman.

The Coptic presence in the Sudan again surged with the imposition of Anglo-Egyptian (q.v.) rule. Favored for their literacy and administrative skills (and according to the Sudanese, their Christianity), the Copts were employed by the Condominium (q.v.) in various branches of government; while in the private sector, Copts were prominent in trade, banking, engineering, and medicine. Some families maintained their prominence through the changes of regime: Tadrus Bey Nakhla (d. 1885), a merchant, served as a financial official under Charles Gordon (q.v.) at Khartoum; his son 'Abd al-Masih Tadrus Nakhla (d. 1933), a merchant and magistrate, became president of the Coptic community of Omdurman. By 1902 a Coptic community school for girls had opened in Khartoum, while the Coptic Secondary School became one of the elite schools in the capital area.

Granted Sudanese nationality and comfortable as a privileged minority, the Copts were an apolitical and contented community during the years of the Condominium and early period of independence. Sudanese demands for an Islamic constitution in the mid-1960s led the Copts to play a more active political role. The left-leaning May Revolution (q.v.) of 1969 was welcomed by many Copts, who initially found an ally in Ja'far al-Nimeiri (q.v.): the Nimeiri regime appointed a Copt to a senior ministry in the early 1970s and donated land and money for Coptic community clubs in Khartoum and Omdurman. However, the introduction of the September Laws of 1983 (q.v.) revealed the fragility of the Copts' situation, as they found themselves with reduced legal status and subject to the rules of Shari'a (q.v.). (No small loss were the Coptic supplies of alcohol, confiscated by the government without compensation.) After the *intifada* of 1985, Copts opposed the National Islamic Front (NIF, q.v.) in the 1986 elections, drawing the wrath of the NIF for a "Communist and Christian attack on Islam."

With the 'Umar al-Bashir (q.v.) coup of 1989, the persecution of Copts in Sudan began in earnest. Hundreds of Copts were soon dismissed from positions in the civil service and judiciary, and in 1990 some Coptic churches were closed. In 1991 a Coptic airline pilot was executed for foreign currency violations after a well-publicized trial trumpeted his Coptic identity. A restriction on rights to Sudanese nationality has hindered Coptic attempts to leave the country, while Coptic merchants have been penalized to force them out of business. Copts complain of an Arabic-Islamic curriculum in the schools, the enforcement of "Islamic" dress for Coptic women, and compulsory military service for men, who are impressed into the popular militia to help wage a *jihad* against the southern Sudanese. There are thought to be approximately 150,000–200,000 Copts remaining in Sudan, with significant communities in the Three Towns, Atbara, Dongola, Wad Medani, Port Sudan, and El-Obeid (qq.v.). *See also* CHRISTIANITY IN NUBIA; CHRISTIANITY IN THE SUDAN; NUBIA.

CROMER, EARL OF. *See* BARING, EVELYN.

– D –

DAFTARDAR. A title for an official responsible for maintaining administrative and financial registers. In Turkish this refers to an "ink-pot carrier," but in Sudanese history, "the Daftardar" usually implies Muhammad Khusraw (q.v.). This particular title-holder was the brother-in-law of Isma'il Pasha (q.v.), the son of Muhammad 'Ali. When Isma'il Pasha was assassinated at Shendi by Mek Nimr (qq.v.) in 1822, the Daftardar went on a two-year punitive campaign in which thousands of Sudanese living from Shendi to Sinnar (q.v.) were beaten and executed.

AL-DAHAB, 'ABD AL-RAHMAN SUWAR. Major general and defense minister in the Ja'afar al-Nimeiri (q.v.) regime who seized power on 6 April 1985 in the wake of massive popular demonstrations to overthrow the Nimeiri dictatorship. On 3 April a Khartoum (q.v.) demonstration estimated at between one and two million formed the immediate backdrop to the coup. General Suwar al-Dahab formed the Transitional Military Council (TMC) with a civilian Council of Ministers that promised to hold popular elections within a year. Contact with the Sudanese Peoples Liberation Army (SPLA, q.v.) was made two months after the new regime took power. One year later Suwar al-Dahab withdrew to the barracks and Sadiq al-Mahdi (q.v.) was elected prime minister.

DAJU. The precise origins of the Daju people are unknown but they may date back even to dynastic Egyptian times. Their position at the southern end of the Forty Days Road (q.v.) to the Selima Oasis is unquestionably ancient. Their language is unique and isolated as the Eastern branch of the Sudanic subfamily to which Nilotic and Nubian (qq.v.) languages also belong. Before the arrival of Islam in Darfur (qq.v.), perhaps as early as the thirteenth century, they established economic and political dominance of trade in Darfur, but were subsequently replaced by Tungur and Keira (qq.v.) dynastic rule after the fourteenth century.

DAMER, AL-. A town about 10 kilometers south of the Atbara-Nile confluence, located on a site where Mesolithic remains dating back 8,000 years have been found, and where a Meroitic settlement probably existed. The present settlement emerged in the seventeenth century as a nomad's "summer camp" (*damar*) and a marketplace adjacent to a peasant hamlet. Security of exchange at this sensitive social boundary was guaranteed by *fuqara'* or religious specialists, whose learning and charisma were thought to give them power beyond that of the ordinary individual. During the eighteenth century one family of *fuqara'* in particular, the Majadhib (q.v.), gained prominence in al-Damer and among the neighboring Ja'aliyin (q.v.). Under their leadership, the prospering market town developed into a partly autonomous entity within the disintegrating Funj (q.v.) state. By the early nineteenth century it had also become a center of learning of regional fame. Hailed by John L. Burckhardt (q.v.) in 1814 for its neatness and good condition, al-Damer's estimated population of 2,000 placed it among the larger Sudanese towns at the time.

In 1823 it was razed to the ground by Turco-Egyptian (q.v.) forces, and the inhabitants fled. Although some of them returned after an amnesty in 1825, al-Damer recovered only slowly and never regained its former form. At the end of the Mahdiya (q.v.) it had only 700 inhabitants. Since 1905 al-Damer has served as a provincial capital instead of Berber (q.v.). Its role as a marketing center for livestock and agricultural products from the Atbara (q.v.) region gave a measure of stability to what remains a quiet town in the shadow of the newly founded industrial city of

Atbara. In 1955 al-Damer's population was 5,600; in 1964, 7,900; by 1990 it was estimated at over 25,000. [by Albrecht Hofheinz]

DANAGLA. Arabized people with many surviving Nubian (q.v.) traits from the region of Dongola (q.v.). They have had long interaction with the Ja'aliyin (q.v.) as both have migrated throughout the Sudan as merchants and traders (Jellaba, q.v.) from at least the days of the Funj (q.v.).

DANCE. *See* MUSIC AND DANCE.

DARFUR. The westernmost region of Sudan, whose name *Dar Fur* (Realm of the Fur) refers to its dominant ethnic group. The Fur (q.v.), based around the heights of Jabal Marra, speak a language that is a separate branch of the Nilo-Saharan family. Islam (q.v.) came here during the late Tungur or early Keira (qq.v.) rule, perhaps the mid-seventeenth century. The latter formed the Fur Sultanate (q.v.), which long controlled trade on the Forty Days Road (q.v.) with Egypt and occupied Kordofan (q.v.) for much of the eighteenth century. Darfur was conquered by the army of Zubayr Rahma Mansur (q.v.) in 1874 and brought under centralized Turco-Egyptian (q.v.) control. In the late nineteenth century cattle-herding Arabs (q.v.) in the southern region formed the nucleus of the Mahdi's (q.v.) following; among their number was the Mahdi's successor, Khalifa 'Abdullahi (q.v.) of the Ta'aisha Baqqara (q.v.). Darfur regained some measure of independence under Sultan 'Ali Dinar (q.v.), who ruled from 1898 until the Anglo-Egyptian (q.v.) conquest of 1916.

The largest of the nine provinces (q.v.) at independence, it comprised 191,650 square miles with an estimated 1970 population of 1,694,000. Its economy was based on pastoralism (chiefly cattle and sheep) and the harvesting of gum arabic, though crops such as durra, fruit, and tobacco were also cultivated. Darfur's principal towns are El-Fasher, the capital; Nyala, connected by rail to El-Obeid (q.v.) and the Nile in 1960; and Geneina near the Chad border, which has a small shoe industry.

DEMOCRATIC UNIONIST PARTY (DUP). Parallel with the Umma Party (q.v.), which was founded upon the religious order of the Mahdiya and its Ansar followers (qq.v.), the DUP was based upon the Khatmiya *tariqa* (qq.v.). Indeed, it was the long opposition of the Khatmiya to the Mahdists that has characterized much of its history since the 1880s. Officially the DUP was formed in 1967 as the result of a merger of the Peoples Democratic Party (PDP) and the National Unionist Party (NUP, qq.v.). Isma'il al-Azhari (q.v.) of the NUP was president and 'Ali 'Abd al-Rahman of the PDP was vice-president. The DUP represented the recreation of the old alliance between al-Azhari and the Khatmiya that had broken up in 1956. The effort to bridge the gap between modern secularists and the traditional Islamic values of the Khatmiya has been both the strength and weakness of the DUP and its allied groupings. In its periods of participation in the democratic process in Sudan, it was common to have internal factional disputes within the DUP over such issues as the future of Sudan.

Seeking to overcome or minimize internal conflicts the DUP, especially under the leadership of 'Uthman al-Mirghani (q.v.), made a number of compromises that gave the party an appearance of hesitation and confusion. Officially the party ended with the 1969 May Revolution (q.v.), but during the Ja'afar al-Nimeiri (q.v.) years the DUP refrained from criticizing the implementation of strict Islamic law (q.v.), which traditionalists supported but secularists opposed. With the brief restoration of democracy in 1986 the DUP regrouped in the parliamentary elections and came in second to the Umma Party, with which it cautiously agreed to form a coalition government with its former rival Prime Minister Sadiq al-Mahdi (q.v.). Since both DUP and the Umma Party had their traditionalist constituencies they were reluctant to discard the Islamic laws of Nimeiri. Meanwhile, a growing group of secularists had so abandoned hope in the stalemated northern political arena that a full-scale armed rebellion had broken out under the leadership of the Sudanese Peoples Liberation Movement/Army (SPLM/SPLA, q.v.).

By 1988, fearing either a divided Sudan or secularists taking power, the DUP leadership finally met with SPLA leader John Garang (q.v.) in Ethiopia. It was agreed that the burning issue of Shari'a must be addressed first with a mutual cease-fire and then abrogation of the Islamic laws. If not, Sudan could not avoid a North-South separation. Also moving toward this policy reversal was the Umma Party. In retrospect, these steps were too little and too late. The paralysis of the traditional northern parties gave an opportunity to Hasan al-Turabi and the National Islamic Front (qq.v) to take power in June 1989 and declare all political parties suspended once again. Al-Mirghani was able to flee to Egypt for a life of exile, where he was later joined by former Prime Minster Sadiq al-Mahdi after his escape from Sudan. The DUP and Umma parties as well as the Sudanese Armed Forces-Legitimate Command (SAF-LC, q.v.), the Beja people (q.v.), the Sudan Alliance Forces (SAF, q.v.), and the SPLA all joined as members of the National Democratic Alliance (NDA, q.v.) based in Asmara in opposition to the Khartoum administration.

Simultaneously, the military groups of the DUP, Umma, Beja, SAF, SAF-LC, and SPLA were all united within the NDA Joint Military Command led by John Garang and his second, Commander-in-Chief General 'Abd al-Rahman Sa'id. The late General Fathi Ahmad 'Ali, the former commander-in-chief of the SAF-Legitimate Command, was the leader of the NDA military forces before his death in April 1997.

When democratic rule is restored to Sudan one may expect that the DUP or some similar organization based on the Khatmiya will continue to be a factor in Sudanese politics. This is especially so because one of the main areas of military opposition to Khartoum is in the eastern Sudan, which has long been a stronghold for the Khatmiya.

DENG AKUIEI AJOU (?–1995). Deng was a chief of the Abiem section of the Malwal Dinka (q.v.) of Aweil in Bahr al-Ghazal; he died at an age of over 100 years. He was active in the resistance against colonial Condominium (q.v.) rule in the early 1920s while his father, Akuei Ajou, was arrested and exiled in Suakin (q.v.) for his own resistance. Once his region was "pacified," the British authorities established "tribal" administration and Chief Deng Akuei was appointed president of the Chief's Court of his section of Abiem Dinka.

After independence the chronic war between North and South left him pessimistic about reconciliation, but it was the Arab militias of the 1980s that forced Deng's emigration to Khartoum (q.v.) where he died in 1995. With his death much of the legacy of traditional regional chieftains also passed. Among his hundreds of children, Aldo Ajou Deng is probably the most prominent, having served in most of the recent governments until the latest regime from which he defected in 1993.

DENG, FRANCIS (1938–). Francis Deng is a southern Sudanese scholar, diplomat, and novelist of Dinka (q.v.) origin. He studied law at the University of Khartoum (q.v.) and at Yale University. He taught at New York University and was a member of the United Nations Human Rights Commission. He has served in important diplomatic posts as ambassador to the United Nations and ambassador to the United States and to Canada. He also served as the minister of state for foreign affairs during the Ja'afar al-Nimeiri regime (q.v.). Deng has written many significant anthropological studies of the Dinka, as well as literary and historical studies, receiving the African Studies Association Herskovits Prize for one of his books. His two novels, *Seed of Redemption* and *Cry of the Owl*, are central to the debate about Afro-Arab relations in Sudan. His latest scholarly work, *War of Visions*, attempts to clarify how the protracted conflict of identities fuels the Sudanese armed struggle for distribution of political power and allocation of resources between the Afro-Arab Islamist northerners and the African-centered, westernized southerners. Deng is currently a senior fellow in the Foreign Policy Studies program at the Brookings Institution. He is also representative of the United Nations Secretary General for internally displaced persons. [by Constance E. Berkley]

DENG, SANTINO (1922–). Southern administrator and politician from the Dinka (q.v.) people. Educated in Catholic mission schools, he became a government agriculturalist and was elected to Parliament in 1953. Deng ran as an independent but joined the National Unionist Party (NUP, q.v.) and received a cabinet post in 1954. He then accepted a ministerial post in the Umma Party (q.v.) government of 1958. Deng remained as minister of animal resources in the Ibrahim Abboud (q.v.) government and was that military regime's sole southerner. After the 1964 October Revolution (q.v.) he formed his own party, the Sudan Unity Party (SUP), which had limited influence. The SUP cooperated with northern policies and was opposed by other southern groups.

DENG, WILLIAM (1929–1968). This southern political leader started in the government administrative service and became an assistant district commissioner. He went into exile during the Ibrahim Abboud (q.v.) era and was one of the founders, in 1962, of the Sudan African National Union (SANU, q.v.). After the 1964 October Revolution (q.v.) he returned to Sudan. In 1965 Deng claimed to lead the southern delegation at the Roundtable Conferences (q.v.). He broke with the leaders of SANU in exile and was elected to Parliament in 1967, where he became chairman of the southern parliamentary group. He was assassinated while traveling in the south in 1968; his death added to southern grievances against the North.

DINKA. The Dinka are the largest single southern Nilotic (q.v.) ethnic group. They are seminomadic cattle-herders by tradition, but are also farmers of millet, corn, and peanuts, and fishermen of the rivers and lakes in their region. They may be Christian or Muslim, but their traditional religion and values are strong, including reverence for ancestors and other aspects of animism. The Dinka may represent 10 percent of the total population of Sudan. Allegedly they numbered two million or more in 1983.

The Dinka are mainly located throughout most of northern Bahr al Ghazal and the areas south and west of the White Nile. Situated at the frontier between Nilotic southerners and cattle-herding Arabs (q.v.), the Dinka were much less isolated than other southern peoples. As a consequence they have produced a number of notable leaders (e.g., Abel Alier, Bona Malwal, Francis Deng, William Deng, and John Garang, qq.v.), playing "brokerage" roles between the two regions and ethnic groups. This region has become a zone of great tension and conflict during the period of the Sudanese Civil War with atrocities reported on all sides.

The Dinka language (q.v.) and its dialects are classified as members of the Nilotic subgroup of the Eastern Sudanic languages. It is thus distinguished from the major Bantu groups farther south and the Afro-Asiatic languages to the North. The Dinka occupy territory that interfaces directly with Arab groups to the North. Linguists conventionally divide them into five regional subgroups: the northeast, the northwest, the southeast, the southwest, and south central.

The northeastern Dinka live along the White Nile, northeast of the *Sudd* swamp lands and along the lower reaches of the Sobat River, where there are also Shilluk and Nuer (qq.v.) peoples. These Dinka are sometimes termed the Padang or Jaang. According to a 1986 missionary linguistic survey there are 320,000 speakers including the following subgroups: 7,200 Abialang, 9,000 Dongjol, 2,500 Luac, 16,000 Ngok-Sobat, 20,000 Jok, 13,500 Ageer, 2,000 Rut, and 400 Thoi. The main dialects represented among the northeastern Dinka include: Abiliang, Ageer, Dongjol, Luac, Ngok-Sobat, Ageer, Rut, and Thoi. The Dongol dialect bears the greatest lexical affinity with the Dinka to the southwest and southeast.

The northwestern Dinka occupy the region farther west and north of the Bahr al-Ghazal River, southern Kordofan (q.v.) and the Abyei region, which is at the frontier between north and south in Sudan. They include 80,000 Ruweng dialect speakers as well as those speaking Alor, Ngok, and Pan Uru dialects. Some linguists consider that this branch of Dinka is linguistically closer to the southern Dinka than the northwestern. Perhaps this reflects an earlier south to north migration pattern for these cattle pastoralists.

The south central Dinka number some 250,000, including 2,000 Aker (Agar), 2,000 Thany, 22,000 Ciec, and 25,000 Gok. They live south of the *Sudd* swamps and to the west of the White Nile, and in the region centered around the town of Bor and in the Lakes District, and as far west as the Jur River near Wau (q.v.). They bear the closest linguistic affinity with southeastern Dinka, from whom they probably descended. They are mainly cattle pastoralists and grain farmers, and there are some fishermen.

The southeastern Dinka also number about 250,000 and include approximately 21,000 Atoc, 9,000 Ghol, 4,000 Nyarueng, 35,000 Twi, and 21,000 Bor-Gok. They live east of the Nile, around Bor, and northward. Their dialects include Athoc, Bor, Ghol, Nyarweng, and Tuic.

The southwestern Dinka number as many as 500,000, including 55,000 Abiem, 15,000 Luac, 40,000 Malual, 17,000 Paliet, 35,000 Palioupiny, and 50,000 Tuic. They are concentrated north of Wau, the provincial capital of Bahr al-Ghazal. Their main dialects include Abiem, Aguok, Apuk, Awan, Lau, Luac, Malwal, Paliet, Palioupiny, Rek, and Tuic.

DINKA FOLKLORE. In their folktales the Dinka (q.v.), construct a world of cosmic totality in which human beings, animals, trees, and spirits not only interact, but also change their forms and perform deeds unnatural to their species. The two main categories governing this world are those of human and nonhuman behavior. The focus tends to be on human interaction with lions, perhaps because lions are what the Dinka fear the most. In the Ngok Dinka dialect, bedtime stories are called *Koor* (i.e., "lions") and lions appear very frequently in them. But the idea is more far-reaching and permits anything to change into anything else. As a Dinka once said about a bedtime story in which such objects as stones, grass, straws, and rafters spoke: "The Dinka want to show that everything has breath and feels pain; everything deserves to be treated like human beings." [by Baqie Badawi Muhammad]

DIQNA. *See* 'UTHMAN DIQNA.

DIU, BUTH (1917–1975). Southern political leader of Nuer (q.v.) origin. He entered government service in 1937, eventually becoming a magistrate. Diu served in the Legislative Assembly (q.v.) and on the Constitutional Commission in 1951. He was also the chairman of the Zeraf Island Rural District Council. Diu was elected to Parliament in 1953 and formed the Southern Party, which became the Liberal Party (q.v.) in 1954 with Diu as secretary-general. He served in many cabinets and was elected to Parliament again in the 1960s. After the 1969 May Revolution (q.v.) he created the Peoples Assembly, and in 1973 was elected to that body.

DONGOLA. It would be easy to confuse Old Dongola (on the east bank) with New Dongola on the west bank of the Nile. Old Dongola of the Christian and Funj (qq.v.) eras is essentially an archaeological site at the center of ancient Nubia (q.v.). On the east bank are the ruins of the Kawa temple of Taharka. To the north one finds the earlier archaeological site of Kerma.

(New) Dongola was founded in 1811 largely by refugee Mameluks who fled the rule of Muhammad 'Ali in Egypt. Dongola's most famous figure is Muhammad Ahmad al-Mahdi (q.v.), son of a Dongolawi boat-builder and founder of the Mahdist movement in 1881. Before the advent of the Wadi Halfa-Abu Hamad railway, Dongola was a common stopover for Nile travelers, but after the construction of the railway, it became substantially isolated and its economy suffered as it still does today.

Dongola was on the path used by the Turco-Egyptians (q.v.) in 1820 and by British General Wolseley (q.v.) in 1884 in his failed attempt to rescue General Charles Gordon (q.v.), and it was occupied by H. H. Kitchener (q.v.) in 1896 on his military push up the Nile. After the British conquest, H. C. Jackson laid out (New) Dongola with a grid of streets, central market, and administrative quarters. At independence in 1956 the population was 3,300; in 1965 it had grown to 5,300. Dongola is still a small town today; its economy rests upon some light industry, the cultivation of date palms, livestock, and irrigated agriculture. Difficult transport is a limiting factor of future growth.

DONGOLAWI (or DUNQULAWI). A person from Dongola (q.v.); plural, Danagla. Dongolawi is sometimes a generic reference to Nubians.

DUEIM, AL- (Arabic, *al-Duwaym*). This town lies on the west bank of the White Nile between Omdurman and Kosti (qq.v.) where the railroad crosses the river. Its growth during the twentieth century has been limited by its much more significant neighbors. Dueim had been a small town before the British conquest in 1898. It functioned as a market town and stood at the eastern end of a trade and pilgrimage route that extended through Kordofan (q.v.) to the Nile.

Immediately to its north is a mountain, Jabal Arishkol, which served as a prominent landmark steering travelers to the river. The nearby hamlet of Shabasha is home to the family of a famous holyman of the Sammaniya *tariqa (qq.v.)*, Shaykh al-Birayr (d.1885), whose tomb is one of al-Dueim's distinguishing features. After the Kosti bridge was built in

1910, real estate prices fell in al-Dueim. At independence its population was less than 13,000, and by 1964 the population had grown only to 16,400. However, by the 1983 census it had reached 39,000.

DUSE MOHAMMED 'ALI. A Sudanese-Egyptian who was a central figure in the early Pan-African movement and an early advocate of Pan Afro-Asian solidarity. Resident in England for many years in the early twentieth century, he was a delegate to the First Universal Races Congress in London in 1911 with W. E. B. DuBois and other prominent African, Afro-West Indian, and Afro-American scholars and activists. As a journalist Duse published the seminal Pan-African literary journal, the *African Times and Orient Review*, from July 1912. As a scholar he published *In the Land of the Pharaohs* in 1911, which was well-received in its day and was self-described as the first history of Egypt written by an Egyptian. In this work he asserts the African basis of the cultural and historical achievement of Egypt.

As a Pan-Africanist Duse advocated various indigenous commercial projects designed to respond to European control over Africa's resources. For his activities he was characterized as "suspect" in a West African British colonial report, who consorted with "undesirable elements in Egypt and India." While in London, he employed the young Marcus Garvey, and later he was a signatory to Garvey's Universal Negro Improvement Association's "Petition to the League of Nations" in 1922 for independence and self-determination of all colonized peoples.

– E –

ECONOMY. Once touted as a potential "breadbasket" due to its fertile Gezira (q.v.) region, Sudan has struggled since independence to maintain a stable economy. Several reasons can be given for Sudan's economic problems. Among them are poor decisions by government planners, corruption and mismanagement, natural disasters (e.g., Nile floods and locust infestations), and an influx of refugees (q.v.) from neighboring countries. Unquestionably, Sudan's economic problems are also linked to its political situation: the protracted civil war is reputed to cost the government an average of $1 million per day, while the casualties of the war seriously erode the country's productive capacity.

The figures for Sudan's economy tell an unhappy story. In a country of enormous size (2.5 million square km), where 35 percent of the GNP comes from agriculture, there is an extremely limited, often seasonally navigable, and poorly maintained infrastructure. Only 5 percent of the country is irrigated farmland, while 24 percent constitutes pastureland, 20 percent woodland, and 51 percent undeveloped or wasteland. Electricity in the capital region—home to the nation's commerce and industry—is sporadic. Per capita income for 1994 was just $870, with a growth rate of 7 percent. Of a labor force of 6.5 million people, 80 percent work in agriculture, 10 percent work in commerce and industry, and 6 percent are employed by the government; meanwhile the unemployment rate hovers around 30 percent and shortages exist for most categories of skilled labor. Emigration of skilled workers, professionals, and intellectuals to the Arab Gulf and elsewhere is a common phenomenon.

Sudan's inflation has soared in recent years: from 70 percent in 1989, the inflation rate rose to 140 percent in 1996 and 100 percent in 1997. Viewed differently, prices rose 70 percent in December 1995 alone and 40 percent in May 1996. The value of the Sudanese currency has accordingly and steadily dropped against the dollar: from an exchange of 0.3 pounds per dollar (ppd) in 1971, the value dropped to 4.5 ppd in 1990, 277.8 ppd in 1994, and an astonishing 2,000 ppd in 1997. November 1998 estimates place the exchange rate at 2,050 ppd. The effect this inflation has had on the Sudanese consumer can only be imagined. In an attempt to inhibit hard currency dealings and shore up the official exchange rate, the government in November 1998 forbade foreign exchange bank accounts of less than $5,000: an amount out of reach to all but the wealthiest Sudanese.

In a country where, according to the World Bank, $800 million of foreign exchange is needed annually to provide basic services and pursue the civil war, revenues in 1994 amounted to only $493 million, against expenditures of $1.1 billion. Defense expenditures alone consumed 7.3 percent of the GDP (approx. $600 million) in fiscal year 1993–1994. Revenue shortfalls are made up by foreign aid, though much economic aid has been reduced since Sudan's support for Iraq in the 1991 Gulf War, while food and medical aid have been interrupted or undelivered as a result of the civil war.

In 1993–1994 Sudan exported $419 million worth of goods, of which 43 percent was cotton, 29 percent gum arabic, and 24 percent meat or livestock. Against this were imports worth $1.7 billion, consisting of foodstuffs, petroleum products, manufactured goods, machinery, medicines, and textiles. The largest share of this trade was conducted with Western Europe.

Sudan's trade imbalance has added to its blossoming international debt, which in 1998 amounted to $20 billion or $531 worth of debt per capita. Its debt to the International Monetary Fund (IMF), which in 1998 amounted to $1.7 billion, has caused particular problems in recent years. In 1984 the IMF froze Sudan's standby credit facilities after it went into arrears on previous debts; and in 1986 the IMF declared Sudan ineligible for new loans. In 1992 the Sudanese government took steps to liberalize its economy, including privatization measures and import-export deregulation, in an effort to improve relations with the IMF. Further economic reforms were undertaken in 1994. Nonetheless in 1995 the Sudan's membership in the IMF was formally suspended over the country's long-standing debt, and it was threatened with permanent expulsion. Negotiations subsequently resulted in a formula for monthly payments of $4 million on Sudan's total debt. However, given the country's colossal debt as well as the domestic problems that sustain it, it came as no surprise in 1997 when the IMF rebuked Sudan for faulting on its monthly payments and again threatened expulsion.

Sudan's response has been to complain that the United States, on behalf of a hostile political agenda against Sudan and the Islamic world, unfairly manipulates the IMF. For its part the United States has claimed that Sudan's sponsorship of international terrorism is an important factor in decisions taken by the IMF and other financial bodies. With the continuation of civil war and drop-off in foreign aid from the Arab Gulf states, it is difficult to imagine how Sudan's economic problems can be resolved. *See also* AGRICULTURE.

EDUCATION. Formal education in Sudan begins with the Islamic schools, the *khalwa* or *kuttab*, which emphasize literacy in Arabic (q.v.) for the purpose of reading the Qur'an. Recitation and memorization of passages of the Qur'an is directed by the Shaykh or Imam (qq.v.) of the school. A boarding school where students pay minimal fees for the school's upkeep and master are key features of this style of education, which still exists and parallels government public schools introduced during British colonial rule. Typically Qur'anic education has been primarily for boys; however, occasionally girls have been accepted as students. Some parents choose to enroll their sons exclusively in Qur'anic schools, or opt for several years in a *khalwa* before entering public schools.

Public education in the Western sense was introduced during the Condominium (q.v.) period and conducted in the English language, primarily for the creation of a literate male population trained for administrative service. Gordon Memorial College (q.v.) was founded by British public subscription in 1902 for this purpose and educated the Sudan's elites for several years until being renamed the University of Khartoum (q.v.) after independence in 1956. Public education for women lagged behind. Babikr Badri (q.v.) founded the Ahfad College for Women (q.v.) in 1907, which his family continues to operate. It is still Africa's only university exclusively for women.

Seven major and many regional universities operate in Sudan, including the University of Khartoum, al-Nilayn University (formerly Cairo University-Khartoum Branch), University of the Gezira, Omdurman Islamic University, Ahfad University for Women, Omdurman Ahlia University, and University of Juba. Five technical institutes also exist, including two in Khartoum (University of Sudan, formerly Khartoum Polytechnic, and Bayan Science and Technology College) plus the Abu Haraz and Abu Na'ama Colleges of Agricultural and Natural Resources and the Mechanical Engineering College of Atbara. Arabic (q.v.) replaced English as the medium of instruction at the University of Khartoum in the early 1990s soon after 'Umar al-Bashir (q.v.) seized power and the National Islamic Front (NIF, q.v.) came to dominate the politics of university education. Islamic-oriented student groups affiliated with the NIF have meanwhile dominated campus politics since this time.

The adult literacy rate in Sudan is roughly 63 percent for men and 38 percent for women. The basic education rate for both sexes is 45 percent. The male-female ratio for primary school enrollment is 57 percent to 48 percent; for secondary school enrollment, 59 percent to 52 percent. In the southern provinces the education rate drops dramatically to 12 percent overall, with 14 percent for males and 10 percent for females. Even these numbers seem inflated with the extreme social upheaval of civil war rendering basic social services virtually nil.

Rural-urban differences in education are quite dramatic, with an overall completion rate for both sexes through grade five at 75 percent in the urban areas and 53 percent in rural areas. The drop-out rate for boys in rural areas is much higher than for girls, which varies from the traditional pattern and is perhaps explained by the greater need for young boys in the economic activities of the countryside as well as their increased conscription into the Sudanese army.

EFFENDI or AFFENDI. A general term of address, often equal to "mister." It also is specifically used to mean an educated person or government official.

EL-. See AL-.

EMIN PASHA (EDUARD SCHNITZER) (1840–1892). A physician of German Jewish background who practiced medicine in the Ottoman Empire where he adopted the name Mehemet Emin (and presumably the religion of Islam, q.v.). Arriving in Khartoum (q.v.) in 1875, he met Colonel Charles Gordon (q.v.) who appointed him medical officer in Equatoria (q.v.). In 1878 he became governor of Equatoria Province, where he remained until 1889. Emin Pasha was best known for his stalwart resistance to both the forces of the Mahdi (q.v.) and slave trader attacks on the Lado Enclave. Isolated from the North by a Mahdist army, he was rescued against his will in 1889 by the explorer H. M. Stanley, with whom he retired to Zanzibar. Emin Pasha traveled and reported extensively about the Sudan and Uganda in the 1870s and 1880s, writing about his colleague George Schweinfurth (q.v.) and about such places as Gondokoro, Khartoum, Lado, and Rumbek. His accounts on the Amadi, Bari, Dinka, and Latuko (qq.v.) peoples of Equatoria were popular nineteenth-century reading.

EQUATORIA PROVINCE. One of the three original southern provinces (q.v.) and the southernmost region of Sudan. Equatoria has a mixed population of Nilotic, Beir, Bari, Azande (qq.v.), and other peoples and a variety of languages is spoken there. It encompasses some 76,495 square miles and a 1970 census estimated its population at 1,303,000. Isolated by the *Sudd* swamps to the north and vast forests to the south, Equatoria was one of the last places reached by European explorers seeking the sources of the Nile or to crush slavery (q.v.). Its provincial capital, Juba (q.v.), is the largest of the southern towns and is central in southern politics, administration, and education.

Prior to the Torit mutiny of 1955 that initiated civil war, Equatoria was the most developed region in the southern Sudan (q.v.), with tobacco and coffee plantations in its southwest portion. Most development has halted due to chronic civil war and Equatoria, as the rest of the South, has suffered enormously. *See also* EMIN PASHA; GORDON, CHARLES; EVIL EYE.

– F –

AL-FAJR MAGAZINE. *Al-Fajr* was a leading literary journal that, like its precursor the journal *al-Nahda* (q.v.), served as a major forum for the articulation of nationalist ideas and the development of modern Sudanese Arabic literature (q.v.). Its title meant "The Dawn" and reflected an optimism in Sudanese social progress and development, shared by young intellectuals of the period. Thus it brought together many different groups of educated Sudanese and provided a vehicle for the expression of their views. It became more overtly political after the death in 1936 of 'Arafat Muhammad 'Abd Allah (1898–1936), who had served as founder and editor-in-chief, and created the journal along with the Hashimab (q.v.) group.

It appeared intermittently, in approximately forty issues, between June 1934 and March 1937. Leading nationalists, poets, and essayists contributed to the journal, such as Muhammad Ahmad Mahjub (q.v.), Yusuf Mustafa al-Tinay, al-Tijani Yusuf Bashir, and the brothers Muhammad and 'Abd Allah 'Ashri Siddiq. At its height *al-Fajr* had about 1,500 subscribers. Notwithstanding its short run, it represents a landmark in the history and literature of the twentieth-century northern Sudan. [by Heather J. Sharkey]

FAMINE. The great Sahelian drought resulting in widespread famine during the mid-1980s affected Sudan, bringing about devastation of animals and crops and causing the death or migration of hundreds of thousands of Sudanese. During this period migration to the cities, especially Khartoum (q.v.), resulted in vast increases in squatter settlements and tremendous pressure on limited relief resources.

Added to the natural, drought-related famine was the increasingly war-induced famine in the southern Sudan (q.v.) that became a national and international political issue when both the Sudanese government and the Sudanese Peoples Liberation Army (SPLA, q.v.) were charged with preventing food relief supplies from getting to the affected areas. Numerous international agencies have been involved in relief efforts, including the United Nations Operation Lifeline Sudan (q.v.), the International Red Cross, US/AID, and others, to get assistance to the estimated 3.5 million people (approximately one and a half million in Khartoum and another two million in the South) who have been displaced by the civil war. UN officials have described the relief effort as one of "Hiroshima proportions."

FARID, NAJWA KAMAL. Appointed by Shaykh Muhammad al-Gizouli (q.v.) in 1971 as the first woman justice in what was then the Shari'a Division of the Sudan Judiciary. Thereafter, three other women justices were appointed during the 1970s to the Shari'a courts. This was a unique step in the Muslim world, since some religious scholars believe that women should be precluded from holding this public office. Indeed, unlike the more numerous women who serve as civil court justices, Shari'a women judges traditionally have not conducted proceedings in public courts, but have worked at various posts in the Judiciary. *See also* IS-LAMIC LAW; ISLAMIZATION; WOMEN.

FARUQ, KING OF EGYPT (1920–1965). Faruq was the son of King Ah-mad Fuad I (q.v.). He came to power as a young man after his father's death in 1936 and reached the throne for the signing of the Anglo-Egyptian Treaty (q.v.) over the Sudan. He was formally coronated in 1937. Faruq's youth and lack of experience may account for his crisis-ridden reign. Initially he, or his advisors, tried to break out of palace isolation: he planned a visit to the Sudan and met with 'Abd al-Rahman al-Mahdi (q.v.) in 1937. He also made efforts to build an alliance with the powerful Wafd party in Egypt. This failed in 1937 when Nahhas Pasha was dismissed, to be replaced with a series of ineffective prime ministers.

As World War II unfolded Faruq expressed concern for the military preparedness of the Sudan to meet the threat from the Italians in Eritrea and Ethiopia. Relations between Faruq and the British High Commissioner Sir Miles Lampson (q.v.) were testy and crisis-ridden, while his views of the Sudanese Governor-General Stewart Symes (q.v.) were generally compatible. In 1942 Lampson surrounded the palace with tanks and called for the king to either abdicate or return to a Wafdist government, which they favored in the war years. In October 1944 Faruq again dismissed the Wafd government and replaced Prime Minister al-Nahhas with Prime Minster Ahmad Mahir, who was assassinated in February 1945. The inclusion of the Wafd once again in 1950 after a strong electoral victory only brought a greater sense of weakness to the king.

During the war and in the postwar years, the movement for Sudanese independence expanded rapidly. Since Faruq was the royal Egyptian head of the Anglo-Egyptian Condominium (q.v.) it was imagined that he might also be the king of the Sudan even in a postcolonial configuration. Indeed, 'Ali al-Mirghani of the Khatmiya (qq.v) sect in the Sudan was so fearful of his rival 'Abd al-Rahman al-Mahdi that he said, according one historian of the Sudan, that he would prefer having a real King Faruq to a "King" 'Abd al-Rahman!

Throughout his reign Faruq's flagrant personal indulgences, political waverings, and threats to break the Anglo-Egyptian accords of 1899 and

1936 exposed him to crises. Meanwhile American Secretary of State Dean Acheson felt that American interests would best be served by strengthening the king, and in early 1952 he proposed to have Faruq recognized as king of the Sudan. Apparently Acheson was oblivious to contemporary Sudanese and Egyptian sentiments and by the summer Cairo was subject to massive riots. In July 1952 the coup of the Free Officer's Movement overthrew Faruq, who was allowed to escape from Alexandria in his royal yacht. He died in exile in 1965.

Al-FASHER. West of the loose sand (*qoz*) and thorny forests of northwestern Kordofan (q.v.) lies al-Fasher, the provincial capital of northern Darfur (q.v.). Al-Fasher came to replace Kobbei (q.v.) to the northwest in the early eighteenth century at the southern end of the Forty Days Road (q.v.). Al-Fasher is situated in a wide valley that provides its supply of water. It is about two-day's camel ride to the east of Jabal Marra in generally open country, which, in normal times, provides sufficient water for rain-fed agriculture. The town lies amidst the territory of the Asirra section of the Hawazma people, but essentially the history of al-Fasher is a history of the Fur ruling class. In al-Fasher one will also find Baqqara (q.v.) from Kordofan and Zaghawa from Darfur (qq.v.).

The name "al-Fasher" means the courtyard in front of the royal palace, as one may also see in the case of its contemporary town of Sinnar (q.v.). The town grew around the palaces of the successive sultans of Darfur. With the passage of time the town itself became known as al-Fasher. Fur hegemony of Kobbei and al-Fasher, emerging in the sixteenth century, resulted in the city serving as a trade center with Egypt to the north, Sinnar to the east, and other Sahelian kingdoms in Chad and Nigeria to the west. Islam (q.v.) entered the region in the sixteenth century following the collapse of Christianity in Nubia (qq.v.). By the early seventeenth century the Islamic Keira Dynasty was established. However, the present town is traced more directly to Sultan 'Abd al-Rahman al-Rashid (1787–1802) during the last decade of the eighteenth century. That the sultan of Darfur was the reigning power is illustrated by a letter he received from Napoleon during the brief French period in Egypt when Napoleon sought the sultan's assistance in pursuing fleeing Mameluks. The English traveler W. G. Greene also reported on life in al-Fasher during the period 1793–1796, and Nubian and Danagla (qq.v.) people established their roots in al-Fasher during this same period. It was a heyday of early trans-Sahelian commerce in cloth, spices, salt, ivory, ebony, livestock, hardware, gum arabic, local handicrafts, and slaves.

Even the Turkish administration, which devastated and transformed the central Nile Valley, especially the Funj (q.v.) state, had little effect in Darfur. Al-Fasher was not brought under Khartoum's (q.v.) administration until October 1874, when the Ja'ali slaver and merchant Zubayr Rahma Mansur Pasha (q.v.) defeated the Fur army, killed the sultan, and occupied al-Fasher. It is not clear if Zubayr was serving the interests of the Turks or his own, but Darfur nominally became a Turkish province. Zubayr's control of al-Fasher was tenuous at best and his first concern was to fortify the town. This was accomplished on a hill just west of the present town, where brick walls, 3-feet thick and 200 feet on a side were constructed with gun emplacements in towers. Inside this wall was a fifteen-foot deep moat some ten feet across and itself surrounded by a palisade of thorns. Troops were garrisoned inside and outside of these fortifications.

Late in the Turkish administration of Darfur, Slatin Pasha (q.v.) was appointed as provincial governor, but this came to an end in November 1884 when, after the fall of el-Obeid (q.v.), he submitted to Mahdist rule and declared his conversion to Islam. Mahdist rule of the Sudan was somewhat more popular than that of the Turks, but the Fur and their Sultans had not lost their sense of history and independence. Such was the case in February 1889 when Khalifa 'Abdullahi (q.v.) had to send his troops to al-Fasher to put down a revolt led by the soldiers of Abu Jummayza, who had seized the town.

At the conclusion of the Mahdiya (q.v.), the British policy of Indirect Rule (q.v.) was applied to Darfur. This led to the revival of the Fur sultanate from 1898 to 1916; however, it was clear that there were two very different perspectives on who should be ruling Darfur. Fur Sultan 'Ali Dinar (q.v.) saw this as the recovery of the independence of Darfur, while the British perceived the sultan as a local instrument of their colonial rule. In early 1916 British troops under Hubert Huddleston (q.v.) assembled in el-Obeid and al-Nahud (q.v.) to prepare to crush 'Ali Dinar's steadfast assertion of his sovereignty.

'Ali Dinar did his best to prepare for the attack and even made "anti-aircraft towers" at his palace to get a clear shot at the light planes that the British employed in their assault. On 21 May 1916 'Ali Dinar fled al-Fasher to make his final stand elsewhere. The troops of Major Huddleston entered al-Fasher a short time later. Huddleston noted that the sultan's palace was a virtual "Alhambra" that put the Khalifa's house in Omdurman (q.v.) to shame. It was well-decorated with ponds, gardens, storerooms, arcades, out-buildings, and flowering trellises. The well-ordered and disciplined clerical staff of Sultan 'Ali Dinar soon had the town functioning once again, but now under British authority. In World War II, the small airbase at al-Fasher was important for American and British air supply missions to North Africa in the struggle against the Germans.

Al-Fasher continued its steady growth as more shops, government buildings, and a larger market appeared. As early as 1940 the population had reached a substantial 23,000. Poor roads to the east to al-Nahud and to the west to al-Geneina had been a problem, but by April 1959 the railway from Khartoum reached Nyala (q.v.) some 200 kilometers south of al-Fasher. Although this has improved transport to al-Fasher it has certainly helped the growth of Nyala even more. Until the 1980s al-Fasher was the largest town in Darfur; this distinction is now held by Nyala. At independence the population was about 28,100 and by 1969 it had reached 51,000. In 1983 it was put at 84,533. These statistics reveal steady population growth, but not a prodigious increase such as in the Three Towns (q.v.) or refugee-filled towns of eastern Sudan or Juba (q.v.).

FASHODA. This village in the southern Sudan (q.v.) on the White Nile, just downstream from the Sobat River, is a political capital for the Shilluk (q.v.). Fashoda was used as a Turco-Egyptian river post in an attempt to control the slave trade (q.v.). In 1898 a French expedition up the Congo River and across the southern Sudan was led by J.-B. Marchand (q.v.). He occupied Fashoda, laying claim to the Upper Nile for France. A major international crisis followed this "Fashoda Incident" when Anglo-Egyptian forces under H. H. Kitchener (q.v.) forced a French withdrawal. Marchand then took his troops eastward to the Abyssinian plateau and exited at Zaila on the Gulf of Aden. Ultimately French claims were withdrawn and the area became part of the Anglo-Egyptian Sudan (q.v.) in 1899. The modern name of Fashoda is Kodok.

FATIH AHMED 'ALI, GENERAL. *See* 'ALI, GENERAL FATIH AHMED.

FATIMA BINT JABIR. *See* AWLAD JABIR.

FEDDAN. A Sudanese unit of land area equal to 1.038 acres.

FEDERAL PARTY. A southern party formed in 1957–1958 by younger men dissatisfied with the Liberal Party (q.v.). It was founded by Ezboni

Mondiri (q.v.) and advocated a federal form of government. It ceased operation with the 1958 military coup.

FEKI. The Sudanese colloquial Arabic term for *faqih* (pl. *fuqaha'*), a Muslim legal scholar or religious teacher. The term was used to refer to a variety of Muslim figures, from local Qur'an teachers and sellers of amulets to the advisors of kings, and from scholars of Shari'a (q.v.) to the leaders of Sufi (q.v.) orders. Indicative of the union in Sudanese Islam (q.v.) between legal and mystical aspects of the religion is the plural form of *feki*, which is *fuqara'* (from *faqir*, meaning "mystic"). *Fekis* were instrumental in the spread of Islam and Sufism in the Sudan, residing along the Nile and as far west as Darfur (q.v.) from at least the seventeenth century. Some came to the Sudan from North Africa or the Middle East, having studied first at al-Azhar (q.v.) or Mecca; others were native-born teachers of Islam. Prominent *fekis* attracted students from far afield to their mosque-schools, and the communities that grew up around them eventually developed into towns. Others lived at the courts of the Sinnar and Keira (qq.v.) rulers, giving legal advice and frequently mediating conflicts. On occasion these *fekis* were given grants of land, exemption from taxes, or other privileges. Ironically, the Shari'a practices they helped to establish contributed to the dissolution of authority of the Sinnar rulers.

A *feki* was sometimes associated with unusual spiritual powers. After their deaths, many *fuqaha* came to be considered saints (*awliya'*, q.v.) and their tombs (*qubbas*, q.v.) became places of pilgrimage, thought to be endowed with supernatural powers. During the time of the Funj Sultanates (q.v.), *fuqaha* were closely associated with the spread of Islam and with giving legal and religious advice. An idea of the range of activity and influence of the *fuqaha* is given by the famous biographical dictionary, the *Tabaqat Wad Dayfallah* (q.v.). *See also* BARAKA.

FELLATA. This is a generic term in the central Sudan for Muslims of West African origin. In West Africa it has the more specific meaning of belonging to the Fulani or Fula (Atlantic subfamily of Niger-Congo languages). Large numbers of Fellata came to the Sudan as agricultural workers in the Gezira (q.v.) or as Muslim pilgrims gradually working their way to Mecca at least since the nineteenth century. In the early twentieth century these were instrumental to the agricultural operations and religious program of Sayid 'Abd al-Rahman al-Mahdi on Aba Island (qq.v.). Economic fortunes in the Gezira have also caused many Fellata to move to the Three Towns (q.v.). In some contexts, the term Fellata can be considered derogatory as most occupy low status, low-paying agricultural jobs.

FEMALE GENITAL MUTILIATION (FGM). Female genital mutilation has begun to replace the term "female circumcision" (q.v.) as a more accurate description of the procedure performed upon young girls in Sudan, other parts of the Nile Valley, northeastern Africa, and West Africa. However, in Sudanese Arabic and localized terminology the use of word "circumcision" (*tahur*) is still common. Three different forms of "circumcision" are recognized: 1) "simple" clitoridectomy, or the excision of the tip of the clitoris only; 2) modified excision, the removal of the clitoris and parts of the *labia majora* and *minora*; and 3) infibulation, excision of the clitoris and all of the *labia majora* and *minora*, leaving a smooth vulva and a small opening for the common flow of urine and menses. The latter, the so-called Pharaonic circumcision, is the most widely practiced type in Sudan. It is estimated that about 90 percent of northern Sudanese Muslim women are circumcised, believing that it is the proper measure to ensure their moral purity and cleanliness. It is clearly a rite of passage for Sudanese girls and the procedure rests largely in the hands of women, although it is a deeply traditional, pre-Islamic custom. FGM is not widely practiced among southern ethnic groups.

During the past decade an international campaign against FGM has focused on the violation of human rights (q.v.) involved in any form of circumcision. A ban or curtailing of FGM has been featured as part of many international human and women's rights agendas, such as the Vienna Human Rights conference in 1993 and the Beijing Women's Conference in 1995. Sudanese and Egyptian human rights organizations have spoken out against the practice and are actively campaigning against FGM. Official Islamic interpretation does not support the continuation of this pre-Islamic practice. Three of the four schools of Islamic jurisprudence opine that circumcision is recommended and not required. Only the Shafi'i school suggests that circumcision is preferred. Thus, Islamic interpretation may be viewed as neutral to the practice.

FILISTS. The Filist group was associated with the *qadi* Shaykh Ahmad al-Sayid al-Fil within the Graduates Club (q.v.) during the 1920s and 1930s. Sayid 'Ali al-Mirghani (q.v.) supported the group, which was in favor of gradual independence and cooperation with Egypt and was opposed to the Ansar-backed Shawqists (qq.v.) within the Graduates Club. Later Shaykh Ahmad al-Fil was among the publishers of the *Sawt al-Sudan* (Voice of the Sudan) newspaper, which supported the Khatmiya (q.v.) program.

FOLK RELIGION. Muslim folk religion is a form of religious practice observed and performed by the common people. It is deeply rooted in the culture, and it reflects the people's cosmological vision as distinct from orthodox Islam (q.v.), derived from the teaching of the Qur'an as well as the sayings and the traditions of the Prophet Muhammad. Myths, legends, and historical narratives exist to legitimize the folk practice of Islam and to provide it with an Islamic origin. The Sudanese cosmology recognizes Allah (God), His messenger, Prophet Muhammad, and the *Awliya* (the saints). It also encompasses aerial spirits, nature, the human world, and the underworld. Allah dominates and controls all of these categories. The Sudanese believe that the realities embraced in these categories are signs of Allah's existence. Their belief in these signs confirms their belief in Allah because the categories reflect Allah's omnipotence. [by Baqie Badawi Muhammad]

FOREIGN RELATIONS: INTERNATIONAL. Sudan's main foreign policy concerns at the time of independence were to preserve its sovereignty and develop economically. The political elites who made up its Foreign Service were naturally shaped by an anticolonial outlook and insistence on social and economic progress, and even before independence had addressed these concerns before the United Nations (q.v.) and the Arab League. Both public pressure and practicality argued for a stance of noninvolvement in the Cold War, and upon independence Sudan opened embassies in both Washington and Moscow, as well as four in Western Europe (Great Britain, France, Federal Republic of Germany, and Italy). Official declarations of neutrality notwithstanding, Sudan's main ties were to the West, with whom Sudan conducted most of its trade and from whom it received most of its foreign aid. Paramount among Sudan's trading partners was of course Britain, which in the first decade of independence supplied about one-third of Sudan's imports and purchased one-fifth of Sudan's exports. Other ties of a social nature cemented Sudan's bond to its former ruler, while both the Sudanese army and civil service were modeled on the British pattern.

Sudanese neutrality in the Cold War made for a difficult balancing act. During the first democratic period of 1956–1958, Sudan's government accepted economic assistance from the United States but not military aid under the U.S. Mutual Security Program. While the government approved of the American position in quelling the Suez crisis of 1956, large crowds protested U.S. Vice-President Richard Nixon's visit to Khartoum (q.v.) in 1957, and Sudan refused to sign the Eisenhower Doctrine offering protection to countries from Communist aggression. Meanwhile, Sudan accepted in principle the technical assistance offered by the Soviet Union, though almost nothing was done to implement cooperation agreements; rather, Sudan seemed to prefer cooperation with Yugoslavia as an East Bloc alternative to the USSR. The U.S. landing of troops in Lebanon in 1958 split Sudan's coalition government, but officially prompted only a noncommittal statement.

Ibrahim Abboud (q.v.) continued this approach when he took power in 1958. One of the first acts of his government was to recognize the People's Republic of China, though as late as 1960 no Sudanese embassy had been established in Beijing. Mainly the Sudan preferred to confine its international political activity to the UN, where it maintained a conservative posture. In matters of aid Sudan preferred international agencies to bilateral relations, hoping to avoid the political implications of technical and economic assistance. Throughout the 1950s and 1960s the UN sent scores of experts to Sudan to advise on matters of administration, development, education, agriculture (qq.v.), and forestry. Meanwhile Sudan's presence in other international bodies was understated. Sudan sent no delegates to the All-African People's Congresses of 1958 or 1960. Though it participated in the two Conferences of Independent African States those same years and joined the Organization of African Unity (OAU) in 1963, little came of this beyond rhetorical support for independence movements and African economic and cultural cooperation. At meetings of the Arab League, Sudan sought only to reconcile differences among member states and lessen the chances of regional conflict.

Sudan's foreign policy changed during the second parliamentary period of 1964–1969, as Middle Eastern and African issues came to dominate the national agenda. In 1965 Sudan severed its relations with Britain over Rhodesia's unilateral declaration of independence, restoring them in 1966. In 1967 Sudan again severed relations with Britain, and this time with the United States as well, in the wake of Israel's defeat of the Arabs in the June war. While relations with Britain, Sudan's most important trade partner, were restored in 1968, relations with the United States remained severed for five years. Meanwhile U.S. and Western support for Israel propelled Sudan into closer military and economic co-operation with the Soviet Union.

The coup that brought Ja'afar Nimeiri (q.v.) to power in 1969 seemed to herald a new era of close Sudanese-Soviet relations. Nimeiri's government appeared distinctly left leaning and contained members of the Sudanese Communist Party (SCP, q.v.), though Nimeiri acted quickly to disband all political parties, including the SCP. In 1970 the government officially recognized East Germany and Nimeiri embarked on trips to Eastern Europe, China, and North Korea. Trade with the East Bloc was subsequently enhanced and Sudan began to seek economic and military aid from the USSR, while political relations with the West steadily declined. However, a failed communist coup against Nimeiri in July 1971 radically reoriented Sudan's foreign relations. As Nimeiri purged his government of all leftists, relations with the East Bloc suffered while those with the West improved. Diplomatic relations were finally restored with Washington in 1972. Though the situation was complicated by continued U.S. support for Israel and by the 1973 assassination of the American ambassador to Khartoum by Palestinians, Nimeiri had decided on a strong bilateral relation with the United States that was to last throughout his regime. American economic and military aid to Sudan arrived steadily, while during the administration of President George Bush a program of biennial joint military exercises (dubbed "Operation Bright Star") was conducted, partly on Sudanese soil. Nimeiri was in Washington on a mission to secure more aid when he was deposed by the Sudanese military in April 1985.

The transitional government that took power after Nimeiri's ouster sought to return Sudan to the earlier nonaligned position. Issues of trade and economic aid, as well as the ongoing problem of civil war in the south, militated against any substantial change in foreign policy. Throughout the premiership of Sadiq al-Mahdi (q.v.) of 1986–1989 Washington continued to enjoy close relations and provide significant aid to Sudan.

The Islamist-backed coup of 'Umar Hasan al-Bashir (q.v.) in 1989 had the most significant effect on Sudanese foreign relations, effectively isolating Sudan from most of its former allies and donor nations. Immediately after the coup the United States terminated its development aid to Sudan, following an American law forbidding aid to a regime that has overthrown a democratically elected government. While the United States continued supplying humanitarian aid to the victims of drought and civil war through the Agency for International Development (AID), it met continued resistance from the Bashir government, which accused the United States of meddling in Sudanese internal affairs. Sudan's decision to support Iraq in the 1991 Gulf War had serious ramifications, as Washington temporarily closed its embassy in Khartoum and withdrew its diplomatic personnel. That same year, the Sudanese government freed five Palestinians who had been convicted in the 1988 terrorist slaying of five Britons in Khartoum, prompting Britain to break diplomatic relations and suspend several million dollars worth of grants and loans. Meanwhile, the twelve-member European Community chastised Sudan's failure to cooperate with international aid organizations, further isolating Sudan diplomatically.

Relations between Sudan and the West worsened throughout the 1990s. In January 1996 the UN Security Council voted to condemn Sudan for its apparent role in the failed assassination attempt on Egyptian President Hosni Mubarak in Addis Ababa in 1995. Three months later the Security Council voted sanctions against Sudan unless it released three suspects in the assassination attempt believed to be in Sudan. In February 1996 the United States again suspended its diplomatic presence in Khartoum, citing fears of terrorism, though a small diplomatic staff was allowed to return in late 1997. In November 1997 Washington announced new sanctions against Sudan in response to Khartoum's alleged sponsorship of terrorism and human rights (q.v.) abuses, including the revival of slavery (q.v.). These sanctions called for barring a wide range of financial and commercial transactions with Sudan as well as blocking all Sudanese assets in the United States. Given America's relatively small share of Sudan's trade ($70 million, including $20 million of imports from Sudan), these sanctions were understood to be mainly a statement of principle. Significantly, U.S. imports of gum arabic from Sudan were exempted from the sanctions. The nadir of U.S.-Sudanese relations occurred in August 1998 when the United States launched a missile strike against a suspected chemical weapons facility in Khartoum North (q.v.), destroying the al-Shifa pharmaceutical factory. Amid heated debate about the factory's actual purpose and Sudan's alleged ties to Saudi terrorist Usama Bin Laden, Britain also suspended diplomatic relations with Sudan, supporting the U.S. decision to bomb the facility.

In the absence of Western ties, Russia has tentatively sought increased cooperation with Sudan in the 1990s. Given Russia's own considerable economic problems, however, it is questionable what fruit such a relationship can bear. Meanwhile, as Sudan's civil war grinds on horribly and inexorably, the UN continues to appeal for aid for the war's victims, propping up an Operation Lifeline Sudan aid mission that the combatants are content to either manipulate or ignore.

FOREIGN RELATIONS: REGIONAL. Sudan, as Africa's largest nation bordering nine other countries, has important and complex foreign relations. The most important regional relationship is that with Egypt to the north. One may say that the thousands of years of political, military, and cultural ties have settled into a relationship of rivals. During the Mahdiya (q.v.), it was from Egypt that the Reconquest was organized and launched. The Umma Party (q.v.), arising from the Mahdiya, favored a greater degree of Sudanese autonomy, while the National Unionist Party (NUP, q.v.) looked for closer union with Egypt. Tensions between the countries have ranged from outright hostility to polite distancing to very close ties: an ancient and continuous theme in Sudanese foreign affairs.

After the 1969 coup d'etat by Ja'afar Nimeiri, the "Arab socialism" upon which it was based led to talk of a projected union among Sudan, Egypt, and Libya, but this was halted by the 1971 coup and countercoup of the Nimeiri regime. Thereafter a joint military pact with Egypt provided protection against future threats to the regime, a security arrangement that proved effective again in a 1976 coup attempt. The ties between Khartoum and Cairo proved strong when Sudan backed Anwar Sadat's unilateral peace agreement with Israel in 1979. Nimeiri's actions in the later years of his regime also found support in Egypt and, when he was ousted, he went into exile there. During the brief democratic period in 1985 calls for his extradition were unheeded by Cairo, and until Nimeiri's return to Sudan in 1999, Egypt hosted the former Sudanese leader.

Since the 'Umar al-Bashir regime came to power in 1989 Sudanese relations with Egypt have worsened. This ranges from expulsion of their respective ambassadors, to a welcome Egyptian reception for virtually all of the diverse opponents of the Bashir regime. Relations worsened even further when Egypt charged Sudan with stationing Iraqi missiles in the Red Sea Hills aimed at Aswan, while Sudan supported Iraq in the Gulf War. A Sudanese-backed assassination attempt against President Hosni Mubarak while he was visiting Addis Ababa in 1995 brought these tense relations to still lower levels. There are endless charges by Mubarak that the National Islamic Front (NIF, q.v.) is backing the Egyptian Islamist movement, *Jama'at Islamiya,* during its campaign of attacks against Egyptian targets such as tourists and police. Moreover, the deliberations over the Egyptian-Sudanese border territory of Halayeb have been terminated by Egyptian military occupation of this disputed triangle along the Red Sea. Finally, it is the failure of the Sudanese to hand over the plotters against Mubarak that has led to the international boycott supported by the United Nations (q.v.) against Sudan.

To the West the al-Bashir regime has proposed a unity agreement with Libya. However, the history of Sudanese-Libyan relations has been very unstable given the changing governments in Khartoum and Libyan pressures in Chad and neighboring Darfur (q.v.). During times of political and military disturbance in Chad, Sudan welcomed refugees from Chad and sometimes was the unofficial host of Chadian opposition movements. In May 1990 Chadian armed forces attacked al-Fasher (q.v.); later they attacked almost a score of nearby border villages in Sudan. These events spawned Zaghawa and Fur (qq.v.) rivalries that destabilized Khartoum. Closer ties between Chad and Sudan have resulted in Chadian authorities denying rear areas to the Sudanese Peoples Liberation Army (SPLA, q.v.) as long as Khartoum blocks Chadian opponents from operating in Sudanese territory. This understanding seems to have resulted in a generally peaceful relationship for most of the 1990s.

Present relations between Sudan and Libya are peaceful but stalemated, especially because Libya is termed another world "pariah nation" because of its refusal to cooperate with the prosecution of the terrorist bombing over Lockerbie, Scotland. Libya is also fearful of the NIF dominance in the Sudanese political arena.

To the East, a special place in Sudanese foreign affairs is held by Ethiopia and Eritrea, due to the continuing military engagement with Sudanese opposition forces, namely the SPLA, National Democratic Alliance (NDA, q.v.), and the Sudan Alliance Forces (SAF, q.v.) hosted in Eritrea and in the southern Sudan (q.v.). The former Sudanese embassy in Asmara has actually been transferred to the opposition. The independence of Eritrea from Ethiopia resulted in slowing the flow of refugees (q.v.) across the borders in both directions, which had been the case for decades. At least some Eritreans are still entering Sudan, and Sudanese opponents to the NIF gathered in Eritrea to carry out military attacks in 1997 and 1998 on the eastern border, including near Kassala and the Roseires Dam.

Ethiopia has hosted numerous peace conferences relating to the Sudanese civil war, including one in 1972 that resulted in the Addis Ababa Agreement (q.v.). In the late 1980s the Sudanese opposition groups, especially the SPLA, began to lose their rear base in Ethiopia with the fall of the Mengistu Haile Mariam regime. But in the later 1990s the

Ethiopian-SPLA relationship improved and the SPLA has been able to renew its military strategy along the Ethiopian-Sudanese border area and adjacent small towns.

Ties with Saudi Arabia, Kuwait, and the Emirates were quite strong in the 1970s, but these have weakened since Sudan supported Iraq in the Gulf War and hosted Usama bin Laden, the Saudi dissident Islamist, for five years under the 'Umar al-Bashir regime. Relations between Khartoum and Riyadh had been deeply embittered but improved slightly when bin Laden was expelled from Sudan in 1996.

To the South, Sudan gave some support to the rebels in Congo in 1964–1965. Sudan is well-known for its liberal refugee policy, which has made it a host for refugees from wars in Uganda and Zaire/Congo. However the political changes in Uganda and Congo in the 1990s put Uganda's Yoweri Museveni and Congo's Laurent Kabila in power after previous periods of violence and corruption. Initially Uganda and Congo had friendly relations with each other, especially when Sudan conducted military attacks against Uganda. The Ugandan government became supportive of SPLA leader John Garang (q.v.). In 1998 Congolese rebels opposed to Kabila engaged in a widespread military uprising in the North and East; in December 1998 they held the main eastern city of Kisangani to organize for a further advance down the Congo River. These rebels received Ugandan support, and it has been alleged that Ugandan troops actually have been present. Other rebel groups, especially Tutsi, are backed by Rwanda and Burundi and sought to seize the rich mining town of Lubumbashi in southeastern Congo. This remarkable turnabout caused Kabila to support Sudan until his death. Meanwhile Sudan is charged with backing the "Lord's Resistance Army" to make border attacks in northern Ugandan territory and Sudanese refugee camps in Uganda. Until 1998 the borderlands of Sudan with Congo, Uganda, Central African Republic, and Kenya were largely under SPLA control and the Sudanese government held only the main towns in the South.

Until 1998 Khartoum's relationship with Congo had been frozen during most of the al-Bashir regime. However, when the Kabila government suddenly faced its own domestic insurgency it sought to undermine the rebels operating from neighboring lands. In desperation to rid himself of this insurgency, Kabila renewed and improved his formerly cool relationship with Khartoum. This fence-mending was done with the understanding that Kabila would not allow SPLA forces to operate from Congolese territory if Khartoum blocked access to Congo by Congolese insurgents. This remarkable political turnabout also caused some additional movement of Congolese Azande refugees to travel to the southern Sudan where they have ethnic ties over the border.

One of the most ominous developments in Sudanese regional relations developed in the wake of the simultaneous bombings of the United States' embassies in Nairobi and Dar es Salaam in August 1998, which took more than 200 lives. Immediately there was talk of links to Osama bin Laden and other extremist Muslims, many of whom have ties to Egypt and Sudan. Later, an attack against the U.S. embassy in Kampala was thwarted. As a result the United States launched several Tomahawk cruise missiles against Sudan, targeting a "pharmaceutical" plant owned by bin Laden in Khartoum North that was alleged to have a role in making biological weapons for use in the civil war.

Thus, foreign relations with virtually all of Sudan's contiguous neighbors have deteriorated recently to the lowest point in the postcolonial period. With Eritrea, Ethiopia, and Uganda there are active military engagements; with Egypt and Libya a tense and vigilant standoff; and with Kenya, a sense of deep suspicion. *See also* ORGANIZATION OF AFRICAN UNITY.

FORTY DAYS ROAD. An ancient trade route across the Sahara linking Kordofen and Darfur (q.v.) and Egypt and known in Arabic as *Darb al-Arba'in*. It is unclear when this route was first opened, though in the seventeenth century the Keira (q.v.) state of Darfur used it to transport slaves (q.v.), ivory, tamarind, and ostrich feathers to Egypt, acquiring in return horses, saddles, weapons, and armor. Trade with Egypt across the Forty Days Road was a chief factor in expanding the authority and institutions of the Keira state. Beginning in the Darfur commercial center of Kobbei (q.v.), it stretched north some 1,787 kilometers through the oases of the Sahara to join the Nile below the town of Assyut, from whence it ran north to Cairo. The name is perhaps misleading, as travel on the route could take as little as two weeks for a fast courier or as much as two months for a large caravan. Despite the route's considerable difficulty it was generally free of banditry, due to the effective cooperation between Darfur and the Bedouin tribes of the Sahara, and hence it was often preferred over the quicker riverine route. The height of trade along the Forty Days Road was reached in the mid-nineteenth century, after which time Nubian merchants began to dominate the trade in slaves and ivory. Trade continued sporadically thereafter, dwindling to insignificance by the end of the century.

FREE NEGROES ORGANIZATION. *See* GABOUSH, PHILLIP ABBAS.

FRONT OF PROFESSIONAL ORGANIZATIONS. An alliance of various groups formed in late 1964 to oppose the Ibrahim Abboud (q.v.) regime. It brought together student and faculty groups with labor unions, peasant representatives, and professional associations like the Sudan Bar Association. It played a significant role in the 1964 October Revolution (q.v.) and was a major force in the transition government of 1964–1965. It encouraged a broader role for women in politics and was closely aligned with the Sudanese Communist Party (q.v.). Popular support for the Front gradually declined as the older parties were reorganized and as public opinion became weary and suspicious of the Front's radical pronouncements. By the 1965 elections the Front had basically broken up into its component parts.

FUAD, KING AHMAD (1868–1936). This king of Egypt ruled from 1917 to 1936, that is during the heyday of imperialism under Condominium (q.v.) rule. Although he was on the throne at the time of the 1924 assassination of Governor-General Lee Stack and of the White Flag revolt (qq.v.), it was mainly after his death under the rule of King Faruq (q.v.) that relations between Egypt and Great Britain deteriorated and Sudanese nationalists began the move for independence. His chief concerns in the mid-1930s were to balance the fluctuating influence of the Wafd party in Egypt and the development of the Sidqi-Bevin Protocol and the Anglo-Egyptian Treaty of 1936 (qq.v.). Indeed much of this negotiation had taken place before his death, but was signed by his son King Faruq when he assumed the throne.

FUNJ SULTANATE OF SINNAR. Following the collapse of the last Christian kingdom at Soba in 1504, a new locus of power in the Sudan was formed. At first the capital shifted from village to village but by the mid-seventeenth century it became situated permanently at Sinnar (q.v.) on the Blue Nile. The ethnic origin of the Funj people is still undetermined, but they were likely derived from Hamaj peoples along the Blue Nile in association with Nubian holymen. The initial Unsab ruling lineage practiced matrilineal descent; this continued until the first decades of the eighteenth century when it was replaced by Arabic record-keeping and patrilineal descent. The traditional founder was Amara Dunqas (1504–1534, q.v.) who was victorious at Soba. The line of direct descent from Amara was broken in 1718 when the Funj nobility deposed Sultan Unsa III.

The Funj Sultanates represented a loose federation of local rulers from Sinnar to Upper Nubia, on the Blue Nile and on the Nile proper. Funj society was structured around a ruling sultan, his religious and political advisors, his bureaucracy of royal staff, soldiers and bodyguards, judges, land surveyors, and tax-collectors. The society was built around agricultural and livestock production, a very substantial slave economy, and a variety of crafts. It was divided into social classes of royalty and their supporters, groups of nobility and provincial authorities, as well as commoners and slaves (q.v.). An important federated group was the 'Abdallab at Qarri, north of Khartoum North (qq.v.). Funj political culture was mixed with a growing Islamic influence over pre-Islamic practices. Thus, the Funj era was a time of increasing Islamization of central Sudanese society.

The Funj were blocked from eastward spread by Christian Ethiopia, while it tolerated the presence of Christian communities stranded in the northern Sudan. To the south, Nilotic and Azande (qq.v.) populations were pushing northward and thereby blocked further Funj expansion southward. To the west there was the Sultanate of Darfur (q.v.). Limited in these ways, the Funj existed under the shadow of Ottoman rule in Egypt that began in 1517.

The Funj sultans reached a peak of power under Badi II Abu Diqn (1644–1681, q.v.) and then faced growing loss of control over vassal princes. At the time of Badi II, Sinnar boasted a palace five-stories tall, a wide plaza (*fashir*), and a huge city wall penetrated by nine guarded gates. Badi IV (1724–1762) faced many challenges to his rule such as the incursion of the Ethiopians in 1744–1745 and the battles of Qihayf and Shamqata in 1747. Sultan Badi IV steadily lost control and was "rescued" from military defeats by Muhammad Abu Likaylik (1716–1774, q.v.). Badi IV finally lost control of the state in 1761 when the powerful and experienced military regent, Abu Likaylik, became the effective ruler and kingmaker. From 1761 until 1821, his people, the Hamaj (q.v.) or "riff-raff," of Fazughli near the Ethiopian border ruled through puppet sultans. In 1772 the Scottish explorer James Bruce (q.v.) visited the central Sudan and Sinnar and reported his observations of the Funj in a fascinating journal of the time.

The final years of the sultanate were filled with revolts and civil wars, which opened the way for the Turco-Egyptian (q.v.) conquest. In 1785 Sultan Adlan II revolted against the followers of Abu Likaylik but was put down. From 1803 to 1809 the rule of the Hamaj regents and their puppet sultans steadily eroded. Thus in 1820, tempted by an easy victory, the Ottoman Egyptians under Muhammad 'Ali (q.v.) sent a military force up the Nile to conquer the Sudan and bring in booty of gold, livestock, and captives to be turned into servants and soldiers. From 1820 to 1822 the Turks fought their way to Sinnar, which readily capitulated and brought an end to Funj rule. Soon after, the Turco-Egyptian administration moved from Sinnar to Khartoum (q.v.). *See also* ALWA; CHRISTIANITY IN NUBIA; AL-FASHER; LIST OF FUNJ SULTANS IN APPENDIX.

FUR. The Fur and their ancestors have long occupied the territory at the southern end of the trans-Saharan Forty Days Road (q.v.), particularly the area around Jebel Marra. This strategic position gave them considerable influence at the eastern end of the Sahel with its east-west trade. Among the earliest inhabitants of this "realm of the Fur" or *Darfur* (q.v.) were the Daju (q.v.) with whom the Fur share membership in the eastern Sudanic language family. However, the Fur are distinguished in some respects and thus qualify as the solitary members of their unique language stock. Although their history goes back to relations with dynastic history, the written record begins with their rule over the Daju in perhaps the fifteenth century. Arabic probably reached them at about this time through contact with Arabized Nubians known as Tungur (q.v.). *See also* 'ALI DINAR; AL-FASHER; FUR SULTANATE; NYALA.

FUR SULTANATE (1650–1916). Western Sudanese kingdom that was contemporaneous with the Funj sultanate (q.v.), established by a powerful branch of the Fur (q.v.) known as the Kunjara. Like the Funj, the Fur are a composite group, historically comprised from northern Nubians, southern "Negroes," and Arabic-speaking groups from the North and West. Its first great ruler was Sulayman Solong (q.v.), who established the Fur sultanate in the seventeenth century in a territory around Jebel Marra that came to be known as *Darfur* (q.v., "realm of the Fur"). Under Sulayman's brother, Musabba, Kordofan (q.v.) became a client state, but this was temporarily ruled by the Funj in the eighteenth century.

The ruling Fur dynasties controlled territory almost to the confluence of the Niles, and west as far as the caravan trade deep into Chad. The basic economy of the state relied upon its strategic position along caravan routes that crossed the sultanate from Wadai and Bornu to the west; from southern Kordofan and Bahr al-Ghazal (q.v.) from whence came ivory and slaves (q.v.) as well as gum arabic, ostrich feathers, and honey that were traded to the east; and to the north along the Forty Days Road (q.v.)

that connected al-Fasher (q.v.) to Egypt. Merchants brought back cloth, gold, silk, and manufactured items. The sultan's personal wealth derived from this trade, on which he levied a 10 percent tax.

The Fur sultanate was committed to the spread of Islam (q.v.) throughout the territory under its rule, and by the end of the eighteenth century, only southern Kordofan had not converted. The Sultanate promoted the construction of mosques and supported religious teachers who applied Shari'a (q.v.) personal law. The number of advanced students that Darfur sent to al-Azhar University (q.v.) in Cairo was so great that they were housed in a special section of the university known as the Darfur cloister.

The Fur government was more centralized than that of the Funj, and the sultan exerted absolute authority. The first capital was at Tagra and later was established at al-Fasher (q.v.). A centralized bureaucracy developed to aid the sultan with a *vizir*, council of state, system of taxation, and regulation of foreign affairs. This system remained in effect until the conquest of Darfur by the Turco-Egyptian (q.v.) invasion after 1821. Later the Darfur state rose against Khedival rule while Charles Gordon (q.v.) was governor-general of the Sudan from 1877 to 1879. This pattern of resistance to foreign domination continued throughout the nineteenth century and well into the twentieth-century colonial period, when the Sudan government formally recognized Darfur as an independent sultanate. The last sultan of Darfur, 'Ali Dinar (reg. 1898–1916, q.v.), was conquered by the British after an attempt to resist Anglo-Egyptian control.

"FUZZY-WUZZY." A somewhat pejorative name for the Beja (q.v.) people of the eastern Sudan, being a reference to their hairstyle. The term was popularized in the writing of Rudyard Kipling. The Beja's fighting ability during the Mahdiya (q.v.) inspired Kipling, especially when they "broke the British square" at the Battle of Tamai in 1884. This term was also used in the 1939 British film *The Four Feathers*, which described the personal lives of four British soldiers fighting in the eastern Sudan.

– G –

GABOUSH, REVEREND PHILLIP ABBAS (ca. 1910–). Nuba (q.v.) politician and revolutionary. Reverend Gaboush was an Episcopal priest, who became a leading figure in the Episcopal Church of Sudan. As a fiery orator not known to mince words, his political career combined the strength of religious conviction with a devotion to the struggles of the Nuba Mountains people over four decades, from the 1960s to 1990s.

Rev. Gaboush was a leader in the General Union of Nubas (GUN, q.v.) and was elected to Parliament in 1965, when GUN won all of the constituencies in the Nuba Mountains in the 1965 elections. He advocated regional autonomy for non-Arabs in the northern Sudan and organized the secret Free Negroes Organization in 1967. He then created the United Front for the Liberation of the African Sudan in 1969 and planned a coup that was preempted by the 1969 May Revolution (q.v.). His concept of "Black Power" and non-Arab autonomy in the North received little public support and was ignored by southern activists. GUN was renamed the Sudan National Party in 1985 and continued its electoral successes. Rev. Gaboush organized the Nuba in the Khartoum (q.v.) outlying districts in the 1986 electoral campaign and won the Hajj Yusuf constituency.

During the visit of the Archbishop of Canterbury, Dr. George Carey, in 1995 Rev. Gaboush was detained by the National Islamic Front (NIF, q.v.) government and reportedly tortured in one of the government's notorious "ghost houses," though a frail man in his eighties. He remains the most respected and prominent leader of national stature from the Nuba Mountains.

GARANG, ENOCH MADENG DE (ca. 1936–?). Southern journalist and political leader. He was a theology student and Presbyterian church official who became the director of the London-based Southern Sudan Association (q.v.) and edited its journal, *Grass Curtain*. He had ties with the Southern Sudan Liberation Movement (q.v.) and was a member of the southern delegation at the Addis Ababa talks. After the 1972 Addis Ababa Agreement (q.v.) he held a number of posts in the Southern Region High Executive Committee.

GARANG DE MABIOR, JOHN (1945–). Founder and leader of the Sudanese Peoples Liberation Army/Movement (SPLA/SPLM, qq.v.) in July 1983, after civil war reignited following the failure of the Addis Ababa Agreement (q.v.). While the SPLA may be considered a descendant of the Anya-Nya II (q.v.), the SPLM is projected as a national rather than regional movement.

Garang is from the hamlet of Wagkulei of the Bor branch of the Dinka (q.v.) people, the most numerous of southern Sudanese. Garang was only nine when his father died and his mother passed away when he was eleven, but he continued his primary school in southern Sudan (q.v.). He was able to travel overland to Tanzania to attend high school where he met Uganda's future President Yoweri Museveni as a fellow classmate. From there he went to the United States to gain his B.S. degree from Grinnell College in 1971. In 1970 he joined the Anya-Nya (q.v.), which was later incorporated into the Sudanese armed forces after the Addis Ababa Agreement of 1972 (q.v.), placing General Joseph Lagu (q.v.) in top southern leadership. Lagu made the twenty-six-year-old Garang his chief aide and, with new relations between North and South, Garang entered the Sudanese Armed Forces as a captain. Returning to the United States in 1974, Garang took a course in military command training at Fort Benning, Georgia. Following that he enrolled in a doctoral program in economics at Iowa State University from 1977 to 1981, where he received his Ph.D. and focused his research on the question of the economic development of the South. Garang's unique combination of formal military and economics training found him teaching at the University of Khartoum (q.v.) and at the Khartoum military school as Ja'afar al-Nimeiri's (q.v.) political crises were mounting. When the 1983 mutinies of Kerubino Kwanyin and William Nyuon Bany (qq.v.) broke out in the South, Garang had already reached the rank of colonel in the Sudanese Armed Forces. In May 1983 Nimeiri sent Garang to Bor in the South to put down these revolts; instead, he joined the revolt and soon came to dominate southern politics as the leader of the SPLA. He came to full national and international attention after the 1985 coup overthrew the Nimeiri regime. Garang refused to negotiate with the Transitional Military Council (TMC) government until the army returned to its barracks. The SPLM program envisioned by him was to go far beyond the secessionist Anya-Nya movement to create a national liberation movement ensuring economic development for all of the poorer regions of Sudan. Another central issue was the abolition of Islamic law (q.v.) and revoking of practices imposed by Nimeiri and maintained by the governments of Sadiq al-Mahdi and 'Umar Hasan al-Bashir (qq.v.). The SPLM considers that the ethnic and religious diversity of Sudan requires a secular national law.

Since 1990 the SPLA has been broadly successful on the military front in the South, as government troops no longer control the rural areas and are confined to provincial capitals currently under siege. Efforts continue to expand the war to southern Darfur and Kordofan (qq.v.), but these have not been so successful on the political front. There are charges and counter charges by both sides regarding atrocities, human rights (q.v.)

violations, and interference with food relief shipments. Despite various attempts by Sudanese political groups, no serious peace talks are underway to negotiate an end to the hostilities. Moreover new fighting broke out after the SPLA split in Nasir on 28 August 1991, shortly after the movement fell into disarray with the fall of Mengistu Haile Mariam in Ethiopia where the SPLA was based.

Open hostilities emerged in October 1991 between these factions. Former SPLA leaders such as Riek Machar, Lam Akol, William Nyuon Bany, Kerubino Kwanyin Bol (qq.v.), and Gordon Kong Col all went different ways after this split, including collaboration with the National Islamic Front (NIF, q.v.) regime in Khartoum. The SPLA-United faction and the Southern Sudan Independence Movement (SSIM) are but two of the groups opposed to Garang's SPLA-Mainstream. The SPLA's battles with internal divisions have been as challenging as the military and political engagement with the forces of Khartoum. However, since the SPLA's "New Sudan" conference in 1994, Garang has been able to maintain his leadership position because of the death of some rivals (Joseph Oduho, William Bany, and Arok Thon Arok) and the side-switching of others (Lam Akol and Riek Machar). Garang's position within the National Democratic Alliance (NDA, q.v.) has continued since 1995, when he was placed in command of the NDA opposition military forces in Ethiopia and Eritrea.

GARANG, JOSEPH (ca. 1930–1971). Southern lawyer, intellectual, and political leader. He held an unusual position as a southern member of the Sudanese Communist Party (SCP, q.v.) and was appointed to cabinet posts during the early years of the Ja'afar al-Nimeiri (q.v.) government, especially minister for southern affairs (1969–1971). The Ministry published the *Nile Mirror,* an English-language weekly concerned with national and southern issues. One of his publications, *The Dilemma of the Southern Intellectual*, was broadly influential and debated.

Garang was central in the drafting of the 9 June 1969 Declaration of Regional Autonomy, which gave rise to a model of negotiated settlement of civil war that was finally achieved with the Addis Ababa Agreement in 1972 (q.v.). He was hanged in Kober Prison in July 1971 for alleged complicity in an attempt to overthrow the Nimeiri regime.

GATKUOTH GUAL, PETER (ca. 1939–1992). One of the most distinguished southern Sudanese political leaders, he was a former president of the High Executive Council for the Autonomous Government of

Southern Sudan from 1979 to 1981. He had previously served the Ja'afar al-Nimeiri (q.v.) government, while it operated in the spirit of the Addis Ababa Agreement of 1972 (q.v.), as vice-president, and as minister of finance and economic planning. He was an overseer of the 1980 elections for the third regional assembly and among the first southerners to report about Sudan's considerable oil finds. When a political settlement was being discussed in 1984 in the wake of renewed fighting, Gatkuoth's name was proposed for governor of Upper Nile province (q.v.) under a federal plan. However, this proposal was derailed by the popular uprising that overthrew Nimeiri in 1985.

After the 1989 coup by 'Umar al-Bashir (q.v.), Gatkuoth was detained in Khartoum (q.v.) by the new regime until 1990, when he left Sudan. He died in London of a brain hemorrhage after suffering a stroke.

GEDAREF. Gedaref, or at least the region including some five villages, was identifiable in the 1820s. Turkish reports in 1824 noted a famine and smallpox epidemic there. Occasionally Gedaref was used as a staging area for slave (q.v.) raids to the southeast, but essentially the town of today did not really emerge until after the British occupation. Gedaref was garrisoned in 1884 with 200 men but fell to the Mahdists in April of that year. Like Kassala (q.v.), Gedaref was populated by a mix of Arab (q.v.) peoples such as the Shukriya (q.v.) and Dubaniya, as well as Hadendowa and Beni Amer.

With Kassala brought under British control in 1897, a military column could venture to Gedaref in 1898 as part of the reconquest campaign. In 1913 the British laid out a surveyed town plan with brick buildings, small shops, and a civil hospital to follow. A raised earthen road made it possible to reach Gedaref in the rainy season. The railway from Kassala to Sinnar (q.v.) passed through Gedaref in 1928 and agricultural production increased with this improved capacity for rail export. During World War II the Mechanized Crop Production Scheme was launched in the adjoining Ghadambaliya Plains. The former market town and military base found new economic life in crops of *durra*, sesame, and other grains. The regional productivity is based in part upon the wide shallow valley, which operates as a catchment basin for rain-fed agriculture. The population statistics for Gedaref are quite phenomenal if one considers its insignificance a century ago. Even by the time of independence this was only a small town of 17,852; by 1964 it jumped to 45,491 and in 1969 it lurched to 70,335 with rates of annual urban growth at 9 to 10 percent. Yet more amazing growth was still ahead when Gedaref leapt to 119,000 in 1983 and to an estimated 220,000 in a 1985 study. This growth in the late 1980s is overwhelmingly attributed to the massive influx of refugees (q.v.) from the various wars and famines (q.v.) within Ethiopia and the southern Sudan. *See also* AGRICULTURE.

AL-GENEINA. Al-Geneina is a border town in Darfur (q.v.) at the western Sudanese frontier with Chad. The "garden" from which its name is derived once represented the residence of the sultan of Massalit who had been installed under the British policy of Indirect Rule (q.v.). Nominally the sultan ruled this territory, which straddled both Chad and Sudan.

Although there is no rail connection to Geneina there is a rough road to al-Fasher (q.v.), which carries considerable traffic in goods and pilgrims. Because of war in Chad, the population of al-Geneina has grown far more than one might expect for a modest border town. At independence its population was 12,300 and by 1969 it had reached 27,800, but in the most recent census in 1983 it suddenly jumped to a substantial 55,996.

GENERAL UNION OF NUBAS (GUN). An organization representing the interests of the Nuba (q.v.) people and southern Kordofan (q.v.). It contested elections and won a few parliamentary seats in the 1960s, when it was led by Phillip Abbas Gaboush (q.v.).

GESSI, ROMOLO (1831–1881). This Italian military officer and multilingual interpreter also held British nationality and served in the Khedival administration of the Sudan during Charles Gordon's (q.v.) first administration as governor-general from 1877 to 1879. Gessi and Gordon were long-standing friends from earlier travels and experiences, and it was natural that the two should serve together in the southern Sudan (q.v.) under the authority of the Khedive. Gessi prided himself on his benevolent rule of Equatoria and Bahr al-Ghazal (qq.v.) in the late 1870s and early 1880s and his effort to suppress the slave trade (q.v.) and liberate thousands of slaves to become soldiers in his army there. Gessi also increased the regional exports of rubber and ivory.

In 1879 the slave trader Sulayman al-Zubayr (son of the notorious slave trader Zubayr Pasha, q.v.) sought to resume his slave raids in Bahr al-Ghazal. In March 1879 Gordon visited the south and sent Gessi to capture Sulayman in June. After protracted pursuit Gessi succeeded; Sulayman and ten collaborators were shot, while Gordon confiscated the possessions of the Zubayr family. Meanwhile Khedive Isma'il (q.v.) had been replaced by Khedive Tewfik (q.v.) in June, and the new Khedive was not pleased with Gessi and Gordon, who was replaced as the governor-general of the Sudan in December 1879 by the slave trader Raouf Pasha. Gessi's territory and soldiers were reduced and he could no longer retain his working relationship with Khartoum under Raouf Pasha. The political situation in the Sudan deteriorated rapidly from 1881 to 1882, when Raouf Pasha was replaced. By 1883 the forces of the Mahdi (q.v.) had positioned themselves to take control of the entire territory.

Gessi resigned in September 1880 and thought to do some mapping of the Bahr al-Ghazal River and the White Nile on his boat the *Saphia*. Instead, his craft was marooned in the vast *sudd* (q.v.) swamp during the dry season. At least 400 of his 600 soldiers and travelers gradually died of starvation. Although Gessi was still alive when he reached Khartoum (q.v.) in January 1881, he died during his evacuation to Suez.

THE GEZIRA. The land between the White and Blue Niles, whose name in Arabic means "island" or "peninsula." At the north end of the Gezira are the Three Towns (q.v.), while on the Blue Nile the main towns are Wad Medani and Sinnar (qq.v.) and on the White Nile the main town is Kosti (q.v.). The Gezira is the agricultural heartland of Sudan; in particular, it produces crops of cotton and sugar cane. While the Gezira has great potential, recent years have seen crop failures and waste, poor transport, agricultural labor shortages, and a general failure to become the "bread basket of the Arab World" as had been prophesied. The spiritual home of Mahdism on Aba Island (qq.v.) in the White Nile is also linked to the agricultural productivity of the Gezira Scheme (q.v.).

GEZIRA SCHEME. A major agricultural project in the Gezira (q.v.) region, which was planned before World War I but only went into full operation in the 1920s. It was originally a joint venture between a private company (the Sudan Plantations Syndicate), the Sudanese government, and local farmers. Its cotton production became a mainstay of the Sudanese colonial economy. After independence the role of the private company was taken over by the government. The area within the Scheme has been used as a model by other African governments impressed by its early success. *See also* AGRICULTURE; HUNT, S. J. LEIGH.

GEZIRA TENANTS UNION. This association was created in 1953 when the representative council for tenants in the Gezira Scheme (q.v.) was recognized as a trade union. The Union was one of the largest and best organized economic interest groups in Sudan. It became involved in national politics, usually in alliance with the more radical parties. Its president was al-Amin Muhammad al-Amin, a member of the Sudanese Communist Party (q.v.) and occasional cabinet member who led the Union to an important role in the 1964 October Revolution (q.v.). After the 1969 May Revolution (q.v.), the Union was subordinated under the Sudanese Socialist Union (q.v.), although the tenants remained active.

GHULAMALLAH IBN 'AYID. *See* AWLAD JABIR.

GILLAN, SIR ANGUS. A Scottish-born member of the Sudan Political Service (q.v.) who served as governor of Kordofan province (q.v.) from 1928 to 1933 and civil secretary from 1934 to 1939 (i.e., under Governor-General Stewart Symes [q.v.]). Were it not for his self-effacing administrative style he may have been elevated to the governor-general position himself. His period as civil secretary might be described as the end of the heyday of colonialism in a still tradition-dominated Sudan. As Symes and Gillan were concluding their terms in office, the nature of ruling Sudan was changing with increasing nationalist agitation and new elite formation, especially in the form of the nascent Graduates Congress (q.v.).

AL-GIZOULI, DAFALLA. Civilian prime minister during the one-year period of the Transitional Military Council (1985–1986), after the overthrow of the Ja'afar al-Nimeiri (q.v.) government. During his tenure he emphasized that a negotiated solution to the civil war was the most critical issue facing the future of Sudan.

AL-GIZOULI, SHAYKH MOHAMMED. Last grand qadi of the Shari'a (q.v.) courts in Sudan, serving from 1972 to 1979. Thereafter, the Civil and Shari'a courts were unified into a single system with a single chief justice. Among his unique achievements was the appointment of four women justices to the Shari'a courts, and a number of important reforms in the practice of Muslim marriage and divorce during his term. *See also* ISLAMIC LAW REFORM.

GLADSTONE, WILLIAM EWART (1809–1898). Gladstone was the British prime minister during the last days of Khedival rule in the Sudan (1868–1874, 1880–1885, 1886, 1892–1894). Though he should have recognized that the British position was deteriorating by the fate of Romolo Gessi (q.v.) in 1881 and the disastrous Hicks Pasha (q.v.) expedition in 1883, Gladstone persisted in thinking that the military situation in the Sudan was sustainable. The British and Turkish position only weakened further, and Gladstone was still prime minister at the time of the 1884–1885 siege of Khartoum under Charles Gordon (qq.v.). It was popularly believed that Gladstone's cautious (or hesitating) support in mounting the Khartoum relief expedition by Garnet Wolseley (q.v.)— only in August 1884—was responsible for Gordon's death in January 1885. Gladstone resigned shortly thereafter, though served twice more thereafter.

GONDOKORO. *See* JUBA.

GORDON, CHARLES (1833–1885). British soldier and adventurer of Scottish ancestry. After military service in the Anglo-Chinese war in 1860, and especially for his role in crushing the Taiping Rebellion (1863–1864), Gordon earned his nickname "Chinese" Gordon. He came to the Sudan in 1873 as governor of Equatoria (q.v.) for the Khedival authority of the Turco-Egyptian (q.v.) regime. He replaced the flamboyant hunter-explorer Samuel Baker (q.v.) in Equatoria, where his assignment was to establish a trade bridge to the lacustrine kingdoms and to suppress the local slave trade (q.v.). He resigned in 1876 without having put in place an effective local government or having achieved either objective.

Gordon was replaced in Equatoria by the remarkable Emin Pasha (q.v.), who carried on with the tasks until isolated by the rising force of Mahdism (q.v.). Meanwhile Gordon assumed the new position of governor-general of the Sudan (1877–1879), again with serious problems, including a much-needed settlement of the war with Ethiopia, a revolt in Darfur (q.v.) against Khedival rule, and the control of Bahr al-Ghazal (q.v.), which was in the hands of the son of the infamous slaver Zubayr Pasha (q.v).

Gordon finally resigned from this position in 1880. By 1882 he was engaged in the war with the Sotho in South Africa. He was about to start colonial military service in the Belgian Congo in 1883 when the British began to face the substantial threat of the Mahdist revolt with the annihilation of the British force under Hicks Pasha (q.v.). In desperation, the British recalled their loyal if somewhat idiosyncratic colonial soldier back to the Sudan to withdraw the remnants of the Turco-Egyptian administration. In early 1884 Gordon returned to Khartoum (q.v.) under a steadily tightening siege by the growing force of Mahdist soldiers.

An evangelical Christian, Gordon was nevertheless an ecumenical worshipper in England and in the Sudan; the growing strength of the Mahdist forces hence represented a profound religious as well as political challenge to him. With Khartoum surrounded by the end of 1884, British reinforcements from Egypt became critical to the survival of Gordon as well as foreign interests in the Sudan. Refusing surrender or mercy from the Mahdi, Gordon was killed on 26 January 1885 when the Mahdist forces captured Khartoum. Relief forces arrived just days later, and the death of Gordon set off a wave of popular protest against the government of William Gladstone (q.v.) in England, joined even by Queen Victoria herself.

The dynamic personality and extensive military and political career of Gordon captured the imagination of the British public, and he has been the subject of a large and often romanticized body of literature. A centenary commemoration was held in January 1985 at St. Paul's Cathedral in London, attended by many who had served in the Sudan Political Service (q.v.) as well as participants from Gordon Memorial College (q.v.).

GORDON MEMORIAL COLLEGE. A colonial educational institution in Khartoum (q.v.) that was established by a large public subscription in Great Britain, raised by General Horatio Kitchener (q.v.) who became its first president. The school opened in 1902 and was an important part of the educational system, being both a major training center for the government services as well as the breeding ground for a class of educated Sudanese nationalists. The college program developed and became the core of the University College of Khartoum, which was created in 1951 and later became the University of Khartoum (q.v.).

GRADUATES CLUB. This "Old Boys" club for Gordon Memorial College (q.v.) was formed in 1918. It provided a forum for discussion among the educated Sudanese and was a focus for early factional disputes, especially between the Filists and Shawqists (qq.v.). Its political functions passed to the important nationalist forum known as the Graduates Congress (q.v.).

GRADUATES (GENERAL) CONGRESS. The early nationalist organization in the Sudan that was built upon earlier traditions of the Graduates Club (q.v.) and discussion groups like the Abu Rauf group in Wad Medani (qq.v.). Most had their own histories of merger and division over political issues in the first two decades of the twentieth century. One of the best examples was the Filist and Shawqist factions (qq.v.).

The Graduates Congress was formed in February 1938 by people from different groups among the educated classes in the Sudan. By 1939 it had a monthly publication, *al-Mu'tamar* (The Congress). Early leaders included Isma'il al-Azhari, Muhammad Ahmad Mahjub, and Ahmad Kheir (qq.v.). It sought independence but soon split into more militant nationalist groups supporting Nile Valley unity with Egypt, and those supporting a separate, independent Sudan.

The Congress faced a basic contradiction that it never fully overcame: Its members were being trained for civil and political service under a colonialism to which they owed their loyalty, while at the same time this was the centerpiece for their discussion of self-government and independence, at least among northerners. In the early 1940s members of the Graduates Congress advanced in the first experiments at Sudanization of the civil service in the midst of World War II. The British anxiously rejected a Congress memorandum asking for self-rule in 1942. This hastened an open split between various factions within the Congress, including now-crystallized Ansar, Khatmiya, and Ashigga (qq.v.) groups, as well as the centrist Committee of Fifteen and the grassroots Committee of Sixty. By 1944 these groups and factions became the embryonic secular political parties of the Sudan. Not surprisingly, the first Sudanese prime minister, Isma'il al-Azhari (q.v.), had been the president of the Omdurman Graduates Club, and his faction in the Graduates Congress had been in ascendancy following the 1945 Congress elections through the late 1940s until independence was granted. At this time Ansar influence was most strongly held by the Advisory Council of the Northern Sudan and not in the Congress. After the war the Congress organization was generally under the control of the supporters of Nile Valley unity and behaved as one of many Sudanese political organizations. By 1950 the British considered banning the Congress, but it was too late and it became a part of the National Unionist Party (q.v.) in 1952, when the Congress was formally dissolved.

GRANT, JAMES. *See* BURTON, RICHARD; SPEKE, JOHN.

GRASS CURTAIN. *See* GARANG, ENOCH; SOUTHERN SUDAN ASSOCIATION.

GREEKS. As one might imagine, the presence of Greeks in the Nile Valley, like that of other Mediterranean peoples, is of great antiquity. Certainly Greek people and their civilization had an important influence on ancient Nubia (q.v.). In more recent times Greeks were to be found among the foreign merchant community in Sinnar (q.v.) in the late seventeenth century. There they traded with the Funj (q.v.) state among a community that included Jews, Armenians (qq.v.), Egyptians, Arabs, Ethiopians, and Turks. Under Turco-Egyptian (q.v.) rule the number of Greeks in the Sudan increased considerably, and a substantial Greek community is said to have resided in Khartoum (q.v.) and the provincial towns. El-Obeid (q.v.) and Bara in Kordofan (q.v.) in particular had large and stable Greek populations in the nineteenth century, as did some of the towns on the Nile. While most engaged in commerce, Greeks were also to be found among the Turco-Egyptian military and government. Gheorghios Douloghlu served for years as surgeon-general to the Turco-Egyptian forces until being killed with William Hicks Pasha (q.v.) at Shaykan in 1883.

Greek merchants were among the European population that waited out the siege of Khartoum with General Charles Gordon (q.v.), and many were captured by the forces of the Mahdi (q.v.) on 26 January 1885. One, Dimitri Kokorembas, was made the amir of the Greeks: renamed 'Abdullahi, he served the needs of the Greek section of Muslim-converts (Masalma, q.v.) in Omdurman (q.v.). Like many of this community, he chose to remain in the Sudan after the Mahdiya (q.v.) and died there in 1915.

When Anglo-Egyptian (q.v.) forces entered Omdurman in 1898 they found a Greek community that numbered only eighty-seven individuals, including non-Greek family members. This number was immediately augmented by Greek merchants who entered the Sudan with the invading army, many having served as contractors to the army on the Red Sea or along the Nile. One, Konstantinos Mourikis, set up a shop and ferry on the White Nile and gave his name to the town that developed around him, Kosti (q.v.). Others settled in the Three Towns (q.v.) area, engaging in commercial or financial services, or opened shops around the country. At least some Greeks served in the Anglo-Egyptian administration, including in the Railway and Steamers Department, as clerical and technical staff.

Like the Jews, Armenians, Italians, Syrians, and Egyptian Copts (qq.v.), the Greeks lived as Sudanese nationals under Condominium (q.v.) rule, their community centered around their churches and social clubs. Issued Sudanese nationality certificates after independence in 1956, they thrived in a favorable business and social climate. Their fortunes began to wane with the nationalization policies of the Ja'afar al-

Nimeiri (q.v.) regime in the 1970s. The trend of Islamization (q.v.), beginning with Nimeiri's "September Laws" of 1983 (q.v.) and leading to the coup of 'Umar al-Bashir (q.v.) in 1989, convinced many Greeks to leave Sudan. A small number have remained and continue to do business despite the difficult political and economic conditions.

– H –

HADARAT AL-SUDAN. The first Sudanese-owned and -edited newspaper. It was founded in 1919 by Husayn Sharif (q.v., 1888–1928), who had gained editorial experience working for the Greek-owned Arabic newspaper, *Ra'id al-Sudan* (The Sudan Leader). Sayyid 'Abd al-Rahman al-Mahdi (q.v.) headed the consortium of its ownership. It was a quasi-official newspaper in that it received government subsidies and tended to support the British against Egypt, while nonetheless calling for eventual Sudanese self-determination. The newspaper included regional and world news, articles on social and economic policies and reforms, and poetry and literary essays. At its peak in the mid-1930s it had a circulation of 1,700, 400 of these representing government office subscriptions. It ceased publication in 1938. [by Heather J. Sharkey]

HAGGAR, GEORGE MIKHAIL (1915–1996). Sudanese businessman, industrialist, and philanthropist, founder of the Haggar Group's agro-industrial complex. Born in Cairo he attended the American School in Omdurman (q.v.) and later the Brummana School in Lebanon. In 1932 he returned to Equatoria (q.v.) to help his parents' trading company based in Gondokoro (q.v.). He later started tea and coffee plantations in western Equatoria, and in 1950 he established a cigarette factory at Iwatoka and tobacco growing schemes in eastern and western Equatoria. He set up other commercial and transport enterprises throughout Equatoria, Uganda, and the Belgian Congo. In 1963 he was forced by the Ibrahim Abboud (q.v.) regime to leave southern Sudan for security reasons.

After the Addis Ababa Agreement of 1972 (q.v.), George Haggar's business interests were revived and he returned to Sudan where he established over twenty-five companies in northern and southern Sudan over the next twenty-two years. This gradually expanded internationally to Great Britain, Spain, France, Germany, Egypt, Ethiopia, Kenya, New Zealand, and in recent years South Africa. With this renewed success he established The Haggar Foundation, which made contributions to various charitable endeavors and supported Juba University in its developmental years in the early 1970s. He was one of the first to receive an honorary degree from that institution, which he continued to assist through scholarships for southern students, and also provided funds for schools to meet the needs of displaced southern children.

Haggar was dedicated to a peaceful settlement of the Sudanese conflict, attempting repeatedly until his death to bring the leadership of the National Islamic Front (q.v.) regime, including Hasan al-Turabi (q.v.), together with the Sudanese Peoples Liberation Army (q.v.) leadership, including John Garang (q.v.). His strong and emotional bond to the southern Sudan (q.v.) extended to his final wish that his body be cremated and his ashes scattered over his tea and coffee plantations at Iwatoka and Kapengere in Yei District of eastern Equatoria, where his first home was built.

HAMAD AL-NIL (?–1894). A famous shaykh of the Qadiriya Sufi tariqa (qq.v.) and a member of the 'Arakiyin holy family based in Abu Haraz on the Blue Nile. He succeeded his father Ahmad al-Rayyah after the death of his brother Tirayfi (1857). Early in the Mahdiya (q.v.), Muhammad Ahmad (q.v.) wrote to Hamad al-Nil seeking his support. The shaykh allegedly declined to join the Mahdi, being skeptical of the latter's claims, but his eldest son Abdullah became a loyal Ansari (q.v.), participating in the battle of Qallabat (1889) as *amir* of the 'Arakiyin. The Khalifa Abdullahi suspected the loyalty of Hamad al-Nil, and eventually had the shaykh arrested and brought to Omdurman (q.v.) with many of his 'Arakiyin followers. Kept under house arrest in the capital, he died in 1894. Originally buried by the river, he was later reinterred farther inland away from rising floodwaters. His tomb on the west side of Omdurman is the site of weekly Sufi devotions and a popular tourist attraction.

HAMAD, HAMAD TAWFIQ (1906–1980). Sudanese businessman and political leader. Hamad was educated in Gordon Memorial College (q.v.) and joined the Finance Department in 1924. He later became the first Sudanese to hold the rank of inspector of accounts for the Department of Agriculture. He left government service in 1947 to pursue his business, farming, and political interests. He was one of the founders of the Graduates Congress (q.v.) and he edited and wrote for its magazine, *al-Mu'tamar*. He was the secretary of the National Front Party (q.v.) until it joined the National Unionist Party (NUP, q.v.). Hamad became a member of the NUP executive committee and was elected to Parliament in 1953. He resigned from the NUP in 1956 and helped to create the Peoples Democratic Party (PDP, q.v.), of which he became director-general. He served as a cabinet minister both with the NUP and the PDP, acting as minister of finance (1954–1956), of communications (1956), and of commerce and industry (1956–1958). When the Ibrahim Abboud (q.v.) regime came to power, Hamad became managing director and then chairman of the Agricultural Bank of Sudan. After the dissolution of political parties following the 1958 coup, he continued to serve as the director of the Agricultural Bank until 1962.

HAMAD, KHIDR (1908–1970). A nationalist politician and one of the first to reject ethnic labels and embrace the word "Sudanese" as a term of national identity. As a graduate of Gordon Memorial College (q.v.) in 1928, he found clerical work in the Finance Department as an English-language typist for the colonial regime until 1946. He was a member of the Abu Rawf (q.v.) group of literary intellectuals in the 1930s, a contributor to the newspaper *Hadarat al-Sudan* (q.v.) under the pseudonym "al-Tubji," and a fundraiser (through the staging of theatrical performances) for the Ahliya Schools (q.v.).

In 1946 Khidr joined the Finance Department of the Arab League and then returned to enter politics. He was a member of the Ashigga (q.v.) and became secretary-general of the National Unionist Party (NUP, q.v.) in 1952. He participated in the Graduates Congress and the Unionist Party (qq.v.), campaigned in Egypt for the Palestinian cause, and later served as secretary-general of the NUP in 1952. He was a parliamentary representative (1953–1958) and a member of the Supreme Council (1964–1969). Khidr was elected to Parliament (1953–1958) and served in Isma'il al-Azhari's (q.v.) cabinet. After the 1964 October Revolution (q.v.) he was made a member of the Supreme Council and was reelected to Parliament in 1968. He was not active publicly after the 1969 Ja'afar al-Nimeiri May Revolution (qq.v.). His memoirs appeared posthumously in 1980, entitled *Mudhakkirat Khidr Hamad: al-Haraka al-wataniyya al-sudaniyya, al-istiqlal wa ma ba'duhu* (The Memoirs of Khidr Hamad: The Sudanese Nationalist Movement, Independence, and After). [by Heather J. Sharkey]

HAMAD AL-MAJDHUB. *See* MAJADHIB.

HAMADALLAH, FARUQ 'UTHMAN (?–1971). Sudanese soldier and political leader. He was prematurely retired before the 1969 May Revolution (q.v.) and later restored to active rank by the Council of the Revolution, of which he was a member. Faruq served in the key post of minister of interior until he was dismissed from his civil and military positions in November 1970. He was one of the leaders of the attempted revolution in July 1971, and was executed after that movement's failure.

HAMAJ. A pre-Arab, pre-Funj grouping in the Blue Nile region south of Sinnar (q.v.) near the Ethiopian border. Members of the Koman branch of Sudanic languages, they rose to political and military importance in the Funj Sultanate (q.v.) during the eighteenth century under the leadership of Muhammad Abu Likaylik (q.v.). He and his clan became kingmakers after 1761, ruling through puppet kings while assuming the simple title of *wazir,* or minister. The Hamaj were unable to prevent the disintegration of the sultanate in a series of civil wars. The last Hamaj "regent" was executed during the Turco-Egyptian conquest of 1821. *See also* SHILLUK.

HAMZA, MIRGHANI (1897–1973). Sudanese engineer and leader, of Danagla (q.v.) origin, educated in Gordon Memorial College (q.v.). After entering the Public Works Department he served in a wide variety of posts, eventually becoming the first Sudanese to gain the rank of assistant director of works (1948–1953). He was a founder and president of the Graduates Congress (q.v.) and served on the Advisory Council for the Northern Sudan (q.v.). He was associated with Khatmiya (q.v.) political interests and refused a post in the colonial Executive Council but served as minister of works. In 1947 he was an advocate to increase Sudanization and more educational opportunities for Sudanese. Mirghani was also a leader of the National Front (q.v.) in the 1950s on the eve of independence. Later he was on the Constitutional Commission and served as a member of Parliament. He helped to organize the National Unionist Party (q.v.) and served on its executive committee. He actually nominated Isma'il al-Azhari (q.v.) for the position of the first prime minister of Sudan and was in his cabinet until he broke with him and formed the Independent Republican Party (q.v.), which was dissolved when the Khatmiya-supported Peoples Democratic Party (q.v.) was created in 1956.

HASHIMAB FAMILY. This distinguished family of scholars of Ja'aliyin (q.v.) origin is originally from the Berber (q.v.) area. The family founder, Ahmad Hashim, was a *qadi* in Berber during the Turco-Egyptian (q.v.)

period, and had ties to the Tijaniya Sufi (q.v.) order. His eldest son, Muhammad al-Faki, studied with Muhammad Ahmad (later the Mahdi, q.v.) at the school of Muhammad al-Khayr 'Abdullah Khujali; he was not an Ansari (q.v.), however, and chose to remain in Berber during the Mahdiya (q.v.). During the Condominium (q.v.) he was a *qadi* in Khartoum (q.v.) and operated a school in Burri. Two other sons were prominent Mahdists: Abu'l-Qasim (d. 1934) joined the Mahdi at the siege of Khartoum in 1884, and later served as secretary first to the Mahdi and later to the Khalifa 'Abdullahi (q.v.). Al-Tayyib (d. 1924) served as a tutor to the children of the Khalifa and other Mahdist notables. Both were granted immunity after the battle of Karari (q.v.) by a British leadership eager to forge ties with the Sudanese elite, and thus were spared the looting that befell the rest of the city's inhabitants. Both were prominent judicial officials during the Condominium: Abu'l-Qasim was a *qadi* in the Gezira (q.v.) region (1900–1911), shaykh al-Islam of Sudan (1911–1934), and president of the Board of 'Ulama (1931–1932), as well as founder of the *Ma'had al-'Ilmi* institute in Omdurman (qq.v.). Al-Tayyib was the mufti of the Sudan from 1900 to 1924. Another member of the family was 'Abd al-Halim Musa'id, a nephew of Ahmad Hashim and prominent *amir* of the Mahdiya. He participated in many of the early battles of the period and died with al-Nujumi (q.v.) at the battle of Tushki (q.v.) in 1889. Descendents of the Hashimab have continued the family's scholarly and judicial tradition in Omdurman and elsewhere. A neighborhood in the center of Omdurman is named for them.

HASHIMAB GROUP. This literary society was founded in the late 1920s in the Mawrada neighborhood of Omdurman (q.v.) among a group of nationalist intellectuals. The name "Hashimab" referred to the family lineage of some of its members. It was also known as the Mawrada Group, after the name of the district, or the Fajr Group, after the *Al-Fajr* (q.v.) literary journal to which many of its members contributed. Like the Abu Rawf (q.v.) Group, its members included many graduates of Gordon Memorial College (q.v.) who read English literature and Fabian socialist writings extensively. Unlike the Abu Rawf Group, its members did not favor unity with Egypt but rather advocated Sudanese autonomy and limited cooperation with the British. Although the backgrounds of its members were mixed, most came from families that had sympathized with the Mahdist (q.v.) cause. Prominent members of the Hashimab/Mawrada/Fajr group included Muhammad Ahmad Mahjub (q.v.), 'Abd al-Halim Muhammad, Yusuf Mustafa al-Tinay, and the brothers Muhammad and 'Abd Allah 'Ashri Siddiq. [by Heather J. Sharkey]

HASAN, AHMAD MAHJUB (1925–1997). This educator, administrator, diplomat, and industrialist was a Sudanese nationalist of Nubian extraction. Born the year after the White Flag (q.v.) uprising, he was raised in an atmosphere of growing political consciousness for independence. One of those attending the *Mahad al-Girsh* (One Piastre or Ten Pence Institute) that eventually led to the formation of the Graduates Congress (q.v.), he grew up in the midst of its great revolutionary nationalists. Educated in Khartoum (q.v.) he was employed by the Steamers Department of the Sudan Railways and was posted to England in 1948.

He was press and information officer of the Sudan Gezira (q.v.) Board from 1955 to 1968, when he returned from London to become manager of the Sudan Tractor Company until his retirement in 1985. In 1986 he established *The Sudan Times* with Bona Malwal (q.v.) and Mahjub Mohamed Salih, which they published until it was closed by the National Islamic Front–backed regime of 'Umar al-Bashir (qq.v.) in 1989.

HELM, SIR ALEXANDER KNOX (1893–1964). Sir Helm was the governor-general of the Sudan who succeeded Sir Robert Howe (q.v.) in the spring of 1955 and continued in service until the last day of the Condominium (q.v.) on 31 December 1955. Despite his short service, it was he who faced the August 1955 revolt in the southern Sudan (q.v.) and who presided over the restoration of Sudanese independence after a half century of Anglo-Egyptian (q.v.) colonial rule. Since Helm's interest was a peaceful transition he did little to solve the deeply rooted problems and was mainly concerned with the transfer of power to Isma'il al-Azhari (q.v.). He resigned with some sense of personal dignity under tumultuous conditions, which could have made him a scapegoat for a failed British foreign policy in the Sudan.

HICKS PASHA, WILLIAM (1830–1883). British officer serving the Egyptian army whose disastrous campaign against Muhammad Ahmad al-Mahdi (q.v.) secured the latter's power and reputation in the Sudan. Hicks retired from service in India in 1880 and was appointed chief-of-staff (later, commander-in-chief) of Turco-Egyptian (q.v.) forces in the Sudan in 1883. In September he marched into Kordofan (q.v.) intent on destroying the Mahdist uprising, despite the Mahdi's obvious supremacy in the west. Hicks's force consisted of incompetent European officers and a poorly trained army of demoralized Egyptians, many of whom were veterans of the Ahmad 'Urabi (q.v.) revolt. Lacking knowledge of the territory, including even its water supplies, the force was continually harassed by Mahdists and finally annihilated on November 5 at Shaykan, near el-Obeid (q.v.). Hicks and all of his staff were killed and a small number of Egyptians captured. Shaykan represented the Turco-Egyptians' last chance of a military solution to the Mahdiya (q.v.).

HINDI, 'ABD AL-RAHMAN SHARIF YUSUF, AL- (?–1964). The son of Yusuf al-Hindi (q.v.) and his *khalifa* (q.v.) or successor as leader of the Hindiya *tariqa* (qq.v.). He had local influence in the Blue Nile area, especially in the town of Burri al-Lamaab, where he resided since 1913. His tomb is still a prominent feature of the town. During the process of achieving Sudanese independence he sought to build unity between the Mahdists and the Khatmiya (qq.v.) tariqa, forming the short-lived National Party in 1946. This soon merged with the National Unionist Party (q.v.).

HINDI, HUSAYN SHARIF YUSUF, AL-. Sudanese religious leader and politician. He was a son of Yusuf al-Hindi (q.v.) and entered politics after the 1964 October Revolution (q.v.). He was a member of the National Unionist Party (q.v.) and held many cabinet posts: minister of irrigation (1965–1966), of finance (1966 and 1967–1968), and of local government (1966–1967). After the 1969 May Revolution (q.v.) he was said to be a leading organizer of movements against the revolutionary regime.

HINDI, SHARIF YUSUF IBN MUHAMMAD AL-AMIN, AL-. (ca. 1865–1942). A religious leader whose followers in the Gezira (q.v.) region formed the Hindiya order, an offshoot of the Sammaniya tariqa (qq.v.). The family is recognized as being among the *Ashraf* (q.v.) or descendants of the Prophet Muhammad, and hence their assumption of the honorific title *Sharif*. Yusuf fought on the side of the Mahdists (q.v.) as a young man but after the Anglo-Egyptian (q.v.) conquest he assisted the new regime. He gained numerous followers as a religious leader and had substantial informal political influence. Al-Hindi was a member of the Sudanese delegation that went to London in 1919 to congratulate King George V on Great Britain's victory in World War I. His advice and support was sought in the early days of the Sudanese nationalist movement but he died before the days of formal party politics. His son and *khalifa* was 'Abd Al-Rahman Yusuf al-Hindi.

HINDIYIA. *See* HINDI, YUSUF; HINDI, 'ABD AL-RAHMAN; HINDI, HUSAYN.

HOWE, SIR ROBERT GEORGE (1893–1981). Howe assumed the position of governor-general of the Sudan in April 1947 following the wartime administration of Sir Hubert Huddleston (q.v.). Howe was a somewhat aloof and often absent career diplomat serving the interests of a postwar Great Britain, which had recognized its weaknesses as a global colonial power. Still, it needed the strategic access to Egypt's Suez Canal while not antagonizing Egypt's interests in the Sudan. The way was paved for the decolonization of the Sudan, at a time of rapidly rising nationalist and working-class sentiments expressed by the Workers' Affairs Association (q.v.), especially from 1946 to 1948. Howe presided over the first meeting of the new Executive Council, which had a mix of Sudanese and British officials as a transition to self-government. In it the newly formed Sudanese political parties were already maneuvering for positions in an independent Sudan.

The Egyptian revolution in 1952 gravely complicated this delicate balancing act and the British were moved further toward an independent Sudan. The British attitude weakened a now militant, anti-imperialist Egypt, which Howe ironically feared would dominate the Sudan. Thus, steps were advanced to hold the 1953 parliamentary elections, which resulted in Howe inaugurating the first, rather unstable, Sudanese Parliament in January 1954. The Sudanese perspective was that this was a prelude to the restoration of its independence in January 1956. The British view was that this would break up the Condominium (q.v.) and thereby weaken Egypt. Howe's long term was ended in July 1955 and followed by the brief and unhappy administration of Sir Alexander Knox. Helm (q.v.).

HUDDLESTON, SIR HUBERT JERVOISE (1880–1950). Sir Hubert Huddleston was the British governor-general of the Sudan from October 1940, when he replaced Sir Stewart Symes (q.v.), to April 1947. Huddleston played an important role in Sudanese history in hunting down the sultan of Darfur, 'Ali Dinar (qq.v.), in 1916 and in suppressing the White Flag (q.v.) revolt in Khartoum (q.v.) in 1924. In 1925 he founded the Sudan Defense Force, following the expulsion of Egyptian troops from the country. These credentials made Huddleston popular with British members of the Sudan Political Service (q.v.). As a conservative colonial administrator, Huddleston sought to manage a rapidly rising movement of militant Sudanese nationalism led by the Workers' Affairs Association and theGraduates Congress (qq.v.). Not surprisingly, Huddleston's military background made him apprehensive and alarmed about potential Sudanese revolts and uprisings. He often reminded the Foreign Office of the Mahdist revolt and the assassination of Governor-General Lee Stack (qq.v.).

Huddleston's wartime administration found the Sudan occupying a strategic position in the region. He was particularly concerned with the threat of Italian attacks from their colonies of Libya and Eritrea against the British in the Sudan. The threat was very grave in the eastern Sudan, especially around Kassala (q.v.) and the Ethiopian-Sudanese border region. There were Italian aircraft raids in 1940 against Atbara, Gedaref, Port Sudan, Omdurman (qq.v.), and Khartoum, but they were not pursued militarily. By the following year, the Sudan Defense Forces had managed to drive the Italians from Kassala so it could be restored to British colonial rule.

By 1944 pressure was starting to mount: Even people from traditionally conservative Tuti Island staged a large demonstration in Khartoum (q.v.) opposing British colonial policies. Further expressions of Sudanese nationalism were made evident and the British were compelled to recognize the Advisory Council of the Northern Sudan (q.v.) in a hesitant step toward ultimate decolonization. On 17 April 1946 Huddleston promised the Advisory Council that the Sudan would become independent and established a Sudanization Committee for this purpose. However, he was more a practical than policy person, who favored a go-slow approach; one apparent result of this hesitating move toward liberalization appeared in the October and November riots in Khartoum against the British.

The fact that there was a council only for the northern Sudan was an implicit recognition that British policy favored the political isolation of the South. The reluctance of Huddleston to accept an immediately independent Sudan was tempered with anxieties and power struggles with the Egyptian Condominium (q.v.) partner, and indeed with the British Foreign Office that feared Huddleston's "Messianic" tendencies in ruling the Sudan.

HUMAN RIGHTS. The United Nations (UN, q.v.) led the way in the development of an international discourse linked to practical politics with the Universal Declaration of Human Rights, which was promulgated in 1948. The emphasis was on individual political rights of citizens of nations. In subsequent decades the United Nations has passed complementary declarations and statements dealing with human rights not specifically mentioned in the original Universal Declaration. In 1979 the UN passed the Convention on the Elimination of all Forms of Discrimination Against Women, and in 1989 the United Nations Convention on the Rights of the Child, while a new UN Convention is forthcoming on the Rights of Indigenous Peoples.

Amnesty International, the first private international organization devoted to human rights, was founded in 1961. Human Rights Watch, with special regional branches, such as Africa Watch and Middle East Watch, developed in the late 1980s. The Arab Human Rights Organization (AHRO) was formed in 1983 in Tunis by Middle Eastern intellectuals, and comparable developments occurred in other African nations in the 1980s, so that by the end of the decade human rights organizations had been founded in most African and Middle Eastern countries.

HUMAN RIGHTS: VIOLATIONS. Most human rights organizational activity has occurred since the rise of the 'Umar al-Bashir (q.v.) regime in 1989, though certainly human rights abuses preceded this regime. These include the amputation of limbs under Islamic law during the later years of the Nimeiri (q.v.) regime in 1983–1989, as well as countless acts committed during the civil war beginning in 1955.

The Sudan Human Rights Organization (SHRO, q.v.) was founded in 1993 in Cairo by exiles from the Bashir regime. A prominent founder was activist attorney Amin Makki Madani. The SHRO maintains branches in Cairo and London and has published *The Sudanese Human Rights Quarterly* since 1996.

Both Amnesty International and Africa Watch published monographs in 1995 on the victimization of children in Sudan since the 1983 renewal of civil war. Respectively, these are: "The Tears of Orphans, No Future without Human Rights in Sudan" and "Children of Sudan, Slaves, Street Children and Child Soldiers."

National, regional, and international protests of the continuous and systematic violation of human rights have been raised since 1989. During the first year of the Bashir regime, protests were lodged because the government banned all publications but its own and began purging government positions of all but National Islamic Front (NIF, q.v.) members. "Islamic" policies directed against the dress and activities of women in public places were likewise protested by regional and international human rights organizations such as Africa Watch and Amnesty International. Perhaps most disturbing were reports of government "ghost houses" where suspected NIF opponents were detained and tortured, including some of the country's most respected human rights activists, university professors, and professionals.

Women frequently took the lead in protests of government human rights violations. Female relations of detainees who died under interrogation protested to have their loved ones returned for proper burial. As the number of army recruits dwindled in the mid-1990s, forced conscription of first university and then secondary school boys became common. Mothers and sisters of these young men protested their forced armed service in demonstrations in 1997. One woman, Na'ima 'Ali 'Abd al-Rahman, was arrested, allegedly tortured, and died in government detention.

Recently, official repression of religious freedom has been criticized by human rights organizations. This has included the bulldozing of Christian schools and churches in Omdurman (q.v.) built by refugees (q.v.) and refugee organizations. *See also* WOMEN.

HUNT, S. J. LEIGH (1855–1933). An American entrepreneur and adventurer with experience in the Sudan. Among his Sudanese projects were the Zeidob Irrigation Scheme formed in Berber (q.v.) in 1904. The Zeidob project involved some 11,418 acres of mechanized irrigation agriculture (q.v.) that were supposed to produce long-staple cotton for export. The Zeidob Scheme was later sold to the Sudan Plantations Syndicate, thus becoming a precursor to the huge Gezira Scheme (q.v.) farther south.

Hunt had connections to the American government and once brought President Theodore Roosevelt (q.v.) to the Sudan for a big-game hunting expedition. Hunt also "solved" his labor problems by bringing "a few hundred" African-Americans to the Sudan to pick cotton on the scheme. Apparently labor conditions were oppressive and these workers struck and demanded repatriation to the United States.

HUSAYN SHARIF. *See* SHARIF, HUSAYN.

HUSAYN KAMIL (1854–1917). Husayn was briefly the Ottoman viceroy of Egypt and the Sudan from 1914 to 1917. He was the son of the Khedive Isma'il, son of Ibrahim, son of Muhammad 'Ali (qq.v.), thus Husayn was the great-grandson of the dynastic founder.

– I –

IBN. Arabic for "son of . . .," occurring either between two proper names or preceding a proper name.

IBRAHIM (1789–1848). Ibrahim was viceroy of Egypt from June to November 1848 when he died. He was the son of Muhammad 'Ali (q.v.), the dynastic founder. His brother Isma'il (q.v.) was killed in the Sudan.

IBRAHIM AL-BULAD. *See* AWLAD JABIR.

IBRAHIM, FATIMA AHMAD. This leader of the Sudanese Communist Party (SCP, q.v.) has become the Sudan's "pasionaria" for her passionate speaking and organizing abilities on behalf of Sudanese women (q.v.). Originally a journalist, she was editor and publisher of *Sawt al-Mara* (Women's Voice) throughout the 1950s and 1960s. She was a founder and leader of the Sudanese Women's Union until its dissolution by Ja'afar Nimeiri (q.v.) in 1971. She was one of the significant leaders of the October 1964 Revolution, and became a symbol of the new Sudanese woman as an activist in public political affairs. In 1965, as a Communist Party candidate, she was the first woman elected to Parliament. Her husband, Ahmad Shafi'i al-Shaykh (q.v.), a leading trade unionist (q.v.), was implicated and executed by the Nimeiri regime in 1971 after the abortive Communist-backed coup.

Fatima Ibrahim remained for a time under house arrest and participated in underground activities during the anti-Communist years of Nimeiri's military rule. During the waning years of the Nimeiri regime, she became, once again, one of the few visible faces of the SCP, agitating, as she had frequently done, from a feminist socialist perspective. During the popular revolution against Nimeiri in the spring of 1985, her oratorical skills were again in demand, and after the restoration of democracy, she advocated representation of women in the provisional government.

Forced into exile once again after the National Islamic Front (NIF)–backed 'Umar al-Bashir regime (qq.v.) came to power in 1989, international attention increased for her considerable accomplishments and sacrifice on behalf of women in Sudan. Amnesty International focused on her case. At the United Nations on 10 December 1993 Fatima Ibrahim, while president of the Women's International Democratic Federation, accepted the UN Human Rights Prize on behalf of the Sudanese

Women's Union. The award was presented to her by UN Secretary General Boutros Boutros-Ghali on Human Rights Day in recognition of her personal struggle for human rights, as well as for the historic contribution made by the Sudanese Women's Union to the cause of women's rights. Singled out for recognition was the role of the Women's Union in securing the right to vote and to participate in the economic life of the country, including equal pay and maternity leave benefits, as well as changes in the personal status laws, particularly the requirement of a woman's consent to a marriage and the abolition of the "obedience" law (*bayt al-ta'a*), which ended the forcible return of wives to abusive husbands.

Fatima Ibrahim remains the most visible symbol of Sudanese women's resistance and struggles for democracy in the face of the chronic militarism and social repression that has characterized Sudanese politics in recent decades. Her activism has been unabated while in exile, in written tracts and on the lecture circuit, in Great Britain, the United States, and Canada. *See also* HUMAN RIGHTS; ISLAMIC LAW, REFORM; WOMEN.

IDRIS IBN ARBAB (1507–1650). A religious teacher of great fame during the Funj era who, according to tradition, lived 147 lunar years. He was respected and consulted by the Funj nobility and served as a mediator in major political disputes. He was a leader of the Qadiriya *tariqa* (qq.v.) and his tomb at 'Aylafun became an important religious center. *See also* FEKI; FUNJ SULTANATES.

IDRISIYA. The *tariqa* (q.v.) led by the descendants of Ahmad ibn Idris of Fez (d. 1837, q.v.), also known as the Adarisa. At first Ahmad's sons were associated with his prominent students' orders, especially the Sanusiya and the Rashidiya (qq.v.). Ahmad's son Muhammad established the Idrisiya in Yemen, while another son, 'Abd al-'Al (ca. 1830–1878), studied with Muhammad al-Sanusi in Libya before settling in Upper Egypt. There he established the Idrisiya as a separate *tariqa* and attempted to bring the Sanusiya and Khatmiya (q.v.) *turuq* under his authority. In 1877 he traveled to Nubia (q.v.) en route to Yemen, and died in Dongola (q.v.) shortly thereafter. 'Abd al-'Al was succeeded by his son Muhammad (d. 1936), who married from the local people and made Dongola an important center of the *tariqa*. The Idrisiya family was now very large and influential and enjoyed great prestige, especially in Nubia but also throughout much of the northern Sudan. Competition with the Khatmiya was perhaps inevitable. Muhammad spent most of the Mahdist period in Upper Egypt, returning to Dongola only after the Anglo-Egyptian (q.v.) occupation in 1897. In his lifetime the Idrisiya became well established in both Dongola and Omdurman (q.v.).

IMAM. A Muslim religious leader, especially a leader in prayer, and among Shi'ite Muslims an overtly political leader as well. In the Sudan, the leaders of the Ansar (q.v.) sect in the twentieth century were entitled *Imam*, beginning with Sayyid 'Abd al-Rahman al-Mahdi (q.v.). 'Abd al-Rahman's agents in Darfur, Kordofan (qq.v.), and White Nile provinces in the 1920s were also styled Imams, and vied with local tribal leaders for authority.

INDEPENDENCE FRONT. A coalition of parties favoring an independent Sudan formed in 1945, primarily for purposes of political discussions in Cairo. The parties involved were the Umma, the Republican Party, the Nationalist Party, and the Liberal Party (qq.v.).

INDEPENDENT REPUBLICAN PARTY. A party formed in 1954 by three leaders of the National Unionist Party (q.v.) who were pro-Khatmiya (q.v.): Mirghani Hamza (q.v.), Khalafalla Khalid, and Ahmad Jayli. The first two had been ministers in Isma'il al-Azhari's (q.v.) cabinet but had been dismissed late in 1954. With the support of 'Ali al-Mirghani (q.v.), the three formed the Independent Republican Party, advocating an independent Sudanese republic that would cooperate with Egypt. The party was dissolved when the Khatmiya-supported Peoples Democratic Party (q.v.) was created in 1956.

INDIRECT RULE. A policy developed originally in Nigeria by British administrator Frederick (later Lord) Lugard (1858–1945), whose *Dual Mandate in British Tropical Africa* (1922) was required reading for colonial policy makers throughout the British Empire. Its essence was that tribal leaders and other "traditional" authorities should assume partial responsibility for their own governance. In the Anglo-Egyptian (q.v.) Sudan this was appealing after the 1919 Egyptian uprising, as the British sought to minimize Egypt's role in the Sudan's administration and so avoid the contagion of nationalist ideas. As added benefits, Indirect Rule spared Britain the expense of salaried administrators; strengthened tribal authority against sects like the Ansar (q.v.); undermined and limited the expansion of a distrusted Sudanese educated class (*affandiya*); and freed

British officials from routine duties while allowing them to concentrate on more specialized (and politically sensitive) tasks.

Indirect Rule's beginnings as an enacted statute came in 1922 in the form of the "Power of Nomad Sheikhs Ordinance," which regularized the judicial functions of some 300 tribal shaykhs (q.v.). This was augmented by the "Powers of Sheikhs Ordinance" in 1927. Its principal architects in the Sudan were John Maffey (q.v.), governor-general from 1926 to 1933, and especially Harold MacMichael (q.v.), assistant civil secretary from 1919 to 1925 and civil secretary from 1926 to 1933.

In order to function effectively, Indirect Rule required tribal cohesion and strong tribal leadership. However, by the twentieth century neither was much in evidence in the Sudan, having been weakened and even destroyed by the centralizing policies of the Turkiya and Mahdiya (qq.v.) regimes as well as early Anglo-Egyptian policy. The concern of the British, then, came to be the reversal of this reality, to the extent of creating "traditional" authority where none existed. Ultimately, Indirect Rule (also known as "Native Administration") became a reactionary policy designed to foster tribalism and rebuff the nationalist aspirations of educated Sudanese. As an aspect of "Southern Policy" like the Closed Districts Ordinance (q.v.), it contributed to the isolation and underdevelopment of the southern Sudan (q.v.) and exacerbated the differences between North and South. *See also* SUDAN POLITICAL SERVICE.

ISLAM. Islam spread rapidly across North Africa during the first century after its introduction in the Arabian Peninsula in the seventh century CE. It later spread to the West African Sahel with major Muslim kingdoms established by the tenth century CE. By contrast, the main penetration of Islam into the Sudan did not occur until the fourteenth century CE (eighth century AH), as it was effectively blocked from entering the Sudan by the presence of the Christianized kingdoms of Nubia (q.v.). The spread of Islam up the Nile occurred over two centuries, both by invasion and assimilation of Muslim merchants and teachers who settled and married among the Nubians. The fall of Dongola, Mukkurra, and Nobatia (qq.v.) as Nubian Christian kingdoms in the fourteenth century permitted the Islamic religion to penetrate to the interior of the Sudan. Another important infusion came from West African Muslims who sometimes crossed the Sudanese Sahel on their pilgrimages to Mecca.

After the fall of Dongola in about 1320 CE the spread of Islam and the Arabic language (q.v.) still took almost two centuries in the central Sudan, with the fall of Alwa (q.v.) in 1504 and the establishment of the Funj

Sultanate at Sinnar (qq.v.) and the Darfur Sultanate al-Fasher (qq.v.). The Funj Sultanate at Sinnar in the Gezira became the first Muslim state in the Sudan, and it exerted its influence from the sixteenth to the nineteenth centuries. The Funj attracted holymen from the Arabian Peninsula, Nubia, and Egypt who introduced Islamic theology, Maliki jurisprudence, and Islamic religious practices to the central Sudan. The Turkiya and Mahdiya (qq.v.) regimes in the nineteenth century further encouraged the spread of Islam and the Arabic language, both through their official policies and the socioeconomic changes they wrought. The southern regions of the Sudan, meanwhile, were generally beyond the influence of Islam at these times except as a source of slaves (q.v.).

Orthodox Islam, associated with the rise of states and statecraft, is concerned with the immutable sources of the religion, the Qur'an and Sunna. Folk Islam, however, is associated with the grassroots, popular Sufi brotherhoods (*tariqa*, pl. *turuq*, q.v.), which predate the "official Islam" of various governing regimes. The Sufi orders that have most influenced the Sudan have been the Khatmiya, Shadhiliya, Tijaniya, and Qadiriya *turuq* (qq.v.), the first having a distinct religio-political history in the modern Sudan, especially associated with the Democratic Unionist Party (DUP, q.v.). These religious orders combined with local saint (q.v.) worship to exercise a profound influence in the initial spread of Islam and the rooting of an Islamic-Sudanese lifestyle among the broad masses of northern Sudanese people. The orders tend to be highly localized and generally are not subject to any central religious or political authority. As a result, a certain tension between popular-folk and orthodox-state Islam has often existed.

The veneration of local saints and the performance of a *zikr*, a ritual commemorating the revered local *shaykh* or *feki* (q.v.), are the focal points of Sufi worship, while strict adherence to official Islam, such as the Shari'a (q.v.) courts, may not be observed. A popular *zikr* of the Qadiriya order is performed each Friday on the outskirts of Omdurman (q.v.), known as the *Raqs al-Darawish* (Dervish Dance). The dance and adjoining tomb of Hamad al-Nil (q.v.) are attended regularly by a diverse group of people seeking the saint's blessings (*baraka*, q.v.), and by increasing numbers of tourists because of its proximity to Khartoum. *See also* FOLK RELIGION; ISLAMIC BANKING; ISLAMIC LAW; ISLAMIC LAW, REFORM; ISLAMIZATION.

ISLAMIC BANKING. Islamic banking has developed in Sudan along with the Islamist trend, as is true elsewhere in the Muslim world. Modern Islamic banking offers an alternative to Western banks by observing the Muslim prohibition on interest-taking or usury (*riba*) and providing banking services and investments that are religiously approved. The international success of the Islamic banks has been dramatic although the earliest banks date only from the 1960s and 1970s. Islamic banks comprise the entire banking sector in Iran and Pakistan, and they currently dominate banking interests in Sudan. The Faisal Islamic Bank was introduced in Sudan in 1977, having developed from capital from the wealthy Saudi Faisal family; Faisal Islamic Banks were introduced in Egypt in the same year. They achieved remarkable popular success even prior to the National Islamic Front (NIF, q.v.) takeover of Sudan in 1989, but became even stronger due to their close ties to the Muslim Brotherhood and the NIF.

Banking services are offered for fees rather than being dependent upon interest, and Islamic investments employ a variety of shared risk and profit-taking models to avoid the use of interest-dependent lending. The Islamic banks and investment corporations have succeeded due to a combination of adherence to religious teaching, a continuous flow of Saudi capital, and the favorable return on investments they have engendered. Ironically, Islamic banks are not prominent in the Saudi Arabian economy.

ISLAMIC CHARTER FRONT. *See* MUSLIM BROTHERHOOD; NATIONAL ISLAMIC FRONT.

ISLAMIC JAMHURIYA. The idea of an Islamic "jamhuriya" or republic is very much a part of contemporary Islamist discourse. The call for an Islamic state is mirrored in the slogan *Islam, huwa al-hal* (Islam is the solution).

The main architect of the Islamist government in Sudan, Hasan al-Turabi (q.v.), has promoted the concept of the Islamic state. In his view an Islamic state would be based upon comprehensive Islamic law (Shari'a, q.v.), enshrining Islamic values and building a moral community, while the scope of government itself is more limited than the all-embracing Shari'a. Government leaders are chosen through *shura* or consultation, a unique Islamic democratic concept not to be confused with Western-style democracy. Muslims must work toward a unified community devoid of sectarian divisions, such as with the traditional schools of Islamic jurisprudence.

In a practical political sense the Islamic state has come to mean the Islamization (q.v.) of basic institutions of government and law, a state headed by an Islamic leader guided by Islamic principles, and most importantly a state government by Shari'a that is based on the holy sources of the religion, the Qur'an and Sunna. Criticism of the Islamic state in theory as well as practice comes from Muslims and non-Muslims alike. Fear about any type of religious governance raises basic questions about theocratic rule. Beyond this general fear of the combination of religion with the state are also fears about the status of non-Muslims and women (q.v.) in an Islamic state. The examples of Iran and Afghanistan as models of Islamic republics come to mind and others also use the case of Sudan as a negative example, especially on the matter of the treatment of its non-Muslim minority in the southern region.

For its part the National Islamic Front (q.v.) has offered a solution of federalism as an alternative to the model of an Islamic state in its negotiations with the Sudanese Peoples Liberation Movement (q.v.).

ISLAMIC LAW (SHARI'A). With the first Sudanese Muslim state, the Funj (q.v.), came the first Islamic jurists to the capital city of Sinnar (q.v.) in the sixteenth century. These scholars of religion and law introduced the Maliki school of jurisprudence, which shaped Muslim practice in the Sudan. During the Turkiya (q.v.), the Ottoman state introduced its official Hanafi school of law, and the interpretations of law from these two schools have exerted a continuing influence to the present time.

Under the revivalist Mahdiya (q.v.), the Shari'a was the sole law in effect, basing its decisions upon the strictest interpretation of the Qur'an and Sunna (the practices of the Prophet Muhammad). With the Anglo-Egyptian conquest and establishment of British rule, English civil law and a new penal code (derived from that developed originally for India) were introduced, displacing Islamic law in all matters except family and personal status affairs of Muslims. An autonomous division of the judiciary for the Shari'a was established alongside the Western-derived Civil and Criminal Division. Nonetheless, a distinctive development of the Shari'a took place during this period. Especially noteworthy were innovations in the law of divorce and changes in the law of inheritance.

During the postindependence years, until Ja'afar al-Nimeiri (q.v.) seized power in 1969, the previous administration of the Shari'a in Sudan remained intact. During the years 1977 to 1983, Nimeiri pursued a consistent course of Islamization (q.v.) of government and law. First, legislation introducing the Islamic taxes (*zakat*) as a state levy, and later legislation banning alcohol in every form of sale or use were passed in the People's Assembly of Nimeiri's party, the Sudan Socialist Union (q.v.).

In 1985 Nimeiri introduced the "September Laws" which, in a stroke, made the Shari'a state law. After this, until Nimeiri's overthrow in 1985, some of the harshest applications of Islamic law yet to be observed in the Muslim world took place. Reportedly, over 200 persons had limbs amputated for theft, and countless others were sentenced to public flogging for alcohol-related offenses by the newly created "Courts of Prompt Justice." The abuses were such that they helped to create the context for popular opposition to the regime that culminated in its overthrow in March of 1985.

In the southern Sudan (q.v.), the civil war that had been peaceably negotiated to a close in 1972 was reignited in 1983, primarily because of the significance of the September Laws, and the removal of the Shari'a as the national law remains the central negotiating point between the central government and the southern opposition, the Sudanese Peoples Liberation Movement/Army (SPLM/SPLA, q.v.). These events have politicized the Shari'a more than ever in the history of modern Sudan and placed Sudan in the most recent of its several constitutional crises. The matter of the place and proper role of Islamic law within the nation-state is a key issue in the reconstruction of Sudan after any negotiated end to the civil war.

ISLAMIC LAW, REFORM. The development of Islamic law in the Sudan in the twentieth century has included a number of significant reforms, instituted through the mechanism of the Judicial Circulars issued from the Office of the Grand Qadi, in the following areas of family law.

Divorce: The right to judicial divorce for the woman (q.v.) is extended because of impotence, harm, or abuse (*talaq al-darar*) suffered by the woman, this right being derived from Maliki judicial interpretations. Occurring in 1917, this is among the first such legal innovations in the Muslim world. Restrictions limiting the husband's unilateral right to divorce, the triple pronouncement or *talaq talata*, were instituted in 1935. Judicial grounds for divorce initiated by women extended to include desertion and mental as well as physical harm or abuse (1973).

Consent in marriage: In 1960 the right of refusal of marriage was extended to the bride, and legal proofs were established to ensure her consent in marriage. Using Hanafi interpretations, this restricted the absolute role of the marriage guardian (*al-wali*), usually the father, to negotiate a marriage contract for a woman.

Inheritance law: Changes in the law of inheritance were instituted whereby the spouse, either husband or wife, is entitled to the entirety of the estate if there are no other legal heirs. This particular reform (1925) placed the spouse relict on a par with the other Islamic heirs, and is a modification of classical Muslim inheritance law. Other reforms (1939) equalized the shares of full and half brothers and sisters, and the grandfather (who formerly could take a share greater than the full brothers) was placed on a par with these heirs (1943). Each of these moves served to strengthen the nuclear family over the traditional strength of the patrilineal males (al-'asaba).

Elimination of the practice of bayt al-ta'a: According to this, wives who had fled the houses of their husbands due to abuse were forcibly returned by the police to their husbands. This reform, in addition to increases in amounts and better enforcement of support payments to divorced wives (al-nafaqa), was part of Ja'afar al-Nimeiri's (q.v.) early progressive attitude toward women and the general improvement of their status.

Many of these reforms antedated comparable developments in other Muslim regions by several decades. A reformist group unique to the Sudan, the Republican Brotherhood (q.v.), has focused much of its theory and practice on the reforms of the Shari'a law, especially as it relates to the rights of women and religious minorities in a Muslim state.

The Islamist 'Umar al-Bashir (q.v.) government turned its attention to additional reform of the family law only six months after seizing power in June 1989. A January 1990 Conference on the Role of Women in National Salvation recommended that a code of personal status law be drafted.

A legislative committee drew up the 1991 Act on Personal Law for Muslims, which was passed by the ruling military and its Council of Ministers and came into effect on 24 July 1991. The new code consists of five volumes and represents the first codification of personal status law in Sudan. The major drafter of the code was High Court Justice Shaykh Siddiq 'Abd al-Hai. Although codification of law has generally not been part of the history of Islamic law, it is projected as a modern reform by Islamists; this is strongly rejected by others.

This first codification of family law did not break new ground in legal innovation, but it does summarize and make explicit points of law that had been decided previously in High Court cases. It consistently favors the more indigenous and African Maliki interpretations over Hanafi law, which is associated with Ottoman Turkish rule. For example, it recognizes the increased authority of women in marriage and rejects the six conditions required for a valid marriage in Hanafi law: religion, freedom, job, financial situation, place of residence, and reasonable pedigree. These conditions when formerly applied in the Sudan raised many cases involving ethnic, racial, and class differences as well as objections raised by marriage guardians to grooms with alleged slavery (q.v.) in their backgrounds. The new law requires only mutual respect between the families. The new law widens the concept of *nafaqa* or support to include education and medical treatment of the wife that was previously excluded under Hanafi law. The major accomplishment of the codified family law is the consolidation of nearly a century of applied law in the Sudan and the ending of the conflicts between Hanafi and Maliki interpretations.

Sudanese women activists have strongly criticized the new law. Lawyer Mona Awad stated that the law is largely influenced by a male-dominated ideology that is, in fact, contradictory to true Islamic teachings. In principle, Islam emphasizes egalitarian relations between males and females and urges men to treat women as their sisters. But this legislation ignored the achievements of Sudanese women prior to June 1989, including their participation in government affairs and high-level decision making. It treats women as legal minors who are incapable of deciding upon their own marriages. Women's testimony in courts is also not equal to that of men, and maternal status is eroded as children (especially male) may be easily separated from their mothers. Women activists therefore insist that the Sudanese Personal Status Law must recognize the international *Convention on the Elimination of All Forms of Discrimination Against Women*, as published by the Sudan Human Rights Organization-Cairo (q.v.). *See also* ISLAMIC LAW (SHARI'A).

ISLAMIZATION. The political struggle to Islamize basic institutions of law and government in the Sudan is a major theme in modern Sudanese history. It is profoundly tied to the colonial experience and is one of the most deeply divisive issues in the continuing quest for national unity. The terms "resurgent Islam" and "Islamic fundamentalism," and now "Islamist," have come to characterize Muslim movements after the Iranian Islamic Revolution in 1979. For Sudan, the contemporary expression of Islamic revival is closely associated with the declining years of the Ja'afar al-Nimeiri (q.v.) regime (1977–1985), and the formation of the National Islamic Front (NIF, q.v.) after the toppling of the military dictatorship. However, the Muslim Brotherhood (q.v.), with historical roots in the Sudan traceable to the 1940s and 1950s, set the modern political agenda for the restructuring of state and society on the basis of Islam (q.v.).

British colonial rule sought to secularize Sudanese society in the immediate aftermath of the crushing of the Islamic Mahdist (q.v.) state. The colonial government tightly regulated all major Islamic institutions. At the time of independence in 1956 one of the models for the new nation that was advanced was that of an Islamic Parliamentary Republic, chiefly backed by the Umma and Khatmiya (qq.v.) groups. A military coup in 1958, led by General Ibrahim Abboud (q.v.), ended this political dialogue, and with civil war then in the South over the political exclusion of southerners, the new government sought to "resolve" the conflict through Islamization and Arabization of the South.

The call for Islamization of state and society continued on the political agenda as a background issue through the popular revolution of 1964 and interim governments, until the 1969 coup d'etat led by Ja'afar al-Nimeiri. For nearly a decade Nimeiri pursued an essentially secular course, with the successful negotiated end to the civil war in the South in 1972. However, as different problems beset his regime in the late 1970s, Nimeiri increasingly turned to Islam to solve his political problems. Islamic banking (q.v.) and financial institutions were promoted by Nimeiri and grew rapidly and dramatically to about 40 percent of all capital investments by the early 1980s. Legislation introducing *zakat* and a total ban on alcohol was adopted, and when other, more comprehensive measures failed in the People's Assembly and Nimeiri needed Muslim Brotherhood support, he introduced the all-encompassing "September Laws" (q.v.) in 1983, proclaiming Islamic law (Shari'a, q.v.) as state law for Sudan.

The most serious consequence of this was the resurrection of civil war in southern Sudan (q.v.), wherein the main political grievance cited was the institution of the Shari'a as state law, and the *sine qua non* for the initiation of peace negotiations was its removal.

After the June 1989 coup d'etat, Sudan joined the ranks of nations regarded by the West as Islamic "resurgent" or "revivalist" in the modern sense since Iran's Islamic Revolution of 1979. The term "Islamist" has come to characterize governments that seek to Islamize political and social institutions and favor the establishment of an Islamic state. Dr. Hasan al-Turabi (q.v.) has lent the ideological framework to the military government that moved quickly in 1989 to abolish all parties and all publications except those approved of by the National Islamic Front (q.v.). Although Sudan did not declare itself an Islamic Republic like Iran or Afghanistan, it is widely regarded as such, for it has moved formally to Islamize government institutions, banks, and economic organizations, and has refused to negotiate with the Sudanese Peoples Liberation Movement (q.v.) over the removal of the Shari'a as state law. The forcible Islamization of Sudan's non-Muslims has frequently been alleged by individuals and political groups representing the people of the Nuba Mountains and southern Sudan.

Since 1989, al-Turabi has emerged internationally, as a major figure among Islamic "fundamentalists," having gained prominence from his key role in shaping the 'Umar al-Bashir (q.v.) military regime. His ability to conduct interviews in Arabic, English, and French, his writings and the translations of his works, and his general accessibility to the international press have made him one of Sudan's most recognized personalities on the global scene and a significant voice of Islamic resurgence until his arrest in 2001. *See also* ISLAMIC JAMHURIYA.

ISMA'IL AL-WALI (1793–1863). A religious leader in Kordofan (q.v.) and the founder of the Isma'iliya *tariqa* (qq.v.). He was a descendant of a religious teacher in Funj times, Bishara al-Gharbawi, and his father was a merchant who had settled in Kordofan. Isma'il was a student of Muhammad 'Uthman al-Mirghani, founder of the Khatmiya (qq.v.), but he attained sufficient prestige to be enabled to establish his own religious brotherhood. Isma'il's descendants were active in both religious and political developments in the modern Sudan and include Prime Minister Isma'il al-Azhari (q.v.). *See also* AL-AZHARI.

ISMA'IL KAMIL PASHA (1795–1822). The third son of Muhammad 'Ali (q.v.), the Ottoman governor and viceroy of Egypt. He commanded the Turco-Egyptian (q.v.) armies that conquered the Sudan in 1820–1822. He was killed by Mek Nimr, a Shayqiya (qq.v.) leader, in the town of Shendi (q.v.). Mek Nimr had invited him to a party at his house, which he later surrounded and set afire. Isma'il's assassination prompted a widespread massacre of Sudanese people residing south of the sixth cataract and along the Blue and White Niles. This brutal repression characterized the tense relations between Sudanese and their Turkish rulers, and provided one of the reasons for the rise of Mahdism (q.v.) in 1881.

ISMA'IL, KHEDIVE (1830–1895). Isma'il was the son of Ibrahim, who was the son of Muhammad 'Ali (q.v.). During the reign of Isma'il (1863–1879), large areas in the south and west of the Sudan were added to the Turco-Egyptian (q.v.) holdings, and his armies moved as far east as Harar in Ethiopia. The Khedive attained renown by his employment of large numbers of European administrators and commercial agents, thus providing a major stimulus to westernization of institutions in Egypt and the Sudan. Modern mapping of the Sudan took place in his administration, including the exploration of the southern Sudan (q.v.) and the discovery of the headwaters of the White Nile. This resulted in growing economic and political domination by the Europeans in Ottoman Egypt and the Sudan. When Isma'il resisted British and French dual control over Egypt's bankrupt finances, he was deposed by the Ottoman sultan in 1879 and replaced by his son Muhammad Tawfiq (q.v.).

ISMA'ILIYA TARIQA. A *tariqa* (q.v.) established by Isma'il al-Wali (q.v.) in the nineteenth century. In origin it is related to the Khatmiya (q.v.) but is an independent brotherhood. The leadership of the order passed from Isma'il to his eldest son Muhammad al-Makki (d.1906), who became an active supporter of the Mahdist movement. Another son, Ahmad al-Azhari, opposed Mahdism as did his descendants. After 1906 there was some tension among heads of the family over the leadership of the order. However, the order continued to be active, with most of its followers concentrated in Kordofan (q.v.). *See also* AL-AZHARI.

IYA BASSI ZAMZAM. Iya Bassi was the rank usually held by the sister of the local ruler in the Sultanate of Darfur (q.v.) during the precolonial period. The Iya Bassi was second in status only to her brother the ruler, and she exercised far more actual power than the wives and mothers of the ruler, or indeed than any of the other male officials.

Iya Bassi Zamzam played a crucial role in the history of Darfur in the early eighteenth century. In 1752 Sultan Tirab ordered his defeated brother, Abu al-Qasim, to be strangled. The Iya Bassi Zamzam witnessed the execution of her brother, and she excoriated Tirab in a loud song of lamentation, whereupon he had her executed too. The song texts composed by this remarkable woman still have such an important political function that Zaghawi (q.v.) men must reckon with them before they decide to take any action contrary to the interests of Iya Bassi Zamzam's family. [by Baqie Badawi Muhammad]

– J –

JA'ALIYIN. The Ja'aliyin claim descent from the followers of the Prophet Muhammad in Arabia. They include various people inhabiting the region between southern Nubia and the Gezira (qq.v.). Their core area is the Nile Valley between the fourth and sixth cataracts, where they live mostly as settled, cattle- and camel-herding (qq.v.) agricul- turalists. Despite their claim of an Arab (q.v.) pedigree, the Ja'aliyin may also be considered a southern group of Arabized Nubians. The mixture of Ja'aliyin and Danagla (q.v.) in particular created a category of people known as "Jallaba" (q.v.), who in the nineteenth century be- came merchants along the Nile Valley and led commercial and slave (q.v.) trading ventures throughout the country, especially in the West and South.

During the time of the Funj (q.v.), the local *shaykh* or *mek* of the var- ious Ja'aliyin territories had considerable power and authority. The ex- ample of Mek Nimr (q.v.), who resisted Turkish occupation from his capital at Shendi (q.v.), is a case in point. Shendi and other Ja'ali towns such as al-Damer (q.v.) were also known as regional centers of religious learning, with the tombs (*qubbas*, q.v.) of their holymen becoming places of saintly worship.

Initially the Ja'aliyin offered broad support to the Mahdist (q.v.) movement in the 1880s, both out of religious conviction and the percep- tion of economic advantage in lifting Turkish control. The Mahdi's most prominent general, 'Abd al-Rahman al-Nujumi (q.v.), was one of many important Ja'ali Mahdists. However, during the reign of the Khalifa 'Ab- dullahi (q.v.), many Ja'aliyin became disillusioned with the Khalifa's fa- voring of his Baqqara (q.v.) kinsmen. This disillusionment turned to open rebellion among the people of Matamma, across the Nile from Shendi, who in 1897 were massacred by a Mahdist army led by the Khal- ifa's cousin Mahmud Ahmad. In the twentieth century, and especially since independence, people of Ja'ali origin frequently have been found in the centers of commerce and politics. *See also* FEKI; HASHIMAB; JUHAYNA; MAJADHIB.

JABIR, SONS OF. *See* AWLAD JABIR.

JADEN, AGGREY. Southern political leader. He went into exile during the Ibrahim Abboud (q.v.) era and was a founder of the Sudan African National Union (SANU, q.v.). He was a SANU spokesman at the Round Table Conference (q.v.) in Khartoum (q.v.) in 1965, but returned to exile where he was active in the Sudan African Liberation Front (q.v.), then the Azania Liberation Front (q.v.), and later the Southern Sudan Provi- sional Government (q.v.).

JALLABA. An Arabic term for small-scale merchants and traders who operate throughout Sudan. Historically the term was applied to Arab (and Arabized Nubian) merchants from the northern riverine groups like the Ja'aliyin, Shayqiya, and Danagla (qq.v) who in the nineteenth century were drawn to such areas as Bahr al-Ghazal and Equatoria (qq.v.) in the lucrative ivory and slave trades (q.v.). Their dealings with the local non-Muslim peoples—usually exploitative, often brutal—earned the name Jallaba a negative connotation.

JANDA, CLEMENT (1941–). Canon of the Episcopal Church of Sudan since 1987. He has also served in a variety of ecumenical posts, including secretary-general of the Sudan Council of Churches, associate general secretary of the All Africa Conference of Churches (AACC), executive secretary of the World Council of Churches in Geneva, Switzerland, and finally secretary-general of the AACC in 1997. He is the first Sudanese to be elected to this prestigious post. Janda was born in Yei in 1941 and ordained an Episcopal pastor in 1970; he served the church in Uganda during the early 1970s, and studied in Uganda, the United States, and Canada. *See also* CHRISTIANITY IN THE SUDAN.

JEWS. The earliest known Jewish traveler to the Sudan since the advent of the Islamic period was David Reubeni (ca.1490–1540), who wrote an account of his 1530 trip from the Red Sea coast to Sinnar and Dongola (qq.v.). By the late seventeenth century Jews were to be found among the foreign merchant community in Sinnar. Jews of the Ottoman lands came to the Sudan to trade during the years of the Turco-Egyptian (q.v.) regime, many as representatives of Egyptian trading firms looking to expand their businesses south. Several are known to have established themselves in el-Obeid (q.v.) and along the Nile Valley, from whence they traded north to Cairo. Few Jews served in the Turkiya administration, the only known examples being Emin Pasha (Governor of Equatoria, 1878–1889, q.v.), born to Christian-convert parents and who later converted to Islam; and Emin's pharmacist, Vita Hasan (d. 1893). More typical was Moshe Ben Zion Koshti (1842–1917): born in Palestine and living in the Sudan as the agent for an Egyptian firm, he traded in Khartoum (q.v.) and Masallamiya until the Mahdist (q.v.) revolt. During the siege of Khartoum (1884–1885) he lent money to General Charles Gordon (q.v.) to provision the town. Captured with the fall of the city, he was given the Arabic name Musa Basiyouni by the Mahdi (q.v.) himself, and spent the next thirteen years as a member of the Omdurman Masalma (qq.v.) community. A leader of the small Jewish community as well as a confidante of the Khalifa 'Abdullahi (q.v.), he was allowed to travel north for trade purposes during the years of the Mahdiya (q.v.); like other members of the Masalma, he took a Sudanese wife at the behest of the Khalifa. After the Anglo-Egyptian conquest, Basiyouni (who retained his Mahdist name) remained in Omdurman, building a small synagogue and establishing a Jewish cemetery.

When the British occupied Omdurman in 1898, they found thirty-six Jews (including families) remaining, many of Iraqi and Egyptian origin. Most returned to their native religion. Some, such as Da'ud Mandil (d. 1901) and Isra'il Da'ud Binyami (d. 1915) did not, either out of firm Islamic conviction or fearing for the social status of their children born of Sudanese mothers. Joined by an influx of Jews mainly from Egypt, they resumed their original occupations in the import/export trade, while some established small manufacturing and food processing plants. The Sudan Jewish Community was formally established in 1908 with the arrival of Rabbi Solomon Malka from Egypt, who served as chief rabbi until his death in 1949. Musa Basiyouni, who had established the first synagogue, was Community president until his death in 1917.

After 1918 the Jewish community moved to Khartoum, where its new synagogue was completed in 1926. Jews from a variety of Middle Eastern (and later European) locations settled in the Sudan, serving in government, banking, commerce, manufacturing, education, law, and medicine. With a social life centered around the synagogue and Jewish recreation club, the Jews attained a peak population of approximately 1,000 people in the 1940s–1950s. Most lived in the Three Towns (q.v.), though others were based in Wad Medani and Port Sudan (qq.v.). As Sudanese nationals under Condominium (q.v.) and postindependence rule, the Jews were initially an assimilated and confident minority. Their confidence began to wane with the establishment of Israel in 1948 and subsequent anti-Zionist sentiments in Sudan and throughout the Arab world. Tensions increased after the 1956 Anglo-French-Israeli invasion of Egypt, and Jews began to migrate out of Sudan. By the late 1960s, most of Sudan's Jews had relocated to the United States, Europe, and Israel, though a small number (short of a quorum for prayer services) remained. The Khartoum synagogue was destroyed in 1987 after having been acquired by a Sudanese bank in a shady real estate deal, marking the end of a formal Jewish presence in Sudan. *See also* ARAB-ISRAELI CONFLICT.

JIHADIYA. An Arabic term for slave soldiers, particularly those impressed into the Turco-Egyptian (q.v.) army in the nineteenth century and later utilized by the Mahdist (q.v.) state (1885–1898). The name derives from the Arabic word *jihad,* meaning "a struggle on behalf of the faith," though *jihadiya* were more professional soldiers than the holy warrior of popular conception. The use of slave soldiery in the Nile Valley dates back as far as Pharaonic times and was a common feature of statecraft in both the Sinnar and Darfur (qq.v.) sultanates beginning in the seventeenth century. The Turco-Egyptian invasion of the Sudan (1820–1822) had as its express purpose the acquisition of slaves to serve as soldiers in a new Egyptian army envisioned by the ruler Muhammad 'Ali (q.v.). Though this plan was abandoned by 1824 due to the high mortality rate among slaves, the Turco-Egyptian regime in Khartoum (q.v.) continued to acquire slaves to serve in military units throughout the Sudan.

Most *jihadiya* came from the Upper Blue Nile, Nuba Mountains, or Bahr al-Ghazal region (qq.v.): the same territories that earlier had been raided for slaves by the Sinnar and Darfur states. *Jihadiya* were obtained in organized raids (known as *ghazwat*) conducted by large trading companies, though individual Sudanese also surrendered domestic slaves to the state in lieu of taxes. The status of *jihadiya* was paradoxical: On the one hand, they were legally unfree, deprived of autonomy and most liberties; on the other hand, they were armed with guns and often possessed their own personal servants. Under good conditions, *jihadiya* served well in a variety of capacities, including such noncombative roles as tax collecting, working in hospitals and arsenals, and even in shops in Khartoum. Under poor conditions (which during the Turco-Egyptian period often prevailed), they deserted. The need to constantly replenish the supply of *jihadiya* became an enormous financial burden on the regime.

Egypt's policy of repressing the slave trade (1869) had little effect on the *jihadiya*, who continued to be seized or otherwise obtained for the army. With the rise of the Mahdist movement in 1881 and the creation of the Mahdist state (1885), little about the use of *jihadiya* changed. The Mahdi and his successor Khalifa 'Abdullahi (qq.v.) placed great emphasis on the acquisition of *jihadiya* for their armies. This notwithstanding, the Mahdists were largely unsuccessful in obtaining slave soldiers, being preoccupied with a variety of threats to their authority and ineffective in the southern regions. Moreover, the Mahdist attempt to socially integrate all believers never quite succeeded, the *jihadiya* being regarded with suspicion, if not contempt, by the other Ansar (q.v.). Poor conditions for *jihadiya* continued to lead to desertions, this time to the Anglo-Egyptian (q.v.) army whose cause they next served as willingly as they had the previous two regimes.

After 1898 the Anglo-Egyptian government in the Sudan continued to employ *jihadiya* and even recruited its own. These served with distinction throughout British East Africa, while their descendants have played important roles in colonial and postcolonial Sudanese armies. *See also* SLAVERY.

JONGLEI CANAL. A major development and irrigation scheme along the White Nile, Bahr al-Zeraf, and Sobat rivers. Construction began in the late 1970s, although it had been proposed as early as 1948. The main goals were to keep some fifteen million cubic meters of water from being lost through evaporation in the swamp or *Sudd* (q.v.) regions, as well as to establish flood control, improve river navigation, and develop an extensive agricultural scheme. The conserved water was to be shared by Egypt and Sudan. Questions were raised about climatological change and decreased rainfall to neighboring countries. However, construction by the French Companie de Construction Internationale came to a halt in 1984, after renewed civil war in the South jeopardized the security of foreign and local workers. *See also* AGRICULTURE; MALAKAL.

JUBA. Juba lies about 160 kilometers north of Nimule at the Sudanese-Ugandan border and is the dominant town in Equatoria Province (q.v.). Juba's history is connected to that of the four surrounding towns of Gondokoro, Lado (q.v.), Mongalla, and Rejaf, which over the years took turns as the provincial capital of the South. The region of Equatoria has long been isolated from northern Sudan by great distance, no railway, very poor roads, irregular steamers, and the vast *Sudd* (q.v.) swamps. Indeed Juba and its people have historically been closer to East Africa than to Khartoum (q.v.), with its interests only in the area's slaves and ivory.

The Gondokoro phase (1839–1874) began with the penetration of the southern Sudan (q.v.) by the Turks, led by Salim Qapudan (q.v.), in 1839. The Lado phase (1874–1888) followed when Charles Gordon (q.v.) moved the provincial capital there, seeking in vain to suppress the slave trade. The Rejaf phase was similar to that of Gondokoro and Lado in both history and circumstance: Rejaf had been visited during the 1838 tour of the South by Salim Qapudan, but was a mere cluster of houses of minor consequence. There were brief periods when slave and ivory commerce flourished, but the area's isolation from regular river transport and hostility by local Nuer, Bari, and Dinka (qq.v.) peoples made any serious development impossible. Mahdists occupied the town in 1888, using it as a prison for political opponents and to serve as a frontier garrison guarding the southern border. The Mahdists quickly discovered the problems of their predecessors: there was frequent talk of mutiny, attacks by hostile neighbors, and difficult transport. A new military threat arrived with the establishment of the Belgians, coming north from the Congo Free State, in the "Lado Enclave" in 1890. After the inevitable clashes, the Mahdists were forced to retreat north to Bor. Finally, following the Anglo-Egyptian (q.v.) conquest of 1898 and the clearing of the *Sudd* in 1902, the British established Mongalla as their provincial headquarters in Equatoria. With slaves no longer an export, a new economy developed based on coffee, rubber, sugar, cotton, millet, and ivory as well as crocodile and snake hides. In 1930 the British reversed their decision and moved the capital to Juba, across the river from Gondokoro and north of Rejaf.

From 1930 to the present Juba has played an important role in Sudanese politics, such as hosting the important 1947 conference that determined there would be a united Sudan rather than have its southern provinces join with East African colonies. Juba's future was looking bright until 1955, the eve of independence, when a local revolt led to the civil war that has continued, in various forms, up to the present. Temporary hope came with the Addis Ababa Agreement of 1972 (q.v.) and a plan for southern regional autonomy, and Juba University was founded. When war resumed after the "September Laws" of 1983, Juba was sent on a dizzying path of urban growth without development. It soon reached a population of 84,000 and some estimate that it reached 150,000 by 1986. Throughout the 1990s Juba found itself surrounded by the forces of the Sudanese Peoples Liberation Army (q.v.) and the Sudanese army, and remains a city under siege. Air and river transport can barely function and the connecting roads are often mined or subject to ambush. Food is often in short supply. *See also* ANTISLAVERY MOVEMENT; BAKER, SAMUEL; EMIN PASHA; MALAKAL; SLAVERY; WAU.

JUHAYNA. The largest general grouping of Sudanese "Arabs" (q.v.) as determined by their traditional genealogies. All claim descent from the Arabian peninsula, in successive waves of migration up the Nile and across the Red Sea for the past 1,400 years. In general, Juhayna Arabs have maintained a seminomadic or nomadic lifestyle, herding camels in the drier regions (Kababish, q.v.) and in the eastern grasslands (Shukriya, q.v.), cattle in the western grasslands (Baggara, q.v.), and leading sedentary, agricultural lives in the river valleys (Ja'aliyin, q.v.). Some Nubian groups also claim Arabian origins but from the descendants of the Khazrag. *See also* CAMEL-HERDING ARABS; CATTLE-HERDING ARABS.

JUNKER, WILHELM (1840–1892). This nineteenth-century German explorer left from east Africa in 1879 to take a route similar to that of James Grant and John Speke (q.v.), but when he reached the southern Sudan (q.v.) he set out westward on the north side of the Uélle River in Azande (q.v.) country. He then took a parallel route back to the east to strike the Nile in the northern *Sudd* (q.v.) to the Sobat River. Southern Sudan was a tumultuous place to be in the early 1880s: the Mahdist revolt began and Junker, as well as Emin Pasha (q.v.) and his troops, became trapped in the Lado Enclave (q.v.). It was Junker who traveled through Ugandan territory in 1886 to reach the coast and Zanzibar. From there he sailed to Vienna and began the appeal to rescue Emin Pasha. A mountain in Alur country just north of Lake Albert is named in his honor. *See also* JUBA.

– K –

KABABISH. The Kababish are a large group of camel-herding (Juhayna) Arabs (qq.v.) living to the west of the Nile in northern Kordofan and parts of Darfur (qq.v.). Their livestock production has given them substantial economic power. They represent an image of traditional Arab life less influenced by the more "African" people to the south. Their patrilineal lineages are intact and under the strong influence of their *shaykhs*. Their strong sense of autonomy and self-reliance has sometimes made them opponents to Mahdism and the Ansar (qq.v.). They suffered under the Mahdiya and their leading *shaykh* was executed by the Mahdi in 1883. Their political organization survived, however, and in the twentieth century their leaders were among the most powerful notables in the country. 'Ali al-Tum (d. 1938) was influential during British rule and members of the family still hold positions of some political importance. From the standpoint of the traditional political parties the Kababish, being neither Ansar nor Khatmiya (q.v.), generally supported the National Unionist Party (q.v.).

KAJBAR DAM PROJECT. The Kajbar Dam project is named for the Mahas Nubian village of Kajbar on the west bank of the Nile about 130 kilometers north of Dongola (q.v.) in the Northern Province (q.v.) of Sudan. The official aim of the project was to have a first phase of power generation of 80 megawatts, later expanded to 165 megawatts, and to 300 megawatts in a third stage. Aside from power, the project was supposed to increase the cultivated area from 240,000 feddans (q.v.) to 1 million feddans in the first phase and to 4 million in the final phase. The project would be financed by a levy on domestic sugar sales as well as major government donations. A Chinese company is proposed to organize the construction.

The project began on 2 July 1995 when the government initiated the Kajbar Project Public Corporation. At first this was presented as a shareholding scheme for all citizens, who would have increased agricultural yields and replaced expensive diesel-made electricity with hydroelectric power. Feasibility studies by the Chinese were completed including geological, power transmission, and other engineering aspects of the project. In February 1996 President 'Umar al-Bashir (q.v.) visited the project and started the campaign to raise the 30 billion Sudanese pounds required.

Initially the local Nubian population was supportive of this project but skepticism about government promises, fears of major landowners gaining major shares, and the sad history of forced relocations have made the project less popular. More victimization of Nubian culture and archaeology is also feared, especially for the important sites at Kerma (q.v.). At its full potential, not only will Kajbar village disappear forever, but the new flood could reach more than eight meters above the catastrophic flood levels of 1988. If this is the case, then Ardwan Island, Argon Konj, and even Kerma could be at risk.

KARAMAT AL-AWLIYA. *See* SAINTS.

KARARI. The site of the last decisive battle of the Mahdiya (q.v.), where the Anglo-Egyptian forces of Gen. H. H. Kitchener (qq.v.) destroyed the Mahdist army under Khalifa 'Abdullahi (q.v.). The battle took place on the morning of 2 September 1898 in the Karari plain, approximately six kilometers north of the Omdurman (q.v.) city limits. By 11:00 A.M. the Ansar (q.v.) had been vanquished with a staggering loss of life, due largely to the British use of an early model of machine gun known as the

Maxim gun. Sudanese casualties were conservatively estimated at 10,000 and may have reached 14,000; the combined Anglo-Egyptian casualties were 56 killed, 21 of whom died during the unnecessary but much heralded charge of the 21st Lancers. Ironically, during the early years of the Mahdi's revolt many Sudanese had imagined Karari to be the site of an eventual Armageddon between the Ansar and the British. For many Sudanese today, Karari remains hallowed ground, where martyrs for Sudanese independence fell in a valiant cause. *See also* MAHDI, MUHAMMAD AHMAD, AL-.

KARIMA. A small railhead town just below the Nile's fourth cataract, adjacent to the historically significant ruins of Jabal Barkal. Across the river and farther downstream is the modern town of Merowe (q.v.), which has grown up around the ancient ruins of Sanam. This modern Merowe must be distinguished from the ancient kingdom and townsite of Meroë, located between the fifth and sixth cataracts and long extinct.

Karima's population in 1955 was 6,000 but fell to less than 5,000 by 1965. By 1987 its population had grown to 15,000. A railway spur from Abu Hamad, on the Nile bend below the fifth cataract, serves Karima. There is some slight tourist development in Karima today: one could stay at the "Taharka Hotel," named for the Kushitic king whose palace stood at the foot of Jabal Barkal. Nearby are ancient burial pyramids, while others are upstream at Nuri and downstream at Kurru. A date canning industry is based here.

KASSALA. Perhaps the most salient feature of Kassala is the volcanic outcropping just east of the town. These massive rocks can be seen from eighty kilometers away across the vast Butana plain that stretches west to the Nile Valley. Wells and the seasonal flood of the Gash River always supplied sufficient water for the town, which lies close to the mountainous border with Ethiopia. The region is the home of various Arab (q.v.) groups such as the Hassaniya, Ashraf, Rashayda, and Shukriya (qq.v.) as well as the Beja (q.v.) and Hadendowa. Ties to Eritrean peoples were well established in the past, and were especially important during the Eritrean war of independence when thousands of Eritrean and Ethiopian refugees (q.v.) fled across the border into eastern Sudan.

In the early nineteenth century Kassala was known simply as the village of Awlad Nasir, but soon after it expanded as the followers of Muhammad 'Uthman al-Mirghani (q.v.) established their permanent home for the politically important Khatmiya (q.v.) religious order. For the first half of the Turco-Egyptian (q.v.) period, Kassala was only marginally integrated until it became the provincial capital of Taka province. Two serious revolts in the 1860s in Taka province provided substantial worries for the Turkish rulers. The first telegraph line did not reach Kassala until 1875. The Turks also made some attempts to improve agriculture in the area and even tried unsuccessfully to dam the Gash River.

Thus, Kassala was a comparatively new town even in the 1880s when it met serious attack by the rising forces of the Mahdi (q.v.). In November 1883 it came under siege, supported by a revolt of Mahdist sympathizers. By February 1884 Kassala was cut off from support at Khartoum or Suakin (qq.v.). It held out for seven months after the fall of Khartoum, but in July 1885 it was finally occupied by the Ansar (q.v.). The years of Mahdism were not very welcome in Kassala and the Khatmiya *tariqa* (q.v.) opposed the Mahdi and Khalifa (q.v.) for religious and political reasons. A severe famine in 1889 caused even greater resentment.

Following the Berlin Conference in 1884–1885 in which the leading European powers divided Africa, Italy, and Great Britain contested over rule in the Horn of Africa. Formal agreement was not reached until 1891, but the Italians in neighboring Eritrea saw an opportunity in 1894 when they captured the town in alliance with the Khatmiya. A Mahdist counterattack in 1895 failed to regain Kassala but did manage to destroy the nearby town of Mogado and all of its people. The Italians' defeat at Adowa, in Ethiopia, in March 1896 found them overextended and on 25 December 1897 they gave Kassala back to the British. The remains of the Italian fortress may still be seen to the east of Kassala.

Being a border town, Kassala has a long reputation for smuggling and banditry. The British did their best to control this problem and fostered the support of the Khatmiya leaders by rebuilding their mosque. More significant economic activity became possible after April 1924 when the railway to Port Sudan (q.v.) was connected to Kassala. Even by this time Kassala was a rather large town by contemporary Sudanese standards as the population had reached more than 35,000. The British also began a technical training school for carpenters, blacksmiths, and metal workers, but their main focus was on the development of agriculture based in the production of cotton and cotton seed. As a subsidiary of the Sudan Plantations Syndicate, the Kassala Cotton company was formed in 1929. After getting off to a bad start with little interest shown by the seminomadic peoples and a world economic depression, production substantially improved in the late 1930s. During World War II Italy sought to undermine the British presence in the Sudan and in 1940 it briefly reoccupied Kassala.

By the time of independence, Kassala had shown very modest growth with a population of about 41,000. Now connected to the rest of the nation by rail, truck, bus, car, and plane, Kassala has experienced an even more rapid population increase apart from the huge numbers of Eritrean refugees from war and famine. If estimates are correct, the town now has a population of over 150,000 and one of the most lively and diverse markets in Sudan.

KASSALA PROVINCE. Former province (q.v.) located between the Red Sea and Blue and main Niles, extending from Ethiopia to Egypt. With its capital in Kassala (q.v.), the province was approximately 131,528 square miles and contained the important grazing land of the Butana as well as the Gedaref (q.v.) plains, known for rain-fed cultivation of durra and sesame. Its population, estimated in the 1970 census at 1,629,000, included a variety of Beja and Arab (qq.v.) groups as well as other ethnicities. The region remains primarily agricultural, though the Red Sea coast is of course important for trade.

KEIRA SULTANATE. The ruling dynasty in Darfur (q.v.) from about 1640 until 1916. The Keira were the chief clan in the Kunjara branch of the Fur (q.v.). Power in Darfur passed from the Tunjur (q.v.) to the Keira in a now-obscure manner associated with the legendary figure of a "Wise Stranger," Ahmad al-Ma'qur. Sulayman Solong (q.v.) was the first recognized sultan of the Keira. Placed strategically on east-west and north-south trade routes, the sultans of Darfur were influential in the dispersal of Islam (q.v.) in the region and throughout the eastern Sahel.

Sultan Muhammad Tayrab (ca. 1752–ca. 1786) ruled the Keira Dynasty during the time it annexed Kordofan (q.v.) from 1785 to 1786. His reign was followed by that of Sultans 'Abd al-Rahman (ca.1787–1803) and Muhammad al-Fadl (1803–1838) who continued the Keira rule over Kordofan until 1821. The Sultanate was threatened by the Turco-Egyptian (q.v.) control of Kordofan in 1821, but Darfur remained independent until the defeat of Sultan Ibrahim in 1874 by Zubayr Pasha Rahma (q.v.). Claimants to the throne struggled against Ottoman and then Mahdist (q.v.) control, but they did not succeed until 'Ali Dinar (q.v.) secured autonomy from the British-controlled Sudan after the

1898 Anglo-Egyptian Condominium (q.v.); he continued his control until 1916 when the Keira Dynasty was brought to an end by the British under Hubert Huddleston (q.v.).

KERUBINO KWANYIN BOL. *See* BOL, KERUBINO KWANYIN.

KHALID, MANSOUR (1931–). A well-known Sudanese lawyer and diplomat, Khalid studied at the Universities of Khartoum (q.v.), Pennsylvania, Algiers, and Paris. After practicing as a lawyer in Khartoum (q.v.), he worked in the United Nations Secretariat (1961–1962), and in Algiers with UN Technical Assistance. After the 1969 October Revolution (q.v.) he was active in governmental affairs, especially in foreign policy. He served as minister of youth and sports (1969–1970), at the United Nations as a Sudanese delegate, and then as foreign minister (1971–1975), and as minister of education (1975–1976), all during the Ja'afar al-Nimeiri (q.v.) years.

Khalid played an important role in the negotiations leading up to the Addis Ababa Agreement of 1972 (q.v.). When this agreement ceased to be implemented and civil war broke out afresh in 1983, the newly organized Sudanese Peoples Liberation Movement (SPLM, q.v.) called for a democratic restructuring of the entire Sudan. In this process, Khalid was among the first northern intellectuals and members of the elite to join this new movement dominated by southerners and with a radically new political image of a future Sudan. He continues in his leading role as an advisor to the SPLM while also serving as the vice-chair of the World Commission on Environment and Development. His published works in Arabic and English are very numerous, but his most important certainly include his critique of the Nimeiri years in his *Numayri and the Revolution of Dis-May* (1985) and his book *The Government They Deserve* (1990).

KHALIFA. Arabic word meaning "successor" or "deputy." It can be the title for a delegate or spiritual heir of the founder or leader of a *tariqa* (q.v.). As a political title it refers to the successor of a recognized leader in the Islamic community, most notably, the successors to the Prophet Muhammad. Its common Anglicized form is "caliph." In this usage, Muhammad Ahmad al-Mahdi (q.v.) in the Sudan gave the title of "khalifa" to his political heirs. In Sudanese history reference to "The Khalifa" usually means 'Abdullahi al-Ta'ishi (q.v.), the Khalifa of the Mahdi. *See also* MAHDIYA.

KHALIL, 'ABDALLAH (1888–1971). Sudanese soldier and politician of Kenzi Nubian (q.v.) origin. He served in the Egyptian army (1910–1924) and the Sudan Defense Force (1915–1944) and was the first Sudanese to reach the rank of *Miralai* (Brigadier). In 1944 he was an influential member of the Advisory Council of the Northern Sudan (q.v.), which became a pro-Mahdist organization. Khalil was a founder of the Umma Party (q.v.) in 1945 and became its first secretary-general. In 1947 he was an Umma Party member of the Independence Front in opposition to Khatmiya (q.v.) interests. Colonial administrators J. W. Robertson and Robert Howe (qq.v.) used Khalil as a vehicle to put their views into the Sudanese political environment. Because of the sectarian and sometimes divisive nature of Sudanese nationalism, some have criticized Khalil for playing this role in the waning days of colonialism. An example of this was Khalil being named as the minister of agriculture in 1947; he insisted that this was necessary to balance the strong role of the Khatmiya at that time and to respond to the Sudanization process.

Khalil served as leader of the Legislative Assembly (q.v.) starting in 1948 and the Executive Council, and he was the Umma representative on the Constitutional Commission. He was elected to Parliament in 1953 and became prime minister in the Umma Peoples Democratic Party (q.v.) coalition government that replaced Isma'il al-Azhari's (q.v.) government in 1956. He was prime minister and minister of defense until the military coup by Ibrahim Abboud (q.v.) in 1958.

KHARTOUM. The capital of Sudan. After Sinnar (q.v.) fell in 1821 the Turco-Egyptian (q.v.) rulers began their government known as the Turkiya in Wad Medani (q.v.), but soon found that their strategic interests were better served if they moved their capital to Khartoum. When Muhammad 'Uthman Pasha arrived in 1825 he constructed a fort and garrison to the east of the Mogren village where Shaykh Arbab had built his religious school. As the administration of the Turks strengthened, urban populations began to expand. By 1826 Khartoum was established as the official residence of the government of the Sudan. The rule of 'Ali Khurshid Pasha (q.v.), from 1826 to 1838, was progressive by Turkish standards, and much attention was devoted to the improvement of Khartoum. A mosque was built in 1829 to be replaced with a larger one in 1837; military barracks were constructed in Khartoum in order to have troops stationed more closely than Halfaya (Khartoum North, q.v.). A military storehouse and a dockyard were built. The Turkish administration even provided free materials for Khartoum's inhabitants to build new, more permanent homes.

Under these conditions, trade was protected and commerce was strongly encouraged. As time passed, a variety of Sudanese ethnic groups, especially the Shayqiya, Ja'aliyin, Danagla (qq.v.), and Egyptians comprised much of Khartoum's population. The Khartoum market also grew with a profitable trade in ivory, gum arabic, indigo, sugar, cotton, millet, ostrich feathers, sesame, and especially slaves (q.v.). During Funj (q.v.) times (1504–1821), the slave trade had sent some 1,500 slaves to Egypt each year. After the end of Funj rule this trade was stepped up considerably with some big government raids capturing as many as 5,000 human beings annually. By 1838 the slave trade counted some 10,000–12,000 captives per year. From 1840 to 1860 trade was even more heavily committed to slavery and 40,000–60,000 slaves were said to be sold yearly in Khartoum.

By the 1850s Khartoum had already grown to a town of 3,000 houses. A few Christian missionaries (q.v.) set up their tents along the banks of the Blue Nile in 1848 but disease and isolation took a heavy toll on their spirits. These missionaries joined a few Italian doctors and druggists as well as some Greek (q.v.) traders providing goods such as cloth and beads to Ja'aliyin and Danagla (qq.v.) traders, who would set out south and west to trade in the more remote parts of the Sudan.

In 1862 the Khartoum Chamber of Commerce was formed and in 1866 the governments of Austria, France, Tuscany, Italy, and Persia set up consulates to watch over their commercial and political interests. The Egyptian-owned Banque du Soudan was opened but failed in 1873. The 1860s also saw the creation of a para-military police force for the main towns of the Sudan, the first time such an institution was known to the country. Muhammad Sa'id Pasha, who ruled from 1854 to 1863, made an effort to decentralize the administration of the Sudan to have greater control of the countryside and of the slave traders in particular. Some services in Khartoum did show improvement such as the post office and 270-bed hospital, which were opened in 1873, but effective administration was weak beyond the capital province.

Khartoum's population reached its nineteenth-century height of about 30,000 people, as periodic floods (e.g., 1830, 1866, and 1878) and epidemics of the plague and cholera helped to restrict population growth. While these factors added to the woes of Khartoum, the central problems remained political and economic. In this context the religious movement known as the Mahdiya (q.v.) took root in 1881 and four years later the weak, besieged city of Khartoum fell to the Mahdist soldiers. The representative of the Egyptian Khedive, Gordon Pasha (qq.v.), was killed and

Khartoum was sacked. Much of Khartoum was in ruins and many of its inhabitants were killed or moved elsewhere.

After the death of the Mahdi, his successor, Khalifa 'Abdullahi (q.v.), methodically destroyed the remaining portions of Khartoum in 1886 to put an end to the symbol of the Turco-Egyptian presence in the Sudan. Any people who remained were moved across the White Nile to Omdurman (q.v.), the capital of Mahdism.

With the overthrow of the Mahdist rule in 1898 the entire area was cleared of debris, and under the authority of General H. H. Kitchener (q.v.) the new city of Khartoum was laid out. The streets were long and wide, interlaced with diagonals meeting at round-abouts that Kitchener's military mind saw as points for machine guns to command large areas. The overall pattern of the street layout was in the form of a series of Union Jacks.

Residential areas along the banks of the Blue Nile were surveyed for British occupation. Gordon Memorial College (later The University of Khartoum, qq.v.) was opened in 1903 and a military barracks and "Native Lodging Areas" (at Burri, east of Khartoum) were works in progress. In 1909 the railway bridge crossed the Blue Nile, thus giving the capital a fairly rapid link to the coast at Port Sudan (q.v.). The city grew quickly and it expanded to the south, east, and west. Under the leadership of Governor E. G. Sarsfield-Hall (1929–1936) an industrial area was provided for west of Sharia Qasr (Victoria Avenue) and exigencies of traffic control made some of Kitchener's diagonal streets obsolete. A master plan was designed to account for European and "Native" residential areas, for workshops and factories, for a market center, for "noxious" trades, and for owners of animals and their vehicles. The Khartoum airport lies close to the city and in the path of its constant expansion; it may soon fall victim to the pressures of urban growth. While the city is vastly bigger than in the days of the British, the essential inner form remains the same except for the "New Extensions" to the south.

In the twentieth century Khartoum's population has changed markedly. By 1930, as the British colonial capital, it had reached 50,000 people, but by independence the population had already grown to 96,000. Rural to urban migration resulted in still greater growth after independence. By 1964 Khartoum had reached 185,000 and the 1973 census stated there were 334,000 inhabitants. The most recent population estimates in 1994 suggest that Khartoum may have attained a population of over 2 million. With 22.5 percent of Sudan's total population now living in urban areas, Sudan's primary city may be larger than this figure suggests. For example, this figure underestimates the hundreds of thousands of refugees (q.v.) from the civil war and foreign wars, Sahelian famine (q.v.), drought, and widespread underdevelopment. Such conditions have generated numberless squatters who live at the periphery of this huge capital city agglomeration, which probably numbers 3.5 to 4.0 million for the metropolitan Three Towns (q.v.) area.

KHARTOUM NORTH. The area known collectively as Halfayat al-Muluk, or simply Halfaya, arose around the two hamlets of Hillet Hamad and Hillet Khujali. Both of these hamlets grew around the tombs (*qubbat*, q.v.) of the Tuti Island Mahas holymen. The early eighteenth century saw relative stabilization of these two villages, which lasted until the arrival of Turkish rule. In 1772 the explorer James Bruce (q.v.) passed through Halfaya and termed it a "large, handsome and pleasant town, although built of mud." Khartoum (q.v.) was not mentioned in this account. In the 1820s a battalion of Turkish troops was stationed at Halfaya or, more specifically Khujali, under Mahu Pasha. A number of Shayqiya (q.v.) people who had originally given heavy resistance to Turkish penetration finally joined with the Turks and, as a reward for their alliance, they were given land to farm and occupy in Khartoum North.

By 1885 Khartoum North had been overrun by Mahdist troops and by the beginning of 1887 almost all of the population had been removed to Omdurman (q.v.) or had fled south along the Blue Nile. When the British returned in 1898 there was nothing but a few houses standing in Hillet Hamad and Hillet Khujali. All subsequent development has occurred since. Today Khartoum North, or "Khartoum Bahri," as it is more commonly known, is the portion of the Three Towns (q.v.) showing the most rapid rate of growth, as it is the area for industrialization and for residential occupation by great numbers of migrants. The bridges that connect Khartoum North to Khartoum and now Omdurman will, no doubt, stimulate further expansion. The bridge in the Three Towns that crosses the Blue Nile parallel to the old Blue Nile bridge will provide convenient access to the eastern portions of Khartoum North as it spreads along the north bank of the river. The newest bridge links the city to Tuti Island.

In the twentieth century Khartoum North's population has changed markedly. Even well into the first decades of the twentieth century, Khartoum North was only a cluster of Arab and Nubian (q.v.) hamlets. It was not until 1950 that it reached a population of 31,000. By independence the population had increased to 40,000. Rural to urban migration resulted in still greater growth since independence. By 1964 Khartoum North had doubled to 82,000 and the 1973 census stated there were 151,000 inhabitants. In the 1983 census Khartoum North had doubled again, reaching a population of 341,155, and perhaps this figure seriously underestimates the tens of thousands of refugee (q.v.) squatters who live at the periphery of this city.

KHARTOUM PROVINCE. A former province (q.v.) located around the city of Khartoum (q.v.) and the junction of the Blue and White Niles, it comprised approximately 8,097 square miles. The site of ancient habitation, it has been the Sudan's administrative center since the Turkiya (q.v.) period. It contains Sudan's most important urban area, the Three Towns (q.v.).

KHARTOUM SUMMIT OF 1967. A meeting of Arab foreign ministers and heads of state in Khartoum (q.v.) following the disastrous Arab defeat in the June 1967 Arab-Israeli war. The choice of Sudan for an Arab summit was a political victory for Prime Minister Muhammad Ahmad Mahjub (q.v.), who sought an active role in conciliating Arab disputes; however, the summit itself did nothing to resolve the Arab-Israeli conflict (q.v.). Of the four resolutions passed at the summit, the third was the most significant. It stated: "The Arab heads of state have agreed to unite their political efforts at the international and diplomatic level [to force Israeli withdrawal from occupied territories]. . . . This will be done within the framework of the main principles by which the Arab states abide, namely, no peace with Israel, no recognition of Israel, no negotiations with it, and insistence on the rights of the Palestinian people in their own country." Like many resolutions this was a compromise formula, with the second clause essentially negating the first. Unrealistically, it expected Israel to surrender captured territory without accompanying Arab assurances of peace and security. The summit also resolved differences between Egypt and Saudi Arabia over Yemen, approved Arab subsidies for Egypt, and rejected suspending the pumping of oil as a political strategy.

KHARTOUM UNIVERSITY STUDENT UNION (KUSU). An organization that grew out of the preindependence General Students' Union and was recognized in 1956 at the time of the transformation of Gordon Memorial College into the University of Khartoum (qq.v.). Historically in the forefront of many political movements, KUSU issued the first memorandum against the military regime of Gen. Ibrahim Abboud (q.v.) in December 1959. Likewise, KUSU led the first demonstrations against the same government in the 1964 October Revolution (q.v.). The leadership of KUSU frequently vacillated between the Sudanese Communist Party and Muslim Brotherhood (qq.v.), with the former dominating the university student movement in the 1960s, while the latter tended to dominate in the 1970s and 1980s. As more universities took their place within Sudanese higher education, including Omdurman Islamic University, Ahliya University, University of Gezira, and Juba University, to name the major examples, the central role of the Khartoum University student movement diminished.

KHASHM AL-GIRBA. An agricultural project and resettlement area in the eastern Sudan near Kassala (q.v.). This was developed for Nubians (q.v.) displaced by the inundation caused by the building of the High Dam at Aswan.

KHATMIYA. A *tariqa* (q.v.) established and led by the Mirghani (q.v.) family. The founder was Muhammad 'Uthman al-Mirghani (1792–1853), a student of Ahmad ibn Idris (qq.v.). The order was introduced into the Sudan by Muhammad 'Uthman during a trip at the end of the Funj (q.v.) era. It was firmly established there by his son, Hasan (1819–1869). The order developed branches in Arabia, Egypt, and Eritrea, but its major influence has been in the Sudan where its history is tied to the experience of the Mirghani family. Sometimes called the Mirghaniya, it is strongest in the northern and eastern sections of the Sudan.

KHEIR, AHMAD (1905–1994). Sudanese lawyer and political leader educated at Gordon Memorial College (q.v.) and the Khartoum School of Law. He was active in early intellectual and nationalist discussion groups. As a leader of the Wad Medani (q.v.) Literary Society, he was credited with the idea for the Graduates Congress (q.v.) and was later active in its work. Kheir assisted in the writing of the Congress memorandum in 1942 that set modern Sudanese politics in motion. He favored the idea of unity with Egypt and he joined the Ashigga Party (q.v.) in 1950. He served as foreign minister throughout the Ibrahim Abboud (q.v.) military regime (1958–1964) and did not take an active political role after the 1964 October Revolution (q.v.). Kheir is well known for his important book *Kifah Jil* (Struggle of a Generation).

KHURSHID, 'ALI (ca. 1786–1845). The first governor-general of the Sudan under Turco-Egyptian (q.v.) rule, serving from 1835 to 1838. His short period as governor-general does not accurately reflect his role for a number of years preceding, wherein he developed the political infrastructure of the Sudan with a civil administration, a fiscal bureaucracy, and an Islamic judiciary. His military career spanned more than a decade in the Sudan, where he attempted to bring eastern regions bordering Ethiopia under Turco-Egyptian control. His efforts and those of his successor, Abu Widan, failed to bring the eastern group, the Hadendowa, into submission.

KID, KHALID HUSSEIN AHMED OSMAN AL- (1942–1995). This soldier, politician, and scholar was popularly known to Sudanese as Khalid al-Kid. He was openly a member of the Sudanese Communist Party (q.v.). After completion of secondary school he joined the military academy. Due to his political sympathies he was repeatedly in and out of favor with various national governments and was imprisoned for several years by the Ja'afar al-Nimeiri (q.v.) government and was a detainee in one of the notorious "ghost houses" of the 'Umar al-Bashir (q.v.) regime between 1989 and 1991. He sought political exile in Great Britain, where he obtained political asylum in 1991 and remained until his death from a car accident in 1995.

KIIR, SALVA (MAYAR DIT). Kiir was one of the earliest and most loyal followers of John Garang (q.v.). Kiir and Garang were central in the founding of the Sudanese Peoples Liberation Army (SPLA, q.v.) in Ethiopia in 1984 following the 1983 southern mutinies. However, in the military command structure, Kiir was outranked by Arok Thon Arok (q.v.). All three are of Dinka (q.v.) origin but from different southern provinces. Kiir currently holds the rank of commander, and as the deputy to the SPLA Council, he has key oversight responsibilities in both foreign and domestic policy. In this capacity he was a leader in the failed peace negotiation efforts in 1994. During the times of internal revolt against Garang, Salva Kiir has not swerved from his support of the SPLA-Mainstream.

KITCHENER, LORD HORATIO HERBERT (1850–1916). Kitchener was a British soldier and colonial administrator of the highest order. After service in the Royal Engineers of the British Army in the Middle East and Cyprus, he was attached to the Egyptian army in 1882 and served in a variety of campaigns in the Sudan during the Mahdist (q.v.) era. In 1888 he was appointed as adjutant general of the Egyptian army and was appointed *sirdar* or commander of the Egyptian army in 1892. In this capacity Kitchener launched the mechanized, railway-carried, Anglo-Egyptian "reconquest" of the Sudan from 1896 to 1898, allegedly to avenge the death of Charles Gordon (q.v.). Attending journalists of "The River War" gave fresh accounts of the British advances as the Mahdists were defeated month after month, finally culminating in the massacre at Karari (q.v.) in which at least 10,000 Sudanese were killed in a single morning. Immediately thereafter Kitchener confronted the French forces under Captain Jean-Baptiste Marchand in an incident at Fashoda (q.v.) on the Upper Nile that took place in the context of French rivalry for control of the Sudan. By the next year, the soldiers of Kitchener had hunted down and killed the Khalifa 'Abdullahi (q.v.).

Kitchener served as governor-general of the Sudan from 19 January to 22 December 1899, and was instrumental in raising British funds for the building of Gordon Memorial College (later The University of Khartoum, qq.v.). He left the Sudan to take a military appointment in South Africa during the British war against the Boers. In 1911–1914 he served as British agent and consul-general in Egypt and took an active role in laying the foundations for the future Gezira Scheme (q.v.) in the Sudan. He was drowned at sea during World War I while serving as British secretary of state for war.

KNOBLECHER, IGNAZ (1822–1858). Knoblecher was a Slovenian Austrian missionary active in the Sudan from 1849 to 1857. He worked especially in the South with support from the Mazza Institute. In 1851 he received support from the Austrian Emperor Franz Josef, who also established an Austrian Vice-Consulate in Khartoum (q.v.). Knoblecher bought land from Bari (q.v.) Chief Lutweri to build a mission in Equatoria (q.v.). In 1853 Knoblecher built a mission in Khartoum. He died in Naples in 1858. *See also* JUBA.

KOBBEI (KOBBÉ, COBBE). A now-deserted but formerly important trading town in Darfur (q.v.). At a time when most of Darfur consisted of little more than villages and hamlets, Kobbei was a town of about 6,000 inhabitants, situated at the southern end of the famous Forty Days Road (q.v.) that extended north into Egypt. Kobbei's markets were held twice weekly and caravans as large as 2,000 camels and 1,000 slaves (q.v.) were known in the seventeenth and early eighteenth centuries. Its population was heterogeneous, including *Fellata* (q.v.) migrants from the western Sahel, Fur (q.v.), Kordofani Arabs, Egyptians, and Nubians (q.v.). The site of Kobbei was ringed with mountains, which offered a natural defense and brought water into its wells. However, a superior water supply at al-Fasher (q.v.) contributed to that town's assumption of the functions of Kobbei. When al-Fasher began to grow in the early eighteenth century, Kobbei became superfluous and faded from existence.

KODOK. *See* FASHODA.

KOKA DAM DECLARATION, 24 MARCH 1986. In the post-Nimeiri (q.v.) Sudan, with no meaningful contact between the southern opposition and the new government in Khartoum (q.v.), the National Alliance for National Salvation (NANS), comprised of a broad group of political parties, and the Sudanese People's Liberation Movement (SPLM, q.v.) met for four days coming to agreement that a critical need existed to create a "New Sudan" that would be free from racism, tribalism, sectarianism, and all causes of discrimination and disparity, and that this process could best begin by convening a National Constitutional Convention. The Koka Dam Declaration called for an immediate lifting of the state of emergency; repeal of the "September Laws" (q.v.); adoption of the 1956 constitution, as amended in 1964 with the incorporation of regional government; abrogation of all military pacts between Sudan and other countries that impinge upon Sudan's national sovereignty; and a cease-fire. The Koka Dam Declaration was a significant step in the peace process of the 1980s and was signed by all major Sudanese political parties except the National Islamic Front (q.v.) and the Democratic Unionist Party (DUP, q.v.). Two years later, in November 1988, the DUP issued a joint declaration with the SPLM that contained all of the major points of the Koka Dam Declaration. *See also* ISLAMIC LAW.

KORDOFAN PROVINCE. Region and former province (q.v.) located between the White Nile and Darfur (q.v.), comprising approximately 146,930 square miles with an estimated population (1970 census) of 2,811,000. Ruled by the Fur Sultanate (q.v.) from the seventeenth century and occupied briefly by the Funj Sultanate of Sinnar (q.v.) in the eighteenth, it was brought under centralized control by the Turco-Egyptian army of Muhammad Khusraw the Daftardar (qq.v.) in 1821. In ancient times the Nuba (q.v.) peoples moved into the hill country in the southern region, where they often successfully resisted outside control. The Arab (q.v.) population of Kordofan, especially the cattle-herding Arabs (q.v.) of the south, formed the nucleus of the Mahdi's (q.v.) following in the late nineteenth century, while the Kababish camel-herding

Arabs (qq.v.) to the north opposed the Mahdiya (q.v.) at great expense. Kordofan contains a number of settled Arab peoples, especially around the towns of el-Obeid, al-Nahud (qq.v.), and Bara, and during the Turco-Egyptian and Anglo-Egyptian (q.v.) periods had a small Greek (q.v.) population. Both agricultural and pastoral in economy, Kordofan produces most of the world's supply of gum arabic, and a dairy industry is located in Babanusa in the southwest.

KOSTI. Kosti lies on the west bank of the White Nile south of al-Dueim (q.v.). Much of its existence rests upon its critical location at a point where West African pilgrims would traverse the river on their way to Mecca, and where the British built a railway bridge in 1910 that opened the very first railway west of the White Nile in the Sudan. This railway continues to other parts of Kordofan and Darfur (qq.v.) and has a spur to Wau (q.v.) in the south, the only southern town with rail service, when it is not closed because of military action.

Named for a Greek (q.v.) shopowner even before the railway bridge, Kosti served as a receiving and transporting center for goods and livestock from Kordofan and Darfur as well as the northern parts of the southern provinces. When the river steamer was in operation it often started from Kosti and then went farther south. Efforts have been made to start a meat-processing factory in Kosti, but the railway may ultimately have taken more business out of Kosti than it brought in. In recent decades a great deal of hope has been placed in the large-scale production of sugar in the Gezira (q.v.); the raw sugar cane is processed at the industrial facility at Kenana near to Kosti.

Kosti's population also shows seasonal variation depending upon cycles in herding and needs for agricultural labor in the Gezira. In 1956 Kosti had a population of 23,000 and by 1964 it had reached 39,000. In 1969 there were 49,000 inhabitants and in the last census in 1983 it had reached 91,946. Unlike neighboring al-Dueim, which grew mostly by natural increase, Kosti's population growth involves rather substantial in-migration, especially refugees (q.v.) from the civil war farther south and from drought to the west.

– L –

LADO ENCLAVE. The Lado Enclave played a key, if temporary, role in the colonial history of the southern Sudan (q.v.). Its history is connected with that of the four surrounding towns of Gondokoro, Rejaf, Mongalla, and Juba (q.v.). Charles Gordon (q.v.) made Lado the capital of Equatoria (q.v.) in 1874 when he began his vain attempt to suppress the slave trade. It soon grew to a town of about 8,000, and Emin Pasha (q.v.), governor in 1878, described it as a town of about 2,000 thatched houses, a mosque, Koranic school, and small hospital. With the period of the Mahdiya (q.v.) came the isolation of Lado, and beginning in 1882 Mahdist forces prevented steamers from reaching the town. Though he was able to organize a temporary defense of the town from both Mahdist and local Equatorian threats, Emin's position became untenable and he was rescued in 1888 by the explorer Henry M. Stanley. Mahdist forces arrived at Lado in October 1888 to find an empty town. Lado became the subject of imperialist machinations with the signing of the Mackinnon Treaty of May 1890, whereby Great Britain recognized the authority of King Leopold of the Belgians in the Lado Enclave in exchange for certain trading rights. *See also* ANTISLAVERY MOVEMENT; BAKER, SAMUEL; SLAVERY.

LAGU, JOSEPH (1931–). Southern soldier and political leader, educated at the Sudan Military College and commissioned in the Sudanese army in 1960. In 1963 Lagu left the army and became involved in southern opposition forces. By 1968 he was in command of the Anya Nya I (q.v.) forces in eastern Equatoria (q.v.). In 1971 he formed the Southern Sudan Liberation Movement (SSLM, q.v.) and succeeded in bringing together a wide range of southern guerrilla and political leaders. He was the major southern leader involved in the negotiations leading up to the Addis Ababa Agreement (q.v.) of 1972 and was able to secure the participation of the southern military forces in the cease-fire involved in that settlement. Lagu became inspector-general of the Sudanese Armed Forces and in 1974 assumed the post of Officer Commanding, Sudanese Armed Forces in the Southern Region.

In 1978 Lagu was summarily dismissed from the army by President Ja'afar Nimeiri (q.v.), ending any speculation that he would become the first southern vice-president of the Republic. He was elected president of the High Executive Council governing the South in 1979 during the Addis Ababa peace, but forced out of leadership in 1981 over his inability to unify southern political forces. He was a member of the National Defense Council during the southern uprisings that followed the 1983 Islamization (q.v.) of state laws. Finally appointed vice-president under Nimeiri in 1985, he met U.S. Vice-President George Bush and discussed the danger of extending Islamic law in the South. An opponent of Colonel John Garang (q.v.), Lagu has played no significant role in military or political affairs since Nimeiri's ouster in 1985.

LAM AKOL AJAWIN. Lam Akol was a professor of engineering at the University of Khartoum (q.v.) who had long been sympathetic to southern grievances. By 1985 this Shilluk (q.v.) soldier and politician fled to the South to join the Sudanese Peoples Liberation Army/Movement (SPLA/M, q.v.). In late 1989 he represented the SPLA at the failed Nairobi peace talks with Mansour Khalid (q.v.), an early northern member of the SPLA, and other ranking SPLA members from the South. He broke from the SPLA-Mainstream force following the April 1991 formation of the separatist Southern Sudanese Independence Movement (SSIM, q.v.), but stayed in Nairobi. By April 1992 other divisions appeared among his followers and by January 1994 he was expelled from the SSIM and created the rival SPLA-United force, which he operated in his Upper Nile (q.v.) Shilluk homeland. In January 1997 Lam Akol split once again from the movement he had formed. With his increased isolation, he was a signatory of the Frankfurt statement in February, which aligned him more closely with the National Islamic Front in Khartoum (qq.v). Among the issues of recent concern were blame for the Malakal (q.v.) attacks, which Lam Akol said were either the work of John Garang or Riek Machar (qq.v.).

LAMPSON, SIR MILES WEDDERBURN (1880–1964). High Commissioner of the Anglo-Egyptian (q.v.) Sudan in Cairo from January 1934, when he followed Sir Percy Hyham Loraine. As all High Commissioners, Lampson was in charge of Sudanese foreign affairs while the governor-general was concerned with internal policy. He was inclined to see the independence of the Sudan at an early date. As a result of the Anglo-Egyptian Treaty of 1936 (q.v.) Lampson became the British ambassador to Egypt and was in this position until 1946. His views on the Sudan were partly framed by his concern about a powerful greater Egypt and British interests in the Suez Canal, so that two separate nations would better serve British interests. King Faruq (q.v.) and other Egyptian factions opposed this position, but in 1942 Lampson made it clear by force of arms that the British would be in charge of Egyptian foreign policy relative to the Sudan.

Lampson's term of office was at a period of intense rivalry between 'Abd al-Rahman al-Mahdi and 'Ali Mirghani and the emergent Graduates Congress (qq.v.), but he was more concerned about the defense of the Sudan in the context of World War II. In the postwar period the call for Sudanese independence grew louder and Lampson favored a process of Sudanization of the administration.

LANGUAGES. It is impossible to assert a specific number of languages or cultures for Sudan, as any reckoning depends upon the degree of difference or similarity that a linguist might ascribe to a given people and their sociolinguistic relatives. With this in mind, one might identify more than 100 different subgroups or, more usefully, describe this linguistic diversity as members of the principal language clusters.

Culturally, some consider themselves "Arabs" (q.v.) or simply Sudanese. Arabic (q.v.), a Semitic or Afro-Asiatic language, is the *linga franca* of the country whether one is "Arab," Muslim, or neither. However, Sudan has diverse and numerous representatives of the Sudanic-language subgroups (Nilotic and Nubian serve as examples), as well as pockets of Cushitic, Furian, Kenuric, Kordofanian, and Niger-Congo languages. *See also* RACE; LITERATURE.

LEAGUE OF UNIVERSITY WOMEN GRADUATES. Founded by Mahasin Sa'ad (q.v.) in 1964 in the context of increasing numbers of female university students. The activities of the League focused on research and study of women's (q.v.) problems, but it faltered initially due to small membership. Reactivated in 1970 by Haja Kashif Badri and Fathiya Fadli and renamed League of University and Higher Institutions Graduates, its new focus was on the problems of women and children. In 1972 its activities ceased.

LEGISLATIVE ASSEMBLY. An elected, representative assembly created after World War II as a part of the process leading up to Sudanese self-rule. It succeeded the Advisory Council for the Northern Sudan and met certain objections to that body since it contained southern as well as northern representatives and was more fully elective. It was created by an ordinance in 1948 and had limited powers. Khatmiya (q.v.) leaders and the prounity of the Nile Valley politicians and parties boycotted the Assembly, which meant that it was dominated by Ansar and Umma Party (qq.v.) members. The leader of the Assembly was 'Abdallah Khalil (q.v.). The Assembly was replaced by the self-governing Parliament elected in 1953 following the Anglo-Egyptian Agreement of 1953 (q.v.).

LIBERAL PARTY. A small northern party, formed in 1944 by splitting from the Ashigga Party (q.v.). It split again in 1945 with the group supporting an independent Sudan joining the Independence Front (q.v.) but was gradually absorbed into the Umma Party (q.v.). Those advocating unity with Egypt, the Liberal Unionists, advocated a federal type system and gradual independence. In 1948 the Liberal Unionists joined the Interior Struggle Front, and by 1952 they joined with the National Unionist Party (q.v.). Among the early Liberal Unionist leaders was Hasan al-Tahir Zarruq (q.v.). The other faction was known as the Liberal Secessionists, but it never attracted much following.

LIBERAL PARTY (SOUTHERN). Successor to the Southern Party (q.v.), formed in 1954 with Buth Diu (q.v.) as secretary-general. The party tended to work with the Umma Party (q.v.) and supported a federal system for the Sudan. The party split into wings led by Stanislaus Paysama and Benjamin Lwoki (qq.v.) in 1958. After the 1964 October Revolution (q.v.) Paysama was president of a new Liberal Party that contested elections but did not win many parliamentary seats.

LIBERAL UNIONIST PARTY. *See* LIBERAL PARTY.

LIKAYLIK, MUHAMMAD ABU (ca. 1710–1776). A Funj (q.v.) military commander who became the virtual ruler of the Sultanate of Sinnar (q.v.). He won a series of battles and became the governor of Kordofan (q.v.). In 1761 he was joined by the old Funj nobility and deposed Sultan Badi IV. He and his family ruled through a series of puppet sultans. Although his clan, the Hamaj (q.v.), dominated the state, they were unable to prevent a series of debilitating civil wars.

LITERATURE. Many of the major ethnolinguistic groups in Africa are represented within the borders of Sudan, so Sudanese literature has affinities with much other African literature. However, Sudan's complex ethnic and linguistic character as well as its racial and cultural admixture have sparked heated debates about the national language and literature.

Modern Sudanese literature originated with the spread of the Arabic-Islamic culture that flourished during the Funj Sultanates (q.v.), for which the *Tabaqat Wad Dafallah* (q.v.) is the principal preserved record. During the period of the Turkiya (q.v.) there coexisted the repetitive, decorative poetry of the Egyptian-educated '*ulama* (q.v.) and the colloquial Arabic (q.v.) poetry of ordinary people. Sudanese poetry began to reflect the realities of new political struggles during the Mahdiya (q.v.), when chiefly praise poetry (*madh*) was composed in honor of the Mahdi and Mahdist capital of Omdurman (qq.v.).

Beginning with the Condominium (q.v.) in 1899, the sensibilities of the nationalist intellectuals were conditioned by the imposed English language and style of education. By 1924 the national White Flag (q.v.) rebellion spawned a new patriotic literature and poetry. The songs of Khalil Farah, which were halfway between literary and colloquial Arabic, expressed the fervent nationalist sentiments of the politically conscious, newly educated Sudanese to the nonliterate masses.

During this period short-lived but lively journals such as *al-Sudan, al-Nahda,* and *al-Fajr* (qq.v.) sprang up. Writers like al-Tijani Yusuf Bashir and Muhammad Ahmad Mahjub (qq.v.) made their initial appearance in *al-Fajr*. The *Fajr* group was aware of Sudan's hybrid cultural traditions and the historical currents that made it unique, and they sought to shape the linguistic symbols of a national identity. Muhammad Ahmad Mahjub expressed the idea of a Sudanese literature "written in Arabic but infused with the idiom of our land because this is what distinguishes the literature of one nation from another." The *Fajr* group's rediscovery of the communal roots of identity and creativity found its first real expression in the works of Muhammad al-Mahdi al-Majdhub. He was the first poet whose work reflects the consciousness of belonging to both the "Negro" and "Arab" tradition.

In the 1960s there emerged a new group of poets who spoke to the "authentic voice of Afro-Arabic identity." For these poets there was no longing for a fusion of the twin threads of African and Arabic culture; rather they were convinced that they were reconciled on the poetic level. These poets were finely tuned to the intellectual and cultural currents of the contemporary world, especially Africa, the Arab world, and the Third World. Because they were active politically, including the struggle for independence, the October Revolution (q.v.), and the 1985 *intifada* (q.v.) that toppled Ja'afar Nimeiri (q.v.), many were forced into exile outside Sudan.

Among the more recent group who have had collections of work published are Salah Ahmad Ibrahim, *Ghabat al-Abanus* (The Forest of Ebony); Mustafa Sana, *al-Bahr al-Qadim* (The Ancient Sea); Muhammad al-Mekki Ibrahim, *Ummati* (My Nation); Muhammad 'Abd al-Hayy, *al-'Awda ila Sinnar* (Sinnar, a Homecoming); and al-Nur 'Uthman, *Sahw al-Kalimat al-Mansiya* (The Awakening of the Forgotten Words). Their poetry blends the imagery of Arabia and Africa, the twin origins of the culture.

The literary genre of the novel in Sudan can be divided into pre- and postindependence periods; like other literary works, they have been concerned with the assertion of Sudanese identity both at the individual and collective levels. While the preindependence novels are combative and self-assertive, the postindependence ones are more openly declarative of Sudanese historical identity, with both its positive and negative aspects.

In the first category we find such works as *Innahum Bashir* (They are Men) by Khalil 'Abdullah al-Haj; *Ghurbat al-Ruh* (The Banishment of the Spirit) by Ibrahim Hardello; and *Bida'yat al-Rabi'* (The Beginning of Spring) by Abi Bakr Khalid, published in 1958, just two years after independence. Abi Bakr Khalid's novel presents a history of the beginning of fiction writing in the Sudan during the 1930s and 1940s. It discusses the lives and works of such writers as al-Mahjub Muhammad 'Ashri al-Siddiq, Hamza al-Malik Tambal, al-Tijani Yusuf Bashir, and Mu'awiya Muhammad Nur, all of whom still exert considerable influence on the style and thought of contemporary Sudanese novelists.

Two novels, *Hadatha fi'l-Qariyya* (It Happened in the Village) and *Amal al-Layl wa al-Balda* (Chores of the Night and the Town), by Ibrahim 'Ishaq Ibrahim along with al-Tayyib Salih's (q.v.) *'Urs al-Zayn* (The Wedding of Zein) and *Bandar Shah* (two parts of which have been published) are considered to be those postindependence novels that attempt to project both the negative and positive aspects of the Sudanese identity. Tayyib Salih's novel, *Mawsim al-Hijra ila Shamal* (Season of Migration to the North), perhaps the best-known work by a Sudanese outside of the country, not only deals with the complexity of Sudanese identity, but also is a novel that is concerned with postcolonial issues and, finally, all of humankind.

Sudanese short story writing has been pursued as both explicit and implicit social protest. Most of the short story writers have adopted a form that could demonstrate their political and social views as critical of their own society or the impact of foreign culture. Though most Sudanese short stories are characterized by a certain measure of realism, it is possible that the form of the short story is more akin to the traditional Sudanese narrative, lyric poetry, thus making it more acceptable to the average Sudanese.

Two collections, edited by Osman Hasan Ahmed, *A Short Anthology of Sudanese Literature* (1978) and *Sixteen Sudanese Short Stories* (1981), include short stories from the southern Sudan where creative writing received a new impetus after the Addis Ababa Agreement of 1972 (q.v.).

Finally, southern Sudanese have often written in English, reflecting a rich cultural background significantly different from the Arab-Islamic one. A number of these writers adapted folktales into short stories that appeared periodically in the journal *Sudanow* until 1989. Francis Deng's (q.v.) two recent novels, *Seed of Redemption* and *Cry of the Owl*, might be called political allegories. His major concern in both novels is with the historical difficulties that have characterized relations between the North and South. This creates for the reader an acute moral awareness of the complexity of North-South divisions that have fed the chronic political instability of the nation since independence. Nonetheless, both novels are deeply concerned with attempts to provide insight into how to achieve a positive solution to the conflict. [by Constance E. Berkley]. *See also* BINT AL-MAKKAWI; MADIH NABAWI; SHAGHABA AL-MARGHUMABIYA.

LIVESTOCK. *See* AGRICULTURE.

LOGALI, HILARY PAUL (1930–1998). Sudanese administrator and political leader of Bari (q.v.) origin. He was educated in the University of Khartoum (q.v.) and Yale University, being recalled from Yale after the 1964 October Revolution (q.v.) to become minister of public works. Logali was subsequently minister of communications (1965) and of labor (1967–68). He was secretary-general and later vice-president of the Southern Front (q.v.), and was elected to Parliament in 1968. After the 1969 May Revolution (q.v.) Logali was detained briefly and then named commissioner for Equatoria (q.v.) Province. After the 1972 settlement he served in the Southern Region High Executive Committee, the Regional Peoples Assembly, and the Sudan Socialist Union (q.v.).

LORING, WILLIAM WING (1818–1886). American Civil War veteran who served in Egypt and the Sudan at the invitation of Khedive Isma'il (q.v.). Loring went to Egypt in 1869 and quickly was promoted from *mir liwa* (colonel) to *liwa* (brigadier). His attempt to reform the Egyptian military was stymied, however, by the rampant corruption there.

Meanwhile Egypt's pursuit of slave recruits for its army had resulted in numerous revolts in the Sudan and overextended borders in the South and East. To the west the Turco-Egyptians (q.v.) had stretched their military resources into Darfur (q.v.), then under the control of the slave-trader Zubayr Rahma Mansur (q.v.). Thus the Turco-Egyptians had pursued a military solution everywhere in the Sudan. In 1875 they attempted a full-scale invasion of Abyssinia, which soon bogged down and became a military debacle. Loring, as second-in-command to the *Sirdar* Muhammad Ratib, served as chief-of-staff on the Abyssinian expedition. Though promoted to *farik pasha* (major general) he was blamed for the Turco-Egyptian failure and dismissed, returning home in 1879. His book *A Confederate Soldier in Egypt* was published in 1884. [by Richard Skidmore]

LUO. A variety of groups of Nilotes scattered throughout the southern Sudan (q.v.), with close ties to related groups in Uganda and Kenya. *See* ACHOLI; NILOTIC.

LWOKI, BENJAMIN (1918–). Southern educator and political leader. Lwoki served as a teacher from 1936 to 1948, eventually becoming the first Sudanese headmaster of the Church Missionary Society Primary School in Yei. He was on the boards of the University College of Khartoum and Mundiri Teacher Training College after 1950. He served on the Equatoria Provincial Council and was elected to the Legislative Assembly (q.v.). Lwoki was a founder of the Southern Party (q.v.) and became president of the Liberal Party (q.v.), where he contested leadership with Stanislaus Paysama (q.v.). He served in Parliament from 1954 to 1958.

– M –

MACHAR, RIEK TENY DHURGON (1953–). This southern soldier and politician of Nuer (q.v.) origin was born in Leer to a chiefly line. He attended the University of Khartoum (q.v.) and received his Ph.D. in 1984 from the University of Bedford in England. He was an early member of the Sudanese Peoples Liberation Army (SPLA, q.v.) and regional commander in its western operational zone in Upper Nile Province (q.v.). He commanded the force that attacked Melut in 1989. In 1990 he commanded the SPLA forces along the Ethiopian borderlands from Renk to Ayod. With Gordon Kong Chol, a former Anya-Nya II (q.v.) member, Machar became a leader of the Nasir faction of the SPLA, which broke from the SPLA-Mainstream under John Garang (q.v.) in August 1991. By 1992 the guerrilla forces of Machar and William Bany (q.v.) were engaged in what became a civil war within the SPLA, including a controversial and divisive attack on Malakal (q.v.), probably called by Machar.

Machar became a leader of the Southern Sudan Independence Movement (SSIM) in February 1993, a rival to the SPLM. In the summer of 1994 he agreed to the principles set forth by the Intergovernmental Agency on Drought and Development conference but did not reunite with Garang. In October 1994 this agreement collapsed when soldiers of Machar attacked the Dinka (q.v.) in Rumbek. On 10 April 1996 Machar and Kerubino (q.v.) were signatories of the "Political Charter" sponsored by the National Islamic Front (q.v.) in Khartoum, earning them opprobrium within Garang's SPLA.

In May 1997 Machar's SSIM was attacking SPLA forces in the Upper Nile. Surprisingly, Machar broke with the government in 2000 and formed yet another faction, the Sudanese Peoples Democratic Front (SPDF, q.v.). This Nuer group has sporadically waged war against and formed temporary alliances with progovernment Nuer forces, pro-SPLA Nuer forces, and SPLA-Mainstream Dinka forces. The SPDF's political position, if it has one, does not seem consistent.

MACMICHAEL, SIR HAROLD ALFRED (1882–1969). A figure of towering importance during the Anglo-Egyptian (q.v.) era, MacMichael served in the Sudan from 1905–1933, initially as a field officer in Kordofan and Darfur (qq.v.) and later as assistant civil secretary (1919–1925) and civil secretary (1926–1933) during the important transition to Indirect Rule (q.v.) under Governor-General John Maffey (q.v.). It was expected by some in the Sudan Political Service (q.v.) that the experienced MacMichael would be promoted to governor-general, since few knew the country as well as he. Instead the office was given to Sir Stewart Symes (q.v.) and MacMichael was appointed governor-general of Tanganyika, from whence Symes had just come. It is speculated that MacMichael had simply become too good at his job in the Sudan, and that the Foreign Office sought a more pliant figure; yet his tireless and superior service could not be ignored. He later served as British High Commissioner for Palestine and Transjordan (1938–1944).

MacMichael was the author of many influential books and articles on Sudanese history and anthropology, especially his *Tribes of Northern and Central Kordofan* (1912) and two-volume work, *History of the Arabs in the Sudan* (1922). His assertions about the "tribal" nature of northern Sudanese society, now seen as dubious, were long regarded as incontrovertible. In about 1930 MacMichael was instrumental in formulating a policy for the southern Sudan (q.v.) based on the idea of "protective isolation," or the segregation of Arabic language (q.v.), culture, and the Islamic religion (q.v.). In the North education was accelerated, while his policy was only partially implemented in the South, particularly the aspects that tended to hold the South in a state of economic backwardness from which it has not yet fully emerged. The model of Indirect Rule proved to be far more easily implemented in the North than in the acephalous societies found in parts of the South.

MADI. The small numbers of Madi and related Bongo (q.v.) people are the principal Sudanese representatives of the Madi cluster of the Central Sudanic subfamily of the Sudanic language group. They are the easternmost examples of their language group and are found in the southeastern borders of Sudan. Small-scale hoe-cultivation and livestock are the basis of their economy. They were under heavy attack by Arab slavers (qq.v.) during the nineteenth century and have been notably acculturated to Nilotic (q.v.) life ways. Still further impact was felt by the Madi at the time of Azande (q.v.) expansion. The Bongo area was visited by George Schweinfurth (q.v.) in the 1860s.

MADIH NABAWI. The emergence of *Madih Nabawi* (poetry in praise of the Prophet) as a literary genre can be traced to the time of Prophet Muhammad (d. 632 C.E.). Sufism (q.v.) subsequently played a significant role in the elaboration and dissemination of *Madih Nabawi*. The Egyptian Sufi poet al-Busiri (d. ca. 1296 CE), who claimed to have had spiritual contact with the Prophet Muhammad when the latter visited him in a dream and cured him of an illness, was an influential composer of *Madih Nabawi*, and he is important in its development in the Sudan. ‘Abd al-Rahim al-Bura‘i (d. 1400 CE), from Yemen, had a similar impact in the Sudan through his composing of *Madih Nabawi*. The first Sudanese *madih* poet was Isma‘il Sahib al-Rababa ("Isma‘il the guitarist"), who lived during the Funj Sultanates (q.v.) in the sixteenth century.

Sudanese *madih* poets composed poetry imitating the themes and meters used by their Muslim Arab counterparts. The themes of *madih* lyrics include: Prophet Muhammad's image as perceived by the *madih* poet or poetess, his hagiography, his miracles, and his intercession on Judgment Day on behalf of sinners, and the *Hajj* (pilgrimage to the Muslim holy places, Mecca and Medina). Since many *madih* poets are illiterate, their style is closer to colloquial than literary style and characterized by the use of vernacular formulae and idioms. *Madih* poetry is usually composed in seclusion through a painstaking process. Then it is performed by expert singers during community ceremonial and ritual events, such as the celebration of *al-Mawlid al-Nabawi* (birthday of Prophet Muhammad), the *hajj*, and other religious and social ceremonies.

Praise singers go through extensive training in apprenticeship before they are deemed worthy to perform before an audience. Although the audience consists of the community at large, performance participation is by male members only. Dance is performed outside by men; women only sing and dance indoors. The presence of an audience is the key element in guaranteeing the continuity of performance. The performance consists of lyrics, dance, music, and kinesics. The musical instruments are *tars* (framed drums), which accompany the recitation of the lyrics. [by Baqie Badawi Muhammad]

MADUOT, TOBY (1939–). Sudanese doctor and southern political leader who took his medical degree in Prague and had a private practice in Khartoum (q.v.). He was elected to Parliament for a Bahr al-Ghazal (q.v.) district in 1968. Maduot was an active member of the Khartoum-based Sudan African National Union (q.v.), working closely with his brother-in-law, William Deng (q.v.). After the 1969 May Revolution (q.v.) he served in the cabinet and then was named commissioner for Bahr al-Ghazal Province (1971). After the Addis Ababa Agreement of 1972 (q.v.) he became a member of the Southern Region High Executive Council and was elected to the Regional Peoples Assembly.

MAFFEY, SIR JOHN LOADER (1877–1969). Maffey assumed the position of governor-general of the Sudan on 24 October 1926 following the weak and short-lived administration of Sir Geoffrey Archer (q.v.), who had been appointed to fill in for the assassinated Sir Lee Stack (q.v.) in 1924. Thus Maffey had the difficult assignment of bringing a very unstable British rule into more effective control with a heavy reliance on the Sudan Political Service (q.v.). From this base, Maffey was able to construct a system of Indirect Rule (q.v.). This followed from the "pacification" efforts made by his predecessors in the Sudan and operationalized by Frederick Lugard in Nigeria. Thus, "tribalization" was encouraged to serve as a means of local control, facilitating (and sometimes masking) the administration of the Anglo-Egyptian government. Maffey is also credited with effective political relations with the Foreign Office in London and with British authorities in Cairo. By his retirement on 13 November 1933 he had presided over the heyday of "clean colonialism" when military pacification was over and before the major period of Sudanese nationalism had begun. In short, Maffey may be considered a model colonial governor.

MAHAD AL-'ILMI (INSTITUTE OF KNOWLEDGE). This institute was the precursor to Omdurman Islamic University, the major institution of higher learning in the Islamic sciences. The Institute was organized in 1912 by Shaykh Abu'l-Qasim Ahmad Hashim (1861–1934), head of the Board of *'Ulama*. It gathered together members of the *'ulama* (religious scholars) who had been teaching in their homes on an informal basis and centered their instruction around the main mosque in Omdurman (q.v.). Its curriculum was modeled on that of al-Azhar University (q.v.) in Cairo. In 1915 the school had 61 students; by 1935 it had 787. Graduates of the school entered careers as mosque preachers and village *khalwa* (Islamic school) teachers especially. *See also* HASHIMAB. [by Heather J. Sharkey]

MAHDI, AL-. In Islamic eschatology, the Mahdi is the divinely guided leader who will, according to tradition, "fill the world with justice, even as it has been filled with injustice." The idea of a Mahdi originated during the first Islamic century with Shi'ite opposition against the Umayyad Dynasty. Eventually the notion developed of a "rightly guided one" who would return from hiding to champion the cause of the Shi'a party: the "Expected Mahdi" (*al-Mahdi al-Muntazar*). Meanwhile, among mainstream Sunni Muslims the idea was adopted in support of a number of parties to dynastic struggles or tribal disputes. Supporting these claims to the title of Mahdi were a variety of prophetic traditions that described the Mahdi's features, characteristics, and accomplishments. Hence the Mahdi was to be of the Prophet's family, have the Prophet's name, appear at a time of natural calamities, and so on. An important vehicle for the spread of the Mahdi idea was the Sufi (q.v.) orders, which were also instrumental in the spread of Islam (q.v.) in the Sudan. History has witnessed several claimants to the title of Mahdi over the centuries, but the thirteenth Islamic century (1785–1883) was a time of particular messianic expectation. In the Sudan the term Mahdi usually refers to the Dongolawi holyman Muhammad Ahmad al-Mahdi (q.v.). *See also* MAHDIYA; MAHDIYA FOLKLORE.

MAHDI, 'ABD AL-RAHMAN, AL- (1885–1959). Posthumous son of Muhammad Ahmad al-Mahdi (q.v.) and the leader of the Ansar (q.v.) sect in the twentieth century. His mother, Maqbula, is alleged to have been of the royal Keira lineage of the Fur (qq.v.); another theory, unpopular among northern Sudanese, is that she was a southerner of the Dinka people (q.v.). After the defeat of the Mahdist state in 1898, 'Abd al-Rahman and other members of the Mahdi family (q.v.) were kept under close supervision by British authorities. With the outbreak of World War I, the Anglo-Egyptian (q.v.) government came to appreciate his usefulness as an ally and allowed him, with some misgivings, to cultivate a following among the Ansar. For his part, 'Abd al-Rahman expressed firm support for the British in the war and was rewarded for his loyalty with inclusion in a delegation to London to meet King George V in 1919. Later, in 1926, he was awarded the title of Knight of the British Empire and thereafter became "Sir Sayyid 'Abd al-Rahman."

Meanwhile, he had begun cultivating his vast land holdings on Aba Island (q.v.) in the White Nile in 1918, where he built a base of support among his followers and acquired considerable wealth growing cotton. This wealth made possible his many charitable and educational endowments and helped secure his following among the Ansar. In the political realm, 'Abd al-Rahman was seen by the British as a necessary counterweight to Sayyid 'Ali al-Mirghani (q.v.), whose followers favored an eventual union with Egypt. The rivalry between the "Two Sayyids" was more than political, however, dating back to the Mahdi-Mirghani (or Ansar-Khatmiya, q.v.) hostility of the nineteenth century. 'Abd al-Rahman's support for a separate, independent Sudan was furthered with the creation of the Umma Party (q.v.) in 1945, which acted as the political arm of the Ansar. Thereafter, the Umma-Unionist (q.v.) rivalry constituted the main theme in Sudanese politics leading up to independence in 1956.

'Abd al-Rahman cooperated with the formation of the National Front (q.v.) in the nationalist period before independence. On the other hand, he was a loyal colonial subject during the administration of every governor-general, which gained him invitations to London in 1919, 1946, and 1952. This difficult balancing act gave him great political experience and earned him credit as a mediator in both camps, especially at times of political crisis such as the 1924 White Flag revolt (q.v.); the 1930s Graduates Congress (q.v.) activity; support for the British in World War II in the 1940s; and the 1953–1955 riots and southern mutiny on the bumpy transition to independence.

The strength of the Ansar was viewed by the British as a balance to the Khatmiya as they tried to play one against the other. This was especially true in the 1953 elections, which brought a National Unionist Party (q.v.) victory and relative isolation of the Umma Party. The tight balance between Umma and Khatmiya interests in 1954 found a compromise solution on the eve of independence with Isma'il al-Azhari of the Ashigga

Party (qq.v.) becoming the first prime minister. Sayyid 'Abd al-Rahman was at al-Azhari's side at the moment of independence on 1 January 1956. He was profoundly moved by this signal reclamation of Sudanese autonomy: seventy-one years earlier his father, the Mahdi (q.v.), had presided over the fall of Khartoum (q.v.). Until his death in 1959 'Abd al-Rahman was among the most powerful forces in Sudanese politics and religion. *See also* MAHDI, SADIQ, AL-; MAHDI, SIDDIQ, Al-; MAHDIYA.

MAHDI, AL-, FAMILY. One of the most significant religious and political families in the modern Sudan. The larger extended family traces itself to al-Hajj Sharif Satti 'Ali, who lived in the seventeenth century in Dongola (q.v.). From him, three separate branches of the family emerged: the line of 'Abd al-Qadir, which produced the Mahdist *amir* Muhammad 'Abd al-Karim; the line of 'Ali, which produced the family patriarch during the Mahdiya (q.v.), Ahmad Muhammad Sharfi; and the line of Muhammad, which produced Muhammad Ahmad al-Mahdi (q.v.) and his cousin, the junior *khalifa* Muhammad Sharif (q.v.). Countless marriages among these three branches as well as with other families have produced a great many individuals who can claim membership in the extended Mahdi family, or "Dongola Ashraf " (q.v.).

Unquestionably, the family's rise to prominence began with the successful movement of Muhammad Ahmad al-Mahdi (d. 1885). The family's overt political power was reduced somewhat during the time of the Mahdi's successor, Khalifa 'Abdullahi (q.v.), though he too was related to the family through marriage and deferred to its wishes more than is commonly realized. Moreover, the family's religious authority—and hence social and economic influence—was never diminished during the Khalifa's reign. Countless Ansar (q.v.) migrated to Omdurman (q.v.) during the Mahdiya specifically to benefit from the family's considerable *baraka* (q.v.), or blessings. After the Anglo-Egyptian (q.v.) conquest of 1898, the Mahdi's posthumous son 'Abd al-Rahman (q.v.) emerged as the family leader and reorganized the Ansar into an effective organization. As well as being a religious sect, the Ansar became a Sudanese nationalist alternative to the influence of Egypt and thus received some British encouragement.

The family provided leadership for both the Ansar religious organization and the Umma Party (q.v.), which was founded in 1945. 'Abd al-Rahman's son, Siddiq (q.v.), was president of the Umma Party and became the Imam (q.v.) of the Ansar when 'Abd al-Rahman died in 1959.

The family was divided in the 1960s between a more modernist branch led by the Umma Party president, Sadiq (q.v.), Siddiq's son, and a traditionalist branch led by al-Hadi ibn 'Abd al-Rahman (1915–1970), who had become Imam in 1961. Many other members of the family held important positions in postindependence Sudan. After the 1969 May Revolution (q.v.), the Mahdist family opposed the new regime and organized Ansar resistance to it. In the spring of 1970 there was rioting in Omdurman and an open military clash at Aba Island (q.v.), and the Ansar resistance was defeated. Imam al-Hadi was killed while trying to escape to Ethiopia, and many other members of the family fled into exile. Members of the family were often accused of plotting against the Ja'afar al-Nimeiri (q.v.) government (1969–1985). During the military Islamist regime of 'Umar al-Bashir (1989–, q.v.) several family members have been jailed or placed under house arrest.

MAHDI, MUHAMMAD AHMAD IBN 'ABDULLAH, AL- (1848–1885).
Arguably the most significant religious leader of the nineteenth-century Sudan and founder of the Sudanese Mahdist movement. Born on Labab Island in Dongola (q.v.) province in the northern part of Sudan, Muhammad Ahmad ibn 'Abdullah was the son of a boatbuilder from a family that claimed *sharifi* status and received a relatively thorough religious education at the hands of a number of prominent *fekis* (q.v.). He became a pupil of Muhammad Sharif Nur al-Da'im and was initiated into the Sammaniya *tariqa* (qq.v.). His vigorous asceticism eventually brought him into conflict with his teacher, whose presence he left to become a disciple of Shaykh Qurashi wad al-Zayn. He was a strong critic of what he believed was the prevailing immorality of his time; and his own zeal as well as popular messianic expectations combined to create the conviction that he was the anticipated Mahdi (q.v.).

In May 1881 he announced his divine mission to followers at Aba Island (q.v.) on the White Nile, and issued a call to action to fight the corrupt Turks as a first step toward the creation of a society purified by Islamic concepts. A government attempt to arrest him was repulsed in a skirmish that the Mahdi's followers (called Ansar, q.v.) took to be a miraculous event. Immediately thereafter the Mahdi led his followers into Kordofan (q.v.) province in a withdrawal that he termed a *hijra* (flight), emulating the Prophet Muhammad's own famous strategic emigration to Medina in 622 C.E.. His support grew rapidly among many segments of the Sudanese population, including the Baqqara (q.v.) pastoralists of the West, due in part to their experience of the harshness of

Turco-Egyptian (q.v.) rule. Several government attempts to defeat the movement failed, each adding to the Mahdi's allure. A critical turning point was the famed defeat of British General Hicks Pasha (q.v.) in 1883, which allowed the Mahdi and his followers to gain strategic advantage as well as captured arms.

By 1883 he controlled the western provinces of Darfur (q.v.) and Kordofan, and by 1884 most of what had been the Turco-Egyptian Sudan. In late 1884 the Mahdi settled at Omdurman (q.v.) to support his followers' siege of Khartoum (q.v.), which finally fell on 25 January 1885. For the next six months he lived at Omdurman, eschewing the former capital of the Turks and its spiritual contamination. He died there suddenly on 22 June after a brief illness. In his voluminous correspondences he had urged the formation of an idealized Islamic society, based on the model of the early Muslims at Medina. It was left to his successor, the Khalifa 'Abdullahi al-Ta'ishi (q.v.), to put this into effect. The Mahdi's descendants have played important roles in twentieth-century Sudan: his posthumous son 'Abd al-Rahman (q.v.) was the leader of the Ansar sect and patron of the nationalist movement in the form of the Umma Party (q.v.). His great-grandson, Sadiq al-Mahdi (q.v.), was prime minister twice in the postindependence era, in 1966–1967 and 1986–1989, winning democratic elections for the Umma Party. *See also* MAHDI, AL-, FAMILY; MAHDIYA; MAHDIYA FOLKLORE.

MAHDI, SADIQ, AL- (1936–). Sadiq al-Mahdi is a central political and religious leader from the al-Mahdi family and Umma Party (qq.v.). He is the son of Siddiq al-Mahdi (q.v.) and a grandson of Sayyid 'Abd al-Rahman al-Mahdi (q.v.). He was educated at the University of Khartoum (q.v.) and Oxford University and served in the Sudanese Parliament as representative from the Aba Island (q.v.) district. After his father's death in 1961 he became head of the Umma Party, and was elected prime minister in 1966–1967 and again from 1986–1989, after the overthrow of Ja'afar al-Nimeiri (q.v.).

An advocate of greater modernization within the Umma Party and Ansar (q.v.) organization, Sadiq clashed frequently with his uncle, the Ansar Imam al-Hadi (d.1970), and for a time two separate branches of the Mahdi family opposed each other in Parliament. Sadiq was imprisoned at various times during the Nimeiri regime, being an outspoken opponent of it after the massacre at Aba Island in 1970. Sadiq sought political refuge outside of Sudan, most notably in Libya, until a much-touted political reconciliation between him and Nimeiri in 1977 brought him back to the country without a major governmental role. After the overthrow of Nimeiri in 1985, the elections that restored democracy to the Sudan returned Sadiq to office as prime minister in 1986 as head of a coalition government. However, his failures to open serious negotiations with the Sudanese Peoples Liberation Movement (q.v.) to end the civil war, and to deal decisively with the issue of Shari'a and Islamization (qq.v.), led to a weakened prime ministership. Sadiq was overthrown by an Islamist military coup in June 1989 led by the National Islamic Front (NIF, q.v.).

This last move brought periods when he was in and out of jail and under house arrest. He is the brother-in-law of Hasan al-Turabi (q.v.), the NIF ideologue and political power broker. In December 1996 Sadiq managed to escape from Sudan and effectively join the formal opposition of the National Democratic Alliance (q.v.) in Cairo. By 2000 he was back in Sudan, presumably to attempt rapprochement with the NIF regime.

MAHDI, SIDDIQ AL- (1911–1961). Siddiq al-Mahdi was the son of 'Abd al-Rahman al-Mahdi (q.v.). He was active within the Ansar and Umma Party (qq.v.) and in the Sudanese nationalist struggles in the 1930s and 1940s, especially in jockeying for position vis-à-vis the National Unionist Party and Ashigga Party (qq.v.). He was probably involved in the March 1953 Ansar-led protest against the emerging government of Isma'il al-Azhari (q.v.), which he feared would marginalize the Umma Party. *See also* MAHDI, AL-, FAMILY.

MAHDIYA. The name applied to the period of the Mahdist revolt and Mahdist state, from 1881–1898. Over the years the period has been regarded in a number of ways. Contemporary northern Sudanese either supported it out of religious zeal or opportunism, or else opposed it as an un-Islamic movement led by a false Mahdi (q.v.). Southern Sudanese, long the victims of northern-led slave (q.v.) and ivory raiding, mainly saw the Mahdiya as a continuation of former hostilities. Later Sudanese have tended to view the Mahdiya as the first flickerings of Sudanese nationalism and the Mahdi and Khalifa (q.v.) as unintended national leaders.

Among Europeans, the initial reaction to the Mahdiya was not unsympathetic: in 1884 British Prime Minister William Gladstone (q.v.) called the Sudanese a people "struggling rightly to be free." With the heightening of British involvement, this sympathy gave way to a condemnation of the Mahdi's fanaticism and hypocrisy; this later was followed by a grudging admission of the Mahdi's sincerity, as against the

Khalifa's tyranny and personal excesses. Confident European writers in the early twentieth century saw the Mahdiya as a type of Sudanese anti-modernism waged by people fighting against the forces of progress. Modern scholars have variously interpreted the Mahdiya as an African anti-imperialist movement, a messianic movement, and a fundamentalist movement within the context of Islamic reform and renewal. *See also* MAHDI, AL-, FAMILY; MAHDI, AL-, MUHAMMAD AHMAD; MAHDIYA FOLKLORE.

MAHDIYA FOLKLORE. Oral tradition is the source of a variety of narratives illustrating the folk conception of the Mahdiya (q.v.). These include a series of anecdotes about how the Sudanese found the name of the Mahdi (q.v.) written on the leaves of plants, in the eggs of wild birds, and on the skin of newborn animals, accompanied by the *Shahada* (Muslim testimony that "There is no God except the one God, and Muhammad is His messenger"). Also, rumors spread that the Mahdi was fighting with a divine sword, that he transformed the fire from the enemy's weapons into water, and that the Ansar's (q.v.) spears and swords produced fire.

The main natural phenomenon that coincided with the Mahdiya was the appearance of a comet known among the Sudanese as *al-Najma Umm Dhanab* (star with a tail). On 28 September 1882 a star with a ship's sail (as the people described it) appeared in the sky before dawn; it extended its stay until sunrise and continued its appearance for several days. People strongly believed that the appearance of this specific star was a sign of change in the ruling system in the Sudan, hence it predicted Mahdist rule. *See also* BINT AL-MAKKAWI. [by Baqie Badawi Muhammad]

MAHJUB, 'ABD AL-KHALIQ. *See* 'ABD AL-KHALIQ MAHGOUB.

MAHJUB, MUHAMMAD AHMAD (1908–1976). Sudanese political leader and intellectual who graduated from Gordon Memorial College (q.v.) and the Khartoum School of Law. He was active in the early intellectual groups, being a leader of the Hashimab (q.v.) group and writing articles and poetry. He was active in the Graduates Congress (q.v.) following World War II and was secretary-general of the Independence Front (q.v.), but resigned in protest over a government pay raise. Mahjub served on the Constitutional Commission and in local government bodies. In 1953 he was elected to Parliament as an independent and was elected head of the parliamentary opposition by the proindependence supporters. He subsequently became associated with the Umma Party (q.v.). He served as minister of foreign affairs (1956–1958) in the government of 'Abdallah Khalil (q.v.) and in the same post in the transition government after the 1964 October Revolution (q.v.). He was prime minister in 1965–1966 and 1967–1969 and played an active role in Arab world international relations. After the 1969 May Revolution (q.v.) he spent much of his time out of the country writing. See also KHARTOUM SUMMIT OF 1967.

MAJADHIB. One of the leading religious clans of the Ja'aliyin (q.v.), who trace their origins to the sixteenth century when their ancestors emerged as a family of *fuqara'* or religious specialists in the area of al-Damer (q.v.). In 1705–1706 Muhammad al-Majdhub ("The Enraptured"), the first of the family to bear this epithet, may have been involved in the first revolt of the northern Sudanese provinces against their Funj (q.v.) overlords. Under his son Feki Hamad wad al-Majdhub (1694–1776), the family asserted its position by accumulating private land titles, forging links with the old local nobility as well as with newly emerging merchant families, and becoming involved in private long-distance trade. Well-trained in Maliki law, Hamad adopted the Shadhiliya *tariqa* (qq.v.).

He and his sons, known since ca. 1800 as the "Majadhib" or "Sons of Wad al-Majdhub," taught Qur'an and the religious law, provided medical help, and mediated socially and judicially between the sedentary population and the nomads. Both their fame as scholars and their political importance grew rapidly. They maintained contact with al-Azhar (q.v.), and their schools attracted students from as far away as Darfur (q.v.). The Turco-Egyptian (q.v.) conquest, the destruction of al-Damer in 1823, and the economic hardships during the nineteenth century dispersed the Majadhib. Some eventually returned to al-Damer; others remained in the Ethiopian borderlands or else founded settlements in Gedaref (q.v.), the Gezira (q.v.), and later in the western Sudan.

Most important religiously was Hamad's grandson, Muhammad Majdhub (1795/6–1831). He spent about eight years studying and teaching in Medina and was greatly influenced by the Moroccan Sufi (q.v.) reformer Ahmad ibn Idris (q.v.). In 1829 he moved to Suakin where he propagated his *tariqa* for two years. His early death prevented him from becoming *khalifa* (q.v.) of his grandfather in al-Damer. But being the most prolific Sudanese preacher and songwriter up to his time, Majdhub did much to spread Islamic knowledge and responsible Islamic practice beyond the traditional confines of the urban scholar-jurists.

His nephew and *khalifa*, Muhammad al-Tahir Majdhub (1832/3–1890), gained many followers in the eastern Sudan. In 1883 he joined the Mahdist movement, and his influence among the people of the Red Sea Hills was an important factor in their rallying behind 'Uthman Diqna (q.v.), the Mahdist leader in the region, who had himself been a follower of al-Tahir. Al-Tahir's son, al-Shaykh ibn al-Tahir Majdhub (ca. 1860–1930), served as secretary to 'Uthman Diqna and commander in the Mahdist army. Renowned for his poetry, learning, and piety, he succeeded his father as head of the eastern Majadhib. Around 1915, he retired to a remote village on the Atbara River where he was greatly venerated by the nomads. His successors moved the center of the eastern Majadhib to Erkowit.

In twentieth-century al-Damer, the religious heritage of Shaykh Muhammad Majdhub was promoted by Majdhub Jalal al-Din (1887/8–1976). Although his efforts to create a centralized *tariqa* failed, the Shaykh gradually displaced the clan's ancestor, Feki Hamad, as the focal point of communal identification. Majdhub Jalal al-Din's son, Muhammad al-Mahdi al-Majdhub (1919–1982), became one of the most celebrated poets of modern Sudan, and 'Abdallah al-Tayyib (b. 1921, q.v.) the country's leading expert on Arabic language. [by Albrecht Hofheinz]

MAJDHUB, Al-. *See* MAJADHIB.

MAK, 'ALI AL- (1937–1992). Al-Mak was a Sudanese short story writer, poet, and translator. He was born in Omdurman (q.v.) and graduated with honors in Arabic language and literature from the University of Khartoum (q.v.). He was editor of Khartoum University Publishing House from its inception. At the time of his sudden death he was on a Fulbright fellowship in Albuquerque, New Mexico, translating Native American poetry into Arabic while on leave as the director of the Khartoum University Arabic Language Translation Unit. Al-Mak's work reflects a socialist-realist view. His first short story appeared in the Khartoum bi-weekly *al-Saraha* when he was sixteen. His major poetic work, *Madinatun min Turab* (City of Dust), published in Khartoum in 1974, is a long prose poem structurally resembling the classical Arabic *qasida*. Through his eulogy to his beloved, but decaying Omdurman, Sudan's political nerve center, al-Mak fuses modern classicism, romanticism, and realism. [by Constance E. Berkley]

MALAKAL. The capital city of Upper Nile Province (q.v.), just north of the confluence of the Sobat River and Bahr al-Ghazal River, and at the north end of the unfinished Jonglei canal (q.v.). Just north of Malakal was the Shilluk (q.v.) village of Fashoda (q.v.), which was the site of a famous stalemate between France and Great Britain over control of the White Nile. The area around Malakal was heavily slaved during the Turkiya (q.v.) and efforts were made to control the slave (q.v.) trade from Fashoda.

Since independence, Malakal, a gateway to the south, served as a river town for local administration having only a small population. However, because of large numbers of refugees (q.v.) from the war in the South and sometimes being under attack by the Sudanese Peoples Liberation Army (q.v.), the population jumped to 34,000 in 1983 and to 80,000 in a 1986 estimate.

MALWAL, BONA (1938–). Sudanese journalist and political leader of Dinka (q.v.) origin. Before the 1969 October Revolution (q.v.) he was editor of *Vigilant*, a Khartoum English-language newspaper with a southern perspective. After the Addis Ababa Agreement of 1972 (q.v.) he was named deputy minister of information and culture (1972–1973), then minister of state for information (1973–1976), and then minister of culture and information (1976–1977). It was in this last post that he founded the internationally read English-language magazine, *Sudanow*, which sought an independent position in the midst of military rule. At present he edits the *Sudan Democratic Gazette* in exile from London.

MANJIL. A title used by exceptionally important chiefs subject to the Funj sultans (q.v.). The best known *manjils* were the 'Abdallab (q.v.) leaders.

MANUTE BOL. *See* BOL, MANUTE.

MA'QUR, AHMAD, AL-. A person associated in local traditions with the transfer of power in Darfur (q.v.) from the Tunjur to the Keira (qq.v.) dynasties. He is said to have been related through marriage to both dynasties. There is some question as to whether he is a fully historical figure or a mythological figure in whose story a long series of events is subsumed. The events of his life fit into the pattern of the "Wise Stranger," a common theme in the Sudanic belt of Africa, who comes to a barbarous land, introduces new ideas and customs, marries the chief's daughter, and establishes a new dynasty.

MARCHAND, JEAN-BAPTISTE. *See* FASHODA.

MARDI, MUHAMMAD AHMAD, AL- (1902–1966). Sudanese political leader and originally a judge in the Islamic courts. He was elected to Parliament in 1953 with the National Unionist Party (NUP, q.v.) and became minister of local government in Isma'il al-Azhari's (q.v.) cabinet (1954–1956). After the 1964 October Revolution (q.v.) he was secretary-general of the NUP and served in the cabinets of Muhammad Ahmad Mahjub and Sadiq al-Mahdi (qq.v.) as minister of commerce (1965–1966).

MASALMA. The name applied to the European and non-Sudanese converts to Islam (q.v.) during the Mahdist period, from an Arabic word meaning to submit. The *Masalma* (also known as *Muslimaniya*) were Italians, Greeks (q.v.), Cypriots, Armenians (q.v.), Jews (q.v.), Syrians (q.v.), and Copts (q.v.) who, usually unwillingly, adopted Islam during the time of the Mahdist revolt and so were considered members of the Mahdi's Ansar (q.v.). Many joined the Mahdi at el-Obeid (q.v.) in 1882–1883 or at Khartoum (q.v.) in 1884–1885. Their condition was a cause of great concern to the British and other Europeans during the Mahdiya (q.v.), and popular contemporary accounts portrayed their lives as uninterrupted misery. In fact many *Masalma* enjoyed a high degree of autonomy: they tended to settle together in Omdurman (q.v.), in a quarter now known as *Hayy al-Masalma*; they were allowed to practice their trades and crafts; the men were encouraged to marry Sudanese women, but they also took wives from among the *Masalma*; obligations to perform public works, pray in the mosque, or serve in the army could be avoided with a bribe; and some *Masalma* were allowed to travel freely for trade. After the battle of Karari (q.v.) in 1898, most *Masalma* returned to their original faiths, though some remained Muslim. Few left the Sudan, most opting to remain in Omdurman or Khartoum and continue their livelihoods. Virtually all members of the former *Masalma* community left Sudan in the 1970s and 1980s, either in response to the Ja'afar al-Nimeiri (q.v.) government's nationalization policies or imposition of Shari'a (q.v.) law.

MAY REVOLUTION OF 1969. Term applied to the regime begun by the seizure of power on 25 May 1969 by General Ja'afar al-Nimeiri (q.v.) that continued for sixteen years, until 6 April 1985. This was Sudan's longest period of military rule. The revolution brought an end to the period of parliamentary politics that had been initiated by the October Revolution of 1964 (q.v.). Party politics seemed unable to solve the problems of economic development and the war in the South. As a result, Sudanese public opinion accepted the new revolutionary government with little opposition.

Built upon a political philosophy of Arab socialism and single party rule (like that of Egypt), the Sudanese Socialist Union (SSU, q.v.) became the symbolic representative of the popular mass will. The May Revolution's single greatest achievement was peace and regional self-rule for the southern Sudan (q.v.) with the signing of the Addis Ababa Agreement (q.v.) on 3 March 1972. Thereafter this day was celebrated as "Unity Day." Former Anya-Nya leader Joseph Lagu (qq.v.) was elected president of the High Executive Council of the Southern Region.

Under the May Revolution, after the 1971 attempted coup, the indigenous mercantile class began to grow and Sudan's external debt increased. The economy became more dependent on Arab development capital and loans from the World Bank and International Monetary Fund. The Jonglei canal (q.v.) was begun during the May Revolution, as was the exploration and commercial exploitation of oil by Chevron (q.v.). More successful development schemes, like the Kenana sugar project, were carried out under "Five Year" economic plans. Higher education was expanded with the opening of two major universities outside of Khartoum, the University of Juba in 1977, and the University of the Gezira. A number of architectural projects are associated with the May Revolution, like the People's Assembly building in Omdurman (q.v.) and Friendship Hall conference center in Khartoum North (q.v.).

The May Revolution ended in April 1985 after several months of popular, antiregime demonstrations that resulted in the seizure of power by General Suwar al-Dahab (q.v.) who promised to restore civilian rule.

MAYEN, GORDON MUORTAT. Southern political leader. He joined the government service in 1946, eventually serving as an assistant district commissioner. After the 1964 October Revolution (q.v.) he was the first vice-president of the Southern Front (q.v.) and minister of works in the transition government. He was a Southern Front spokesman at the Roundtable Conference (q.v.) in 1965 and then became active in southern exile groups. Mayen served as foreign affairs spokesman for the Southern Sudan Provisional Government (SSPG, q.v.) in 1968 but then formed the Nile Provisional Government (NPG, q.v.) in opposition to the SSPG. He advocated the policy of demanding complete independence for the South. When the NPG broke up, he did not participate in the Anyidi Revolutionary Government (q.v.), nor did he cooperate later with Joseph Lagu (q.v.). He continued to advocate total independence for the South and rejected the Addis Ababa Agreement of 1972 (q.v.). Mayen sought political asylum in Great Britain and tried to create an African National Front.

MBORO, CLEMENT. Sudanese administrator and southern political leader. He joined the government service in 1940 and was the senior southern Sudanese official in the administration when Sudan became independent. By 1964 Mboro had become the deputy governor of Darfur (q.v.) Province. After the 1964 October Revolution (q.v.) he was a founder and the president of the Southern Front (q.v.) and was minister of interior in the transition government (1964–1965). He later served as minister of industry (1968–1969) and was elected to Parliament in 1968. Mboro was jailed briefly following the 1969 May Revolution (q.v.) but was named president of the Relief and Resettlement Commission after the Addis Ababa Agreement of 1972 (q.v.). He was elected to the Southern Regional Peoples Assembly in 1973 and was speaker in 1978. Mboro was ousted as speaker in 1979 after opposing Joseph Lagu (q.v.) and failed to be reelected to the Fourth Regional Assembly in 1982. He opposed Ja'afar al-Nimeiri's (q.v.) redivision of the South after 1982, but failed to regain his political influence after the revival of civil war in 1983.

MEDIA. Just six months after the Anglo-Egyptian (q.v.) conquest of the Sudan, in March 1899, the Sudan government began publishing an occasional, bilingual (English and Arabic) paper known as *The Sudan Gazette*. This was less a proper newspaper than an official organ of the government that publicized decisions of administration, taxation, land ownership, and so on for those who could read and afford the two piastre price. The first independent newspaper was *The Sudan Times*, a bilingual Egyptian publication founded in 1903 and edited by the Lebanese journalist Labib Juraydini until 1925. At roughly the same time a Greek-owned publication, *The Sudan Herald* (and its weekly Arabic supplement, *Ra'id al-Sudan*), began publication, closing in 1919. The first Sudanese-owned and -edited paper was *Hadarat al-Sudan* (q.v.), a weekly (later bi-weekly) founded in 1919 by the journalist Husayn Sharif (q.v.), who had earlier edited *Ra'id al-Sudan*. Owned by Sayyid 'Abd al-Rahman al-Mahdi (q.v.) and others, *Hadarat* espoused the view of "Sudan for the Sudanese." Until its closure in 1938 it was an important counterpoint to the Unionist arguments of the Egyptian-owned or -edited papers, and served as the organ of both the Sudan government and the Sayyid.

Until 1945 there were only two Arabic newspapers published in Sudan: *al-Nil* (est. 1935) and *Sawt al-Sudan* (est. 1940), owned respectively by 'Abd al-Rahman al-Mahdi and 'Ali al-Mirghani (q.v.). While independent they were hardly objective, reflecting the views of the country's two chief sects, the Ansar and Khatmiya (qq.v.). Both papers were published in Khartoum (q.v.) and had limited influence outside the capital area and urban areas of the North in general, as indeed is the case with the press today. There are three reasons for this centralization. First, all Sudanese governments since the creation of the Condominium (q.v.) have mistrusted the political influence of the press, often exercising a high degree of control over who can publish and what is printed. Second, the vastness of the country and limitations of transport make circulation of newspapers difficult. Third, the low degree of literacy outside the capital area limits the appeal of newspapers: in 1942 only 4 percent of the Sudanese population was literate, while in 1998 the figure was approximately 32 percent.

The number of Sudanese newspapers increased considerably with the movement for independence. By 1960 there existed seven daily papers, four semiweekly papers, and fifteen weekly papers. The estimated total circulation of daily newspapers was at least 20,000. Additionally some seventeen weekly and monthly periodicals were published at this time, in Arabic and in English; all but seven were published in Khartoum. Many of these were specialized publications concerned with social or cultural issues, such as *Sawt al-Mar'a* (Women's Voice), established in 1955 by Fatima Ahmad Ibrahim (q.v.), and *Sports and Cinema*, established in 1948 by Ibrahim al-Maghribi. Among the daily newspapers, the two most influential were *al-Rai al-Amm* (est. 1945), edited by Isma'il Atabani, and *al-Ayyam* (est. 1954), edited by Beshir Mohammed Said (q.v.).

From 1958 to 1964 the military government of Ibrahim Abboud (q.v.) subjected the press to rigid censorship. As all political parties were banned, many of their corresponding papers were suspended, including *al-Nil* and *al-Ummah* (organs of the Ummah Party, q.v.), *al-'Alam* and *al-Ashigga* (organs of the National Unionist Party, q.v.), and *al-Midan* and *al-Taliya* (organs of the Sudan Communist Party, q.v.). The Ministry of Information reserved the right to license all newspapers and censor all news, and even the important daily *al-Ayyam* was suspended twice for contradicting the government in its editorials. From 1969–1985 this policy was essentially followed by the regime of Ja'afar al-Nimeiri (q.v.), as it has been by the present regime of 'Umar Hasan al-Bashir (q.v.).

By early 1999 seven daily papers were in circulation. Six of these are independents: *al-Rai al-Amm, Alwan, Akhbar al-Yom, al-Shari' al-Siyasi, al-Rai al-Akhar*, and *al-Wifaq*. The seventh daily, *al-Anbaa*, is edited by the State Minister of Information and replaces the now-defunct official papers *al-Inqaz al-Watani* and *al-Sudan al-Hadith*. All papers are subject to the rulings of the National Council of the Press and Publications, which monitors the papers' adherence to the Law of Press and Publications. Temporary suspension of papers and the arrest of editors are not uncommon. In July 1998 editions of *al-Shari' al-Siyasi* and *al-Rai al-Akhar* were confiscated by government security forces, presumably for criticizing Sudan's new constitution; later that month the National Council ordered dailies to increase their number of pages, in an apparent attempt to drive some of the independents out of business. All reporting on the civil war requires the clearance of the Sudanese army, which has vowed to apply military law to media that transgress this rule. Obviously no Khartoum paper publishes from a southern Sudanese (q.v.) perspective. The former *Sudan Times* published by Bona Malwal (q.v.) is defunct, replaced by *The Sudan Democratic Gazette* published in London.

The official news agency in Sudan is Sudan News Agency (SUNA), which distributes news bulletins taken from Reuters, UPI, AP, and other foreign news services. SUNA is a branch of the Ministry of Information, as is Sudan TV and Radio Omdurman, and all three have government-appointed directors who report to the Ministry. The content of Sudan TV since its inception in 1963 was largely drama, music, and comedy shows (many imported from Egypt), sports, and current affairs/news programs; while Radio Omdurman broadcast a variety of news, music, dramatic shows, and educational programs since 1940. Since the Bashir coup of 1989 and rise in influence of the National Islamic Front (q.v.), the quantity of religious programming has increased considerably.

Despite the Bashir regime's efforts to control the news, many Sudanese are able to receive broadcasts from the opposition National Democratic Alliance's (q.v.) radio station in Eritrea or from the Sudanese Peoples Liberation Movement (q.v.). Somewhat contradictorily, those Sudanese who can afford satellite dishes are allowed to receive foreign television broadcasts in exchange for an annual payment to the government. Finally, the advent of the Internet—however limited still—has made it possible for Sudanese to gain access to virtually endless sources of information and debate on national issues.

MEK (MAK). A title used by some traditional chiefs in the Sudan. Among the most famous was Mek Nimr of Shendi (qq.v.).

MEK NIMR. Ja'ali leader and ruler of Shendi (q.v.) who, in 1822, killed Isma'il Kamil Pasha (q.v.) and some of his associates by luring them into a building for a party and then burning the structure. As a result, Isma'il's successor, Muhammad Khusraw al-Daftardar (q.v.), set about a campaign of both revenge and repression in the region. Mek Nimr and many of the Ja'aliyin (q.v.) fled to al-'Atish, east of Gedaref (q.v.), where they took refuge with others who had sought asylum from Turco-Egyptian (q.v.) rule and taxation.

MEKKI, YUSUF KUWA (1945–2001). An important champion of Nuba (q.v.) culture and leader of the Sudanese Peoples Liberation Army (SPLA, q.v.). Born into a Muslim family in the Nuba mountains, Yusuf Kuwa developed a distinctly African identity in reaction to prevalent Arab (q.v.) cultural biases. Educated at the University of Khartoum (q.v.), he returned home to teach and cofound a Nuba youth and cultural organization, *Komolo* (Youth). In 1981 he won election to the regional assembly where he tried unsuccessfully to advance Nuba causes. With the revival of civil war in 1983 and suppression of *Komolo*, Yusuf Kuwa joined the SPLA, where he assumed command of a division in the Nuba Mountains from 1984–2000. Revered by his followers, he had little success resisting the depredations of government troops.

MEROWE (SANAM). A town opposite Karima (q.v.) below the Nile's fourth cataract, which marks the location of ancient Napata, the sometime capital of Kush. Modern Merowe must be distinguished from its ancient namesake Meroë, far across the Bayuda desert near the modern town of Shendi (q.v.). In 1955 its population was not even 2,000 and by 1965 it had reached only 2,700. It is a river fording, and has a small airport for domestic flights.

MIHERA BINT ABBOUD. Mihera was the daughter of Shaykh Abboud, the Suwarab Shaykh in *Diyar al-Shayqiya* (region of the Shayqiya, q.v.). Her legend turned her into a Sudanese folk heroine. When the Turco-Egyptian troops of Muhammad 'Ali Pasha (qq.v.) invaded the northern riverine Sudan in 1820, their invasion met with resistance despite their advanced weaponry. After conquering the people in the far north, they proceeded south, and rumors of the arrival of Muhammad 'Ali's troops spread among the Shayqiya. The rumors described the troops as powerful and armed with advanced weapons, and they were said to be heading south toward the Shayqiya land. Hearing these rumors, the Shayqiya men seemed reluctant to face the invaders. The unmarried Mihera, in a very theatrical act, stood up for her people. She mounted her *hajeen* (camel), dressed in men's clothes and carried a sword. She said to the men, "Here we are, our clothes are for you." This reversal was effective; the Shayqiya men responded positively and Mihera composed this song:

Alayla al-iyal rikbu khayl al-kar
Giddamon 'aqidun bi'l-aghar daffir
Genyatna al-'usud alayla titnatir.
Ya'l-Pasha al-ghashim gool le jedadak kar.

Translation:

Today our men all on their horses
In front of them their commander
On his beautiful horse struts.
Our men are like lions when they roar
Oh, fool Pasha, just let your chickens go away.

[by Baqie Badawi Muhammad]

MILNER MISSION REPORT. The policy endorsing a transition from military to civilian rule in colonial administration and the application of indirect rule was officially accepted in the Milner Mission report of 1921 during the rule of Governor-General Lee Stack (q.v.). Lord Milner was Colonial Secretary who headed a Royal Commission that undertook a mission to the area in 1919–1921 and recommended virtual independence for Egypt. This was rejected by the British Cabinet and he resigned. In one form or another this policy continued through World War II until active steps were taken toward the full decolonization of the Sudan.

MIRGHANI, SAYYID 'ALI IBN MUHAMMAD 'UTHMAN, AL- (1878–1968). Sayyid 'Ali al-Mirghani was a major religious and political leader in twentieth-century Sudan. He was a member of the Mirghani family (q.v.) and leader of the Khatmiya *tariqa* (qq.v.), which dominated the politics and economy of the eastern Sudan. He lived in Cairo during the Mahdist era and was a vigorous opponent of the Mahdi's (q.v.) movement. Likewise he was a lifetime rival of 'Abd al-Rahman al-Mahdi (q.v.), the Madhi's posthumous son. Sayyid 'Ali cooperated with the British in the Anglo-Egyptian (q.v.) "reconquest" and was, in the early twentieth century, considered by the British to be the chief spokesman for local opinion. His rivalry with 'Abd al-Rahman al-Mahdi in the Graduates Congress (q.v.) in the 1930s and 1940s, in the Khatmiya (q.v.) newspaper *Sawt al-Sudan* (Voice of the Sudan), and in elections and the struggle for independence in the 1940s and 1950s led him to be more sympathetic to Egyptian nationalism in contrast to the Mahdist position of independence. At heart 'Ali al-Mirghani was as great a Sudanese nationalist as 'Abd-Rahman, but his fears of a Mahdist return to power in the Sudan were still fresh and real, thus the temptation for alliance with Egypt was great because both shared this apprehension.

While the British were apprehensive about recurrent Mahdism, they supported the Mirghani position, and when the British grew fearful of a strong Nile Valley alliance of Egypt and the Sudan, they became more favorable to the Mahdists. Likewise, when the Mahdist strength in the Graduates Congress was growing, as seen in the 1943 elections, the Khatmiya swung its tactical support behind the small Ashigga Party (q.v.) in 1944 to block 'Abd al-Rahman's Ansar (q.v.) and the influence they were having within the Advisory Council for the Northern Sudan (q.v.). Clearly this basic sectarian division of northern elites was a great advantage for the British colonial administration.

During World War II Sayyid 'Ali was the major patron for the emerging parties supporting unity of the Nile Valley, especially with the National Front (1949–1952, q.v.) and later through their National Unionist Party (NUP, q.v.). Ever cautious but effective political maneuvering put the NUP in the dominant position after the 1953 parliamentary elections. Even though the first prime minister was to emerge from the Ashigga Party it was the NUP that controlled the political landscape. After independence al-Mirghani still had a major influence on the political health of Isma'il al-Azhari (q.v.) and his Ashigga Party. In 1956 some Khatmiya elements broke away from the NUP to form the Peoples Democratic Party (PDP, q.v.). An objective of this was to form a broad coalition including even the Umma Party (q.v.) to bring down the al-Azhari government.

All political parties were banned during the Ibrahim Abboud (q.v.) era after 1958, but the personal prestige of al-Mirghani among the military leaders meant that he maintained a degree of political influence. Following the 1964 October Revolution (q.v.) overthrowing Abboud, illness reduced al-Mirghani's direct involvement but he continued to be an important focus of political action in the 1965 elections. In 1967 the NUP and PDP regrouped to form the Democratic Unionist Party (DUP, q.v.). Al-Mirghani died in 1968, nine years after his rival 'Abd al-Rahman al-Mahdi. Political parties were again abolished by the Ja'afar al-Nimeiri (q.v.) government in 1969 until 1985. The DUP still exists today within the National Democratic Alliance (NDA, q.v.), which is battling against the National Islamic Front (NIF, q.v.) in Khartoum.

MIRGHANI, HASAN IBN MUHAMMAD 'UTHMAN, AL-. *See* KHATMIYA; MIRGHANI.

MIRGHANI, MUHAMMAD 'UTHMAN, al- (and MUHAMMAD 'UTHMAN II). *See* KHATMIYA; MIRGHANI.

MIRGHANI, MUHAMMAD 'UTHMAN IBN AHMAD, AL-. A member of the Mirghani family (q.v.) who assumed a leadership role in the family's center in Kassala (q.v.) after his father Ahmad's death in 1928. In national politics he usually accepted the leadership of his uncle, 'Ali al-Mirghani (q.v.). Muhammad 'Uthman was active in the early days of nationalist party politics and helped to organize the National Front (q.v.) in 1949, and was also the publisher of an independent newspaper later. However, he retired from public life in the 1950s because of ill health and some disagreements with other Khatmiya (q.v.) political leaders.

MIRGHANI, MUHAMMAD 'UTHMAN IBN 'ALI, AL- (1936–). The leader of the Khatmiya (q.v.) after the death of his father, Sayyid 'Ali al-Mirghani (q.v.) in 1968. As a young man he took part in the religious and political activities of the order. Following the October Revolution (q.v.) of 1964 he participated more directly in the Peoples Democratic Party (PDP, q.v.) and was named to the Executive Committee of the Democratic Unionist Party (q.v.) when it was formed in 1968 through the merger of the PDP and the National Unionist Party (q.v.). After the 1969 May Revolution (q.v.) he gave his support to the Ja'afar al-Nimeiri (q.v.) government in its conflict with the Ansar (q.v.) but had no official political role.

MIRGHANI FAMILY. A prominent family with religious prestige in the Sudan. In the eighteenth century the family, residing in Mecca, was among the recognized descendants of the Prophet Muhammad. Muhammad 'Uthman al-Mirghani (1793–1853, q.v.) was a student of Ahmad Ibn Idris (q.v.) and established the Khatmiya *tariqa* (qq.v.). Muhammad

'Uthman preached in the Sudan around 1817–1821, where he married a local woman. Hasan (1819–1869), his son by this marriage, returned to the Sudan and firmly established the family and order as an influential force in the Sudan. The family and order also had branches in Arabia, Egypt, and Eritrea. The Mirghanis in the Sudan worked closely with the Turco-Egyptian (q.v.) regime and were vigorous opponents of the Mahdi (q.v.). Hasan's son, Muhammad 'Uthman II (1848–1886), was an effective mediator and organizer. He died in Cairo after leading an ultimately unsuccessful resistance to the Mahdist movement in the Nile Valley and Kassala (q.v.) area. His sons, Ahmad (1877–1928) and 'Ali (1878–1968), lived outside the Sudan until the Anglo-Egyptian (q.v.) conquest.

In the twentieth century many members of the family, from different branches, were active in religious and political affairs. They quite consistently opposed revived Mahdist influence. At first they cooperated with the British but then became more pro-Egyptian, fearing that British cooperation with 'Abd al-Rahman al-Mahdi (q.v.) would lead to a Mahdist-dominated Sudan. They aided parties supporting Nile Valley unity. Muhammad 'Uthman ibn Ahmad helped organize the National Front (q.v.) in 1949, and the family, especially 'Ali, was identified with the Peoples Democratic Party (q.v.) formed in 1956. The family exercised some influence on the Ibrahim Abboud (q.v.) regime and was relatively active in party politics in the 1960s. At 'Ali al-Mirghani's death in 1968, his son, Muhammad 'Uthman (q.v.), succeeded him in family and *tariqa* leadership. The family cooperated with the Ja'afar al-Nimeiri (q.v.) government after the 1969 May Revolution (q.v.) and was active again in party politics during the most recent period of democracy, 1986–1989. *See also* ASHRAF.

MIRGHANIYA. *See* KHATMIYA.

MISSIONARIES IN SUDAN. The European commercial stronghold in Upper Nile (q.v.) was achieved in part through missionary pressure. The Vicarate Apostolic of Central Africa was established in 1846 as a first step toward establishing a mission to the now accessible territories. A group of Catholic missionaries established their headquarters at Khartoum (q.v.) in 1848, and sent Ignaz Knoblecher (q.v.) to Upper Nile as head of the mission. The first missionaries arrived at Gondokoro (q.v.) in 1853 to missionize among the Bari (q.v.). Unsuccessful, the last surviving missionary withdrew in 1854 to found the station of the Holy Cross among the Dinka (q.v.) farther north, led by Monsignor Daniele Comboni (q.v.). Holy Cross and the Gondokoro missions were abandoned in

1859 and 1860 respectively, and Comboni withdrew to Khartoum (q.v.) with a small retinue of Dinka converts. The fate of these failed mission attempts convinced Comboni that Christianity could best be spread in Africa by Africans. Caterina Zeinab (q.v.), baptized in Egypt in 1860, became the first Dinka evangelist, returning to Khartoum to teach at the mission and assist with baptisms.

Comboni, with his philosophy of native evangelization, founded a seminary in 1867 at Verona for this purpose, and in the course of his efforts established the Catholic Church in the Sudan. Having achieved limited success, Christian evangelizing came to a halt during the Mahdiya (q.v.). After the "reconquest," Comboni missionaries returned to the Sudan, and in 1900 the Comboni Sisters established their first school for girls in Omdurman (q.v.) and another in Khartoum. In 1903 the Sudanese government allotted to the missionary societies applying for permission to work in Sudan separate territories for evangelization:

Upper Nile Province (q.v.), from the east bank of the Nile to the Sudan-Ethiopian border, was assigned to the United Presbyterian Church of America; west of the Nile and the whole of Bahr al-Ghazal (q.v., except Rumbek) was allotted to the Catholic Mission; and Equatoria (q.v.) west of the Nile (Yei, Yambio, Moru) was allotted to the Church of England.

In 1957, one year after Sudanese independence, the mission schools in the South were taken over by the Ministry of Education. In 1962 the government forbade all missionary activity without permission from the Council of Ministers; and in 1964 all foreign missionaries were expelled from the South, leaving the Sudanese clergy in control of church activities there. In 1974 the Holy See set up a local hierarchy in Sudan with two ecclesiastical provinces and bishops administering each, consisting of all dioceses of the northern and southern Sudan. The fear of Christian evangelization grew during the period of Islamic resurgence after 1977. With the renewal of civil war in the South in 1982, and Islamization (q.v.) of Sudan's laws in 1983, the tensions between Christianity (q.v.) and Islam (q.v.) became more politicized. Relief efforts in the war-ravaged southern Sudan (q.v.) were often hampered by government suspicion of the Christian relief agencies' motives. There are currently no active missionaries in Sudan, although a number of Christian-based relief organizations have resumed operations after international pressure was exerted on the 'Umar al-Bashir (q.v.) regime.

MONDIRI, EZBONI. Southern political leader. He was active in southern party affairs in the 1950s, forming the Federal Party (q.v.) in 1957–1958 as a result of a split within the Liberal Party (q.v.). He was elected to Parliament in 1958 but was jailed for incitement when he worked to rally support for a federal form of government. After the 1964 October Revolution (q.v.) he was named minister of communications in the transition government but left the country in 1965 to work with southern opposition groups. Mondiri was a leader in the Azania Liberation Front (q.v.) and was a prominent commander of southern forces in Equatoria (q.v.). He was active in the Southern Sudan Liberation Movement (q.v.) and played a key role in the negotiations leading up to the Addis Ababa Agreement of 1972 (q.v.). After the settlement Mondiri served in the Southern Region High Executive Council (1973–1975).

MUFTI, IBRAHIM, AL- (1913–). A nationalist and political leader. He was educated in the Sudan and became a lawyer. He was one of the founders of the Graduates Congress and the Ashigga Party (qq.v.), and was generally active in pro-Nile unity nationalism. Al-Mufti became a member of the executive committee of the National Unionist Party (NUP, q.v.) after it was formed in 1952 and was then elected to Parliament. He served in the cabinet of Isma'il al-Azhari (q.v.) as minister of commerce and then of finance. After the 1964 October Revolution (q.v.) he was again a major NUP leader, serving at various times as minister of finance, of foreign affairs, and of irrigation. He was no longer active in politics after the 1969 May Revolution (q.v.). Al-Mufti is a descendant of a nineteenth-century religious leader, Isma'il al-Wali (q.v.), and a cousin of Isma'il al-Azhari (q.v.).

MUHAMMAD 'ABD AL-RAHIM (1878–1966). Amateur historian who wrote numerous books and articles on the history and cultures of the Sudan. Born outside el-Obeid (q.v.), as a young boy he accompanied his father to the Mahdist siege of Khartoum (q.v.), and later participated in the famous battle at Tushki in 1889. During the later years of the Mahdiya (q.v.) he served in the Khalifa's (q.v.) bodyguard and was wounded in the final battle at Karari (q.v.) in 1898. After the establishment of Anglo-Egyptian (q.v.) rule Muhammad studied in Omdurman (q.v.) and at al-Azhar (q.v.) in Cairo, finally joining the Condominium (q.v.) administration as an accountant. His travels throughout the Sudan allowed him the opportunity to collect oral histories, which he used in his many writings. Regrettably only four of his books have yet been published, as well as several articles that appeared in a journal he published *(Majallat Umm Durman)* from 1936 to 1937. Some fifteen unpublished manuscripts cover a wide variety of subjects on the history of the Sudan.

MUHAMMAD ABU LIKAYLIK. *See* LIKAYLIK, MUHAMMAD ABU.

MUHAMMAD AHMAD AL-MAHDI. *See* MAHDI, MUHAMMAD AHMAD, AL-.

MUHAMMAD 'ALI (1769–1849). An Albanian soldier who was the Ottoman governor of Egypt between 1805 and 1811 and who ruled as Pasha (q.v.) from 1811 to 1848. He instituted modernizing reforms there and became virtually independent from his Ottoman overlords. In 1820, he sent military forces into the Sudan and conquered most of the northern part of the country. In 1822 his son Isma'il Kamil Pasha (q.v.) was assassinated by Mek Nimr (q.v.). This precipitated a sustained punitive expedition by Muhammad Khusraw (q.v.). In 1838–1839 Muhammad 'Ali visited the Sudan. At his death in 1849 he was interred at the mosque atop the Moqattam Hills in Cairo, which has become a major urban landmark.

MUHAMMAD AL-MAHDI AL-SANUSI. *See* SANUSIYA.

MUHAMMAD AL-MAJDHUB AL-KABIR. *See* MAJADHIB.

MUHAMMAD AL-MAJDHUB AL-SUGHAYYIR. *See* MAJADHIB.

MUHAMMAD BADR AL-UBAYD (ca. 1810–1884). A prominent religious leader in the Blue Nile area in the nineteenth century. He was famous as a teacher and *tariqa* (q.v.) leader and established an important religious center at Umm Dubban. His sons gave strong support to the Mahdist (q.v.) movement.

MUHAMMAD IBN SARHAN AL-SUGHAYRUN. *See* AWLAD JABIR.

MUHAMMAD KHUSRAW AL-DAFTARDAR (?–1833). A Turkish soldier in Muhammad 'Ali's (q.v.) service in Egypt and married to the Pasha's daughter. He was originally a financial officer—his title *Daftardar* refers to the keeper of tax registers—and later an officer in the armies that conquered the Sudan in 1820–1822. He was responsible for the conquest of Kordofan (q.v.) and also led a long-term punitive expedition in 1822 following the murder of the son of Muhammad 'Ali, Isma'il Kamil Pasha, by Mek Nimr (qq.v.). He returned to Egypt in 1824, leaving his name and mark in the Sudan to connote the worst of Turkish repression.

MUHAMMAD SHARIF IBN HAMAD (ca. 1870–1899). A cousin of Muhammad Ahmad al-Mahdi (q.v.), appointed by the Mahdi to be the successor to the Khalifa (q.v.) 'Ali or *Khalifat al-Karrar*, and chief rival to the Khalifa 'Abdullahi (q.v.). Though a young man at the beginning of the Mahdiya (q.v.) and very much junior to the two other Khulafa (pl.), Muhammad Sharif was given command of one of the three divisions of the Mahdist army, the Red Flag, which consisted of the Dongola Ashraf (qq.v.) and Ansar (q.v.) of riverine origins (known as *awlad al-balad,* or "townspeople"). Upon the Mahdi's death in 1885 he challenged 'Abdullahi for leadership of the movement, only to be overruled by a moderate faction led by Khalifa 'Ali al-Hilu (q.v.) and the Ashraf patriarch, Ahmad Muhammad Sharfi. An uneasy truce between the two followed, while their mutual antagonism was all but public: Muhammad Sharif felt entitled to leadership as the Mahdi's kinsman and regarded 'Abdullahi as an uncouth westerner; 'Abdullahi for his part regarded Muhammad Sharif as a pampered young upstart.

Tensions rose in 1886 when Khalifa 'Abdullahi seized control of the valuable *jihadiya* (q.v.) soldiers, leaving Muhammad Sharif with little visible authority. In November 1891 Muhammad Sharif led an open revolt against the Khalifa in Omdurman (q.v.), occupying the Mahdi's tomb with an armed band and threatening a bloody confrontation. This again was mediated by a moderate faction and the Ashraf grievances were temporarily acceded to; shortly thereafter, Muhammad Sharif's Danagla followers were detained and divested of many of their goods, while the junior *khalifa* himself was tried for acts against the faith and imprisoned. He was released only in 1896 when the Anglo-Egyptian (q.v.) invasion threatened the Mahdist state. Muhammad Sharif was captured after the battle of Karari (q.v.) while fleeing west. Sent to live in Shukkaba near Wad Medani (q.v.), he was arrested in August 1899 on suspicion of subversion and promptly executed along with the Mahdi's sons al-Fadl and al-Bushra. *See also* MAHDI, AL-, FAMILY.

MUHAMMAD SHARIF NUR AL-DA'IM (?–1908). Leader of the Sammaniya *tariqa* (qq.v.) in the nineteenth century and grandson of Ahmad al-Tayib, who introduced the order into the Sudan. Muhammad Sharif was a prominent religious notable in the time of Turco-Egyptian (q.v.) rule. His most famous student was Muhammad Ahmad al-Mahdi (q.v.), whom he initiated into the Sammaniya. Although Muhammad Sharif quarreled with his student and initially opposed the Mahdist movement—he in fact wrote a pamphlet denouncing Muhammad Ahmad as a false Mahdi (q.v.)—he later joined the Mahdist side after the fall of Khartoum (q.v.).

After the Anglo-Egyptian (q.v.) conquest, Muhammad Sharif lived as a respected figure in the village surrounding the tomb of Shaykh Ahmad al-Tayib. He was succeeded in the Sammaniya leadership by his son, 'Abd al-Mahmud.

MUHAMMAD TAJ AL-DIN AL-BAHARI. *See* QADIRIYA.

MUHAMMAD TAWFIQ, TEWFIK (1852–1892). Muhammad Tawfiq was the son of Isma'il, the son of Ibrahim, the son of Muhammad 'Ali (qq.v), all sovereigns of Egypt. Muhammad Tawfiq ruled Egypt and, nominally, the Sudan, from 1879 to 1892, thus during the last days of Turco-Egyptian (q.v.) rule as well as for the largest part of the Mahdiya (q.v.). It was under Muhammad Tawfiq that Charles Gordon (q.v.) formally served.

MURLE. *See* BEIR CLUSTER.

MUSA, 'UMAR AL-HAJ. Sudanese soldier and political leader. He completed training at the Officers Training School in Omdurman (q.v.) in 1944 and began a military career. During the Ibrahim Abboud era he was appointed officer commanding the Signal Corps and was a senior officer at the time of the 1969 May Revolution (q.v.). Soon after the revolution he was minister of defense briefly and then was named minister of national guidance (1969–1971), becoming minister of information and culture in the first Sudanese Socialist Union (SSU, q.v.) cabinet in 1971, remaining in the post until 1975. In 1975 Musa was made assistant secretary general of the SSU.

MUSIC AND DANCE. The extreme cultural heterogeneity of Sudan embraces the musical traditions of ancient Nile societies, of Christianity and Islam (qq.v.). It includes the diversity of Arabo-Islamic, African, ancient, and syncretic traditions and today includes the penetration of Western styles as well as the popularization of modern electronic Sudanese music and tapes.

Each ethnic group and region has musical and dance traditions that are unique. They may exist as pure entertainment, festivities, rites of passage, or somber religious and funerary functions. A wedding in any region of Sudan is unthinkable without music of varying forms. The famed *dhikr* or Dervish dance serves as a religious invocation and remembrance of founding religious figures. The proto-martial stick fighting and wrestling of some regions have sometimes evolved into a rhythmic dance form. Many Sudanese went to battle with the booming war drum exhorting them to still higher levels of bravery. Modern political demonstrations have rhythmic chants and poetic slogans.

Individual soloists may be highly renowned in a village or on a cassette player. Other songs and dances should only be performed as a group activity. Groups are often broken down by age and gender as they reinforce these primary social values in Sudanese society in all regions. Music and dance solidifies society and helps to record and commemorate historical events and personages.

The percussive patterns of polyrhythms and call-and-response are also popular in many regional forms and variations. A central role of drums, sistrums, clappers, scrapers, bells, and gongs is deeply rooted in Sudanese history, but no less than equally ancient reed flutes, horns, and complex woodwinds. Stringed instruments also range from the simple Nubian *rababa*, to the complex Arabic *oud*, and the four-, five-, or six-string lyres and harps of the southern Sudanese groups such as the Madi, Shilluk, Dinka, and Nuer (qq.v.), where one also finds the *mbira* sounding board activated by vibrating metal strips or xylophones made of hardwoods resonating over graduated gourds. Some instruments and musical traditions may appear throughout the country in clubs or on national television.

MUSLIM BROTHERHOOD. A militant religious and political organization formed in Egypt in 1928 by Hasan al-Banna (d. 1949) and known in Arabic as *al-Ikhwan al-Muslimun*. It advocates government and laws based directly on the Qur'an and works for fundamentalist Islamic revival. The Brotherhood recruited individual Sudanese in the 1940s but a branch was not established in the Sudan until the early 1950s. At that time the Brotherhood came together with the Islamic Liberation Movement (ILM), a Sudanese group with similar aims formed in 1949.

Among the founders of the ILM were the "Hantoub Group" from Wad Medani (q.v.), including al-Saim Muhammad Ibrahim, Babikr Karrar, and Muhammad Yusuf Muhammad. The ILM drafted a constitution and set as its goals the revival of Islam (q.v.) and the establishment of a new world order transcending the East-West dichotomy. Gradually ILM members established contact with the Brotherhood in Egypt, which formalized the evolution of the ILM into a Sudanese branch with a 21 August 1954 conference at the Omdurman Cultural Club that officially adopted the name. Inevitably nationalist sentiments developed and in early 1955 a new leadership structure was devised designating *al-Muraqib al-'Amm* (the general supervisor) as a Sudanese elected leader of the Brotherhood. Thereafter the Brotherhood could devote its energies to the domestic agenda of combating the communist movement that had captured the interest and support of so many of Sudan's nationalist intellectuals.

The Muslim Brotherhood came under the leadership of al-Rashid al-Tahir who had proven himself as a student leader at Gordon Memorial College in Khartoum (qq.v.). As a distinct politico-religious movement it had little time for the traditional leadership of the two *sayyids* of the Mahdi and Mirghani (qq.v.) families, and shaped its own political program of anticommunism, proindependence, and an ultimate goal of establishing an Islamic order. The organizational structure of the Brotherhood inherited from Egypt included: at the lowest level, the *usrah* or cell, usually of five members, which acted as a unit for indoctrination; above that was the *shu'ba*, or branch in the neighborhood or town; then a constituent assembly comprising members who had completed four years membership and were over twenty years of age; and an Executive Bureau from the constituent assembly. In 1962 the constituent assembly was replaced by an elected *shura* (consultative) council. This coincided with the shift in leadership from al-Tahir to Hasan al-Turabi (q.v.), another dynamic leader from the postindependence University of Khartoum (q.v.). He became especially prominent after his return to Sudan from studying abroad in 1964, by that time a ten-year veteran of the movement with a new prestigious Ph.D. degree.

Al-Turabi became secretary general of the Brotherhood in 1964 while also dean of the Faculty of Law at Khartoum University. Under al-Turabi's influence the Islamic Charter Front (q.v.) was organized in November 1964 for the purpose of participating in the post-October Revolution (q.v.) democratic elections in April 1965. Under this banner 100 candidates were fielded, including 15 in the special graduates constituencies. The Islamic Charter Front won seven seats, including the election of al-Turabi to the Parliament.

The Brotherhood was popular among students and recent graduates. There were some divisions among the leadership in the 1960s, reflecting tensions between leaders of the original ILM the Brotherhood. All of these groups were initially outlawed after the 1969 May Revolution (q.v.) but continued to be active in opposing the revolutionary regime.

After Ja'afar al-Nimeiri (q.v.) crushed the communist-backed coup attempt of 1971, the Brotherhood was in less jeopardy and eventually individual Muslim Brothers came to play an active role in the regime, especially as it began to pursue a policy of Islamization (q.v.) after 1977. By the end of the 1970s the Brothers controlled most of the university student unions. Al-Turabi was made attorney general after the "September Laws" (q.v.) were introduced in 1983, and the Brotherhood remained allied with the May Revolution until its last days in 1985. In the wake of the new democracy that Sudan experienced after sixteen years of military rule, the Muslim Brotherhood developed a more broadly based political organization, the National Islamic Front (NIF, q.v.), in 1985.

The broader international Islamist trend crystallized in Sudan with the NIF, which moved beyond the traditional Brotherhood to include broader social elements, such as religious scholars (*'ulama)*, Sufi (q.v.), and tribal leaders, as well as women (q.v.). After 1989, with the effective coming to power of the NIF, the former elements of the Muslim Brotherhood organization were absorbed by the NIF.

MUSLIM BROTHERHOOD, WOMEN'S BUREAU (MUSLIM SISTERS). The Women's Bureau of the Muslim Brotherhood (q.v.) is known popularly as *al-Akhwat al-Muslimun* (Muslim Sisters). The first woman to join the Muslim Brotherhood was Fatima Talib in 1949. Su'ad al-Fatih and Thuraya Umbabi broke with the leftist Sudanese Women's Union (q.v.) and joined in 1951. Following the organizational Congress of the Muslim Brotherhood (q.v.) in 1954 a Women's Bureau was established. In 1956 it began to publish a weekly woman's magazine, *Al-Manar*, edited by Su'ad al-Fatih, but it folded within a year. In 1964 *Al-Manar* was published again, responding to activism by women (q.v.) in the October Revolution (q.v.) who organized as the Patriotic Women's Front and were led by al-Fatih. Its declared goals were the "formation of the believing individual" and the development and education of women so as to give them a larger social and political role. *Al-Manar* supported the right of women to vote, and competition for the woman's vote became intense in the 1965 democratic elections. The Islamist women's movement never rivaled in numbers or influence the mass democratic women's movement, the Sudanese Women's Union, and the female vote was largely anti-Brotherhood. Held back by the tradition of religious activism being the province of males, the modern mobilization of Sudanese Islamist women was not to materialize until after the successful emergence of the more broadly based National Islamic Front (q.v.), especially after 1989.

MUSLIM FOLK RELIGION. *See* FOLK RELIGION; ISLAM.

MUSLIM SISTERHOOD. *See* MUSLIM BROTHERHOOD, WOMEN'S BUREAU.

MUSTAFA, ZAKI. Sudanese lawyer and legal scholar. He served as dean of the Law Faculty at the University of Khartoum (q.v.) and was named attorney general in 1973. In 1975 he became a part-time legal advisor to Ja'afar al-Nimeiri (q.v.) and was appointed secretary-general of the joint Saudi-Sudanese authority for exploitation of Red Sea resources.

– N –

NACHTIGAL, GUSTAVE (1834–1885). This German (Prussian) physician and explorer of the Sahara and Sahel set out from Tripoli, Libya, in 1869. His trip was largely scientific and funded by the Prussian king. Nachtigal traveled southward to the town of Murzuk and took a side trip to the Tibesti plateau region in southern Libya. From there he passed on to the kingdom of Bornu in Nigeria and rounded the southern shore of Lake Chad and on to Wadai. He entered Darfur via al-Fasher (qq.v.), followed the caravan route to el-Obeid in Kordofan (qq.v.), and headed for Khartoum (q.v.). He traveled down the Nile in 1874 and returned to Europe by 1875. His work *Sahara and Sudan*, published in three volumes from 1879 to 1889, gives important observations of the region.

NAHDA MAGAZINE, AL-. This literary journal blazed trails in the development of modern Sudanese Arabic literature (q.v.). Its title meant "The Resurgence" and reflected a faith in Sudanese social progress and development held by many young intellectuals of the period. Thirty issues of the journal appeared in 1931 and 1932. Publication came to a stop with the untimely death of its founder and editor-in-chief, Muhammad 'Abbas Abu al-Rish (1908–1933). Contributors, including a large number of Gordon Memorial College (q.v.) graduates, used the journal to experiment with literary forms both new, such as the short story and play in prose, and old such as the use of poetry. These writers came from across the political spectrum and included those who sympathized with Egyptian unity as well as others who favored an independent Sudan. Among them were Muhammad Ahmad Mahjub (q.v.), Isma'il al-Atabani (q.v.), Makkawi Ya'qub, Yusuf Mustafa al-Tinay, and others. One of its contributors, 'Arafat Muhammad 'Abd Allah (1898–1936), went on to found the journal *al-Fajr*. *See also* MEDIA. [by Heather J. Sharkey]

AL-NAHUD. This town on the western side of Kordofan (q.v.) is about 144 kilometers west of el-Obeid (q.v.). Its Arabic name, meaning "breasts," is said to refer to the abundant supply of wells in the town and vicinity or to the twin peaks visible from outside of the town. It was from al-Nahud that the British made their final moves to conquer Darfur (q.v.) in 1916, and its history is often associated with events farther west. In 1901 Sultan 'Ali Dinar (q.v.) stayed briefly in al-Nahud and his cousin/representative met British officials there in 1903. By 1910 the British had constructed a telegraph line there as they strengthened their presence in Kordofan. During this period the British also developed anxieties about Fur (q.v.) expansion over the Humr people of al-Nahud and subsequently used them in their attack on Darfur. In 1915 the British added to the defense of al-Nahud fearing an attack by 'Ali Dinar. More wells were dug and supplies of *durra* and sorghum were accumulated. By March 1916, at the time of the inspection by General F. R. Wingate (q.v.), al-Nahud held some 2,000 Anglo-Egyptian (q.v.) troops. In May 1916 Major Hubert Huddleston (q.v.) took this army to al-Fasher (q.v.) to consolidate the control over Darfur.

Following the conquest of Darfur the local trade in gum arabic, cattle, camels, hides, and cotton allowed for a steady, but modest increase in the population and commerce of al-Nahud. At the time of the conquest of Darfur al-Nahud had about 7,500 people. Although the town is situated in Humr territory, it was Jallaba and Greek (qq.v.) merchants from the Nile Valley who controlled the local commerce. Once the railway passed to the south of al-Nahud at Abu Zabad, the future growth of al-Nahud became limited, and while it has developed it is certainly not keeping the same pace as other towns of the western Sudan. By the time of independence it had reached 17,300, but by 1969 it had only grown to a modest 22,000; by 1983 the population was only 30,000.

NATIONAL DEMOCRATIC ALLIANCE (NDA). In the wake of the thwarted democratization process that occurred in the post-Ja'afar al-Nimeiri (q.v.) Sudan (1985–1989) and the effective coming to power of the National Islamic Front (q.v.) in 1989, the NDA was organized on 21 October 1989 to restore national democracy and form a united front to oppose the NIF-backed 'Umar al-Bashir (q.v.) regime. After 1989 democratic parties and institutions, other than those approved by the NIF, were banned and forced underground or into exile. The democratic opposition in exile organized the united opposition comprised of all banned parties, including, after 1993, the important tactical alliance with the southern movement, the Sudanese Peoples Liberation Army/Movement (SPLA/SPLM, q.v.). The NDA has drawn its support from exile communities, especially in Egypt, in Europe, and in North America.

Declaring its total rejection of the al-Bashir military regime, the NDA proposed a program of internal and external resistance, a transitional period of the restoration of democracy and the rule of law, cancellation of the 1983 "September Laws" (q.v.) on Islamization (q.v.), the convening of a National Constitutional Conference establishing representative regional government, and full restoration of the Addis Ababa Agreement of 1972 (q.v.).

A vision for the "New Sudan" began to be articulated by the NDA that spoke of governmental forms that promote a just society protecting the legitimate rights of every citizen in a secular state free from racism, religious discrimination, or any other prejudice based upon creed, color, or ethnic origin. The new Sudan would be built upon the construction of a lasting peaceful solution to the civil war waged especially since 1983.

The SPLM/SPLA formally joined the NDA on 17 April 1993 in Nairobi. In so doing it reaffirmed its commitment to a united Sudan, thus opposing the separatist elements that had reemerged in the southern movement since 1989. Agreement was reached with this historic alliance of northern opposition forces and the dominant southern movement that international and regional human rights (q.v.) instruments shall be an integral part of the laws of the Sudan; and that full equality of all citizens with respect to religion, race, gender, and culture shall be respected. Thus joint agreement on the basics of a new Sudanese constitution was reached. The signatories to the 1993 Nairobi expansion of the NDA included: the SPLM/SPLA, Umma Party (q.v.), Democratic Unionist Party (q.v.), Sudan Communist Party (q.v.), Union of Sudan African Parties, and the Sudanese Armed Forces-Legitimate Command (q.v.).

The NDA remains the sole broadly based opposition to the Islamist al-Bashir regime in Khartoum and as such it stands to play the most significant role in any post-Islamist Sudan.

NATIONAL FRONT (1949–1952). A political grouping formed in 1949 by members of the Khatmiya (q.v.) that received support from 'Ali al-Mirghani (q.v.). It opposed the more extreme positions of the Ashigga Party (q.v.), favoring dominion status for the Sudan in unity with Egypt. The leader of the Front was Muhammad 'Uthman ibn Ahmad al-Mirghani (q.v.), a nephew of Sayyid 'Ali, and its major political spokesman was Mirghani Hamza. The party was weakened by the illness of Muhammad 'Uthman in 1952 and was dissolved when the Front participated in the creation of the National Unionist Party (q.v.).

NATIONAL FRONT (1957–1958). A coalition of organizations opposed to the pro-Western and conservative policies of the 'Abdallah Khalil (q.v.) government. It was formed in 1957 and included the National Unionist Party (q.v.), the Anti-Imperialist Front (q.v.), and the National Union of Students. The Front came to an end with the military government of Ibrahim Abboud (q.v.) in 1958.

NATIONAL FRONT (1974). A combination of Muslim Brotherhood, Umma Party (qq.v.), and other politicians opposed to the Ja'afar al-Nimeiri (q.v.) regime, accused of antigovernment plots.

NATIONAL ISLAMIC FRONT (NIF). An Islamist political group organized after the April 1985 coup that overthrew the Ja'afar al-Nimeiri (q.v.) regime. An outgrowth of the Muslim Brotherhood (q.v.), it represents a broader base for popular mobilization toward a political agenda of Islamization (q.v.). Its program for the future political direction is summarized in the *Sudan Charter, National Unity and Diversity* 1987, which emphasizes freedom of religious choice. Islamic jurisprudence would be the general source of law, reflecting the Muslim majority population, while minority populations would have personal law and customs recognized by the Shari'a (q.v.), which recognizes the principle of religious freedom. Further, Sudan is conceived of as a single country wherein Arab (q.v.) and African origins have blended. Power-sharing is envisioned as taking place within a political system of constitutional decentralization.

Despite the latter position, the NIF stood outside of the major peace initiatives taken since the mid-1980s, being the only major political grouping not to sign the watershed Koka Dam Declaration of 1986 (q.v.), as well as other similar attempts to institute peace talks. The NIF backed the military regime of 'Umar al-Bashir (q.v.) after it toppled the Sadiq al-Mahdi (q.v.) government.

Since 1989 the NIF has effectively ruled Sudan with the 'Umar al-Bashir military regime under the political direction of Dr. Hasan al-Turabi (q.v.), founder and chief theoretician of the NIF. Banning all other non-NIF parties has resulted in their monopoly of official politics with the opposition forces silenced or forced into exile. The National Democratic Alliance (q.v.) is the main opposition movement to the NIF.

In the NIF program, the unity of Sudan is underscored, while a federal system is preferred that envisions power-sharing between the national center and the federated regions. Federalism is the hallmark of the NIF policy solution to the question of national unity and the civil war. A general constitutional conference is conceived of as an integral part of the transition to peace and a new federal constitution, predicated upon a cease-fire agreement.

Since a mutual cease-fire agreement has not been achieved by this or any other government since the Addis Ababa Agreement of 1972 (q.v.), continuation of the protracted and unresolved civil war has meant that the proposals regarding a negotiated federal system have not been realized. However, the policy of Islamic law being the only law in force has been enforced, although the Islamization of law took place in September 1983, six years before the NIF seized power. It sees itself as practicing an Islamic form of democracy based upon the concept of *shura*, or consultation, where an Islamic leader takes advice from elected officials or from the religious scholars, the *'ulama*.

The NIF sees itself as a part of the international Islamic revival restoring to the state and social and political institutions their Islamic heritage denied by decades of colonialism and Western or other foreign influence. Indeed, during the present Islamist period, one of Sudan's most consistent allies has been Iran. The Sudanese NIF has also allied itself with Islamist movements in Egypt and Algeria, and has welcomed American Nation of Islam leader Louis Farrakhan. *See also* FOREIGN POLICY.

NATIONAL UNIONIST PARTY (NUP). The NUP was formed late in 1952 as a merger of a variety of groups favoring unity of the Nile Valley. It received the support of 'Ali al-Mirghani (q.v.) and was led by

Isma'il al-Azhari (q.v.). It won a majority of seats in the Parliament elected in 1953 and formed the government that proclaimed the independence of Sudan. However, in 1956 the Khatmiya (q.v.) wing of the NUP left to form the Peoples Democratic Party (PDP, q.v.), leaving the NUP as the party of al-Azhari. It was outlawed during the Ibrahim Abboud (q.v.) regime and joined in the opposition. After the 1964 October Revolution (q.v.), al-Azhari allied his party with the Umma Party (q.v.), with al-Azhari acting as head of state and the Umma providing the prime ministers. The NUP merged with the PDP to form the Democratic Unionist Party (q.v.) in 1967.

NATIONALIST PARTY. A short-lived party created in 1946 supporting independence for the Sudan. It participated in the National Front (q.v.) and soon merged with the Umma Party (q.v.).

NAZIR. The Arabic term applied to an official in local government appointed to represent a region or a traditional ethnic group. This position was an important link to the colonial policy of indirect rule (q.v.).

NDOGO. *See* AZANDE.

NEGUIB, GENERAL MUHAMMAD (1901–1984). This Sudanese-born Egyptian was a professional soldier with distinguished service in Palestine in 1948. As a result of the antimonarchist coup d'etat in Egypt on 23 July 1952, Muhammad Neguib became the formal leader of the Egyptian Free Officers Movement organized by Gamal 'Abd al-Nasser. In filling this power vacuum, he was appointed as the first Egyptian prime minister on 7 September 1952 after millennia of foreign rulers. These events were the result of postwar nationalism in the Nile valley and a failed British colonialism, as well as the rise of the state of Israel in 1948 that provoked Arab hostility. In retrospect this was a turning point not only for Egyptian independence but also for Sudanese independence and a reduced role for the British in this process.

Despite their long-standing support of King Faruq (q.v.) the British now hoped that a somewhat more conservative Neguib would bring some stability in these tumultuous times. The Anglo-Egyptian agreement of 1953 (q.v.) was the result of these rapidly changing alliances at this transitional period. However, the 1953 agreement was only an interlude with more negotiations in Cairo and Khartoum still to come in the process of decolonization and self-rule in 1953 and 1954. Given thoughts of Mahdism only a half century earlier, both the British and Egyptians tilted toward support of the Khatmiya (q.v.) in the Sudan and of opposition to the growth of the Ansar (q.v.) and neo-Mahdism.

In March 1953 Neguib went to Khartoum (q.v.) for a state visit. He anticipated a warm reception because he was born in the Sudan and was a well-known figure of Arab nationalism, not to mention his considerable popularity among his Khatmiya supporters. However, the Mahdists organized sustained rioting and protests that briefly resulted in the declaration of a state of emergency and an aborted visit for Neguib. In February 1954 struggles between Neguib and the more radical Gamal 'Abd al-Nasser brought his dismissal and very brief reinstatement. Neguib's position weakened again following an October 1954 attempt on Nasser's life by Muslim Brothers who were supported by Neguib. By November 1954 Nasser had full control of the government once again and Neguib was put under house arrest for almost a decade. He played no further public role in Egyptian politics.

NEWBOLD, SIR DOUGLAS (1894–1945). Newbold had a long service to British colonial government in the Sudan, first joining the Sudan Political Service (q.v.) in 1920. During the John Maffey, Stewart Symes, and Hubert Huddleston (qq.v.) governorships, Newbold served as political officer in the Red Sea Hills and in Kordofan (q.v.), later becoming the governor of Kordofan from 1932 to 1938, where he toured extensively. He was appointed civil secretary, succeeding Angus Gillan (q.v.) in 1939, and proceeded to refine the practice of "Native Administration." By 1940 Newbold was much engaged in enforcing the Closed Districts Ordinance (q.v.) that had been designed to isolate the South, but was now applied to buttress the East against the threat of Italian attacks from Eritrea. He was almost appointed as acting governor general in 1940 upon the hesitating departure of Symes.

As the war worsened, Newbold was compelled to gut the Sudan Political Service for military assignments elsewhere and he worried that this would have a negative effect on the colonial administration he had carefully built. In response, from 1942 to 1944 he accelerated the infant policy of Sudanization of the local administration, especially for the North, for which the Advisory Council of the Northern Sudan (q.v.) was created in 1943. With the appearance of so many Sudanese faces there was some backlash amongst conservative elements in the Sudan Political Service, especially as the urgency of the war and the opposition to traditional leaders by the Graduates Congress (q.v.) mounted. The steady growth of the rivalries in the 1940s between the Khatmiya and Ansar (qq.v.) made the British position stronger in the short term, but more unmanageable for the longer term.

Newbold discovered that the task of balancing the personal and political issues of the governor-general and the institutional interests of the Sudan Political Service was a complex business. Such was his topic of reflection as he sought to appraise and practically implement the policy of indirect rule (q.v.) during his term of office. Among his colleagues, his effectiveness and stature is often favorably compared to that of Harold MacMichael (q.v.). Newbold's term as civil secretary ended with his death in March 1945. With his departure the heyday of colonial rule slipped away and the clock of decolonization began to tick.

NIAM-NIAM. This archaic and pejorative term was used to suggest cannibalism. Such references are found on nineteenth-century maps of the southern Sudan (q.v.) and were based upon hearsay accounts rather than substantive observation. Since the term "Niam-Niam" was sometimes applied to the Azande (q.v.), it may have been that this regional conquest state generated such rumors to instill fear among the neighboring ethnic groups.

NILE PARTY. A small party formed in 1967. It had some following in Bahr al-Ghazal (q.v.) and won one seat in the 1968 parliamentary elections.

NILE PROVISIONAL GOVERNMENT (NPG). A southern political group. It was formed in Uganda in 1969 when the Southern Sudan Provisional Government (q.v.) broke up. Its main leaders were Gordon Mayen (q.v.) and Maro Morgan. The NPG was soon split with the formation of the Anyidi Revolutionary Government (q.v.). The NPG dissolved in 1970 but Mayen refused to accept the leadership of Joseph Lagu (q.v.) in the Southern Sudan Liberation Movement (q.v.). Mayen formed the African National Front, which opposed the 1972 settlement.

NILO-HAMITIC. *See* NILOTIC.

NILOTIC. All Nilotes belong to the eastern group of Sudanic language speakers. Most are cattle, sheep, and goat pastoralists by tradition. They arrived from southeastern Sudan sometime before AD 1000. Some scholars suggest that they retreated southward from Nubia (q.v.) in more ancient times, but the documentary and archaeological investigation of these people in such early times is very sparse. The extent of greater Nilotic territory also includes the Luo, Masai, Karamajong, Jie, and Turkana of Kenya. At the northeastern peripheries of their territory they came into contact with Cushitic or Hamitic influences through Ethiopia and are sometimes called Nilo-Hamitic people.

In the Sudan, after reaching superior grazing lands to the east and west of the Bahr al-Jabal, Nilotic people dispersed in all directions. The best-known Sudanese Nilotes are the Dinka and Nuer (qq.v.). Elsewhere, they spread over a group of earlier inhabitants, the pre-Nilotes, and transferred their linguistic system to them. To the southwest their spread was checked by the Azande (q.v.) people and on the north their expansion was blocked by cattle-herding Arabs (q.v.) and the pre-Nilotic Shilluk (q.v.).

NIMEIRI, JA'AFAR (NUMAYRI) (1930–). Nimeiri was a Sudanese military leader and head of state who graduated from the Sudan Military College in 1952 and took military training courses in Germany and the United States. He became an officer commanding the 1st Battalion, Khartoum (q.v.) in 1964 and was arrested for his opposition to the Ibrahim Abboud (q.v.) regime shortly before the outbreak of the October Revolution of 1964 (q.v.). Later he commanded the military training camp at Gebeit in the Red Sea and in 1966 was arrested on suspicion of complicity in an aborted coup attempt. He was the recognized leader of the May Revolution (q.v.) in 1969, and became the chairman of the Council of the Revolution and minister of defense in the new government. In October 1969 Nimeiri became prime minister and held that post along with a variety of ministerial positions. In 1970 the Revolutionary Council named him supreme commander of the armed forces. In July 1971 he was briefly dismissed during an abortive coup attempt, but soon regained his position. In the fall of 1971 he was elected president in a special national referendum and held the positions of president, prime minister, and minister of planning in the first government formed after the adoption of the new national constitution. Nimeiri was also a member of the Political Bureau of the Sudanese Socialist Union (SSU, q.v.). He was recognized as the leading figure in the creation of the new constitutional regime, the organization of the SSU, and in bringing about the negotiations that led to a settlement of the conflict in the southern Sudan (q.v.).

Surviving a second major coup attempt in 1976 Nimeiri was again "elected" president of the republic by national plebiscite in 1977 in which he gained over 95 percent of the vote. Thereafter he turned increasingly to Islam (q.v.) for political leverage and personal comfort. He began to appear in public in *jallabiya* and turban, and was frequently photographed praying in a mosque. His regime undertook a number of moves toward Islamization (q.v.) of state and society after 1977, the most controversial of which was declaring Islamic law (q.v.) to be state law with the "September Laws" (q.v.) of 1983, which introduced the harsh *hudud* punishments into civil and criminal law. With a regime that was perceived as ever more dictatorial, and with Nimeiri declaring himself Imam (q.v.), he became isolated politically and the object of antigovernment demonstrations in 1984–1985. While on an official visit to the United States Nimeiri was overthrown on 6 April 1985 by General Suwar al-Dahab (q.v.) who promised to restore Sudan to civilian rule within a year. Nimeiri spent fourteen years in exile in Egypt, where his extradition became a minor political irritant between the two countries. He returned to Sudan in 1999 with the aim of creating a new political movement, though his presence there is strictly at the sufferance of the ruling National Islamic Front (q.v.). In the December 2000 presidential election Nimeiri managed to attract 9.6 percent of the vote, coming in a distant second to military ruler 'Umar al-Bashir (q.v.). *See also* FOREIGN RELATIONS.

NIMR MUHAMMAD NIMR ("MEK NIMR") (ca. 1785–ca. 1846). The last of the autonomous *Meks* of the Ja'aliyin in Shendi (qq.v.). He rose to power in the warfare of the last days of the Funj (q.v.) and unwillingly submitted to the Turco-Egyptian (q.v.) army in 1821. In 1822 he trapped and killed Isma'il Kamil Pasha (q.v.), the Turco-Egyptian commander, but his revolt was short-lived. He fled to the Ethiopian borderlands and continued to conduct small raids on the eastern Sudan. *See also* MUHAMMAD KHUSRAW.

NINTH OF JUNE DECLARATION, 1969. One of the earliest and most far-reaching programs of the May Revolution (q.v.). The declaration recognized the historical and cultural differences between North and South Sudan and stated that the unity of Sudan must be built upon these objective realities. It added that the southern people have the right to develop their respective cultures and traditions within a united, socialist Sudan. "Regional Autonomy" was offered to the South as a means of fulfilling these goals while providing a mechanism for unity within the democratic structures of the North. In this first statement a four-point program was offered, including a general amnesty; promise of economic, social, and cultural development of the South; appointment of a minister for southern affairs; and provision for the training of personnel. Ultimately, the spirit of this declaration led to the Addis Ababa Peace Agreement of 1972 (q.v.) and a decade of peace, thus providing a model for any future Sudanese reconciliation. *See also* GARANG, JOSEPH; NIMEIRI, JA'AFAR.

NORTHERN PROVINCE. Former province (q.v.), the second largest after Darfur (q.v.). With an approximate size of 184,200 square miles and a relatively small population (1,133,000 in the 1970 census), Northern Province stretched along the Nile from Wadi Halfa (q.v.) in the north to Shendi (q.v.) in the south, including also the towns of Dongola, Merowe, Berber, and Atbara (qq.v.). It is what in ancient times was known as Nubia (q.v.). Inhabited by a variety of Arab and Nubian (qq.v.) groups, including camel-herding Arabs (q.v.), it was always an important trade route. In Anglo-Egyptian (q.v.) times the first pump irrigation cotton scheme, the Zeidab Scheme, was located here in 1904 and served as a forerunner to the Gezira Scheme (q.v.). Dates are currently the region's most important crop and a canning industry is based in Karima (q.v.).

NUBA. Residents of the hill country of southern Kordofan (q.v.), who must be distinguished from the northern Sudanese Nubians (q.v.), even though some Nubian refugees have also found their homes in the Nuba Hills. The Nuba proper speak Kordofanian languages, while the Nubians are from the Nubian portion of the Nile where they speak languages of the eastern branch of the Sudanic family. The similarity of their names is explained by the origin of the word "Nuba," an ancient and pejorative term of no geographical or ethnic precision referring to the enslaveable peoples upriver from Egypt. As political frontiers shifted over the centuries, notions of who was enslaveable (or "uncivilized") tended to change; thus northern riverine peoples were "Nubian" relative to ancient Egypt, while Kordofanian hill peoples were "Nuba" with respect to eighteenth-century Sinnar (q.v.). Meanwhile the exact origins of the Nuba are unclear, and the archaeology of their region is poorly developed.

The Nuba are "Negroid" rather than "Arab" (q.v.) by conventional classification and probably had a much more extensive territory until they were pushed into their mountain retreat by cattle-herding Nilotics (q.v.) to the south in the tenth century or before, by cattle-herding Arabs to the north from the sixteenth century onward, and by relentless predations of Jallaba (q.v.) slavers in the eighteenth and nineteenth centuries.

The Nuba have maintained distinctive linguistic and cultural traditions but have been increasingly incorporated into northern Sudanese life. Nuba have been particularly active in and against the Sudanese military. Occasional Nuba political activism can be seen in movements like the General Union of Nubas led by Phillip Abbas Gaboush (q.v.). *See also* HUMAN RIGHTS.

NUBIA. Nubia is the general name for the area of the Nile Valley south of Aswan in Egypt, at the first cataract on the Nile, extending into the northern Sudan at the third or fourth cataracts. This is the land of the ancient kingdoms of Kush and the various small ancient states such as Yam and Irtet. After the fall of the medieval Christian kingdoms of Nobatia, Mukuria, and Alwa (fourteenth to sixteenth centuries), the population became almost completely Muslim. Although many Nubians speak Arabic (q.v.), the Nubian languages have been maintained, including a number of local dialects such as Sukot, Halfawi, Mahas, and Dongolawi (q.v.). Nubians have been active in trade and politics since ancient times; more recently in the nineteenth century, they formed an important component of the Jallaba (q.v.) merchants who operated in the Bahr al-Ghazal, Upper Nile, and Equatorial (qq.v.) regions. Wherever they resettled, Nubians tended to maintain a close sense of community.

Nubians and their subgroups have a very long history linked to the rise of Nile Valley agriculture, states, and urbanism. This parallels their association with ancient Egyptians, and continues to this day with the leading role of Nubians in contemporary Sudanese society. While a mixture of "Arab" (q.v.) or Arabized peoples predominate in the northern riverine areas, the Nubians are one of the most important minority ethnic groups. This fact is made more significant when it is understood that Nubians only constitute 3 to 4 percent of the national population.

Racially, Nubians have a phenotypic diversity that is in harmony with the complex history of their territory: Arabs, autochthonous Nubians, southern slaves, North Africans, and European conquerors have all left their genetic imprints. Nubians of the northern Sudan are distinguished from the peoples of the Nuba (q.v.) hills, who appear to have been isolated in southern Kordofan (q.v.) before the main penetration of Islam (q.v.) into the Sudan.

As bearers of Islam to the Funj (q.v.) sultanate, Mahas Nubians in particular provided *fekis* (q.v., religious sages) and advisors to the rulers at Sinnar (q.v.). The religious schools of Feki Hamad wad Maryam, Shaykh Khujali, and Shaykh Arbab al-Ajayid were established at the confluence of the two Niles, on Tuti Island, and along the Blue Nile up to Sinnar. The mosque and school of Shaykh Arbab, built in 1691, was said to be the first permanent structure in Khartoum (q.v.).

More recently, much of Nubia was flooded in the 1960s by the rising waters of Lake Nasser, formed by the construction of the Aswan High Dam. Most traditional townsites were affected. This compelled Kenuz Nubians to move to villages in Egypt, especially Kom Ombo. Sukkot, Mahas, and Halfawi Nubians were relocated to towns in the eastern Sudan such as New Halfa and Khashm al-Girba (q.v.). Some Nubians remained but moved their homes to higher elevations. *See also* CHRISTIANITY IN NUBIA; MEROË.

NUER. The Nuer and their associated subgroup, the Atuot, are among the most numerous of southern Sudanese Nilotic (q.v.) people speaking their branch of Sudanic language. They are expansive, seasonally migrating pastoralists as are most Nilotic people. They are relatively homogenous in language and culture, but without political centralization or formal regional integration. Various types of livestock are held, and cattle convey a profound measure of wealth, status, and personal influence. Their political organization has been termed "ordered anarchy" as they mostly lack a permanent chief. Their patrilineal system of descent is built around a segmentary lineage principle that keeps a high degree of mobility and political autonomy for each segment. Age grades are common but there are no classes and essentially no hereditary chiefs.

The Nuer strongly resisted British control early in the twentieth century. They were less active in later political developments, although Buth Diu (q.v.), an important southern politician after World War II, was a Nuer. Since the revival of the civil war in 1983, political leaders such as Riek Machar (q.v.) have played a significant role on both the regional and national fronts. Within the Sudanese Peoples Liberation Movement/Army (SPLM/SPLA, q.v.), Machar led the breakaway Nasir faction in 1991 that created a nearly fatal split within the SPLA, and from which it proved difficult for the SPLM to recover. Machar's opposition to the SPLA and John Garang (q.v.) made him a favorite of the 'Umar al-Bashir (q.v.) regime and he held several appointments in Khartoum (q.v.), including assistant to the President of the Republic and chairman of the Southern States Coordinating Council, before rejoining the SPLM in 2001. Machar returned to Nuer territory in eastern Upper Nile (q.v.) in 2001 but the southern movement remained divided and dominated by the Dinka (q.v.) ethnic majority, making it difficult for the Nuer or Machar to play a decisive brokering role in the SPLM or national politics. The Nuer remain a minority ethnic group who can be opportunistically used by either regional southern or northern leaders as leverage in opposition politics. Ethnographic aspects of the Nuer have been described by the anthropologist E. E. Evans-Pritchard.

NUGDALLAH, SARA. Senior female member of the Umma Party (q.v.), who was arrested and detained without charge several times after the 1989 Islamist coup led by General ʿUmar al-Bashir (q.v.). One of the many symbols of female resistance by parties in opposition to the Bashir regime, she was arrested in April 1994 and held for ten weeks in Omdurman (q.v.) prison.

NUJUMI, ʿABD AL-RAHMAN WAD AL- (?–1889). A Mahdist commander of Jaʿali (q.v.) origin, who joined the Mahdi (q.v.) in 1881, was present at the fall of Bara (1883), and served as supreme commander at the siege of Khartoum (1884–1885, q.v.). Titled *Amir al-Umara* (commander-in-chief), al-Nujumi was one of the most capable of all Mahdist leaders; still, he did not enjoy the trust of Khalifa ʿAbdullahi (q.v.), whose claim to leadership had been challenged by some of the riverine Sudanese. Al-Nujumi was based in the North from 1886, preparing for the Mahdist invasion of Egypt. Added to the logistical problems of planning an invasion, he had to contend with the Khalifa's political intrigues and insufficient material support. By the time his expedition finally departed it was seriously compromised. Undermanned and undersupplied, his army was destroyed by that of the Egyptian Sirdar, F. W. Grenfell, at Tushki on 3 August 1889. Al-Nujumi was killed there with many of his followers, while thousands of Sudanese were taken into captivity. Some Jaʿaliyin placed the blame for Tushki directly on the Khalifa and consequently became disaffected with the Mahdiya (q.v.).

NUQRASHI, AL. *See* BEVIN, ERNEST.

NUR AL-DIN, MUHAMMAD (ca. 1894–1964). Economist and political leader from Sudanese Nubia (q.v.). He worked for the National Bank of Egypt, serving in various branches in the Sudan from 1925–1947. He was active in early nationalist politics, acting as president of the Graduates Club in el-Obeid (q.v.) and helping to found the Graduates Congress (q.v.). He was vice-president of the Ashigga Party (q.v.) when it was formed and then led a faction of that party that disagreed at times with

Isma'il al-Azhari (q.v.). Nur al-Din became an officer of the National Unionist Party (q.v.) when it was formed and was elected to Parliament in 1953. He was active in supporting unity with Egypt and opposed Azhari's movement toward an independent Sudan.

NYALA. A town in western Darfur (q.v.). Nyala was the sometime capital of the Fur Sultanates (q.v.), though this function was more often filled by al-Fasher (q.v.), which remained the larger town until the 1980s. After the railway reached Nyala in 1960, its rate of population growth outpaced al-Fasher. Not only does Nyala serve as the western terminus for rail traffic, but it is also the place for people to start treks to the marvelous volcanic mountains of Jabal Marra (3,071 meters) and explore the prehistoric rock paintings at Jabal Dagu.

At independence Nyala's population was barely 14,000 people but it had more than doubled by 1964 to 27,100 and in 1969 it reached 38,800, rising to 60,000 by 1973. Since then it has experienced a rapid rate of urban growth of more than 8 percent per year. Since 1983 thousands of refugees (q.v.) of the wars in the southern Sudan (q.v.) and Chad, as well those fleeing severe ecological degradation, have swollen the population still further to 114,000. *See also* DAJU; KOBBEI.

– O –

EL-OBEID. The major city of Kordofan (q.v.) region. Two features of el-Obeid that account for its very significant growth and regional prominence are the numerous water sources and its strategic location on important regional and east-west trade routes. A variety of peoples are found in el-Obeid including the Badariya, Kababish (q.v.), Jawama'a, Kawahla, Humr, Baqqara (q.v.), and Lagowa as well as Jallaba (q.v.) and other merchants from the Nile Valley. Traditionally many of these semi-nomadic people were found around wells in the area and would come to el-Obeid to trade. El-Obeid's trade with Shendi, al-Fasher, and Sinnar (qq.v.) can be dated back many centuries.

During most of the Turkiya (q.v.), the effective administration stopped at el-Obeid, but in the 1870s a postal and telegraph system linked el-Obeid to Khartoum and al-Fasher (qq.v.). This did not last long because the rise of the Mahdiya (q.v.) was centered in Kordofan and by 1881 the forces of the Mahdi (q.v.) had cut the telegraph lines as he began his siege of el-Obeid. Only that town and the satellite town of Bara were not under his control by the end of 1882. In September 1882 the Mahdist army camped close to el-Obeid and launched a strong attack that was repulsed with heavy loss to his men. He then changed his strategy to a prolonged siege to starve the town into submission. The Turkish commander of el-Obeid, Muhammad Sa'id Pasha, strengthened his defenses, a move that was countered by Mahdist sympathizers in the city. Many of the influential Jallaba traders, especially those trading in slaves, felt constrained by the Turkish administration and believed that Mahdism might be more favorable to their interests. The lively exchange in slaves, gum arabic, ostrich feathers, livestock, local produce and handicrafts, and hides was of significant scale. A secret alliance between the wealthy merchant Ilyas Umm Birayr and the Mahdi helped to seal the fate of el-Obeid.

By the end of 1882 hundreds of inhabitants of the besieged city were forced to eat dogs, cats, mice, and insects while thousands died. By the middle of January 1883, both the nearby town of Bara and el-Obeid fell and many of the weary defenders were executed. When this news reached Khartoum, the expedition of Hicks Pasha (q.v.) was mounted to recapture the town. Hicks and his 10,000 men were stopped southeast of el-Obeid and almost completely wiped out on 5 November 1883. In the same month, the governor of Darfur (q.v.), Slatin Pasha (q.v.), submitted to Mahdist rule and declared his conversion to Islam (q.v.). El-Obeid thus became the first provisional capital of Mahdism, though to the Mahdi and his Ansar (q.v.) it was simply one more "spot" (*buq'a*) en route to total victory. In the spring of 1884 the Mahdi left el-Obeid to prepare for his long and successful siege of Khartoum.

Despite the expectations of the Jallaba merchants, the economy of el-Obeid deteriorated under the Mahdi and his Khalifa (q.v.). The famine of 1889–1890 only made a bad situation worse. When Khalifa 'Abdullahi's relative, Mahmud Ahmad, arrived in el-Obeid in 1890 to become the governor of Darfur and Kordofan, he discovered that the lively market was only a glimmer of its former self and common products were nowhere to be found.

British troops reoccupied el-Obeid on 17 December 1899 and Slatin Pasha returned a year later to make contact with Sultan 'Ali Dinar (q.v.), who came as far as al-Nahud (q.v.) in 1901. Facing resolute resistance from 'Ali Dinar, the British moved ahead to consolidate their control of Kordofan. The railway crossed the White Nile at Kosti (q.v.) in 1910 and a railway spur from al-Rahad was sent north to reach el-Obeid in 1912, thereby providing a direct link over the 685 kilometers between Khartoum and el-Obeid. The improvement in security and commerce can be seen in the establishment of a National Bank of Egypt in el-Obeid during this period.

Through the 1920s the population began to grow and the residential and commercial sections expanded; a small population of Greeks (q.v.), Italians, and Syrians (q.v.) appeared. In 1956 the population was put at 54,000 and by 1969 it reached 68,700. These figures represent steady but not exceptional rates of growth. However, since that time, el-Obeid's population has surged massively because of the regional problems with civil war, famine (q.v.), and drought. A conservative figure for 1983 puts the population at 139,446, but other estimates state that 200,000 or even 250,000 are more realistic.

OCTOBER REVOLUTION OF 1964. This revolution resulted in the ouster of General Ibrahim Abboud (q.v.), putting an end to the first period of military rule in independent Sudan. It was accomplished through civilian demonstrations expressing general dissatisfaction with the Abboud regime. This popular revolution showed a spirit of self-sufficient democracy in Sudanese political socialization. The "spirit" of October was recalled in a second mass revolutionary movement in 1985, which toppled another military ruler, Ja'afar al-Nimeiri (q.v.).

ODUHO, JOSEPH H. (ca. 1930–1993). Oduho was born in Lobira, Equatoria (q.v.), of Latuka origins. He attended high school in Uganda and at Rumbek, Sudan, began teaching in 1952, and led a demonstration against the 1953 agreement between northern Sudanese politicians and Egypt, which appeared to disenfranchise the South. Oduho advanced in his teacher training at the Bakht al-Ruda school in 1953–1954 and became involved in the 1955 mutiny in the South, during which time he very narrowly escaped execution. He continued to teach school in Equatoria and then was elected to Parliament in 1958. Oduho fled Sudan immediately after the coup of Ibrahim Abboud (q.v.), which pursued a military "solution" for the South. By 1960 his exile continued in Uganda, Kenya, Congo-Brazzaville, Congo-Kinshasa, and Tanzania. In 1962 he and William Deng, Father Saturnino, and Clement Mboro (qq.v.) formed a precursor of the Sudan African National Union (SANU, q.v.) and Oduho became its president. SANU was accorded guest status at the Pan-African conference in Leopoldville, Congo, in January 1963 and Oduho returned to Kampala to gain political asylum. In Uganda, he established the office of SANU and its Anya-Nya I (q.v.) military wing under the command of Lt. Joseph Lagu (q.v.).

In 1964 SANU presented its case to the Organization of African Unity (q.v.), but Oduho was removed from the position of president partly over the issue of his participation in the 1965 Round Table Conference in Khartoum (qq.v.), which resulted in a division within SANU. As SANU broke up into William Deng and Aggrey Jaden (q.v.) factions, Oduho helped to form the Azania Liberation Front (ALF, q.v.) in 1965 and continued to be active in southern resistance. The Aggrey faction then became known as the Sudan African Liberation Front (q.v.) and reunited with the ALF under Oduho's leadership in January 1966. With great tensions between Israel and the Arab world at this time, the ALF met with Israeli officials to plan for their support and training. From 1966 to 1967 rival southern organizations proliferated and any unity of southern political movements collapsed.

In May 1969 the Ja'afar al-Nimeiri (q.v.) government came to power in Khartoum, but Oduho and the Anya-Nya saw nothing new in his program at first. Israeli military assistance and training by the West German mercenary Rolf Steiner (q.v.) began in 1970–1971, especially at Owing-Kibol in the southern border area. Oduho and his second-in-command Joseph Akwon, an Anuak (q.v.), worked to build military and political ties with Israel and correctly perceived that the new Khartoum regime was hostile to Israeli interests. Oduho and Akwon discovered that Israeli interests were not committed to secession but only to destabilization of Khartoum, and Oduho quit Anya-Nya in 1971. Meanwhile, Akwon was killed in early 1972 near Malakal (q.v.).

With these opponents to peace negotiations gone, events accelerated and the Nimeiri government aggressively pursued peace with the South in the Ninth of June Declaration (q.v.) of Regional Autonomy in 1969 and then in the Addis Ababa negotiations in 1971–1972, which were finally signed in March 1972. Prolonged peace came to the Sudan for the first time since 1955. After the Addis Ababa Agreement of 1972 (q.v.) Oduho returned to Sudan to serve as a member of the Southern Region High Executive Council (1972–1975) and the Sudan Socialist Union (q.v.) Political Bureau (1974–1975). He was also elected to the Southern Regional Peoples Assembly in 1973 and was the minister of housing in Juba (q.v.).

The culturally heterogeneous South proved difficult to rule even by southerners and ethnic divisions continued to inhibit progress from 1973 to 1977. A new rebel force called Anya-Nya II (q.v.) was built from southern troops who were originally loyal to Akwon. By 1980 the ineffective southern government was dissolved and a call for new elections was made for 1982. Fear of a return to military "solutions" rather than political ones moved the recently formed Sudanese Peoples Liberation Movement (SPLM, q.v.) into armed resistance in 1983. Oduho sought to make the SPLM a civilian force with a subordinate military wing, the Sudanese Peoples Liberation Army (SPLA, q.v.). He became head of the Political and Foreign Affairs Committee of the SPLM in 1984 and his son, Casito Oduho, continues to be active in the SPLM.

Factional disputes persisted among the southern guerrillas, evidenced by the 1991 divisions within the SPLM. In an apparent effort to resolve such a dispute between the forces of Riek Machar and John Garang (qq.v.), Oduho was killed on 27 March 1993 at Konjor in circumstances that are still debated, but probably relate to an SPLA attack on Southern Sudan Independence Movement (SSIM) soldiers.

OMDURMAN. One of the three cities that form the "Three Towns" metropolitan capital of Sudan. Very little is known about Omdurman prior to the Mahdiya (q.v.); however, archaeological evidence suggests some type of human settlement there as far back as the Neolithic era, and oral traditions claim it as the home of the so-called Anaj people. The actual origins of the site, as well as the meaning of the name Omdurman (Umm Durman), are likely to remain a mystery. The first settlement at Omdurman for which historical evidence exists is the Qur'an school of the Mahasi holyman Hamad wad Umm Maryam (d. 1730), who moved there from nearby Tuti Island. A number of references to Omdurman appear in the travel literature of the eighteenth and nineteenth centuries, though it is clear that as late as the mid-nineteenth century it was sparsely populated, consisting of a number of dwellings and perhaps a small market, as well as being a grazing and watering site for the herds of the local Jamu'iya Arabs.

The first substantial structures to be built there were the earthworks and camp erected in 1883 for the soldiers of Gen. William Hicks Pasha (q.v.), whose expedition to destroy the Mahdi (q.v.) was annihilated at Shaykan in November 1883. After the arrival of Gen. Charles Gordon (q.v.) in the Sudan in 1884, Omdurman became the site of an important fortress guarding the west flank of Khartoum (q.v.). In October 1884 the Mahdi arrived at Omdurman to support the siege of Khartoum. The fortress at Omdurman was compelled to surrender in January 1885; two weeks later, on 25 January Khartoum fell to the Mahdists.

It is clear from the Mahdi's numerous writings that he had no intention of creating a capital, but rather of waging a movement of Islamic reform throughout the world. To him, Omdurman was merely a spot (*al-buq'a*), one of many along his path to an ultimate Islamic victory; consequently the site of the Mahdi's last camp was known throughout the Mahdist period as "the Mahdi's spot" (*Buq'at al-Mahdi*). As circumstances would have it, the Mahdi died there suddenly in June 1885. His successor, the Khalifa 'Abdullahi (q.v.), chose it as the capital of his militant state, mindful of the great symbolism and sanctity that the Mahdi's tomb lent the location.

Over the next two years Khartoum was completely emptied of its residents, while Omdurman rose to become the premier city of the Sudan. Apart from its important association with the Mahdi, Omdurman had several other advantages as a capital: its superior drainage made it a far healthier site than Khartoum; it lay astride trade routes to the west, while its natural harbor and access to the two Niles made it the ideal site for an entrepot; finally, it provided the Khalifa the strategic depth of the western hinterland, to which he could retreat in the event of a river-based attack.

Few of these considerations mattered to the Ansar (q.v.), who began to pour into Omdurman by the thousands in 1885 to swear oaths of allegiance to the Khalifa as well as to visit the Mahdi's grave. By mid-1886 the city stretched almost four miles along the Nile and perhaps a mile into the interior; by the completion of the great period of emigration to the capital in 1890, it may have extended as much as two miles into the interior. Certainly not all of the inhabitants of Omdurman were there willingly: the Baqqara Arabs (qq.v.) in particular were compelled to emigrate to the capital, both because the Khalifa needed their support and didn't trust them in faraway Darfur (q.v.). On the other hand, many thousands of Ansar journeyed there as a pilgrimage to a holy city, anxious to live in the shadow of the Mahdi's tomb (*al-Qubba*, q.v.) and profit from its *baraka* (q.v.).

The various ethnic groups that settled Omdurman resided in distinct quarters, each with its own local authorities and basic amenities, thus giving the city the appearance of an agglomeration of villages. The symbolic as well as geographic center of the city was the Great Mosque, built next to the Khalifa's house and in front of the Mahdi's tomb. Reports suggest that it could hold as many as 70,000 worshippers. To the west stood the vast public market, divided according to the wares sold and services offered; along the river were the public treasury, prison, boatyards, and port; to the south, the old Omdurman fortress, reconstituted as the garrison of the professional soldiers (*jihadiya*, q.v.). All else was residential space. Over the years, difficult conditions of crowding, poor sanitation, and irregular food supply sometimes taxed the city to its limits; consequently, diseases spread easily. The famine of 1889 forced the Khalifa to carry out unpopular raids on the countryside for food supplies and livestock to provision his soldiers; nevertheless, thousands of people in Omdurman perished.

In 1896 the Anglo-Egyptian (q.v.) invasion of the Sudan commenced. By August 1898 its forces reached the Karari (q.v.) hills north of Omdurman where, on 2 September, a savage massacre of the Mahdist soldiers took place. Ansar zeal was no match for the British machine guns, which in the space of a few hours cut down at least 10,000 Sudanese. Omdurman meanwhile was shelled and the tomb of the Mahdi deliberately damaged. Survivors who remained loyal to the Khalifa fled to the south or west, where they were pursued or disappeared in harsh terrain. The population of Omdurman fell back abruptly, as the British forcibly emptied the city of much of its population. In the early twentieth century people began to return and reestablish Omdurman as the Sudan's largest city and commercial and residential center. Khartoum became the formal governmental capital under the Anglo-Egyptian Condominium (q.v.), but Omdurman remained the thriving cultural nexus for all of the Sudan. Until present Omdurman has usually contained more inhabitants than Khartoum. In 1928 a bridge from Khartoum to Omdurman made the link between the two cities more convenient, while a trolley line carried workers and civil servants between the two cities. Today the old bridge has been widened to accommodate the rush of traffic in mornings and afternoons. A crude lorry road was opened from Omdurman to Dongola (q.v.) in 1948, draining most of the river transport. In the 1970s a modern bridge from Omdurman to Khartoum North (q.v.) was opened, linking the Three Towns area with surfaced roads.

The population of Omdurman has varied markedly during its history. From a cluster of riverside hamlets before the Mahdiya, its population soared to as many as 250,000 during its time as the Mahdist capital. The population fell drastically after the conquest in 1898, perhaps by as much as 75 percent, but by 1930 it had returned to 103,600, more than twice the size of Khartoum. By 1964 it had reached 193,000, while a rapid rate of increase resulted in a population of 300,000 by 1973. The population census in 1983 estimated Omdurman to hold 526,000 inhabitants. By the 1990s the population almost certainly reached a million, including the hundreds of thousands of squatters, refugees (q.v.) from the civil war, and others living at the city's periphery.

OMDURMAN AHLIA UNIVERSITY. Founded in 1986 as an independent, nonsectarian, coeducational institution, this university took its inspiration from the early "*ahliya* schools" or "*ahli* education" movement, which began in the late 1920s. Omdurman Ahlia University offers a broad range of degrees in finance, Arabic and English literature, medical laboratory studies, business management, library science, computer science, and so on. By 1996 it had an enrollment of approximately 15,000 students. [by Heather J. Sharkey]

OPERATION LIFELINE SUDAN (OLS). Launched in 1989 as a multinational relief operation to the war-torn southern region where civil war had resumed in 1983, Operation Lifeline Sudan has continued to the present time, unfortunately with little effect. During the 1989–1998 period an estimated 1.2 million lives were lost while more than two billion dollars have been spent to alleviate human suffering. In 1998 it was estimated that one million dollars per day was being spent on the relief effort. Each year since 1989 the United States has declared Sudan an "emergency," thus ensuring that $70–100 million in American disaster aid can be sent. U.S. officials are now hard-pressed to explain how an "emergency" can last for more than a decade. For the past decade OLS has been the main nonreligious relief funnel into the southern Sudan, while the Christian group World Vision has also been a major contributor, assisted by the U.S. Agency for International Development (AID). As the virtually unwinnable war has dragged on the relief agencies themselves have been criticized, in effect, for helping to continue the war of attrition by virtue of their humanitarian aid.

ORGANIZATION OF AFRICAN UNITY (OAU). This modern Pan-African organization was formed in Addis Ababa, Ethiopia, on 25 May 1963 in the context of the rapid decolonization of Africa. It carried on the long political tradition of Pan-Africanism developed by W.E.B. DuBois, Marcus Garvey, C.L.R. James, Jomo Kenyatta, Kwame Nkrumah, George Padmore, Haile Sellasie, and others, who put forward many of the concepts without the fact of decolonization. Although there have been many setbacks and failed dreams, the OAU provided legitimacy and support for continued struggles against colonial rule and white supremacy on the continent. The OAU also serves as a forum for

negotiating intra-African disputes such as border issues, natural resource and environmental issues, refugee (q.v.) concerns, international
postal and transport topics, and human rights (q.v.). The OAU has been
guided by a principle that the colonial borders should not be challenged
for fear of opening many problematic issues. It has also sought to address issues of democratic transition and multiparty secularism while
many African nations were suffering from genocide and military rule.
Naturally there have been shortcomings: even the host nation of the
OAU, Ethiopia, has faced serious political issues domestically and especially internationally with Eritrea. Despite this, the OAU has survived
four decades and remains the chief means for African nations to bring
attention to their dreams and discuss their grievances in a peaceful and
diplomatic manner.

With Sudan's early independence in 1956 it quickly became a leader
and founder nation of the OAU. Sudan was long a liberal receiver of
refugees from conflicts in Uganda, Zaire, Chad, Ethiopia, and Eritrea
and it followed OAU and United Nations High Commissioner for
Refugees guidelines rather well. It was the OAU that provided the opportunity for the Addis Ababa Agreement of 1972 (q.v.) that brought almost ten years of peace to Sudan's civil war; this has been much heralded despite Sudan's return to another long period of war. In July 1978
the OAU held its annual meeting in Khartoum (q.v.). In 1987 the OAU
adopted the Charter on Peoples Rights that added to the legitimacy of
African human rights issues.

Prime Minister Sadiq al-Mahdi (q.v.) reluctantly met with Sudanese
Peoples Liberation Army leader John Garang (qq.v.) at an OAU Summit
in July 1986 to discuss peace in Sudan, but these talks failed. When
'Umar al-Bashir (q.v.) came to power in 1989 he attended an OAU Summit while Egyptian President Hosni Mubarak was the OAU Chairman;
Mubarak also met with John Garang. Various other cease-fires and peace
talk initiatives for Sudan have passed through the offices of the OAU.
Notable among these efforts were the OAU-sponsored Abuja conferences (q.v.) in Nigeria in December 1991 that brought the conflicting
parties to the negotiating table, but without resolution.

President Mubarak was attending an OAU summit in June 1995 when
an assassination attempt against him narrowly failed. It was believed that
the assassins were backed by Khartoum, and this led to Sudan's political
isolation and an international air boycott.

OSMAN DIGNA. *See* 'UTHMAN IBN ABI BAKR DIQNA.

– P –

PAPAL VISIT TO SUDAN. In an unprecedented act, Pope John Paul II visited the Sudanese capital city on 10 February 1993, stopping in Khartoum (q.v.) for nine hours and conducting an open air mass. Accompanied by Khartoum's Archbishop Gabriel Zubeir Wako, the Pope publicly criticized the Islamist government for persecuting its Christian minority. The Vatican claims that there are two million Roman Catholics among Sudan's population of twenty-six million. In his comments to President al-Bashir (q.v.) he said, "No group should consider itself superior to another. The state has a duty to respect and defend the differences existing among its citizens." This was described by the Vatican as the strongest statement made by the Pope on behalf of Christians at risk since his first trip to Poland as Pope. Al-Bashir in a public meeting with the Pope denied Sudan violated the rights of Christians and said its problems result from foreign interference and the Western press. *See also* CHRISTIANITY IN THE SUDAN.

PASHA. The highest title or rank in the old Turkish or Egyptian court and military hierarchy, equivalent to a governor-general.

PAYSAMA, STANISLAUS (1903–). Sudanese political leader and administrator. He was born in al-Fasher, Darfur (qq.v) and educated in mission schools. He entered government service in 1927, serving in a variety of administrative posts. After World War II Paysama assisted in the formation of the Southern Sudan Welfare Committee and was in the Legislative Assembly for Bahr al-Ghazal (q.v.). He served on the Constitutional Commission (q.v.), helped to organize the Southern Party (q.v.), and became president of the party after it changed its name to the Liberal Party (q.v.) in 1954. Paysama became involved in a leadership contest in the party with Benjamin Lwoki (q.v.) but retained control. He served in Parliament from 1954 to 1958. After the 1964 October Revolution (q.v.) he formed a new Liberal Party, which had little success in elections and minimal political influence.

PEACE NEGOTIATIONS. Since 1989 major peace talks have been conducted at Addis Ababa, Ethiopia (1989); Nairobi, Kenya (1990); Abuja, Nigeria, from 1991 to 1992; and at the Intergovernmental Agency on Drought and Development (IGADD, q.v.) meetings in Addis Ababa (September 1993 and March 1994) and Nairobi (July and September 1994,

January 1995, November 1997, March 1998, and April 1999). None of these has achieved a lasting cease-fire or even the beginning of serious negotiations between the Sudanese government of 'Umar al-Bashir (q.v.) and the Sudanese Peoples Liberation Movement (SPLM, q.v.).

It was agreed at Abuja (q.v.) I and II in 1991–1992 that self-determination for the South is a recognized right to be carried out within a limited two-year period allowed for the transition from war to peace. However, the talks broke down in a context of mutual distrust and disunity within the ranks of the SPLM. Further, talks between the National Islamic Front (NIF, q.v.) government in Khartoum (q.v.) and SPLM have never involved the broad opposition forces of the National Democratic Alliance (NDA, q.v.). Comprehensive peace talks based upon the NDA Asmara Declaration of June 1995 (q.v.) would accept separation for the South if the southern people choose this in a referendum; confederation also could be considered as an option on the referendum.

The IGADD-hosted talks in Nairobi in 1997 yielded nothing, a result anticipated by the Sudanese government that sent low-level representation. The opposition took the occasion to reiterate its main Declaration of Principles, first adopted on 21 April 1997 in Nairobi, which included: a referendum in the South on self-determination; the type of government remains open, but the SPLM favors confederation within a government of national unity in which all parties, including the NIF, take part; the conflict is understood as that which has existed between the geographical North and South as they stood in 1956. There is some disagreement with the Asmara NDA Declaration of 1995 that "marginalized" people of Nuba Mountains (q.v.), Abyei, and the Ingessana Hills are also to be included as part of the South.

The NIF is uncompromising on the issue of religion, that Islam (q.v.) must remain the state religion, and this continues to be the major stumbling block to progress in peace negotiations.

PEOPLES DEMOCRATIC PARTY (PDP). A party formed in 1956 by Khatmiya (q.v.) elements in the National Unionist Party (NUP, q.v.). It received the support of 'Ali al-Mirghani (q.v.) and was led by 'Ali 'Abd al-Rahman (q.v.). Later in 1956 it joined with the Umma Party (q.v.) to form a coalition government replacing that of Isma'il al-Azhari (q.v.). This coalition continued until the Ibrahim Abboud (q.v.) coup in 1958, after which all parties were outlawed. The PDP included a wide spectrum of political views, ranging from those of conservative rural leaders to some of the most radical politicians in Sudan. The PDP leadership participated in opposition to Abboud and in the 1964 October Revolution (q.v.), but it then boycotted the 1965 elections. In 1967 the PDP merged with the NUP to form the Democratic Unionist Party (DUP, q.v.).

PETHERICK, JOHN (1813–1882). In 1845 this Welshman was employed as a mining engineer by Muhammad 'Ali Pasha (q.v.) of Egypt. This brought him to Khartoum (q.v.) and later el-Obeid (q.v., 1848–1853), where he traded in gum arabic. Later he traveled to Gondokoro (q.v.) in the southern Sudan to engage in the ivory trade. His interests in commerce resulted in his appointment as the British vice-consul from 1858–1864. As a related concern, Petherick was much fascinated with the exploration of the headwaters of the White Nile, which had not yet been discovered. From 1861 to 1865 Petherick explored along the Bahr al-Ghazal (q.v.) into Mitoo, Bongo, and Madi country, thus laying a geographical foundation for the travels of George Schweinfurth (q.v.) a few years later. He was greatly interested in supporting the efforts of Samuel Baker, Richard Burton, and John Speke (qq.v.) in their explorations of Lake Victoria, although he did not travel there himself. Relieved of his post amidst accusations of slave trading, Petherick left the Sudan 1865.

POETRY. *See* ARABIC LANGUAGE; BINT AL-MAKKAWI; MADIH NABAWI; SHAGHABA AL-MARGHUMABIYA; LITERATURE.

PONCET BROTHERS. French explorers Ambroise (1835–1868) and Jules (1838–1873) Poncet traveled in the Sudan from 1851 to 1868, originally with their uncle Alexandre Vaudey, who was killed in a trading dispute with the Bari (q.v.) people in 1854. Departing from Khartoum (q.v.) they went up the White Nile through Shilluk and Nuer (qq.v.) country, on toward the southwest through Dinka (q.v.), Djior, and Dor lands. Their route was about the same as that taken in 1869–1870 by George Schweinfurth (q.v.). The brothers' ivory trading firm in Khartoum, A. & J. Poncet Freres, was dissolved in 1872.

PORT SUDAN. The history and growth of Sudan's only seaport is both relatively brief and rapid. The harbor and town were officially opened in 1905 when the railway arrived and the port of Suakin (q.v.), about forty-six kilometers south, was closed. Merchant vessels first entered the harbor in 1907. The larger, natural harbor of Shaykh al-Barqut in Amarar territory is the heart of the economy. It has berths for ships up to 125 meters, large electric loading cranes, warehouses, and provisions for some ship repair. Railway lines west to Atbara (q.v.) and south to Kassala (q.v.) provide Sudan's only link by rail to the ocean.

At first water supplies were a serious limiting factor and adequate amounts could only be obtained by desalination-condensation. In 1925 a water pipeline was installed in Khor Arba'at that collects water during the rainy season. This additional supply makes it possible to tender water for docking ships.

Major commercial fishing is not well developed, but some tourist sport-fishing and scuba-diving takes place as well as a minor industry of oyster shells used for buttons and jewelry. Salt is also collected and sold. These industries are all subsidiary to the central shipping function of Port Sudan, which handles almost 90 percent of Sudan's bulk items in foreign trade. As a result of this primary importance Port Sudan grew from 50,000 inhabitants in 1955 to 104,000 in 1969. By 1990 it was estimated that this urban area contained over 215,000 people, while a government-owned journal suggests that Port Sudan may now have some 500,000 inhabitants if all of the refugees (q.v.) from decades of war in Eritrea are included.

Certainly Port Sudan plays a unique role in the economy of Sudan. Connections to Khartoum (q.v.) by rail, truck, bus, airplane, and the all-weather road completed in 1980 all aided Port Sudan's development. There is also a steamer service to Suez about four times a month. Port Sudan's grand scale of streets and parks has been matched by the burgeoning population, but the impoverished Sudanese economy has left a great deal of the city in disrepair.

PROFESSIONAL FRONT. *See* FRONT OF PROFESSIONAL ORGANIZATIONS.

PROVINCES. Over the past 200 years the Sudan's administrative provinces have varied considerably. At independence in 1956 Sudan was divided into nine provinces, including six northern provinces (Blue Nile, Darfur, Kassala, Khartoum, Kordofan, and Northern, qq.v.) and three southern provinces (Bahr al-Ghazal, Equatoria, and Upper Nile, qq.v.). These were further divided into eighty-four administrative districts. In territory the northern provinces covered nearly two-thirds of Sudan and contained most of the urban areas. The borders of the nine provinces somewhat approximated the administrative boundaries recognized during the Turkiya and Mahdiya (qq.v.) periods, while the internal district divisions followed the administrative practice of the Anglo-Egyptian Sudan (q.v.).

In 1972, following on the Addis Ababa Agreement (q.v.), President Ja'afar al-Nimeiri (q.v.) granted a measure of regional autonomy to the South, creating a "Southern Region" with its own representative assembly. This ended the period of civil war that had begun in 1955. In May 1983 Nimeiri redivided the South into three subregions as he embraced a staunch Islamist position imposing Islamic law (Shari'a, q.v.) throughout the country. The Addis Ababa Agreement and self-government for the South were formally abrogated in June 1985. The provinces of Sudan now included the three southern ones (Bahr al-Ghazal, Equatoria, and Upper Nile) plus twelve northern ones (Blue Nile, Kassala, Khartoum, Gezira, Nile, Northern, Northern Darfur, Northern Kordofan, Red Sea, Southern Darfur, Southern Kordofan, and White Nile).

This administrative situation continued through the prime ministership of Sadiq al-Mahdi (q.v.) as the problems of Islamic law and civil war went unresolved. In 1991 the regime of 'Umar al-Bashir (q.v.) introduced a federal style of government with 9 states, 66 provinces and 281 local government districts. These nine states overlapped the original nine provinces.

In February 1994 a constitutional decree redivided Sudan into twenty-six states. This arrangement was confirmed in a new constitution, drafted by a presidential committee, and approved by a "national" referendum, which took effect in June 1998. These are as follows: Bahr al-Jabal, Blue Nile, Eastern Equatoria, Gedaref (q.v.), Gezira (q.v.), Junqali, Kassala, Khartoum, Lakes, Nile, Northern, Northern Bahr al-Ghazal, Northern Darfur, Northern Kordofan, Red Sea, Sinnar (q.v.), Southern Darfur, Southern Kordofan, Upper Nile, Wahda, Warab, Western Bahr al-Ghazal, Western Darfur, Western Equatoria, Western Kordofan, and White Nile. Overall, the politics of administrative and legislative districts can be seen as another symptom of Sudan's national identity crisis, which has led to chronic civil war.

– Q –

QADAH AL-DAM (ca. 1862–1925). Nickname of the *shaykh* of the Fellata (q.v.), Ahmad Muhammad, who originally was known as *Qadah al-'Asha'* (Dinner Bowl) for his habit of inviting passersby to join him for dinner. Upon returning from the battle of Karari (q.v.) in a blood-soaked cloak, he was renamed *Qadah al-Dam* (Bowl of Blood). Ahmad Muhammad was born in al-Fasher (q.v.) to Muhammad Koyranga, of the family of Fulani rulers of Katagum in northern Nigeria, and Maryam Fatima Abu Bakr, a member of the Keira (q.v.) dynastic clan of Darfur (q.v.). He was raised in Katagum and married locally, emigrating to the Sudan with his wives in 1882. He joined the Mahdi (q.v.) before the battle of Shaykan (1883) and took part in the siege of Khartoum (q.v.), settling thereafter in Omdurman (q.v.). During the Mahdiya (q.v.) he served as an *amir* (commander) under the Ta'aishi commander al-Zaki Tamal, and his home was a frequent resting place for visitors of the Fellata, Fur (q.v.), and other western peoples. In 1899 Ahmad Muhammad was chosen by the Fellata notables of Omdurman to be their *shaykh*; this appointment was officially confirmed by the government in 1901. He was recognized for his services to the Anglo-Egyptian (q.v.) regime by Governor-General F. R. Wingate (q.v.) in 1908, and died in Omdurman in 1925. The Fellata quarter of Omdurman is named for him.

QADI. A Muslim judge who administers Islamic law. The *qadi* represents official, state-supported Islam (q.v.) and is generally associated with Shari'a (q.v.) courts in the cities and towns. In some rural areas of Sudan there is a traveling circuit *qadi*.

QADIRIYA. The oldest and possibly most widespread *tariqa* (q.v.) in the Islamic world, and certainly in Africa. It is traced back to 'Abd al-Qadir al-Jaylani (d. 1166) in Baghdad. The order is decentralized with local leadership having independence regarding rules and practices. The order is traditionally said to have been brought to the Sudan in the sixteenth century by Muhammad Taj al-Din al-Bahari (ca. 1520–ca. 1600). He came from Baghdad and taught for seven years. The *khalifas* (q.v.) that he appointed became major religious leaders in the Sudan and their descendants include prominent holy families like the Arakiyin and the Ya'qubab (qq.v.). Other famous Qadiriya saints, like Idris ibn al-Arbab (q.v.), affiliated with the order through their own travels or experience. The *tariqa*'s influence in the Sudan is tied to the prestige of individual local leaders. It is strongest in the Gezira (q.v.) area, where the clans of early saints are located, but it is also important in some areas of nomadic people. Its flexibility of organization has sometimes made the order an effective missionary group through its ability to adapt to local conditions.

One of the better known *zikrs* (religious remembrance ceremonies) is performed at the tomb of Hamad al-Nil (q.v.), on the outskirts of Omdurman (q.v.). It is commonly known as the "Dervish Dance," but is typical of the syncretic forms of folk Islam (q.v.) that perpetuate many of the *tariqas*.

QARIB ALLAH SALIH AL-TAYIB (1866–1936). A leader of the Sammaniya *tariqa* (qq.v.) in the twentieth century. He was a descendant of Ahmad al-Tayib who brought the order to the Sudan in 1800. He succeeded his cousin, 'Abd al-Mahmud, the son of Muhammad Sharif Nur al-Da'im (q.v.), as *khalifa* (q.v.). Qarib Allah had studied in Egypt and the Hijaz (Arabia) and was widely respected for his piety. His personal followers came to comprise a special branch of the Sammaniya *tariqa* known as the Qaribiya.

QARIBIYA. *See* QARIB ALLAH SALIH AL-TAYIB.

QUBBA. The Arabic name for the tomb of a holyman, which serves as a repository for his *baraka* (q.v.), or blessings, and a place of *ziyara* (visitation) for his followers and their descendants. A *qubba* is usually erected over the grave of a holyman identified variously as *wali* (saint), *faki* (q.v.), or *shaykh* since, according to folk Islam (q.v.) this is where his *baraka* is believed to be strongest; otherwise a *qubba* can be simply a memorial shrine. Distinguished by their tall, egg-shaped domes rising above a square building, *qubbas* are found throughout the Nile Valley, particularly along the Blue Nile, though some are scattered throughout Kordofan (q.v.) and other regions of Sudan.

Visitors may come simply to honor the memory of the holyman and to bring offerings of food or money, which are distributed among the tomb's custodians, or else to request the holyman's protective or curative powers. Pregnant women might visit a *qubba*, for instance, to seek an easy delivery, or the birth of a son. The vicinity of a *qubba* is often considered a "protected space" (*haram*), and people may seek asylum there from enemies or the authorities. Binding oaths can be sworn there or personal goods stored there, and even wild animals should not be slain there. As well as personal visits, *qubbas* are also a place for regular Sufi (q.v.) devotions, particularly on the anniversary of the holyman's birth. Several *qubbas* dot the landscape of the capital area, including most prominently those of the Mahasi holyman Shaykh Khujali (d.1743) in Khartoum North (q.v.) and the Mahdi's (q.v.) *qubba* in Omdurman (q.v.). Other prominent *qubbas* are those of Idris wad Arbab (q.v., d.1650) at 'Aylafun and Hasan al-Mirghani (d. 1869) at Khatmiya (q.v.) near Kassala (q.v.).

– R –

RABIH ZUBAYR (1845–1900). Slave trader and adventurer. He was born in Khartoum (q.v.) and worked in the southern provinces as a slave trader. He gradually moved westward, later claiming to be a follower of the Mahdist (q.v.) movement, and attempted to establish states in Chad and Bornu. After a series of wars he was killed by the French in 1900 near Lake Chad. *See also* SLAVERY.

RACE. Most racially derived terms are lacking in Sudan and the Nile Valley, a region of great antiquity and diversity of interactions. There are hundreds of distinct languages and cultures in Sudan that do not fit easily into racial categories. The people of Sudan are certainly African in the continental sense, but they can also include people of Middle Eastern, Asian, and European origins as well. Ideas of being "Arab" (q.v.) are also confusing, as this term has special sociopolitical connotation in the twentieth century, and the precise meaning in Arabic, "nomad," is anachronistic in the modern world. If one uses the term "Negroid" with its connotations of blackness, many Sudanese do not fit this stereotypical phenotype, nor is the term applied today inside Sudan. Some Sudanese writers employ the term "Afro-Arab" for northern Sudanese and a variety of Nilotic (q.v.) people in the South.

In recent years the term "Arabized" has been used in conjunction with various ethnic groups of Muslim northerners, such as Arabized Nubians (q.v.). This has been especially applied by both southern and northern intellectuals who are questioning the Arab identity of Sudan's central riverine peoples and traditionally dominant social and political groups. At any rate, "Arab" does not cover many other groups such as Nubians, Nuba (q.v.), some Bantu, Adamawa, pre-Nilotes, Nilo-Hamites, Fellata (q.v.), Fur (q.v.), and Sudanic groups. Indeed, at this level, there is confusion between language and race. In Sudan there has been such admixture between indigenous and exogenous ethnic and linguistic groups, combined with an extremely long history, that racial phenotypes become challenging to apply scientifically.

The issue of race has moved closer to the center of Sudanese politics in the years of protracted civil war since 1983, with questions of national identity still unresolved. Northern intellectuals are self-critically examining their purported Arab pedigrees, while some southern intellectuals, such as Francis Deng (q.v.), assert the hybrid blend of race and culture that comprises the Sudanese people. Deng's novels, *Seed of Redemption* and *Cry of the Owl*, explore these themes. The official position of the Sudanese Peoples Liberation Movement (SPLM, q.v.) to the transitional government of 1987 was that Sudan must be a "secular, multiracial state." Since the 'Umar al-Bashir (q.v.) regime came to power in 1989 there have been allegations of intensified racialism, especially in editorial caricatures of Southern SPLM activists in official government publications. The government's apparent sanctioning of ethnic cleansing in the Nuba Mountains (q.v.) has reinforced this view. Open discussion of the issue of race with some appropriate legislation and guarantee of nonracialism in any future Sudan is now a fundamental part of the agenda for a new, democratic Sudan. *See also* HUMAN RIGHTS; LANGUAGE.

RASHAYDA. A community of nomadic pastoralists who specialize in camel breeding and subsistence agriculture. They graze their livestock in the interior desert pastures of eastern Sudan and cultivate sorghum when feasible in shallow *wadis* during the rainy season. Most live along the Red Sea coast, in the region west and south of Kassala (q.v.), and on the banks of the Atbara River; some have tenancies in the New Halfa scheme. The Rashayda emigrated from the Arabian peninsula to the Sudan in about 1865 and speak a distinctive, north-west Arabian dialect of Arabic (q.v.). During the chaos of the Mahdiya (q.v.) in the eastern Sudan they sought refuge in Eritrea, returning to their present locations after 1900. Because they are in competition with other pastoralists for scarce pasture and water their relations with the neighboring Hadendowa have been tense. They consider themselves members of a single political unit (*qabila*) that is not dominated by any single lineage or family; sociopolitical stratification is minimal, although a distinction is made between "free" Rashayda and those descended from "slaves." Their women veil strictly, covering their faces with a loose *mungab* before marriage, a tight mask (*gina'*) after marriage, and a brilliantly decorated *burqa'* on festive occasions. In the 1970s many Rashidi men went to Saudi Arabia as labor migrants and rediscovered kindred groups in Kuwait and near Medina and Ha'il. [by William C. Young]. *See also* CAMEL-HERDING ARABS.

RASHID, IBRAHIM, AL-. *See* RASHIDIYA.

RASHIDIYA. A *tariqa* (q.v.) founded by Ibrahim al-Rashid al-Diwayhi (d. 1874). Ibrahim came from a Shayqiya (q.v.) branch near Dongola (q.v.)

and was a disciple of Ahmad ibn Idris (q.v.). He claimed to be the true *khalifa* (q.v.) of his teacher but this claim was disputed by leaders of the Khatmiya (q.v.) and other followers of Ibn Idris. Ibrahim won some followers in the Sudan; however, his most successful ministry was among pilgrims in Mecca. The order gained adherents from India, Arabia, Syria, and Somalia, where it was reported to be the order of the reformist Muslim leader, Muhammad ibn 'Abdallah (pejoratively called the "Mad Mullah" in some Western literature), early in the twentieth century. Ibrahim died in Mecca but the order continued in the Sudan on a small scale under local leadership.

RATIB. The collection of prayers and other religious texts, including selections from the Qur'an and Hadith, compiled by the Mahdi (q.v.) for his followers' use. During the Mahdiya (q.v.) it was recited twice daily, after the morning and afternoon prayers, and was the only text (apart from the Qur'an) approved for the Ansar (q.v.). The Ratib was banned by the Anglo-Egyptian (q.v.) government, which feared its potential to revive Mahdist sentiment. This position weakened with the forging of an alliance between the government and 'Abd al-Rahman al-Mahdi (q.v.) during World War I. By the 1930s copies of the Ratib, published in Egypt, were being openly distributed in the Sudan.

REFUGEES. Of the current population of Sudan, estimated at 25 million in 1994, a growing percentage now resides externally. Sudanese nationals living outside of Sudan fall into three categories: refugees and asylum-seekers, labor migrants, and settlers in immigrant communities. Refugees comprise the largest group of Sudanese abroad. An estimated total of 433,700 Sudanese refugees live in camps monitored by international relief agencies in neighboring countries. Most of these have been displaced by Sudan's ongoing civil war. Uganda hosts the largest number, with over 200,000 Sudanese refugees, while the Republic of the Congo (formerly Zaire) hosts nearly 100,000 and Ethiopia 70,000. Close to 30,000 Sudanese refugees reside in both Kenya and the Central African Republic. Smaller numbers of asylum seekers have been granted refugee status in Eritrea (1,000), Lebanon (200), and Egypt (1,500), this latter figure being actively questioned.

Egypt's formerly close political unity with Sudan is reflected in the large, but contested, number of Sudanese who, until recently, were eligible for permanent residency. This special status was rescinded for all Sudanese nationals entering Egypt following the attempted assassination of

President Hosni Mubarak in July 1995, allegedly by Sudanese militants. The UNHCR now puts the number of Sudanese in a refugee-like situation in Egypt at 50,000, though informally many agree that the actual number is much higher, perhaps as high as a half-million, while refugee status continues to be granted at a rate of only 15 percent. Egypt also hosts a community of labor migrants that dates from the 1940s and whose members still maintain Sudanese nationality. This community has faced difficulties since the 1995 change in residency status.

A growing number of Sudanese nationals have been accepted for resettlement in the Netherlands, the United States, and Canada. Between 1990 and 1997, the United States extended Temporary Protected Status (TPS), a provision that provides temporary protection to *de facto* refugees, to Sudanese already residing in that country. More and better work opportunities abroad have encouraged Sudanese to leave Sudan. Labor migration to oil-rich Arab countries, particularly among Sudanese professionals, has been a major source of brain drain, a process dating from the 1970s but exacerbated by political and economic crisis in the 1990s. There is anecdotal evidence that Sudanese who traveled to Egypt, the Gulf, Europe, and North America for advanced studies tended to seek professional positions outside of Sudan, particularly as conditions within Sudan deteriorated. Sudan has also lost several of its ambassadors and other government officials to exile.

Sudan also has received refugees from neighboring countries afflicted by environmental problems or embroiled in regional and internal conflicts, at one point hosting the largest number of such refugees on the African continent. For instance the Sahelian drought of 1983 brought millions of refugees from Chad and Ethiopia into Sudanese refugee camps. Others have arrived from Eritrea, Central African Republic, Republic of the Congo, and Uganda. [by Anita Fabos]. *See also* FAMINE.

REJAF. *See* JUBA.

RELIGION. Sudan is a country of enormous cultural, linguistic, and religious diversity. That said, Islam (q.v.) predominates in the northern two-thirds of the country, with more formal and literate expressions in the cities and towns and "folk" or popular expressions in the rural areas. For instance, Islamic law (Shari'a, q.v.) courts may be found in the larger towns and cities, while the tombs (*qubbas*, q.v.) of holymen dot the rural Gezira (q.v.) region and elsewhere. Sufi *tariqas* (qq.v.), a decidedly popular feature of Islam, may, however, be found among any northern population, urban or rural.

Islam came relatively late to the Sudan, becoming established from the fourteenth to the sixteenth centuries; Nubia (q.v.) was then eastern Orthodox Christian, while much of the rest of the north practiced indigenous religions. The Nuba (q.v.) mountains and southern Sudan (q.v.) were home to indigenous religions (often misidentified as "animist") until the Turkiya and Anglo-Egyptian (qq.v.) periods, when Christianity was encouraged through missionary (q.v.) activities. In the postindependence period of civil war, Islam and Christianity have often confronted one another on several fronts, as North and South have been locked in chronic conflict. There are allegations that government troops in the 1990s attempted to spread Islam in the South by force, which, if true, would be in direct violation of Qur'anic injunction.

Statistically about 70 percent of all Sudanese practice mainstream (i.e., Sunni) Islam, and these are overwhelmingly in the North; another 25 percent practice indigenous beliefs, and these are in the South; while a final 5 percent practice Christianity in the South and vicinity of Khartoum (q.v.). While the North is almost entirely Muslim, the South is approximately 25 percent Christian and 75 percent indigenous religions. It must be noted that the practices of both Islam and Christianity in Sudan are often highly syncretic. *See also* CHRISTIANITY IN NUBIA; CHRISTIANTY IN THE SUDAN; FEKI; FOLK RELIGION.

REPUBLICAN BROTHERHOOD. The Republican Brotherhood was an Islamic social reform movement founded in the early 1950s by Mahmud Muhammad Taha (q.v.) following on the efforts of the Republican Party (q.v.). The Republican Party had been founded in 1946 by a group of men, including Taha, to participate in the Sudan's independence movement, with a goal of establishing a Republic of Sudan, rather than a religious monarchy or a union with Egypt. The party was dissolved when it became clear that Sudan's sectarian parties, based on connections with the Ansar or Khatmiya (qq.v.) religious sects, would dominate the years leading up to independence.

The Republican Brotherhood was the popular name for what Taha had called the "New Islamic Mission" when he redirected his political efforts toward developing a new consciousness about a modern vision of Islam and Islamic law (qq.v.). This religious ideology is based on an interpretation of the Meccan and Medinan texts of the Qur'an. Taha's "Second Message of Islam" views the earlier Meccan texts of the Qur'an as holding a universally observable message for contemporary humankind—and which guided the Prophet's personal practice—while the Medinan revealed texts were meant to construct and reform Arabian society of the seventh century. Taha advocated that Islamic law and practice be based on the meaning of the Meccan texts.

Initially Taha was the sole force behind this movement as he undertook speaking engagements all over Sudan and wrote and published extensively. As the numbers of his followers grew, drawing from intellectual groups, disaffected Sufis (q.v.), and members of sectarian organizations, they took on more responsibility in propagating the message of the movement. Taha and his followers produced more than 200 books on topics ranging from prayer in Islam to the role of women (q.v.) and education in society.

The movement had a progressive stance on social issues such as women and marriage. Women played a strong role in the organization, engaging in the writing of the Brotherhood's books and speaking about them on the streets of the major towns and on university campuses. Marriage was seen as a partnership with both parties pledging that there would be equal rights to divorce and the husband would remain monogamous. Particularly emphasized is the Republican Brotherhood claim of the lack of human rights (q.v.) and equity regarding the treatment of women and non-Muslims in modern Islamic societies. A pragmatic rendering of the program of the Republican Brotherhood would involve the specific revision of the Shari'a law regarding marriage and divorce, with equal rights to contract the marriage and to divorce and the prohibition of polygamy. Under a revised constitution, based on the true principles of Muslim equity and justice, non-Muslims would be treated on a par with Muslims, and religious freedom would be absolutely protected.

While the politics of the Republican Brotherhood were generally moderate, tacitly supporting the Ja'afar al-Nimeiri (q.v.) regime in its early years due to Nimeiri's efforts to control Islamic forces in politics, there were nonetheless a number of clashes with the government over the role of Shari'a and freedom of speech issues. Mahmud Muhammad Taha spent brief periods in jail during the 1960s and 1970s, while the membership in his organization grew to approximately 1,000 active men and women by 1980. In 1983 the Republican Brothers launched a major speaking and writing campaign against Nimeiri's imposition of the "September Laws" (q.v.) in the country, which led to the arrest of more than seventy members of the organization, including four Republican Sisters and Taha himself. No charges were brought against the group until a final pamphlet was issued at the end of 1984 demanding that Islamic law be dropped as the only state law in force. Taha was charged with apostasy, convicted and sentenced to death. He was hanged on 18 January

1985 and the movement disbanded. Many of its members live in exile in Great Britain and the United States. [by W. Stephen Howard]

REPUBLICAN PARTY (1). A small but relatively long-lived party founded in 1945 by Mahmud Muhammad Taha (q.v.). It favored Sudanese independence but did not ally itself with any other party or front. The party had no electoral success but continued to be represented in all-party consultative groups like the National Constitutional Committee in 1956. During the Ibrahim Abboud (q.v.) regime the party's founder and leader became more active in the cause of Islamic reform and the movement emerged in nonparty form following the 1964 October Revolution (q.v.). Taha wrote a number of books on religious and social subjects, providing the basis for the group's programs that came to be known as the "Second Message of Islam." For these works, Mahmud was judged as an "apostate" from Islam (q.v.) in 1984 and ordered executed by Ja'afar al-Nimeiri (q.v.) in 1985 for his views. *See also* REPUBLICAN BROTHERHOOD.

REPUBLICAN PARTY (2). During 1946 a second party named the Republican Party was created by Yusuf al-Tinay, but it was very short-lived.

RIEK. *See* MACHAR, RIEK.

ROBERTS, DAVID (1796–1864). This remarkable English artist had formal training in painting at the Royal Academy in London, but it was his travels in the Middle East from 1838 to 1839 that led him to create beautiful lithographs and paintings of the region. These were highly popular in the nineteenth century and are presently undergoing a revival. His three volume work *Egypt and Nubia* (1846–1849) provided some images of the colors of ancient Nubian temples that are now lost. His work also shows these monuments on their original sites before being submerged by Nile flooding or relocated. His work *The Holy Land, Syria, Egypt and Nubia* (1842–1849) also offers images of some of the main Islamic features of the region at this time.

ROBERTSON, JAMES WILSON (?–1983). Scottish member of the Sudan Political Service (SPS, q.v.) from 1926–1953, who served in various posts along the White and Blue Niles, in Kordofan (q.v), and finally Khartoum (q.v.). Robertson was elevated to the post of civil secretary in March 1945 following the death of Sir Douglas Newbold (q.v.), retiring in 1953. His appointment by Governor-General Hubert Huddleston (q.v.) was made to appease conservatives in the SPS who had felt marginalized by Newbold. While Newbold's policies persisted in general, Robertson was less flexible and accommodating, and his sometimes-abrasive style encouraged Sudanese resentment of British rule. Nonetheless, he did call a constitutional conference in 1946 to discuss devolution of power and the inclusion of Sudanese in central and local governments. Recognizing that the separation of North and South was impracticable, he held another conference in Juba in June 1947 to attract southern Sudanese representation to a new legislative assembly.

In the postwar period in which Robertson served, Great Britain was less able to staff its colonial governments and resources were limited. Robertson and others saw their ability to manipulate local Sudanese politics slipping away, while Britain's strategic concerns with Egypt preoccupied its Foreign Office. Ultimately, Robertson's role in the transition to Sudanese self-government was a crucial one. Upon leaving the Sudan he served as the last British governor-general in Nigeria, from 1955 to 1960. He recorded his experiences in a memoir, *Transition in Africa* (1974).

ROOSEVELT, THEODORE (1858–1919). Roosevelt was governor of New York from 1898 to 1900 and served as the 26th (Republican) President of the United States from 1901 to 1909. An avid hunter, he set off for Africa at the conclusion of his presidency, eventually shooting hundreds of animals in the Sudan.

Entering the country near Juba (q.v.), Roosevelt took a British government steamer down the White Nile to Khartoum (q.v.). There he was hosted by S. J. Leigh Hunt (q.v.), an American entrepreneur and agricultural investor. From Khartoum, Roosevelt took the British military railway through Berber (q.v.) and Abu Hamad to Wadi Halfa (q.v.), returning by rail and steamer to Cairo.

ROUND TABLE CONFERENCE OF 1965. This historic conference was held in Khartoum (q.v.) from 16 to 25 March 1965 in the wake of the October Revolution (q.v.), and was the first such meeting in postindependence Sudan to confront directly the issue of the future of the southern Sudan (q.v.) within the Republic of Sudan. Since civil war had already been waged for a decade, the question of separation or integration of the South was inevitably at the center of discussions. All of the northern parties present, including the Umma Party, Peoples Democratic Party, Sudan Communist Party, the National Unionist Party (NUP), and Islamic

Charter Front (qq.v.), refused to accept the separation of the South; while the southern parties, including the Southern Front and the Sudanese African National Union (SANU, qq.v.), were divided over the issue. While the Sudan Unity Party, a wing of SANU led by Santino Deng (q.v.), stood for a united Sudan, the Southern Front, members of SANU in exile, and Anya-Nya (q.v.) favored separation.

There was no resolution at the conclusion of the conference. However, political lines had been clearly drawn regarding both the issue of separation or unity and the peaceful or military solution to the conflict. The final proposals of the northern parties included: recognition of the right to self-determination in the South, but not secession or the right to pursue an agenda leading to a sovereign southern state; advocacy of the principle of regional government and rejection of both highly centralized and federated forms of government as inappropriate to the realities of the Republic of Sudan; and implementation of an immediate cease-fire. By way of comparison, the final proposals of SANU and the Southern Front included: a program of southernization of politics and administration with a division of powers and institutions between the northern and southern regions; integrated transport, post, and telegraph services to serve as points of articulation with the North; a Council of Ministers, twelve from each territory, selected to govern the Republic. Finally, six resolutions to attempt to normalize the situation in the southern Sudan were jointly signed by the aforementioned eight political parties or organizations that were represented at the conference.

These resolutions had little effect; in the months following the conference the newly elected government coming to power in July 1965 pursued a military offensive against Anya-Nya and worked with those southerners who favored unity. The failure of the Round Table Conference to arrive at political consensus meant little change in official policy regarding the South, and a new Parliament was elected without any southern representatives since the Supreme Council had ruled that elections should not be conducted in the South. Nevertheless, twenty-one people, mostly northerners, appeared in Parliament claiming that they had been elected by southern constituencies, arguing the decision of the Supreme Council was illegal. Events worsened with the negative southern reaction to the seating of these "representatives," most of whom were NUP and Umma party members who had not been duly elected, and led to further distrust by southerners of northern motives.

The historical significance of the Round Table Conference is that it represented an initial effort by the Sudanese to resolve their internal conflict in the absence of any colonial or international context. Likewise, it supported the remedy of regional self-rule that came to be a hallmark of the Addis Ababa Agreement of 1972 (q.v.), which ended the war and promoted unity for about a decade during the Ja'afar al-Nimeiri (q.v.) years. However, its failure to achieve consensus is significant, as the fundamental issues of economic equity and political representation have still not been resolved over three decades later, and civil war is still chronic and endemic in the country.

ROWLAND, ROLAND "TINY" (1917–1998). Rowland was the chief executive of the British conglomerate Lonrho, which invests heavily in Africa and the Arab world. He was particularly interested in Kenya, Ethiopia, and Sudan for its great, but largely unrealized, agricultural potential. Perhaps even before the collapse of the Ja'afar al-Nimeiri (q.v.) government in 1985, Rowland was sympathetic to the Sudanese Peoples Liberation Movement (SPLM, q.v.) and became a formal member shortly afterward. By 1993 his great wealth put him in position to support and influence southern Sudanese politics, especially through John Garang (q.v.) and within American and British diplomatic circles. His private "Gulfstream" aircraft were used to shuttle SPLM officials to various negotiations in the region.

RUPPELL, EDUARD WILHELM (1794–1884). German naturalist and explorer who traveled widely in the northern Sudan. From 1823 to 1824 he visited Korti, Dongola, Meroë, Shendi, and Sinnar (qq.v.), and from 1824 to 1825 he went from Dongola to el-Obeid (q.v.) and possibly to southern Kordofan (q.v.).

– S –

SA'AD, MAHASIN. Sa'ad was a founder of the League of University Women's Graduates (q.v.) and Secretary of the Umma Party's (q.v.) Women's Association. An activist for women's rights, she was also an early pioneer in the family planning movement in Sudan.

SA'ID, BESHIR MOHAMED (1921–1995). Sa'id was born in Omdurman (q.v.) and educated in private schools before gaining a place at Gordon Memorial College (q.v.). Upon graduation he became a secondary school teacher from 1947 to 1954 but changed to journalism during the final stages of the nationalist movement and was employed by *The Sudan Standard*, the only newspaper at the time. In 1954 Sa'id started *al-Ayyam* press, which published a major independent newspaper in the significant two years before independence. He served for a time as president of the Sudanese Press Association and also worked in the Office of Public Information in the United Nations Secretariat (1961–1963).

After the 1969 May Revolution of Ja'afar al-Nimeiri (qq.v.), Sa'id was held in detention for a time. His commercial and printing business expanded to include other Arabic and English language publications. Later he became a governor of the University of Khartoum (q.v.) and was awarded an honorary doctorate by that institution. He was visiting professor of history at the University at the time of his death.

Sa'id published several books, including biographies of the nationalist politicians Ahmad Khayr and Isma'il al-Azhari (qq.v.) and a historical study of the twentieth-century Sudan titled *al-Sudan min al-Hukm al-Thuna'i ila Intifadat Rajab* (The Sudan from Condominium Rule to the October Revolution). He was the author of numerous articles and several books, including *Sudan at the Crossroads* published in the late 1960s, and he translated Abel Alier's (q.v.) *Southern Sudan: Too Many Agreements Dishonored*, which he published at his own cost. Throughout his career he developed a reputation for balance and fair-mindedness regarding some of the most difficult issues of the day, including the growing divide between the northern and southern regions. [by Heather J. Sharkey]. *See also* MEDIA.

SA'ID, MUHAMMAD (1822–1863). Ottoman viceroy of Egypt and the Sudan and youngest son of Muhammad 'Ali Pasha (q.v.). During his reign (1854–1863) a concession was granted to Ferdinand de Lesseps to construct the Suez Canal from the Mediterranean to the Red Sea. The flourishing slave trade in the Sudan and the pressure put on the Turco-Egyptian (q.v.) administration from European quarters to end the trade led Sa'id to extend governmental control over the White Nile and to forbid the export of slaves to Egypt. Although the official antislavery (q.v.) policy had limited effect on the trade, at least official Ottoman opposition to slavery (q.v.) could be claimed to the Europeans.

SAINTS. Orthodox Islam recognizes the concept of sainthood for someone chosen and blessed by Allah. The cult of the saints is part of the sociocultural life of the Sudanese, although as such it is discouraged in Orthodox Islam (q.v.). Most Sudanese believe that a saint or a *wali* (sing. of *'Awliya*) has the power to perform *karama* (a miraculous act) to satisfy people's needs. The genuine proof of a person's sainthood rests on the number and strength of the legends that show his/her miraculous manifestations, most of which occur after death. *'Awliya* provide spiritual inspiration and various services for their followers and the community at large by means of saintly intervention in times of need. Also, through their undisputed authority and judgment, they help people in resolving social conflicts arising from ordinary life situations. By virtue of his/her *baraka* (q.v.) a *wali* can ward off the malevolent power that affects human life negatively, or he/she can perform a *karama* to save a disciple in a desperate situation. [by Baqie Badawi Muhammad]

SALIH, AL-TAYYIB (1929–). This Sudanese novelist and short story writer has gained considerable renown in the Arab world and in the English-speaking world through translations of his works. Born in al-Debba in northcentral Sudan, his works have focused on Sudanese village life and how the true Sudanese ethos is preserved by the people of the village. His works have had profound artistic and structural influence upon many other contemporary Arabic writers. The artistry and linguistic structure of *Season of Migration to the North* earned him praise as "a new genius of the Arab novel" as early as 1968. The novel differs from other Arab novels about the encounter between East and West in that it deals with the experiences and traumas of an East African, born of an Arab father and southern Sudanese slave mother who, after spending a large portion of his youth and adulthood in England, returns as a stranger to the Nile village of Wad Hamad, where he attempts to give back to the villagers that knowledge that he has learned abroad. The novel portrays much of the complexity of the psyche of the contemporary African and Arab Sudanese society that can be broadly understood by a wider audience in the translated work.

Al-Tayib Salih resides in London and is a regular contributor to the Arabic language journal *Al-Majalla*. He has been an active participant in the international conferences of Sudanese Studies, and in the national meetings of the Sudan Studies Association (q.v.) based in the United States and the Sudan Studies Society of the United Kingdom (q.v.). Both his novel *Bandar Shah* and several of his short stories have been translated into English and widely reprinted. His *Wedding of Zein* has also been made into a feature-length film. [by Constance E. Berkley]. *See also* LITERATURE.

SALIM QAPUDAN. A Turco-Egyptian sailor and explorer who commanded three expeditions attempting to discover the source of the White Nile in 1839–1842. Rapids in the southernmost Sudan proved to be a barrier.

SAMMANIYA. A *tariqa* (q.v.) organized by Muhammad al-Samman (1718–1775) in Arabia. It was brought to the Sudan by Ahmad al-Tayyib al-Bashir (1742–1824), a member of a Sudanese holy family who had traveled and studied in Egypt and the Hijaz. He built a large following for the *tariqa* in the central Sudan. His grandson, Muhammad Sharif Nur al-Da'im (q.v.), was a teacher of Muhammad Ahmad al-Mahdi (q.v.), who was a recognized member of the order. The Sammaniya provided many followers for the Mahdi, but the *tariqa* did not dissolve or simply become a branch of the Mahdist movement. In the twentieth century the order continued to have a large number of followers in the central Sudan and also developed branch orders that became influential. The most notable of these are the followers of Yusuf al-Hindi and Qarib Allah Salih (qq.v.).

SANUSIYA. A *tariqa* (q.v.) established in the eastern Sahara ca. 1841 by Muhammad Ibn 'Ali al-Sanusi (1791–1859). Al-Sanusi had been a student of Ahmad ibn Idris (q.v.), whom he met in Mecca in 1826, and they continued as collaborators for many years. Al-Sanusi was originally from western Algeria, but he created a strong base for religious and political influence in Libya, where he died in Jaghbub in 1859. Upon the death of Ibn Idris, several of his students set up independent Sufi *turuq*, such as the Khatmiya (q.v.) established by Muhammad 'Uthman al-Mirghani (q.v.). Sanusi went to Cyrenaica, Libya, to start his order. Initially he was joined by Ibrahim al-Rashid, who returned to the Sudan to begin his own Rashidiya (q.v.) *tariqa*.

The Sanusiya *tariqa* was an order that aimed at raising the level of Islamic knowledge among the Bedouin. However, it also facilitated and participated in the trans-Saharan trade. At the onset of colonialism in the early twentieth century the Sanusiya sometimes became a focal point of militant resistance to French and Italian rule. Thus it served as a Pan-Islamic force believed to be a factor behind a number of revolts in Sudan, where its influence was primarily among immigrants from West Africa and Darfur (q.v.).

At the death of al-Sanusi, his son Muhammad al-Mahdi al-Sanusi (1844–1902) assumed leadership of the *tariqa* and was invited by the Sudanese Mahdi (q.v.) to be one of his four high officers, or *khalifas* (q.v.).

This offer was declined and there was no real center of Sanusiya following in Sudan, although its economic and religious relations with Darfur persisted. The Sanusiya leadership maintained considerable correspondence with 'Ali Dinar (q.v.) and with neighboring Wadai in Chad. Despite French fears, the Sanusiya's role was essentially limited to arbitration and conciliation, aimed at safeguarding their commercial and religious objectives. [by Knut S. Vikor]

SAQIYA. For many centuries, regions along the Nile Valley have known mechanized irrigation by means of the *saqiya* (water wheel, or *eskalay*, in Kenzi Nubian), a very sophisticated example of ancient technology in the Nile Valley. Irrigation devices other than the *saqiya* have been used to cultivate the crops near the Nile, but the *saqiya* was until recently the basis of irrigation and agriculture (q.v.) in the Nile Valley. It is constructed by local experts from local materials such as wood and ropes made from palm trees. The *saqiya* is powered by animals. The farmers take care of minor repairs and provide regular servicing; however, major repairs are performed by a traditional specialist who is responsible for the maintenance of a number of *saqiyas,* and who is paid in crops at the end of the harvesting season. Traditionally, six farmers share one *saqiya*. They operate by rotation, using six cows, and they work under one leader called *Samad,* who is the sole agricultural, technical, and administrative director. He acquires his position by virtue of his recognized experience. This group of six adopts a system of two or three shifts, although two shifts are more common. They work usually in the morning and at night, resting during the hot afternoon. [by Baqie Badawi Muhammad]

SATURNINO, LOHURE (?–1967). Southern political leader and Roman Catholic priest. He was named to the constitutional committee in 1957 and elected to Parliament in 1958, becoming a leading member in the southern parliamentary bloc. After the Ibrahim Abboud coup in 1958 he returned to the South and then fled the country in 1961. He was one of the creators of the Sudan African National Union (SANU, q.v.) and helped to organize Anya-Nya (q.v.) activities. After SANU broke up, he became one of the prominent members of the Azania Liberation Front (q.v.). He was killed early in 1967 near the Uganda border.

SAYYID (SAYID, SAYYED). A title or form of address, usually denoting a position of religious prestige but also common in polite usage as the equivalent of "Sir" or "Mister." Descendants of the Prophet Muhammad always are addressed as Sayyid (fem. Sayyida); hence the Mahdi's (q.v.) formal name was Muhammad Ahmad al-Mahdi ibn al-Sayyid 'Abdullah, consisting of his given name, his title ("the Mahdi"), and his father's title and name (al-Sayyid 'Abdullah). The two paramount religious leaders of twentieth-century northern Sudan, 'Abd al-Rahman al-Mahdi and 'Ali al-Mirghani (qq.v.), respective leaders of the Ansar and Khatmiya (qq.v.) sects, were frequently referred to as "the two Sayyids." *See also* ASHRAF.

SELIM I, SULTAN (1470–1520). The forces of this Ottoman Sultan (reg. 1512–1520) were sent to the Sudan in the early sixteenth century after he brought the Mamluk period in Egypt to a close in January 1517 and initiated the era of Ottoman rule in the Nile Valley. Selim I actually left Egypt by September 1517 but appointed Governor Khayr Bey to rule in his name. With the Mamluk rivals vanquished the Turkish forces marched to Nubia (q.v.) where they defeated the local representatives of the Funj Sultanates (q.v.) at Hannek in 1520 and then withdrew. No further Turkish attacks were notable in the Sudan until the early nineteenth century when a full-scale Turkish invasion was mounted in 1820. *See also* TURKIYA.

SCHNITZER, EDOUARD. *See* EMIN PASHA.

SCHWEINFURTH, GEORG AUGUST (1836–1925). This German scientist was an avid scholar of the natural history and paleontology of the Nile Valley, the Red Sea coast, and Abyssinia during the time of the Turkiya (q.v.). He traveled in Egypt, the Sudan, and Ethiopia from 1863 to 1866 until his funds were exhausted. In 1868 he undertook a second trip that was to be a botanical exploration of the Equatorial (q.v.) regions west of the Nile. He sailed down the Red Sea to Suakin (q.v.) and traveled overland to the Nile, which he reached on 1 November 1868. During his three-year travels he went to the lands of the Dinka and Shilluk (qq.v.) and farther south into central Africa. At that time the Shilluk were just concluding a war with the Turkish rulers of the Sudan. Schweinfurth visited their capital at Fashoda (q.v.), where he almost lost his life in an attack by swarming bees.

By February 1869 he left Fashoda and went on to the Sobat River where he met the ivory trader Muhammad Abu Sammat. Upstream he entered the northern section of the vast *Sudd* (q.v.) swampland. At last on 25 March he reached the Dinka area at Port Rek where he turned westward to Dyoor and Bongo territory, little known to Westerners, where he stayed until November 1869. From there he went on to "Mittoo" and "Niam-Niam" country from the camp of Abu Sammat for an additional three months. All the while he made ethnographic notes and botanical collections. On 20 March 1870 he reached "Monbuttoo" country and its capital town south of the west-flowing Welle River where King Munza resided. Schweinfurth was received at the immense lodge of King Munza on 22 March 1870. Although he did not travel farther south he heard of the "Akka" pygmy people living in that direction. On 12 April 1870 he began his return to the North through the rival "Niam-Niam" kingdom under chief Wando.

Great misfortune lay just ahead when he and his party were trapped in their *zariba* (thorn enclosure) by a rapidly spreading brush fire. Although Schweinfurth did not lose his life, most of his specimens were lost, though his journals were preserved and constitute one of the first botanical records of the region. His disappointment was huge but he finally determined to continue northward rather than spend more exhausting months rebuilding his collection. At last he reached Khartoum (q.v.), and from there Suakin and Europe, returning home in November 1871 after an historic trip to places previously unknown to Europeans. In the 1870s and 1880s he explored the Libyan and Arabian deserts, and Fayum west of the Nile.

Schweinfurth contributed greatly to the natural history of Saharan, Equatorial, and Central Africa. His main published work on these travels is his *Im Herzen von Afrika*, translated into many languages and published in English as *The Heart of Africa* (1874). He died in Berlin on 19 September 1925. A mountain just north of Lake Albert was named in his honor.

"SEPTEMBER LAWS." On 8 September 1983 President Ja'afar al-Nimeiri (q.v.) decreed that henceforth Islamic law (Shari'a, q.v.) would be the sole state law in force in Sudan. This occurred after the 1980 move to unify the previously separated civil and Islamic courts into a single system administered by the Sudan judiciary. Shortly after this merger Hasan al-Turabi (q.v.) was appointed attorney general and the judiciary fell under the direct influence of the ideology of the Muslim Brotherhood (q.v.).

Along with this decree, Nimeiri also called for a restructuring of the Sudanese legal system, which included giving a stronger hand to the attorney general; revising court procedures in order to attain prompt justice by simplifying the legal process; and establishing the application of

Islamic laws in all fields (in addition to the former jurisdiction that administered personal status laws only), including the concept of aggravated theft punishable by *hadd* punishments ("to the limit," such as limb amputation; flogging for defamation, drinking, possession, manufacture, or sale of alcohol; and the death penalty for adultery and armed robbery).

Fair trials and irrefutable proof, or admission of guilt, along with the nonapplicability to non-Muslims, were to be guaranteed in the implementation of the new laws. However, within a year of their promulgation, it was clear that these guarantees were not being met. "Courts of Prompt Justice" replaced the previous courts along with a large portion of the trained judicial officials who were purged if not supportive of the changes. Non-Muslims were charged and punished for alcohol-related offenses, while Muslim and non-Muslim alike had limbs amputated after the "Prompt Justice" courts determined their guilt for property crimes. Several hundred amputee victims, primarily between 1983 and 1985, organized themselves into a social welfare society after democracy was restored with the overthrow of Nimeiri in April 1985. The *hadd* punishments were discontinued during the period of democracy from 1985 to 1989, and were not initially resumed after the National Islamic Front (NIF, q.v.) seized power in the June 1989 coup d'etat.

National and international criticism of the punishment of amputation especially, as a violation of human rights (q.v.), is probably responsible for their effective elimination. However, the "September Laws" have not been abrogated, and Islamic law remains the sole law in force in Sudan. This is a central issue in the civil war between northern and southern parties. The National Democratic Alliance (q.v.) has called for a secular, democratic state where no religious law is in effect, while the Sudanese Peoples Liberation Movement (q.v.) says the removal of the "September Laws" is a *sine qua non* for any negotiated peace.

SHADHILIYA. One of the chief traditions of Islamic mysticism, traced back to the teachings of Abu'l-Hasan 'Ali al-Shadhili (ca. 1197–1258). The founder, a Moroccan who taught in Tunis and Alexandria, was a key figure in carrying mystical ideas out of the hermit circles where they had developed and introducing them to urban artisans and scholars. In the Sudan, the Shadhili tradition dates to at least the fifteenth century, when it was represented by a number of *shaykhs* (q.v.) who nonetheless were overshadowed by the dominant brotherhood, the Qadiriya (q.v.). The Shadhiliya gained ground in the eighteenth century, mainly through the spread of the *Dala'il al-Khayrat*, a famous set of prayers emphasizing the centrality of the Prophet as mediator of the revealed Truth.

The Shadhiliya is often portrayed as being more "learned" and "refined" than the Qadiriya, which is viewed as the common person's *tariqa (q.v.)*, and this image no doubt contributed to its success. The Majadhib (q.v.) became the best-known representatives of the Shadhiliya in the Sudan, but many other *turuq* also use Shadhili prayers. One such group, the Burhaniya, has played a leading role in the twentieth century in the defense of Sufism among modernizing groups. [by Albrecht Hofheinz]

SHAFI' AHMAD AL-SHAYKH, AL- (?–1971). Al-Shafi' was an influential pioneer of the Sudanese Communist Party (SCP, q.v.) and was one of the major leaders of the militant tendency within the labor and nationalist movement in the late 1940s. He served in critical positions as the secretary of the powerful Sudan Railway Workers Union (SRWU, q.v.), and as the secretary-general of the Sudanese Workers Trade Union Federation (SWTUF, q.v.).

Al-Shafi' was convicted of "defaming a colonial official" in the Sudan Political Service (q.v.) in 1950 and sent to jail for one month. This caused a three-day solidarity strike of the SRWU, which led to more political charges by the colonial government and then to a general strike in the Sudan in 1951.

For much of the postcolonial period, political parties, trade unions (q.v.), and the SCP in particular, were banned by military regimes, so al-Shafi' spent considerable time trying to avoid arrest and repression. During democratic periods he reappeared in an active public life and especially in the early years of Ja'afar al-Nimeiri (1969–1971, q.v.) he was very active. In the wake of the Hashim al-Atta coup of July 1971, he and other leading members of the SCP were alleged to have backed the plot and he was hanged. He was the husband of Fatma Ahmad Ibrahim (q.v.), one of the most stalwart Sudanese feminists and SCP member of the Sudanese Parliament.

SHAGHABA AL-MARGHUMABIYA. Shaghaba was known among the Marghumab, a people of the eastern Sudan, as the most famous poetess of her time (18th century CE). She recorded in poetry the battles of her people with others in the region, especially the Batahin (an ethnic group of the Butana region between Kassala (q.v.) province in eastern Sudan, the northern region of the Sudan, and the Blue Nile).

Shaghaba was a public figure whose role was to ridicule the one who dishonored his *qabila* (ethnic group) and to praise heroic acts. The purpose of the poems that she composed was to send a provocative message to the cowardly person, not to expel him, but to encourage him to join the group and protect the *qabila*.

In a very passionate poem with a surprisingly acerbic tone, Shaghaba humiliated her son Husayn, who had never participated in a battle. She disowned him and she said that she felt ashamed that her son was a grown man who lived without any scars on his skin. His belly was getting big because he had never experienced a passionate relation with a woman; if he had a lover, he would fight to protect her and the whole *qabila* from their enemies. Indeed, this was what a woman asked for from her man. Being a warrior, his body would be handsomely shaped; but such was not the case with Husayn. Shaghaba wished her son to be a warrior, to see his body marked with scars; what pride and joy would be hers when she treated his wounds. But Husayn was so lazy and reckless that he didn't finish his studies. His *loh* (the student's board for writing) was never hung or displayed as a sign of his scholarly achievement.

This kind of poetry reveals group solidarity and the spirit of communal will. These themes are displayed in Shaghaba's desire to sacrifice her son in order to protect the whole *qabila*. [by Baqie Badawi Muhammad]

SHANNAN, 'ABD AL-RAHIM MUHAMMAD KHAYR. Sudanese soldier and political figure. During the government of Ibrahim Abboud (q.v.), Shannan was active in the Revolutionary Command Council and then was arrested and jailed for plotting against Abboud. He was released after the 1964 October Revolution (q.v.) and was elected to Parliament (1965–1968) and formally retired from the army. In 1973 he was arrested for plotting against the regime of Ja'afar al-Nimeiri (q.v.) in association with conservative opposition to the regime. He was convicted but given a light sentence because of poor health and advanced age.

SHARI'A. *See* ISLAMIC LAW.

SHARIF, HUSAYN (HUSAYN AL-KHALIFA MUHAMMAD SHARIF) (1888–1928). Sharif was a pioneer in Sudanese journalism. He was a grandson of the Mahdi (q.v.) and the son of the Mahdist Khalifa Muhammad Sharif (qq.v.), though he went by the shortened name "Husayn Sharif." He represented a young generation of Western-educated and politically moderate Mahdist intellectuals. After graduating from the Gordon Memorial College (q.v.) around 1912, he worked as a correspondent for the Greek-owned Arabic newspaper, *Ra'id al-Sudan* (*The Sudan Leader*), and then assumed its editorship from 1915 until its closure in 1919. In 1919 Sharif founded the first Sudanese-owned and -edited newspaper, *Hadarat al-Sudan* (q.v.), on the grounds that "a country without a newspaper is like a heart without a tongue." He participated actively in philanthropic projects such as the Ahliya Schools Movement (q.v.), and was a president of the Graduates Club of Omdurman (qq.v.). Husayn Sharif died in 1928, but the newspaper that he founded continued publication until 1938. *See also* MEDIA. [by Heather J. Sharkey]

SHAWQISTS. The group associated with the judge Muhammad 'Ali Effendi Shawqi in the Graduates Club (q.v.) during the 1920s and 1930s, when he played a pivotal role in the 1931 strike at Gordon Memorial College (q.v.). By 1932 factional politics began to appear within the Graduates Congress (q.v.). The major opponents of the Shawqist faction in the Graduates Club were the Filists (q.v.). 'Abd al-Rahman al-Mahdi (q.v.) supported the Shawqist faction, which mistrusted Egypt and favored the idea of a separate, independent Sudan. Shawqi resigned in 1943 after the Graduates Congress elections and became a founding member of the Umma Party (q.v.) in February 1945.

SHAYKH (SHEIKH). A traditional lineage or family branch leader. The title is also used for religious leaders and teachers.

SHAYKH OMER 'ABD AL-RAHMAN (1938–). This shadowy figure was born in Egypt and earned a Ph.D. in Islamic jurisprudence from the famed al-Azhar University (q.v.) in Cairo. It is said by Col. Abboud al-Zoumur that he was inspired by Shaykh Omer to carry out the assassination of Egyptian President Anwar Sadat in 1981. Shaykh Omer was found not guilty of complicity and released in 1982, but he remained an inspirational figure for the Islamic *jihad* movement in Egypt. In its various forms, known as *Jama'at Islamiya* ("Islamic Groups"), it has conducted a campaign of terror against Copts (q.v.), Egyptian police, and foreign tourists.

Travels by the Shaykh to Iraq and Sudan were mounted to gain political and financial support for his activities. It is believed that support from Iran and the Saudi extremist Osama Bin Laden was delivered to him through Sudan under the National Islamic Front (NIF, q.v.) backed government of General 'Umar al-Bashir and Hasan al-Turabi (qq.v.).

Shaykh Omer likely admired the present Sudanese government as a model Islamic state. In fact it was on a Sudanese passport that Shaykh Omer received a tourist visa to the United States "by mistake" from the U.S. Embassy in Khartoum (q.v.).

His published work *The Absent Duty* offered guidelines for killing Copts and looting their property to finance the Islamic Group's activities. Blind from diabetes, Shaykh Omer made use of tape cassettes of his sermons, which were smuggled in from Sudan and elsewhere. Shaykh Omer is critical of Egyptian President Hosni Mubarak's opposition to Iran and Iraq, which have been kind to him.

Shaykh Omer arrived in New York in May 1990 and lived in Brooklyn, although steps were taken to have his visa revoked in November 1990. In March 1992 his green card was revoked, but this was appealed. Meanwhile he was linked to provocative sermons inciting violence, such as the case of Sayid Noseir now serving a life sentence for murder. The murder of Farag Foda is also believed to be linked with Shaykh Omer's followers. Most notorious of all was the first bombing of the World Trade Center in New York as well as a plan to blow up the United Nations Building and key traffic tunnels serving the city. In the subsequent trials for his ten conspirators, Shaykh Omer was found guilty.

In November 1997 one of the "Islamic Groups" in Egypt attacked a prominent tourist site in Luxor, killing sixty and calling for the release of Shaykh Omer as well as the release of their colleagues in Egyptian jails and courts. The possibility of more terrorist attacks is high since it is unlikely that the prisoners will be released. The association with these people and events with Sudan is not clear, but much feared. This is especially the case after Khartoum's alleged involvement with the attempted assassination of President Mubarak in Addis Ababa in 1995. Shaykh Omer has said that it is an "Islamic duty" to oppose the "corruption and tyranny" of "Pharoah Mubarak" and his "gangs of cowards." This attempt on the life of Mubarak and the refusal of Sudan to extradite the plotters resulted in a United Nations partial boycott of Sudan, which was extended and expanded by the United States in November 1997 because of Sudan's support for international terrorism.

SHAYQIYA. A major camel-herding Arab (q.v.) group usually said to be related to the Ja'aliyin (q.v.). Essentially both are Arabized Nubians (q.v.). The Shayqiya are centered in the Nile Valley south of Dongola (q.v.) and established a series of independent sultanates in the later period of the Funj Sultanates (q.v.). After vigorously resisting the Turco-Egyptian (q.v.) invasion, the Shayqiya cooperated with the new rulers and spread throughout the Sudan as irregular soldiers and Jallaba (q.v.) traders. As with many riverine Arabs, the Shayqiya initially opposed the Mahdiya (q.v.) and suffered great losses, though eventually many served as Ansar (q.v.). As a people they were too dispersed to have much power, but as individuals and families they have been prominent in twentieth-century history.

SHENDI. Prior to Turco-Egyptian (q.v.) rule, Shendi was one of the main commercial towns of the northern Sudan and the home of many Jallaba (q.v.) merchants. Shendi lies just upstream from the ancient Meroitic capital and its neighboring pyramid fields. To the southeast of Shendi are the important Meroitic ruins at Naqa and Mussawarat al-Sufra. Across the Nile is the town of Metemma. In the early eighteenth century Shendi may have had a population of about 5,000, surpassed only by its contemporaries, the towns of Sinnar, Suakin, and perhaps al-Fasher (qq.v.).

Trade routes from Shendi went up and down the Nile; to the Gezira (q.v.) and the south; and to Kobbei in Darfur (qq.v.). Trade items included those from Venice, Egypt, Arabia, and Ethiopia, and the market was daily, unlike that of smaller towns. Local produce of pottery, baskets, livestock, rope, grains, wood, and dates made for a lively exchange. Slavery (q.v.) was another important aspect of Shendi's trade in the eighteenth and nineteenth centuries. Shendi slave merchants were mostly middlemen and a few slave hunters, but in 1814 it was estimated that as many as 5,000 slaves passed through Shendi each year.

Shendi established itself in nineteenth-century Sudanese history in 1823 when Isma'il Kamil Pasha (q.v.), fresh from his conquest, went to Shendi to procure taxes and otherwise express his authority. The ruler of the time, Mek Nimr (q.v.), was deeply insulted and provoked, and organized a conspiracy to kill Isma'il and his men while they were lulled by drink and sleep. Although their plot was successful it brought more than a year of retribution by Isma'il's brother-in-law, Muhammad Khusraw al-Daftardar (q.v.), who carried out massacres at dozens of Nile Valley towns and villages, killing up to 50,000 people.

When order had been restored, 'Ali Khurshid Pasha (reg. 1826–1838) arranged to construct a summer palace at Shendi. But peace was not to last, as the Mahdiya (q.v.) and British conquest again brought destruction upon this town. In 1955 Shendi's population was put at 11,500; by 1969 it reached about 21,000; a report for 1973 indicated a population of over 24,000. This steady growth rate suggests a role of regional migration and by 1990 Shendi's population may have exceeded 37,000.

SHIBEIKA, MEKKI (1905–1980). Sudanese intellectual leader and university professor who graduated from the American University of Beirut and received his doctorate from London University in history. He taught at Gordon Memorial College (q.v.) and then in the University of Khartoum (q.v.). He was active in the organization of the Graduates Congress (q.v.) and served as its secretary for a time. After independence he became professor of history at the University of Khartoum and then served as dean of the Faculty of Arts and also as president of the Philosophical Society of the Sudan. He wrote many important studies of Sudanese history in both English, e.g., *The Independent Sudan: The History of a Nation* (1959), and Arabic, *al-Sudan 'abra al-Qurun* (Sudan Across the Centuries). Shibeika is widely considered to be one of the notable intellectual figures of the twentieth-century Sudan.

SHIBLI, AMIN. Sudanese lawyer and political leader who was active in the 1964 October Revolution (q.v.) and served for a number of years as president of the Sudan Bar Association (q.v.). He was an organizer of a new Socialist Party in 1967 that hoped to be able to attract a broader basis of public support than the Sudanese Communist Party (q.v.) had won. He served briefly as minister of justice after the 1969 May Revolution (q.v.) and then in a variety of posts representing Sudan in the Arab League and other organizations.

SHILLUK (CHULLA, COLO, DHOCOLO, SHULLA). An ethnic group of the southern Sudan (q.v.) concentrated along the western banks and islands of the White Nile, especially between Renk and Malakal (q.v.), as well as on the lower thirty-two kilometers of the Sobat River. Their ancestral homeland is unknown, but they are thought to have displaced an earlier hunting and gathering population. Shilluk traditions of a royal throne, semidivine kingship, dynastic rule, social hierarchy, sororal marriage, oppositional division of the kingdom, water purification ritual, and origin myths resemble those of the ancient Egyptians, though the direction of cultural borrowing has not been determined. A pre-Nilotic (q.v.) people, the Shilluk are related to the Hamaj (q.v.) and distinguished by their Sudanic rather than Semitic language and the persistence of matrilineal forms of organization.

Arab travelers in the ninth century documented pre-Nilotic peoples in the area. During the Funj Sultanates (q.v.) from 1504 to 1821 slave raiders attacked Shilluk lands, leading to some southward migration in the sixteenth century and a more concentrated village pattern. Perhaps reflecting this time, their mythology records that Nyakang was the first *reth* or king to unify the Shilluk in a proto-state formation. The area was reached by European explorers in the eighteenth century. Slave raids in the early nineteenth century again victimized the Shilluk, and the Turkiya (q.v.) administration took hold in 1867. Mahdist rule (1885–1898) was generally resisted, though in the early twentieth century a sustained British colonial administration and missionary (q.v.) presence was established.

The Shilluk ecosystem is mainly grasslands, swampy riverbanks and islands, but *sunt* trees appear in places. There are approximately a 150 compacted hamlets (*myer*) constituting their domain. The Shilluk are predominantly sedentary farmers. Their economy is based on the Sudanic food complex of millet (*durra*) or sorghum, but other foods such as corn, melons, okra, sesame, and beans are also known. The *durra* is fermented to make an alcoholic drink. As farmers they are endowed with livestock, including sheep and goats, but especially cattle, which play important roles in religion and kinship. However, cattle for the Shilluk are not nearly as significant as they are for the neighboring Nuer and Dinka (qq.v.). Shilluk men are in charge of milking and do not make use of fresh cattle blood, as their neighbors do. Being riverfolk their foods are diversified by hunting and fishing.

For the Shilluk the election of a *reth* integrates the society with its traditions, provides for political leadership and continuity, and presents the greatest opportunity for public oratory and group confirmation. Unlike Sudanese Arabs (q.v.), few Shilluk girls are subject to female circumcision (q.v.) as a rite of prepubescence. The practice of removing the lower incisor teeth is common for Shilluk youths, as is ethnic scarification, which consists of making a series of raised bumps across the forehead just above the eyebrows. Other decorative cicatrices are known. Traditional religious beliefs are still strongly held, though some few Shilluk have turned to Islam and Christianity (qq.v.).

The population of the Shilluk has not been properly counted for years, but early in the postcolonial period there were at least 110,000 Shilluk speakers who shared a common cultural heritage. An estimate in 1982 by the Summer Institute of Linguistics placed their number at 175,000. During the current civil war in Sudan the Shilluk and other southern ethnic groups have often spent as much time quarreling among themselves as against their perceived common enemies in the northern Sudan. For example, the Dinka-led Sudanese Peoples Liberation Movement (q.v.) does not have strong appeal among the Shilluk, who tend to be allied with the Shilluk rebel Lam Akol (q.v.).

SHINGETTI, MUHAMMAD SALIH (1898–1968). This Sudanese political leader and businessman served for many years in the administrative service and was active in early nationalist movements. He was a part of the Sudan Union Society (q.v.) and was active in the formation of the Graduates Congress (q.v.). He was a political independent but usually worked closely with 'Abd al-Rahman al-Mahdi (q.v.). Shingetti was speaker of the Legislative Assembly (q.v.) and the House of Representatives in the first Parliament, elected in 1953. During the Ibrahim Abboud (q.v.) era he was actively involved in agricultural businesses and other commercial ventures. After the 1964 October Revolution (q.v.) he worked with the Umma Party (q.v.) but was not as directly involved in politics as before. He was nominated by Sadiq al-Mahdi's (q.v.) wing of the Umma Party to the Supreme Council but was not elected. He died returning from pilgrimage to Mecca in 1968.

SHUKRIYA. A great section of the Juhayna Arabs (qq.v.). They are concentrated in the Blue Nile and Kassala (q.v.) areas and are a major camel-herding Arab (q.v.) people. The fortunes and history of the Shukriya are reflected in the experiences of the leading Abu Sinn (q.v.) family.

SHUQAYR, NA'UM BISHARA (1863–1922). A Lebanese historian of the Sudan. Born in al-Shuwayfat, Lebanon, Shuqayr attended the Syrian Protestant College (later the American University in Beirut) and graduated with a B.A. degree in 1883. He spent his career in the Egyptian army, joining the Nile expedition in 1884, serving on the Sudan frontier until 1887, and working in intelligence after 1890. In 1891 he accompanied General H. H. Kitchener to Suakin (qq.v.) and witnessed the battle of Tokar. He helped to arrange the escape of Rudolf von Slatin (q.v.), a prisoner of the Mahdists, from Omdurman (q.v.) in 1895, and was awarded the title of Bey (q.v.) for his efforts.

On the basis of documents that he and Col. F. R. Wingate (q.v.) seized from the homes of Mahdist commanders and scribes after the battle of Karari (q.v.) in 1898, he wrote a history of the Sudan, entitled *Tarikh al-Sudan al-Qadim wa'l-Hadith wa-Jughrafiyatuhu* (A History of the Ancient and Modern Sudan, and Its Geography), published in 1903. An abridged version was issued in 1967 under the title *Jughrafiya wa-Tarikh al-Sudan.* The book was the first full history of the Sudan in Arabic and offered a shrewd analysis of the Mahdist revolution and its causes. Na'um Shuqayr published at least two other works. One, a history of the Sinai, entitled *Tarikh Sina'*, appeared in 1916. The other, a volume of Egyptian, Sudanese, and Levantine proverbs, entitled *Amthal al-'Awamm fi Misr wa'l-Sudan wa'l-Sham*, appeared in 1894, and was reissued in a 1995 edition prepared by the Sudanese historian Muhammad Ibrahim Abu Salim. [by Heather J. Sharkey]

SIDQI, ISMA'IL; SIDQI-BEVIN PROTOCOL. *See* BEVIN, ERNEST.

SIHR, AL-. The evil eye is a folk belief complex widespread in Northeast Africa and the Middle East. A person with the power can cause harm voluntarily or involuntarily merely by looking enviously, or praising, another person or his/her possessions. In northern Sudan among the Muslim Arab Rubatab, the *Sihr* (evil eye) is a speech event during which a speaker (*sahhar*) allegedly attempts to cast the evil eye on an object or a person by comparing them metaphorically to something else. While the victims of the metaphors attribute subsequent misfortunes to this casting of the evil eye, the *sahhars* claim to be merely entertainers, and not evildoers. Among the Shilluk (q.v.), people believe that the evil eye is something that can be inherited.

The Sudanese believe that evil forces can only be defeated by saying *"Ma Sha Allah,"* which literally means "This is what Allah willed!" The person who might otherwise be affected by the evil eye, by reciting this phrase, will resist the evil forces and release himself/herself from their power. In so doing, the person will find refuge with Allah while also suppressing the forces that might harm other people. A victim also might be protected by uttering a traditional expression, such as *"Ya 'Ayn Qaharik Allah."* This literally means, "Oh eye, Allah suppressed you." These words will ward off the evil eye or *sihr* through the force of Allah. Reciting some verses from the Qur'an, or saying *"Allahu Akbar"* (which, when used in this context, means "Allah is greater" and able to suppress the devil's work), plays the same role in protecting the person. [by Baqie Badawi Muhammad]

SINNAR (SENNAR). Sinnar entered history in the sixteenth century when it became the capital of the Funj Sultanates (1504–1821, q.v.). During this period it served both commercial and administrative interests in its trade with Darfur, Shendi, Suakin (qq.v.), and Ethiopia. When visited by

T. Krump in 1701 it was described as "one of Africa's most important trading centers, certainly the largest in the Sudan at that time."

Just before the Turco-Egyptian (q.v.) conquest in 1816, Sinnar was visited by Muhammad 'Uthman al-Mirghani (q.v.) who was looking for a home base for his Khatmiya (q.v.) religious order, but even by that time Sinnar had deteriorated very significantly. When it was occupied by Mahu Bey in 1821 it did not take long to realize that a better location and conditions would be found at Wad Medani and Khartoum (qq.v.) for the Turkish rulers. The old royal palace was derelict, and the mosque in bad repair. Turkish slaving interests kept some economic activity in Sinnar, but by 1860 its population was a mere 4,000.

In April 1882 the rising forces of Mahdism (q.v.) attacked Sinnar, which still supported the Khartoum government. In February 1883 the siege was lifted by 'Abd al-Qadir Hilmi, and General Charles Gordon (q.v.) was just able to send heavily armed steamers to Sinnar until September 1884 to collect grain and food for his hard-pressed troops. Even after Khartoum fell in January 1885, Sinnar was able to hold on for a few more months.

When the British returned, a completely new site for the town of Sinnar was established and old Sinnar awaits future archaeological inquiry. In 1919 the British began the construction of a large dam at Sinnar to control the Blue Nile and develop a water supply system for the cotton fields of the Gezira Scheme (q.v.). Once this project was in production a railway line reached Sinnar in 1929 for the export of cotton. By the time of independence Sinnar's population had grown to 8,600 people and by 1970 it was 26,000, giving it the highest rates of urban growth in the Gezira (q.v.) region. By 1990 Sinnar had certainly passed 45,000 inhabitants. Its position on the railway lines to the north, west, and east give it continued importance, but the all-weather road to the east only passes through Wad Medani (q.v.) and diverts a measure of potential commerce.

SLATIN PASHA, BARON RUDOLF VON (1857–1932). Austrian officer who served in the Egyptian and Sudanese services. After a varied military career he became an administrator in the Turco-Egyptian (q.v.) government in the Sudan. In 1879 he was promoted to governor of Dara province in southern Darfur (q.v.). The Mahdist (q.v.) revolt broke out while he was governor of Darfur in 1881, and in 1884 he surrendered to the Mahdists, having already adopted Islam (q.v.). For the next eleven years he served the Khalifa 'Abdullahi al-Ta'aishi (q.v.) as an attendant in Omdurman (q.v.). This was a position of considerable prestige, and it is clear that the Khalifa favored him; moreover, Slatin was apparently on close terms with many of the Ansar (q.v.), who knew him by his Arabic name of 'Abd al-Qadir Salatin.

Escaping from Omdurman to Egypt in 1895 Slatin went to work for the Anglo-Egyptian (q.v.) military intelligence. He repaid the Khalifa's trust by depicting him as an oppressive tyrant in his book *Fire and Sword in the Sudan* (1895), ghostwritten by F. R. Wingate (q.v.), which helped to incite popular support for a British conquest of the Sudan. After the establishment of Anglo-Egyptian control he was named inspector-general (1900–1914) and had great influence over policies relating to local affairs. Because of his Austrian nationality he resigned his post at the beginning of World War I and left the Sudanese government service. In his later years he softened his public statements about the Khalifa 'Abdullahi.

SLAVERY. In one form or another, slavery has been a feature of society in the Nilotic Sudan from earliest recorded times. The region was a source and supplier of slaves for successive civilizations from the ancient dynastic Egyptians, through Greco-Roman times, during the Christian kingdoms and Funj Sultanates (q.v.), and on to the Ottoman Turks. Slavery persisted in the early decades of British colonialism and has been renewed on a small scale in the context of the present civil war in the southern Sudan (q.v.).

Slavery as an aspect of Islamic statecraft began with the rise of the Sinnar and Darfur sultanates (qq.v.) in the sixteenth and seventeenth centuries respectively. During Funj times (1504–1821) some 1,000–1,500 slaves were sent annually to Egypt from large-scale slave raids (*razzias*) to the south and east of Sinnar. With the development of long-distance trade with Egypt and other territories, these states came to rely heavily on the services of professional slave soldiers to procure slaves for trading as well as domestic labor. "Nubian" (q.v.), i.e., Sudanese, slaves were a highly valued luxury commodity in eighteenth-century Cairo, and it is from this context that the West came to associate Nubians with slavery. The most common source of slaves for Sinnar and Darfur were the non-Muslim stateless peoples settled on the states' borders, especially in the Upper Blue Nile, Nuba Mountains, and Bahr al-Ghazal (qq.v.) regions. Slave raiding could be a large, well-organized affair, as in the case of Darfur, which exported slaves to Egypt over the trans-Saharan Forty Days Road (q.v., *Darb al-Arba'in*).

Reports from Lewis Burckhardt (q.v.), who visited Shendi (q.v.) and the Blue Nile in 1814, noted a brisk trade from Upper Nile (q.v.) and

Ethiopia to Shendi, which was the major regional slave trade center. His reports indicated that it was common for some 5,000 slaves to pass through that town annually. Ethiopians (especially women) were particularly valued. From Shendi they were shipped to Suakin (q.v.) for sea transport to Arabia and Egypt, or they were walked and shipped by river to Egypt. It was common for slaves to be sold and resold many times as they became more removed from their homelands and their prices steadily increased.

A majority of the slaves were under fifteen years of age and brought about $15 each for males and about $25 for females. Allegedly, few females left Shendi as virgins. Slaves showing some smallpox scars commanded a higher price. This feature assured they had had the disease and survived; it only strikes once. During the reign of Muhammad 'Ali (q.v.) about 150 slaves were exported annually to Egypt as eunuchs; in 1812 he sent out a special order for 200 eunuchs as a royal present to his associates. Slaves were widely considered non-Muslim (even with Muslim names) and they were treated as livestock or children; cases of manumission were rare.

Generally slave trading remained a sporadic and inefficient affair until the Turco-Egyptian (q.v.) conquest of the Sudan (1820–1822). In fact, one of the Egyptians' primary goals in invading Sudan was the acquisition of slaves to serve as soldiers (*jihadiya*, q.v.) in the army of Muhammad 'Ali. Though this plan was short-lived (most slaves succumbed to disease or ill-treatment before arriving in Egypt), the expansion of Egyptian control together with the exploration of the White Nile encouraged a new trade in ivory. This in turn led to greater slave raiding among the Nilotic and Equatorian (qq.v.) peoples of the south in Upper Nile and Bahr al-Ghazal as well as southern Darfur, the Nuba Mountains, and the Ethiopian borderlands.

While the trade in ivory soon proved inconsistent and unprofitable, the trade in slaves did not. European, Egyptian, Levantine, and Sudanese merchants quickly developed notorious reputations for their predatory slaving. Typical of slavery practices elsewhere, slaves often were used in a variety of ways. They could be bartered to pay wages (especially for the soldiers in slave raiding), be made as gifts, or loan collateral. Mainly they served as laborers, soldiers, or even as tax collectors for the Turco-Egyptian regime. Taxes collected by slave soldiers could sometimes be paid in slaves to keep this vicious cycle turning.

The business of procuring slaves for the Turco-Egyptian government and marketplace eventually became the monopoly of private trading companies. Based in fortified encampments (*zara'ib*, sing. *zariba*) throughout the Upper Nile and Bahr al-Ghazal, these provided valuable employment opportunities for northern Sudanese displaced by government tax policies. These included the feeder and transit towns of Deim Zubayr or Fertit, Fashoda (q.v.), and later Wau, and Lado (qq.v). Armed with huge private slave armies, they were almost impossible to resist. At least the Dinka and Azande (qq.v.) peoples, among many other victims of the slavers, were able to mount effective resistance and avoid being conquered.

By the end of the reign of the Egyptian Khedive Abbas (reg. 1848–1854), northern Sudanese merchants (*Jallaba*, q.v.) and Levantines began to take the place of Europeans in the trading companies. From the 1840s to 1860s the slave trade increased hugely with 40–60,000 slaves sold annually in Khartoum (q.v.). Two particularly notorious slavers were the Egyptian Muhammad Ahmad al-'Aqqad and Sudanese Zubayr Rahma Mansur (q.v.), who maintained their commerce with private armies of slaves and Danagla and Shayqiya (qq.v.) soldiers. Zubayr Pasha settled in Bahr al-Ghazal in 1856 and became a virtually independent ruler of the territory. In 1873 the government was forced to recognize him as governor of the province; one year later he conquered what remained of the state of Darfur.

Although the slave trade was officially abolished during the reign of the Khedive Muhammad Sa'id (q.v.) in 1856, it effectively continued in the Sudan until the end of the Turkiya (q.v.). The trade was fueled by the continuing need for rank-and-file soldiers in the armies of the Ottoman rulers and for use as domestic servants throughout the middle and upper strata of Ottoman society, in Egypt, and for export to Turkey. Their annual numbers included scores of castrated slaves for use as harem eunuchs. The castration was often carried out by Copts (q.v.) in Middle Egypt.

Two European administrators for the Turco-Egyptian administration, Samuel Baker and Charles Gordon (qq.v.), were employed in the 1870s to suppress the slave trade; both enjoyed only modest and temporary success. Bowing to necessity, Gordon revoked the earlier ban on slave trading during his last mission to the Sudan in 1884. The very political and economic support Gordon needed was from the major *Jallaba* slave traders he sought to control.

Before the Mahdiya (q.v.) Sudanese slaves performed agricultural and manual labor and domestic service, were hired out as laborers, and assigned as prostitutes. With the rise of the Mahdist state (1885–1898), some slave soldiers who had formerly served the Turco-Egyptians took up service with the Mahdists as *jihadiya*. These served effectively for the most part, though the Mahdist state's limited ability to procure new slave soldiers limited their military significance. Thus the practice of slavery continued but the export slave trade diminished, as the fate of the slave companies was disrupted with the Egyptian regime.

The Anglo-Egyptian (q.v.) conquest of the Sudan (1896–1898) was launched in part on behalf of suppressing slavery, and the Condominium (q.v.) Agreement of 1899 officially abolished the slave trade. At the same time, the new British rulers were mindful of their tenuous hold on power. Hesitant to disrupt the economy of the land, they tended to ignore most evidence of slavery, even employing government personnel to help recover "run-away servants." The occasional exposure of the continuation of slavery in the Sudan caused them no small amount of discomfort.

Sudanese independence in 1956 brought promises of socioeconomic progress and national unity and a brief respite from slavery. Nonetheless, the resurgence of civil war in 1983 led to a revival of acts of enslavement, usually by western pastoralists (armed by the Khartoum government) against their non-Muslim neighbors to the south. Accompanying the economic competition between these two groups is deep-seated antipathy borne of racism and fueled by the long history of the slave trade, xenophobic religious ideology, and cultural intolerance.

The general Arabic reference to southerners as '*abid* (slaves) by some northern Sudanese remains a painful insult that surfaced in the context of strife in the southern Sudan in the 1980s and 1990s. There are substantiated reports of persistent slavery in southern Kordofan (q.v.), Darfur, and other North-South borderlands. The documentation of slavery in contemporary Sudan was made in a report by Ushari Ahmad Mahmud and Suleiman Baldo in their account of the al-Da'in (Darfur) massacre of 1988, and the reports of slaves captured in the aftermath. This was brought to the attention of international human rights (q.v.) groups, such as the Anti-Slavery Societies of London and Boston and the UN Working Group on Contemporary Forms of Slavery. Reports of the revival or continuation of slavery, especially in war-torn areas, continued after the 1989 Islamist coup of 'Umar al-Bashir (q.v.).

In 1993 a UN Special Rapporteur, Gaspar Biro, was appointed to investigate these reports and he substantiated the charges of slavery. This was immediately challenged by the Sudanese government as "totally false and baseless." The government has contended that lawlessness is a consequence of civil war and that cattle raiding by the Nuer (q.v.) has been more common. Louis Farrakhan, leader of the African-American

Muslim group, Nation of Islam, defended Sudan against the charge of slavery in a visit to the country in 1995. The United States has been critical of the apparent tolerance of slavery in Sudan, but it did not change its fundamental foreign policy that continues to infuse aid to the victims of the protracted civil war.

Slavery's presence is justified by custom, not formally opposed by religion, and is tolerated as a by-product of war and historic hostilities. It is an embarrassing reminder of the inability or unwillingness of the government to eradicate it, while it is morally condemned by the outside world as intolerable in this day and age. Antislavery activities have been waged on behalf of Sudanese victims by numerous human rights organizations and concerned journalists.

SOCIALIST PARTY OF THE SUDAN. *See* SHIBLI, AMIN; SUDANESE COMMUNIST PARTY.

SOCIALIST REPUBLICAN PARTY (SRP). A small political party formed in 1951 by traditional leaders and moderate intellectuals. The SRP supported independence but feared a Mahdist (q.v.) "monarchy." It also opposed direct political involvement by the religious organizations. The SRP cooperated with the British and was believed by some Sudanese to have been, in fact, a British creation to help block the Mahdists and support the Khatmiya (q.v.) groups in the period just prior to independence. Its leadership included a number of important traditional and rural leaders. The SRP secretary was the moderate intellectual Ibrahim Badri. However, the party was opposed by the Umma Party (q.v.), the pro-Egyptian groups, and the religious leaders. In November 1952 the SRP made a tactical alliance with the National Unionist Party and Isma'il al-Azhari (qq.v.) to further its objectives. A failed effort by the Mahdists to link with the SRP supports the speculation that it might have been backed by the British facing a critical time in their colonial administration. It won only three parliamentary seats in the House elections of 1953 and none in the Senate. Soon after, the SRP ended its activity.

SOUTHERN FRONT. A coalition of southerners formed in 1964. It drew upon southern civil servants and operated within Sudan rather than in exile. It had three ministerial posts in the 1964–1965 transition government and won ten seats in the 1968 parliamentary elections. Front leaders included Clement Mboro and Hilary Logali (qq.v.). The Front was dissolved after the 1969 May Revolution (q.v.).

SOUTHERN LIBERAL PARTY. *See* LIBERAL PARTY; SOUTHERN PARTY.

SOUTHERN PARTY. A party formed by educated southerners just prior to the 1953 elections. It had broad support in the South, winning twelve of the twenty-two southern seats in the House of Representatives in those elections. In 1954 the party changed its name to the Liberal Party (q.v.).

SOUTHERN SUDAN. The Southern Sudan has been defined geographically as the historical three southern provinces, Bahr al-Ghazal, Upper Nile, and Equatoria (qq.v.), but has also included the border areas of Abyei, the Nuba Mountains (q.v.), and Ingessana Hills in recent peace negotiations. The question of self-determination, or the principle that the South has the right to choose whether it wants to be independent of the Sudanese nation-state or federated with it, was agreed upon in the 1995 Asmara Agreement (q.v.) signed by all Sudanese political parties except the Islamic National Front (q.v.).

The South was administered separately during colonial rule, formally from 1933 to 1956, with the Closed Districts Ordinance (q.v.) that forbade Arabic (q.v.) language or customs to be used in the southern provinces. Failure to achieve an independent Sudan in 1956 that fairly represented the southern region resulted in the first period of civil war from 1955 to 1972, when the Addis Ababa Peace Agreement (q.v.) ended the war and solved the "southern problem" by implementing a policy of regional autonomy for the South, along with other guarantees of regional self-rule.

The movement toward state Islamization (q.v.), from the 1983 September Laws (q.v.) to the 1989 Islamist coup d'etat, led to a revival of the civil war in 1983 and renewed calls for separation and/or self-determination for the southern Sudan. A federated Southern Sudan has become a major feature of the "New Sudan" envisioned by the National Democratic Alliance (NDA, q.v.) and the Sudanese Peoples Liberation Movement (SPLM, q.v.).

SOUTHERN SUDAN ASSOCIATION. A London-based organization of southern Sudanese formed in 1970. It published the *Grass Curtain,* a magazine that hoped to influence Western opinion in favor of the southern cause. It was associated with the Anya-Nya (q.v.) and was dissolved after the Addis Ababa Agreement of 1972 (q.v.). Its director, Madeng de Garang (q.v.), became a member of the new Southern Region High Executive Committee, which was created as a result of the settlement.

SOUTHERN SUDAN INDEPENDENCE MOVEMENT (SSIM). *See* RIEK MACHAR.

SOUTHERN SUDAN LIBERATION MOVEMENT (SSLM). The political wing of the Anya-Nya (q.v.) and the forerunner of the Sudanese Peoples Liberation Movement (q.v.) and Sudanese Peoples Liberation Army (q.v.). It was most active politically during the period prior to the Addis Ababa Agreement of 1972 (q.v.).

SOUTHERN SUDAN PROVISIONAL GOVERNMENT (SSPG). A southern political organization created in 1967. It basically replaced the Azania Liberation Front (ALF, q.v.) and was an attempt to bring together all the southern groups existing outside the Sudan. It opposed southern groups that participated in the Sudanese political system. Aggrey Jaden (q.v.) was president of the SSPG. The SSPG disintegrated by March 1969 due to personality conflicts and ethnic rivalries. It was succeeded by the Nile Provisional Government (NPG, q.v.).

SOUTHERN SUDAN WELFARE COMMITTEE. An early southern organization formed in 1946–1947 by Stanislaus Paysama (q.v.) and others. It was primarily composed of southerners in government services concerned about equal pay and opportunity with northerners.

SOUTHERN WOMEN'S LEAGUE. Organized in 1965 after the upsurge of political activity after the October 1964 Revolution (q.v.). All members were southern women (q.v.), many of whom were originally school mistresses, but by 1969–1970 the League made inroads among university students. Its founding leaders were 'Alawia 'Abd al-Farag, Hudda Zayn al-'Abdien, and Elizabeth Morgan. After Ja'afar al-Nimeiri's May Revolution of 1969 (qq.v.) announced the Ninth of June Declaration (q.v.) making peace and regional autonomy the professed solutions to conflict in the southern Sudan (q.v.), the Southern Women's League was absorbed into the national Sudanese Women's Union and became the Southern Women's Union in 1970. After the Addis Ababa Agreement of 1972 (q.v.), a desk for Southern women within the framework of Regional Government was established, which was comprised of Mary Sirsio Edrro as president, with other members including 'Alawia 'Abd al-Farag, Bothina Doka, Salwa Gibril, Sothan Abatrisio, and Victoria Ayar. *See also* WOMEN'S RIGHTS.

SPEKE, JOHN HANNING (1827–1864). Born in England, John Speke developed an early interest in foreign travel and adventure. His real fascination lay in the exploration and discovery of the headwaters of the White Nile. Joining Richard Burton (q.v.), who had similar interests, the two traveled to Somalia in 1855. In 1857 Burton and Speke departed from Zanzibar and penetrated the East African coast, reaching Lake Tanganyika after seven months. Exhausted but still eager, a sick Burton halted while Speke marched alone with his small party for three more weeks to the north, becoming the first European to see Lake Nyanza (Lake Victoria) on 3 August 1858.

Speke called upon his former army colleague, James W. Grant, to join a second trip in 1860 that was to travel around Lake Victoria until the Nile was discovered leading out. So sure were they of success that they sent an ivory merchant named John Petherick (q.v.) up the Nile to Gondokoro (q.v.) to await their exit on the White Nile with new supplies. On 17 November 1861 Speke and Grant entered Karagwe near the western shore of Lake Victoria, and later Speke discovered Rippon Falls and thus the outflow of the Lake.

From the Falls Speke traveled northward to reunite with Grant and slowly advance toward Gondokoro, which they reached on 26 February 1863. There they met Petherick as well as Samuel and Florence Baker (q.v.), who had set out from Khartoum (q.v.) southbound. The Bakers continued their travels southward into central Africa while Speke and Grant returned to Khartoum.

Burton had already published *The Lakes Regions of Central Africa* in 1860 and Speke followed with *What Led to the Discovery of the Source of the Nile* in 1864. A public debate in London on the source of the Nile was set for 16 September 1864, with each man making his claims. The day before the event Speke was killed in a shooting accident that raised allegations of either murder or suicide.

STACK, SIR OLIVER FITZ MORRIS LEE (1868–1924). Stack assumed office as governor-general of the Sudan on 1 January 1917 and, in only two years, the Egyptian revolution of 1919 provided Stack with a foretaste of turbulent events to come. These early days of colonial rule were essentially a highly centralized military administration in the cities and towns of the Sudan and an indifferent rural administration that had not yet evolved into Indirect Rule (q.v.).

The most significant event to unfold in the Sudan during the Stack governorship was the 1924 revolt organized by Sudanese officers and soldiers, which has come to be known as the White Flag League (q.v.). Sudanese protonationalists seized a number of strategic points in Khartoum (q.v.) and were awaiting reinforcements from like-minded Egyptians. At a critical turning point the Egyptians hesitated and the leaders of the revolt, 'Ali 'Abd al-Latif and 'Abd al-Fadil al-Maz (qq.v.), were killed. The revolt was put down in part by the military command of Sir Hubert Huddleston (q.v.).

Riots in Atbara (q.v.) by Egyptian workers and the pro-Wafd elections in Egypt in 1924 only further weakened the British position throughout the Nile Valley. By September, Stack was getting desperate to regain control of the resistance in both Egypt and the Sudan. However, on 19 November 1924 Stack was assassinated in Cairo. In the wake of the events in Khartoum, the British determined that although the failure of the Egyptian troops to join the revolt was decisive, the evacuation of Egyptian troops from the Sudan would be prudent to avoid further threats.

STANLEY, HENRY M. *See* EMIN PASHA.

STEINER, ROLF (1933–). German soldier who had been in the French Foreign Legion and was involved in a wide variety of military ventures in Africa as a mercenary. He was arrested in 1971 in Uganda and turned over to the Sudanese government to stand trial as a mercenary because of his alleged ties to Israel in aiding the southern Anya-Nya and their Anyidi Provisional Government (qq.v.). He was convicted and sentenced to death, but this was later commuted to twenty years' imprisonment. Steiner was released and deported from Sudan in 1974.

STONE, CHARLES POMEROY (1824–1887). An American Civil War veteran offered military service in Egypt under Khedive Isma'il (q.v.), who was aggressively expanding the Turco-Egyptian (q.v.) presence in the Sudan following the opening of the Suez Canal in 1869. Stone went to Egypt in 1870 to become the chief of General Staff of the Khedive and attained the rank of lieutenant-general. He survived the political turbulence of 1879 and continued in Khedival service under Tawfiq (q.v.), who replaced Isma'il. In 1882 Tawfiq faced the Ahmad 'Urabi revolt (q.v.), which was put down at the battle of Tel al-Kebir by the British General Garnet Wolseley (q.v.). Stone was outraged that the British had bombarded Alexandria with little warning, resulting in the deaths of many Europeans, but after the evacuation of British citizens. He returned to the United States in 1883 to resume his career as an engineer, which included his design for the foundation for the Statue of Liberty. [by Richard Skidmore and Richard Lobban]

SUAKIN. A fascinating but essentially abandoned town on the Red Sea. Its history probably dates back to Pharaonic times when New Kingdom pharaohs used this area in their trading and exploring missions along the Red Sea and to the "Land of Punt." The immediate hinterland was occupied by the Blemmyes (q.v.) from the very earliest times. In the Christian era Suakin's strategic location also attracted both Axumites from Ethiopia and their Sabaen relatives from Yemen.

The main part of the town is located on an island connected by a short causeway to the mainland. This was guarded by a fortified gate and could offer a good defense to the inhabitants, traders, and pilgrims to Mecca. For much of this millennium Suakin was the main point of access to the interior of Africa from Arabia. The famed Arab historian Ibn Battuta (1303–1377 CE) reported that the Sultan of Suakin had a Beja (q.v.) mother and a father who was the Amir of Mecca. Such notes help to place Suakin in its historical and social context.

Certainly by the thirteenth century, and perhaps much earlier, Suakin was also an important outlet for the export of slaves (q.v.) from the Sudan. It was faster to come down or across the Red Sea and enter the Sudan from Suakin than to go overland or upstream along the Nile. After the sixteenth century Muslim pilgrims from West Africa also came to Suakin on their way to Mecca. During the Ottoman rule in Egypt, particularly the reign of Sultan Sulayman (1520–1566), control was exercised over Suakin's shipping and commercial interests, especially that derived from the trade in slaves coming from Shendi and Sinnar (qq.v.). In later times Suakin would see merchants from India, China, and Portugal coming to purchase slaves, ivory, ebony, incense, gum arabic, and other goods.

In the early eighteenth century Suakin was a town of about 8,000 people and functioned as the main ocean port for the Funj Sultanate (q.v.) at Sinnar. But in the nineteenth century Sinnar collapsed, Turkish oppression was instituted, Red Sea pirates were active, and Suakin's merchant role was seriously undermined. The journal of John Burckhardt (q.v.) in 1814 noted Suakin's stagnation. In 1843 the Turco-Egyptian governor of the Sudan, Abu Widan Pasha, sought to make Suakin a direct tributary to Khartoum (q.v.). In 1857 increased freight traffic from the Alexandria-Suez railway in Egypt brought further improvement to Suakin's economy. A telegraph line was established in 1857 and in 1863 a regular steamship service connected Suez and Suakin. A post office was built in 1867 and railway routes were surveyed to Kassala, Berber, and Shendi (qq.v.), but no tracks laid. Formal authority from Istanbul was transferred to Egyptian Khedive Isma'il (q.v.) in May 1866, so that the Egyptians would have complete control of Suakin and nearby Massawa. This picture brightened further with the opening of the Suez Canal in 1869.

Ironically, the official end to the slave trade helped Suakin's economy as it made slaves more scarce, and the slaves who passed from Suakin to Arabia commanded a higher price. These "boom" years from 1857 to 1884 came to a halt with the rise of the Mahdiya (q.v.). General Charles Gordon (q.v.) was under Mahdist pressure in February 1884 when General Valentine Baker set out from Suakin to relieve the garrisons at Tokar and Sinkat from Mahdist attack. Only one third of Baker's men were able to return from the battlefield. The fall of Khartoum in January 1885 was followed by the removal of the civilian population of Suakin in July. British General H. H. Kitchener (q.v.) strengthened his defenses and repeatedly came under attack by the great Mahdist military tactician 'Uthman Diqna (q.v.). In 1888 Suakin almost fell under his close siege. Even when 'Uthman Diqna was captured in 1891 in Tokar, he soon escaped and resumed his attacks on Suakin. The economic life of Suakin was only that of a garrisoned town.

When Anglo-Egyptian (q.v.) rule was established in January 1899 under the Condominium Agreement (q.v.), it was only Suakin where the Egyptian flag flew alone; elsewhere the British and Egyptian colors flew together. The forty-year-old dream of a railway to Suakin was realized in 1905 and the population was rebuilt to about 10,500 with two Egyptian banks and a cotton ginning factory all making their contributions. However, this second very brief period of growth also demonstrated the geographical limitations of Suakin. The tiny defensive island harbor could not accommodate expansion and the narrow, coral-infested channel could not accept the much larger steamers of the twentieth century. A radical decision was taken in 1909 when construction began on a new town at Port Sudan. By 1920 many of Suakin's buildings had fallen down and the city was reduced to a desolate prison and pilgrims' quarantine station. At present hardly a building stands.

SUDAN AFRICAN CLOSED DISTRICTS NATIONAL UNION (SACDNU). *See* SUDAN AFRICAN NATIONAL UNION.

SUDAN AFRICAN LIBERATION FRONT (SALF). A southern political organization formed by Aggrey Jaden (q.v.) in 1965 following the
breakup of the Sudan African National Union (q.v.). Later in the year
SALF merged with the Azania Liberation Front (q.v.).

SUDAN AFRICAN NATIONAL UNION (SANU). A southern liberation
movement formed in exile during the Ibrahim Abboud (q.v.) period.
William Deng, Joseph Oduho, and Father Saturnino (qq.v.) were among
the organizers in 1962. It was originally called the Sudan African Closed
Districts National Union and changed its name to SANU in 1963. SANU
leadership split during and after the Roundtable Conference of 1965 in
Khartoum (qq.v.). At issue was the degree of compromise possible with
the Sudanese government. William Deng remained in the Sudan. His
SANU-Inside contested elections and won ten southern seats in Parliament in 1967 and fifteen seats in the 1968 elections, with its support concentrated in Bahr al-Ghazal (q.v.). In 1967–1968 SANU-Inside split into
factions led by William Deng and Alfred Wol. The murder of Deng in
1968 reduced the influence of SANU-Inside. After 1965 most of the
leaders of SANU-In-Exile formed the Azania Liberation Front (q.v.).

SUDAN ALLIANCE FORCES (SAF). The Sudan Alliance Forces is a
group of broadly based resistance parties and individuals that emerged in
the wake of the National Islamic Front (NIF, q.v.) coup in 1989. The
roots of the SAF are found within the trade unions (q.v.), professional organizations, secular students, and progressive military. Indeed, it was
this coalition that first emerged in the movement that brought down the
military government of Ja'afar al-Nimeiri (q.v.) in 1985. Many members
of the SAF are veterans of this struggle and regrouped in 1994 as a new
coalition with a similar purpose, but now are facing a military/Islamist
regime.

The SAF is a member organization within the National Democratic
Alliance (NDA, q.v.) and is committed to the overthrow of the Islamist
regime in Sudan and its replacement with democratic governance. Officially they call for the acceptance of a Bill of (Human) Rights, fair and
free elections, and the rule of law by an independent judiciary.

To further these goals, the SAF has engaged in armed struggle like the
allied Sudanese Peoples Liberation Army (SPLA, q.v.). While the larger
and older SPLA has waged war against the central government in the
southern regions, the SAF has fought along the eastern border of northern Sudan. Its military force is second only to the SPLA in size. Like the

SPLA and other forces united under the NDA umbrella, the SAF accepts the ultimate command of Col. John Garang (q.v.).

The SAF is governed by its own eight-person Executive Committee that is linked to the larger structure of the NDA, which, in 1995, united a still wider range of all Sudanese political formations, except of course the NIF. The Asmara Declaration (q.v.) of that year pledged all NDA members to a democratic, secular state that accepted the right of self-determination. The SAF specifically believes that two Sudanese nations at peace are better than one nation at war, as has been the case for most of the postindependence period. A four-year transitional period is envisaged by the SAF at which time the southern or other regions could freely determine their own fate and future, vis-à-vis their relation to northern Sudan.

The umbrella structure of the SAF also includes *Amal* (Sudan Future Care), its civilian charitable trust organization founded in 1996. Amal is responsible for legal, educational, health, humanitarian, and reconstruction projects in the areas it controls in the eastern Sudan and from its present headquarters in Asmara, Eritrea. In 1997, with military and political advances, the SAF added a Human Rights Monitoring Group to promote such concerns within the liberated zones. This was followed in 1998 with its Sudan Trust for Education, Rehabilitation, and Research to restore educational and food delivery services in the areas it controls in Kassala, Red Sea, and Blue Nile provinces (q.v.).

SUDAN BAR ASSOCIATION (SBA). The Sudan Bar Association was originally formed under Anglo-Egyptian (q.v.) rule, and was organized constitutionally in its present form at the time of independence in 1956. It has sought to play an important oversight role in postindependence Sudan, especially monitoring the protection of civil liberties and human rights (q.v.) during the predominantly military form of governance that has characterized Sudanese politics. It has tried to ensure the independence of the Sudan Judiciary under challenging periods of the lack of democracy.

In 1985 the SBA protested the charge of apostasy leveled against Mahmud Muhammad Taha (q.v.), leader of the Republican Brotherhood (q.v.), who was subsequently executed. The SBA argued that this was a flagrant violation of fundamental judicial principles. The SBA also opposed the imposition of the Islamic penal code, which it considered to be opposed to basic human rights. After the National Islamic Front (q.v.) seized power in June 1989 the SBA was dissolved and its assets confiscated. The SBA nonetheless continued its human rights activism, receiving the American Bar Association's International Human Rights Award in 1991.

SUDAN HUMAN RIGHTS ORGANIZATION (SHRO). The Sudan Human Rights Organization was established in 1983 by Professor Mohammed Omer Beshir (q.v.) as a branch of the Arab Organization for Human Rights (AOHR). Legally recognized by the Transitional Military Council under General Suwar al-Dahab (q.v.) in 1985, the SHRO continued to maintain a national membership and a great concern for peace, democratic rule, national unity, the right to religious beliefs, and other international human rights (q.v.) norms.

In response to SHRO human rights campaigns, Sudan ratified the International Convention on Political and Civil Rights, the International Convention on Economic, Social, and Cultural Rights, and signed the International Convention Against Torture. The SHRO launched a fearless campaign to repeal the "September Laws" (q.v.) of the Ja'afar al-Nimeiri (q.v.) government and played a significant role in the fact-finding committee following the massacre of Dinka (q.v.) people at al-Da'in, Darfur, in 1988. The SHRO also hosted the annual meeting of AOHR in Khartoum (q.v.) in 1988.

Banned in Sudan by the National Islamic Front (NIF, q.v.) government in June 1989, the SHRO relaunched its activities in Cairo in 1991 under the leadership of attorney Amin Mekki Medani to monitor human rights violations with the African Commission on Human and Peoples' Rights. Its founding members were Mutassim Hakim of the Democratic Unionist Party (q.v.), Hamuda Fath al-Rahman (trade unionist, doctor, and human rights activist), Zaynab 'Uthman al-Husayn (human rights activist), Mahgoub al-Tigani Mahgoub (q.v.), and Amin Mekki Medani (then president of the SHRO-London). The first board of trustees also included Abedon Agaw, Kamal Ramadan, Salah Jalal, Huriya Hakim, Mohamed Hassan Da'ud, Ahmed al-Sayyid Hamad, Muhammad Mustafa al-Hori, Suliman Bakheit, and Sayf al-Din al-Jami'a.

Chaired by Mahgoub al-Tigani Mahmoud, SHRO-Cairo spearheaded a popular campaign against NIF rule; published comparative research on Sudan laws and human rights, a book on trade unionism and human rights, and a book on torture under NIF rule, the *Sudanese Human Rights Quarterly*; and trained members of the National Democratic Alliance (q.v.), which adopted international human rights norms as a major source for Sudanese future governance. [by Mahgoub al-Tigani Mahmoud]

SUDAN MOVEMENT FOR NATIONAL LIBERATION. *See* SUDANESE COMMUNIST PARTY.

SUDAN PARTY. A short-lived political party formed in 1952 by Muhammad Ahmad 'Umar. Its platform was unique in that it called for an independent Sudan as a member of the British Commonwealth.

SUDAN POLITICAL SERVICE (SPS). Elite British administrative corps comprised of athletically inclined university graduates that ruled the Sudan during the Condominium (q.v.) period. Wielding absolute authority yet known for their integrity, highly paternalistic yet exceptionally dedicated, members of the Sudan Political Service embodied the great contradiction that was the Anglo-Egyptian (q.v.) Sudan.

Initially British administrators were drawn from military ranks, though as early as 1901 some few civilians were also recruited. Lord Cromer (Evelyn Baring, q.v.), the British agent in Egypt, conceived of a cadre of "active young men endowed with good health, high character and fair abilities." By 1905 a system of recruitment had been established. Members of the SPS (officially the "Sudan Civil Service") came mainly from elite public schools and Oxford and Cambridge Universities; most had graduated with second- and third-class honors; and most were "Blues" (i.e., recognized for athletic prowess): hence the Sudan's nickname as "The land of Blacks ruled by Blues." Given the distinction of its members, the SPS's reputation quickly equaled that of the prestigious Indian Civil Service.

The responsibilities of young SPS officers were enormous, especially given their limited experience, profound isolation, and vast territory to administer. Rarely did even 125 govern the entire Sudan at once, and less than 400 total were recruited. In the face of tremendous challenges they performed admirably; they may not, however, have been well-suited to confront the challenge of nationalism following World War I. Among their luminaries were Sirs Harold MacMichael and James Robertson (qq.v.), both civil secretaries. Many produced memoirs and important works of scholarship. *See also* INDIRECT RULE.

SUDAN STUDIES ASSOCIATION (SSA). Founded in the United States and officially incorporated in 1981 as an association to promote the scholarly study of the Sudan, the SSA's membership grew from a North American base to include international members from Africa, the Middle East, Asia, and Europe. The SSA has held annual conferences since 1981 and has published occasional volumes of selected conference papers as well as a quarterly newsletter. It has been the co-organizer of four international conferences on the Sudan: in 1988 with the Institute of African and Asian

Studies at the University of Khartoum (q.v.); in 1991 with the Sudan Studies Society of the United Kingdom (SSSUK, q.v.) and Institute of African and Asian Studies at the University of Durham; in 1994 with Boston University in Boston; and in 1997 with The American University in Cairo.

The SSA has cooperative relations with the University of Khartoum's Institute of African and Asian Studies and the SSSUK. The SSA has supported various educational and flood relief projects in Sudan, and with other Sudan studies associations has created a forum where Sudanese scholarship and debate can take place in a nongovernmental context, at a time when such freedoms have been curtailed in Sudan.

SUDAN STUDIES SOCIETY OF THE UNITED KINGDOM (SSSUK). Founded as a registered charity, the SSSUK began publication in 1987 of its official newsletter, *Sudan Studies*, first produced at the University of Durham's Department of Geography. Fittingly, the University of Durham houses the main archival record of the British colonial period in the Sudan. Scholars regard the Sudan Archive at Durham, founded by the late historian of the Sudan, Richard Hill, as the most important Sudan studies resource outside Khartoum (q.v.).

The main goals of the society are to promote Sudan studies in the United Kingdom and to disseminate news of Sudan in Europe, North America, and elsewhere. It has held annual conferences and cooperated with the Sudan Studies Association (q.v.) and the Institute of African and Asian Studies, Khartoum, in international conferences. It was the host of the second international conference on Sudan studies at the University of Durham in 1991.

SUDAN UNION SOCIETY. An early nationalist organization formed in Omdurman (q.v.) around 1920. It was a secret group containing men like 'Abdallah Khalil and Muhammad Salih Shingeiti (qq.v.), who were later important political leaders. It opposed the British administration and worked for Sudanese self-determination. Some members eventually left the Union and joined the more militant White Flag League (q.v.). Most of the Union's activities ceased as a result of the suppression of nationalism after 1924.

SUDAN UNITED TRIBES ASSOCIATION. An association formed by 'Ali 'Abd al-Latif (q.v.) advocating Sudanese independence. When he was jailed in 1922 the Association came to an end. After his release from jail in 1923, 'Ali formed the White Flag League (q.v.).

SUDAN UNITY PARTY (SUP). *See* DENG, SANTINO.

SUDAN WORKERS TRADE UNION FEDERATION (SWTUF). A congress of trade unions in Sudan formed in 1950 as an outgrowth of the Workers Congress of 1949. It was an activist in nationalist causes, organized many strikes before independence, and continued to represent militant and radical unionism after independence. The SWTUF came into conflict with the Ibrahim Abboud (q.v.) regime but survived the first era of military rule. Official government recognition was granted in 1966 but was withdrawn after 1969, although combined union action continued. The SWTUF had a long and close association with the Sudanese Communist Party (q.v.), especially through the long-term secretary-general of SWTUF, Shafi' Ahmad al-Shaykh (q.v.). His execution in 1971 formally suspended the SWTUF, but the trade union (q.v.) movement continues in various underground formations that are opposed to military rule.

SUDANESE ARMED FORCES—LEGITIMATE COMMAND (SAF-LC). A military faction formed after 1989 to oppose the Islamist government of 'Umar al-Bashir (q.v.). The SAF-LC is a member of the umbrella resistance organization, the National Democratic Alliance (NDA, q.v.), based in Asmara, Ethiopia. Like other member groups, including the Umma Party, Democratic Unionist Party, the Beja, Sudan Alliance Forces, and Sudanese Peoples Liberation Army (qq.v.), the SAF-LC is under the ultimate authority of SPLA leader Col. John Garang (q.v.). The late commander of the SAF-LC, General Fathi Ahmad 'Ali (d.1997), was the previous leader of the NDA Joint Military Command.

SUDANESE COMMUNIST PARTY (SCP). The roots of the Sudanese Communist Party were planted in the Sudan by at least 1944, although there was scattered activity by individual Communists before World War II. Possibly some of the junior officers in the Sudan Political Service (q.v.) had Communist leanings, though if so their influence can only be guessed at. Sudanese certainly had been affected by the earlier evolution of the Egyptian Communist Party, established in 1922. In 1945 a formal organization arose called the Sudan Movement for National Liberation, which was an offshoot of the Egyptian Communist Party. Later called the SCP, its base resided in the universities, schools, trade union (q.v.) movement, among professional workers, and Gezira Scheme (q.v.) tenants. Early Sudanese founders included 'Abd al-Wahab Zayn al-Abdin, the first chairman; 'Awad Muhammad 'Abd al-Raziq, the second chairman; and 'Abd al-Khaliq Mahgoub (q.v.), who became the SCP secretary-general in 1949 until his death in 1971.

During the 1940s and 1950s the SCP operated through various front organizations. It was especially important among students at Gordon Memorial College (q.v.) and Cairo University-Khartoum extension. A youth group was started in 1948, a Students Congress in 1949, and the Democratic Front in 1954, which contested elections through the Anti-Imperialist Front (q.v.). Although relatively small, the SCP was extremely well-organized and probably the largest Communist Party in the Middle East and Africa during its heyday. As such it played a significant role in the movement to achieve national independence in 1956. The party developed an orthodox, Moscow-oriented wing, led by 'Abd al-Khaliq Mahgoub, and a wing emphasizing local Sudanized Marxism.

After independence the SCP joined in opposition to the Ibrahim Abboud (q.v.) regime and played an important role in the 1964 October Revolution (q.v.) and the subsequent transitional government. Of the essentially northern parties, the SCP was also rare in recruiting among southerners. In the 1960s the SCP openly contested elections but came into conflict with the Umma-National Unionist Party (qq.v.) coalition governments. Since most traditional northern parties were founded among Muslims, the SCP was always a thorn in their side since it did not endorse a Muslim viewpoint and advocated secular rule. Even in periods of democracy the SCP had to fight for its political place in Sudanese Parliaments. Communist party influence during the 1964 October Revolution was reflected in subsequent elections when Fatma Ahmed Ibrahim (q.v.) became the first woman elected to the Sudanese Parliament, Ahmad Sulayman (q.v.) was elected from a territorial constituency, and 'Abd al-Khaliq Mahgoub was elected as an independent. A major constitutional crisis was formed in 1965–1967 in an attempt to outlaw the parliamentary participation of the SCP. In this, some members created a more broadly conceived Socialist Party of the Sudan (1967–1969), while others advocated operating underground.

After the 1969 October Revolution of Ja'afar al-Nimeiri (qq.v.) the SCP gained its most central influence. The policy of the SCP on regional autonomy for the South was adopted as the Ninth of June Declaration (q.v.) in 1969 and under the leadership of Joseph Garang (q.v.), minister of southern affairs and a SCP member, the path was open to the Addis Ababa Agreements of 1972 (q.v.).

The nationalist wing of the party, led by Ahmad Sulayman and Faruq Abu Issa (q.v.), cooperated with the new regime but the Mahgoub faction was less supportive. Mahgoub was arrested in 1970 and jailed for a time. The major crisis came in July 1971, when pro-Communist officers led by Hashim al-Atta (q.v.) briefly overthrew the government. As much as the 1969–1971 period had seen the SCP's greatest political strength, the post-1971 period proved to be its greatest catastrophe. In the aftermath of the coup hundreds of Communists were arrested, including Mahgoub and other long-time SCP leaders such as Joseph Garang and Shafi' Ahmad al-Shaykh (q.v.). After extremely brief "trials" they were executed along with the dissident officers, and the party organization was crushed for many years to come. After the fall of Nimeiri in 1985, the SCP, now led by Ibrahim Nugud, was able to resume its activities and participate in the democratic process, with Fatma Ibrahim resuming her legendary oratory.

As before, this period was short-lived and it was only from 1986 to 1989 that the party could openly and actively participate in the national elections. Three SCP members appeared in the new Parliament for the important debates of the time. As soon as the democratic process was interrupted again in 1989 by the military coup of 'Umar al-Bashir (q.v.), the SCP was immediately banned and top leaders were jailed.

Long accustomed to an underground existence the SCP was able to offer the Bashir government its strongest opposition in organizing protests and demonstrations. The underground periodic SCP newsletter *al-Midan* is circulated and read far beyond party members, although at great risk within Sudan under National Islamic Front (q.v.) rule. In November 1990 the new secretary-general of the SCP, Babikr al-Tigani al-Tayib, managed to escape from house arrest to flee to neighboring Ethiopia and then to Eritrea. There, the SCP functions as a member of the National Democratic Alliance (NDA, q.v.) against the Bashir government. In keeping with its long advocacy for the South, the SCP also gives critical support to many of the policies and positions of the Sudanese Peoples Liberation Movement (q.v.), which is also a central member of the NDA.

SUDANESE CONSCRIPT BATTALION (1863–1867). In December 1862 French Emperor Napoleon III requested 500 troops from Ottoman Egypt to assist him in his ill-fated attempt to established French control over Mexico. His own French troops had been decimated by war injuries and disease, especially yellow fever. Responding to this request the Egyptian authorities conscripted 446 officers and men from their slave reserves (*jihadiya*, q.v.), emancipated them by proclamation, "converted" them to Islam (q.v.), and quickly committed them to this novel military adventure.

The soldiers were of various southern origins including Shilluk, Dinka, Nuer, Jur, Bari, and Nuba (qq.v.). On 7 January 1863 the group departed from Alexandria for Veracruz, Mexico, with scores dying along the way. After rapid training they showed exemplary service with action at numerous battles. Additionally they served in defensive capacities (e.g., sentry duty and railroad guards) and with the mounted troops. Their general commander Muhammad al-Mas Pasha (d.1878) later became governor of Khartoum (q.v.) and his tomb (*qubba*, q.v.) is still a prominent feature of the city.

With a major counteroffensive by Mexican Republicans in 1867, the remaining members of the Battalion were evacuated from their Mexican service in March 1867, arriving back in Egypt on 27 May 1867. They had lost 133 of their original number. In the Sudan they saw further military service, especially in the late 1860s and 1870s in the southern Sudan (q.v.) as part of efforts by Samuel Baker and Charles Gordon (qq.v.) to curb the slave trade and establish Turco-Egyptian (q.v.) rule. Some also served in the exploratory expedition by American Col. Charles Chaillé-Long (q.v.) from 1874 to 1876. Later, others served in the Turco-Egyptian army against the Mahdi (q.v.) in the XII Sudanese Regiment in 1883, and at least two veterans supported the Mahdist cause. Many were killed in loyal service to Gordon during the siege of Khartoum in 1885 and in the fall of Kassala (q.v.). Though their service in Mexico was unique, the Battalion's experience as professional "slave" soldiers mirrors that of other southerners throughout the nineteenth century. Their story has come to wider attention through the work of Richard Hill and Peter Hogg in their book *A Black Corps d'Elite* (1995).

SUDANESE PEOPLES DEMOCRATIC FRONT (SPDF). Nuer (q.v.) faction formed in 2000 by the mercurial rebel leader Riek Machar (q.v.), who has supported and opposed both the Sudanese Peoples Liberation Army (SPLA, q.v.) and Sudan government since the 1990s. The SPDF initially sought arms from the SPLA, but later received support from the government. In early 2001 it was fighting progovernment Nuer militias and the Sudan army in eastern Upper Nile (q.v.), while in central Upper Nile it was fighting pro-SPLA Nuer forces. It is still unclear what, if anything, the SPDF stands for.

SUDANESE PEOPLES LIBERATION MOVEMENT (SPLM), SUDANESE PEOPLES LIBERATION ARMY (SPLA).

The SPLM is the major resistance movement based in the southern Sudan (q.v.) and neighboring Ethiopia; its armed wing is the SPLA. With the failure to continue the Addis Ababa Agreement of 1972 (q.v.) that ended an earlier period of civil war, the goodwill between North and South began to break down. This happened for a number of reasons: the discovery of oil in the South and a maneuver to channel profits to the North; the increasing political manipulation of the South by the Ja'afar al-Nimeiri (q.v.) regime; and a growing list of grievances on the part of southerners. Hostilities resumed on 16 May 1983 when soldiers of Major Kerubino Kwanyin Bol (q.v.) attacked government forces. In June further attacks were led by William Nyon Bany (q.v.) at Ayod. As a result Lieutenant Colonel John Garang (q.v.), then of the Sudanese Armed Forces, was sent to Bor to suppress a mutiny of southern troops who opposed their reassignment to the North.

These events preceded the introduction of the "September Laws" (q.v.) in 1983 and are considered a signal event in the second major round of civil war. Instead of crushing the mutinies, Garang encouraged other acts of resistance with himself at the head of a full-scale rebellion against the northern government. The SPLA was officially founded on 3 March 1984 under his leadership. Unlike previous southern movements the SPLA clarified at the outset that it was not a separatist movement, but that its role was the liberation of the whole of the Sudanese people from the "tyranny of military dictatorship," uneven economic development, and chronic civil war. Thus, the movement represented a new stage in the political development of the South, and the SPLM has attracted to its cadre some northern Sudanese intellectuals. Since the renewal of civil war the SPLA has brought under its control major regions of the southern Sudan, including the cities of Malakal in Upper Nile (qq.v.) and Wau in Bahr al-Ghazal (qq.v.), and has threatened Juba in Equatoria (qq.v.). The SPLM maintains an active radio service that is monitored in Uganda and Ethiopia and received in Khartoum (q.v.), and which has commented extensively on the unfolding political events in Khartoum.

In 1985 the Nimeiri government was overthrown after massive popular demonstrations in the North, but due also in no small part to the successes of the SPLA in the South. Garang eschewed meeting with the new government, since it was still technically a military regime under the command of Maj. Gen. Suwar al-Dahab (q.v.), although with a civilian prime minister. When Sadiq al-Mahdi (q.v.) was elected prime minister in 1986, his coalition government failed to successfully initiate talks with the SPLM, and his use of government-backed militias perpetuated the war against the SPLA, which may have reached a total force of some 12,500 soldiers. Also in 1986 the Shilluk leader Lam Akol (qq.v.) broke with the North and joined the SPLA. At least by 1988 the key SPLA leadership was solidly built around Garang, followed by Kwanyin Bol, Bany, Salva Kiir, and Arok Thon Arok (q.v.). Under this group commanders from various southern regions were also established. However, this watershed period of southern unity, from 1986 to 1989, did not last. The civilian leadership of the SPLM was still considered to be under the veteran southern leader Joseph Oduho (q.v.), but as the war continued the SPLA militarists steadily became the more influential body.

When the government of Sadiq al-Mahdi was overthrown in June 1989, the new Islamist regime at first refused to recognize or meet with the rebel group. The SPLM sees the fundamental issues between North and South as uneven economic development and a history of sectarian and religious bigotry. With the civil war estimated to cost the Sudanese people an average of one million dollars per day, SPLM-Sudan government talks are an essential prerequisite to Sudan's economic recovery. By 1989 the SPLA troops were better armed, much more experienced and motivated, and may have reached 25,000 soldiers.

The SPLM/SPLA was a signatory to the Koka Dam Declaration of 1986 (q.v.) and the National Democratic Charter of 1989 (q.v.) with all major political parties except the National Islamic Front (q.v.). The SPLM sees itself in alliance with all democratic opposition forces in Sudan. In the early 1990s the SPLA was recognized at an organizational meeting of the National Democratic Alliance (q.v.) as the major armed force of resistance, which could potentially mobilize 50,000 soldiers with the capacity to attack all southern provinces, southern Darfur and Kordofan (qq.v.), and eastern borderlands, in concert with such northern allies as the Sudan Alliance Forces (q.v.). However, by 1993 some southern elites, fearing marginalization within the SPLA leadership, introduced internal divisions and rivalries contesting Garang's leadership. Oduho and Bany sought a more civilian-based SPLM, while Lam Akol and the Nuer leader, Riek Machar (q.v.), had their strengths in the region between the White Nile, Sobat, and Nasir area. Kerubino Kwanyin Bol was based in the frontier zone of Bahr al-Ghazal and Arok Thon Arok found his supporters in the area around Bor.

This unstable mixture of regional and ethnic groups soon dissolved into further factionalism. In 1996 Oduho was killed in a failed effort to moderate the forces. In the same year Bany was also killed seeking a rival position for his Southern Sudan Independence Movement (q.v.) against the SPLA. Riek Machar and Arok Thon Arok shifted their allegiances to Khartoum in April 1996 when they signed a "Political Charter," but in February 1998 Arok Thon was killed in a plane crash in Nasir, which also took the life of Sudanese Vice-President Zubayr Muhammad Salih. This process of elimination has left Khartoum still backed by Riek Machar, Lam Akol, and Kerubino Kwanyin Bol, while the SPLA leadership under Garang appears relatively stronger with some forty battalions now under his command.

The military structure of the SPLA includes Garang in the top position with his chief-of-staff for logistics and administration, the Military High Command, and the Convention Organizing Committee. Under these bodies are other regional battalion and zonal commanders and alternates and an American system for the other officer ranks. The named battalions include the Abu Shawk, Bee, Crocodile, Eagle, Fire, Hippo, Kalashnikov, New Cush, New Funj, Nile, Nuba Mountain Task Force, and Tiger. These battalions have been mobilized for both offensive and defensive actions, mining operations, and ambushes as well as sieges of the provincial capitals.

Nominally the SPLA is just the armed wing of the SPLM, but in the context of widespread military engagement it is clear that the SPLA is dominant. The SPLM has ministers for political and foreign affairs, legal affairs, environment and tourism, and human affairs, as well as its own Central Committee and its liaisons with the Military High Command.

SUDANESE SOCIALIST UNION (SSU). The sole legal political party that functioned as the primary political apparatus of the Ja'afar al-Nimeiri (q.v.) regime and his "May Revolution" (q.v.). Established in January 1972 along the lines of the socialist unions in Egypt and Syria, its philosophy envisioned a single political organization based upon an alliance of workers, farmers, intellectuals, national capitalists, and soldiers. During its early years of development the SSU formed its own popular organizations, such as the Sudanese Youth Union and the Sudanese Women's Union (q.v.), and it fostered its own brand of single party democracy with a People's Constituent Assembly. Rarely did this Assembly disagree with Nimeiri's policies. By the time of its First National Congress in January 1984, it had organized 6,381 basic SSU units nationally, primarily at the village and town quarter levels. These community units sometimes initiated self-help projects, such as health clinics or schools, but with limited government support, as the SSU functioned primarily as a political entity. In the waning years of the Nimeiri regime, the SSU and the People's Assembly became discredited by their uncritical support of the increasingly dictatorial policies of the government. Consistent opposition also came from southern representatives. With the overthrow of the Nimeiri government in April 1985, the SSU came to an end.

SUDANESE WOMEN'S JOURNALISTS LEAGUE. One of the effects of the participation of women (q.v.) in the 1964 October Revolution (q.v.) was that each magazine and journal devoted a page or section to women's affairs, written or edited by a woman journalist. The League was organized in 1968, after being rejected by the national Journalists Union, and it promoted journalism by and about women until its dissolution in 1970.

SUDANESE WOMEN'S UNION (SWU). The Sudanese Women's Union, the first organized group of women, was formed in 1946 as an outgrowth of the Sudanese Communist Party (q.v.), with an eye toward the creation of the new Sudanese woman in an independent Sudan. The Sudanese Women's Union focused its early activities on organizing trade unions (q.v.) in economic sectors in which women were primarily employed, such as teaching and nursing, as well as on nationalist activities.

After independence, through the decades of the 1950s and 1960s, the SWU published its *Sawt al-Mara* (Voice of Women), where numerous issues relating to the political and social status of women were raised, such as polygamy, divorce reform, and female circumcision (q.v.). Suffrage was extended to women, not at the time of independence, but after the 1964 October Revolution against the Ibrahim Abboud (qq.v.) regime, when women openly and enthusiastically demonstrated for popular democracy. Fatma Ahmad Ibrahim (q.v.), a founder of the SWU, was the first woman elected to Parliament in 1965. The SWU was also influential in agitating for the reforms in the Shari'a (q.v.) law of marriage and divorce that took place in the 1960s and early 1970s.

With the coming to power of Ja'far al-Nimeiri (q.v.) in 1969, the women's movement achieved certain new gains and higher visibility in government, and initially the SWU was supportive of the "May Revolution" (q.v.). However, the gains for women were mainly confined to the appointment of northern Sudanese women to ministerial, judicial, and other official posts, and southern women were not included, despite the positive approaches the regime took regarding the resolution of the southern problem. Thus, the SWU grew increasingly critical and after July 1971 it was banned. Under severe repression, the original Union went underground, along with many other progressive organizations, and became the Democratic Women's Union. A new Sudanese Women's Union was organized as a branch of the Sudanese Socialist Union (SSU, q.v.), and its leaders, Dr. Fatma 'Abd al-Mahmud and Nafisa Ahmad al-Amin (qq.v.), became leading women figures in a variety of other posts in the political apparatus of the May Revolution and SSU. Thus the original autonomy and effectiveness were lost, and attempts to construct a national organization for women through the SSU foundered and devolved to traditional northern dominance and close alliance with the Nimeiri regime.

By way of consolation, Fatma Ahmad Ibrahim accepted a United Nations Human Rights Award in 1994 on behalf of the SWU for its consistent work in support of women's rights since the 1940s.

SUDANESE WORKERS TRADE UNION FEDERATION. *See* TRADE UNIONS.

SUDD. The large swamp "barrier" region in the southern Sudan (q.v.), mainly in the Bahr al-Jabal part of the White Nile. This huge flat area of swamp vegetation makes navigation of the river difficult without constant clearing activity. Early explorers and Arab slavers were often blocked by this protective barrier from the southern people. A project to drain the *Sudd* by digging the lengthy Jonglei canal (q.v.) has been advanced. The current war in the southern Sudan has suspended this huge project, which intends to penetrate the Sudan and divert additional waters to the northern Sudan and Egypt.

SUFI. The Arabic term for a Muslim mystic, one who seeks an ecstatic or personal experience of God. Sufi brotherhoods, originally derived from Turkey, mainly entered the Sudan from the northern and western parts of Africa. Some Sufi leaders established their own following or *tariqa* (q.v.), which could wield considerable political influence. The term Sufi is thought to derive either from the Arabic *suf* (wool), as many Sufi leaders wore woolen scarves or clothing, or from the Greek *salaf*, meaning wisdom. Sufi orders were instrumental in the political and social development of the Sudan in the eighteenth and nineteenth centuries, and Sufism continues to play an important role in Sudan through such *tariqas* as the Qadiriya, Tijaniya, Sammaniya, Shadhiliya, and especially Khatmiya (qq.v.). While Sufism shaped the character and movement of Muhammad Ahmad al-Mahdi (q.v.) in the 1880s, his Ansar (q.v.) followers of the twentieth century do not, strictly speaking, constitute a Sufi order.

SUGHAYARUN, MUHAMMAD, Al-. *See* AWLAD JABIR.

SULAYMAN, AHMAD. Sudanese lawyer and political leader who was an active member of the Sudanese Communist Party (SCP, q.v.), serving at times on its Executive Committee. He was minister of agriculture in the transition government after the 1964 October Revolution (q.v.) and was elected to Parliament in a by-election in 1967. He was the first member of the SCP to be elected to Parliament from a territorial constituency rather than the special constituencies assigned at various times for graduates. Sulayman became involved in a constitutional crisis when Sadiq al-Mahdi (q.v.) as prime minister worked to bar members of the SCP from Parliament. After the 1969 May Revolution (q.v.) he held a variety of cabinet posts, including minister of economics (1969–1970), of industry (1970–1971), and of justice (1971–1972). He was known to be part of the nationalist group within the SCP and disagreed with 'Abd al-Khaliq Mahjub (q.v.).

SULAYMAN SOLONG. Solong was the first of the known historical rulers of the Keira Dynasty in Darfur (qq.v.). He probably reigned between 1640 and 1680 and is credited with the formal introduction of state-supported Islam (q.v.) into Darfur. Little is known of his actual life or rule, but he, his son, and his grandson transformed their small kingdom into a multiethnic successor state to the Tunjur (q.v.) empire.

SYMES, SIR GEORGE STEWART (1882–1962). A former British governor of Tanganyika who became the governor-general of the Sudan on 10 January 1934. He replaced Sir John Maffey (q.v.), who had introduced an effective system of Indirect Rule (q.v.) or "native administration." Many had expected Harold MacMichael (q.v.) to replace Maffey as governor-general, so the arrival of Symes was not greeted with much enthusiasm by the now-entrenched and clubbish Sudan Political Service (q.v.). The Symes regime sought to introduce reforms and a merger of some of the top positions in the colonial government, and by 1936–1937 he elevated the position of civil secretary to greater stature. Native administration was considered to be functioning well and was little changed. As with previous governors, the South was treated with broad indifference. The merger of some provincial governments was not popular with those who lost positions, and Symes was reluctant to bring in Egyptian administrators despite the fact that this was projected in the Anglo-Egyptian Condominium (q.v.) and in the Anglo-Egyptian Treaty of 1936 (q.v.). Moreover, the Egyptians were providing a major part of the revenue for colonial rule and in the provision of Egyptian soldiers.

Sudanese members of the administration were rare, and their exclusion increased their frustration with the British colonial occupation. Symes' desire for great colonial autonomy in Cairo may have also played a subsequent role in shaping the Sudanese nationalist movement away from Egypt. This trend was easily seen in the formation of the Graduates General Congress (q.v.) in 1938. Meanwhile, the fears of a new Mahdist (q.v.) movement had abated and Symes saw that he could balance the political ambitions of the Khatmiya (q.v.) by relaxing restraints placed upon Mahdists. The regime mostly operated in the post-Depression era in which the Sudan gradually restored its economy, particularly in the productive Gezira Scheme (q.v.). Practical technological, agricultural, and educational opportunities for Sudanese did improve in this period.

By 1935 regional military matters related to World War II began to preoccupy Symes. He strengthened the Sudan Defense Force in various ways with expanded officer training, modest troop recruitment and modernization of military technology. He retired in October 1940 and was replaced by Hubert Huddleston (q.v.).

SYRIANS. Merchants and traders from the Levantine region of Syria (today, Syria and Lebanon) began arriving in the Sudan during the Turco-Egyptian (q.v.) period, playing important roles in the ivory and slave (q.v.) trade on the Upper Nile and Bahr al-Ghazal (qq.v.) in the 1850s–1860s. At least some Syrians served the Turkiya (q.v.) regime, e.g., Muhammad Ma'ni Bey, who was vice-governor of Khartoum (q.v.) from 1860 to 1870 and later governor of Khartoum until 1878; while another, Elias Debbas (1846–1927), introduced cotton ginning at Suakin (q.v.) in 1876. Syrians caught up in the Mahdist (q.v.) revolt of the 1880s bowed to circumstances and joined the Mahdi's movement, either at el-Obeid (q.v.) or after the fall of Khartoum. For the remainder of the period they supported themselves by trade or else served as clerks in the Mahdist regime. The Christians among them converted to Islam (q.v.), mostly of necessity, and they formed part of the "foreigner" community at Omdurman (q.v.) known as the Masalma (q.v.). At the urging of the Khalifa 'Abdullahi (q.v.), many took Sudanese wives; Syrian women, meanwhile, were highly prized as wives by the Sudanese for their "civilized" ways. When the British occupied Omdurman in 1898, they found fifty Syrians (including families) remaining.

The British effort to reconquer the Sudan had meanwhile been aided immeasurably by Syrians in the employ of the Egyptian Military Intelligence (EMI). Prominent among these were Na'um Bey Shuqayr (d. 1922, q.v.), who served in intelligence from 1890 to 1900 and later wrote an important history of the Sudan, and Milham Bey Shakur (d. 1911), who served from 1884 to 1898 and was assistant director of EMI from 1896 to 1898.

Syrians arrived in large numbers after the imposition of Anglo-Egyptian (q.v.) rule, filling the junior ranks of the Condominium (q.v.) administration during its early years. Particularly after the departure of Egyptian military doctors in 1924, most doctors in the Sudan were Syrians. These were almost entirely graduates of the Syrian Protestant College, later the American University in Beirut. Throughout the 1940s the government's Department of Finance was also heavily staffed by Syrians. Others pursued various trades, particularly in the Three Towns area and Port Sudan (qq.v.). A Syrian, Labib Juraydini (d. 1938), was editor of the *Sudan Times* newspaper from 1906 to 1925, while Aziz Kfuri (d. 1942) helped in the rebuilding of Khartoum in 1899 and founded the Sudan Chamber of Commerce. A Syrian community, comprised of Catholics, Orthodox, Protestants, and Muslims, thrived in Khartoum in the 1940s and 1950s, their social life revolving around a Syrian community club. All were given Sudanese passports during the Condominium period, as well as Sudanese Nationality Certificates after independence. The destruction of the Syrian community began with the Ja'afar al-Nimeiri (q.v.) regime's policy of nationalization in the 1970s, and intensified with the "September Laws" (q.v.) of 1983 and rise of political Islam. Few Syrians have remained in Sudan since the 'Umar al-Bashir (q.v.) coup of 1989. *See also* ATIYAH, EDWARD.

– T –

TABAQAT WAD DAYFALLAH. A biographical dictionary of Sudanese holymen (*fuqaha*) compiled early in the nineteenth century by Muhammed al-Nur Wad Dayfallah (d. 1809). The author was a Sudanese historian-jurist. The book is a primary source for the religious and social history of the Sudan during the Funj (q.v.) era. A partial translation into

English appears in Sir Harold MacMichael's (q.v.) *History of the Arabs in the Sudan. See also* FEKI.

TAFENG, EMIDIO. Southern soldier and political leader. He was a commander in the Anya-Nya (q.v.) rebel force. After the breakup of the Southern Sudan Provisional Government (q.v.) and its successor, the Nile Provisional Government (q.v.), Tafeng announced the creation of the Anyidi Revolutionary Government (q.v.) because of the disunity among the civilian southern political leaders. The Anyidi Revolutionary Government was soon absorbed by the Southern Sudan Liberation Movement of Joseph Lagu (q.v.).

TAHA, MAHMUD MUHAMMAD (ca. 1912–1985). A philosopher, religious leader, and prolific author who founded the Republican Party (q.v.) in 1945 and the New Islamic Mission or Republican Brotherhood (q.v.) in 1952. Taha was born into a devout family in Hijaleej, a small eastern Gezira (q.v.) village north of Rufa'a on the Blue Nile. He studied agricultural engineering at Gordon Memorial College (q.v.) and became a member of the Graduates Congress (q.v.). Taha practiced agricultural engineering in Kosti (q.v.) and the Gezira and grew increasingly interested in the politics surrounding the independence movement in the late 1930s and early 1940s. He founded the Republican Party in 1945 to move toward the establishment of a Republic of Sudan, rather than a monarchy or merger with Egypt. His first arrest was by the colonial authorities in 1946 for leading a demonstration to release a midwife who was detained for performing circumcision on a young girl. Taha's point was that the colonial authorities could not legislate morality and that morality would not change until women (q.v.) were treated as equals in society.

While major parties took over the independence movement, Taha became increasingly interested in modernizing Sudan's Islamic vision. He spent two years in isolation following his first imprisonment, a time in which he produced the outline for his major book, *The Second Message of Islam.* This book describes the difference between the earlier revealed Meccan texts of the Qur'an and the later revealed Medinan texts. The latter, in which most details of Shari'a (q.v.) and a circumscribed role for women are described, were considered by Taha to be temporal and to speak to the followers of the Prophet Muhammad at that time alone. Taha felt that it was time to follow the Meccan texts of the Qur'an in daily practice, in order to imitate the personal practice of the Prophet and bring the world to the modern place that God had intended.

Mahmud Muhammad Taha married Amna Lutfi of Rufa'a and had two daughters, Asma and Sumaya, and a son Muhammad, who died as a teenager. He conducted a national speaking campaign throughout the 1950s and 1960s, attracting a following of intellectuals, disaffected Sufis (q.v.), and exiles from other political orientations. Eventually more than 1,000 men and women were active participants in Taha's Republican Brotherhood. From a base in his home in Omdurman (q.v.), Taha provided the spiritual leadership for an organization that produced and published books on a variety of social and moral topics, engaged in speaking tours throughout Sudan, and lived communally to some extent in order to practice the social principles that he felt were at the heart of Islam (q.v.). In 1983 Taha directed a campaign against Ja'afar al-Nimeiri's (q.v.) imposition of the "September Laws" (q.v.) making Islamic law the sole state law in force. This resulted in the harassment of Republican Brothers in mosques and the eventual arrest of Taha and more than seventy of his followers, including four women. Taha was put on trial for apostasy in January 1985, convicted, and sentenced to death. He was executed on 18 January 1985. [by W. Stephen Howard]

TAHIR AL-MAJDHUB, AL-. *See* MAJADHIB.

TAJ AL-DIN AL-BAHARI. *See* QADIRIYA.

TAJA. The theme of a Sudanese woman who heroically stood up for her people during a crucial time has frequently repeated itself in Sudanese history. When the British invaded Darfur (q.v.) in 1916, Sultan 'Ali Dinar (q.v.) was given the choice between facing the invaders, who were well equipped with sophisticated weapons, or surrendering. He consulted his sister Taja, who became outraged and insisted that her brother must face the infidels. If men refused to fulfill their responsibilities, she threatened that women would take their place. According to Sudanese values this would be a deep humiliation for the men, because warfare is men's duty. Taja offered to exchange her clothes with her brother if he surrendered to the infidels. 'Ali Dinar faced his responsibility, and he was killed outside al-Fasher (q.v.), the capital of Darfur. [by Baqie Badawi Muhammad]

TAMBAL, HAMZA AL-MALIK (alt. TANBAL) (1898–1951). Tambal was a poet and literary critic born in Aswan, Egypt, to a family that had fled their native Argo, near Dongola (q.v.), during the Mahdiya (q.v.). He was educated in Aswan schools and then returned to the Sudan to serve as a government sub-*mamur* (i.e., district officer) from 1923 to 1932. Tambal is credited with having first suggested the idea of a distinctly Sudanese Arabic literature (q.v.) in a series of essays published as *Al-Adab al-Sudani wa ma Yajib an Yakuna 'Alayhi* (Sudanese Literature and What It Ought to Be) in 1927. His essays spawned a debate among early nationalists on the relation of Sudanese literature to the Sudanese national identity. He applied his ideas on Sudanese literature in an equally influential book of poetry titled *Diwan al-Tabi'a* (Nature Anthology) in 1931. [by Heather J. Sharkey]

TAMBURA (?–1913). A major chief of the Azande (q.v.), captured in the 1870s as a boy by slave traders who killed his father. He served in the Egyptian army and was rewarded by being sent back to his home country with arms. He fought Mahdist (q.v.) forces and established a broad area under his control in southwestern Sudan. Tambura recognized the superiority of European technology and cooperated with the French and then the British. This served to strengthen his own position in his kingdom. He was succeeded by his son Renzi. *See also* SLAVERY.

TARIQA (TURUQ, pl.). The Arabic word for "path" or "way." In Islamic society a *tariqa* is a set of devotional exercises established by a respected Sufi (q.v.) or mystic. The term is also used for the organization, order, or brotherhood of followers of such a respected teacher. *See also* KHATMIYA; MIRGHANIYA; QADIRIYA; SAMMANIYA; SANUSIYA; SHADHILIYA.

TAQIYA. The Sudanese have long considered head covers to be significant. These take different forms and designs that have religious, socioeconomic, political, and cultural associations. They also have different names: *taj* (crown), *imma* (turban), and *taqiya* (skull cap). Sometimes head covers may have accessories attached to them such as feathers, horns, and decorated bands. In addition, Cobra snakes, sun-discs, and stars are the motifs that ornament head covers and indicate specific status. These kinds of head covers are for deities, kings, sultans, shaykhs, and royal families. But common people usually wear a head cover made of cloth or plated grass that is known as a *taqiya*.

The *taqiya* has been known by the Sudanese for 4,000 years. The kings of the Kushite dynasties wore a version of the *taqiya*. Among the characteristics of this *taqiya* is that it covered all of the forehead. A band decorated with a cobra shape centered the front. The *taqiya* worn by the Nubian Christian kings of the Middle Ages was known as the *taqiya umm qarnayn* ("*taqiya* with two horns"). It had the shape of a ram's head, which resembles the god Amun. The horn motif continued to be used by the Funj Sultans of Sinnar and the 'Abdallab (qq.v.) shaykhs, and evidence of its use by Sudanese leaders is found as late as the nineteenth century during the Mahdiya (q.v.).

The *taqiya* is also significant from a Sufi (q.v.) perspective. It is a symbol of spiritual status, and when the Sufi lost his *taqiya*, his rank was endangered. The *taqiya* for the Sufi is like a shield that prevents him from being consumed by Allah's power.

The common *taqiya* is worn for religious and social purposes. It is decorated with embroidery, and the decorations are characterized by three main properties: repetition, similarity, and variety. There are several common colors: white, red, orange, and green. These colors are a manifestation of the concept of color as it appears in other aspects of the cultural heritage of Sudanese life. [by Baqie Badawi Muhammad]

TAYYIB, 'ABDALLAH, AL-. *See* 'ABDALLAH AL-TAYYIB.

THREE TOWNS. The Three Towns area is composed of Khartoum (q.v.), the capital, Khartoum North (q.v.), an industrial and residential area, and Omdurman (q.v.), the commercial city and Islamic center. It is located at the confluence (*mogren*) of the White and Blue Niles. More specifically, Khartoum is at the northern tip of the Gezira (q.v.), Khartoum North borders the Blue Nile and east bank of the Nile proper, and Omdurman is on the west bank of the Nile proper. Amidst this conurbation is Tuti Island, an old residential and agricultural settlement of Mahas Nubians (q.v.). Khartoum was the Sudan's capital during the Turkiya (q.v.), while Omdurman served as the capital during the Mahdiya (q.v.), and in 1898 the British rebuilt Khartoum as the capital of the Anglo-Egyptian (q.v.) Sudan. The new Khartoum was a planned city, designed with specific quarters and laid out in regular blocks in a series of "Union Jack" shapes to facilitate Britain's tenuous control over the newly conquered territory. Omdurman on the other hand had evolved rapidly around family and ethnic neighborhoods, all radiating out from a center that contained the Mahdi's tomb (*al-Qubba*, qq.v.), Khalifa's (q.v.) house, and main mosque.

Today, the Three Towns represent around 7–10 percent of the national population, yet this is where 50 percent of all doctors, 70 percent of the consumption of electricity, and 70 percent of national industry are concentrated. Estimates for the late 1980s suggest a total population of well over a million and a half, with some 500,000 in each of the three towns. Without accurate census data we must rely on the estimates of demographers and aid workers, who have suggested a total population of anywhere from two and a half to over three million. In any case, the Three Towns is clearly the most heavily populated area in the country.

The technological base of the Three Towns is the most advanced in Sudan, and printing, light manufacture, repair, and processing industries can all be found there. Trade for most of the country passes through the capital area, which controls virtually all of Sudan's commerce. Moreover, since independence in 1956 the Three Towns have experienced unprecedented growth. The recent expansion of slum and squatter housing and a rise in upper-class housing points to the fact of growing socioeconomic distinctions. Residential patterns by class are incorporated into the zoning systems of the major towns. The core areas of these cities have evolved to include the businesses and markets and some higher-class residential units. At the peripheries of the towns there is the greatest horizontal growth of both working-class and upper-class housing. A sector of the urban population also includes teachers, professionals, and technicians, but there are more rapidly increasing numbers of poorer workers and large numbers of refugees (q.v.).

Although there is a multiethnic component in urban life, those close to the center of power are primarily of riverine Arab (q.v.) groups. Arabs of Egyptian, Lebanese, and Syrian (q.v.) descent also predominate in these sectors of the commercial elite, in association with certain Greek (q.v.) and Italian families that are also involved in commerce. English, French, American, German, eastern European, and Asian commerce is usually handled through governmental and banking offices or through Sudanese agents. A marginal foreign community of teachers, technical advisers, and diplomatic staff occupies the better housing, but these people are usually self-contained in their social lives. Southern Sudanese are conspicuously absent from the upper socioeconomic levels of the urban areas.

The Three Towns area in general has been the center for national political and military activities, be they the anticolonial revolt of the White Flag League (q.v.) in 1924, or coups in 1958, 1969, and 1989, or popular revolts against military governments in 1964 and 1985. Khartoum's importance, as the center of government and military command, is obvious. Omdurman, meanwhile, contains not only Parliament but also, more significantly, the national marketplace and popular capital. Associated with the Mahdiya of the nineteenth century and early nationalist activity (e.g., Graduates Club, q.v.) of the twentieth, Omdurman has come to symbolize Sudanese national aspirations to a broad range of people, Khatmiya as well as Ansar (qq.v.), southerners as well as northerners.

Population Changes in the Three Towns

Year	Khartoum	Khartoum North	Omdurman
1800	small hamlet	small hamlet	small hamlet
1840(a)	30,000	——	——
1862(a)	30,000	——	——
1870(a)	20,000	——	——
1887(b)	evacuated	——	c. 250,000
1925(a)	32,211	——	——
1930(a)	50,463	——	103,569
1934(a)	46,776	——	110,959
1950(c)	62,000	31,000	——
1955(d)	95,493	40,187	116,231
1964(d)	185,398	81,654	192,925
1969(e)	244,482	118,105	244,588
1973(f)	333,921	150,991	299,401
1983(d)	476,000	341,000	526,000
1990(g)	600,000	480,000	700,000

Sources: a) Hamdan 1960; b) Kramer 1991; c) Hodgkin 1951; d) Sudan Census; e) Bushra 1972; f) Provisional 1973 Sudan Census; g) Lobban projection. *See also* URBANIZATION.

TIGANI, MAHGOUB MAHMOUD AL-. This Sudanese sociologist and demographer was a founding member of the Sudan Human Rights Organization (SHRO, q.v.) and elected president of SHRO-Cairo in 1991. After exile in The Gambia where he was head of the research unit of the African Centre for Democracy and Human Rights (1991–1994), his exile continued in Cairo until he was granted political asylum in the United States.

While in Cairo he worked closely with the National Democratic Alliance (q.v.) and with the Sudanese Armed Forces-Legitimate Command (q.v.). Tigani has published works in Arabic and English on human rights (q.v.) issues and has translated a number of scholarly works on Sudan from English into Arabic.

TOM, 'ALI AL- (1874–1938). A leading *shaykh* and *nazir* (qq.v.) of the Kababish Arabs (qq.v.), whose family had been opponents of the Mahdiya (q.v.). He was one of the most influential notables in the Condominium (q.v.) era and was knighted by Britain's King George V in 1925. The British policy of Indirect Rule (q.v.) helped him unify the Kababish. He was succeeded by his son, al-Tom 'Ali al-Tom (1897–1945), and his family continues to have influence in local and national politics.

TOPOSA (TOPOTHA, AKARA, KARE, KUMI). An ethnic group of Equatoria (q.v.) in the extreme southeastern Sudan, who number approximately 100,000 according to a 1984 estimate. They are found alongside the Singaita, Lokalyen, and Loyooro rivers. The Toposa migrate east to Moruangipi and into the Ilemi Triangle at the Ethiopian border when seeking land for their cattle, but they have only nomadic cattle camps in these easterly locations. Their linguistic relatives and territorial neighbors, the Jie, live farther north.

The eastern Toposa and Jie are closely related to the Turkana, while the western Toposa are linked linguistically to the Karamajong, with whom they have a nonaggression treaty. The relations between the western Toposa and the Jie living in Sudan are often hostile, as is their relationship with the Turkana and Murle-Didinga peoples.

Because of isolation and intergroup rivalries over cattle-herding territories, each of these groups has a strongly developed identity including a high incidence of monolingualism, which is overcome to a limited degree by creolized Arabic.

TOSKHI. *See* TUSHKI.

TRADE. *See* ECONOMY.

TRADE UNIONS. The history of the Sudanese trade union movement may be said to have started in the mid-1930s in response to demographic transformations and capitalist economic development under British colonialism. Workers' clubs began in some of the railway towns like Atbara and Khartoum (qq.v.). These railway workers' clubs formed the basis of the Sudan Railway Workers' Union (SRWU) and the Workers' Affairs Association (WAA), which was established in 1946, the same year as the founding of the Sudanese Communist Party (SCP, q.v.). The colonial government faced a major challenge that year with a strike of the Gezira Scheme (q.v.) tenants union.

On 9 July 1947 the WAA organized another demonstration resulting in the arrest of sixty leaders, which, in turn, stimulated a strike by all railway workers. At the conclusion of the strike on 18 July 1947 the WAA became officially recognized. In January and April 1948 the WAA called more strikes and forced the colonial government to set up a wage study commission.

In the late 1940s the British published a Trade Union Ordinance that granted legal recognition to properly registered trade unions; several union groups did receive recognition at this time. By 1950 the WAA had evolved into the Sudanese Workers Trade Union Federation (SWTUF) but it was denied full legal status, no doubt because of its constitutional opposition to imperialism and to the goal of achieving self-determination. At first the SRWU was not a member of the SWTUF but later brought its influential membership into the federation. As the nationalist fervor grew, a United Front for the Liberation of the Sudan was set up, thereby providing a structure in which the SWTUF played a militant and leading role. The SCP-backed Movement for the National Liberation cooperated with the SWTUF and also added considerable political orientation.

After assisting in the achievement of national independence the trade unions were kept at the periphery of governmental policy making, but they continued to reflect the working-class outlook of the membership of industrial and manual workers. Pushed from the center of the political arena, the trade unions formed a left opposition to the other parties. The stance of left opposition of the SWTUF was reinforced by the SCP influence, which opposed crossing class lines in the political struggle. Not only did this ideology stress union autonomy, but also such parties of the traditional elite like the Umma (q.v.) essentially ignored the trade union movement.

Even though the SWTUF had formed in 1950 it was not until 1957, one year after independence, that the legal right to form trade union federations was granted. At this time there were two main labor federations: one was the International Confederation of Free Trade Unions (ICFTU), which was pro-West, and the other was the SWTUF, which maintained links with the prosocialist World Federation of Trade Unions (WFTU). The SWTUF influence and size was much greater than that of the ICFTU and was no doubt related to the leadership of Shafi' Ahmad al-Shaykh (q.v.) as its secretary-general.

This period of legality also saw the emergence of the Sudan Government Workers Trade Union Federation (SGWTUF), which successfully applied for legal registration while the SWTUF fought a continual court battle to prevent its being banned altogether. By 1958 some 160 workers' and employers' unions had been registered but most had fewer than 100 members. Alarmed by this active labor organizing, a Western-backed military junta led by General Ibrahim Abboud (q.v.) seized power in November 1958 and promptly suspended trade unions and the right to strike. The SWTUF offices were raided, its newspaper was suspended, and several leaders were placed under arrest. The SWTUF organization was transferred overseas to continue its publications and one SWTUF member, Ibrahim Zakaria, became a secretary for the WFTU. Although illegal, protests continued and in 1960 General Abboud introduced his own Trade Union Ordinance, which was similar to that of the British except that its provisions were more restrictive and were aimed particularly at the SWTUF by prohibiting all federations of trade unions and banning the SGWTUF. The remaining legal unions were compelled to register with the Ministry of Information and Labor. Another special provision prohibited unionization in firms of less than fifty workers, thus excluding almost 60 percent of all workers from trade union representation.

Repressive policies forced the labor movement underground and ultimately made it more difficult to control. The 1961 strike of railway workers protested the military junta's rejection of the call for a return to civilian rule. The massive and better coordinated demonstrations in 1964 again cut off Khartoum (q.v.) and were this time successful in toppling the military government in alliance with university students and other forces. The fall of General Abboud brought SWTUF Secretary General Shafi' Ahmad al-Shaykh to a ministerial rank and he was made chief representative of the workers' movement.

In 1965 a right-wing government was elected and the trade unionists were returned to their position at the periphery as a political opposition and focal point of workers' discontentment and alienation. In May 1969 the military junta of Ja'afar al-Nimeiri (q.v.) came to power and its initial leftward orientation gained it a large measure of support from the SWTUF. Policy differences in Nimeiri's Revolutionary Command Council in late 1970 resulted in a rift and a rightward drift of the government until the abortive July 1971 coup, which, during its three days of power, saw huge worker demonstrations in the capital city. The collapse of this ill-fated effort sent the trade union movement deep into the underground except for the labor bodies that are currently recognized by the Ministry of Labor. In short, since independence the trade union movement has had only a few years of full legality. *See also* URBANIZATION.

TRADE UNION FOR WOMEN. Established originally as a union of school mistresses in 1949, it developed into the first trade union (q.v.) of women (q.v.) in 1953. While still under colonial rule it agitated for equality in wages, promotion, and pension rights with male teachers. The union also demanded greater opportunities for women to study abroad. Although harassed, members continued their work until the union was abolished, with all other popular organizations, during the Ibrahim Abboud (q.v.) regime in 1959. During the 1964 October Revolution (q.v.) the union was active and after the revolution the Women Teachers' Trade Union joined with the Teachers' Trade Union to form one body.

TRIAD. A Saudi Arabian-based company with substantial investments in Sudanese agricultural and industrial development.

TUMBURA. *See* ZAR.

TUNGUR. The Tungur arrived in northern Darfur (q.v.) in about the fourteenth century and spread west into Wadai. It is not clear whether they were Arabized Berbers, Nubian (q.v.) refugees, related to the Daju (q.v.), or perhaps "Africanized" Danagla (q.v.). In any case, they intermarried or replaced the Daju whom they came to rule. They accepted Islam (q.v.), but relatively late. Their territory was based in northern Darfur with clashes and claims to control Wadai and Kanem. Sometime after 1600 the last leader of the Tungur, Ahmad al-Ma'qur (q.v.), was replaced by the Keira dynastic line of Fur (qq.v.) sultans.

AL-TURABI, HASAN (1932–). Dr. Hasan al-Turabi was a prominent leader and prime mover behind the Sudanese Muslim Brotherhood (q.v.) and the chief architect of its political descendant, the National Islamic Front (NIF, q.v.), which has in effect ruled the Sudan from 1989 to the present. His association with the Muslim Brotherhood began in his student years when he was the leader of its university branch, and he guided many changes in the direction of this Islamist movement.

Turabi was born in Kassala (q.v.) in 1932 and is a descendant of a famous eighteenth-century religious scholar, Shaykh Hamad al-Turabi. He first studied Islam (q.v.) with his father, Shaykh 'Abdullah al-Turabi, who was a judge in Sudan for thirty years. Turabi graduated from the University of Khartoum (q.v.) in 1955 with a B.A. in law, pursued a Master's degree in law in London in 1957, and later earned his Ph.D. from the Sorbonne in Paris in 1962. His activism as a Muslim Brotherhood leader and spokesman caused him to be in and out of favor with various Sudanese governments over the decades. He was elected to Parliament after the 1964 October Revolution (q.v.) as a Muslim Brotherhood candidate, but later arrested in 1970 and spent the next seven years in and out of prison.

Turabi served as dean of the Faculty of Law of the University of Khartoum, and was appointed attorney general in 1979 during the Ja'afar al-Nimeiri (q.v.) regime while it was experimenting with various ways of Islamizing law and government in Sudan. He served in that key position until 1982 while also acting as an adviser to Nimeiri. He was a member of the Sudan Socialist Union (q.v.) politburo during the Nimeiri years from 1977–1985. With the overthrow of the Nimeiri regime by a combination of popular protest and military coup d'etat, Turabi and the Muslim Brotherhood were stigmatized to a degree, due to their collaboration with Nimeiri during the last years of his rule. Seeing an opportunity in the new power vacuum, Turabi founded the National Islamic Front in April 1985. The strategy worked and the NIF emerged as the third strongest party, after the traditional parties, the Umma and Democratic Unionist Party (qq.v.), in the 1986 elections.

Emboldened, the NIF under Turabi's leadership sought the very center of power. However, the leader of the Umma Party, Sadiq al-Mahdi (q.v.), emerged as prime minister and the NIF was excluded from the new government. That government collapsed in 1988 and the NIF joined the government formed in July, with Turabi as attorney general and minister of justice. The NIF continued its push to Islamize basic institutions, including continuing to implement the Shari'a (q.v.) as the sole law in force in Sudan. The period of democracy from 1985 ended in 1989 when the government of Sadiq al-Mahdi was overthrown by General 'Umar Hasan al-Bashir (q.v.) in June. Turabi is widely regarded as having played key roles in both the planning of the 1989 coup as well as the subsequent Islamist direction that the Bashir government took.

Turabi had no official role in the regime until he became the speaker of the National Council of the regime. Nonetheless, he has long been its leading exponent and theoretician. Since 1989 he has traveled extensively outside of Sudan, including trips to Islamic conferences in Algeria and elsewhere. He traveled on an ill-fated trip to the United Kingdom and North America in 1992, where many of his appearances were met with protests by Sudanese exiles and human rights (q.v.) activists. His testimony before the U.S. Congress was met with hostile questioning, and he was physically assaulted in Toronto by an angry Sudanese in exile.

Turabi remains a controversial figure. He is regarded as an original and innovative thinker and a charismatic leader among his own supporters inside and outside Sudan, and his writings in Arabic have been widely read and translated into many languages. Meanwhile his critics revile him as an opportunist, terrorist, and political extremist, charging that he has ruthlessly purged Sudan's governmental institutions of opposition. Even within the ruling Islamist government in Khartoum he has fallen in and out of favor: after considerable parliamentary maneuvering to increase his power vis-à-vis the president in 2000, Turabi was placed under arrest in Kober prison in Khartoum North (q.v.) in early 2001 by the Bashir regime, which sought to charge him with "inciting hatred against the state" and sedition. Both counts are punishable by death or life imprisonment. Certainly his future is uncertain, but this has been the hallmark of his career since its inception. *See also* ISLAMIZATION.

TURCO-EGYPTIAN REGIME. *See* TURKIYA.

TURKIYA. The name given to the Turco-Egyptian regime ruling the Sudan from 1821 to 1881, as well as the period of Turco-Egyptian rule. It was Egyptian in the sense that the Sudan was formally ruled by the governor of Egypt, and it was Turkish in the sense that Egypt itself was still formally a part of the Ottoman Turkish Empire. Turco-Egyptian personnel were drawn from a variety of countries, including the Ottoman Empire (Turks, Egyptians, Armenians, Circassians), Britain, Austria, Italy, and America. In popular usage, the term has at times been used for any foreign regime in the modern era.

This historical period can be said to mark the beginnings of the modern Sudan, in the sense that its foreign rule (and Sudanese resistance to it) helped to forge a sense of national identity. Together with its collaborator and successor colonial power, Great Britain, these foreign powers drew the boundaries of what would become the modern nation-state of Sudan.

The Turkiya was ushered in with the invasion of northern Sudan in 1821 by the Ottoman armies of Muhammad 'Ali (q.v.) under the command of his son, Isma'il Kamil Pasha (q.v.), which struck at Dongola (q.v.), driving out the last of the Mamluks. It reached as far south as Sinnar (q.v.) in the same year and encountered the strongest resistance among the Shayqiya (q.v.). The last Sultan of the Funj (q.v.), Badi VI, submitted to this armed invasion in June 1821.

A second army, under Muhammad Bey Khusraw, "the Daftardar" (q.v.), struck southwest and conquered Kordofan (q.v.), but was unable to bring Darfur (q.v.) under Turkish rule. The invasion of the Sudan was undertaken for the usual reasons, the promise of gold, slaves (q.v.), gum arabic, and livestock, all of which contributed to the empire. The recruits for Muhammad 'Ali's army were typically Sudanese slaves from the non-Muslim regions who were trained at Manfalut in Upper Egypt from as early as 1823. The heavy taxation of subjects, characteristic of Turkish rule, was frequently paid in slaves by free Muslim Sudanese. A high mortality rate and frequent episodes of resistance by the Sudanese slave-soldiers (*jihadiya*, q.v.) led Muhammad 'Ali to recruit among the Egyptian peasantry, whose reaction was bitterness and unrest, but without the same consequences as the Turks encountered in the Sudan.

The Turkiya brought to the Sudan its first interregional government bureaucracy that was staffed by some Turkish-speaking officials, but largely run by Arabic-speaking locals. Fiscal administration was entrusted to Copts (q.v.), with forty Coptic clerks being sent to the Sudan in 1839. Long staple cotton, introduced from the Sudan into Egypt, became a significant export, and the empire secured a regional monopoly on this trade with the control it took of the Red Sea ports of Suakin (q.v.) and Massawa.

Periodic uprisings took place against the Turks, from the murder of Isma'il Pasha in 1822 to the revolt of the Ja'aliyin (q.v.) that was suppressed by the Daftardar in 1823, but there was no general Sudanese rising until Muhammad Ahmad al-Mahdi (q.v.) coalesced and unified this resistance beginning in 1881. The major response to the Turkiya was flight from regions under Turco-Egyptian rule, often to avoid the onerous burden of taxes. Many riverine Sudanese were thus led to become itinerant merchants or *jallaba* (q.v.), especially in the slaving and ivory-hunting regions of the south and southwest. Especially remembered was the harshness of rulers such as the Daftardar and his successor, 'Uthman Bey, the Circassian. *See also* BAKER, SAMUEL; CHAILLE-LONG, CHARLES; GORDON, CHARLES.

TUSHKI. This site on the right bank of the Nile in Lower Nubia (q.v.) across the Egyptian border represented the northernmost military initiative of Mahdism (q.v.) during the rule of the Khalifa 'Abdullahi (q.v.). The amir 'Abd al-Rahman al-Nujumi (q.v.) was selected to lead this attack on 3 August 1889, which failed disastrously. It is thought that the Khalifa sought a victory at Tushki to boost flagging spirits and isolate his domestic opponents. Many Ja'aliyin (q.v.) felt that the Khalifa deliberately sent Nujumi to a certain death at Tushki to rid himself of a potential competitor.

– U –

UBAYD HAJ AL-AMIN (1898–1933). A Sudanese nationalist leader. Ubayd was a founder of the Sudan Union Society (q.v.) and later of the White Flag League (q.v.). He worked in government departments but was dismissed and then imprisoned for his role in the 1924 nationalist uprisings. He died in jail.

'ULAMA ('ULEMA). Muslim religious scholars, who interpret the Islamic holy sources (the Qur'an and Sunna, or practices of Prophet Muhammad) and make determinations in religious and legal matters in public *fatwas* (judgments) or in Islamic courts of law. They may be appointed members of Islamic or secular governments, or act as public religious advisers in other capacities. *See also* ISLAM; ISLAMIC LAW.

UMARA DUNQAS. *See* AMARA DUNQAS.

UMMA PARTY. The political party supported by the Ansar (q.v.) organization. It was formed in 1945 in reaction to the emergence of more radical groups like the Ashigga Party (q.v.), and with the support and patronage of 'Abd al-Rahman al-Mahdi (q.v.). The Umma advocated a separate, independent Sudan and was always associated with Ansar interests. Its main base of support was (and remains) Darfur and Kordofan (qq.v.), where the greatest number of Ansar are found. Umma's president was 'Abd al-Rahman's son, Siddiq al-Mahdi (q.v.), until his death in 1961. The party won twenty-three out of ninety-seven seats in the 1953 parliamentary elections and became the major opposition party. After independence it formed a coalition with the Peoples Democratic Party (q.v.) and 'Abdallah Khalil (q.v.) of the Umma became prime minister (1956–1958). This government was overthrown in 1958 by the coup of Ibrahim Abboud (q.v.), and all parties were outlawed.

The Umma reemerged after the 1964 October Revolution (q.v.) under the leadership of Siddiq's son, Sadiq al-Mahdi (q.v.), and won 76 out of 173 seats in the 1965 elections. The party allied itself with Isma'il al-Azhari (q.v.) to form the government with Muhammad Ahmad Mahjub (q.v.) as prime minister from 1965 to 1966 and 1967 to 1969 and Sadiq al-Mahdi as prime minister from 1966 to 1967. In 1966–1969 the party was split by a clash between Sadiq and the Ansar religious leader al-Hadi al-Mahdi (q.v.). The latter died in 1971 while trying to escape to Ethiopia after Ja'afar al-Nimeiri's (q.v.) bombing of Aba Island (q.v.). With the recognized successor Imam al-Hadi gone the party's leadership fell to Sadiq al-Mahdi.

Following a brief reconciliation with Nimeiri in the mid-1970s, Sadiq was imprisoned for his opposition to the government's imposition of the "September Laws" (q.v.), which he denounced as "un-Islamic." Despite Sadiq's criticisms of Nimeiri's brand of Islam (q.v.), the Umma remained an Islamic party dedicated to achieving its own Islamic political agenda for Sudan. This accounts for Sadiq's equivocation on the issue of Shari'a (q.v.) and the removal of the "September Laws," which he was loathe to abrogate while prime minister from 1986 to 1989 during another interlude of democratic party politics. Failing to appreciate the reasons for non-Muslims' antipathy toward the Shari'a, Sadiq cooperated with his brother-in-law Hasan al-Turabi (q.v.), leader of the National Islamic Front (q.v.), to draft Islamic legal codes for the country. Although during the last period of parliamentary democracy (1985–1989) the Umma Party was the largest in the country, by the time Sadiq realized that ending the civil war and retaining the Shari'a were incompatible, public confidence in his government had dissolved, setting the stage for military intervention.

Following the June 1989 coup of 'Umar al-Bashir (q.v.), Sadiq al-Mahdi was arrested and kept in solitary confinement for several months. He was not released from prison until early 1991. Sadiq gave his approval of positions adopted by the Umma Party during his detention, including joining the Sudanese Peoples Liberation Movement (q.v.) and northern political parties in the National Democratic Alliance (NDA, q.v.), the main opposition group. After several years in exile, Sadiq returned to Sudan in 2000. The degree to which his political thinking has evolved since the 1989 coup is unknown; at least officially, he and the Umma Party support the NDA's position that the "September Laws" must be revoked and the Addis Ababa Agreement of 1972 (q.v.) fully restored.

UNIONIST PARTY. A small but influential party formed in 1944. The leaders of the party, including Hamad Tawfiq Hamad and Khidr Hamad (qq.v.), were well-known intellectuals who had been active in the Abu Rawf (q.v.) literary group in the 1930s and had been prominent in the Graduates Congress (q.v.). They continued to be active in politics after the party was dissolved by participating in the creation of the National Unionist Party (q.v.) in 1952. The Unionists supported unity with Egypt on the basis of dominion status for the Sudan. The leaders also hoped to avoid the involvement of religious organizations in politics, although some had close ties to the Khatmiya (q.v.).

UNITED FRONT FOR SUDANESE LIBERATION. A group coordinating the efforts of pro-unity parties (excluding the National Front, q.v.), Communist groups, students and tenants associations, and the Sudanese Worker's Trade Union Federation (q.v.) for a brief period in 1951–1952. The association demanded immediate termination of the Condominium (q.v.) government and a United Nations (q.v.) plebiscite for Sudanese self-determination, and refused any cooperation with the British. The United Front soon broke up and its constituents joined other coalitions ranging from the National Unionist Party (q.v.) to the Anti-Imperialist Front (q.v.).

UNITED FRONT FOR THE LIBERATION OF THE AFRICAN SUDAN. *See* GABOUSH, PHILLIP ABBAS.

UNITED NATIONS (UN). As a member of the United Nations and one of the poorest countries in the world, Sudan has been the recipient of considerable UN aid through the World Health Organization (WHO), the UN Capital Development Fund (UNCDF), and the Food and Agricultural Organization (FAO). Sudan has also played host over the years to large groups of refugees (q.v.), especially from Ethiopia, Eritrea, Uganda, Republic of Congo (formerly Zaire), and the Central African Republic. The United Nations High Commission for Refugees (UNHCR) has assisted Sudan while the country has hosted, at times, Africa's largest number of refugees.

All of this aid has doubtless saved many lives; however, the continuation of civil war in Sudan has undermined any hope of the country making reasonable progress in its social, economic, and physical development. Since the 1990s Sudan has been the recipient of large amounts of humanitarian assistance, particularly through Operation Lifeline Sudan (q.v.). With allegations of human rights (q.v.) violations on both sides of the civil war, the UN appointed a Special Observer for Human Rights, Mr. Gaspar Biro, who produced a comprehensive human rights document. This was rejected by the Sudan government as biased. Since the 1989 Islamist coup of 'Umar al-Bashir (q.v.), Sudan has been isolated from many other member states of the UN. In 1996 the UN Security Council approved Resolution 1044, which imposed economic sanctions on Sudan in response to its being identified with international terrorism.

Later the United States was able to block Sudan from taking its seat as a member of the Security Council in October 2000. *See also* FOREIGN RELATIONS.

UNITY OF THE NILE VALLEY PARTY. A small political party formed in 1946 advocating the complete integration of Egypt and the Sudan. Its leader was Dardiri Ahmad Isma'il. The party dissolved when it participated in the creation of the National Unionist Party (q.v.) in 1952.

UNIVERSITY OF KHARTOUM. The University of Khartoum was first established as Gordon Memorial College (q.v.) in 1902. In 1924 it was expanded to become a secondary educational institute. Just before independence, in 1947, it was upgraded still further to become a university college affiliated with the University of London. At independence it assumed the basic form it has today, although there have been repeated expansions including a Faculty of Medicine and Faculty of Law as well as research institutes such as the Institute of African and Asian Studies (IAAS). The IAAS descended from the former Sudan Research Unit (SRU) formed in the 1960s. Sudanist scholars have often been associated with the SRU/IAAS and the Sudan Library at the University of Khartoum. These facilities have generated large numbers of wide-ranging studies and publications. Of these, the journal *Sudan Notes and Records* has special significance.

The University of Khartoum has been central in many of the political movements in Sudan and was important in the 1964 October Revolution (q.v.) against the military government of Ibrahim Abboud (q.v.). Since 1989 the government has built numerous provincial universities in support of its decentralization strategy, which seeks to reduce the historic political dominance of the University of Khartoum. Other important institutes of higher education included Ahfad University College for Women (q.v.), Juba University, Gezira University, the Islamic University of Omdurman, and the Khartoum Branch of Cairo University.

UPPER NILE PROVINCE. One of the three original southern provinces (q.v.), Upper Nile includes land along the White Nile, Bahr al-Jabal, Bahr al-Ghazal and Sobat rivers, stretching east to the border with Ethiopia, with an approximate size of 91,190 square miles. A 1970 census estimated its population at 1,282,000, of whom the majority are Nuer (q.v.) with a sizable Shilluk (q.v.) population and some Dinka (q.v.). Dominated by Nilotic (q.v.) peoples, it has always been a place of cattle pastoralism.

Upper Nile was raided for slaves and ivory by Jallaba (q.v.) merchants in the nineteenth century and was the scene of unsuccessful efforts by antislavery (q.v.) forces. Minimally controlled by the Turkiya and Mahdiya (qq.v.) regimes, it saw an important confrontation between General H. H. Kitchener (q.v.) and French forces in 1898 at Fashoda (q.v.) to determine British control. Attempts have been made to develop agricultural and fishing industries in Upper Nile, and the proposed Jonglei Canal (q.v.) runs through its vast *Sudd* (q.v.) swamp. Malakal (q.v.), its most important town, lies on the White Nile just north of the Sobat River. Like the rest of the South, Upper Nile has been devastated by years of chronic civil war.

'URABI, AHMAD (1840–1911). An Egyptian army officer and nationalist leader whose revolt against khedivial authority was defeated by the British military at the battle of Tel al-Kabir in September 1882. 'Urabi represented the large class of native Egyptian, mid-level officers in the Egyptian army whose promotions were blocked by the Ottoman ruling class of Turks, Albanians, and Circassians. In February 1881 these officers mutinied and forced Khedive Muhammad Tawfiq (q.v.) to appoint an Egyptian minister of war; later, in coalition with civilian nationalists, they demanded a constitution and parliamentary government.

As threatening as this revolt was to khedivial authority, it was equally so to Great Britain and France, whose program of Dual Financial Control (begun in 1878) sought to reform the Egyptian economy and protect Anglo-French investments. Also of great concern to Britain was control of the Suez Canal, which was vital to British trade. Rioting in Alexandria in 1882 precipitated an Anglo-French naval bombardment of the city, followed by a landing of British troops and defeat of 'Urabi's army. 'Urabi and his colleagues were convicted of treason and exiled, their nationalist cabinet dismissed, the constitution suspended, and the army disbanded.

The significance of the 'Urabi revolt to Sudan was that it led to the British military occupation of Egypt in 1882 and a more overt British role in Egyptian affairs. The Anglo-Egyptian army created after British occupation was used by Gen. H. H. Kitchener (q.v.) from 1896 to 1898 to conquer the Mahdiya (q.v.).

URBANIZATION. Sudan's urban experiences are among the earliest for Africa and the world. However, the ancient history of the Sudan—or more properly, Nubia (q.v.)—is beyond the scope of this work. During

Islamic times the former Christian capital of Dongola (q.v.) was transformed into a Muslim town, while Soba was destroyed and replaced by the new center of power of the Funj Sultans, Sinnar (qq.v.). Regional trading towns were important in late medieval and precolonial times, including Arbagi in the Gezira (q.v.), Kobbei and al-Fasher in Darfur (qq.v.), Bara and el-Obeid in Kordofan (qq.v.), Shendi (q.v.) along the Nile, and especially Suakin (q.v.) on the Red Sea. Such towns were centers of regional subsistence trade as well as long distance trade in ivory, gold, slaves (q.v.), incense, animal products, pottery, baskets, mats, and foodstuffs.

Division of labor, craft specialization, and religious shrines at the tombs (*qubbas*, q.v.) of religious leaders and mosques gave rise to urban quarters as well as districts for nobility and areas for seasonal populations. Few of these towns, except perhaps Sinnar, had more than 5,000–10,000 permanent inhabitants. To an extent one might refer to them as small-scale administrative centers or royal cities but there was little attention to defensive structures or manufacture. All substantial towns would have had main mosques for collective prayer along with market and residential areas. Urban quarters were subdivided along family or descent lines. In the South the degree of urbanization was substantially less, with some limited forms of collective settlement known only among the Azande and Shilluk (qq.v.).

Not until the Turkiya (q.v.) period did larger-scale urbanization begin to take place in the Sudan. After their conquest of the Funj Sultanate of Sinnar in 1821 the Turco-Egyptians created Khartoum (q.v.) as their military and political center, along with a new town at Wad Medani (q.v.), while strengthening their strategic base at Suakin. Other Sudanese towns during the Turkiya could be considered military and trade outposts, but hardly "urban" in any meaningful sense. Many were largely devoted to the supply of slaves and other raw and natural materials while giving some base for their forward military forces to collect taxes and tribute and explore more remote regions.

Sudanese resistance to Turco-Egyptian rule launched the movement of Muhammad Ahmad al-Mahdi (q.v.) in 1881, which led to the fall of Khartoum in January 1885. Shortly thereafter the Mahdi (q.v.) died and his successor, Khalifa 'Abdullahi (q.v.), ordered Khartoum abandoned as he expanded the Mahdist camp across the river into his capital city of Omdurman (q.v.). During the thirteen years of the Mahdist state, Omdurman grew into a sprawling city of perhaps 250,000 people, encompassing a huge variety of Sudanese ethnic groups and foreign nationalities.

Simultaneously, other cities in the Sudan, such as el-Obeid, Kassala (q.v.), and Shendi, experienced significant decline as the Khalifa developed Omdurman into the central market and concentrated resources and manpower in the capital.

In 1898 the Anglo-Egyptian (q.v.) army conquered the Sudan with a decisive battle at Karari (q.v.), and Khartoum was quickly rebuilt as the colonial capital of the Sudan. A substantial out-migration from Omdurman back to the regional towns and villages followed, in accordance with an Anglo-Egyptian policy to "empty the capital area of useless mouths." Towns in Kordofan and the Gezira experienced a particular resurgence. Gradually the town of Khartoum North (q.v.) was added as an industrial and residential base. Together with Khartoum and Omdurman, this urban area became known as the Three Towns (q.v.).

In general the model of Sudanese urbanization is that of the "primary city" in which a hugely disproportionate concentration of national resources is located in one area, the Three Towns, at the expense of most other towns or cities. This imbalance is exacerbated by the huge influx of refugees (q.v.) fleeing war in the south, west, and east along with regional economic underdevelopment. Migrants to the city far exceed its natural growth by the excess of births over deaths. Moreover, the migrants are mostly young and male, making for a volatile political mixture. Refugees from Kordofan, Darfur, and the three southern provinces are now very numerous and the sparse financial resources of the government are grossly inadequate to meet their basic needs. In exasperation the military government of 'Umar al-Bashir (q.v.), in power since 1989, has sometimes resorted to bulldozing informal squatter settlements in a vain effort to eradicate this aspect of Sudan's civil strife. As for the country as a whole, data from the 1994 Population Reference Bureau estimate that the total urban population of Sudan is 6,339,000 with 22.5 percent of the nation's people living in urban areas.

Primary cities are a typical result of colonialism where the interest of the colonial power was military and political administration and control of the flow of natural resources. Little investment was made in the manufacturing sector, but rather in the primary production of agricultural and natural resources to develop the colonial economy. Similarly the service sectors of primary cities are not in such lucrative domains as banking and credit, but rather in menial wage jobs of domestic service and low-paid clerical work. Thus, the distorted colonial inheritance of Sudan's urban structure is very much a part of its present legacy. True, more diversification is taking place and a Sudanese urban, commercial, and military elite has replaced that of the British. More towns and cities are experiencing growth than was the case under British colonial rule. However, much of the secondary urbanization is not motivated by healthy economic reasons, but rather in response to ecological and military uncertainty.

At the same time, other lesser processes of urbanization in Sudan are underway. In the north the towns of Dongola and Karima, Shendi and Atbara (q.v.) are growing modestly, while Port Sudan (q.v.) has had remarkable growth as the nation's sole maritime port linked to the national rail and road system. Refugees from conflict in the Horn of Africa have boosted the population of Port Sudan significantly. Kassala too has grown due to its position as a refugee transit point; in 2000 this city was the site of a rebel incursion followed by a brutal punitive mission by the Khartoum government.

Along the Blue Nile the process of urbanization has also been unfolding, especially at Wad Medani, now a center for regional trade of agricultural goods. Most cities also having banking, health, and educational facilities as some measure of a decentralization policy. In the South the provincial capitals of Wau, Juba, and Malakal (qq.v.) have exploded with massive and sudden population growth due to the great military insecurity in their immediate hinterlands. In fact the central government has no consistent control over the southern countryside and its forces are frequently under attack by the rebel Sudanese Peoples Liberation Army (q.v.). These southern cities have become garrison towns under military rule, with their inhabitants living a precarious and isolated existence.

'UTHMAN IBN ABI BAKR DIQNA (1840–1926). Mahdist military leader in the eastern Sudan, known as *Amir al-Sharq* (Commander of the East). Diqna was born into a prominent merchant family in Suakin (q.v.) and engaged in trade, including slaves (q.v.), between the towns of Berber (q.v.) and Jidda in Arabia. In 1877 he was arrested during the antislavery (q.v.) campaigns and lost a significant part of his fortune. He joined the Mahdi in el-Obeid (qq.v.) and on 8 May 1883 was sent to lead the Beja (q.v.) people of his native region in a rebellion against government troops. He successfully enlisted the support of his spiritual mentor, al-Tahir al-Majdhub of the Majadhib (q.v.), and so found acceptance among the Beja peoples.

In 1884 Diqna captured Sinkat and Tokar, but was unable to take Suakin from the British. In the following years he had numerous problems with rival commanders sent by the Khalifa (q.v.) to assist him. The loss of Tokar in February 1891 marked the effective end of the Mahdiya (q.v.) in the east, and he retreated to Adarama on the Atbara River. Diqna survived the battle of Karari (q.v.) in 1898 and fled south with the Khalifa 'Abdallahi (q.v.); in 1900 he was the last leading Mahdist to be captured. He was imprisoned first in Egypt and then in Wadi Halfa (q.v.), where he was held until his death in 1926. His reputation for having never been defeated in a decisive battle made him a venerated figure of national resistance in the twentieth century. During the Ja'afar al-Nimeiri (q.v.) regime his remains were exhumed and reburied in Erkowit in the Red Sea Hills, where he lies in a small domed tomb widely visible across the hills. [by Albrecht Hofheinz]

– V –

VERONA FATHERS. *See* CHRISTIANITY IN THE SUDAN; COMBONI, DANIELE.

– W –

WAD. In Sudanese Arabic (q.v.) this means "son of . . ." Thus, Wad Ahmad means "son of Ahmad." "Walad" (sing.) and "Awlad" (pl.) may be used in a similar fashion.

WAD AJIB. Literally means "Son of Ajib" and refers to the descendants of Ajib, the son of 'Abdallah Jama'a (q.v.), who held the title of *manjil* (q.v.) during the Funj sultanates (q.v.).

WAD AL-NUJUMI. *See* 'ABD AL-RAHMAN WAD AL-NUJUMI; MAHDIYA.

WAD DAYFALLAH. *See* TABAQAT WAD DAYFALLAH.

WAD HABUBA. *See* 'ABD AL-QADIR WAD HABUBA.

WADI HALFA. Urban life in Nubia (q.v.) is extremely ancient, but the history of this important border town is more recent, dating to the nineteenth century when it served as a river port for steamers from Aswan,

Egypt, and as a railhead for trains going south to Khartoum (q.v.). The original town was completely destroyed by the rising waters of Lake Nasser in 1964, and thus modern Wadi Halfa dates only to the 1960s.

In 1820 Wadi Halfa featured in the Turco-Egyptian (q.v.) conquest of the Sudan, with troops massing there on their way south. Talk of building a railroad from Wadi Halfa to Khartoum was heard in the 1850s, but nothing happened until 1873 when track was laid about fifty-three kilometers toward Kerma, but not completed. In 1866 a telegraph line was strung between Wadi Halfa and Egypt. After the collapse of the Turkiya (q.v.) in 1885, Wadi Halfa entered a period of insecurity for much of the Mahdist rule. Border skirmishes were common during the early years of the Mahdiya (q.v.). In 1889 the army of 'Abd al-Rahman al-Nujumi (q.v.) passed by Wadi Halfa on its way to defeat at the battle of Tushki (q.v.).

In 1896 General H. H. Kitchener (q.v.) began his plans for the Anglo-Egyptian (q.v.) conquest of the Sudan and arrived in Wadi Halfa amidst a cholera epidemic. His engineers abandoned the idea of continuing the railroad along the Nile and selected a direct route across the desert to Abu Hamad following the way of camel trekkers. The military function of the railroad gave it a high priority and by July 1897 Anglo-Egyptian troops were transported from Wadi Halfa to Abu Hamad.

The economy of Wadi Halfa was built upon its role as a frontier post and transport center. A small agricultural economy, a small fishing and fish processing industry, and remittances from Nubians (q.v.) elsewhere were the principal sources of income. At the end of the nineteenth century Wadi Halfa had a population of only a few thousand. In 1956 it reached 11,000, but by 1965 it had fallen to only 3,200 as many left to go to the resettlement communities for Nubians in Egypt and Sudan. Today, the newly sited town only has a few thousand people, mostly working in support services for Wadi Halfa's main role as a transit point.

WAD MEDANI. Wad Medani is the first large town south of Khartoum (q.v.) along the Blue Nile. Reputedly it was founded in the seventeenth century by Muhammad wad Medani, a grandson of the Islamic judge Dushayn, who was buried in this hamlet and whose tomb (*qubba*, q.v.) was erected there. Throughout the eighteenth and nineteenth centuries it remained a typical small town with a market for food, leather, knives, spears, livestock, mats, and baskets. The first substantial expansion took place in 1905 when the British established Wad Medani as the provincial headquarters of Blue Nile Province (q.v.). In 1909 the railway passed through between Sinnar (q.v.) and Khartoum. From 1911 to 1914 the British established the Wad Medani Experimental Farm, which proved the potential of irrigated agriculture in the Gezira (q.v.).

It is worth noting that it was in the 1920s Wad Medani Literary Society that the seeds were sown for the Sudan Graduates General Congress (q.v.). This group was central to the nationalist agitation of the 1930s and 1940s. In the years before independence the British forced this group to dissolve because of the political pressure it generated in the Gezira and elsewhere.

Wad Medani also showed its interest in education by creating a Qur'anic Girls' School as early as 1928. Wad Medani has been the largest town in the Gezira for all of this century. Even at independence it was relatively large at 50,200 and by 1969 it had reached 74,500; by 1987 the population had grown to 145,000.

WAU. The capital of Bahr al-Ghazal (q.v.) province and the only southern provincial capital that does not lie on the Nile. It is also the only southern capital served by the railway coming from Muglad in southern Kordofan (q.v.). As with other towns in the southern Sudan (q.v.), transport has long been poor and under the conditions of civil war has become worse.

Wau is situated on the west bank of the Jur River, which is formed by the confluence of the Sueh and Wau Rivers. In the 1860 travels of Georg Schweinfurth (q.v.) the town was not even noted on his maps. Throughout the nineteenth century slave hunters used the Wau area to raid for slaves (q.v.). In December 1878 Charles Gordon (q.v.) sent the Italian Romolo Gessi (q.v.) to Wau to rout a group of slavers with a barrage of rockets. Thus, the earliest historical references to Wau are filled with violent images and the town often served as a remote post for military administration. It was from Wau in 1882 that the Turco-Egyptians (q.v.) launched their attack on the last independent Azande ruler, Yambio (qq.v.). Throughout the Turkish administration much of Bahr al-Ghazal province was in revolt by Dinka (q.v.) people and others.

In 1898 the French, under Jean-Baptiste Marchand, were stationed briefly at Wau (Fort Desaix) on their way to challenge the British at Fashoda (q.v.), but any local administration was still tenuous at best. It was not until 1901 under the William Sparkes expedition that the British presence could even be considered to begin seriously, but Wau had only 1,000 inhabitants. Sickness and transport, supply, and communication problems were a persistent frustration. For example, the railway to Wau was proposed in the 1920s but not realized until forty years later.

In 1904 a Roman Catholic Mission School was built to help produce a small group of literate civil servants. This was followed in 1905 by another school built by the Verona Fathers (q.v.). Thus the first decades of British rule saw education in the hands of European missionaries (q.v.) and commerce controlled by Jallaba and Syrian (qq.v.) merchants; southerners were not in control of their own fate. The town of Wau showed barely any growth at all. The Closed Districts Ordinance (q.v.) of 1922 sought to maintain this regional isolation, as the British feared the spread of Islam and Arabic language (qq.v.), culture, and dress. This policy was brought into effect and at least partially contributed to the 1955 revolt in Wau and other southern towns, which essentially began the current widespread conflict. In 1964 a southern rebel group, the Anya-Nya (q.v.), attacked Wau and almost seized it from Sudanese regular troops. Tensions mounted and in August 1965 a wedding party attended by the southern elite was attacked and large numbers of people were killed. The Addis Ababa Agreement of 1972 (q.v.) finally brought the fighting to an end until the early 1980s, when it resumed under the banner of the Sudanese Peoples Liberation Movement (SPLM, q.v.).

Amidst the severe military insecurity in Wau and in Bahr al-Ghazal, the population soared to about 50,000 by 1970, 58,000 in 1983, and some claim that it has reached as much as 100,000 today. However, since the resumption of civil war in 1983, severe population dislocation has been experienced due to the hostilities and war-induced famine. Under these conditions, economic, industrial, and transport development has been suspended.

WERNE, FERDINAND. German explorer who served with Ahmad Pasha Abu-Widan (q.v.) on an expedition to Taka and Kassala (q.v.) in 1840, and later on an expedition to the southern Sudan (q.v.) to discover the headwaters of the Nile from 1840 to 1841. Werne may not have gone beyond nine degrees latitude, i.e., Nuer (q.v.) country in the northern *sudd* (q.v.). The expedition, led by the Turkish officer Salim Qapudan (q.v.), reached the southern portion of Bari (q.v.) country.

WHITE FLAG LEAGUE. An early nationalist organization founded in 1924 by 'Ali 'Abd al-Latif and Ubayd Haj al-Amin (qq.v.) to overthrow British colonialism in the Sudan. It advocated a unified opposition with Egypt and drew support from younger educated Sudanese. It was the central force in the nationalist unrest, demonstrations, and armed resistance of 1924. Although the leaders were jailed or killed and the organization dissolved after 1924, the White Flag League laid the foundation for Sudanese nationalism in the twentieth century.

WILSON, SALIM. Born in the mid-nineteenth century, Atobhil Macar Kathish, a Ngok Dinka (q.v.), became known as "the Black Evangelist of the North" because he lived for some time in England. Captured and enslaved as a youth, he was emancipated by an invading Egyptian army in 1878–1879 and persuaded to join two British missionaries (q.v.) on their return to England. Baptized in 1881, he chose to retain Salim as his Christian name and Wilson from the name of his English benefactor. At the time of the Mahdist (q.v.) takeover of the Sudan, Salim Wilson toured England as a Sudanese redeemed by Christ, wearing *jallabiya* (q.v.), turban, and a leopard skin. Although it was his greatest desire to return to the Dinka as an evangelist, he was never assigned to the Sudanese mission. He did, however, correct the Dinka translation of the Gospel of St. Luke for the British and the Foreign Bible Society. He published three books in English giving various accounts of his life and religious outlook.

WINGATE, SIR FRANCIS REGINALD (1861–1953). This British administrator and soldier was attached to the Egyptian army in 1884. He served in the office of Egyptian Military Intelligence during the Mahdiya (q.v.), becoming its director in 1889. Wingate was highly influential in the development of British policy regarding the Sudan and, through his writings, helped to shape the popular British view of the Mahdiya. He had a hand in the writing of three books: his own *Mahdiism and the Egyptian Sudan* (1891); *Ten Years' Captivity in the Mahdi's Camp, 1882–1892* (1892), based on the memoirs of Fr. Joseph Ohrwalder; and Rudolf Slatin's (q.v.) *Fire and Sword in the Sudan* (1896).

As a military man he was given the highest position in the colonial service as the governor-general of the Sudan from 23 December 1899 to 31 December 1916. He was the principal architect of the Anglo-Egyptian Condominium (qq.v.) administration, though his actual activities may have been more social than administrative. Wingate used the services of Zubayr Rahma Mansur (q.v.) to assist him in repressing Mahdist sentiments. On the other hand Zubayr was a persistent slave trader who ran afoul of Wingate's effort to bring the widespread practice of slavery (q.v.) to an end in the Sudan. Such a delicate balance was also seen in Wingate's need for a Sudanese clerical class to serve the colonial administration, while also fearing the creation of an educated group that might oppose the Anglo-Egyptian military occupation of the country.

By 1910 Wingate instituted a governor's Advisory Council, which would later evolve into the important positions of civil secretary, financial secretary, and legal secretary. Wingate's private secretary was Stewart Symes (q.v.), who was himself installed as governor-general of the Sudan in 1934. Distracted by World War I, Wingate was virtually abandoned by the Foreign Office but he served briefly as high commissioner in Egypt (1917–1919) and then retired from public life.

WOL WOL, LAWRENCE (?–1996). Southern Sudanese political leader of western Dinka (q.v.) origin. He studied and received advanced degrees in Germany and France and then became active in a number of southern organizations. He was an officer in the Sudan African National Union (q.v.) and served as European representative of the Nile Provisional Government (q.v.) in 1969 and the Southern Sudan Liberation Movement of Joseph Lagu (qq.v.) in 1971. For a time he was editor of *Voice of the Southern Sudan* published in London. Wol Wol participated in the negotiations leading up to the Addis Ababa Agreement of 1972 (q.v.). After the settlement he was named minister of state for planning and then minister of planning in the Sudanese government. He was elected to the Southern Regional Peoples Assembly in 1973 and served in the Southern High Executive Committee. In 1976 he was named Sudanese ambassador to Uganda.

In 1981, after Ja'afar al-Nimeiri (q.v.) abrogated the terms of southern autonomy and appointed his own southern government, Wol Wol was made the minister of finance. Later he became the first governor of Bahr al-Ghazal (q.v.) under the reorganization. Wol Wol was diagnosed with diabetes in 1978 and he finally succumbed to the disease in January 1996 in Khartoum (q.v.).

WOLSELEY, VISCOUNT GARNET JOSEPH (1833–1913). Distinguished British military officer who fought in Europe and Asia and began colonial service in Africa with an attack against the Asante people of the Gold Coast (1873–1874), followed by action against the Zulu of South Africa in 1879. In the Middle East Wolseley saw service in Cyprus in 1878 and was in charge of suppressing the nationalist Ahmad 'Urabi (q.v.) revolt in Egypt in 1882.

In 1883 the British situation was rapidly deteriorating in the Sudan with the defeat of Hicks Pasha (q.v.). General Charles Gordon (q.v.) was sent to withdraw the remaining Turkiya (q.v.) administration in 1884, but instead found himself trapped in the siege of Khartoum (q.v.). Urgent appeals for rescue went out to a reluctant and unsure British Foreign Office, and it was very late when Wolseley was asked to lead an undermanned Gordon Relief Mission.

Funds were authorized in August 1884 by Prime Minister William Gladstone (q.v.) and Wolseley reached Cairo in September. He left Korti on the Nile on 30 December and engaged Mahdist (q.v.) forces at Abu Tulayh on 17 January 1885, al-Qubba on 19 January 1885, and al-Matamma on 21–22 January. Meanwhile the siege of Khartoum was tightening. Gordon was killed in the dawn of 26 January and Wolseley's small advance force arrived at the city two days late; he and his troops had to fight their way back up the Nile to Egypt. In 1894 Wolseley was made a Field Marshal and in 1895 became commander-in-chief of the British army, but was forced out in an early phase of the Boer War in 1899.

WOMEN. The conditions of women in Sudan are as variable as its many ethnic groups, religions, and languages. The analysis is made more complex by factors of regional diversity, rural and urban differences, and by more recent developments in class stratification. Like Sudanese society itself, the subject of women can be differentiated regionally between North and South, or religiously between Muslims, Christians, and practitioners of traditional religions, all with varying degrees of social status.

In the North marriage and divorce are generally governed by Islamic law (Shari'a, q.v.), while customary and civil law prevail in the South. Women's access to political power has of course not been equal to men in either North or South, but women have served as judges and government ministers in the towns of the North since the 1960s. Southern women have been the most profoundly affected by chronic civil war, and its accompanying famine and population displacement make any improvements in their status unlikely. While equal rights for women were protected in the Permanent Constitution of 1973, a great deal remains to be addressed in practice, including a national approach to family law reform, increased political participation of women at all levels, and a concerted effort to include women in development planning and economic development.

Since the National Islamic Front (NIF, q.v.) came to power in 1989 there have been reports of human rights (q.v.) violations against non-NIF women, who are alleged to have lost government positions. Meanwhile women in public have been harassed for wearing "improper" (i.e., non-Islamic) dress: the wearing of the *hijab* (Islamic head covering), while not formally mandated by law, has been imposed by police and courts since the 1990s. Women supporters of the NIF have had greater opportunities and have defended the regime's policies toward women both internally and in external media outlets. Sudanese Islamist feminists were especially active at the 1995 Fourth International Congress on Women held in Beijing, raising challenges to the human rights criticism of Islamic regimes. They argue that Islam (q.v.) and Shari'a provide comprehensive legal, political, and religious rights for women. Their critics respond that excluding women from high government positions and the lack of equal rights in divorce and inheritance are a violation of women's human rights.

Education for girls and women lagged behind that for males in the Anglo-Egyptian (q.v.) period but has become more equalized in the postindependence period. Nearly half of all university graduates are women, and Sudan boasts Africa's only women's university, the Ahfad University in Omdurman (qq.v.) founded in the early twentieth century by Babikr Badri (q.v.) and maintained since by his family. Education for southern girls and women has of course been interrupted by civil war, and there are few southern women leaders known outside the region in any field.

During the past decades publications on women in Sudan have increased tremendously, as evidenced in the separate bibliographic entry on women in this dictionary. This entry may be consulted to ascertain the scope of this new arena of scholarship. *See also* 'ABD AL-MAHMUD, FATMA; AMIN, NAFISA AHMAD AL-; FEMALE GENITAL MUTILATION; IBRAHIM, FATIMA AHMED; ISLAMIC LAW; ISLAMIC LAW REFORM; LEAGUE OF UNIVERSITY WOMEN GRADUATES; MUSLIM BROTHERHOOD, WOMEN'S BUREAU; NUGDULLAH, SARA; SOUTHERN WOMEN'S LEAGUE; SUDANESE COMMUNIST PARTY; SUDANESE WOMEN'S JOURNALIST LEAGUE; SUDANESE WOMEN'S UNION; TRADE UNION FOR WOMEN; WOMEN'S FRONT; WOMEN'S UNION.

WOMEN'S FRONT. Organized by a group of Muslim Sisters in the surge of political activity after the October 1964 Revolution (q.v.). It promoted social and educational goals for women (q.v.) from the standpoint of the Muslim Brotherhood (q.v.). A political goal was to offer a counterpoint to the growth and influence of the secular Sudanese Women's Union (q.v.), which it perceived to be led by Communist party members. *See also* MUSLIM BROTHERHOOD, WOMEN'S BUREAU.

WOMEN'S LEAGUE: SOUTHERN SUDAN. *See* SOUTHERN WOMEN'S LEAGUE.

WOMEN'S LEAGUE OF UNIVERSITY GRADUATES. *See* LEAGUE OF UNIVERSITY WOMEN GRADUATES.

WOMEN'S LEAGUE OF JOURNALISTS. *See* SUDANESE WOMEN'S JOURNALIST LEAGUE.

WOMEN TEACHERS' TRADE UNION. *See* TRADE UNION FOR WOMEN.

WORKERS' AFFAIRS ASSOCIATION. *See* TRADE UNIONS.

WORKERS' FORCE. A political group formed in 1967. It was led by radical union leaders, especially from the Sudan Railway Workers. It won one seat in the parliamentary elections of 1968 in the railroad center of Atbara (q.v.). *See also* SUDANESE COMMUNIST PARTY; SUDANESE WORKERS TRADE UNION FEDERATION.

– Y –

YAMBIO (ca. 1820–1905). A major chief of the Azande (q.v.) who assumed control over his father's kingdom in the 1860s. He was famed for his resistance to Europeans and was generally hostile to newcomers, fighting the notorious slave trader Zubayr Rahma Mansur (q.v.) in the 1870s and the Turco-Egyptian (q.v.) government in 1881. In 1884 he was captured but subsequently freed by the Mahdists (q.v.), who soon came to power and sought to forge an alliance with Yambio to extend their influence to his region of southwestern Sudan. However, the tradition of resistance continued with only a loose alliance between the Mahdists and Yambio, who preferred to be autonomous. In the late 1890s he was compelled once again to resist Mahdist forces.

No sooner were the Mahdists toppled by General H. H. Kitchener (q.v.) in 1898 than Yambio found himself trapped between British and Belgian imperial aspirations. Both European powers wanted to control Azande land for themselves in 1903–1904. Once British colonial rule was consolidated in the central Sudan, the British (and the Belgians in the Congo) were able to attack peripheral peoples such as the Azande.

The British found Yambio in their joint pincer movement and in early 1905 mercenary Sudanese troops fighting for the British were able to defeat him on the battlefield. After the war the British applied their system of Indirect Rule (q.v.) and used various rival Azande princes for their colonial administration. Generally this system was not successful among egalitarian acephalous southern Sudanese, but the hierarchical Azande state made it function rather effectively.

YA'QUBAB. A major religious family with branches in the Sinnar and Shendi (qq.v.) areas. The founder, Muhammad ibn Hamad Ban al-Naqa (fl. ca. 1550), was an early leader of the Qadiriya *tariqa* (qq.v.) in the Sudan. Salih Ban al-Naqa (1681–1753) established the Shendi branch and had religious prestige in the northern Funj (q.v.) areas, as did his son, 'Abd al-Rahman (b. 1709). The Ya'qubab affiliated with the Sammaniya *tariqa* (q.v.) around 1800 under the leadership of Shaykh al-Tom Ban al-Naqa. The line of *khulafa* (q.v., khalifa) of the Ya'qubab was interrupted briefly during the Mahdiya (q.v.) but was reestablished in the twentieth century.

– Z –

ZAGHAWA (SOGHAUA, ZEGGAOUA, ZORHAUA, ZAUGE). An ancient Nilo-Saharan language. The main subgroups of Zaghawa speakers are the Kobbe, Dor, and Anka, which have mutually intelligible dialects. Today most Zaghawa are bilingual in Arabic (q.v.) and virtually all are Muslim, but with a degree of syncretism with their pre-Islamic traditions. Their agrarian economy is founded on seminomadic herding and agriculture as well as trade of their farm produce including milk, cream, cheese, hides, and butter. According to the 1982 Summer Institute of Languages classification and statistics, there are 102,000 Zaghawa in Sudan, 17,500 in Chad, 35,000 in Niger (1991), 7,000 in Libya (1993), or 161,500 for all countries. They are located mainly in northwest Darfur (q.v.), though some are distributed farther south and others are found in northern Kordofan (q.v.) and adjacent Libya. *See also* BERTI.

ZANDE. Singular of Azande. *See* AZANDE.

ZANDE SCHEME. A major development effort in the southwestern Sudanese borderlands begun after World War II. It was an attempt to create another large-scale agricultural scheme and processing industry like the huge Gezira Scheme (q.v.). In this case, following the military defeat of Yambio (q.v.) and the insertion of a system of Indirect Rule (q.v.), the British hoped to achieve agricultural development in the Azande (q.v.) region. Transportation and other costs as well as the growing civil war in the South brought much of the operation to an end.

ZAR. A spirit possession cult found in Sudan, Egypt, the Horn of Africa, the Arabian Peninsula, and Iran, and also known as "Bori" in West Africa. Its immediate aim is curing illness and general misfortune caused by the possession of a type of spirit also called "Zar." In Sudan there are different kinds of Zar practices, the two better-known ones being *Bori* practiced by northern Sudanese women and the less widespread *Tumbura* practiced by male and female slave descendants from the South and Nuba Mountains (q.v.).

In Bori, the manifestations that the Zar takes when possessing its hosts are seen as distinct spirits that represent "the other," i.e., all that is foreign to the northern Sudanese cultural context of the cult's clientele. Thus a Bori devotee may be possessed by the Zar spirit of an Ethiopian prostitute, Turkish or European officials, West Africans, or cannibal sorcerers from the southern Sudan. In the case of Tumbura, the manifestations of Zar are often seen as facets of a single Zar spirit and represent the devotees' collective self, such as the Banda people from the South, warriors from the Nuba Mountains, British and Egyptian officers of the nineteenth century, ex-slave soldiers, and Gumuz people from the Ethiopian borderlands who suffered from slavery (q.v.).

In both practices, the external appearance and attributes of Zar manifestations are staged in a theatrical manner during the cult's rituals. Clad in the style of dress and acting out the stereotypical behavior of their Zar, such as brandishing a spear when possessed by a Nuba (q.v.) warrior, or wearing sunglasses and smoking a pipe when possessed by a European, the devotees dance ecstatically, induced by special kinds of incense and music associated with their possessing agents. Bori and Tumbura nowadays share many traits, and many of their previous differences are far less pronounced.

The result of the Zar's possession is that the spirit establishes itself in its host's body permanently, causing a variety of disturbances ranging from headaches and listlessness to serious psychological disorders, hemorrhaging, paralysis, and blindness. As the Zar does not respond to exorcism, the only way to treat these problems is to come to terms with the spirit. The host is initiated into the Zar cult under the tutelage of its (usually female) leader, known as a *shaykha*, celebrating a number of ceremonies and offering the spirit small presents. Satisfied, the Zar "sleeps" and the symptoms of illness disappear. In Bori, the illness may reoccur periodically; the only recourse for the possessed is to remain a lifelong member of the cult and to continue appeasing the spirit. However, in Tumbura, after the patient's initiation into the cult, the Zar is transformed into a protective agent conflated with the personality of the Sufi shaykh (qq.v) 'Abd al-Qadir al-Jaylani. Participation in Tumbura ceremonies ensures that the shaykh's benevolence will remain with the devotee. In some Tumbura groups this process has become blurred and the logic of Bori partially adopted.

Sociologically, possession by the Zar spirit has been interpreted as a way for "subordinate" individuals—women (q.v.), homosexuals, slave descendants, and other marginalized people—to protest their oppression. In this view, Zar rituals are seen as occasions when subordinates can speak the unspeakable with impunity. Other approaches, which do not deny the general logic of this hypothesis, have seen Bori as a female practice through which women may express their concerns regarding fertility and hopes for the future; or as a female counterhegemonic practice that enables devotees to see their cultural categories and constraints as "constructs" rather than as "natural facts." Meanwhile Tumbura has been analyzed as a counterdiscourse through which slave descendants and other non-Arab Muslim subalterns might articulate a positive self-identity based on an alternative history that is narrated in the songs of the cult. [by Gerasimos Makris]

ZARRUQ, HASAN AL-TAHIR (1916–1980). Sudanese political leader and teacher who was educated at Gordon Memorial College (q.v.), graduating from the teachers section in 1935. He taught in various schools until he was dismissed from government service in 1948 for political activities. Zarruq was a founder of the Liberal Party (q.v.) in 1944, leading the Liberal Unionist section that favored unity with Egypt. He was active in party alliances after World War II, helping to lead opposition to the Legislative Assembly (q.v.) and serving as assistant secretary to the United Front for Sudanese Liberation (q.v.). Rather than joining the National Unionist Party (q.v.) he was one of the founders of the Anti-Imperialist Front (q.v.) in 1953 and was elected to Parliament in that year. Zarruq was associated publicly with the Sudanese Communist Party (q.v.) as the editor of *Al-Midan*, a communist newsletter in Khartoum (q.v.). He was elected to Parliament in 1965 from the special graduates constituency.

ZARRUQ, MUBARAK (1916–1965). Sudanese political leader who graduated from Gordon Memorial College (q.v.) and was active in early nationalist and intellectual organizations. He was on the Executive Committee of the first Students' Union in 1940 and was active in the Graduates Congress (q.v.). He worked with the Sudan Railways (1934–1939) and then entered law school, setting up practice as an attorney in 1943. Zarruq also served on the Executive Committee of the Ashigga Party (q.v.) and was a close friend and associate of Isma'il al-Azhari (q.v.). After World War II he was active in a number of organizations, being elected to the Omdurman Municipal Council (1950) and acting as secretary of the United Front for Sudanese Liberation (q.v.). He became a member of the National Unionist Party (q.v.) when it was created in 1952 and was elected to Parliament in 1953. Zarruq was named minister of communications in al-Azhari's first cabinet and joined al-Azhari in opposition after 1956. He took part in the 1964 October Revolution (q.v.) and was minister of finance in the transitional government (1964–1965), but died suddenly just before the 1965 elections.

ZENAB, CATARINA (1848–1921). The first Dinka (q.v.) Catholic evangelist. Born at the Kic Dinka village of Gog and a student of Daniele Comboni (q.v.) at the Holy Cross Mission, she traveled with him to Khartoum (q.v.) in 1860. An energetic Christian, she assisted Father Beltrame in Egypt in compiling a Dinka dictionary and grammar. Fluent in both Dinka and Arabic, she was sent to the Seminary at Verona, Italy, where she was trained to be a missionary to the Dinka people. She returned to Khartoum where she taught at the mission and assisted at baptisms. Catarina and her son remained in Khartoum during the Mahdiya (q.v.), and after the Anglo-Egyptian (q.v.) conquest of the Sudan she acted as interpreter for the revived Catholic mission. She died in Khartoum in 1921. *See also* MISSIONARIES IN SUDAN.

ZUBAYR (ZUBEIR) RAHMA MANSUR (1830–1913). Zubayr was a Jallaba (q.v.) merchant, slave trader and adventurer from a branch of the Ja'aliyin Arabs (qq.v.) who established himself as a major commercial and military force in southern Sudan (q.v.) by 1856. In 1865, with a private army and tactical alliances with compliant chiefs, Zubayr became the virtual ruler of Bahr al-Ghazal (qq.v.) province. However, the disruption he caused was halted by the effective resistance of King Yambio of the Azande (qq.v.), who was only beginning a long history of resistance to northern Arab slave traders. Blocked from spreading to the south, Zubayr conquered much of Darfur (q.v.) in 1874. Turco-Egyptian (q.v.) governors mistrusted him but were powerless to oppose him, and thus officially cooperated with his regional control. His role in maintaining slavery (q.v.) in the Sudan was and remains controversial.

Nursing a grievance against the Turco-Egyptian regime, Zubayr traveled to Cairo in 1875. There he was detained by Khedive Isma'il (q.v.), himself under pressure from British Prime Minister William Gladstone (q.v.), whose antislavery (q.v.) campaign was being led in the Sudan by Charles Gordon and Romolo Gessi (qq.v.). Zubayr's son, Sulayman, was executed by Gessi for slave raiding in 1879. In 1884 Zubayr was suggested by Gordon as a natural leader who might be sent to the Sudan to oppose the Mahdi (q.v.), but this idea was rejected by British politicians because of Zubayr's past as a notorious slave trader. In 1899 the governor-general, F. R. Wingate (q.v.), secured Zubayr's return to the Sudan where he functioned as a counselor to the new Anglo-Egyptian (q.v.) government and maintained a large farm. He died in his home village of al-Jayli north of Khartoum (q.v.).

Appendix

1. CURRENT SUDAN FACTFILE
   A. ECONOMIC DATA:
   GDP/capita: $250 USD (1997)
   GDP purchasing power parity $23.7 billion (1994 est.)
   GNP/capita: $641 USD
   National product real growth rate: 7% (1994 est.)
   National product per capita: $870 (1994 est.)
   Currency: 1 Sudanese pound (#Sd)=100 piastres
   Inflation rate (CPI): 70%/yr. (1989 est.)
                   100%/yr. (1997)
                   140%/yr. (1996)
   Exchange rates: official rate Sudanese pounds/USD
       $1/1,301–2,000 (1997)
       $1/1,450 (1996)

$1/1,280 (January 1995)
$1/277.8 (1994)
$1/153.8 (1993)
$1/ 69.4 (1992)
$1/ 5.4 (1991)
$1/ 4.5 (1990)
$1/.3 (1971)
Debt/capita: $531 USD
Debt to IMF: $1.7 billion (1997–1998)
Total debt: $20 billion (1997–1998)
  $17.0 billion (1993 est.)
  Debt service $97,000,000 (1989, actual)
  Debt service $1,202,000,000 (1990, obligation)
Labor force: 6,500,000 (1994, est.)
(Note: labor shortages for most categories of skilled
  employment.)
Agriculture, 80%
Industry and commerce, 10%
Government, 6%
Other, 4%
Unemployment rate: 30% (FY92/93 est.)

Budget:
  Revenues: $493 million (1994 est.)
  Expenditures: 1,100 million (1994 est.)

Defense: 7.2% of GDP or ca. $610 million (1989)
  Economic aid recipient: (FY 70–89)
    $1.5 billion; Western Europe (non-U.S.)
    $5.1 billion; ODA and OOF bilateral
    $3.1 billion; OPEC bilateral aid (1979–1989)
    $0.6 billion; Communist countries (1970–1989)

Production:
  Agriculture: 80% (35% of GNP)
  Industry/commerce: 11% (FY 1992/93)
  Government: 6%
  Industrial growth rate 6.8% (FY 92/93 est.)
  Industries: cotton ginning, textiles, cement, edible oils, sugar,
    soap distilling, shoes, petroleum refining

Agriculture: cotton, oilseeds, sorghum, millet, wheat, gum
arabic, sheep; marginally self-sufficient in most foods

Trade:
Exports: $419 million (f.o.b., FY93/94)
cotton 43%, gum arabic 29%, livestock/meat 24%, sesame,
peanuts
Trade partners: Western Europe 46%, Saudi Arabia 14%,
Eastern Europe 9%, Japan 9%, US 3% (FY87/88)
Trade with U.S. (1997): Sudanese imports from U.S. $50 mil-
lion; Sudanese exports to U.S. $20 million; total trade with
U.S. $70 million
Imports: $1.7 billion (c.i.f., FY93/94)
Commodities: foodstuffs, petroleum products, manufactured
goods, machinery and equipment, medicines and chemicals,
textiles
Trade partners: Western Europe 32%, Africa and Asia 15%, U.S.
13%, Eastern Europe 3% (FY87/88)

Electricity:
500 million kwh produced (1993)
37 kwh/capita (1989)
42 kwh/capita (1993)
Transport and communication:
Railroads: 5,500 km narrow gauge
4,800 km 1.067 m gauge
716 km 1.6096 m gauge plantation line
Highways: 20,703 km
tarmac: 2,000 km
gravel: 4,000 km
dirt: 2,304 km
track: 12,399 km
Waterways: 5,310 km navigable
Pipelines: 815 km
Merchant Marine: 5 ships (1,000 GRT or over) cargo 3;
roll-on/roll-off cargo 2
River ports: Juba, Khartoum, Kosti, Malakal, Nimule
Seaports: Port Sudan, Suakin
Civil air: 14 major aircraft

Airports: total: 70

with paved runways over 3,047 m	1
with paved runways 2,438 to 3,047 m	5
with paved runways 1,524 to 2,437 m	3
with paved runways under 914 m	13
with unpaved runways 2,438 to 3,047 m	1
with unpaved runways 1,524 to 2,438 m	14
with unpaved runways 914 to 1,523 m	33

Land use: arable land; irrigated land (1989) 18,900 sq. km; 5%; permanent crops, 0%; meadows and pastures, 24%; forest and woodland, 20%; other, 51%

Communications:

radio:	11 AM stations
satellites:	INTELSAT and ARABSAT
telephones:	73,000
television:	3 stations

Military:

Branches: Army, Navy, Air Force, Popular Defense Force, Militia.

Number in Armed Forces: 57,500

Manpower availability:

males at age 15–49 6,806,588;

males fit for military service 4,185,206;

males at military age (18)/year 313,958 (1995)

Defense expenditures: $600 million, 7.3% of GDP (FY 93/94 est.)

B. DEMOGRAPHIC DATA

Area:	2,505,810 km2; 967,500 mi2
Coastline:	853 km
Population:	24,971,806 (July 1990)
	27,361,000 (1994, est.)
	29,419,798 (1994)
	30,120,420 (1995)
	43,045,000 (projected for 2010)
	60,602,000 (projected for 2025)

Age structure:

0–14 years, 46.0%

female 6,801,001; male 7,124,892 (1994)

15–64 years: 52.0%
 female 7,706,864; male 7,830,980 (1995)
Over age 65, 2.3%
 female 280,297; male 376,386 (1995)
Population growth rate: 2.90% (1990)
 3.10% (1994)
 2.35% (1995 est.)
Crude birth rate #/1,000: 44.00 (1990)
 44.20 (1994)
 41.29 (1995)
Crude death rate #/1,000: 14.00 (1990)
 13.20 (1994)
 11.74 (1995 est.)
Infant death rate #/1,000: 107.0 (1990)
 84.8 (1994)
 77.7 (1995 est.)
Life expectancy at birth:
 All: 53.00 (1994)
     54.71 (1995)
 Males: 51.00 (1990)
     52.20 (1994)
     53.81 (1995)
 Females: 55.00 (1990)
     53.80 (1994)
     55.65 (1995)
Fertility rate (children/woman): 6.50 (1990)
    (children/woman): 6.37 (1994)
        6.00 (1995 est.)
Contraceptive prevalence (percent-all types) 8.7
Contraceptive prevalence (percent-modern types) 5.5
Last contraceptive survey (year) 1989
Literacy: age 15 and over can read and write (1994)
 total population: 27%
 male: 43%
 female: 12%
 percent urban, 22.50% (1994)
 total urban population 6,339,000 (1994)

Sources: The 1994 Data are from the Population Reference Bureau. The 1995 data are from the World Wide Web from Muaz M. Ata Al-Sid

<muaz@sudan.net> so can disting. based on July 1995 estimates. Other data from Keesings Historisch Archief, Inter-Parliamentary Union, 1997. Note that the current conditions in the Sudan make it impossible for a proper national census to be conducted, thus these statistics are estimates and approximations based on best projections. Variations in rates should not be taken as changes in trends but possible ranges.

2. ETHNO-LINGUISTIC GROUPS IN OR ADJOINING SUDAN *

I. Afro-Asiatic (Hamitic) Languages:
    A. Semitic: Arabic (Juhayna Group):
        1. Camel-Herders: Batahin, Dubaniya, Humr,
            Kababish, Shukriya, Shayqiya
        2. Cattle-Herders: Baqqara, Bidayria, Habbania,
            Hasaniya, Hawazma, Kawahla, Rizayqat, Ta'isha
        3. Settled: Ja'aliyin, Jamuiya, Mirafab, Rubatab,
            Mesalamiya, Rufa'a, Abdallab, Kinana
    B. Cushitic (Northern Branch):
        Beja, Ababda, Amarar, Beni Amer, Bisharin,
        Hadendowa
II. Sudanic Languages (Eastern Group):
    A. Pre-Nilotic:
        1. Barea Branch: Barea only
        2. Bertan Branch: Berta, Beni Shangul
        3. Koman Branch: Gule, Hamaj (founders of Funj),
            Gumuz, Kadallu, Koma, Uduk, Mao
        4. Ingassana Branch: Ingassana and others
        5. Kunama Branch: Kunama only
    B. Nilotic
        1. Bari, Karamojong, Nandi, and Masai Clusters
            (strongly Cushitized): Karamojong, Turkana, Bari,
            Kakwa, Kuku, Latuka, Mondari, Sere, Fajulu
        2. Dinka and Luo Clusters (weakly Cushitized):
            Dinka, Jur, Nuer, Atwot, Acholi, Luo; and Pre-
            Nilotic: Shilluk, Anuak, and Meban
        3. Beir Branch (on Ethiopian border): Didinga, Murle,
            Masongo
    C. Daju Branch: Daju
    D. Nubian Branch: Mahas, Sukkot, Kenuz
III. Kordofanian Languages (the Nuba Hills): Katla, Koalib,
    Tagali, Talodi, Tumtum, Temein

IV. Furian (of Darfur)

V. Niger-Congo (Nigritic) Languages (N.B. main family of Bantu
    language group):
    Eastern Subfamily (Equatorial Cluster): Azande, Banda,
        Ndogo, Mundu
    Central Subfamily (Madi Cluster): Madi, Bongo

VI. Kanuric (Central Saharan) Languages:
    Berti, Zaghawa, Bideyat

* This chart is inspired by G. P. Murdock, *Africa: Its Peoples and Their Culture History* (New York: McGraw Hill, 1955), but has been adapted and revised by R. A. Lobban, 1998, for this publication. Official Sudanese sources provide the following proportions for ethnicities: "Black" 52%; "Arab" 39%; Beja 6%; Foreigners 2%; Other 1%. Religions: Sunni Muslim, 70% (in north); Animism, 25%; Christian, 5% (most in south and Khartoum).

3A. FUNJ SULTANS OF SINNAR

1. Amara Dunkas	1504–1534
2. Nayil ibn Amara	1534–1551
3. 'Abd al-Qadir I ibn Amara	1551–1558
4. Amara II Abu Sakikin ibn Nayil	1558–1569
5. Dakin al-'Adil ibn Nayil	1569–1586
6. Dawra ibn Dakin	1586–1587
7. Tabl ibn 'Abd al-Qadir I	1587–1591
8. 'Abd al-Qadir II, ibn Unsa I	1592–1604
9. 'Abd al-Qadir II, ibn Unsa I	1604–1606
10. 'Adlan I, ibn Unsa I	1606–1611
11. Badi I, ibn 'Abd al-Qadir II, Sid al-Qawm	1611–1617
12. Rubat I, ibn Badi I	1617–1645
13. Badi II Abu Diqn ibn Rubat I	1645–1681
14. Unsa II, ibn Nasir ibn Rubat	1681–1692
15. Badi III al-Ahmar ibn Unsa II	1692–1716
16. Unsa III ibn Badi II	1716–1720
17. Nul (not of the old royal line)	1720–1724
18. Badi IV Abu Shulukh ibn Nul	1724–1762

3B. SULTANS OF THE HAMAJ REGENCY (following Spaulding, *Heroic Age*, 1985, 303):

19. Nasir ibn Badi IV	1762–1768
(Regent: Muhammad Abu Likaylik)	

20. Isma'il ibn Badi IV   1768–1769
21. 'Adlan II, ibn Isma'il   1775–1776
    (Regent: Rajab wad Muhammad)   1780–1786
22. Awkal   1787–1788
    (Regent: Nasir wad Muhammad)
23. Tabl   1788–1789
24. Badi V, Ibn Tabl   1789–1790
25. Hasab Rabihi   1790–1791
26. Nuwwar   1791–1792
27. Badi VI, ibn Tabl   1792–1793
28. Ranfa   1798–1805
    (Regents: Idris wad Muhammad, 'Adlan
    wad Muhammad, Muhammad wad Rajab)
29. *Interregnum*, Badi VI (second reign), 'Ajban   1805–1807
    (Regent: Husayn wad Muhammad)
30. *Fall of Sinnar*   1820–1821

4. KEIRA SULTANS OF DARFUR (following O'Fahey, *State and Society*, 1980, 16):
  1. Sulayman Solong   ca. 1650–1680
  2. Musa ibn Sulayman   1680–1700
  3. Ahmad Bakr ibn Musa   1700–1720
  4. Muhammad Dawra ibn Ahmad Bakr   1720–1730
  5. 'Umar ibn Muhammad Dawra ("Lele")   1730–1739
  6. Abu al-Qasim ibn Ahmad Bakr   1739–1752
  7. Muhammad Tayrab ibn Ahmad Bakr   1752–1786
  8. 'Abd al-Rahman al-Rashid ibn Ahmad Bakr   1787–1803
  9. Muhammad al-Fadl ibn Abd al-Rahman   1803–1838
    Darfur loses control over Kordofan   1821
10. Muhammad Husayn ibn Muhammad Fadl   1838–1873
11. Ibrahim ibn Muhammad Husayn   1873
Pretenders to the throne during the period of Turco-
  Egyptian and Mahdist rule in Darfur (1874–1898):
12. Hasab Allah ibn Muhammad Fadl   1874
13. Bosh ibn Muhammad Fadl   1874
14. Muhammad Harun Sayf al-Rashid ibn Bosh   1875–1880
15. Abdallah Dud Banja ibn Bakr   1880–1884
16. Yusuf ibn Ibrahim   1884–1888
17. Abu al-Khayrat ibn Ibrahim   1889

The revived sultanate:

18. 'Ali Dinar ibn Zakariya ibn Muhammad Fadl	1898–1916

5. TURCO-EGYPTIAN GOVERNORS OF THE NINETEENTH
   CENTURY (following Na'um Shuqayr, *Ta'rikh al-Sudan*, 1903):

1. 'Uthman Bey	1825–1826
2. Mahu Bey	1826
3. Khurshid Pasha	1826–1839
4. Ahmad Pasha Abu Widan	1839–1844
5. Ahmad Pasha al-Manikli	1844–1845
6. Khalid Pasha	1846–1850
7. 'Abd al-Latif Pasha	1850–1851
8. Rustum Pasha	1851–1852
9. Isma'il Pasha Abu Jabal	1852–1853
10. Salim Pasha	1853–1854
11. 'Ali Pasha Sirri	1854–1855
12. 'Ali Pasha Jarkis	1855–1857
13. Arakil Bey al-Armani	1857–1859
14. Hasan Bey Salamah	1859–1862
15. Muhammad Bey Rasikh	1862–1863
16. Musa Pasha Hamdi	1863–1865
17. Ja'far Pasha Sadiq	1865
18. Ja'far Pasha Mazhar	1866–1871
19. Mumtaz Pasha	1871–1873
20. Isma'il Pasha Ayyub	1873–1877
21. Gordon Pasha	First time: 1877–1879
22. Ra'uf Pasha	1879–1882
23. 'Abd al-Qadir Pasha Hilmi	1882–1883
24. 'Ala al-Din Pasha Siddiq	1883
25. Gordon Pasha	Second time: 1884–1885

6A. BRITISH GOVERNORS-GENERAL OF THE ANGLO-
    EGYPTIAN SUDAN:

Anglo-Egyptian Conquest	1898
Anglo-Egyptian Conventions	1899
1. H. H. Kitchener	1898–1899
2. F. Reginald Wingate	1899–1916
3. Lee Stack	1916–1924

4. Geoffrey Archer	1924–1926
5. John Maffey	1926–1933
6. Stewart Symes	1934–1940
7. Hubert Huddleston	1940–1946
8. Robert Howe	1947–1955
Egyptian Revolution	1952
9. Alexander Knox Helm	1955–1956
Sudanese Elections	1953
Sudanese Independence	1956

6B. HIGH COMMISSIONERS OF THE CONDOMINIUM (resident in Cairo):

Sir Eldon Gorst	1907–1911
Lord Horatio Kitchener	1911–1914
Sir Reginald Wingate	1917–1919
Lord Allenby	1919–1925
Lord Lloyd	1925–1929
Sir Percy Loraine	1930–1933
Sir Miles Lampson	1934–1946

6C. HEADS OF GOVERNMENT OF THE INDEPENDENT SUDAN:

Isma'il al-Azhari (Prime Minister)	1954–1956
Abdallah Khalil (Prime Minister)	1956–1958
Ibrahim Abboud (President, Supreme Military Council)	1958–1964
Sirr al-Khatim al-Khalifah (Prime Minister)	1964–1965
Muhammad Ahmad Mahjub (Prime Minister)	1965–1966
Sadiq al-Mahdi (Prime Minister)	1966–1967
Muhammad Ahmad Mahjub (Prime Minister)	1967–1969
Babiker Awadallah (Prime Minister)	1969–1971
Ja'afar al-Nimeiri (Prime Minister and President)	1969–1985
Suwar al-Dhahab (Head, Transitional Military Council)	1985–1986
Dafalla el-Gizouli (Prime Minister)	1985–1986
Sadiq al-Mahdi (Prime Minister)	1986–1989
Gen. 'Umar Hasan al-Bashir (President)	1989–present

7. 1890 AGREEMENT FOR THE ADMINISTRATION OF THE SUDAN

Agreement between Her Britannic Majesty's Government and the Government of His Highness the Khedive of Egypt relative to the future administration of the Sudan.

Whereas certain provinces in the Sudan which were in rebellion against the authority of His Highness the Khedive have now been reconquered by the joint military and financial efforts of Her Britannic Majesty's Government and the Government of His Highness the Khedive;

And whereas it has become necessary to decide upon a system for the administration of and for the making of laws for the said reconquered provinces, under which due allowance may be made for the backward and unsettled condition of large portions thereof, and for the varying requirements of different localities;

And whereas it is desired to give effect to the claims which have accrued to Her Britannic Majesty's Government by right of conquest, to share in the present settlement and future working and development of the said system of administration and legislation;

And whereas it is conceived that for many purposes Wadi Halfa and Suakin may be most effectively administered in conjunction with the reconquered provinces to which they are respectively adjacent;

Now it is hereby agreed and declared that by and between the undersigned, duly authorized for that purpose, as follows;

ARTICLE I

The word 'Sudan' in this agreement means all of the territories south of the 22nd parallel of latitude, which:

(1) have never been evacuated by Egyptian troops since the year 1882: or

(2) which having before the late rebellion in the Sudan been administered by the government of His Highness the Khedive were temporarily lost to Egypt and have been reconquered by her Majesty's Government and the Egyptian Government, acting in concert: or

(3) which may hereafter be reconquered by the two Governments acting in concert.

ARTICLE II

The British and Egyptian flags shall be used together both on land and water, throughout the Sudan, except in the town of Suakin, in which locality the Egyptian flag alone shall be used.

ARTICLE III

The supreme military and civil command in he Sudan shall be vested in one officer, termed the 'Governor-General of the Sudan'. He shall be appointed by Khedival Decree on the recommendation of Her Britannic Majesty's Government, and shall be removed only by Khedival Decree, with the consent of Her Britannic Majesty's Government.

ARTICLE IV

Laws, as also Orders and Regulations with the full force of law, for the good government of the Sudan, and for regulating the holding, disposal and devolution of property of every kind therein situated may from time to time be made altered or abrogated by Proclamation of the Government. Such Laws, Orders, and Regulations may apply to the whole or any named part of the Sudan, and may, either explicitly or by necessary implication, alter or abrogate any existing Law or Regulation.

ARTICLE V

No Egyptian Law, Decree, Ministerial Arrete, or other enactment hereafter to be made or promulgated shall apply to the Sudan or any part thereof, save in so far as the same shall be applied by Proclamation of the Governor-General in manner hereinafter provided.

ARTICLE VI

In the definition by Proclamation of the conditions under which Europeans, of whatever nationality shall be a liberty to trade with or reside in the Sudan, or to hold property within its limits, no special privileges shall be accorded to the subjects of any one or more Power.

ARTICLE VII

Import duties on entering the Sudan shall not be payable on goods coming from Egyptian territory. Such duties may however be levied on goods coming from elsewhere than Egyptian territory, but in the case of goods entering the Sudan at Suakin or any other port on the Red Sea littoral, they shall not exceed the corresponding duties for the time being leviable on goods entering from abroad. Duties may be levied on goods leaving the Sudan, at such rates as may from time to time be prescribed by Proclamation.

ARTICLE VIII

The jurisdiction of the Mixed Tribunals shall not extend, nor be recognized for any purpose whatsoever, in any part of the Sudan, except in the town of Suakin.

ARTICLE IX
Until, and save so far as it shall be otherwise determined by Proclamation, the Sudan, with the exception of the town of Suakin, shall be and remain under martial law.

ARTICLE X
No Consuls, Vice-Consuls, or Consular Agents shall be accredited in respect of nor allowed to reside in the Sudan, without the previous consent of Her Britannic Majesty's Government.

ARTICLE XI
The importation of slaves into the Sudan, as also their exportation, is absolutely prohibited. Provision shall be made by the Proclamation for the enforcement of this Regulation.

ARTICLE XII
It is agreed between the two Governments that special attention shall be paid to the enforcement of the Brussels Act of the 2nd of July 1890, in respect of the import, sale, and manufacture of firearms and their munitions, an distilled or spirituous liquors.
Done in Cairo, the 19th January 1890.
Signed: (Boutros Ghali; Cromer)

8. POLITICAL STRUCTURE AND ADMINISTRATION
Structure of Military Government:
Chief of State/Head of Government:
Chairman of the RCC, Prime Minister, and Minister of
Defence
First Vice-President
Second Vice-President
Cabinet appointed by the president
Legislative branch: 300-member Transitional National Assembly
Judicial branch: Supreme Court, Special Revolutionary Courts
Political parties: none
Flag: three equal horizontal bands of red (top), white, and black
with a green isosceles triangle based on the hoist side
National Assembly (*Majlis Watani*) has 400 members, 275
directly elected for a 4-year term in single seat constituencies
and 125 indirectly elected by national conference. Under

complete control of the National Assembly President, i.e, The National Islamic Front.

9. EDUCATIONAL INSTITUTIONS

Universities:
1. Ahfad University, P.O. Box 167, Omdurman, Sudan,
   TEL: 249-11-553363
2. Ahlia University, P.O. Box 786, Omdurman, Sudan,
   TEL: 249-11-551489/553447
3. Atbara University, P.O. Box 1843, Khartoum, Sudan
4. Bahr al-Ghazal University, Wau Town, Sudan
5. University of al-Gezira, P.O. Box 20, Medani, Sudan
6. University of Juba, P.O. Box 321/1, Juba, Sudan
7. University of Khartoum, P.O. Box 321 Khartoum, Sudan
8. Al-Nilayn University, P.O. Box 1055, Khartoum, Sudan
9. Omdurman Islamic University, P.O. Box 382, Omdurman, Sudan
10. Sudan University for Science and Technology, P.O. Box 407, Khartoum, Sudan

Secondary schools:
1. Comboni College, Director, Int'l Programs, Shari' 'Ali Abdel Latif, Khartoum, Sudan
2. Khartoum American School, c/o American Embassy Khartoum, Dept. of State Washington, DC, 20521-2200, USA
3. Unity High School, P.O. Box 85, Khartoum, Sudan

10. SUDAN-RELATED WEB SITES

http://www.intifada.org (The site of the NDA democratic opposition movement.)

http://www.sudan.org (Sudan discussion forum on culture, history, politics, human rights, women and gender issues, and constitutional matters.)

http://safsudan.com (A Web site with links to many Sudan-related issues.)

http://members.tripod.com/~adaraweesh/start (A Sudanese Arabic online magazine, "al-Daraweesh.")

http://i-cias.com/abubakr.htm

http://www.achiever.com/freehmpg/nubian

http://www.linnet.com/~richchar/Nubia (Nubian-related Web sites.)

http://www.info.usaid.gov/HORN/sudan (Country profile with links to aid-related sites.)

http://www.arab.net/sudan (Part of the larger Arabnet, this site provides basic information with numerous links to other sites, particularly relating to business and travel.)

http://www.1001sites.com/ (News, discussion, and analysis of Middle Eastern and North African affairs, with numerous links to Sudan-related sites.)

http://www.elshaab.com/ (Site of the Egyptian Labor Party, with some Sudan-related news and opinion.)

http://www.sas.upenn.edu/African_Studies/Newsletters/ssa.html (Site of the Sudan Studies Association of North America.)

http://www.sudan.net/ (Sudan page of Muaz M. Ata al-Sid, with many links to Sudan-related sites.)

http://www.sudaneseonline.com/ (Up-to-date news on Sudan from a variety of news sources.)

Bibliography

ABBREVIATIONS

IJAHS   *International Journal of African Historical Studies*, Boston
IJMES   *International Journal of Middle East Studies*, Cambridge
JAH   *Journal of African History*
JARCE   *Journal of the American Research Center in Egypt*, Cairo
JAS   *Journal of African Studies*
JEA   *Journal of Egyptian Archaeology*, London
JMAS   *Journal of Modern African Studies*
JRAI   *Journal of the Royal Anthropological Institute*, London
MEJ   *Middle East Journal*, Washington, DC
SNR   *Sudan Notes and Records*, Khartoum

INTRODUCTION

A wide variety of information on Sudan is available to the English-language reader. Both Sudanese and Western scholars have written valuable works that both analyze and interpret the history and culture of Sudan. It is thus possible to learn about major aspects of the Sudanese experience from a variety of perspectives. (Note that references and entries on prehistoric and ancient Nubia to the end of Christianity can be found in the forthcoming *Historical Dictionary of Ancient Nubia.*)

General reference works of special value are Richard Hill, *A Biographical Dictionary of the Sudan*, which covers ancient times to the twentieth century and Mandour el-Mahdi, *A Short History of the Sudan,* which presents a summary of Sudanese history from antiquity to present times; two general, multidisciplinary descriptions are H. D. Nelson, *Area Handbook for the Democratic Republic of the Sudan*, published by the U.S. Government Printing Office, and *Sudan Today*, prepared by the Sudanese Ministry of Information and Culture.

339

For the early Islamic era, two works are very useful. They are Yusuf Fadl Hasan, *The Arabs and the Sudan: From the Seventh to the Early Sixteenth Century,* and R. S. O'Fahey and J. L. Spaulding, *Kingdoms of the Sudan and the Tabaqat Wad Dafalla.* An older, but still useful, reference work is H. A. MacMichael's *A History of the Arabs in the Sudan.*

For the modern era a variety of sources are available. A helpful general introduction is P. M. Holt, *A Modern History of the Sudan,* which is now available in a newer version coauthored with M. W. Daly, *The History of the Sudan from the Coming of Islam to the Present Day.* A. B. Theobald's *Ali Dinar, Last Sultan of Darfur, 1898–1916* captures the spirit of the last sultanate of Sudan in the twentieth century. Richard Hill's *Egypt in the Sudan, 1820–1881* gives an account of the Turco-Egyptian period and P. M. Holt's *The Mahdist State in the Sudan, 1881–1898* is the standard work on the Mahdist period. The latter can be supplemented with the exciting, but Eurocentric, literature of "the prisoners of the Mahdi" genre, e.g., Rudolf von Slatin's *Fire and Sword in the Sudan.* It should be remembered, additionally, that much of this genre's material originated as anti-Mahdist war propaganda, and many of these same biases also appear in the writings about Charles "Chinese" Gordon. For an insider's view of the Mahdiya, one can read *The Memoirs of Babikr Bedri.* A growing Sudanese scholarship on the Mahdist period has also been inspired by Muhammad I. Abu Salim's organization of the documentation sources at the Dar al-Watha'iq in Khartoum.

A variety of perspectives are now available on the history of the Anglo-Egyptian period (1899–1956). Many British administrators wrote accounts of their experiences, as in H. C. Jackson, *Sudan Days and Ways,* and others wrote more general accounts. One of the more interesting accounts is *The Sudan,* which was written by a former civil secretary H. A. MacMichael, and another account centered around the life of another civil secretary, namely *The Making of the Modern Sudan: The Life and Letters of Sir Douglas Newbold* by K. D. D. Henderson. The period of the Anglo-Egyptian Sudan is also given comprehensive treatment in a two-volume history by Martin W. Daly, namely *Empire on the Nile: The Anglo-Egyptian Sudan, 1898–1934* and *Imperial Sudan: The Anglo-Egyptian Condominium, 1935–1956,* published in 1986 and 1991, respectively, by Cambridge University Press.

For Sudanese perspectives, one should read the scholarly accounts in M. Abd al-Rahim, *Imperialism and Nationalism in the Sudan*; M. O. Beshir, *Revolution and Nationalism in the Sudan*; and the recent work by Robert Collins and Francis Deng, *The British in the Sudan, 1989–1956.* The literature by Sudanese scholars on anticolonial and nationalist activities during the Condominium has increased since the first edition. This is reflected in the bibliographical section on the Anglo-Egyptian period.

A number of valuable works on Sudan since independence have appeared since Mekki Shibeika's *The Independent Sudan*, 1959, and Peter Bechtold's *Politics in the Sudan*, 1976. These include special issues of *Africa Today* (N.B.: 1981), *Arab Studies Quarterly* (N.B.: 1999), and *Sudan since 1989: The Turabi al-Bashir Years*, which was edited by Richard Lobban and Carolyn Fluehr-Lobban. One might also examine Peter Woodward's *Condominium and Sudanese Nationalism* published in 1979 and *Sudan, 1898–1989: The Unstable State*, 1990. *Sudan Since Independence: Studies of Political Development since 1956* is an excellent collection of essays, which was edited by Muddathir Abdel Rahim and others in 1986.

The issue of the history of the independent Sudan that is, perhaps, most critical is the "Southern Problem." An excellent summary of both the southern conflict and southern history can be found in Robert O. Collins, *The Southern Sudan, 1883–1898: A Struggle for Control*, 1962. A variety of southern perspectives can be found in O. Albino's *The Sudan: A Southern Viewpoint*, which was written before the settlement of 1972, and Dunstan Wai's *The Southern Sudan: The Problem of National Integration*, 1973. Mansour Khalid's *John Garang Speaks*, 1987, and G. Sorbo and Abdel Ghaffar M. Ahmed's *Management of the Crisis in the Sudan*, 1989, will bring the reader up to date in regard to the renewal of conflict and civil war since 1983. Historical coverage is provided in two books by the northern Sudanese writer M. O. Beshir, namely *The Southern Sudan: Background to Conflict* and *The Southern Sudan: From Conflict to Peace*.

Many of the now classical ethnic studies concern Sudan. The best known are the works of E. E. Evans-Pritchard, e.g., *The Nueri* and *Witchcraft, Oracles, and Magic Among the Azande*. Studies of the Dinka by Francis Deng, especially *Tradition and Modernization: A Challenge for Law among the Dinka of the Sudan*, *Africans of Two Worlds: The Dinka in Afro-Arab Sudan*, and *The Man Called Deng Majok: A Biography of Power, Polygyny and Change*, 1987, have enriched ethnographic knowledge of the southern region. While earlier studies during the colonial period tended to concentrate on southern groups, studies of northern peoples are more common since the outbreak of civil war in 1955, and its renewal in 1983, made research in the southern region all but impossible. Some of the better-known postcolonial studies of northern ethnic groups are Talal Asad's *The Kababish Arabs*; Ian Cunnison's *Baggara Arabs*; and Harold Barclay's *Burri al-Lamaab*. An exciting new dimension in the ethnographic literature of Sudan has been the documentation of the lives of women and their participation in history and culture, which is reflected in new sections in the bibliography as well as the dictionary itself.

Other fields reflect the diversity that has come to characterize the growing scholarship of Sudan. In the realm of economics there are valuable special studies, such as J. D. Tothill, *Agriculture in the Sudan;* A. Gaitskell, *Gezira: A Story of Development in the Sudan*; Sa'd al-Din Fawzi, *The Labour Movement in the Sudan, 1946–1955*; and Mohamed Abdel Rahman Ali, *Government Expenditure and Economic Development: A Case Study of the Sudan*. In the area of religion, there is the still useful *Islam in the Sudan* by J. S. Trimingham and G. Vantini's *Christianity in the Sudan*, 1981, which covers ancient as well as contemporary history. The area of law has seen some important works emerge, such as *Islamic Law and Society in the Sudan*, 1987, by Carolyn Fluehr-Lobban, and a new section entitled Law and Islamization, especially since Ja'atar al-Nimeiri proclaimed Shari'a to be state law in 1983, can be found in the bibliographic section on politics.

Since 1989, when allegations of a revival of slavery and human rights abuses directed against non-Muslim minorities began to surface under the 'Umer al-Bashir regime, a growing literature has developed, which is reflected in a new sections on human rights. The issue of refugees fleeing from Sudan's chronic civil war is also covered in a new section of the bibliography.

To follow current affairs in Sudan, people can use the chronologies in the *Middle East Journal,* published in Washington, DC, by the Middle East Institute and in *Africa Report,* published in New York. The annual reviews in *Africa Contemporary Record* are also helpful.

The following are occasional publications, documentation sources, or distribution outlets that publish materials relating to the study of Sudan:

- The *Sudan Studies Association Newsletter*, a publication of the Sudan Studies Association (USA), is a quarterly publication that includes organizational and member news, recent publications, book and film reviews, and current affairs. The current editor (1990–1992) is Isma'il 'Abdalla of the College of William and Mary, Williamsburg, Virginia. (N.B.: Vol. No. 1, 1981–present.)

- *Sudan Studies* is the official newsletter of the Sudan Studies Society of the United Kingdom and includes news, reports of research in Sudan, and current affairs, and it is published twice a year. Inquiries can be addressed to the following: Hon. Editor, Justin Wills, 43 North Bailey, Durham DH1 ZEX, England. (N.B.: 1987–present.)

- The Centre of Middle Eastern and Islamic Studies' Documentation Unit at the University of Durham has numerous Sudanese government and occasional publications relating to Sudan. The Sudan Collection at the University of Durham is overseen by Lesley Forbes and contains unique documents and memorabilia related to the British colonial experience in the Sudan. Ithaca Press (8 Richmond Road, Exeter EX4 4JA, United Kingdom) has undertaken the copublication along with the Graduate College and the University of Khartoum of many monographs and books that would ordinarily only appear in Sudan. These monographs cover a wide range of subjects in the sciences, social sciences, and humanities. They are primarily related to Sudanese studies.

- The Middle East Bibliographic Services (12077 Wilshire Boulevard, Suite 605, Los Angeles, California 90025, USA) distributes a number of titles relating to Sudan that, likewise, would not ordinarily be available in North America.

1. GENERAL REFERENCES

Adams, William Y. *Nubia: Corridor to Africa*. Princeton, N.J.: Princeton University Press, 1976.

Arkell, A. J. *A History of the Sudan to 1821*. London: Athlone Press, 1961.

Butzer, Karl W., and Carl L. Hansen. *Desert and River in Nubia*. Madison: University of Wisconsin Press, 1968.

The Cambridge History of Africa, ed. J. D. Fage and Roland Oliver. 8 vols. Cambridge: Cambridge University Press, 1986.

Collins, Robert O., and Robert L. Tignor. *Egypt and the Sudan*. Englewood Cliffs, N.J.: Prentice-Hall, 1967.

Gailey, Harry A. *History of Africa from Earliest Times to 1800*. Hinsdale, Ill.: Dryden Press, 1970.

Gleichen, A., ed. *The Anglo-Egyptian Sudan: A Compendium Prepared by Officers of the Sudan Government*. 2 vols. London: H.M.S.O., 1985.

Hasan, Yusuf Fadl, ed. *The Arabs and the Sudan*. Edinburgh: Edinburgh University Press, 1967.

——, ed. *Sudan Republic*. New York: Praeger, 1965.

Hill, Richard. *A Biographical Dictionary of the Sudan*. 2nd ed. London: Frank Cass, 1967.

Holt, Peter M. *A Modern History of the Sudan: From the Funj to the Present Day*. New York: Grove Press, 1961.

——. "The Sudan." In *The Arab World: A Handbook*, ed. Haddad and Nijim. Chicago: Medina Press, 1978.

Mackie, Ian. *Trek into Nubia*. Edinburgh: Pentland Press, 1994.

MacMichael, H. A. *A History of the Arabs in the Sudan*. 2 vols. New York: Barnes and Noble, 1967. (Original ed., 1922.)

el-Mahdi, Mandour. *A Short History of the Sudan*. London: Oxford University Press, 1965.

Said, Beshir Mohammed. *The Sudan: Crossroads of Africa*. London: Bodley Head, 1965.

"The Sudan: Twenty-Five Years of Independence." Lobban, Richard, and Carolyn Fluehr-Lobban, eds. *Africa Today* (Special Issue) 28, no. 2 (1981).

General Bibliographies

Ahmed, Osman Hassan., ed. *Sudan and Sudanese: A Bibliography of American and Canadian Dissertations and Theses on the Sudan*. Sudan Publication Series. Vol. 9. Washington, DC: Embassy of the Democratic Republic of the Sudan, 1982.

El-Beshir, Ahmed al-Amin, ed. *The Democratic Republic of the Sudan in American Sources*. Washington, DC: Office of the Cultural Counselor, Sudan Embassy, 1983.

Dagher, Joseph Assaad. *Sudanese Bibliography, Arabic Sources (1875–1967)*. Beirut: Librairie Orientale, 1968.

Evans-Pritchard, E. E. *Bibliographies on Modern Egypt and the Sudan*. Denver, Colo.: American Institute of Islamic Studies, 1972.

Hill, Richard L. *A Bibliography of the Anglo-Egyptian Sudan: From the Earliest Times to 1937*. Oxford: Oxford University Press, 1939.

el-Nasri, Abdel Rahman. *A Bibliography of the Sudan, 1938–1958*. London: Oxford University Press, 1962.

Nur, Qasim Osman. *Sudan: Bibliography of Bibliographies*. Khartoum: Economic and Social Research Council, 1982.

Zahlan, A. B., ed. *Agricultural Bibliography of Sudan 1974–1983*. London: Ithaca Press, 1984.

Travel and Description

al-Adawi, Ibrahim. "Description of the Sudan by Muslim Geographers and Travelers." *SNR* 35 (1954): 5–16.

Baker, Anne. *Morning Star: Florence Baker's Diary of the Expedition to Put Down the Slave Trade on the Nile, 1870–1873*. London: Kimber, 1972.

Baker, Sir Samuel White. *The Albert N'Yanza: Great Basin of the Nile and Explorations of the Nile Sources*. Detroit: Negro Universities Press, 1970. (Original ed., 1869.)

——. *In the Heart of Africa*. Westport, Conn.: Negro Universities Press, 1970.

——. *The Nile Tributaries of Abysinnia and the Sword Hunters of the Hamran Arabs*. New York: Johnson Reprint Corp., 1971. (Original ed., 1867.)

Budge, Ernest Alfred. *The Nile*. Westport, Conn.: Negro Universities Press, 1970. (Original ed., 1912.)

Clayton, Peter A. *David Roberts' Egypt*. London: Henry Sotheran, 1990.

Craig, Hugh. *Great African Travelers*. London: George Routledge and Sons, 1890.

Hall, Richard. *Lovers on the Nile*. New York: Quartet Books, 1981. (This work is an account of the travels of Samuel and Florence Baker.)

James, Frank. *The Wild Tribes of the Sudan*. New York: Negro Universities Press, 1969. (Original ed., 1883.)

Junker, Wilhelm. *Travels in Africa During the Years 1875–1878*, trans. A. H. Keane. London: Chapman and Hall, 1890.

Kinross, Lord. "The Nile." *Horizon* 8, no. 3 (1966): 80–99.

Langley, Michael. *No Woman's Country: Travels in the Anglo-Egyptian Sudan*. London: Jarrolds, 1950.

Ludwig, Emil. *The Nile: The Life-Story of a River*, trans. M. H. Lindsay. New York: Viking Press, 1937.

Petherick, John. *Travels in Central Africa and Explorations of the Western Nile Tributaries*. Farnborough: Gregg, 1968. (Original ed., 1869.)

Schuver, Juan Maria. *Juan Maria Schuver's Travels in Northeast Africa, 1880–1883*. London: Hakluyt Society, 1996.

Speke, John H. *What Led to the Discovery of the Source of Nile*. London: Cass, 1967. (Original ed., 1864.)

Taylor, Bayard. *A Journey to Central Africa: Or Life and Landscapes from Egypt to the Negro Kingdoms of the White Nile*. New York: Negro Universities Press, 1970. (Original ed., 1854.)

Ward, John. *Our Sudan, Its Pyramids and Progress*. London: Murray, 1985.

Audio-Visual Information

Ahmed, Osman Hassan. *A Bibliography of Documentary and Education Films on Sudan*. Washington, DC: Office of the Cultural Counselor, Sudan Embassy, 1982.

Anon. *Action Sudan: The Church and the Peace*. Toronto: Religious Television Associates for the Interchurch Committee for World Development and Relief, Canada, and Church World Service, 1974. Videocassette.

The Forgotten Kingdom. London: BBC-TV, 1971. (Released in the USA by Time-Life Films.) Videocassette.

Khartoum. England: Julian Blaustein Productions, 1966. (Released in the United States by United Artists Corp.) Videocassette.

Michael, Barbara, and Anne Kocherhaus. *Nomads of the Savanna*. 30 mins. Pennsylvania State University Audio-Visual Services, 1994. Videocassette.

The Nuer. 75 mins. Film Study Center, Peabody Museum, Harvard University, 1971. Videocassette.

Republic of Sudan. London: Eye Gate House, 1962. Filmstrip.

The Shilluk of Southern Sudan. 52 mins. Granada Television International, Ltd., 1976. Videocassette.

For Younger Readers

Burdett, Langley. *Discover Our Heritage*. Boston: Houghton Mifflin, 1997.

Bianchi, Robert Steven. *The Nubians: People of the Ancient Nile*. Brookfield, Conn.: Millbrook Press, 1994.

Caputo, R. "Sudan: Arab-African Giant." *National Geographic* 161, no. 3 (1982): 346–379.

Drower, Margaret. *Nubia: A Drowning Land*. London: Longmans, 1970.

Henderson, Larry. *Egypt and the Sudan: Countries of the Nile*. New York: Nelson, 1971.

Hodgkin, Robin A. *How People Live in the Sudan*. London: Educational Supply Association, 1963.

Hyslop, John. *Sudan Story*. London: Naldrett Press, 1952.

Langley, Andrew. *Explorers on the Nile*. Morristown, N.J.: Silver Burdette, 1982.

Mann, Kenny. *Egypt, Kush, Aksum: Northeast Africa*. Parsippany, N.J.: Dillon Press, 1997.

Roddis, Ingrid, and Miles Ingrid. *Let's Visit Sudan*. Bridgeport, Conn.: Burke Publishing, 1985.

Sudan. Enchantment of Africa Series, ed. Allan Carpenter. Chicago: Children's Press, 1972.

2. CULTURAL

Arts and Architecture

Anon. "Painter from the Sudan: El Salahi." *African Arts* 1, no. 1 (1967): 16–26.

——. "Traditional Music Archives, Institute of African and Asian Studies, University of Khartoum." *Africa* 65, no. 4 (1995): 611–612.

Diab, Rashid. "Contemporary African Art from the Sudanese Perspective." *Atlantica: Internacional Revista de las Arte* 8 (1994): 12–18; 126–129.

Hale, Sandra. "Arts in a Changing Society: Northern Sudan." *Ufahamu* (UCLA Journal of African Studies) 1, no. 11 (1970): 64–79.

——. "Sudanese Cultural Renaissance: Social Themes Have Brought About a Flowering of Written, Sung, and Spoken Word." *Africa Report* 15, no. 9 (1970): 29–31.

El-Hakim, Omar M. *Nubian Architecture: The Egyptian Vernacular Experience*. Cairo: Palm Press, 1993.

Lee, David R. "Mud Mansions of Northern Sudan." *African Arts* (1971–72): 60–62.

Mahgoub, Yasser Osman Moharam. "The Nubian Experience: A Study of the Social and Cultural Meanings of Architecture." Ph.D. diss., University of Michigan, 1990.

Semple, Clara. *Traditional Jewelry and Ornament of the Sudan*. London: Routledge, Kegan Paul International, 1990.

Shaddad, Muhammad Hamid, Kamala Ibrahima Ishaq, and Naiyla al-Tayib. "The Crystalist Manifesto (Al-bayan al-kristali)." In *Seven Stories About Modern Art in Africa*, ed. Clementine Deliss, 242–313. Paris and New York: Flammarion, 1995.

Spring, Christopher. "Beyond the Loom, Non-woven Designs, and Techniques." In *North African Textiles*, 99–117. Washington, DC: Smithsonian Institution Press, 1995.

Wenzel, Marian. *House Decoration in Nubia*. London: Duckworth, 1972.

Languages and Literature

Abbas, Ali Abdalla. "Notes of Tayeb Salih: *Season of Migration to the North* and *The Wedding of Zein*." *SNR* 55 (1974): 46–60.

——. "The Strangled Impulse: The Role of the Narrator in Tayeb Salih's *Season of Migration to the North*." *SNR* LX (1979): 56–85.

Abdul-Hai, Muhammad. *Conflict and Identity: The Cultural Poetics of Contemporary Sudanese Poetry*. African Seminar Series. Vol. 26. Khartoum: Institute of African and Asian Studies, Khartoum University, n.d.

Ahmed, Osman Hassan, ed. *A Short Anthology of Sudanese Literature, Selections from Sudanese Literature*. Vol. 5. Washington, DC: Office of the Cultural Counselor, Sudan Embassy, 1982.

——, ed. *Sixteen Sudanese Short Stories*. Sudanese Publication Series. Vol. 6. Washington, DC: Office of the Cultural Counselor, Sudan Embassy, 1981.

——, ed. *Tayeb Salih's Season of Migration to the North: A Casebook*. Beirut: American University in Beirut, 1985.

Bell, Herman. "An Extinct Nubian Language from Kordofan." *SNR* 54 (1973): 73–80.

Berkley, Constance E. "Artistry in El Tayeb Salih's Short Stories." *Northeast African Studies* 5, no. 1–2 (1983).

——. "The Contours of Sudanese Literature," *Africa Today* 18, no. 22 (1981): 109–119.

——. "'The Cypriote Man' and 'El Tayeb Salih'." *Pacific Moana Quarterly* 6, no. 3/4 (July/Oct. 1981): 176–189.

——. "Six Sudanese Poets." In *Encyclopedia of Arabic Literature*, ed. J. S. Meisami and Paul Starkey. London: Routledge, Fall 1997.

——. "The Sudanese Short Story: A Suspended View of Transitional Movements." *Africa Research & Publications Project* 6, no. 1 (1983).

——. "Systems of Thought in El Tayeb Salih's *Al-Rajul Al Qubrosi*." *The Search, Journal for Arab & Islamic Studies* 4, no. 1 and 2 (Winter 1983): 77–89.

Berkley, Constance E., and Osman Hassan Ahmed, eds. *Anthology of Modern Sudanese Poetry*. Sudanese Publication Series. Vol. 10. Washington, DC: Cultural Counselor's Office, Embassy of The Democratic Republic of the Sudan, August 1982.

Berkley, Constance E., and Osman Hassan Ahmed, eds. and trans. *Tayeb Salih Speaks: Four Interviews with the Sudanese Novelists*. Sudanese Publication Series. Vol. 8. Washington, DC: Cultural Counselor's Office, Embassy of The Democratic Republic of the Sudan, 1982.

Boullata, Issa J. "Encounter between East and West: A Theme in Contemporary Arabic Novels." *MEJ* 30, no. 1 (1976): 49–62.

Deliss, Clementine, ed. "The School of the One (Madrasat al-Wahid) Founding Manifesto." In *Seven Stories about Modern Art in Africa*, 244–246. Paris and New York: Flammarion, 1995.

Douglas, Dan. "From School to University: Language Policy and Performance at the University of Khartoum." *International Journal of the Sociology of Language* 61, no. 112 (1988): 89.

Elias, Edward E. *Practical Dictionary of the Colloquial Arabic of the Middle East*. Cairo: Elias' Modern Press, n.d.

Evans-Pritchard, E. E. "Azande Slang Language." *Man* 54 (1954): 185–186.

——. "Sanza: A Characteristic Feature of Zande Language and Thought." *Bulletin of The School of Oriental and African Studies* 18 (1956): 161–180.

Greenberg, J. H. "Nilotic, Nilo-Hamitic and Hamito-Semitic." *Africa* 27 (1957): 364–378.

——. *Studies in African Linguistic Classification*. New Haven, Conn.: Compass, 1955.

Hadra, Tawheeda Osman. "The Relative Clause in English and Sudanese Spoken Arabic." *SNR* LIX (1978): 24–46.

Horan, Hume A. *To the Happy Few: A Story of Death, Love, and Loss in the Sudan*. Washington, DC: Electric City Press, 1996.

Hurriez, Sayyid H. *Ja'aliyyin Folktales: An Interplay of African, Arabian, and Islamic Elements*. Bloomington: Indiana University Press, 1977.

Ibrahim, Abdullahi Ali. "Sudanese Historiography and Oral Tradition." *History in Africa* 12 (1985): 17–130.

Jernudd, Bjorn. "Phonetic Notes on Tone and Quality in the Fur Language." *SNR* LVIII (1977): 159–179.

Kohler, O. "The Early Study of the Nilotic Languages of the Sudan." *SNR* 51 (1970–1971): 56–62; 85–94.

Kojo Fusu. *Magdoub Rabbah and 'The Solar Engraving'*. Washington, DC: Office of the Cultural Counselor, Sudan Embassy, 1977.

Layton, Robert. "Creativity of the Artist." In *The Anthropology of Art*, ed. Robert Layton, 228–239. New York: Cambridge University Press, 1991.

Al-Mak, 'Ali. *A City of Dust*, trans. Al-Fatih Mahjoub and ed. Constance E. Berkley. Sudanese Publication Series. Vol. 11. Washington, DC: Cultural Counselor's Office, Embassy of The Republic of the Sudan, 1982.

Muhammad, Bagie Badawi. "The Role of Oral Poetry in Reshaping and Reconstructing Sudanese History (1820–1956)." *Folklore Forum* (1996): 60–74.

——. "The Sudanese Concept of Beauty, Spirit Possession, and Power." *Folklore Forum* (1993): 43–67.

Muhammad Hamid Shaddad, Kamala Ibrahim Ishaq, and Naiyla Al Tayeb. "The Crystalist Manifesto (al-Bayan al-Kristali)." In *Seven Stories about Modern Art in Africa*, ed. Clementine Deliss, 242–318. Paris and New York: Flammarion, 1995.

Murray, G. W. "An English-Nubian Comparative Dictionary." *Harvard African Studies* 4 (1923).

Nasr, Ahmad A. "Popular Islam in al-Tayib Salih," *Journal of Arab Literature* 11 (1980): 88–104.

Nebel, A. *Dinka Grammar*. Verona, Italy: Missioni Africane, 1948.

Sandell, Liza. *English Language in Sudan: A History of its Teaching and Politics*. London: Ithaca Press, 1982.

Shinnie, P. L. "The Ancient Languages of the Sudan." In *Language in the Sudan: A Symposium,* ed. R. W. Thelwal. London: Hurst, 1975.

al-Shoush, Mohammed Ibrahim. "In Search of Afro-Arab Identity: The Southern Concept of the Northern Sudan as Seen through the Novels of Francis Deng." *British Journal of Middle Eastern Studies* 18, no. 1 (1991): 67.

Struck, B. "A Bibliography of the Languages of the Southern Sudan." *SNR* 11 (1928).

Svoboda, Terese, trans. *Nuer Song Cleaned the Crocodile's Teeth*. Greenfield Center, N.Y.: Greenfield Review Press, 1985.

Trimingham, J. S. *Sudan Colloquial Arabic*. London: Oxford University Press, 1946.

'Ushari Ahmad, Mahmud. "Arabic in the Southern Sudan: History and Spread of Pidgin Creole." *International Journal of the Sociology of Language* 61 (1986): 113–116.

Sudan-Related Fiction in English

Atiyah, E. *Black Vanguard*. London: Davies, 1952.

Barry, Milo. *Bondage: Dervishes in the Sudan*. Van Nuys, Calif.: United Service, 1956.

Deng, Francis Mading. *The Cry of the Owl*. New York: Lilian Barber Press, 1989.

——. *Seed of Redemption: A Political Novel*. New York: Lilian Barber Press, 1986.

Gartner, Chloe. *Drums of Khartoum*. New York: Morrow, 1967.

Henriques, R. D. Q. *No Arms, No Armour*. London: Collins, 1951.

Kipling, R. *The Light That Failed*. London: Macmillan, 1898.

Sawkins, J. *Jangara*. London: Longmans, 1963.

Tayeb Salih. "The Doum Tree of Wad Hamid." In *Everyday Life in Muslim Society*, ed. D. Bowen and E. Early. Bloomington: Indiana University Press, 1995.

——. *Season of Migration to the North,* trans. Denys Johnson-Davies. London: Heinemann Educational Books, 1967.

——. *The Wedding of Zein and Other Stories*, trans. Denys Johnson-Davies. London: Heinemann, 1968.

3. SCIENTIFIC

Geography

Abdel Mageed, A. "Plant Domestication in the Middle Nile Basin." *Cambridge Monographs in African Archaeology* 35 (1989).

Abdel Mageed, Yahia. "Integrated River Basin Development: A Challenge to Nile Basin Countries." *SNR* LXII (1981): 69–81.

Ali, A. I. M. "A History of European Geographical Exploration of the Sudan, 1820–65." *SNR* 55 (1974): 1–15.

Babiker, Ahmed Abdalla Ahmed. "The Land Rotation Cultivation System and its Effects on Woody Vegetation Suppression in the Jebal Marra Area of Sudan." *SNR* LXII (1981): 108–122.

Bein, F. L. "Land Use Patterns along the Nile." *SNR* LIX (1978): 180–189.

el-Bushra, el-Sayed. "Towns in the Sudan in the Eighteenth and Early Nineteenth Centuries." *SNR* 52 (1971): 63–70.

Haynes, Kingsley E., and Dale Whittington. "International Management of the Nile, Stage Three?" *Geography Review* 71 (1901):17–32.

Ibrahim, Fouad N. *Ecological Imbalance in the Republic of the Sudan, with Reference to Desertification in Darfur.* Bayreuth, Germany: Bruckhaus, 1984.

Mahmoud, Abdel Salam. "Vegetational Dynamics in the Semi-Desert of Khartoum Province," *SNR,* LVIII (1977): 205–216.

Roden, David. "Regional Inequality and Rebellion in the Sudan." *Geographical Review* 64, no. 4 (1974): 498–516.

El-Sammani, M. O. "Gaps in the Water Provision Map of the Sudan." *SNR* LIX (1978): 97–106.

———. "The Impact of Water-Supply Centres on Ecosystems with a Suggested Strategy for Action." *SNR* LXII (1981): 123–146.

El-Tom, Mahdi Amin. *The Rains of the Sudan.* Khartoum: Khartoum University Press, 1975.

———. "The Relative Dryness of the White Nile." *SNR* 55 (1974): 161–166.

———. "Toward a Rational Estimation of Average Rainfall in the Sudan." *SNR* 53 (1972): 123–151.

Van Arsdale, Peter W. "The Ecology of Survival in Sudan's Periphery: Short-Term Tactics and Long-Term Strategies." *Africa Today* 36, nos. 3–4 (1989): 65–79.

Geology

Ahmed, Farouq. "The Sileitat es-Sufur Subvolcanic Intrusion, Northern Khartoum Province." *SNR* LVIII (1977): 226–233.

Almond, D. C. "New Ideas on the Geological History of the Basement Complex of North-East Sudan." *SNR* LIX (1978): 107–136.

el-Boushi, Ismail Mudathir. "The Shallow Ground Water of the Gezira Formation at Khartoum and the Northern Gezira." *SNR* 53 (1972): 152–161.

Hussein, Mohammed Tahir. "Reconstitution of the Paleogeography of the Delta Tokar." *SNR* LIX (1978): 145–165.

Mula, Hafiz G. "A Geophysical Survey of J. Aulia Region." *SNR* 53 (1972): 162–166.

Omer, M. K., and J. Perriaux. "Gedaref Sandstones vs. Nubian Sandstones: A Comparative Study." *SNR* LIX (1978): 137–144.

Shepherd, A., et. al. *Water Planning in Arid Sudan.* London: Ithaca Press, 1987.

Vogt, Kees. *A Field Worker's Guide to the Identification, Propagation, and Uses of Common Trees and Shrubs of Dryland Sudan.* London: SOS Sahel, 1995.

———. *The Geology of the Sudan Republic.* Oxford: Clarendon Press, 1971.

Medicine and Health

Bayoumi, Ahmed. *The History of Sudan Health Services.* Nairobi, Kenya: Literature Bureau, 1979.

Constantinides, P. "Ill at Ease and Sick at Heart: Symbolic Behavior in a Sudanese Healing Cult." In *Symbols and Sentiments*, ed. I. M. Lewis, 63–84. London: Academic Press, 1977.

Erwa, Hashim H., M. H. Satti, and A. M. Abbas. "Cerebrospinal Meningitis in the Sudan." *SNR* 52 (1971): 101–109.

Gruenbaum, Ellen. "The Islamist Movement, Development, and Health Education: Recent Changes in the Health of Rural Women in Central Sudan." *Social Science and Medicine* 33, no. 6 (1991): 637–646.

———. "Medical Anthropology, Health Policy, and the State: A Case Study of Sudan." *Policy Studies Review* 1 (1981): 47–65.

Hartwig, Gerald W. "Smallpox in the Sudan." *IJAHS* 14, no. 1 (1981): 5–33.

Khalifa, M. A. "Age Pattern Fertility in the Sudan." *Journal of Biosocial Science* 15 (1983): 317–323.

Lowenstein, L. F. "Attitude and Attitude Differences to Female Genital Mutilation in the Sudan: Is there Change on the Horizon?" *Social Science and Medicine* 12 A, no. 5 (1978): 417–421.

Osman, Abdel A 'al Abdalla. "Milestones in the History of Surgical Practice in the Sudan." *SNR* 54 (1973): 139–152.

Rushwan, Hamid E. "Epidemiological Analysis and Reproductive Characteristics of Incomplete Abortion Patients in Khartoum, the Sudan." *Journal of Biosocial Science* 11, no. 1 (1979): 65–75.

Rushwan, Hamid E., J. G. Ferguson, and R. P. Bernard Jr. "Hospital Counseling in Khartoum: A Study of Factors Affecting Contraceptive Acceptance after Abortion." *International Journal of Gynaecology and Obstetrics* 15, no. 5 (1978): 440–443.

Schwabe, Calvin, and Isaac Makuet Kuojok. "Practices and Beliefs of the Traditional Dinka Healer in Relation to Provision of Modern Medical and Veterinary Services for the Southern Sudan." *Human Organization* 40 (1981): 231–238.

El Tahir, Taha. "Family Planning Practice in Central Sudan." *Social Science and Medicine* 37, no. 5 (1993): 685–690.

Takasaka, Kouichi. "Postpartum Amenorrhea: Waiting Time to Conception and Prevalence of Pregnancy in a Sudanese Agricultural Community." *Human Biology* 58 (1996): 933–944.

El-Tom, A. R., et al. "Introducing Integrated Health Services in a Traditional Society: The Sudan Community-Based Family Health Project." *International Quarterly of Community Health and Education* 5, no. 3 (1984–5): 187–202.

Yousif, Yousif Babiker, Kalyan Bagchi, and Abdel Gadir Khattab. "Food and Nutrition in the Sudan." In *Proceedings of the First National Food and Nutrition Seminar 1972*. Khartoum: National Council for Research, 1973.

4. SOCIAL ANTHROPOLOGY

Abdalla, Isma'il Hussein. "The Choice of Khashm al-Girba Area for the Resettlement of the Halfawis." *SNR* LI (1970): 56–74.

Abd al-Rahim, Muddathir. "Arabism, Africanism, and Self-Identification in the Sudan." In *Sudan in Africa*, ed. Y. F. Hasan, 228–239. Khartoum: Sudan Research Unit, Sudan Studies Library, 1971.

Ahmed, Abdel Ghaffer M. "The State of Anthropology in the Sudan." *Ethnos* 47, nos. 1–2 (1982): 64–80.

Ali-Dinar, Ali Bahr Aldin. "Contextual Analysis of Dress and Adornment in Al-Fashir, Sudan." Ph.D. diss., University of Pennsylvania, 1995.

'Ali El-Dawi, Taj El-Anbia. "El-Obeid: A Sudanese Urban Community in Kordofan Province." *African Urban Notes* 6, no. 2 (1971): 99–107.

Anon. "Traditional Music Archives, Institute of African and Asian Studies, University of Khartoum." *Africa* 65, no. 4 (1995): 611–612.

Arens, W. "The Divine Kingship of the Shilluk: A Contemporary Reevaluation." *Ethnos* 44, nos. 3–4 (1979): 167–181.

Asad, Talal. *The Kababish Arabs*. London: C. Hurst, 1970.

Andretta, Elizabeth. "Symbolic Continuity, Material Discontinuity, and Ethnic Identity among Murle Communities in the Southern Sudan." *Ethnology* 28, no. 1 (1989): 17–31.

Awad, Mohamed Hashim. *Socio-economic Change in the Sudan*. Khartoum: Graduate College, University of Khartoum and London: Ithaca Press, 1983.

Barclay, Harold B. *Buuri al Lamaab: A Suburban Village in the Sudan*. Ithaca, N.Y.: Cornell University Press, 1964.

Baumann, Gerd. *National Integration and Local Integrity: The Miri of the Nuba Mountains in the Sudan*. Oxford: Oxford University Press, 1988.

Bernal, Victoria. *Cultivating Workers: Peasants and Capitalism in a Sudanese Village*. New York: Columbia University Press, 1991.

el-Bushra, El-Sayed Mohammed. "The Definition of a Town in the Sudan." *SNR* 54 (1973): 66–72.

——. "Sudan's Triple Capital: Morphology and Functions." *Ekistics* 39 (1975): 246–250.

Burton, John W. "The Creation and Destruction of Nilotic Sudan." *Journal of Asian and African Studies* 29, nos. 1–2 (1994): 1–9.

——. "The Ghost of Malinowski in the Southern Sudan: Evans-Pritchard and Ethnographic Fieldwork." *Proceedings of the American Philosophical Society* 127, no. 4 (1983): 278–289.

——. "When North Winds Blow: A Note on Small Towns and Social Transformation in the Nilotic Sudan." *African Studies Review* 31, no. 3 (1988): 49.

Connick, Roxanne. "Woman Singer in Darfur, Sudan Republic." *Anthropos* 68 (1973): 785–800.

Cunnison, Ian. *Baggara Arabs*. Oxford: Clarendon Press, 1966.

Cunnison, Ian, and Wendy James, eds. *Essays in Sudan Ethnography Presented to Edward Evans-Pritchard*. New York: Humanities Press, 1972.

Deng, Francis Mading. *Africans of Two Worlds: The Dinka in Afro-Arab Sudan*. New Haven, Conn.: Yale University Press, 1978.

——. *Dinka Folktales: African Stories from the Sudan*. New York: Africana Publishing, 1974.

——. *The Dinka of the Sudan*. New York: Holt, Rinehart, and Winston, 1972.

——. *The Man Called Deng Majok: A Biography of Power, Polygyny, and Change*. New Haven, Conn.: Yale University Press, 1987.

——. *Tradition and Modernization: A Challenge for Law among the Dinka of the Sudan*. New Haven, Conn.: Yale University Press, 1971.

Duffield, Mark. *Maiurno: The Transformation of a Peasant Society in Sudan*. London: Ithaca Press, 1981.

Evans-Pritchard, Edward Evan. *The Azande, History, and Political Institutions*. Oxford, England: Clarendon Press, 1971.

——. *Man and Woman among the Azande*. London: Faber and Faber, 1974.

——. *The Nuer*. Oxford: Clarendon Press, 1940.

——. *Nuer Religion*. Oxford: Clarendon Press, 1940.

——. *Witchcraft, Oracles, and Magic among the Azande*. Oxford: Clarendon Press, 1937.

Faris, James C. *Southeast Nuba Social Relations*. Aachen: Alano, 1989.

Fernea, Elizabeth Warnock. *Nubian Ethnographies*. Prospect Heights, Ill.: Waveland Press, 1991.

Fernea, Robert A. *Nubians in Egypt, Peaceful People*. Austin: University of Texas Press, 1973.

Fluehr-Lobban, Carolyn. "An Anthropological Analysis of Homicide in the Afro-Arab Sudan." *Journal of African Law* 20, no. 1 (1976): 20–38.

——. "Josina's Observations of Sudanese Culture." *Human Organization* 40 (1981): 177–179.

——. *Law and Anthropology in the Sudan*. Sudan Research Unit, 13. Khartoum: University of Khartoum Press, 1973.

——. *Islamic Law and Society in the Sudan*. London: Frank Cass, 1987.

——. *Islamic Society in Practice*. Gainesville: University Press of Florida, 1994.

Fluehr-Lobban, Carolyn, and Richard Lobban. "Families, Gender, and Methodology in the Sudan." In *Self, Sex, and Gender in Cross-Cultural Fieldwork*, 182–96. Urbana: University of Illinois Press, 1986.

Grawert, Elke. *Making a Living in Rural Sudan: Production of Women, Labour Migration of Men, and Policies for Peasants' Needs*. New York: St. Martin's Press, 1998.

Haaland, R. "Archaeological Classification and Ethnic Groups: A Case Study from Sudanese Nubia." *Norwegian Archaeological Review* 10 (1977): 1–31.

Hale, Sondra. *Nubians: A Study in Ethnic Identity*. Vol. 17. Khartoum: Institute of African and Asian Studies, 1971.

Holy, Ladislav. *Neighbors and Kinsmen: A Study of the Berti People of Darfur*. New York: St. Martin's Press, 1974.

Huffman, Ray. *Nuer Customs and Folklore*. London: Frank Cass, 1970.

Jok, Jok Madut. "Women, Sexuality, and Social Behavior in Western Dinka: The Impact of War on Reproductive Health in South Sudan." Ph.D. diss., UCLA, 1996.

James, Wendy R. *Kwanim-Pa—The Making of the Uduk People: An Ethnographic Study of Survival in the Sudan-Ethiopian Borderlands*. Oxford: Clarendon Press, 1979.

——. "Social Assimilation and Changing Identity in the Southern Funj." In *Sudan in Africa*, ed. Yusuf Fadl Hasan, 197–211. Sudan Research Unit: Khartoum University Press, 1971.

Johnson, Douglas H. "C. A. Willis and the 'Cult of Deng': A Falsification of the Ethnographic Record." *History in Africa* 12 (1985): 117–130.

Karp, Ivan, and Kent Maynard. "Reading the Nuer." *Current Anthropology* 24, no. 4 (1983): 481–492.

Kelly, Raymond C. "A Note on Nuer Segmentary Organization," *American Anthropologist* 85, no. 4 (1983): 905–906.

Kleppe, Else Johansen "The Debbas on the White Nile, Southern Sudan," In *Culture History in the Southern Sudan: Archaeology, Linguistics, and Ethnohistory*, ed. J. Mack and P. Robertshaw, 59–71. Nairobi: British Institute in East Africa, 1982.

Lewis, B. A. *The Murle, Red Chiefs, and Black Commoners*. Oxford: Clarendon Press, 1972.

Lienhardt, G. *Divinity and Experience: The Religion of the Dinka*. London: Oxford Press, 1961.

Lobban, Richard A., Jr. "Class, Endogamy, and Urbanization in the Three Towns of the Sudan." *African Studies Review* XXII, no. 3 (1979): 99–114.

——. "Class and Kinship in Sudanese Urban Communities." *Africa* 52, no. 2 (1982): 51–76.

——. "The Dialectics of Migration and Social Association in the Urban Sudan." *International Journal of Sociology* XX (1977): 99–120.

——. "A Genealogical and Historical Study of the Mahas of the Three Towns, Sudan," *IJAHS* 16, no. 2 (1983): 231–262.

———. "Sudanese Class Formation and the Demography of Urban Migration." In *Arab Society: Social Science Perspectives*, ed. N. S. Hopkins and S. E. Ibrahim, 163–176. New York: Columbia Nadel University Press, 1985.

———. "Urbanization and Malnutrition in the Sudan." *Northeast African Studies* (1982).

Lobban, Richard A., and C. Fluehr-Lobban. "Drink from the Nile and You Shall Return: Children and Fieldwork in the Sudan and Egypt." In *Children in the Field*, ed. J. Cassell, 237–255. Philadelphia, Penn.: Temple University Press, 1987.

MacMichael, Harold A. *The Tribes of Northern and Central Kordofan*. London: Frank Cass, 1967. (Original ed., 1912.)

Makris, G. P. "Slavery, Possession and History: The Construction of the Self among Slave Descendants in the Sudan." *Africa* 66, no. 2 (1996): 159–182.

Mohammed, Abbas Ahmed. *White Nile Arabs, Political Leadership and Economic Change*. London School of Economics, Monographs on Social Anthropology. Vol. 53. London: The Athlone Press, 1980.

Nadel, S. F. *The Nuba: An Anthropological Study of the Hill Tribes of Kordofan*. London: Publisher, 1947.

O'Brien, Jay. "The Calculus of Profit and Labour-Time in Sudanese Peasant Agriculture." *The Journal of Peasant Studies* 14, no. 4 (1987): 454–468.

———. "Toward a Reconstitution of Ethnicity: Capitalist Expansion and Cultural Dynamics in Sudan." *American Anthropologist* 88, no. 4 (1986): 898–907.

Ogot, B. A. *History of the Southern Luo*. Nairobi: East African Publishing House, 1967.

Paul, A. *A History of the Beja Tribes of the Sudan*. London: Frank Cass, 1968. (Original ed., 1954.)

Payne, W. J. A., and Mustafa Khogali. "Notes on the Occurrence of Gizu in Northern Darfur Province." *SNR* LVIII (1977): 217–225.

Poeschke, Roman. *Nubians in Egypt and Sudan: Constraints and Coping Strategies*. Saarbrucken: Verlag für Entwicklungs Politik, 1996.

Rehfisch, Famham. "A Study of Some Southern Migrants in Omdurman." *SNR* 43 (1962): 50–104.

Riefenstahl, L. *The Last of the Nubia*. New York: Harper and Row, 1974.

Saleh, Mohammed Hassan. "Hadanduwa Traditional Territorial Rights and Inter-Population Relations within the Context of the Native Administration System (1927-1970)." *SNR* LXI (1980): 118–133.

Seligman, C. G. "The Early History of the Anglo-Egyptian Sudan." *Scientific American* 81 (1916).

———. "The Hamitic Problem in the Sudan." *Journal of the Royal Anthropological Institute* 42 (1913).

Seligman, C. G., and B. Z. Seligman. *Pagan Tribes of the Nilotic Sudan*. London: G. Routledge and Sons, 1932.

al-Shahi, Ahmed, ed. *Themes from Northern Sudan*. London: Ithaca Press, 1986.

Singer, Andre, and Brian V. Street. *Zande Themes*. Totowa, N.J.: Rowman & Littlefield, 1972.

Stevenson, R. C. *Nuba People of Kordofan Province: An Ethnographic Survey.* Khartoum: University of Khartoum Press, 1984.

Tubiana, Marie-Jose. "Power and Confidence: The Mother's Brother-Sister's Son Relationship and the Zaghawa Political System (Chad-Sudan)." *Cahiers d'Etudes Africaines* 19, no. 1–4 (1979): 73–76.

Tully, Dennis. *Culture and Context in Sudan: The Process Market Incorporation in Dar Masalit.* Albany: State University of New York Press, 1988.

Verdon, Michel. "Where Have all the Lineages Gone? Cattle and Descent among the Nuer." *American Anthropologist* 84, no. 3 (1982): 566–579.

Wall, L. L. "Anuak Politics, Ecology, and the Origins of Shilluk Kingship." *Ethnology* 15 (1976): 151–162.

Zahir, Fahima. "Khartoum North Squatter Settlements." In *Proceedings of the 17th Annual Conference of the Philosophical Society of the Sudan*, 222–243. Khartoum: University of Khartoum Press, 1972.

Demography and Population

Abusharaf, Rogaia M. "Sudanese Migration to the New World: Socio-Economic Characteristics." *International Migration* 35, no. 4 (1997): 513–535.

Abu Sin, M. E. "Environmental Causes and Implications of Population Displacement in Sudan." In *War and Drought in Sudan*, ed. E. Eltigani, 11–22. Gainesville: University Press of Florida, 1995.

el-Agraa, Omer, et al. *Popular Settlements in Greater Khartoum.* London: International Institute for Environment and Development, 1985.

Balamoan, G. Ayoub. "Migration Policies and the Shaping of the Sudanese Society." In *Policy Sciences and Population,* ed. W. F. Ilchman, et al., 193–216. Lexington, Mass.: Lexington Books/D. C. Heath, 1975.

——. *Migration Policies in the Anglo-Egyptian Sudan, 1884–1956.* Cambridge, Mass.: Harvard University, Center for Population Studies, 1976.

Birks, Stace J. "Migration, A Significant Factor in the Historical Demography of the Savannas: The Growth of the West African Population of Darfur, Sudan." In *African Historical Demography*, 195–210. Edinburgh: University of Edinburgh, 1977.

Birks, Stace J., and Clive Sinclair. *Human Capital on the Nile: Development and Emigration in the Arab Republic of Egypt and the Democratic Republic of the Sudan.* Geneva: International Labour Office, 1978.

Dafallah, Hassan. *The Nubian Exodus.* Khartoum: Khartoum University Press, 1975.

Demeny, Paul. "The Demography of the Sudan, An Analysis of the 1955–56 Census." In *The Demography of Tropical Africa,* ed. W. Brass, et al., 466–514. Princeton, N.J.: Princeton University Press, 1968.

Eltigani, Eltigani E., ed. *War and Drought in Sudan: Essays on Population Displacement.* Gainesville: University Press of Florida, 1995.

Fahim, Hussein M. *Nubian Resettlement in the Sudan.* 13th ed. Cairo: Social Research Center, American University in Cairo, 1972.

Farah, Abdul-Aziz, and Samuel H. Preston. "Child Mortality Differentials in Sudan." *Population and Development Review* 8, no. 2 (1982): 365–383.

Farah, Abdul-Aziz , et al., eds. *Aspects of Population Change and Development in the Sudan.* Khartoum: Khartoum University Press, 1982.

Fourth Population Census of Sudan, 1993: Advance Sample Tabulations, Northern State. Khartoum: Department of Statistics, Census Office, 1994.

Fourth Population Census of Sudan, 1993: Final Tabulations, Northern State. Khartoum: Department of Statistics, Census Office, 1994.

Hassaballa, Hassaballa O., and E. Eltigani. "Displacement and Migration as a Consequence of Development Policies in Sudan." In *War and Drought in Sudan,* ed. E. Eltigani, 23–34. Gainesville: University Press of Florida, 1995.

Henin, Roushdi. "The Level and Trend of Fertility in the Sudan." In *Population Growth and Economic Development in Africa,* ed. S. H. Ominde and C. N. Ejiogu. London: Heinemann, 1972.

Jalal el-Deen, Mohamad al-Awad. "Birth Control Trends and Preference for Male Children in Jordan and Sudan." *Population Bulletin of ECWA* 22/23 (1982): 71–91.

Khalifa, Mona. "Birth Control Practice in Khartoum." *Egyptian Population and Family Planning Review* 15, no. 1 (1981): 10–21.

Khogali, Mustafa Mohammed. "Western Sudanese Migrants to Khasm el-Girba Agricultural Region." In *Redistribution of Population in Africa,* ed. J. I. Clarke and L. Kosinski, 166–175. London: Heinemann, 1982.

Krotki, Karol J., ed. "The Population of Sudan in the 19th Century and the Beginning of the 20th." *Annuaire de Demographie Historie* (1979): 165–193.

——. *Travellers' and Administrators' Guesses of Population Size in XIX and XX Century, Sudan, Contrasted with Quasi-Stable Estimates.* Edmonton: University of Alberta, 1975.

Lobban, Richard A. "Sudanese Class Formation and the Demography of Urban Migration." In *Toward a Political Economy of Urbanization in Third World Countries,* ed. H. I. Safa, 67–83. Oxford: Oxford University Press, 1982.

Mahmoud, Mahjoub El-Tigani. "Sudanese Emigration to Saudi Arabia." *International Migratio* 21, no. 4 (1983): 500–514.

el-Mustafa, Mohamed Yousif Ahmed. "Fertility and Migration: A Preliminary Analysis of Dynamics of Urban Growth (Sudan)." Khartoum: National Council for Research, 1981.

Sid Ahmed, Galal el-Din. "The First Year at Khashm al Girba." *SNR* XLVIII (1967): 160–166.

"The Sudan Fertility Survey, 1979: A Summary of Findings." *World Fertility Survey Summary of Findings* 36 (1982): 1–17.

The Sudan. Chapel Hill: Carolina Population Center Library, University of North Carolina, 1977.

Sociology and Social Conditions

Abdelrahman, A. I., and Morgan S. Philip. "Socioeconomic and Institutional Correlates of Family Formation: Khartoum, Sudan, 1945–75." *Journal of Marriage and the Family* 49, no. 2 (1987): 401–412.

Ahmed, Abdel Ghaffar M., and Mustafa Abdel Rahman. "Small Urban Centres: Vanguard of Exploitation; Two Cases from Sudan," *Africa* 49, no. 3 (1979): 258–271.

el-Arifi, Salih Abdalla. "Urbanization in the Gezira Scheme." *SNR* LXI (1980): 47–64.

Awad, M. "The Evolution of Landownership in the Sudan." *MEJ* 25, no. 2 (1971): 212–228.

Cederblad, Marianne, and Sheikh Idris A. Rahim. "Effects of Rapid Urbanization on Child Behavior and Health in a Part of Khartoum, Sudan I. Socio-Economic Changes, 1965–1980." *Social Science and Medicine* 22, no. 7 (1986): 713–721.

Fluehr-Lobban, Carolyn. "Women and Social Liberation: The Sudan Experience." In *Three Studies on National Integration in the Arab World.* Vol. 12. North Dartmouth, Mass.: Arab-American University Graduates, 1974.

Hale, Sondra. "Nubians in the Urban Millieu: Great Khartoum." *SNR* 54 (1973): 57–73.

Herbert, D. T., and Naila B. Hijazi. "Urban Deprivation in the Developing World: The Case of Khartoum/Omdurman." *Third World Planning Review* 6, no. 3 (1984): 263–281.

Lobban, Richard A. "Alienation, Urbanization, and Social Networks in the Sudan." *JMAS* 13, no. 3 (1975): 491–500.

———. "The Historical Role of the Mahas in the Urbanization of the Sudan's Three Towns." *African Urban Notes* (1971): 24–38.

———. "Two Urban Communities in the Three Towns." *African Urban Notes* 6, no. 2 (1972).

———. "Urban Studies and Bibliography on Urbanization in the Sudan." *African Urban Notes* (1970): 37–46.

Nordenstam, Tore. *Sudanese Ethics.* Uppsala: Scandinavian Institute of African Studies, 1968.

Rahim, Sheikh Idris A., and Marianne Cederblad. "Effects of Rapid Urbanization on Child Behavior and Health in a Part of Khartoum, Sudan II. Psycho-Social Influence on Behavior." *Social Science and Medicine* 22, no. 7 (1986): 723–730.

Salih, Mohamed, and Margaret Salih, eds. *Family Life in the Sudan.* Khartoum and London: University of Khartoum Press and Ithaca Press, 1986.

Wolfers, Michael. "Race and Class in the Sudan." *Race and Class* 23, no. 1 (1981): 65–79.

Refugees

Akol, Joshua Otor. "Refugee Migration and Repatriation: Case Studies of Some Affected Rural Communities in Southern Sudan." Ph.D. diss., University of Manitoba, 1985.

Asher, Michael. "Sudan Sends Hungry Home to Starve: After Ethiopia, the Drought in Sudan is Gathering Pace." *African Business* (Feb. 1985): 16–18.

Hagos, H. "Refugees as a Resource for Development: A Case Study of Eritrean and Ethiopian Refugees in the Sudan, 1967–1992." Ph.D. diss., Manchester University, UK, 1995.

Karadawi, Ahmed. "Constraints on Assistance to Refugees: Some Observations from the Sudan (Ethiopian Refugees in the Sudan)." *World Development* 11 (1983): 537–547.

Kilgour, Mary C. "Refugees and Development: Dissonance in Sudan." *MEJ* 44 (1990): 638–649.

Kuhlman, Tom. *Burden or Boon? Eritrean Refugees in the Sudan.* London: Zed Books, 1991.

Luling, Virginia. "Oromo Refugees in a Sudanese Town." *Northeast African Studies* 8, nos. 2–3 (1986): 131–142.

Nobel, Peter. "Refugee Law in the Sudan: With the Refugee Conventions and the Regulation of Asylum Act of 1974." *Scandinavian Institute of African Studies* 64 (1982).

el-Nur, Ibrahim. *Resource Guide to Displaced and Refugee Studies in the Sudan: An Annotated Bibliography.* Khartoum: Khartoum University Press, 1994.

Rogge, John R. *Too Many, Too Long: Sudan's Twenty-Year Refugee Dilemma.* London: Rowman and Allanheld, 1985.

———. "Urban Refugees in Africa: Some Changing Dimensions to Africa's Refugee Problem with Special Reference to Sudan." *Migration World Magazine* 14, no. 4 (1986): 7–13.

Weaver, Jerry L. "Searching for Survival: Urban Ethiopian Refugees in Sudan." *Journal of Developing Areas* 22 (1988): 457–475.

———. "Sojourners along the Nile: Ethiopian Refugees in Khartoum" *JMAS* 23, no. 1 (1985): 147–156.

Wilson, Ken. "The Impact of Refugees." *Horn of Africa* 8, no. 1 (1985): 73–78.

Woldegabriel, Berhane, et al. "Food: Our Daily Bread." *Sudanow* 6 (1981): 6–10.

Woodward, Peter. "Political Factors Contributing to the Generation of Refugees in the Horn of Africa." *International Relations* 84 (1985): 15–38.

Religion

el-Affendi, Abdelwahab. *Turabi's Revolution, Islam and Power in the Sudan.* London: Grey Seal Books, 1991.

Beidelman, Thomas O. "The Nuer Concept of Thek and the Meaning of Sin: Explanation, Translation, and Social Structure." *History of Religion* 21 (1981): 126–155.

Burton, John W. "Christians, Colonists, and Conversion: A View from the Nilotic Sudan." *JMAS* 23, no. 2 (1985): 349–369.

Cudsi, Alexander S. "Islam and Politics in the Sudan (From 'Abbud Regime, 1958–64, to President Ja'far Numayri)." In *Islam in the Political Process*, ed. J. Piscatori, 36–55. 1983.

Daly, Martin W., ed. *Al-Majdhubiyya and al-Mikashfiyya: Two Sufi Tariqas in the Sudan.* Khartoum and London: Ithaca Press, 1985.

Dekmejian, R. Hrair. "Charismatic Leadership in Messianic and Revolutionary Movements: The Mahdi (Muhammad Ahmad) and the Messiah (Shabbatai Sevi)." In *Religious Resurgence*, ed. R. Antoun and M. E. Hegland, 78–107. Syracuse: Syracuse University Press, 1987.

Delmut, Christian. "Islamization and Traditional Society and Culture of Jabal Quli (Dar Funj)." *SNR* LXII (1981): 25–46.

Deng, Francis M. "Dinka Response to Christianity: The Pursuit of Well Being in a Developing Society." In *Vernacular Christianity*, ed. W. James and D. Johnson, 157–169. New York: Lilian Barber Press, 1988.

———. *Dinka Cosmology.* London: Ithaca Press, 1980.

Elayeh, E. H. "The Second Message of Islam: A Critical Study of the Islamic Reformist Thinking of Mahmoud Muhammad Taha (1909–1985)." Ph.D. diss., Manchester University, 1995.

Esposito, John L. "Sudan's Islamic Experiment." *Muslim World* 76, nos. 3–4 (1986): 181–202.

Fluehr-Lobban, Carolyn. "Islamization in the Sudan: A Critical Assessment" *MEJ* 44, no. 4 (1990): 610–623.

al-Gaddal, Mohammed Said. "Religion in a Changing Socio-Political Structure: A Case Study of Islam in the Nineteenth Century Sudan." *Mawazo* 5, no. 4 (1984): 23–30.

Gafour, Ayyoub-Awage Bushara. *My Father the Spirit Priest.* Lewiston, N.J.: Edwin Mellen Press,1987.

Grandin, Nicole. "Le Shaykh Muhammad 'Uthman al-Mirghani (1793–1853): Une Double Lecture de ses Hagiographies." *Archives de Sciences Sociales de Religions* 58, no. 1 (1984): 139–155.

Hale, Sondra. "Sudan Civil War: Religion, Colonialism, and the World System." In *Muslim-Christian Conflicts*, ed. S. Joseph, 157–182. Boulder, CO: Westview Press, 1978.

Hamoudi, Salah el-Tigani. "Arab and Islamic Origins of the Tomb and Sacred Enclave in the Sudan." *SNR* LVIII (1977): 107–116.

Hasan, Yusuf Fadl. "The Penetration of Islam in the Eastern Sudan." In *Islam in Tropical Africa*, ed. I. M. Lewis 112–123. London: Oxford University Press, 1966.

Hill, R. L. "Government and Christian Missions in the Anglo-Egyptian Sudan." *MES* 1, no. 2 (1965): 113–34.

Hofheinz, Albrecht. "Internalizing Islam, Shaykh Muhammad Majdhub: Scriptural Islam and Local Context in the Early Nineteenth Century Sudan." Ph.D., diss., University of Bergen, 1996.

Holt, Peter M. *Holy Families and Islam in the Sudan.* Princeton, N.J.: Princeton University Program in Near Eastern Studies, 1967.

———. "The Islamization of the Nilotic Sudan." in *Northern Africa: Islam and Modernization*, ed. M. Brett, 13–22. London: Frank Cass, 1973.

Holy, Ladislav. *Religion and Custom, In a Muslim Society: The Berti of the Sudan.* Cambridge: Cambridge University Press, 1991.

Jacobs, Scott H. "The Sudan's Islamization." *Current History* 84 (1985): 205–208.

James, Wendy. *The Listening Ebony: Moral Knowledge, Religion, and Power among the Uduk of Sudan*. Oxford: Clarendon Press, 1988.

James, Wendy, and Douglas H. Johnson, eds. *Vernacular Christianity: Essays in the Social Anthropology of Religion Presented to Godfrey Lienhardt*. New York: Lilian Barber Press, 1988.

Johnson, Douglas H. "Divinity Abroad: Dinka Missionaries in Foreign Lands." In *Vernacular Christianity,* ed. W. James D. Johnson, 170–182. New York: Lilian Barber Press, 1988.

Johnson, Nels. "Religious Paradigms of the Sudanese Mahdiyah." *Ethnohistory* 25, no. 25 (1978): 159–178.

Jombi, Caesar Lukudu. *Juridic Structure of the Christian Church in the Sudan: From the Origin of Christianity in Nubia Before and After the Diffusion of Islam.* Rome: Pontificia Universita Lateranense, 1987.

Kaba, Lansine. "The Politics of Quranic Education among Muslim Traders in the Western Sudan: The Subbanu Experience." *Canadian Journal of African Studies* 10, no. 3 (1976): 409–421.

Kapteijns, Lidwien. "Mahdist Faith and the Legitimation of Popular Revolt in Western Sudan." *Africa* 55, no. 4 (1985): 390–399.

——. *Mahdist Faith and Sudanic Tradition: The History of Masalit Sultanate, 1870–1930.* London: Kegan Paul, 1985.

al-Karsani, Awad al-Sid. "The Establishment of Neo-Mahdism in the Western Sudan, 1920–1934." *African Affairs* 86 (1987): 385–404.

Kleppe, Else Johansen. "Religion Expressed through Bead Use: An Ethnoarchaeological Study of Shilluk, Southern Sudan." In *Words and Objects*, ed. G. Steinsland, 78–90. Oslo: Norweigen University Press: Institute for Comparative Research in Human Culture. 1986.

Lewis, I. M., ed. *Islam in Tropical Africa.* Oxford: Oxford University Press, 1966.

——. "Spirit Possession in North-East Africa." In *Sudan in Africa*, ed. Yusuf Fadl Hasan, 212–227. Sudan Research Unit, Khartoum: Khartoum University Press, 1971.

Magnarella, Paul J. "The Republican Brothers: A Reformist Movement in the Sudan." *Muslim World* 72 (1982): 14–24.

Malka, Eli S. *Jacob's Children in the Land of the Mahdi: Jews of the Sudan.* Syracuse, N.Y.: Syracuse University Press, 1997.

An-Na'im, Abdullahi Ahmed. "Christian-Muslim Relations in the Sudan: Peaceful Coexistence at Risk." In *The Vatican, Islam, and the Middle East*, ed. K. Ellis, 265–276. Syracuse, N.Y.: Syracuse University Press, 1987.

——. "The Islamic Law of Apostasy and its Modern Applicability: A Case from the Sudan." *Religion* 16, no. 3 (1986): 197–224.

——. "Mahmud Muhammad Taha and the Crisis in Islamic Law Reform: Implications for Interreligious Relations." *Journal of Ecumenical Studies* 25 (1988): 1–21.

——. *The Second Message of Islam: Writings of Mahmoud Muhammad Taha*, trans. A. A. An-Na'im. Syracuse, N.Y.: Syracuse University Press, 1987.

al-Naqar, 'Umar. *The Pilgrimage Tradition in West Africa.* Khartoum: Khartoum University Press, 1972.

O'Fahey, R. S. "Islam, State, and Society in Darfur." In *Conversion to Islam*, ed. N. Levtzion, 189–206. New York and London: Holmes and Meier, 1979.

Pitya, Philip Legge. "History of Western Christian Evangelism in the Sudan, 1898–1964." Ph.D. diss., Boston University, 1996.

Sanderson, Lilian. "Sudan Interior Mission and the Condominium Sudan, 1937–1955." *Journal of Religion in Africa* 8, no. 1 (1976): 13–40.

al-Shahi, Ahmed S. "Northern Sudanese Perceptions of the Nubian Christian Legacy." In *Vernacular Christianity*, ed. W. James and D. Johnson, 31–39. New York: Lilian Barber Press, 1988.

——. "Sufism in Modern Sudan." In *Islam in the Modern World*, ed. D. Maceoin and Al-Shahi, 57–72. New York: St. Martin's Press, 1983.

Sidahmed, Abdel Salam. *Politics and Islam in Contemporary Sudan.* Richmond, UK: Curzon, 1997.

el-Tom, Abdullahi Osman. "Drinking the Koran: The Meaning of Koranic Verses in Berti Erasure." *Africa* 55, no.4 (1985): 414–431.

Trimingham, J. S. *Islam in the Sudan.* London: Frank Cass, 1968. (Original ed., 1949.)

——. *The Sufi Orders in Islam.* Oxford: Clarendon Press, 1971.

Vantini, G. "Christian Relicts in Sudanese Traditions." In *Nubia Christiana*, 25–42. Vol. 1. Warsaw: Akademie Teologii Katolickiej, 1982.

Voll, John O. "Effects of Islamic Structures on Modern Islamic Expansion in the Eastern Sudan." *IJAHS* 7 (1974): 85–98.

——. "Islam: Its Future in the Sudan." *Muslim World* 63, no. 4 (1973): 280–296.

——. "Mahdis, Walis, and New Men in the Sudan." In *Sufis, Saints, and Scholars*, ed. N. Keddie, 367–384. Berkeley: University of California Press, 1972.

——. "The Sudanese Mahdi: Frontier Fundamentalist." *IJMES* 10, no. 2 (1979): 145–166.

Warburg, Gabriel R. "Islam in Sudanese Politics." In *Religion and Politics in the Middle East*, ed. M. Curtis, 307–321. Boulder, Colo.: Westview Press, 1981.

——. "The Sharia in Sudan: Implementation and Repercussions, 1983–1989." *MEJ* 44, no. 4 (1990): 624–637.

Zubeir Wako, Gabriel. "The Role of Missionaries in the Local Church (The Sudan)." *Afer* 25 (1983): 204–208.

Education

Ali, Mohamed Adam. *Development and Problems of Girls' Education in Northern Sudan.* A History of Girls' Education. Vol. 113. Khartoum: Economic and Social Research Council, 1983.

el-Amin, Nafissa Ahmed. "Sudan: Education and Family." In *Change and the Muslim World*, ed. P. Stoddard, et al., 87–94. Syracuse: Syracuse University Press, 1981.

Beshir, Mohamed Omer. *Educational Development in the Sudan, 1898 to 1956*. Oxford: Clarendon Press, 1969.

Hajjar, Habib. "Surveying the Context for the Implementation of UPE in the Sudan." *International Review of Education* 29, no. 2 (1983): 179–191.

Sandell, Liza. *English Language in Sudan: A History of its Teaching and Politics*. London: Ithaca Press, 1982.

Sanderson, L. *Education, Religion, and Politics in Southern Sudan, 1899–1964*. London: Ithaca Press, 1981.

Sanyal, B. C., L. Yaici, and I. Mallasi. *From College to Work: The Case of the Sudan*. Paris: UNESCO, International Institute for Educational Planning, 1987.

el-Tayeb, Salah el-Din el-Zein. *The Students' Movement in the Sudan,1940–1970*. Khartoum: Khartoum University Press, 1971.

Women

Abusharaf, Rogaia. "Unmasking Tradition: A Sudanese Anthropologist Confronts Female 'Circumcision' and its Terrible Tenacity." *The Sciences* (March/April 1998): 23–27.

Ali, Nada Mustafa. "The Invisible Economy, Survival, and Empowerment: Five Cases from Atbara, Sudan." In *Middle Eastern Women and the Invisible Economy*, ed. R. Lobban, 96–112. Gainesville: University Press of Florida, 1998.

Amyuni, Mona Takieddine. "Images of Arab Women in *Midaq Alley* by Naguib Mahfouz and *Season of Migration to the North* by Tayeb Salih." *IJMES* 17 (1985): 25–36.

Anon. "Sudanese Men against Female Circumcision." *Africa Currents* 14 (1979): 31–32.

Badri, Aliya B. "A Comparison of Sudanese Male Children's Cultural Orientation and Intelligence." *The Ahfad Journal* 7, no. 1 (1990): 51–61.

Badri, Hagga Kashif. "The History, Development, Organisation, and Position of Women's Studies in the Sudan." In *Social Science Research and Women in the Arab World*, 94–112. Paris: UNESCO, 1985.

——. *Women's Movement in the Sudan*. New Delhi: Asia News Agency, n.d.

el-Bakri, Z. B., and E. M. Kameir. "Aspects of Women's Political Participation in Sudan." *International Social Science Journal* 35, no. 4 (1983): 605–623.

Boddy, Janice. *Wombs and Alien Spirits: Men, Women, and the Zar Cult in Northern Sudan*. Madison: University of Wisconsin Press, 1989.

——. "Womb as Oasis: The Symbolic Context of Pharaonic Circumcision (Infibulation) in Rural Northern Sudan." *American Ethnologist* 9 (1982): 682–698.

Bristow, Stephen. *Women's Extension Forestry Manual: A Methodology from Northern Sudan*. London: S. O. Sahel International (UK), 1997.

Burton, John. "Independence and the Status of Nilotic Women." *Africa Today* 28, no. 2 (1981): 54–60.

——. "The Moon is a Sheep: A Feminine Principle in Atuot Cosmology." *Man* 16 (1981): 441–450.

——. "Nilotic Women: A Diachronic Perspective." *JMAS* 20, no. 3 (1982): 467–491.

Cloudsley, Anne. *Women of Omdurman, Life, Love, and the Cult of Virginity.* New York: St. Martin's Press, 1984.

Constantinides, Pamela. "Women Heal Women: Spirit Possession and Sexual Segregation in a Muslim Society (Sudan)." *Social Science and Medicine* 21, no. 6 (1985): 685–692.

——. "Women's Spirit Possession and Urban Adaptation in the Muslim Northern Sudan." In *Women United, Women Divided: Comparative Studies of Ten Contemporary Cultures*, ed. P. Caplan and B. Bujva, 185–205. Bloomington: Indiana University Press, 1979.

Coughenour, C. Milton, and Saadi Nazhat. "The Process of Agricultural Change among Women Farmers of North Kordofan, Sudan." *The Ahfad Journal* 3, no. 1 (1986): 19–29.

Delmet, Christian. "Islamization and Matriliny in the Dar-Fung, Sudan." *L'Homme* 19 (1979): 33–52.

el-Dareer, Asma. *Woman, Why Do You Weep? Circumcision and its Consequences.* London: Zed Press, 1982.

el-Din Osman, Dina. "The Legal Status of Muslim Women in the Sudan." *Journal of East African Research and Development* 15 (1985): 124–142.

Fluehr-Lobban, Carolyn. "Agitation for Change in the Sudan." In *Sexual Stratification*, ed. A. Schlegel, 127–143. New York: Columbia University Press, 1977.

——. "Challenging Some Myths: Women and Islamic Law in the Sudan." *Expedition* 25 (1983): 32–39.

——. "The Women's Movement in the Sudan and Its Impact on Law and Politics." *The Ahfad Journal* 2 (1985): 53–62.

Gruenbaum, Ellen. "The Islamist State and Sudanese Women." *Middle East Report* 179 (1992).

——. "Reproductive Ritual and Social Reproduction: Female Circumcision in Sudan." In *Economy and Class in Sudan*, ed. Norman O'Neill and Jay O'Brien, 308–325. London: Gower, 1988.

Hale, Sondra. *Gender Politics in Sudan: Islamism, Socialism, and the State.* Boulder, Colo.: Westview Press, 1997.

——. "The Rise of Islam and Women of the National Islamic Front in Sudan." *Review of African Political Economy* 54 (1992): 27ff.

——. "The Wing of the Patriarch: Sudanese Women and Revolutionary Parties." *MERIP Report* 16, no. 1 (1986): 25–30.

Hall, Marjorie J., and Bakhita Amin Ismail. *Sisters under the Sun: The Story of Sudanese Women.* New York: Longman, 1981.

Hayes, Rose. "Female Genital Mutilation, Fertility Control, Women's Role, and the Patrilineage in Modern Sudan." *American Ethnologist* 2, no. 4 (1975): 617–633.

——. "The History, Development, Organization, and Position of Women's Studies in the Sudan." In *Social Science Research and Women in the Arab World*. Dover, N.H.: Longwood Publishing, 1984.

Hosken, Fran P. "Women and Health: Genital and Sexual Mutilation of Females." *International Journal of Women's Studies* 3 (1980): 300–316.

House, William J. "The Status of Women in the Sudan." *JMAS* 26, no. 2 (1988): 277–302.

Hutchinson, Sharon. "Relations between the Sexes among the Nuer: 1930." *Africa* 50, no. 4 (1980): 371–388.

Ibrahim, Fatma Ahmed. "Every Moment That I Live." *Connexions* 9 (1983): 3–4.

——. "I Will Take You along to the Living Quarters of the Poor." *Off Our Backs* 13 (1983): 10–11.

Ismail, Ellen T. *Social Environment and Daily Routine of Sudanese Women: A Case Study of Urban Middle Class Housewives*. Berlin: Dietrich Reimer Verlag, 1982.

Jennings, Anne. "Nubian Women in the Shadow Economy." In *Middle Eastern Women and the Invisible Economy*, ed. R. Lobban, 45–59. Gainesville: University Press of Florida, 1998.

Kenrick, Rosemary, ed. *Sudan Tales: Recollections of Some Sudan Political Service Wives, 1926–56*. Cambridge: Oleander, 1987.

Kenyon, Susan M. *Five Women of Sennar: Culture and Change in Central Sudan*. Oxford: Clarendon Press, 1991.

——, ed. *The Sudanese Woman*. London: Ithaca Press, 1986.

——. *Women and the Urban Process: A Case Study from El-Gal'a*. Khartoum: University of Khartoum Press, 1984.

Khalifa, Mona A. "Age Pattern of Fertility in the Sudan." *Journal of Biosocial Science* 15 (1983): 317–324.

——. "Characteristics and Attitudes of Family Planners in Khartoum, Sudan." *Journal of Biosocial Science* 14, no. 1 (1982): 7–16.

——. *The Marriage Pattern in Sudan and its Interrelationship with Fertilization*. Wad Medani: Population Studies Centre, Faculty of Economics and Rural Development, University of Gezira, 1983.

Lewis, I. M., Ahmed al-Safi, and Sayyid Hureiz, eds. *Women's Medicine: The Zar-Bori Cult in Africa and Beyond*. Edinburgh: Edinburgh University Press, 1991.

Lobban, Richard A., ed. *Middle Eastern Women in the 'Invisible' Economy*. Gainesville: University Press of Florida, 1998.

Lowenstein, L. F. "Attitudes and Attitude Differences to Female Genital Mutilation in the Sudan: Is There Change on the Horizon?" *Social Science and Medicine* 12 (1978): 417–421.

Madut, Chan Reech. *Some Aspects of Bridewealth among the Dinka with Special Reference to the Twich Dinka of Kongor District, Southern Sudan*. Khartoum: University of Khartoum Press, 1984.

Michael, Barbara. "Baggara Women as Market Strategists." In *Middle Eastern Women and the Invisible Economy*, ed. R. Lobban, 60–73. Gainesville: University Press of Florida, 1998.

Muludiang, Venansio Tombe. "Urbanization, Female Migration and Labor Utilization in Urban Sudan: The Case of the Southern Region." Ph.D. diss., Brown University, 1983.

Mustafa, Mutasim Abu Baker, and Stephen D. Mumford. "Male Attitudes Toward Family Planning in Khartoum, Sudan." *Journal of Biosocial Science* 16, no. 4 (1984): 437–450.

Sanderson, Lilian Passmore. *Against the Mutilation of Women.* London: Ithaca Press 1981.

——. *Female Genital Mutilation.* London: Anti-Slavery Society, 1986.

Spaulding, Jay. "The Misfortunes of Some—the Advantages of Others: Land Sales by Women in Sinnar." In *African Women and the Law: Historical Perspectives*, ed. M. J. Hay and M. Wright, 3–18. Vol. VII. Boston: Boston University African Studies Center, 1982.

Spaulding, Jay, and Stephanie Beswick. "Sex, Bondage, and the Market: The Emergence of Prostitution in the Northern Sudan, 1750–1950." *Journal of Sexuality* 5, no. 4 (1995): 115–141.

Toubia, Nahid. "The Social and Political Implications of Female Circumcision." In *Women and the Family in the Middle East: New Voices of Change.* Austin: University of Texas Press, 1985.

——. "Women and Health in the Sudan." In *Women of the Arab World*, ed. N. Toubia, trans. Nahed El Gamal, 98–109. London: Zed Books, 1988.

Washi, Siddiga, Donna Cowan, and R. Terry. "The Impact of Mother's Education on Indicators of School Performance of First through Third Grade Primary School Children Living in Low Socio-Economic Areas of Khartoum, Sudan." *The Ahfad Journal* 10, no. 1 (1993): 44–55.

el-Wathig Kamier, et al. *The State of Women's Studies in the Sudan.* Development Studies and Research Centre, Faculty of Economic and Social Studies, Khartoum: University of Khartoum Press, 1985.

Zumrawi, F., J. P. Hassan, and S. Harison. "Characteristics of Mothers and Children Attending MCH Clinics in Khartoum Province, Sudan." *SNR* LXII (1981): 154–160.

Human Rights

Anon. *Civilian Devastation: Abuses by All Parties in the War in Southern Sudan.* New York: Human Rights Watch/Africa Watch, 1994.

——. *Denying the "Honor of Living": Sudan, A Human Rights Disaster.* New York: Human Rights Watch/Africa Watch, 1996.

——. *A Desolate "Peace": Human Rights in the Nuba Mountains, Sudan.* London: African Rights, 1997.

——. *Eradicating the Nuba.* New York: Human Rights Watch, 1992.

——. *Food and Power in Sudan: A Critique of Humanitarianism.* London: African Rights, 1997.

——. *The Ghosts Remain: One Year after an Amnesty is Declared, Detention and Torture Continue Unabated.* New York: Human Rights Watch, 1992.

——. *Imposing Empowerment? Aid and Civil Institutions in Southern Sudan.* London: African Rights, 1995.

——. *"In the Name of God": Repression Continues in Northern Sudan.* New York: Human Rights Watch, 1994.

——. *Justice in the Nuba Mountains of Sudan: Challenges and Prospects, a Report on African Rights' Involvement with Access to Justice in the Nuba Mountains, 1995–7.* London: African Rights, 1997.

——. *Living on the Margin: The Struggle of Women and Minorities for Human Rights in Sudan, a Series of Reports.* New York: The Fund for Peace, Human Rights/Horn of Africa Program, 1995.

——. *The Lost Boys: Child Soldiers and Unaccompanied Boys in Southern Sudan.* New York: Human Rights Watch, 1994.

——. *New Islamic Penal Code Violates Basic Human Rights.* New York: Human Rights Watch, 1991.

——. *Outcry for Peace in the Sudan.* Washington, DC: Centre for the Strategic Initiatives of Women, 1996.

——. *Refugees in Their Own Country: The Forced Relocation of Squatters and Displaced People from Kordofan.* New York: Human Rights Watch, 1992.

——. *The Secret War against the Nuba.* New York: Human Rights Watch, 1991.

——. *Sudan: Human Rights Violations in the Context of Civil War.* London: Amnesty International, 1989.

——. *Sudan: Imprisonment of Prisoners of Conscience.* London: Amnesty International, 1990.

——. *Sudanese Human Rights Organizations.* New York: Human Rights Watch, 1991.

——. *Torture in Sudan.* London: Sudan Human Rights Organization, 1993.

——. *Violations of Academic Freedom.* New York: Human Rights Watch, 1992.

——. *War in the South Sudan: The Civilian Toll.* New York: Human Rights Watch, 1993.

Deng, Francis M., and Larry Minear. *The Challenges of Famine Relief: Emergency Operations in the Sudan.* Washington, DC: Brookings Institution, 1992.

——. *Protecting the Dispossessed: A Challenge for the International Community.* Washington, DC: Brookings Institution, 1993.

Duffield, Mark. "Absolute Distress: Structural Cases of Hunger in Sudan." *Middle East Report* 166 (1990): 4–11.

Keen, D. "Benefits of Famine: A Political Economy of Famine and Relief in Southwest Sudan, 1983-1989." Ph.D. diss., Oxford University, 1995.

Kibreab, Gaim. *People on the Edge in the Horn: Displacement, Land Use and the Environment in Gedaref Region, Sudan.* Lawrenceville, N.J.: Red Sea Press, 1996.

Lawyers Committee for Human Rights. *Beset by Contradictions: Islamization, Legal Reform, and Human Rights in Sudan*. New York: The Committee, 1996.

Mahmud, Ushari, and Suleiman Baldo. *The Diein Massacre: Slavery in the Sudan*. Khartoum: Khartoum University Press, 1987.

Minear, Larry. *Humanitarianism Under Siege*. Trenton, N.J.: Red Sea Press, 1990.

Prendergast, John. *Diplomacy, Aid, and Governance in Sudan*. Washington, DC: Center of Concern, 1995.

———. *"For Four Years I Have No Rest": Greed and Holy War in the Nuba Mountains of Sudan*. Washington, DC: Center of Concern, 1994.

———. *The Struggle for Sudan's Soul: Political and Agrarian Roots of War and Famine*. Washington, DC: Center of Concern, 1995.

Rone, Jemera. *Behind the Red Line: Political Repression in Sudan*. New York: Human Rights Watch, 1996.

Slavery in Mauritania and Sudan: Joint Hearing before the Subcommittees on International Operations and Human Rights and Africa. 104th Cong., 2nd sess., 13 March 1996. Washington, DC: Supt. of Docs, 1996.

Verney, Peter, ed. *Sudan, Conflict, and Minorities*. London: Minority Rights Group, 1995.

5. HISTORICAL

Survey Works

Alexander, John A. "The Saharan Divide in the Nile Valley: The Evidence from Qasr Ibrim." *African Archaeological Review* 6 (1988): 73–90.

Arkell, A. J. *History of the Sudan: From the Earliest Times to 1821*. 2nd ed. London: Athlone Press, 1961.

Collins, Robert O. "Egypt and the Sudan." In *The Historiography of the British Empire—Commonwealth Trends, Interpretation, and Resources*, ed. R. W. Winks, 281–291. Durham, N.C.: Duke University Press, 1961.

Daly, M. W., and L. E. Forbes. *Sudan in Original Photographs (From 1884–1954)*. London: Routledge and Kegan Paul International, 1990.

Ewald, Janet J. *Soldiers, Traders, and Slaves: State Formation and Economic Transformation in the Greater Nile Valley, 1700–1885*. Madison: University of Wisconsin Press, 1990.

Grabler, Susan. "Government Archives in Northern Sudan." *History in Africa* 12 (1985): 363–368.

Hill, Richard L. "Historical Writing on the Sudan since 1820." In *Historical of the Middle East*, ed. B. Lewis and P. M. Holt, 357–366. London: Oxford University Press, 1962.

Holt, P. M. *A Modern History of the Sudan*. New York: Grove Press, 1961.

Holt, P .M., and M. W. Daly. *The History of the Sudan: From the Coming of Islam to the Present Day*. London: Weidenfeld, 1979.

Kapteijns, Lidwien. "The Historiography of the Northern Sudan from 1500 to the Establishment of British Colonial Rule: A Critical Overview." *IJAHS* 22, no. 2 (1989): 251–267.

El Mahdi, Mandour. *A Short History of the Sudan.* London: Oxford University Press, 1965.

Sanderson, G. N. "The Modern Sudan, 1820–1956: The Present Position of Historical Studies." *JAH* 4 (1963): 432–461.

Stianson, Endre, and Michael Kevane, eds. *Kordofou Invaded: Peripheral Incorporation and Social Transformation in Islamic Africa.* Leiden, Netherlands: Brill, 1998.

Udal, John O. *The Nile in Darkness: Conquest and Exploration, 1504–1862.* London: Michael Russell, 1998.

Islamic Sultanates

Adams, William Y. "Islamic Archaeology in Nubia: An Introductory Survey." In *Nubian Culture Past and Present: Main Papers Presented at the Sixth International Conference for Nubian Studies in Uppsala,* ed. Tomas Hagg, 327–364. Stockholm: Almquist & Wiksell International, 1987.

Adams, William Y., J. A. Alexander, and R. Allen. "Qasr Ibrim 1980 and 1983." *JEA* 69 (1983): 43–60.

Crawford, O. G. S. *The Fung Kingdom of Sennar.* Gloucester: John Bellows, 1951.

Ewald, Janet. "Speaking, Writing, and Authority: Explorations in and from the Kingdom of Taqali." *Comparative Studies in Society and History* 30, no. 2 (1988): 199–224.

Hasan, Yusuf Fadl. *The Arabs and the Sudan.* Edinburgh, Scotland: Edinburgh University Press, 1967.

———. "External Islamic Influences and the Progress of Islamization in the Eastern Sudan between the Fifteenth and the Nineteenth Centuries." In *Sudan in Africa,* ed. Y. F. Hasan, 73–86. Khartoum: Khartoum University Press, 1971.

Jedrej, M. Charles. *The Southern Funj of the Sudan under Anglo-Egyptian Rule, 1900–1933.* Edinburgh, Scotland: Centre for African Studies, Edinburgh University, 1996.

Jombi, Caesar Lukudu. *Juridic Structure of the Christian Church in the Sudan: From the Origin of Christianity in Nubia before and after the Diffusion of Islam.* Rome: Pontificia Universita Lateranense, 1987.

MacMichael, H. A. *A History of the Arabs in the Sudan.* 2 vols. London: Frank Cass, 1962.

Nachtigal, Gustav. *Sahara and Sudan: Wadai and Darfur.* London: G. Hurst, 1971.

al-Naqar, 'Umar. "The Historical Background to the 'Sudan Road'." In *Sudan in Africa,* ed. Y. F. Hasan, 98–108. Khartoum: Khartoum University Press, 1971.

O' Fahey. "Kordofan in the Eighteenth Century." *SNR* 54 (1973): 32–34.

———. "Religion and Trade in the Kayra Sultanate of Dar Fur." In *Sudan in Africa*, ed. Y. F. Hasan, 87–97. Khartoum: Khartoum University Press, 1971.

———. "Saints and Sultans: The Role of Muslim Holy Men in the Keira Sultanate of Dar Fur." In *Northern Africa: Islam and Modernization*, ed. M. Brett, 49–56. London: Frank Cass, 1973.

———. *State and Society in Dar Fur*. New York: St. Martin's Press, 1980.

———. *States and State Formation in the Eastern Sudan*. Khartoum: Khartoum University Press, 1970.

———. "The Tunjur: A Central Sudanic Mystery." *SNR* LXI (1980): 47–60.

O' Fahey, R. S., and J. L. Spaulding. *Kingdoms of the Sudan*. Studies in African History. Vol. 9. London: Methuen, 1974.

O' Fahey, R. S., and M. I. Abu Salim. *Land in Dar Fur: Charters and Related Documents from the Dar Fur Sultanate*. New York: Cambridge University Press, 1983.

Osman, Ali. "Islamic Archaeology in the Sudan." In *Nubische Studien*, ed. M. Krause, 223–229. Mainz am Rhein, Germany: P. von Zabern. 1986.

Onwubuemeli, Emeka. "Early Zande History: The Origins of the Avungara." *SNR* 53 (1972): 36–66.

Spaulding, Jay L. "Farmers, Herdsmen, and the State in Rainland Sinnar." *JAH* 20, no. 3 (1979): 329–347.

———. "The Funj: A Reconsideration," *JAH* 13 (1972): 39–53.

———. "Toward a Demystification of the Funj: Some Perspectives on Society in Southern Sinnar, 1685–1900." *Northeast African Studies* 2, no. 1 (1980): 1–18.

Theobald, A. B. Ali Dinar. *Last Sultan of Darfur, 1898–1916*. London: Longmans, 1965.

Trimingham, J. S. *Islam in the Sudan*. London: Frank Cass, 1965.

Turco-Egyptian Period

Ali, Abbas Ibrahim Muhammad. *The British: The Slave Trade and Slavery in the Sudan, 1820–1881*. Khartoum: Khartoum University Press, 1972.

Gray, Richard. *A History of the Southern Sudan, 1839–89*. London: Oxford University Press, 1961.

———. "Some Aspects of Islam in the Southern Sudan during the Turkiya." In *Northern Africa: Islam and Modernization*, ed. M. Brett, 65–72. London: Frank Cass, 1973.

Hasan, Yusuf Fadl. "Some Aspects of the Arab Slave Trade from the Sudan in the 7th–19th Centuries." *SNR* LVIII (1977): 85–106.

Hill, Richard L. *A Biographical Dictionary of the Sudan*. 2nd ed. London: Frank Cass, 1967.

———, ed. and trans. *On the Frontiers of Islam: Two Manuscripts Concerning the Sudan under Turco-Egyptian Rule, 1822–1845*. Oxford, England: Clarendon Press, 1970.

———. *Egypt in the Sudan, 1820–1881*. London: Oxford University Press, 1959.

Hill, Richard, and Peter Hogg. *Black Corps d'elite: An Egyptian Sudanese Conscript Battalion with the French Army in Mexico*. East Lansing: Michigan State Press, 1995.

Hill, Richard, and Elias Toniolo, eds. *The Opening of the Nile Basin: Writings by Members of the Catholic Mission to Central Africa on the Geography and Ethnography of the Sudan, 1842–1881*. New York: Barnes and Noble, 1975.

Hofheinz, Albrecht. "Internalizing Islam, Shaykh Muhammad Majdhub: Scriptural Islam and Local Context in the Early 19th Century." Ph.D. diss. Bergen, Norway: University of Bergen, 1996.

Holt, Peter M. "Egypt and the Nile Valley." In *The Cambridge History of Africa*, 13–39. Vol. 5. London: Cambridge University Press, 1976.

Ibrahim, H. A., and B. A. Ogot. "The Sudan in the Nineteenth Century." In *General History of Africa*. Vol. 6, *Africa in the 19th century until the 1880's*, ed. J. F Ade Ajayi, 356–375. Berkeley: University of California Press, 1989.

Jackson, H. C. *Black Ivory and White: The Story of El Zubeir Pasha Slaver and Sultan as Told by Himself.* New York: Negro Universities Press, 1970.

Kapteijins, Lidwien. "Dar Sila: The Sultanate in Precolonial Times, 1870–1916." *Cahiers d'Etudes Africaines* 23, no. 4 (1983): 447–470.

———. "The Emergence of a Sudanic State: Dar Masalit, 1874–1905." *International Journal of African Historical Studies* 16, no. 4 (1983): 601–630.

———. "The Use of Slaves in Precolonial Western Dar Fur: The Case of Dar Masalit, 1870–1905." *Northeast African Studies* 6, nos. 1–2 (1984): 105–126.

Kapteijns, Lidwien, and Jay Spaulding. *After the Millenium: Diplomatic Correspondence from Wadai and Dar Fur on the Eve of Colonial Conquest, 1885–1916*. East Lansing: Michigan State University, 1988.

Makris, Gerasimos. "Creating History: A Case from the Sudan." *Sudanic Africa* 5 (1994): 111–148.

———. "Slavery, Possession, and History: The Construction of Self among Slave Descendants in the Sudan." *Africa* 66, no. 2 (1996): 159–182.

Mercer, P. "Shilluk Trade and Politics from the Mid-Seventeenth Century to 1861." *JAH* 12, no. 3 (1971).

Moore-Marrell. *Gordon and the Sudan: Prologue to the Mahdiyya*. London: Frank Cass, 2000.

Moorehead, Alan. *The White Nile*. London: Hamish Hamilton, 1960.

———. *The Blue Nile*. New York: Harper & Row, 1962.

Santi, Paul, and Richard Hill. *The Europeans in the Sudan: 1834–1878*. Oxford: Clarendon, 1980.

Shibeika, Mekki. "The Expansionist Movement of Khedive Isma'il to the Lakes." In *Sudan in Africa*, ed. Y. F. Hasan, 142–155. Khartoum: Khartoum University Press, 1971.

Spaulding, Jay. "The Birth of an African Private Epistolography, Echo Island 1862–1901." *JAH* 34 (1993): 115–141.

———. "Slavery, Land Tenure, and Social Class in the Northern Turkish Sudan." *IJAHS* 15, no. 1 (1982): 1–20.

Talhami, Ghada Hashem. *Suakin and Massawa under Egyptian Rule, 1865–1885.* Washington, DC: University Press of America, 1979.

Toniolo, Elias, and Richard Hill, eds. *The Opening of the Nile Basin, 1842–1881.* New York: Barnes and Noble, 1975.

Tubiana, Joseph. "Autobiography and the Sense of History: Two Sudanese Examples." *Revue de l'Occident Musulman et de la Mediterranee* 34 (1982): 135–143.

Mahdiya

Brown, L. Carl. "The Sudanese Mahdiya." In *Rebellion in Black Africa*, ed. R. I. Rotberg, 3–23. London: Oxford University Press, 1971.

Chenevix Trench, Charles. *The Road to Khartoum: A Life of General Charles Gordon.* New York: W. W. Norton, 1979.

Churchill, Winston L. S. *The River War.* 3rd ed. London: New English Library, 1973.

———. *Young Winston's Wars: The Original Dispatches of Winston S. Churchill, War Correspondent, 1897–1900*, ed. F. Woods. London: L. Cooper, 1972.

Collins, Robert O. *The Southern Sudan, 1883–1898, A Struggle for Control.* New Haven, Conn.: Yale University Press, 1962.

Gessi Pasha, R. *Seven Years in the Sudan.* London: Gregg, 1967. (Original ed., 1892.)

al-Hajj, Muhammad A. "Hayatu b. Sa'id: A Revolutionary Mahdist in the Western Sudan." In *Sudan in Africa*, ed. Y. F. Hasan, 128–141. Khartoum: Khartoum University Press, 1971.

Hill, Richard. *Slatin Pasha.* London: Oxford University Press, 1965.

Hill, Richard, and Thirza Kupper. *The Sudan Memoirs of Carl Christian Giegler Pasha.* New York: Oxford University Press, 1984.

Hodgkin, Thomas. "Mahdism, Messianism, and Marxism in an African Setting." In *Sudan in Africa*, ed. Y. F. Hasan, 109–127. Khartoum: Khartoum University Press, 1971.

Holt, P. M. *The Mahdist State in the Sudan, 1881–1898.* 2nd ed. Oxford: Clarendon Press, 1970.

———. "The Source Materials of the Sudanese Mahdiya." *Middle Eastern Affairs* 1 (1958).

Ibrahim, Ahmed Uthman. "Some Aspects of the Ideology of the Mahdiyya." *SNR* LX (1979): 15–27.

Ibrahim, Hassan Ahmed. "Imperialism and Neo-Mahdism in the Sudan: A Study of British Policy towards Neo-Mahdism, 1924–1927." *IJAHS* 13, no. 2 (1980): 214–239.

———. "Mahdist Risings against Condominium Government in the Sudan, 1900–1927." *IJAHS* 12, no. 3 (1979): 440–471.

Johnson, Nels. "Religious Paradigms of the Sudanese Mahdiyah." *Ethnohistory* 25, no. 2 (1978): 159–178.

Konczacki, Janina. "The Emin Pasha Relief Expedition (1887–1889): Some Comments on Disease and Hygiene." *Canadian Journal of African Studies* 19, no. 3 (1985): 615–625.

Kramer, Robert S. "The Capitulation of the Omdurman Notables." *Sudanic Africa* 3 (1992): 41–55.

——. "Holy City on the Nile: Omdurman, 1885–1898." Ph.D. diss., Chicago, Northwestern University, 1991.

Mahmoud, Mahgoub el-Tigani. "The Mahdist Correctional System in the Sudan: Aspects of Ideology in Politics." *Africa Today* 28, no. 2 (1981): 78–86.

Malka, Eli S. *Jacob's Children in the Land of the Mahdi: Jews of the Sudan.* Syracuse, N.Y.: Syracuse University Press, 1997.

Nakash, Yitzhak. "Fiscal and Monetary Systems in the Mahdist Sudan, 1881–1898." *IJMES* 20, no. 3 (1988): 365–385.

Santandrea, S. *Ethno-Geography of the Bahr el Ghazal (Sudan): An Attempt at a Historical Reconstruction.* Bologna, Italy: Missionaria Italiana, 1981.

Shaked, Haim. *The Life of the Sudanese Mahdi.* Edison, N.J.: Transaction, 1976.

——. *The Presentation of the Sudanese Mahdi in a Unique Arabic Manuscript.* Tel Aviv, Israel: Tel Aviv University Press, 1971.

Shibeika, Mekki. *British Policy in the Sudan, 1882–1902.* London: Oxford University Press, 1952.

Slatin, Rudolf Carl von. *Fire and Sword in the Sudan*, trans. F. R. Wingate. New York: Negro Universities Press, 1969. (Original ed., 1898.)

Warburg, Gabriel R. "British Policy toward the Ansar in Sudan: A Note on an Historical Controversy." *Middle Eastern Studies* 33, no. 4 (1997): 675–692.

——. "From Revolution to Conservatism: Some Aspects of Mahdist Ideology and Politics in the Sudan." *Der Islam* 70, no. 1 (1993): 88–111.

——. "Ideological and Practical Considerations Regarding Slavery in the Mahdist State and Anglo-Egyptian Sudan: 1881–1918." In *The Ideology of Slavery in Africa*, ed. Paul Lovejoy, 245–269. Beverly Hills: Sage, 1982.

Wingate, F. R. *Mahdism and the Egyptian Sudan.* 2nd ed. London: Frank Cass, 1968. (Original ed., 1891.)

Wright, Patricia. *Conflict on the Nile: The Fashoda Incident of 1898.* London: Heinemann, 1972.

Ziegler, P. *Omdurman.* London: Collins, 1973.

Zulfo, 'Ismat Hasan. *Karari: the Sudanese Account of the Battle of Omdurman*, trans. Peter Clark. London: Frederick Warne, 1980.

Anglo-Egyptian Sudan

Abbas, Mekki. *The Sudan Question.* London: Faber and Faber, 1952.

Abd al-Rahim, Muddathir. *Imperialism and Nationalism in the Sudan: A Study in Constitutional and Political Development, 1899–1956.* Oxford: Clarendon Press, 1969.

Abdin, Hasan. *Early Sudanese Nationalism, 1919–1925.* Sudanese Library Series. Vol. 14. Khartoum: Khartoum University Press, n.d.

Abu Hasabu, Afaf A. *Factional Conflict in the Sudanese Nationalist Movement, 1918–1948.* London: Ithaca Press, 1985.

El-Amin, Mohammed Nuri. "Britain: The 1924 Sudanese Uprising and the Impact of Egypt on the Sudan." *IJAHS* 19, no. 2 (1986): 235–260.

———. "The Impact of the Fajr School on Sudanese Communism." *SNR* LXII (1981): 1–24.

Bakheit, Ja'far M. A. *Communist Activities in the Middle East between 1919–1927: With Special Reference to Egypt and the Sudan.* Khartoum: University of Khartoum, 1968.

Beshir, Mohamed Omer. *Revolution and Nationalism in the Sudan.* New York: Barnes and Noble, 1974.

Collins, Robert O., and Francis M. Deng. *The British in the Sudan, 1898–1956.* London: Macmillan, 1985.

Daly, M. W. *British Administration and the Northern Sudan.* Leiden, Netherlands: Brill, 1979.

———. "The Development of the Governor-Generalship of the Sudan: 1899–1934." *SNR* LXI (1980): 27–46.

———. *Empire on the Nile: The Anglo-Egyptian Sudan, 1898–1934.* Cambridge: Cambridge University Press, 1986.

———. *Imperial Sudan: The Anglo-Egyptian Condominium, 1934–56.* Cambridge: Cambridge University Press, 1991.

———. "Principal Office-Holders in the Sudan Government, 1895–1955." *IJAHS* 17, no. 2 (1984): 309–316.

———. *The Sirdar: Sir Reginald Wingate and the British Empire in the Middle East.* Philadelphia, Penn.: American Philosophical Society, 1997.

Deng, Francis M., and Martin W. Daly. *"Bonds of Silk: The Human Factor in the British Administration of Sudan.* East Lansing: Michigan State University Press, 1989.

Garretson, Peter P. "The Southern Sudan Welfare Committee and the 1947 Strike in the Southern Sudan." *Northeast African Studies* 8, no. 2–3 (1986): 181–191.

Grabler, Susan. "European Capital Exports and the Concessions Policy in the Sudan, 1898–1913." *Northeast African Studies* 8, nos. 2–3 (1986): 95–109.

———. *The Sudan and British Administration, 1898–1956: Elements of a Social Historical Interpretation of a Colonial Experience.* Leiden, Netherlands: Brill, 1982.

Hail, J. A. *Britain's Foreign Policy in Egypt and Sudan, 1947–1956.* Reading, England: Ithaca Press, 1996.

Hamad, Bushra. "Sudan Notes and Records and Sudanese Nationalism, 1918–1956." *History in Africa* 22 (1995): 239–270.

Hino, Abannik O. "Latuka Country: An Outline of the Process of Colonial Encroachment and Reaction to It, 1840–1900." *Northeast African Studies* 4, no. 3 (1982–1983): 39–49.

Jedrej, M. Charles. *The Southern Funj of the Sudan under Anglo-Egyptian Rule, 1900–1933.* Edinburgh, Scotland: Centre for African Studies, Edinburgh University, 1996.

Johnson, Douglas H. "The Death of Gordon: A Victorian Myth." *Journal of Imperial and Commonwealth History* 10, no. 3 (1982): 285–310.

————. "Tribal Boundaries and Border Wars: Nuer-Dinka Relations in the Sobat and Zaraf Valleys, c.1869–1976." *JAH* 23, no. 2 (1982): 183–203.

Kelly, Harry Holdsworth. *Imperial Boundary Making: The Diary of Captain Kelly and the Sudan-Uganda Boundary Commission of 1913.* Oxford: Oxford University Press, 1997.

Lobban, Richard A., Jr. "The Law of the Monkeys and the Justice of Elephants." *Africa Today* 28, no. 2 (1981): 87–95.

MacMichael, H. A. *The Anglo-Egyptian Sudan.* London: Faber and Faber, 1934.

Mangan, J. A. "The Education of an Elite Imperial Administration: The Sudan Political Service and the British Public School System" *IJAHS* 15, no. 4 (1982): 671–699.

Mawut, Lazarus Leek. *Dinka Resistance to Condominium Rule, 1902–1932.* Khartoum and London: Khartoum University Press and Ithaca Press, 1983.

Mills, David Eugene. "Dividing the Nile: The Failure to Strengthen Egyptian-Sudanese Economic Bonds, 1918–1945." Ph.D. diss., University of Utah, 1997.

Mohammed, Ahmed al-Awad. "Militarism in the Sudan: The Colonial Experience." *SNR* LXI (1980): 15–26.

Nasr, Ahmed Abd al-Rahim. "British Policy towards Islam in the Nuba Mountains, 1920–1940." *SNR* 52 (1971): 23–32.

Perkins, Kenneth J. "The Best Laid Out Town on the Red Sea: The Creation of Port Sudan, 1904–09." *Middle Eastern Studies* 27, no. 2 (1991): 283–303.

Powell, Eve Marie Troutt. "Colonized Colonizers: Egyptian Nationalists and the Issue of the Sudan, 1875–1919." Ph.D. diss., Harvard University, 1995.

Salih, Kamal Osman. "British Policy and the Accentuation of Inter-ethnic divisions: The Case of the Nuba Mountains Region of Sudan 1920–40." *African Affairs* 89, no. 356 (1990): 417–437.

Sanderson, G. N. "Sudanese Nationalism and the Independence of the Sudan." In *Northern Africa: Islam and Modernization*, ed. M. Brett, 97–109. London: Frank Cass, 1973.

Seligman, C. G., and Brenda Z. Seligman. *Pagan Tribes of the Nilotic Sudan.* London: Routledge and Kegan Paul, 1932.

Sikainga, Ahmad Alawad. *The Western Bahr Al-Ghazal under British Rule, 1898–1956.* Athens: Ohio University Press, 1991.

Tosh, John. "The Economy of the Southern Sudan under the British, 1898–1955." *Journal of Imperial and Commonwealth History* 9, no. 3 (1981): 275–288.

Voll, John O. "The British, the Ulama, and Popular Islam in the Early Anglo-Egyptian Sudan." *IJMES* 2 (1971): 212–218.

Voll, Sarah P. "The Introduction of Native Administration in the Anglo-Egyptian Sudan." *Al-Abhath* 24 (1971): 111–123.

Warburg, Gabriel. "From Ansar to Umma: Sectarian Politics in the Sudan, 1914–1945." *Asian and African Studies* 9 (1973): 101–153.

——. "Religious Policy in the Northern Sudan: Ulama and Sufism, 1899–1918." *Asian and African Studies* 7 (1971): 89–119.

——. "Slavery and Labour in the Anglo-Egyptian Sudan." *Asian and African Studies* 12, no. 2 (1978): 221–245.

——. "The Sudan, Egypt, and Britain, 1899–1916." *Middle East Studies* 6 (1970): 163–178.

——. *The Sudan under Wingate: Administration in the Anglo-Egyptian Sudan, 1899–1916*. London: Frank Cass, 1971.

Williams, C. R. *Wheels and Paddles in the Sudan (1923–1946)*. Edinburgh, Scotland: The Pentland Press, 1986.

Wingate, Ronald. *Wingate of the Soudan: The Life and Time of General Sir Reginald Wingate*. Westport, Conn.: Greenwood Press, 1975. (Original ed., 1955.)

Woodward, Peter. *Condominium and Sudanese Nationalism*. New York: Barnes and Noble, 1979.

——. "In the Footsteps of Gordon: The Sudan Government and the Rise of Sayyid Sir Abd Al-Rahman, 1915–1935." *African Affairs* 84 (1985): 39–51.

——. "The South in Sudanese Politics, 1946–56." *Middle Eastern Studies* 16, no. 3 (1980): 178–192.

Wright, Patricia. *Conflict on the Nile: The Fashoda Incident of 1898*. London: Heinemann, 1972.

Independent Sudan

Abdalla, I. "The 1959 Nile Waters Agreement in Sudanese-Egyptian Relations." *Middle East Studies* 7 (1971): 329–342.

'Abdel Rahim, M., et al. *Sudan since Independence: Studies of Political Development since 1956*. London: Gower, 1986.

'Abdel Rahim, Muddathir. *Imperialism and Nationalism in the Sudan*. Oxford: Clarendon Press, 1969.

——. "The Choice of Khashm al-Girba Area for the Resettlement of the Halfawis." *SNR* 51 (1970): 56–75.

Allum, Percy. "The Sudan: Numeiry's Ten Years of Power." *Contemporary Review* 235 (1979): 233–42.

Barbour, K. M. "The Sudan since Independence." *JMAS* 18, no. 1 (1980): 73–97.

Bechtold, Peter. "Military Rule in the Sudan: The First Five Years of Ja'far Numayri." *MEJ* 29 (1975): 16–32.

——. *Politics in the Sudan: Parliamentary and Military Rule in an Emerging African Nation*. New York: Praeger, 1976.

Collins, C. "Colonialism and Class Struggle in Sudan." *MERIP Reports* 46 (1976): 3–17.

Crawford, R. "Sudan: The Revolution of October, 1964." *Mawazo* 1, no. 2 (1967): 47–60.

Dafalla, Hassan. *The Nubian Exodus*. London: Hurst, 1975.

Daly, M. W. *Modernization in the Sudan: Essays in Honor of Richard Hill*. New York: Lilian Barber, 1985.

Hinkel, F. *Exodus from Nubia*. Berlin: Akademia-Verlag, 1978.

Legum, C. "Sudan's Three-Day Revolution." *Africa Report* 16, no. 7 (1971): 12–15.

Niblock, T. "A New Political System in Sudan." *African Affairs* 73, no. 293 (1974): 408–418.

Sabry, H. Zulfakar. *Sovereignty for Sudan*. Sudan Studies Series. London: Ithaca Press, 1982.

Shibeika, Mekki. *The Independent Sudan*. New York: Speller, 1959.

Al-Teraifi, Al-Ayub. "Sudanisation of the Public Service: A Critical Analysis." *SNR* LVIII (1977): 117–134.

Voll, John O. "The Sudan after Nimeiry." *Current History* 85 (1986): 213–216.

———, ed. *Sudan: State and Society in Crisis*. Bloomington: Indiana University Press, 1991.

Warburg, Gabriel R. *Egypt and the Sudan: Studies in History and Politics*. London: Frank Cass, 1985.

6. POLITICAL

Government and Administration

Abd al-Rahim, Muddathir. "Arabism, Africanism, and Self-Identification in the Sudan." *JMAS* 8, no. 2 (1970): 233–250.

———. *Changing Patterns of Civilian-Military Relations in the Sudan*. Uppsala, Sweden: Scandinavian Institute of African Studies, 1978.

———. *Imperialism and Nationalism in the Sudan: A Study in Political Constitutional Development*. Sudan Studies Series. London: Ithaca Press, 1986.

Abdelkarim, Abbas, Abdallah al-Hassan, and David Seldon. "The Generals Step In." *MERIP Reports* 135 (1985): 19–24.

Abu Affan, Bodour. "A Missed Opportunity? Sudan's Stabilization Program, 1979–82." In *Sudan: State and Society in Crisis*, ed. John O. Voll. Bloomington: Indiana University Press, 1991.

Abu Hasabu, Afaf Abdel Magid. *Factional Conflict in the Sudanese Nationalist Movement, 1918–1948*. Graduate College Publications. Vol. 12. Khartoum: Khartoum University Press, 1985.

Aguda, O. "Arabism and Pan-Arabism in Sudanese Politics." *JMAS* 11, no. 2 (1973): 177–200.

Ahmad, Abd al-Ghaffar Muhammad. *Shaykhs and Followers: Political Struggle in the Rufa'a al-Hoi Nazirate in the Sudan*. Khartoum: Khartoum University Press, 1974.

Ahmed, Rafia Hassan. *Critical Appraisal to the Role of the Public Service Commission in the Sudan, 1954–1969*. Khartoum: Tamaddon Printing Press, 1974.

Alier, Abel. *Southern Sudan: Too Many Agreements Dishonoured.* Exeter: Ithaca Press, 1990.

El-Amin, Mohammed Nuri. "The Impact of the Sudanese Unionists on Sudanese Communism." *Middle Eastern Studies* 22, no. 3 (1986): 418–434.

———. "A Leftist Labour Movement in the Sudan in the Early 1920s: Fact or Fiction?" *Middle Eastern Studies* 20, no. 3 (1984): 370–378.

———. "The Role of the Egyptian Communist Party in Introducing the Sudanese to Communism in the 1940's." *IJMES* 19, no. 4 (1987): 433–454.

Anon. "Sudan's Revolutionary Spring." *MERIP Reports* 15 (1985): 3–28.

Babiker, Mahjoub Abd al-Malik. *Press and Politics in the Sudan, 1920–1945.* Graduate College Publications. Vol 14. Khartoum and London: Khartoum University Press and Ithaca Press, 1985.

Bechtold, Peter. "More Turbulence in Sudan: A New Politics This Time?" *MEJ* 44, no. 4 (1990): 579–595.

———. *Politics in the Sudan: Parliamentary and Military Rule in an Emerging African Nation.* New York: Praeger, 1976.

———. "The Sudan Since the Fall of Numayri." In *The Middle East from the Iran-Contra Affair to the Intifada*, ed. R. O. Freedman, 367–389. New York: Syracuse University Press, 1991.

Beshir, Mohammed Omer. *Terramedia: Themes in Afro-Arab Relations.* London: Ithaca Press, 1982.

Bienen, Henry, and Jonathan Moore. "The Sudan: Military Economic Corporations." *Armed Forces and Society* 13, no. 4 (1987): 489–516.

Burr, J. Millard, and Robert O. Collins. *Requiem for the Sudan: War, Drought, and Disaster Relief on the Nile.* Boulder, Colo.: Westview Press, 1994.

Chiriyankandath, James. "The 1986 Elections: Tradition, Ideology and Ethnicity." In *Sudan after Nimieri*, ed. P. Woodward, 76–91. London: Routledge, 1991.

Collins, Robert O. *The Waters of the Nile: Hydropolitics and the Jonglei Canal 1900–1988.* Oxford: Oxford University Press, 1990.

Daly, M. W., and Ahmad Alawad Sikainga, eds. *Civil War in the Sudan.* London: British Academic Press, 1993.

Deng, Francis Mading. *Dynamics of Identification: A Basis for National Integration in the Sudan.* Khartoum: Khartoum University Press, 1973.

———. *The Recollections of Babo Nimir.* London: Ithaca Press, 1982.

———. "War of Visions for the Nation." *Middle East Journal* 44, no. 4 (1990): 596–609.

First, Ruth. *Power in Africa: Political Power in Africa and the Coup d'Etat.* Baltimore, Md.: Penguin, 1970.

Gandy, Christopher. "Sudan 1972: Pragmatism Replaces Ideology." *New Middle East* 42–43 (1972): 14–16.

Garang, John de Mabior. *The Call for Democracy in Sudan*, ed. Mansour Khalid. London and New York: Kegan Paul International, 1992.

Greenfield, Richard. "Two Months That Shook Sudan." *Horn of Africa* 8, no. 1 (1985): 5–20.

Gresh, Alain. "The Free Officers Face-to-Face, 1969–71." *IJMES* 21 (1989): 393–409.

Gurdon, Charles. *Sudan at the Crossroads.* New York: Lynne Reiner, 1984.

Hale, Sondra. "Sudan Civil War: Religion, Colonialism, and the World System." In *Muslim-Christian Conflicts*, ed. S. Joseph and B. Pillsbury, 157–184. Boulder, Colo.: Westview Press, 1978.

Hamad, Mohammed Beshir. *The Politics of National Reconciliation in the Sudan: The Numayri Regime and the National Front Opposition.* Center for Contemporary Arab Studies, Washington, DC: Georgetown University, 1984.

El-Hassan, Omer El-Beshir. "Representative Bureaucracy and Public Policy Responsiveness in the Sudan." Ph.D. diss., University of Mississippi, 1994.

Hodgkin, Thomas. "Mahdism, Messianism and Marxism in the African Setting." In *Sudan in Africa*, ed. Y. F. Hasan, 109–127. Khartoum: Khartoum University Press, 1970.

Howell, John, ed. *Local Government and Politics in the Sudan.* Khartoum: Khartoum University Press, 1974.

Jamal, Sadia. "Under Bashir's Boot." *New African* 274 (1990): 9–10.

Kelly, Raymond C. *The Nuer Conquest: The Structure and Development of an Expansionist System.* Ann Arbor: University of Michigan Press, 1985.

Khalid, M. "Ethnic Integration in the Sudan." *Review of International Affairs* 24, no. 548 (1973): 22–26.

Khalid, Mansour. *The Government They Deserve: The Role of the Elite in Sudan's Political Evolution.* London: Kegan Paul, 1990.

——. *Nimeiri and the Revolution of Dis-May.* London: KPI Ltd., 1985.

——. "Sudan: A Plea for Pluralism; Northern Politicians Must Share Responsibility for Sudan's Current Political Crisis." *Africa Report* 30 (1985): 53–57.

Khalifa, Babiker. "Sudan: Recent Developments." *Africa Today* 36 (1989): 3–4; 5–11.

Kirk-Greene, A. H. M. "The Sudan Political Service: A Profile in the Sociology of Imperialism." *IJAHS* 15, no. 1 (1982): 21–48.

Kramer, Robert S. "Political Parties of the Sudan." In *Political Parties of the Middle East and North Africa*, ed. Frank Tachau, 476-99. Westport, Conn.: Greenwood Press, 1994.

Lavrencic, K. "Interview with President Jaafar Nemeiry." *Africa* 21 (1973): 24–27.

Lesch, Ann Mosley. "A View from Khartoum." *Foreign Affairs* 65, no. 4 (1987): 807–826.

——. "Khartoum Diary." *Middle East Report* 161 (1989): 36–38.

——. *The Sudan: Contested National Identities.* Bloomington: Indiana University Press, 1998.

Mahjub, Muhammad Ahmad. *Democracy on Trial: Reflections on Arab and African Politics.* London: Deutsch, 1974.

Mahmoud, Fatima Babiker. "Some Aspects of the Political Economy of the Sudan." *SNR* LXII (1981): 47–68.

——. *The Sudanese Bourgeoisie: Vanguard of Development?* Khartoum: Khartoum University Press, 1984.

Malwal, Bona. *People and Power in Sudan: The Struggle for National Stability*. Sudan Studies Series. London: Ithaca Press, 1981.

———. *The Sudan: A Second Challenge to Nationhood*. New York: Lilian Barber Press, 1985.

———. "The Sudan: The Unsettling Political Future." *Middle East Insight* 4 (1985): 9–14.

Mazrui, Ali. "The Multiple Marginality of the Sudan." In *Sudan in Africa*, ed. Y. F. Hasan, 240–255. Khartoum: Khartoum University Press, 1971.

Medani, Khalid. "Sudan's Human and Political Crisis." *Current History* 92, no. 574 (1993): 203–208.

Al-Na'im, Abdullahi Ahmed. "Constitutionalism and Islamization in the Sudan." *Africa Today* 36, nos. 3–4 (1989): 11–29.

———. "Constitutional Discourse and the Civil War in the Sudan." In *Civil War in the Sudan*, ed. M. W. Daly and A. A. Sikainga, 97–116. London: British Academic Press, 1993.

———. *An Islamic Reformation?* Syracuse: Syracuse University Press, 1997.

Niblock, Tim. "The Background to the Change of Government in 1985." In *Sudan after Nimieri*, 34–44. London: Routledge, 1991.

———. *Class and Power in Sudan: The Dynamics of Sudanese Politics, 1898–1985*. Ithaca: State University of New York Press, 1988.

Nimeiri, Sayed. *Taxation and Economic Development: A Case Study of the Sudan*. Khartoum: Khartoum University Press, 1975.

O'Brien, Jay. "Understanding the Crisis in Sudan." *Canadian Journal of African Studies* 20, no. 2 (1986): 275–279.

O'Neill, Norman. "Imperialism and Class Struggle in the Sudan." *Race and Class* 20, no. 1 (1978): 1–19.

Ottaway, Marina. "Post-Numeiri Sudan: One Year On." *Third World Quarterly* 9, no. 3 (1987): 891–905.

Petterson, Donald. *Inside Sudan: Political Islam, Conflict, and Catastrophe*. Boulder, Colo.: Westview, 1999.

Rouleau, Eric. "Sudan's Communists: Routed by Arabism." *Le Monde* (Weekly English Edition), 28 August 1971, 11–13.

Salih, Kamal Osman. "The Sudan, 1985–89: The Fading Democracy." In *Sudan after Nimieri*, ed. Peter Woodward, 45–75. London and New York: Routledge, 1991.

Al-Shahi, Ahmed. "Response to Nimieri's Policies: Some Observations on Social and Political Changes in Northern Sudan" In *Sudan after Nimieri*, ed. P. Woodward, 144–159. London and New York: Routledge, 1991.

Shaked, Haim, Esther Souery, and Gabriel Warburg. "The Communist Party in the Sudan, 1946-1971." In *The USSR and the Middle East*, ed. M. Confino and S. Shamir, 335–374. New York: Wiley, 1973.

Sinada, Mamoun. "Constitutional Development in the Sudan Contemporary with the Evolution of the University of Khartoum." *SNR* LXI (1980): 77–88.

Stevovic, Mihailo. "Sudan: After the Coup." *Review of International Affairs* 34 (1985): 24–26.

Sylvester, Anthony. "Muhammad Versus Lenin in Revolutionary Sudan." *New Middle East* 34 (1971): 26–28.

——. *Sudan under Nimieri*. London: The Bodley Head, 1977.

al-Teraifi, Al-Agab Ahmed, ed. *Decentralisation in Sudan*. Khartoum and London: University of Khartoum Press and Ithaca Press, 1987.

Voll, John O. "Political Crisis in Sudan." *Current History* 89 (1990): 153–156; 178–180.

——. "The Sudan after Nimeiry." *Current History* 85 (1986): 213-16.

——. *Sudan: State and Society in Crisis*, ed. John Voll. Bloomington: Indiana University Press, 1991.

Wai, Dunstan M. *The African-Arab Conflict in the Sudan*. New York: Holmes and Meier, 1981.

——. "Revolution, Rhetoric, and Reality in the Sudan." *JMAS* 17, no. 1 (1979): 71–93.

Wai, Dunstan, and U. M. Kupferschmidt, eds. *Islam, Nationalism, and Radicalism in Egypt and the Sudan*. New York: Praeger, 1983.

Warburg, Gabriel R. "Democracy in the Sudan: Trial and Error." *Northeast African Studies*, 8, nos. 2–3 (1986): 77–94.

——. *Egypt and the Sudan: Studies in History and Politics*. London: Frank Cass, 1985.

——. *Islam, Nationalism, and Communism in a Traditional Society: The Case of the Sudan*. London: Frank Cass, 1978.

Waterbury, John. *Hydropolitics of the Nile Valley*. Syracuse: Syracuse University Press, 1979.

Woodward, Peter. *Condominium and Sudanese Nationalism*. Totowa, N.J.: Barnes and Noble, 1979.

——. "Nationalism and Opposition in Sudan." *African Affairs* 80 (1981): 379–388.

——. *Sudan, 1898–1989: The Unstable State*. Boulder, Colo.: Lynne Reiner, 1990.

International Relations

Aregay, Merid Wolde, and Sergew Hable Selassie. "Sudanese-Ethiopian Relations before the Nineteenth Century." In *Sudan in Africa*, ed. Y. F. Hasan, 62–72. Khartoum: Khartoum University Press, 1971.

Bechtold, Peter K. "New Attempts at Arab Cooperation: The Federation of Arab Republics, 1971–?" *MEJ* 27, no. 2 (1973): 152–172.

Beshir, Mohammed Omer. *Sudan: Aid and External Relations*. Khartoum and London: Khartoum University Press and Ithaca Press, 1984.

Brewer, William D. "The Libyan-Sudanese 'Crisis' of 1981: Danger from Darfur and Dilemma for the United States." *MEJ* 36 (1982): 205–216.

Diriage, Ahmed Ibrahim. "A New Political Structure for the Sudan." In *Management of the Crisis in the Sudan*, ed. A. Ghaffar M. Ahmed and G. Sorbo, 91–107. Bergen, Norway: University of Bergen, 1989.

Fabunmi, L. *The Sudan in Anglo-Egyptian Relations: A Case Study in Power Politics, 1800–1956.* Westport, Conn.: Greenwood Press, 1973.

Hail, J. A. *Britain's Foreign Policy in Egypt and Sudan, 1947–1956.* Reading, England: Ithaca Press, 1996.

Kasfir, Nelson. "One Full Revolution: The Politics of Sudanese Military Government, 1969-1985." In *The Military in African Politics*, ed. J. W. Harbeson, 141–162. New York: Praeger, 1987.

Kheir, A. "Chinese in the Sudan." *Eastern Horizons* 12, no. 3 (1973): 45–47.

Lesch, Ann Mosley. "Sudan's Foreign Policy: In Search of Arms, Aid, and Allies." In *Sudan: State and Society in Crisis*, ed. John O. Voll. Bloomington: Indiana University Press, 1991.

Taha, Faisal Abdel Rahman Ali. "The Boundary between the Sudan, Chad, and Central African Republic." *SNR* LX (1979): 1–14.

———. "The Sudan-Libyan Boundary." *SNR* LVIII (1977): 65–72.

———. "The Sudan-Uganda Boundary." *SNR* LIX (1978): 1–23.

———. "The Sudan-Zaire Boundary." *SNR* LVIII (1977): 73–84.

Voll, John O. "Northern Muslim Perspectives." In *Conflict and Peacemaking in Multiethnic Societies*, ed. J. V. Montville, 389–400. Lexington, Mass.: Lexington Books, 1990.

———. "Unity of the Nile Valley: Identity and Regional Integration." *JAS* 3, no. 2 (1976): 205–228.

Wai, Dunstan M. "The Sudan: Domestic Politics and Foreign Relations under Nimeiry." *African Affairs* 78 (1979): 297–317.

Woodward, Peter. "External Relations after Nimieri." In *Sudan after Nimieri*, ed. P. Woodward, 207–217. London: Routledge, 1991.

———. "Some Dimensions of Neighbor-State Relations in the Nile Valley." *SNR* LXI (1980): 110–117.

Law and Islamization

Al-Affendi, Abdelwahab. *Turabi's Revolution, Islam and Power in the Sudan.* London: Grey Seal, 1991.

Akolawin, Natale Olwak. "Islamic and Customary Law in the Sudan." In *Sudan in Africa*, ed. Y. F. Hasan, 279–301. Khartoum: Khartoum University Press, 1971.

An-Na'im, Abdullahi Ahmed. "Constitutionalism and Islamization in the Sudan." *Africa Today* 36, no. 3 (1989): 11–29.

De Waal, Alex. "Some Comments on Militias in the Contemporary Sudan." In *Civil War in the Sudan*, ed. M. W. Daly and A. A. Sikainga. London: British Academic Press, 1993.

Flint, Julie, "Sudan: Under Islamic Siege." *Africa Report* 38, no. 5 (1993): 24–27.

Fluehr-Lobban, Carolyn. "An Anthropological Analysis of Homicide in the Afro-Arab Sudan." *Journal of African Law* 20 (1976): 20–38.

———, ed. "Circulars of the Shari'a Courts in the Sudan, 1902–1979," trans. Hatim Babiker Hillawi and C. Fluehr-Lobban. *Journal of African Law* 27, no. 2 (1983): 79–140.

———. "A Comparison of the Development of Muslim Family Law in Tunisia, Egypt, and the Sudan." In *Law and Anthropology*. Vol. 7. Dordrecht, Netherlands: M. Nijhoff Publishers, 1994.

———. *Islamic Law and Society in the Sudan.* London: Frank Cass, 1987.

———. "Islamization in Sudan: A Critical Assessment." *MEJ* 44, no. 4 (1990): 610–623.

———. "Islamization of Law in the Sudan." *Legal Studies Forum* 10, no. 2 (1987): 189–204.

———. "Issues in the Shari'a Child Custody Law in the Sudan." *Northeast African Studies* 4, no. 1 (1982): 1–9.

———. "Shari'a Law in the Sudan: History and Trends since Independence." *Africa Today* 28, no. 2 (1981): 69–77.

Gordon, Carey N. "The Legal Regime of Public Finance in the Sudan: The Legacy of Nimeiri." *Journal of African Law* 30 (1986): 20–50.

———. "Recent Developments in the Land Law of the Sudan: A Legislative Analysis." *Journal of African Law* 30 (1986): 143–174.

Howell, P. P. *A Manual of Nuer Law, Being an Account of Customary Law: Its Evolution and Development in the Courts Established by the Sudan Government.* London: Oxford University Press, 1970.

Johnson, Douglas H. "Judicial Regulation and Administrative Control: Customary Law and the Nuer, 1898–1954." *JAH* 27, no. 1 (1986): 59–78.

El-Mahdi, Saeed M. A. *A Guide to Land Settlement and Registration.* Khartoum: Khartoum University Press, 1971.

———. "Limitations on the Ownership of Land in the Sudan." *SNR* LVIII (1977): 152–158.

Makinda, Samuel. "Iran, Sudan, and Islam." *The World Today* 49, no. 6 (1993): 108–112.

Moussalli, Ahmad S. "Hasan al-Turabi's Discourse on Democracy and *Shura.*" *Middle Eastern Studies* 30, no. 1 (1994): 52–64.

Mustafa, Zaki. *The Common Law in the Sudan: An Account of the "Justice, Equity, and Good Conscience" Provision.* Oxford: Clarendon Press, 1971.

Riad, Ibrahim. "Factors Contributing to the Rise of the Muslim Brethern in Sudan." *Arab Studies Quarterly* 12, nos. 3–4 (1990): 33–53.

Runger-Gabelmann, Mechthilde. *Land Law in Western Sudan: The Case of Southern Darfur.* London: Ithaca Press, 1987.

Rycx, Jean François. "The Islamization of Law as a Political Stake in Sudan." In *Sudan after Nimeiri*, ed. Peter Woodward, 139–143. London: Routledge, 1991.

Salim, Abdalla Hassan. *Rights of the Accused in the Sudan.* Khartoum and London: University of Khartoum and Ithaca Press, 1983.

Vasdev, Krishna. "Laws Relating to Trade Marks, Patents, and Copyright in the Sudan." *SNR* LX (1979): 38–55.

Warburg, Gabriel. "The Sharia in Sudan: Implementation and Repercussions, 1983–89." *MEJ*, no. 4 (1990): 624–637.

Southern Sudan Conflict and Resolution

Abu Eissa, F. "Revolution Relieved Sudan's Southern Problem." *Middle East International* 3 (1971): 50–52.

Adams, M. "Settlement in the Southern Sudan." *Middle East International* 12 (1972): 2–3.

el-Affendi, Abdelwahab. "Discovering the South: Sudanese Dilemmas for Islam in Africa." *African Affairs* 89, no. 356 (1990): 371–409.

Ahmed, Abdel Ghaffar Mohammed. "Management of the Crisis in the Sudan: Some Basic Issues." In *Management of the Crisis in the Sudan*, ed. A. Ghaffar, M. Ahmed, and G. Sorbo, 5–9. Bergen, Norway: Centre for Development Studies, University of Bergen, 1989.

Albino, Oliver. *The Sudan: A Southern Viewpoint.* London: Oxford University Press, 1970.

Alier, Abel. *Southern Sudan: Too Many Agreements Dishonoured.* Sudan Studies Series. London: Ithaca Press, 1990.

Assefa, Hizkias. *Mediation of Civil Wars: Approaches and Strategies: The Sudan Conflict.* Westview Studies in Peace, Conflict, and Conflict Resolution. Boulder, Colo.: Westview Press, 1987.

Bagadi, Hamad O. "A Review of the Peace Efforts since April 1985." In *Management of the Crisis in the Sudan*, ed. A. Ghaffar, M. Ahmed, and G. Sorbo, 108–113. Bergen, Norway: Centre for Development Studies, University of Bergen, 1989.

Burton, John W. "The Sudanese War, the Peace, and the Pastoralists: An Anthropological View." *Northeast African Studies* 4, no. 2 (1982): 47–55.

Beninyo, B. K. "Evaluation of the Educational Policies of the Sudan, 1972–92: Impact and Implications in Educational Development in the Southern Sudan." Ph.D. diss., Leeds University, Leeds, UK, 1996.

Beshir, Mohamed Omer. "Ethnicity, Regionalism, and National Cohesion in the Sudan." *SNR* LXI (1980): 11–14.

———. *The Southern Sudan: From Conflict to Peace.* London: Hurst, 1975.

———. *Southern Sudan: Regionalism and Religion, Selected Essays.* Graduate College Publications. Vol. 10. Khartoum and London: University of Khartoum and Ithaca Press, 1984.

Betts, Tristram. *The Southern Sudan: The Ceasefire and After.* London: Africa Publication Trust, 1974.

Burr, J. Millard. "Quantifying Genocide in the Southern Sudan, 1983–1993." Washington, DC: USA Committee for Refugees, October 1993.

Chand, David. "The Sudan Civil War: Is Negotiated Peace Possible." *Africa Today* 36, nos. 3–4 (1989): 55–63.

Collins, Robert O. "Pounds and Piastres: The Beginnings of Economic Development in the Southern Sudan." *Northeast African Studies* 5, no. 1 (1983): 39–65.

——. *Shadows in the Grass: Britain in the Southern Sudan, 1918–1956.* New Haven: Yale University Press, 1983.

——. "The Toposa Question, 1912–1927." *Northeast African Studies* 3, no. 3 (1981): 81–82; 87–88.

Deng, Francis Mading. "Cultural Dimensions of Conflict Management and Development: Some Lessons from the Sudan." In *Culture and Development in Africa: Proceedings of an International Conference Held at the World Bank*, ed. Ismail Serageldin and June Taboroff, 2–3. Washington, DC: World Bank, 1994.

——. *Dynamics of Identification: A Basis for National Integration in the Sudan.* Khartoum: Khartoum University Press, 1973.

——. "Hidden Agendas in the Peace Process." In *Civil War in the Sudan*, ed. M. W. Daly and A. A. Sikainga, 186–215. London: British Academic Press, 1993.

——. "The Identity Factor in the Sudanese Conflict." In *Conflict and Peacemaking in Multiethnic Societies*, ed. J. V. Montville, 343–362. Lexington, Mass.: Lexington Books, 1990.

——. *War of Visions: Conflict of Identities in the Sudan.* Washington, DC: Brookings Institution, 1995.

——. "War of Visions for the Nation." *MEJ* 44, no. 4 (1990): 596–609.

——. "What is Not Said is What Divides Us." In *Management of the Crisis in the Sudan*, ed. A. Ghaffar, M. Ahmed, and G. Sorbo, 10–18. Bergen, Norway: Centre for Development Studies, University of Bergen, 1989.

Deng, Francis M., and Larry Minear. *The Challenges of Famine Relief: Emergency Operations in the Sudan.* Washington, DC: Brookings Institution, 1992.

De Waal, Alex. "Starving Out the South." In *Civil War in the Sudan*, ed. M. W. Daly and A. A. Sikainga, 157–185. London: British Academic Press, 1993.

Eltom, Akram A. "Operation Life-Line Sudan and the UNDP Programs for the Displaced." In *War and Drought in Sudan*, ed. E. Eltigani, 87–96. Gainesville: University Press of Florida, 1995.

Eprile, Cecil. *War and Peace in the Sudan, 1955–1972.* London: Newton Abbot, David and Charles, 1974.

Fluehr-Lobban, Carolyn. "Protracted Civil War in the Sudan." *The Fletcher Forum of World Affairs* 16, no. 2 (1992): 67–80.

Garretson, Peter P. "The Southern Sudan Welfare Committee and the 1947 Strike in the Southern Sudan." *Northeast African Studies* 8, nos. 2–3 (1986): 181–191.

Hargey, T. M. "The Suppression of Slavery in the Sudan 1898-1928." Ph.D. diss., Oxford University, 1981.

Heraclides, Alexis. "Janus or Sisyphus? The Southern Problem of the Sudan." *JMAS* 25, no. 2 (1987): 213–231.

Hodnebo, Kjell. "A Report on Some Archives in Equatoria Province, Sudan." *History in Africa* 8 (1981): 327–332.

Ibrahim, Salah El-Din El Shazali. "War and Displacement: The Sociocultural Dimension." In *War and Drought in Sudan*, ed. E. Eltigani, 35–46. Gainesville: University Press of Florida, 1995.

Johnson, Douglas H. "The Fighting Nuer: Primary Sources and the Origins of a Stereotype." *Africa* 51, no. 1 (1981): 508–527.

———. "The Future of Southern Sudan's Past." *Africa Today* 28, no. 2 (1981): 33–41.

———. "North-South Issues." In *Sudan after Nimieri*, ed. Peter Woodward, 119–138. London: Routledge,1991.

Johnson, Douglas, and Gerard Prunier. "The Foundation and Expansion of the Sudan People's Liberation Army." In *Civil War in the Sudan*, ed. M. W. Daly and A. A. Sikainga, 117–141. London: British Academic Press, 1993.

Kasfir, Nelson. "Peacemaking and Social Cleavages in Sudan." In *Conflict and Peacemaking in Multiethnic Societies*, ed. J. V. Montville, 363–387. Lexington, Mass.: Lexington Books, 1990.

Keen, David. *The Benefits of Famine: A Political Economy of Famine and Relief in Southwestern Sudan, 1983–93.* Princeton: Princeton University Press, 1994.

Kibreab, Gaim. *Ready and Willing—But Still Waiting*. Uppsala, Sweden: Life and Peace Institute, 1996.

Lagu, Joseph, and Abel Alier. "A Protest by Former Southern Leaders." *Horn of Africa* 8, no. 1 (1985): 47–51.

Lesch, Ann Mosely. "Confrontation in the Southern Sudan." *MEJ* 40, no. 3 (1986): 410–428.

Lobban, Richard A. "National Integration and Disintegration: The Southern Sudan." In *Three Studies on National Integration in the Arab World*. Information Papers. Vol. 12. North Dartmouth, Mass.: Arab-American University Graduates, 1974.

Lowrey, William Olson. "Passing the Peace—People to People: The Role of Religion in an Indigenous Peace Process among the Nuer People of Sudan." Ph.D. diss., The Union Institute, 1996.

Mahran, Hatim A. "The Displaced, Food Production, and Food Aid." In *War and Drought in Sudan*, ed. E. Eltigani, 63–74. Gainesville: University Press of Florida, 1995.

Mawut, L. L. *Dinka Resistance to Condominium Rule, 1902–1932.* Khartoum: Khartoum University Press, 1983.

Morrison, G. *The Southern Sudan and Eritrea: Aspects of Wider African Problems.* London: Minority Rights Group, 1971.

Musa, O. "Reconciliation, Rehabilitation, and Development Efforts in Southern Sudan." *MEJ* 27, no. 1 (1973): 1–7.

An-Na'im, Abdullahi Ahmed. "Constitutional Discourse and the Civil War in the Sudan." In *Civil War in the Sudan*, ed. M. W. Daly and A. A. Sikainga, 97–116. London: British Academic Press, 1993.

O'Ballance, Edgar. *The Secret War in the Sudan: 1955–1972.* Hamden, Conn.: Archon Books, 1977.

O'Brien, Jay. "Sudan's Killing Fields." *Middle East Report* 161 (1989): 32–35.

Oduho, Joseph, and William Deng. *The Problem of the Southern Sudan.* London: Oxford University Press, 1963.

Sanderson, Lilian Passmore, and Neville Sanderson. *Education, Religion, and Politics in Southern Sudan, 1899–1964.* London and Khartoum: Khartoum University Press and Ithaca, 1981.

Scott, P. "The Sudan People's Liberation Movement (SPLM) and Liberation Army (SPLA)." *Review of African Political Economy* 33 (1985): 69–82.

Sikainga, A. A. "Northern Sudanese Parties and the Civil War." In *Civil War in the Sudan*, ed. M. W. Daly and A. A. Sikainga, 78–96. London: British Academic Press, 1993.

Thomas, Graham F. *Sudan: Death of a Dream.* London: Darf, 1990.

Van Voorhis, Bruce. "Food as a Weapon: Operation Lifeline Sudan." *Africa Today* 36, nos. 3–4 (1989): 29–43.

Voll, John O. "Reconciliation in the Sudan." *Current History* 80 (1981): 422–425.

Wai, Dunstan M. *The African-Arab Conflict in the Sudan.* New York: Africana Publishing Co., 1981.

———. "Pax Britannica and the Southern Sudan: The View from the Theater." *African Affairs* 79 (1980): 375–395.

———, ed. *The Southern Sudan, The Problem of National Integration.* London: Frank Cass, 1973.

Wako, Gabriel Zubeir. "How Can Christian Intellectuals Contribute to the Peace Effort in the Country?" *Afer* 29 (1987): 51–57.

Wakoson, Elias Nyamlell. "The Politics of Southern Self-Government, 1972–83." In *Civil War in the Sudan*, ed. M. W. Daly and A. A. Sikainga, 27–50. London: British Academic Press, 1993.

Wol, Stephen A. "Education of Displaced Southern Students in Northern Sudan." In *War and Drought in Sudan*, ed. E. Eltigani, 47–51. Gainesville: University Press of Florida, 1995.

Woldemikael, Tekle M. "Southerners in a Northern City." *Horn of Africa* 8, no. 1 (1985): 26–31.

Yongo-Bure, B. "The Underdevelopment of Southern Sudan since Independence." In *Civil War in the Sudan*, ed. M. W. Daly and A. A. Sikainga, 51–77. London: British Academic Press, 1993.

7. ECONOMIC

Agriculture and Environment

Ahmed, Medani Mohammed. *Indigenous Farming Systems: Knowledge and Practices in the Sudan.* Khartoum: Khartoum University Press, 1994.

———. *Indigenous Knowledge for Sustainable Development in the Sudan.* Khartoum: Khartoum University Press, 1994.

Ali, Ali Abdel Gader. "Productivity of Labour in Sudanese Traditional Agriculture: Some Exploratory Results." *SNR* LVIII (1977): 142–151.

Ali, Ali Abdel Gader, and Huda Abdel Sattar. "On Production Relations in Sudanese Irrigated Agriculture." *SNR* LXII (1981): 15–27.

Ali, Taisier Mohammed. "The Road to Juba." *Review of African Political Economy* 26 (1983): 4–14.

Briggs, John A. "Problems of Agricultural Planning: Observations from the Jamu'iya Development Scheme in the Central Sudan." *SNR* LXII (1981): 98–107.

Bunting, A. H. "Agricultural Research at the Sudan Central Rainlands Station, 1952–56." *Nature* 178 (1985): 1103–1104.

Croydon, Blanche. *Sudan and the Manchester Connection: The Impact of the Manchester Cotton Trade on Sudan's Socio-Economic Structures.* Exeter Middle East Monographs. London: Ithaca Press, 1990.

Crul, R. C. M., and F. C. Roest. *Current Status of Fisheries and Fish Stocks of the Four Largest African Reservoirs: Kainji, Kariba, Nasser/Nubia, and Volta.* Rome: Food and Agriculture Organization of the United Nations, 1995.

Daumont, Roland, et al. *Sudan, Recent Economic Developments.* Washington, DC: International Monetary Fund (Middle Eastern Department and the Policy Development and Review Department), 1997.

De Waal, Alexander. *Famine That Kills, Darfur, Sudan, 1984–85.* New York: Oxford University Press, 1989.

Duffield, Mark. "Change among West African Settlers in Northern Sudan." *Review of African Political Economy* 26 (1983): 45–59.

Frankenberger, Timothy R. "Integrating Livestock into Farming Systems Research: An Example from North Kordofan, Sudan." *Human Organization* 45, no. 3 (1986): 228–238.

Grawert, Elke. *Making a Living in Rural Sudan: Production of Women, Labour, Migration of Men, and Policies for Peasants' Needs.* New York: St. Martin's Press, 1998.

Hag Elamin, Nasredin A. *Adjustment Programmes and Agricultural Incentives in Sudan: A Comparative Study.* Nairobi, Kenya: African Economic Research Consortium, 1997.

Jedrej, M. C., and G. Stremmelaar. "Guneid Sugar Scheme: A Sociological Consideration of Some Aspects of Conflict between Management and Tenants." *SNR* 52 (1971): 71–78.

Kameir, El Wathiq, and Ibrahim Kursany. *Corruption as the "Fifth Factor" of Production in the Sudan.* Uppsala, Sweden: Scandinavian Institute of African Studies, 1985.

Kibreab, Gaim. *People on the Edge in the Horn: Displacement, Land Use, & the Environment in the Gedaref Region, Sudan.* Lawrenceville, N.J.: Red Sea Press, Inc., 1996.

Kursany, Ibrahim. "Peasants of the Nuba Mountain Region." *Review of African Political Economy* 26 (1983): 35–44.

O'Brien, Jay. "Sudan: An Arab Breadbasket?" *MERIP Reports* 99 (1981): 20–26.

Osman, M. Shazali, and H. E. El Hag. "Irrigation Practices and Development in the Sudan." *SNR* 55 (1974): 96–110.

Saab, R. "A Basic Programme for the Development of Sudanese Agriculture." *Arab Economics* 6, no. 68 (1974): 24–25.

Saeed, Abdalla Babiker Mohamed. *The Savanna Belt of the Sudan: A Case Study.* Khartoum: Ministry of Cooperation and Rural Development, 1971.

Salih, Siddig A. *Sustainable Ecosystem in Africa: Managing Natural Forest in Sudan.* Helsinki, Finland: World Institute for Development Economics Research, 1994.

Shaaeldin, Elfatih. *The Evolution of Agrarian Relations in Sudan.* London: Ithaca Press, 1986.

Strachan, Peter. *Empowering Communities: A Casebook from West Sudan.* London: Oxfam UK and Ireland, 1997.

Zahlan, A. B., ed. *The Agricultural Sector: Policy and System Studies.* Middle East Science Policy Series. London: Ithaca Press, 1986.

Gezira and Zande Scheme

Abdelkarim, Abbas. "The Development of Sharecropping Arrangements in Sudan Gezira: Who is Benefitting?" *Peasant Studies* 13, no. 1 (1985): 25–37.

Adam, Mohamed Abdelgadir. *The Policy Impacts on Farmers' Production and Resource Use in the Irrigated Scheme of Gezira, Sudan: A Case of Change from a Controlled Subsidised System to a Free Market Mode of Production.* Koln, Germany: Wissenschaftsverlag Vauk, 1996.

Affan, Khalid. "Why Do Gezira Tenants Withhold Their Households' Labour?" *Journal of Asian and African Studies* 20, nos. 1–2 (1985): 72–88.

Barnett, Tony, and Abbas Abdelkarim. *Sudan: The Gezira Scheme and Agricultural Transition.* London: Frank Cass, 1991.

Hassan, Farah, and William Andrea Apaya. "Agricultural Credit in the Gezira." *SNR* 54 (1973): 104–115.

Medani, A. I. "Consumption Patterns of the Gezira-Managil Tenants." *SNR* 52 (1971): 79–87.

Onwubuemeli, E. "Agriculture: The Theory of Economic Development and the Zande Scheme." *JMAS* 12 (1974): 569–587.

Reining, Conrad. "Resettlement in the Zande Development Scheme." In *Involuntary Migration and Resettlement: The Problems and Responses of Dislocated Peoples*, ed. A. Hansen and A. Oliver-Smith, 201–224. Boulder, Colo.: Westview Press, 1982.

———. *The Zande Scheme: An Anthropological Case Study of Economic Development in Africa.* Evanston, Ill.: Northwestern University Press, 1966.

Taha, T. "The Gezira Scheme Extensions: A Case Study." *Journal of Administration Overseas* 14, no. 4 (1975): 240–250.

Thornton, D. S. "Agricultural Development in the Gezira Scheme." *SNR* 53 (1972): 98–113.

Development, Economics, and Business

Abedin, Najuml. "Job Evaluation and Classification in Sudan: A Case Study of Mismanagement." *Northeast African Studies* 7, no. 1 (1985): 65–70.

Abdelrahman, Ali Hasabelrasoul. "Agricultural Cooperatives and Community Economic Development: A Case Study of Western Sudan." Ph.D. diss., Pennsylvania State University, 1995.

Abdelrasoul, Abdelrasoul Abdelghauom. "Dividing the Sudan into Homogeneous Regions for Development." M.A. thesis, Clark University, 1996.

Abu Affan, Bodour Osman. *Industrial Policies and Industrialization in the Sudan.* Khartoum and London: Khartoum University Press and Ithaca Press, 1985.

Adams, Martin. "The Baggara Problem: Attempts at Modern Change in Southern Darfur and Southern Kordofan." *Development and Change* 13, no. 2 (1982): 259–289.

Adams, Martin E., and Elizabeth Hawksley. "Merging Relief and Development: The Case of Darfur." *Development Policy Research* 7 (1989): 143–169.

Adams, Martin E., and John Howell. "Developing the Traditional Sector in the Sudan." *Economic Development and Cultural Change* 27, no. 3 (1979): 505–518.

Affan, Bodour O. *The Impact of Private Foreign Investment on the Future Development of the Sudan Economy.* Khartoum: Economic and Social Research Council, 1980.

Ahmed, Abdel Ghaffar M., and Mustafa Abdel Rahman. *Urbanisation and Exploitation: The Role of Small Centres.* Khartoum: University of Khartoum, 1979.

Ahmed, Hassan A. Aziz. "Aspects of Sudan's Foreign Trade during the 19th Century." *SNR* 55 (1974): 16–32.

Ahmed, Medani Mohammed, ed. *Indigenous Knowledge for Sustainable Development in the Sudan.* Khartoum: Khartoum University Press, 1994.

Ali, Ali Abdalla. "The Sudan's Invisible Trade, 1956–1969: A Brief Survey." *SNR* 54 (1973): 124–138.

Ali, Mohamed Abdel Rahman. "Calculating the Contribution of a Structural Shift to Economic Growth in the Sudan, 1955–1967." *SNR* 54 (1973): 116–123.

———. *Fluctuations and Impact of Government Expenditure in the Sudan, 1955–1967.* Khartoum: Khartoum University Press, 1974.

———. "The Propensity to Consume and Economic Development in a Dual Economy: Sudan, 1955–1967." *SNR* 53 (1972): 114–122.

Ali, Mohammed Abdel Rahman, and Kamal Abdel Gadir Salim. "Export Taxes and Fiscal Policy in Developing Countries with Special Reference to the Sudan." *SNR* 55 (1974): 111–122.

Awad, Mohamed Hashim. *Socio-Economic Change in the Sudan.* Khartoum: Khartoum University Press, 1983.

———. "The Southern Sudan: Planning for National Integration." *SNR* 55 (1974): 88–95.

Barnett, Tony, and Abbas Abdelkarim, eds. *Sudan: State, Capital, and Transformation.* London: Croom Helm, 1988.

Blakely, Edward J., and Charles E. Hess. "Designing a National System for Development: A Role for the University in the Sudan." *Community Development Journal* 12, no. 3 (1977): 191–200.

Burton, John W. "Development and Cultural Genocide in the Sudan." *JMAS* 29, no. 3 (1991): 511–521.

Bushra, F., el-. "Population Growth and Economic Development in the Sudan." *Bulletin of Arab Research and Studies* 5 (1974): 3–11.

Cole, David Chamberlain. *Between a Swamp and a Hard Place: Developmental Challenges in Remote Rural Africa*. Cambridge, Mass.: Harvard Institute for International Development, 1997.

Due, John F., and Jean M. Due. "The Financing of the Southern Region and Other Regional Governments of the Sudan." *Bulletin of International Fiscal Documentation* 36 (1982): 4–14.

Ebrahim, Mohammed H. S. "Irrigation Projects in Sudan: The Promise and the Reality." *JAS* 10, no. 1 (1983): 2–13.

Fruzetti, Lina, and Akos Ostor. *Culture and Change along the Blue Nile: Courts, Markets, and Strategies for Development*. Boulder, Colo.: Westview Press, 1989.

Grabler, Susan. "European Capital Exports and the Concessions Policy in the Sudan, 1898–1913." *Northeast African Studies* 8, no. 2–3 (1986): 95–108.

Hansohm, Dirk. "The 'Success' of IMF/World Bank Policies in Sudan." In *The World Recession and the Food Crisis in Africa*, ed. Peter Lawrence, 148–156. London: James Currey, 1986.

Hansohm, Dirk, and Karl Wohlmuth. "Promotion of Rural Handicrafts as a Means of Structural Adjustment in Sudan." *Scandinavian Journal of Development Alternatives* 6 (1987): 170–190.

El Hassan, Ali Mohamed, ed. *Essays on the Economy and Society of the Sudan*. Khartoum: Economic and Social Research Council, National Council for Research, 1977.

Kaikati, Jack G. "The Economy of the Sudan: A Potential Breadbasket of the Arab World." *IJMES* 11, no. 1 (1980): 99–123.

Kontos, Stephen. "Farmers and the Failure of Agribusiness in Sudan." *MEJ* 44, no. 4 (1990): 649–667.

Lako, George Tombe. "The Impact of the Jonglei Scheme on the Economy of the Dinka." *African Affairs* 84 (1985): 15–38.

Lees, Francis A., and Hugh C. Brooks. *The Economic and Political Development of the Sudan*. Boulder, Colo.: Westview Press, 1977.

Mahmoud, Abdelrahim Elrayah. *Social Administration and Social Policies in Sudan*. Khartoum: Economic and Social Research Council, National Council for Research, 1987.

Manger, Leif. *Trade and Traders in the Sudan*. New York: Lilian Barber Press, 1984.

Mirghani, Abdel Rahim. *Development Planning in the Sudan in the Sixties*. Khartoum and London: Khartoum University Press and Ithaca Press, 1983.

Morton, James. *The Poverty of Nations: The Aid Dilemma at the Heart of Africa.* New York: St. Martin's Press, 1996.

Mustafa, Mohamed El Murtada. "Development Planning and International Migration in the Sudan." *Labour and Society* 5, no. 1 (1980): 85–98.

Nimeiri, Sayed M. "Tax Incentives for the Promotion of Private Industry in the Sudan." *SNR* 55 (1974): 123–133.

Oesterdiekhoff, Peter, and Karl Wohlmuth. "The 'Breadbasket' is Empty: The Options of Sudanese Development Policy." *Canadian Journal of African Studies* 17, no. 1 (1983): 35–67.

Omer, El Haj Abdalla Bilal. *The Danagla Traders of Northern Sudan.* Sudan Studies Series. London: Ithaca Press, 1985.

——. "Rural Traders and Socioeconomic Transformation in the Dongola Areas of Sudan's Northern Province." *International Review of Modern Sociology* 12, no. 1 (1982): 133–146.

Plater, Terry Denise. "Forced Migration and Resettlement as a Strategy for Development: An Analysis of Implications Based on a Study of the New Halfa Scheme in Eastern Sudan." Ph.D. diss., University of Pennsylvania, 1994.

Prendergast, John. "Blood Money for Sudan: World Bank and IMF to the 'Rescue'." *Africa Today* 36, nos. 3–4 (1989): 43–55.

Rondinelli, Dennis A. "Administrative Decentralization and Economic Development: The Sudan's Experiment with Devolution." *JMAS* 19, no. 4 (1981): 595–624.

Roy, Delwin A. "Development Policy and Labor Migration in the Sudan." *MES* 25, no. 3 (1989): 301–323.

Saeed, Osman Hassan. *The Industrial Bank of Sudan, 1962–1968: An Experiment in Development Banking.* Khartoum: Khartoum University Press, 1971.

——. *The Jonglei Canal.* Khartoum and London: University of Khartoum Press and Ithaca Press, 1984.

——. "Marketability of Securities as an Incentive for Voluntary Savings: A Case Study of the Sudan." *SNR* 52 (1971): 88–100.

Sammani, Mohamed Osman. "A Study of Central Villages as Planning Units for the Sudan." *Ekistics* 32, no. 189 (1971): 124–133.

Shaaeldin, Elfatih. *The Evolution of Agrarian Relations in Sudan.* The Hague, Netherlands: Institute of Social Studies, 1986.

Al-Shahi, Ahmed. "Economic Change and Individual Initiative: The Case of the Development Community in Northern Sudan." *SNR* LXI (1980): 61–76.

Speece, Mark, and Thomas Gillard-Byers. "Government Market Intervention in Kordofan, Sudan." *Northeast African Studies* 8, nos. 2–3 (1986): 111–129.

Strachan, Peter. *Empowering Communities: A Casebook from West Sudan.* London: Oxfam UK and Ireland/LOC, 1997.

Taha, El Waleed Mohamed. "From Dependent Currency to Central Banking in the Sudan." *SNR* 51 (1970): 95–105.

El-Terefi, El Agab. *Decentralisation and Devolution in Sudan.* London: Ithaca Press, 1991.

Tignor, Robert L. "The Sudanese Private Sector: An Historical Overview." *JMAS* 25, no. 2 (1987): 179–212.

Van der Wel, Paul, and Abdel Ghaffar M. Ahmed. *Perspectives on Development in Sudan*. The Hague, Netherlands: Institute of Social Studies, 1986.

Voll, Sarah P. "Cotton in Kassala: The Other Scheme." *JAS* 5, no. 2 (1978): 205–222.

Wilson, R. T. "Temporal Changes in Livestock Numbers and Patterns of Transhumance in Southern Darfur, Sudan." *Journal of Developing Areas* 11, no. 4 (1977): 493–508.

Woldegabriel, Berhane. "Rahad: A Model for Development." *Sudanow* 3 (1978): 47–51.

World Bank. *Sudan: Pricing Policies and Structural Balances*. Washington, DC: 1985.

Wynn, R. "The Sudan's 10-Year Plan of Economic Development, 1961/62–1970/71: An Analysis of Achievement to 1967–68." *Journal of Developing Areas* 5, no. 4 (1971): 555–576.

Yacoub, el Sammani A., and Fouad A., Agabani *Scientific and Technical Potential (STP) in the Sudan*. Khartoum: Khartoum University Press, 1974.

Labor

Abu Sharaf, Rogaia Mustafa. "Sudanese-New World Migration: The Social History of Sudanese International Migration to the United States and Canada." Ph.D. diss., University of Connecticut, 1994.

Ahmed, Ahmed Salim. "The Manpower Situation in the Sudan." *Labour and Society* 5 (1980): 291–308.

Ali, Mohamed Adham. *Some Reflections on Manpower Waste in the Sudan*. Khartoum: Economic and Social Research Council, National Council for Research, 1977.

Bernal, Victoria. *Cultivating Workers, Peasants, and Capitalism in a Sudanese Village*. New York: Columbia University Press, 1991.

Faaland, Just. "Growth, Employment, and Equity: Lessons of the Employment Strategy Mission to the Sudan, Undertaken within the Framework of the World Employment Programme of the International Labor Organization." *International Labour Review* 114 (1976): 1–10.

McLoughlin, P. F. M. "Labour Market Conditions and Wages in the Three Towns, 1900–1950." *SNR* 51 (1970): 105–118.

Milne, Janet C. M. "The Impact of Labour Migration on the Umarar in Port Sudan." *SNR* 55 (1974): 70–87.

Oberai, A. S. "Migration, Unemployment and the Urban Labour Market: A Case Study of the Sudan." *International Labour Review* 115 (1977): 211–223.

O'Brien, Jay. "Formation of the Agricultural Labour Force." *Review of African Political Economy, Special Issue on Sudan* 26 (1983): 15–34.

Sheehan, Glen. "Labour Force Participation Rates in Khartoum." In *Labour Force Participation in Low-Income Countries*, ed. G. Standing and G. Sheehan, 165–175. Geneva, Switzerland: International Labour Office, 1978.

Taha, Abdel Rahman E. Ali. "Reflections on the Structure and Government of the Sudan Railway Workers' Union." *SNR* 55 (1974): 61–69.

Taha, A. R. E. A., and Ahmed H. el Jack. *The Regulation of Termination of Employment in the Sudanese Private Sector.* Khartoum: Khartoum University Press, 1973.

About the Authors

Richard Andrew Lobban Jr. is Professor of Anthropology and African Studies at Rhode Island College where he served as Director, Program of African and Afro-American Studies. His Ph.D. in anthropology is from Northwestern University in 1973 from his research on Mahas Nubians in the Sudan. His M.A. on African anthropology is from Temple University (1968), and he earned his B.S. in biology from Bucknell in 1966. He has taught, lectured, and researched in the United States, Canada, Europe, and Africa and was the distinguished Thorp Professor at Rhode Island College. He serves as a member of the graduate faculty as Tufts University, School of Veterinary Medicine. In 1978 he was consultant to Brooklyn Museum's international exhibition entitled *Nubia: Africa in Antiquity*. He was a founder and first president of the Sudan Studies Association in 1981. In 1993 and 1994 he lectured at the Nubia Institutes of the Boston Museum of Fine Arts. In 1994 he was an organizer of the Third International Meeting of Sudan Studies in Boston. In 1998 he was a guest lecturer at the Kerma exhibit at the National Museum of African Art at the Smithsonian Institution. He is a member of the African Studies Association and the Middle East Studies Association and is the Vice-President for the Rhode Island Black Heritage Society. His publications on the Sudan range from Nubian and Sudanese ethnography in Islamic times to research and writing on Nubian and Egyptian antiquity. His interests include comparative urban and complex societies, gender studies, research theory and methods, slavery, and African cartography. Dr. Lobban is a frequent visitor and resident in Egypt and Sudan, including frequent study tours of Egyptian Nubia. Dr. Lobban also has published extensively on Cape Verde, Guinea-Bissau, and Tunisia.

Carolyn Fluehr-Lobban is Professor of Anthropology and Director of General Education at Rhode Island College. She received her B.A. and M.A. degrees in anthropology from Temple University and her Ph.D. in anthropology and African studies from Northwestern University in 1973. She joined Rhode Island College in 1973 and received the Maixner Award for Distinguished Teaching in 1990 and the Thorp Award for Distinguished Scholar in 1998. She has spent six years living and conducting her fieldwork in the Sudan, Egypt, and Tunisia and has traveled extensively in the Middle East, including Algeria, Israel, Lebanon, Morocco, Syria, Turkey, and Yemen. Her research has covered Islamic law and society, Muslim women's social and legal status, ethics and anthropological research, human rights and cultural relativism, and comparative legal studies. She has been the recipient of numerous grants and four post-doctoral fellowships. She is a founder and twice past president of the Sudan Studies Association, and has served on the Ethics Committees of the Middle East Studies Association and the American Anthropological Association. She is the author or editor of seven books, including a general introduction to Muslim society to a Western audience, *Islamic Society in Practice* (1994), and *Islamic Law and Society in the Sudan* (1987), which should soon appear in Arabic translation. Her most recent work has brought the writings of Egyptian liberal-humanist intellectual, Muhammad Sa'id al-Ashmawy from Arabic to English in her 1998 publication of his works entitled *Against Islamic Extremism*.

Robert S. Kramer is Associate Professor of History at St. Norbert College in Wisconsin, where he teaches courses on Africa and the Middle East. He received his B.A. degree in history from Bard College in 1979 and studied Arabic at the American University in Cairo from 1980 to 1982. His M.A. is in Middle East studies from the University of Chicago (1984) and his Ph.D. is in African history from Northwestern University (1991). He has researched and written on Muslim societies in the Sudan and Ghana, as well as other topics relating to Islam in general. He is a member of several scholarly organizations.